An eyewitness account of lessons not learned **Why**

VIETNAM MATTERS

RUFUS PHILLIPS

NAVAL INSTITUTE PRESS
Annapolis, Maryland

Naval Institute Press
291 Wood Road
Annapolis, MD 21402

Library of Congress Cataloging-in-Publication Data
Phillips, Rufus.
 Why Vietnam matters : an eyewitness account of lessons not learned / Rufus Phillips.
    p. cm.
 Includes bibliographical references and index.
 ISBN 978-1-59114-674-2 (alk. paper)
 1. Vietnam War, 1961–1975—United States. 2. Vietnam—History—1945–1975. 3. Phillips, Rufus.
I. Title.
 DS558.P49 2008
 959.704'3—dc22

                              2008023335

Printed in the United States of America on acid-free paper

14 13 12 11 10 09 08   9 8 7 6 5 4 3 2
First printing

For my wife, Barbara, our children, and our grandchildren.

For the 1954–56 Saigon Military Mission.

For the volunteers of USOM Rural Affairs,

Americans and Vietnamese.

And for all those who died for a just but

imperfectly pursued cause.

Contents

Maps

Foreword

By Richard Holbrooke

In 1951, at the height of the Cold War, the CIA spotted a talented young man at its favorite recruiting grounds, Yale University. Thus began the saga of Rufus Phillips, one of the most remarkable figures of America's tortured involvement in Vietnam. Rufus got to Saigon in August 1954, shortly after the French defeat in Indochina. It was a critical time for the region. The United States was replacing the French as the major outside power, and the Viet Minh (the Vietnamese communists, led by Ho Chi Minh), who already controlled the northern half of the nation, were soon to begin a twenty-year drive to unify Vietnam under their control. Working under the legendary and controversial Edward Lansdale (the model for the character of Colonel Hillandale in the bestselling book *The Ugly American*), Rufus rose rapidly. He was intelligent, energetic, and charismatic.

Eight years later he was back in Vietnam, running a groundbreaking division of the United States foreign aid mission called the Office of Rural Affairs, dedicated to what would be called today "nation building." (In those days it was usually referred to as "pacification"—a word no longer politically correct.) And one year after that, Rufus Phillips became my first boss.

I had joined the Foreign Service in 1962, drawn to it by President John F. Kennedy's stirring calls to public service. Others in my generation went into the Peace Corps, or rode freedom buses south to fight segregation. As for me, in part because my best friend in high school had been David Rusk, whose father, the future secretary of state, had talked to our senior class about something called the Foreign Service, I took and passed the Foreign Service exam when I was a senior in college. I entered the Foreign Service one month after graduating. Less than a year later, after language training and area studies, I was sent to Vietnam along with several other young diplomats, including Vladimir Lehovich, to whom I owe many things, including years of friendship and his advice and assistance for this foreword.

Unknown to Vlad and me, the undersecretary of state for political affairs, U. Alexis Johnson, wanted to try a small experiment and give a few young Foreign Service officers (FSOs) field experience, outside embassies. Almost by chance, partly because we were bachelors, Vlad and I were the first selected. There were about ten thousand to twelve thousand American military personnel, mostly as advisers to the Vietnamese armed forces, in Vietnam when we arrived. American deaths in Vietnam had reached about fifty. Both numbers seemed enormous to us. As I recall, we were not in the slightest bit concerned about our own safety. We were young and indestructible. Bad things happened to other people. Soon we would be joined by some of the best young diplomats of our generation, many of whom went on to stellar careers: Frank Wisner, Tony Lake (who joined the Foreign Service with Vlad and me), Peter Tarnoff, John Negroponte (with whom I would eventually share a house), and Les Aspin (then an Air Force captain who never wore a uniform), were among the tight group of junior officials who came to Vietnam and became, in many cases, lifelong friends. Not everyone survived intact. One of our group, Doug Ramsey, was captured by the Viet Cong and spent years in hellish conditions before coming home in the early 1970s with other prisoners. There were others who died, at least one by his own hand. Tony Lake and a colleague, Edie Smith, barely survived a bomb attack just outside their offices in the U.S. embassy.

For Vlad and me, Rufus was at the center of this exciting time in our lives. There was something slightly mysterious about him. He was young enough to be our older brother, but he was respected by everyone, including the ambassador. He was close to senior Vietnamese officials. His past was the subject of whispers, but he was said to be a personal protégé of the great Lansdale. He had briefed Kennedy personally!

All of this turned out to be true. But what I remember most was his inspirational style of leadership, his endless energy, and his boundless optimism about his mission and its importance to the nation. He believed, as did other members of his generation, that America could accomplish almost anything, if we did it right. In the early 1960s, especially right after Kennedy's extraordinary achievement in the Cuban Missile Crisis, our slightly younger group believed the same thing. Rufus gave this belief shape and substance.

Why Vietnam Matters is a major contribution to the history of Vietnam. It contains important lessons for the wars America is currently fighting in Iraq and Afghanistan. So much of what the current generation of military and civilian officials claim are new doctrines and ideas are identical to programs and strategies that were virtually all tried in Vietnam. Gen. David Petraeus' much-praised counter-insurgency handbook, for example, bears a strong (and not accidental) resemblance to the manuals we studied in the Vietnam era.

Vlad reminds me that, with the creation of Rural Affairs, Rufus Phillips "turned the traditional U.S. aid effort on its head." The aid mission was, he recalls, "a headquarters-focused, capital-oriented organization that helped ministries in Saigon and had no presence in the countryside. Suddenly Rufe grafted onto that bureaucratic mission a group of creative, problem-solving, often strikingly young and highly motivated Americans, most not career-AID, who went into the country's provinces to work with Vietnamese on vital local needs like schools, wells, refugees, and rice and pig culture, as well as more basic issues of physical security and representative local government."

The reader may well ask what possible qualifications two young men from New York City, educated at Ivy League colleges, had for such work. The truth is that we had none. This was not, of course, true of most of our colleagues, who were not FSOs and did know a thing or two about pigs and wells. Anyway, Rufus understood our limitations and assigned us at first to work under other people. But when he thought we were ready (of course we were not), he sent us into two neighboring provinces in the Mekong Delta to oversee the distribution of American aid funds and supplies and assist the local government. Our work has distinct echoes of today's provincial reconstruction teams (PRTs) in Afghanistan, although we had none of the heavy security structure that surrounds Americans in today's even more dangerous war zones. When I visited the PRT in the province of Khost, in eastern Afghanistan, in April 2008 and watched Kael Weston, a career diplomat working closely with local tribal leaders, mullahs, and police officials, I felt I was watching someone who could have stepped right out of Rural Affairs/Vietnam.

The Rural Affairs philosophy was not always pleasing to the Saigon government or other American officials. It cut bureaucratic corners and reduced corruption. What Rufus cared about most was defeating the Viet Cong, and he sometimes broke crockery to do the job.

In late 1963, Rufus left Vietnam for family reasons. To him Rural Affairs was "the most dedicated bunch I had ever seen in government or elsewhere"—a comment that still resonates with me over forty years later. "Everyone was treated as an equal," Rufus said. "We were all on a first-name basis." In 2007, Lang Ha, one of Rural Affairs' first local employees who was forced to stay behind in Vietnam for seventeen years after North Vietnam's victory in 1975, remembered,

> We were different. Yes, we were not only colleagues—we were brothers and sisters in the big family of Rural Affairs. . . . We worked together, we were happy when there was success, unhappy when we met failure, but we were all the time together. I remember when our staff would come back from the field, the main office in Saigon was like a beehive. With Rural Affairs, the interaction between American staff and local employees also changed completely, and for the better.

Rufus was the best informed American about the situation in rural Vietnam, but not until this book has it been understood that for several crucial years in the 1960s he was probably the best informed American on events in the country as a whole, and perhaps the American most trusted and listened to by the Vietnamese. In this book he brings new detail to such well-studied subjects as the 1963 coup against President Diem and the work of General Lansdale.

Why Vietnam Matters will probably be the last insider book written by an important participant in that now-distant war. When Rufus started it years ago, every publisher and agent told him that no one wanted another Vietnam memoir. In this case they were wrong; this is an important book. The reader may not agree with everything in this book, especially some of its conclusions. But for those of us who served under him, and for whom Vietnam was a seminal and shaping experience, that is not the point. We are heartened to know that, after all these years, Rufus Phillips has not lost his fire, his conviction, his belief in the possibility of American greatness and leadership. In that sense, he remains our leader.

Preface

This is an inside history of what really happened in Vietnam and why it matters. The important lessons we should have learned were obscured by the conventional wisdom that we should never have been there in the first place. In the context of the Cold War and of communist objectives in Asia, we had good reasons for our presence. This book examines what we did with that presence, from the point of view of an engaged actor during the most critical years from 1954 through 1968. This was the time when we simultaneously lost our way and the support of the American people. What happened after 1968 is also addressed, but it was too little, too late; the support of the American people could not be retrieved.

At the highest levels we approached the Vietnam conflict with excessive hubris, convinced we knew best how to win, with little understanding of the enemy or of our South Vietnamese allies. We became obsessed with a big-army war when the real war, a people's war—mainly political and psychological in nature—went largely unnoticed. This story is being told now to add to the historical record and because of its relevance to our conduct in Iraq, Afghanistan, and the "war on terror."

No one associated with Vietnam was more guilty of hubris than Secretary of Defense Robert S. McNamara. With his assembly-line mindset, he established much of the tone and direction for our involvement during the Kennedy and Johnson administrations. In early 1962, not long after the United States had begun an intensified effort to help the South Vietnamese confront the Vietcong insurgency, McNamara asked Air Force brigadier general Edward G. Lansdale to look over a graph of evaluation factors he was preparing with which to measure progress in the war against the Vietcong insurgents. McNamara's factors were all numerical: numbers of operations, numbers of enemy killed, numbers of captured weapons. When McNamara asked what he thought of the list, Lansdale replied that it wouldn't give him an honest picture of progress. Another column was needed, Lansdale said: "You might call it the 'x factor'; it's missing." McNamara, while jotting it down, asked what it meant. The "x factor," Lansdale said, represented the feelings of the Vietnamese people. Without that all the other tallies would be false and misleading. McNamara grimaced, asked sarcastically how anyone could get a reading on people's feelings, and erased his "x factor" notation. Lansdale begged him not to codify the war, but he had lost the secretary's attention.[1]

McNamara's attitude, lack of understanding, and managerial approach symbolized the disconnect between our top leadership in Washington and Saigon and reality on the ground. Amplifying official ignorance of the "x factor" was the communications gap between top Americans and the Vietnamese. Bui Diem, former South Vietnamese ambassador to the

United States and a keen observer of both sides, called it a "very powerful explanation of what went wrong in Vietnam.... [T]he lack of understanding between the United States and South Vietnam. American military and diplomatic strategy was shaped by a profound misunderstanding of the Vietnamese—both friends and foe—of their culture as well as their view of the fundamental issues."[2] Some of us struggled against this fog of incomprehension, but the chasm between American official views and Vietnamese realities and aspirations could not be overcome.

The "*x* factor" was about the human, political side of the war—about which, Dan Van Sung, a perceptive Vietnamese nationalist, has said, "The anti-Communist fight in Vietnam is seventy-five percent political and twenty-five percent military. Yet, everything American is directed to the twenty-five percent and nothing to the seventy-five percent."[3] In juxtaposition, McNamara and other key officials thought of the war mainly in terms of statistics, such as body counts, quantities of supplies, and bureaucratic actions, not the human factor, not intangibles of the spirit. Winning the war by a superior application of men, money, and materiel became the dominant American theme. If the South Vietnamese were not up to the task, we would do it ourselves by bombing the North and killing enough Vietcong in the South to force the communist side to quit; then we would turn the country back over to the South Vietnamese. Thus, the official American view of the war missed its single most influential component—a South Vietnamese political cause worth fighting for—while the enemy, the Vietcong, framed every action as furthering its political cause against "colonialism and feudalism" and for unification. Missed opportunities to focus on the "political seventy-five percent," while changing the "military twenty-five percent," to include the human factor are recounted in this book. Some of these missed opportunities could have been turning points away from eventual disaster.

There was a way to help the South Vietnamese fight their war against a North Vietnamese communist–supported, –inspired, and –controlled insurgency, a way that held a chance of success. This had to do with helping the noncommunist Vietnamese take back their nationalist political revolution by developing a positive political cause worth fighting and dying for, beyond fear of communism. Critics have argued that the North Vietnamese cause of unification and patriotism, wrapped in a hatred of foreign domination, was too strong for the South Vietnamese ever to have mounted a countervailing cause of democratic self-government and the freedom and opportunity that came with it. In particular, they have argued that the North Vietnamese with the Ho Chi Minh Trail and bases in Cambodia were in a position to exert so much military pressure there was no room, no breathing space, for democratic self-government to develop. The notion that the South Vietnamese might mount a serious challenge to the Vietcong insurgency on political grounds was not considered practical. Yet that idea would have struck at the insurgency where it was politically weakest—its totalitarianism.

Unfortunately, we never made a sustained effort to give the South Vietnamese that support. Our indifference to their nationalist aspirations, as well as our massive troop intervention and inattention to its destructive impact on the structure and culture of Vietnamese society, damaged South Vietnamese opportunities to try that course. Much of the failure to coalesce around a political cause was clearly theirs. But we failed to recognize the revolutionary nature of the Vietnamese situation, of its defining nationalist and anticolonial characteristics. By the very nature of our intervention, we undercut that noncommunist political cause by becoming, in the eyes of too many Vietnamese, a highly destructive replacement for the French, never mind that our motives were quite the opposite. In failing to recognize the ultimate political nature of the war during the critical years 1963 to 1968, we had such a visibly destructive impact that we undermined our cause with the South Vietnamese and the American public at the same time. We changed course after 1968, by helping the Vietnamese fight a people's war to pacify the countryside. That was largely successful. But we still failed to support the political reforms necessary to achieve a unified democratic political cause outmatching the Vietcong and showing the American people something worthy of their support.

The missing political and psychological component of the Vietnam War remained buried in the rush to forget about the whole thing. Mainly we remember finally honoring our soldiers who fought and died there. As the more than one million "boat people" fleeing the communist takeover touched our consciences, recognition dawned that trying to help the South Vietnamese resist was in retrospect a worthier cause than many had thought. Then the Berlin Wall fell, the Cold War was over, and it was on to the "New World Order," until the roof fell in on September 11, 2001. This put us back into fighting insurgencies in distressed countries against mainly ideological (this time religiously motivated) foes while simultaneously helping build reasonably coherent and democratic nations within the same lands. The cultures, the histories, the religions, and the peoples of these countries may be very different from those of Vietnam, but our misconceptions, errors, and dysfunctional, bureaucratic approaches display dismaying similarities. The failure to give trustworthy and understandable explanations, warts and all, to our own people of what we are doing and what success might reasonably look like have compounded our missteps.

This book results from a journey through some intensively formative years of direct exposure to the Vietnamese and their strategically critical neighbors, the Lao—their hopes, their aspirations, their fears, and the cruel and uncertain set of circumstances in which they found themselves. Starting that journey in 1954 as one of a handful of assistant midwives at the hazardous birth of the Republic of Vietnam, south of the seventeenth parallel, I was there trying to help the South Vietnamese salvage it in 1962 and 1963, when the coup and Diem's assassination became, instead of a new beginning, the beginning of the end. I continued to be involved in that rescue effort until 1968.

During part of that time I was fortunate to serve under that same singular American who tried to educate McNamara. Lansdale was something of an eighteenth-century American revolutionary operating in the bureaucratic second half of the twentieth century; a uniquely skilled but controversial practitioner of the art of "nation building."[4] He transmitted a wide-angle view of how best to help the Vietnamese construct a cohesive nation out of a traditional but highly nationalistic and individualistic society, in the midst of revolutionary change and against hostile competing forces. I was pretty much an average American, with perhaps an above-average sensitivity and ability to listen and understand, to earn the trust of, and work with the Vietnamese as a partner and friend in a common cause.

Looking back at what happened in Vietnam will, I trust, throw light on our recent attempts at countering insurgencies in Iraq and Afghanistan while promoting democracy and "nation building," under the trying circumstances of civil conflict and upheaval. The challenge we faced in Vietnam was not just trying to help a beleaguered and politically divided nation resist an internal takeover backed by external support; it was a challenge within ourselves to listen to the people we were trying to help and not to think we always knew better.

Whatever the merits of having gone into Iraq in the first place, until recently we have performed so badly that the support of the American people has been lost, as it was in the Vietnam years. Recent course corrections and leadership changes on the ground, if pursued over time, may provide a breathing space for civil accommodation, with a chance of leaving behind a tolerably dysfunctional country. However, popular support for American persistence has pretty much run dry. This is a dilemma for which there is no easy prescription. If we are not careful, we may repeat it in Afghanistan. That we find ourselves where we are is due to an even greater degree of arrogance, ignorance, and incompetence than afflicted us over Vietnam. The end of this book extracts some lessons from Vietnam and applies them to Iraq, Afghanistan, and the "war on terror." Also raised is the moral question of what we, as a great nation, owe the Iraqi people, bearing as we do a significant measure of responsibility for what has happened there.

This book also sets out to tell the Vietnamese side of the story, to correct the caricature found in much of our literature of the Vietnamese as one-dimensional, cardboard characters, difficult to relate to or understand and deep in the background, obscured by what Americans thought and did. Some of us saw the Vietnamese differently, as flesh-and-blood human beings whose hopes for a better future we shared. Victims of forces and events often beyond their control, they could have risen above their limitations had they received better, and more understanding assistance than we were able to give, and had we and they acted in a way that told a different story to the Vietnamese and American people. This account attempts to let them speak for themselves.

It has long been my ambition to tell this story. I started on it over twenty-five years ago but was discouraged by a publisher's advice that few would be interested in yet another book about Vietnam, no matter how different the story. What has happened in Iraq and Afghanistan and the relevance of what we should have learned from Vietnam impels me to finish what I began a quarter-century ago. This account is as true and accurate as I could make it from my memory and the record, and it is wholly mine; I take full responsibility for any sins of commission or omission in these pages.

Part 1
THE BIRTH OF
SOUTH VIETNAM
1954–56

Prologue

The United States parachuted OSS agents into northern Vietnam in 1945, before the end of World War II in Asia. The agents supported the Vietnamese resistance against the Japanese, mainly Ho Chi Minh's nationalist front movement, the Vietnamese Independence League (Vietminh). However, substantial U.S. engagement did not begin until later.

In 1949, China fell to the communists. The Cold War was at its peak in Europe, with the Berlin Airlift under way and the United States desperately trying to weld Western Europe into a common defense pact. Of critical concern were France and Italy, which had strong domestic communist parties. The French had returned to Indochina in 1945 to reassert colonial control and were now caught in a deepening military struggle involving ever-growing numbers of troops against the communist-controlled Vietminh. President Truman came under increasing pressure to provide military assistance in Indochina, to shore up the French against the communists in Europe. Moreover, the fall of China in 1949 made it appear likely that all of Southeast Asia might go the same way, beginning with the "Associated States" of Indochina: Vietnam, Cambodia, and Laos (so designated by the French in 1950). Thus, in March 1950, President Truman approved an initial fifteen-million-dollar military aid program for Indochina and Thailand, most of the aid going directly to the French armed forces in Indochina. Our involvement had taken a significant step.

By early 1954, after eight years of struggle, Indochina's future hung in the balance. France's war against the Vietminh was not going well. A plan to prevent a Vietminh takeover of Laos by creating a redoubt in the northern Vietnam valley of Dien Bien Phu, blocking the main route of invasion and luring Vietminh forces into a decisive confrontation with superior French firepower, proved a dismal failure.

By the spring of 1954, it appeared the French might lose the battle for Dien Bien Phu, and with it support for the war. Officials within the Eisenhower administration became frantic. The question at hand was: Should the United States directly intercede militarily to prevent a French defeat? President Eisenhower strongly resisted the idea of directly intervening with U.S. troops or bombers.

Even before disaster loomed at Dien Bien Phu, French public pressure had grown for an end to the war, with the result that France had welcomed an international conference on Indochina to seek a negotiated end to the conflict. The Geneva Conference opened on April 26, 1954; France, the United Kingdom, the Soviet Union, China, and the United States were the great-power participants, attending with the Vietminh and the state of Vietnam (ruled by Bao Dai), as well as the states of Laos and Cambodia. On May 7, eleven days later, Dien Bien

Phu fell to the Vietminh forces of Gen. Vo Nguyen Giap, severely undercutting any prospect of concessions for the French.

On May 4 the Saigon newspaper *Le Journal d'Extreme Orient* published a declaration by Maurice Dejean, the French commissioner general, that there was no "intention of" partitioning Vietnam, but in June the idea of dividing Vietnam into two territories became the centerpiece of secret discussions between the French and the Vietminh.[1] Although the bulk of regular Vietminh forces were in the North, the combined French and Vietnamese forces controlled almost as much territory in the North as in the South. Moreover, a substantial part of the population in the North was Catholic, had strongly resisted the Vietminh, and was certain to be a target for retaliation should the communists rule that region.

Noncommunist Vietnamese were left in the dark until the deal was cut. As the conference droned into June a framework of understanding was reached: Vietnam would be separated at the seventeenth parallel, French forces and their Vietnamese allies would evacuate the North to regroup in the South, and Vietminh forces would evacuate from the South to the North—all this to be accomplished by May 1955. An International Control Commission composed of Poles, Indians, and Canadians was to supervise the cease-fire agreement in the Associated States of Indochina. An unsigned protocol at Geneva proposed national elections covering all of Vietnam within two years.

The Eisenhower administration internally viewed Geneva as a disaster.[2] Particularly exasperating was the French failure to train more Vietnamese soldiers or give the noncommunist Vietnamese real independence in the past. Bao Dai reigned as emperor from the Riviera; his regime, a member of the French Union, had no truly independent status. The French still issued Vietnam's currency, ran its national bank, operated the public utilities, and effectively controlled the national army and police, whose only source of gasoline for its vehicles and airplanes, or other logistical support, was the French Expeditionary Corps.

The noncommunist Vietnamese lapsed into severe shock, depression, and anger at the news. Given the political vacuum in the South, a communist takeover of all of Vietnam within two years, or even less, seemed unavoidable. Beyond vague ideas of somehow rallying the Vietnamese in the South and contingency plans for leaving agents behind to conduct guerrilla warfare against the Vietminh, the United States had little idea how to prevent a complete communist takeover.

As a desperate measure, Col. Edward G. Lansdale, then assigned to the Central Intelligence Agency (CIA), had been asked back in January 1954, when the odds against the French were already lengthening, to try to work in Vietnam the same "magic" he had in the Philippines. There, as an advisor, he had helped the Filipinos defeat the communist Hukbalahaps and elect Ramon Magsaysay as president in a clean election. The decision to send him was a joint one by Secretary of State John Foster Dulles, his brother Allen Dulles, director of the CIA, and the Defense Department. Gen. John "Iron Mike" O'Daniel, head of the American Military Advisory Group (MAAG) in Saigon, and Ambassador Donald Heath also asked for him.

When Secretary Dulles informed him that President Eisenhower wanted him to go, Lansdale said he would but only to help the Vietnamese, not the French. That was the idea, he was told. This became an important basis for his mission, which was to influence for a time the course of history. It also changed the course of my life and those of others. Lansdale did not receive orders to go to Vietnam until the end of May, when the outcome of Geneva was clear; those orders ended with an unusual personal note, "God bless you," from Allen Dulles.[3] On

June 1, 1954, Lansdale arrived in Saigon, where he assembled a team, known as the Saigon Military Mission. It had two daunting purposes: prevent the North Vietnamese from taking over the South and prepare stay-behind resistance, not only in the North but in the South as well, in case it too fell.[4]

Emperor Bao Dai represented the thirteenth generation of the Nguyen dynasty, founded when Gia Long united the country in 1802. The French leadership had so committed to the self-justifying myth that Vietnam had never been a nation that Foreign Minister Bidault solemnly told Secretary Dulles in April 1954, "Independence was not a key to courage. Vietnam was a country, which, for 1,500 years, has never had any sovereignty."[5] And now, with teeth-gnashing reluctance, the French high commissioner refused until September to move out of Norodom Palace to make room for its new occupant, Prime Minister Ngo Dinh Diem, who arrived in July.

Appointed by Bao Dai as a last hope for South Vietnam, Diem was viewed by many American officials as a cipher with little chance of generating popular support.[6] Typical of American opinion were the views of the American embassy in Paris that Diem was "a Yogi-like mystic. . . . [H]e appears too unworldly and unsophisticated to be able to cope with the grave problems and unscrupulous people he will find in Saigon."[7] Diem found himself something of a prisoner in Gia Long Palace, where he was first installed. His palace guard was provided by the National Police, who were in turn controlled by the Binh Xuyen, a gangster sect (about which more later).

The French liked to describe South Vietnam after Geneva as a *panier de crabes* (basket of crabs). French interests competed with those of the Americans. The Vietnamese were divided between Prime Minister Diem, Emperor Bao Dai, the religious sects of the Cao Dai and Hoa Hao, the Binh Xuyen, and the Vietnamese army, as well as displaced political parties and refugees from the North. The French policy of divide-and-rule had left the various Vietnamese groups with little trust in each other. The question on American minds now was how any coherent government or country could be wrung out of this mess.

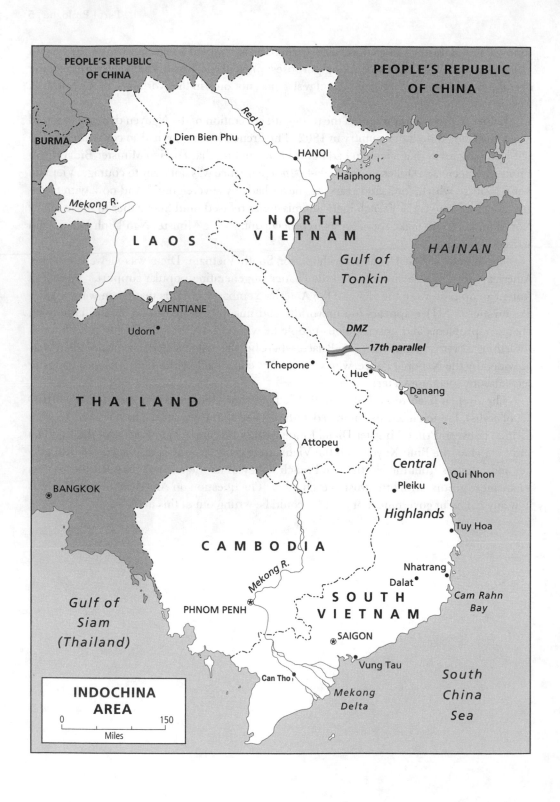

PEOPLE'S REPUBLIC
OF CHINA

BURMA

Dien Bien Phu

HANOI

Haiphong

PEOPLE'S REPUBLIC
OF CHINA

Red R.

Mekong R.

L A O S

N O R T H
V I E T N A M

*Gulf of
Tonkin*

HAINAN

VIENTIANE

Udorn

T H A I L A N D

DMZ
17th parallel

Tchepone

Hue

Danang

Attopeu

Central

Pleiku

Qui Nhon

BANGKOK

Highlands

Tuy Hoa

C A M B O D I A

Mekong R.

Nhatrang

Dalat

*Cam Rahn
Bay*

PHNOM PENH

S O U T H
V I E T N A M

*Gulf of
Siam
(Thailand)*

SAIGON

Can Tho

Vung Tau

*Mekong
Delta*

*South
China
Sea*

**INDOCHINA
AREA**

0   150
Miles

Chapter 1

Saigon—*Panier de Crabes*

Our plane for Saigon, a U.S. Air Force C-47 with ten people on board, took off around eight in the morning from Clark Air Force Base in the Philippines. It was August 8, 1954; I was twenty-four years old. I had awakened early that morning—maybe because of my sense of anticipation, of excitement generated by my sudden reassignment to Indochina. I showered, dressed in fresh khakis, and went outside the barracks. The air was fragrant and smelled different than the tropics I remembered from my wartime youth in Florida. Dawn began to break with violent streaks of purple and violet behind a volcanic cone that rose abruptly above the plain beyond the flight line, coloring the tips of white puffy clouds. The light gradually grew into the most magnificent sunrise I had ever seen. I was to see others like it during the many rainy seasons I spent in Indochina, but none as memorable.

A CIRCUITOUS PATH

As the six-hour flight to Saigon wore on, I reflected on the path that had brought me, a U.S. Army second lieutenant detailed to the Central Intelligence Agency, to this place and time. It was certainly not preordained, nor what my parents had expected for me.

My childhood was spent in Virginia on a five-hundred-acre farm called Gravel Hill, about thirty miles from Appomattox, where the surrender of Lee's army had effectively ended the Civil War. When I was barely two, my father—a successful partner in a New York City brokerage firm—had lost everything in the 1929 stock market crash. He had been faced with a choice of either going back to his native Middletown, Ohio, with his tail between his legs and using family connections to find a job with Armco Steel or moving to my mother's ancestral home in rural, Southside, Virginia, where he would be poor but independent. He chose the latter. We arrived in the summer of 1931 in a secondhand Essex. My grandmother and step-grandfather lived in the antebellum Greek Revival mansion that dominated Gravel Hill; we moved into a two-story, pre–Civil War former overseer's log cabin, down behind the barn.

My father put whitewashed wood siding over the logs for additional insulation, added abbreviated porticos over two doors in front to dress the cabin up and an enclosed back porch to serve as a kitchen, as well as a tin roof, but there was no electricity or running water. We used a hand-drawn well on one side and a privy out back. My parents' upstairs bedroom was decorated incongruously with art nouveau furniture (from the fancy Long Island apartment we had lost) and rugs on the floor. Above the bed on the wall of logs hung an expressionistic mural of New York City painted by my father. But as a child, I was conscious of no particular hardship. Except for the paintings and bedroom furniture, little set us apart from other families in that era and place.

Robbie Foster was black and my best friend. His family were tenants on Gravel Hill, living nearby in another old cabin more run down than ours. He and his brothers were my only companions until I was six. We went barefoot in the summer and spent endless days playing with a homemade car that Robbie's older brother, Matthew, put together using planks for a chassis and sawed-off logs with tacked-on pieces of tire for wheels. An antebellum distillery pond on one of the two streams on the place, blasted out of rock, was our swimming hole. Growing up with only black friends was formative in ways I would not recognize until much later, when empathy for people vastly different in appearance, culture, and language seemed to come naturally. Later, after Robbie's family moved, I went by school bus to an all-white public grammar school in Charlotte Court House. The separation of the races seemed very strange at first. I didn't share the active prejudice of many of my new white friends. But I accepted segregation; I wouldn't begin to question it actively until I got to college. For the time being it just seemed to be the way things were, although I was certainly influenced by the enlightened outlook of my parents.

The Charlotte County I knew as a child was in the depths of the Great Depression. Like many areas in the South, it had yet to recover psychologically or economically from the Civil War. The ethos of our corner of the world was expressed in ways that northerners found hard to understand. My grandmother, born in 1875, was unreconstructed. She never referred to Abraham Lincoln as "President Lincoln," only with asperity as "Mr. Lincoln." She had five uncles who had fought for the Confederacy, one dying during the siege of Richmond, another marching out with the Cadet Corps of the Virginia Military Institute to the battle of New Market. The Fourth of July was observed as a national holiday in Southside Virginia, but not visibly, with parades or fireworks. Because my father was from Ohio and favored the Union, we were the only family in Charlotte County who made a big thing out of it. When I was almost five, my father took a photograph of Robbie Foster and me on the Fourth, wearing cocked paper hats and waving American flags. He got it published in the *Richmond Times Dispatch* as a message. Only later would I become aware of its import.

As a child, I was fascinated by Kipling's tales of India, the G. A. Henty series of historical novels, and by the comic strip *Terry and the Pirates.* Through an uncle by marriage who handled foreign sales for the American Tobacco Company in Richmond, I began collecting stamps from all over the world. Dreaming about adventures in faraway, mysterious places, never thinking I might actually ever get there, I developed a vivid imagination in a family atmosphere of personal independence, egalitarianism, and patriotism. There was also a rejection of arbitrary authority, a skepticism that my father combined with political cynicism, a hangover from his disillusionment at the First World War's aftermath. I absorbed his patriotism, egalitarianism, and some of his rebelliousness, without the cynicism.

December 7, 1941, sticks in my mind as it does for most of my generation. My father found me that Sunday in our front yard playing after lunch with our English setter, Pete. It was a sunny and unusually warm day for December. He and mother had been listening to the radio. "The Japs just bombed Pearl Harbor," he said excitedly. "I'm going to volunteer." Patriotism had clearly taken over. Soon he was off for officer training in the Army Air Corps, where he was commissioned a captain. Turned down for pilot training because of his age, he took charge of a basic training squadron for Air Corps cadets at Miami Beach. Moving there in the fall of 1942 was a sea change from rural Charlotte County.

We returned to Virginia before the war ended, when more than enough pilots had been trained. The county schools lagged, so my parents scraped together the money to send me on a partial scholarship to Woodberry Forest, a private school in Orange, Virginia, where I played football, got decent grades, and made lifelong friends. My time at Woodberry got me into Yale, where two of my father's brothers had gone. The Yale I entered in 1947, however, was no longer the largely "preppy" university of the prewar years. Most students in the upper classes were World War II veterans, considerably older than the others, many on the GI Bill. My 1951 class was still about 20 percent veterans.

The summer of my senior year, 1950, when I was working as a laborer building a pumping station in Mississippi for Tennessee Gas Transmission, the North Koreans invaded South Korea. The war became a call to arms for my Yale class. More than four hundred went into the various services after graduation. Some saw combat; one, Peter Braestrup, later a *Time* correspondent and the *Washington Post's* Saigon bureau chief, became a Marine and was wounded. A few died there. The Cold War was very much with us. A poll taken of my class for our yearbook as we were about to graduate found that 87 percent thought we would be at war with the Soviet Union within five years.[1]

During the spring of graduation, a CIA recruiter challenged me with the question, "Would you be willing to jump behind enemy lines?" I rose to the bait; this was an exciting way to serve. But my parents talked me into studying law at the University of Virginia, on a deferment from the draft; I entered that fall. In the meantime Jack Downey, one of my closest friends and a fraternity brother, volunteered for the Agency and went for special paramilitary training. By the end of the year Jack was in Japan, where, as I could tell from his occasional, cryptic letters, he was directly involved in the conflict.

Law school bored me. At midyear I contacted the CIA: Did they still want me? They did, so I left school, much to the dismay of my parents. I had grown up in the ethos of World War II; now it was the Cold War. While waiting for my security clearance, I spent most of my time in the Library of Congress reading through a long list of books about communism. They gave me a grasp of its ideology and operations; my exposure to that pernicious, quasi-religious doctrine only increased my desire to get into the fight. But missing from the reading list was Mao Tse-tung and his peasant-based theories about communist revolutionary warfare in Asia. There was nothing about Ho Chi Minh either.

Finally, in March 1952, I was cleared and came "on board." After initial orientation and general training in intelligence operations, I was sent to "the Farm," the Agency's paramilitary training center set up on part of an old army camp near Williamsburg, Virginia. I thoroughly enjoyed the four-month course, which included Jump School and covered all aspects of guerrilla warfare and intelligence operations behind enemy lines, as the CIA's forerunner, the Office of Strategic Services, or OSS, had learned in supporting guerrillas in World War II. My roommate was Tony Poshepny, later to achieve notoriety as "Tony Po" working with the Hmong (Meo) in Laos in the 1960s and early 1970s, before we withdrew and that country collapsed. As an eighteen-year-old Marine Tony had fought on Iwo Jima, where he was wounded, had attended college on the GI Bill, and then had joined the Agency. We worked together on several tactical exercises, his combat experience making up for my lack of it; I was good at map reading, which he was not. On one exercise we managed to infiltrate "enemy" headquarters, manned by the training staff, and captured its head (whose improbable name was Bert Courage), much to his chagrin and our class's delight.

On graduation in October 1952, I felt ready for my upcoming assignment to a secret paramilitary base in West Germany, where Eastern European émigrés were being trained for reinfiltration as guerrilla assets to be activated when the shooting war started. War seemed imminent then, with the Soviet Union still threatening Berlin and actively supporting the Korean conflict. I would have preferred to join my classmate Jack Downey in the Far East, but there were no slots available.

Not long after I returned to Washington word came that the covert training base in West Germany had been "blown" (compromised). My assignment was canceled. Then in late November, the Agency learned that Jack Downey had been shot down and was presumed dead on a secret mission over the Manchurian part of Communist China.[2]

At the end of 1952, I was still without a definite assignment. Downey's fate affected me more deeply than I realized. What was I doing, twiddling my thumbs in Washington, when a close friend had died for his country? I could have remained in the Agency as a civilian, taking a nonparamilitary job and so been deferred from the draft indefinitely, but this was not what I had signed up for. I decided to enlist in the army to serve in the infantry, which was most compatible with my paramilitary training.[3]

Inducted at Camp Meade in Maryland in January 1953, I went through basic training during a very cold winter at Indiantown Gap, Pennsylvania. The training officers and drill sergeants were mainly Korean War veterans. Shortly afterward I reported to Fort Benning, Georgia, for Officers Candidate School. It was a shock from the first day. The army dictum was that the only way to make officers was to break them down first, then reassemble the parts. Harassment by supervisory "tactical officers" was constant. Initially I rebelled against its arbitrariness—a surplus of "chicken shit" inspections and what I took to be senseless bullying. Eventually I found my balance and graduated with a sense of satisfaction as well as pride. I was commissioned in early November and went on to finish Jump School, also at Fort Benning. This added a not-to-be-sneezed-at $110 a month to my paycheck.

After Jump School graduation I was assigned to an administrative pool at the Pentagon, on detail to the Agency, which had no place to send me. When an opening (though no definite assignment) in Korea appeared in late January, I took it because it would take me to Asia. Maybe the Chinese or the North Koreans would violate the truce, or something might develop in Indochina, where I really wanted to go, because that's where the action seemed to be. I made sure the Agency's Indochina desk was aware that I was interested and knew French (how little, I did not say).

Arriving in Korea in early April 1954, I worked first with a group of North Korean refugees who had been writing, printing, and distributing propaganda by balloon flights over North Korea. My job was to terminate the Korean employees, disassemble the printing plant, and ship it back to America—a sad job not made any easier by Seoul's war-ruined state, where no jobs were available for the Koreans I was about to discharge. The sight sticks vividly in my mind of a Korean on a bicycle hanging frantically to the rear of a moving rice truck, sticking a hollowed-out bamboo pole into one of the sacks and draining the contents into a container on the handlebars. South Korea looked like a basket case, without a future, and I was making it worse.

The deteriorating situation in French Indochina, gleaned daily from the Armed Forces newspaper, the *Stars and Stripes,* did nothing to cheer me up. As the French plight at Dien Bien Phu worsened and the United States did not intervene, my hopes for getting there evaporated. With Dien Bien Phu's fall, the cessation of combat, and the Geneva Conference, I gave up, resigned to remaining in Korea.

Then in late July, the station chief, John Hart, waved a recently received cable at me. "You're being reassigned to Saigon on a priority basis," he said. I couldn't contain my excitement. Hart took it in stride and wished me well. Shortly thereafter I received formal military orders assigning me on temporary duty to the American Military Assistance Advisory Group (MAAG) in Saigon. Flights were arranged from Seoul to Tokyo and from there to Clark Field in the Philippines.

My recollections faded as the flight continued. I wondered instead about the immediate future. What would I be facing? Would I measure up? What if I had to work in my less-than-fluent French right off the bat? I seemed the most junior officer on the plane. Going into the unknown I felt alone, inexperienced, and vulnerable.

SAIGON

A shout above the din of the engines broke into my anxious musing. One of the passengers pointed to a porthole. Peering through the scratched glass, I made out the sweep of green plain beyond a hilly coast. As we began to pass over land, the air got bumpy. We were following the winding course of a river, which faded from view toward the northwest. Sooner than expected, as we turned on the approach to Saigon's airport, Tan Son Nhut, I caught my first glimpse of the tall trees and wide avenues of the city. The plane rolled to a stop in front of a squat, yellowish, stucco terminal. We emerged blinking into the blazing heat of the early afternoon and were ushered into the terminal, where a French officer, accompanied by a short, slight, white-uniformed Asian whom I assumed was Vietnamese, looked at our orders perfunctorily and waved us through. A major from the MAAG met us. There were no military quarters available, he said; we would have to stay at a hotel, the Majestic, for the time being.

I felt particularly lost as he waved me into the back of his jeep with my duffle bag. We entered the city proper on Boulevard Charles de Gaulle. The traffic swelled with the greatest variety of vehicles I had ever seen—bicycles; mopeds; pedicabs called "cyclos," with passengers seated in front; motorized pedicabs with passengers also in front; scooters; scooters pulling two-wheeled covered platforms for passengers or flatbeds carrying bananas, rice, or other goods; small French taxicabs; larger French cars, Citroens and Peugeots, carrying mainly French civilians and military; and military jeeps and trucks carrying Vietnamese and French troops, including Senegalese, Algerians, and Moroccans, each with distinctive head coverings, as well as Foreign Legionnaires with their white kepis. Only the military vehicles seemed familiar. "American aid," said the major. It was about 2:30 in the afternoon, and the streets were jammed. I was about to ask the cause when the major said that it was near the end of the siesta hour, people were going back to work—an introduction to an unfamiliar way of life.

The white and yellow stucco bungalows and two- and three-story houses with tile roofs along the main street into town were reminiscent of the Spanish colonial style so common in south Florida. With the exception of the coconut palms and bougainvillea vines draped over walls and facades, the trees and shrubbery were unfamiliar. Even stranger were the smells of ripe and rotten tropical fruit, coconut oil, and the pungent scent of Vietnamese fish sauce, *nuoc mam*. As we turned onto Rue Catinat in the direction of the Saigon River, I was struck by the sight of a sidewalk cafe in front of what was labeled the Hotel Continental. The cafe was completely enclosed from the sidewalk by a screen of closely spaced steel bars to keep Vietminh grenades out—a terrorism remnant of the guerrilla war which I presumed had stopped.

Finally, dodging more cyclos on the way, we reached our destination, the Hotel Majestic, by the Saigon River waterfront. As we climbed out of the jeep our escort warned us to be careful. The war was still on; the day before, five French outposts had fallen south of Saigon to Vietminh attack.[4] The cease-fire in the South would not go into effect officially until 8:00 AM Saigon time on August 11, two and half days from now. Nobody knew for sure, he said, if the Vietminh would honor it.

The Majestic was a five-story building with a pale yellow stucco façade. One entered an open lobby with ceiling fans. Excruciatingly slow iron-cage elevators took you up to musty rooms without air conditioning. At night, lizards called "geckos" clustered around the light wells of the lobby and the dining room on the top floor to catch insects, while ceiling fans circulated the humid air with a gentle *whop-whop*. My roommate, army first lieutenant Edward Williams, was about my height but slim, with a reserved and impassive air. We shared a tiny room with two mosquito net–enshrouded single beds, an overhead fan, two wooden chairs, a small table, a wooden armoire, and a bathroom with a sink and a bathtub with an attached telephone-type shower. It was the rainy season, so the bed sheets were perpetually damp, and the room had a moldy smell that I would forever associate with that time of year in Vietnam.

The climate took some getting used to. Midday was blazing hot. As the typical afternoon wore on, huge thunderheads accumulated, giving some relief from the sun but adding to the atmosphere's stickiness. Near or after sundown, intense downpours, usually finishing in the evening, lowered the temperature and left the streets glistening. Early mornings were the best time, a breath of fresh coolness before the fumes from vehicles engulfed the streets and the heat began to climb.

After settling into our room, Williams and I went up to the bar on the top floor to have a beer. I knew nothing of his background, so I gave him the same cover story I was supplied before leaving Korea: I had been transferred to MAAG in Saigon because of my proficiency in French and the need for any additional American military to arrive in Saigon before August 11, when a cap on personnel imposed by the Geneva cease-fire agreements supposedly went into full effect. I was to say nothing more. After hearing my recitation, he laughed.

Williams came from Washington, where he had seen my name on orders. We were members of a covert group called the Saigon Military Mission, entirely separate from the regular CIA station. I questioned him intensely about what we might be doing, but he said he had no better idea than I. It would be up to our new boss, Colonel Lansdale. All he knew about Lansdale was thirdhand. He was reported to be very unorthodox. Some of the intelligence types thought he was overrated and didn't like him. He had been very successful in the Philippines, but no one seemed to know exactly why or how. It was said he had high-level backing within the Agency and even from the State Department and the Pentagon.

For the next several days we hung around the hotel. Through Williams I identified eight others who had been sent as part of the special mission under Lansdale. We gradually became acquainted, being careful to talk only at the bar or out on the sidewalk, thinking the rooms were probably bugged. I did get permission to write my parents to let them know I was in Saigon, with the caveat that this was not to be revealed to anyone outside my immediate family.

Our group's contact with the rest of Saigon at this point was very limited. We had no passports. Military orders in English were our only identification in a strange city where almost no one spoke that language. I tried out my spoken French on the waiters at the hotel and was discouraged by how rudimentary it was, but my reading was better. From copies of *Le Journal d'Extrême Orient,* the Saigon French language newspaper, I began to get a limited feel for what was going on. There was a nearby bookstore on Rue Catinat where it was possible to buy the *Journal* and a local weekly magazine, *Indochine Sud-Est Asiatique,* with interesting cultural articles on Vietnam. The news and articles focused mainly on the French. Its July 1954 issue carried only a small paragraph announcing Diem's accession to the office of prime minister, with a snapshot of his face, under the "*Actualité Indochinois*" (Indochina News) section.

My twenty-fifth birthday on August 10 passed with a quiet celebration. Somebody had slipped the word to one of the waiters, who presented me with a surprise mocha cake—the de facto Franco-Vietnamese national dessert. I was obliged to consume it at practically every Vietnamese formal luncheon or dinner thereafter; it seemed to be the only recipe for cake the French ever brought to Indochina. To reassure my parents and retain some tangible link with home, I wrote them that American girls at the embassy had baked me a birthday cake: "It was a lousy cake but a nice gesture."

COLONEL LANSDALE

Reading about South Vietnam was helpful, but I was impatient to know some real Vietnamese. After a week Lansdale came to the hotel. Those who made up Lansdale's initial team crowded into one of the larger bedrooms, which had been searched for hidden microphones. He was forty-six years old, of medium height and build, and was dressed in khaki shorts, knee socks, and a short-sleeved uniform shirt with an air force officer's hat worn at a slightly rakish angle. I noticed crew-cut hair, a high forehead, penetrating eyes, a throat with a prominent, slightly swollen Adam's apple, and a brush mustache. He seemed very military yet accessible at the same time.

Born in 1908 in Dayton, Ohio, Edward Geary Lansdale was a regular air force colonel who had had a singular career, starting in World War II as an army intelligence (G-2) officer in the Pacific. His significant service began as the war ended, first in G-2 and then as public information officer in the American Military Command in the Philippines. In the process he had switched his commission to the air force, which he hoped would be less tradition bound than the army. Underneath a natural friendliness, which attracted Filipinos, lay a purposeful and dedicated approach to discovering what made the Philippines tick. He focused on the growing communist Hukbalahap rebellion. Unconventional, he would go into the countryside alone, post himself on likely "Huk" trails, meet guerrillas, give them cigarettes, and engage them in conversation. He learned firsthand their political motivation, their tactics, and why they were winning support in the backcountry Filipino villages, the *barrios*.[5]

Characteristically, Lansdale had run his Agency mission in the Philippines outside the normal American diplomatic, military, economic, and intelligence bureaucracy, with a small supporting staff of "operators" and a direct channel of communications to the top in Washington. He had enjoyed sympathetic support from strong American ambassadors, such as Myron Cowen and Adm. Raymond Spruance, who were not jealous of his influence and kept bureaucratic rivalries at bay. He sought to understand Filipino aspirations and motivations and to discern the complete range of political, psychological, military, and even economic and social actions that would be needed to defeat the Huks. His main weapons were imaginative but practical ideas about how to make democratic self-government work and how to create conditions that fostered the emergence of effective national leadership. He often generated these ideas in informal brainstorming sessions of Americans and Filipinos, civilian and military, in the living room of his house. These sessions became known as "Lansdale's coffee klatches," and he was known affectionately as "Uncle Ed."

During the height of the 1953 presidential campaign of Ramon Magsaysay, the former defense secretary, who had achieved great success against the Huks, Lansdale consumed a month touring Indochina as part of a small survey group headed by Lt. Gen. John W. "Iron Mike" O'Daniel. Lansdale spent most of his time in Vietnam. He was fascinated by the complexity and difficulty of the situation facing the Vietnamese and the French. The only hope, he concluded, lay in giving the noncommunist Vietnamese real independence.

In 1954 he was told to get ready to go to Vietnam; Allen Dulles asked him to "find another Magsaysay." But Lansdale knew that Vietnam would be even more difficult and complicated than the Philippines. He spent hours reading everything available and talking to anyone with firsthand experience, but information was meager. He began distilling what had worked in the Philippines into basic principles that he thought could be applied in any country.[6]

Since arriving in Vietnam on June 1, Lansdale had spent his time talking to as many Vietnamese as he could, using embassy and U.S. Information Service (USIS) personnel as interpreters. When Diem arrived in late June, Lansdale was prepared. He drafted a political plan for Diem and proposed it at their first meeting, using George Hellyer, the chief of the local USIS, as an interpreter. Lansdale found Diem overwhelmed by the tasks confronting him and with little experience in running a national government or in open political leadership. But he also saw an honest patriot, obviously devoted and not afraid. Lansdale was determined to help Diem try to build on his natural strengths, but he was not at all sure Diem would make it.[7]

We in his Saigon group were totally unaware of all this at our first meeting. After shaking hands with each of us, Lansdale spoke quietly in his throaty voice. He apologized for the delay; operational problems had kept him completely occupied. (Later I learned that in fact he had been puzzled by what to do with us. We all had paramilitary or counterintelligence backgrounds, which didn't fit into what he saw as his most urgent needs—for political action, military civic action, and psychological warfare support.)[8] He couldn't tell us what we would be doing yet. He had no office and was operating out of a small house. Soon he would interview us individually to begin making assignments. In the meantime, arrangements had been made through MAAG to get us local identity cards, so we could move around more freely. Our job was to save South Vietnam, but he couldn't tell us exactly how we were going to do that. The present situation was very confused. We had to be patient. With these cryptic statements he gave us a half-smile and was gone. I didn't know what to make of him or our situation, and neither did anyone else. I had expected a clear-cut mission; it was a disappointing start. "Save South Vietnam"—how in the world were we going to do that?"

I struck up a friendship with Marine captain Arthur "Nick" Arundel, part of our group. Nick had graduated the same year as I but from Harvard, had majored in journalism, gone through Marine Corps officers training at Quantico, and then through CIA paramilitary training. During the Korean War he had been involved in supporting guerrilla raids into North Korea from coastal islands. Nick was sandy haired, intense, and fairly short. His size helped him to blend in with the Vietnamese; as for me, towering over them at about six foot two, I felt myself sticking out like a sore thumb.

Arundel and I began to explore the city. Its population swollen to about two million by refugees fleeing eight years of war in the countryside, Saigon was a sprawling metropolis composed of two cities, Saigon and Cholon, located mainly along the north bank of the Saigon River. Cholon was populated extensively by overseas Chinese, whose presence was advertised by the Chinese characters over their shops and restaurants and by the way their women dressed, most often in plain, white blouses over loose, black pajamalike slacks, and without the Vietnamese conical hat.

Often referred to as the "Paris of the East," Saigon had broad avenues lined with tall, straight mahogany and gnarled tamarind trees, interspersed with flame trees that flowered red in the dry season. There was a languorous air about the place; no one seemed to be in a hurry to do anything. Underneath the sophisticated French veneer was the real Vietnam, on the side streets—the vendors with their stalls, pushcarts, and unintelligible cries; Vietnamese women shopping in their graceful gowns, *ao dai*s, over pantaloons and their straw hats; the Chinese; villagers in black pajamas with headcloths instead of hats; dark-skinned Cambodians with checkered headcloths—an astonishing and, to us, mysterious variety of human beings. Particularly eye-catching in the early morning were the young girls riding bicycles to school, glossy black hair flowing down the backs of their fluttering, gossamer-white *ao dai*s, one girl pedaling and another gracefully balanced sidesaddle on the rear fender. On first contact, the Vietnamese were pleasant and courteous but remote and evasive. How were we ever going to understand them?

Emblematic of our confusion during the first weeks in Saigon were the street demonstrations along Rue Catinat. The speeches and banners were all in Vietnamese; we wondered what it was about. The demonstrations, we soon learned, were against the Geneva Accords, particularly against dividing the country in two, but we still had no idea if they were led by nationalists unwilling to lose the North or communist sympathizers who felt the same about the South. There we were, working for the Agency, and we couldn't decipher a street demonstration.

As Nick and I began to circulate more, we met other Americans in the embassy, the Special Technical and Economic Mission (STEM), and MAAG. We also ran into French officers at the bars, restaurants, and the Cercle Sportif (the French version of an in-town country club), some of whom were willing to talk about their experiences. The French were exceedingly bitter about their leaders, especially over Dien Bien Phu. I, and others, had to restrain a French major I met in a bar from physically attacking Brig. Gen. Christian de Castries, the commander at Dien Bien Phu, who walked into the same bar. The major, who had been captured at the battle and recently repatriated, claimed de Castries had ordered air drops of champagne and strawberries into the besieged fort instead of ammunition and medical supplies. The French were also bitter at the Americans, for not coming to their aid directly, and at the Vietnamese they commanded, for being "cowardly."[9]

The Americans were frustrated by the fact that their previous attempts to help the Vietnamese had been channeled almost exclusively through the French. The MAAG was accredited solely to the French and had no direct training or advisory relationship with the Vietnamese. A common American complaint was that the French never really gave the Vietnamese a chance to run their own show. Still, most Americans seemed to accept the French view that the Vietnamese were incapable of running a government and lacked the will to fight. Most of our economic assistance had gone into the North. Why should we help the South, some argued, when it too would soon be down the drain?

In fact, the collective American opinion in Saigon was that it would all be over within a few months: either the South would collapse in a struggle between noncommunist Vietnamese sects and factions, or the Vietminh, seeing their chance to take the whole country, would renew the war against a demoralized and much smaller French Expeditionary Corps. Many thought we should draw the line farther west, in Thailand. The only ones who seemed to express some hope were General O'Daniel and Lansdale. O'Daniel had taken a reduction in rank to serve in Vietnam, and was confident he could transform the Vietnamese into a capable fighting force, just as he had the South Koreans.

FIRST ASSIGNMENT

After about two weeks, word came we were to be interviewed by Lansdale—"the Colonel," as we referred to him. Nick Arundel was first, and he returned with a big smile. Lansdale had asked him about his experience in Korea and then told him he would soon go to Hanoi on a secret mission. In the meantime he was to work with the local Vietnamese newspapers and a journalist and "revolutionary" who had contacted Lansdale.

In the afternoon, I walked over to the single-story, four-room bungalow on Rue Miche that doubled as Lansdale's office and living quarters. The bungalow was set back from the street, its only entrance and exit off a narrow alley between the high walls of two adjacent houses. It seemed vulnerable to attack. Navy lieutenant Joe Redick—Lansdale's principal assistant and interpreter—ushered me in. Joe, a professor of French prior to joining the CIA, was very protective of Lansdale. Joe had a precise and fussy manner, and he was also an expert pistol shot, which I didn't know. He told me, implying that my presence was inconvenient, that I would have to wait; a Vietnamese group had suddenly appeared, demanding to see Lansdale. From outside Lansdale's office I could hear excited, high-pitched voices in French and Vietnamese. After a half-hour the door opened, and a group of grim-faced Vietnamese filed out of the house, accompanied by Lansdale, who briefly introduced me. Among them was Bui Diem, who would become a lifelong friend and eventually the Vietnamese ambassador to the United States.

After saying goodbye to the Vietnamese, Lansdale returned to the house with his characteristic lope, beckoning me to follow. As soon as we were face to face, I saluted and said I was reporting for duty. He smiled and waved me informally into an easy chair. It was the first and last time I ever gave him a formal salute. He read the questions on my mind and explained that the Vietnamese who had just left had requested arms to fight the Vietminh, and the French if necessary. In July the French had begun evacuating two mainly Catholic provinces in the North without warning the inhabitants. Local militias in these provinces had resisted the Vietminh tooth and nail during the war and were now being abandoned. Already refugees were reported to be streaming out, and there were unconfirmed reports of militia leaders and priests being murdered by the Vietminh. One Catholic militia unit had actually fired on the departing French.

While the refugees were mainly Catholic, the group who had just asked for help were mainly Buddhists and members of the Dai Viet, a nationalist political party from the North not inclined to support Diem. There were no differences among the noncommunist Vietnamese, however, on the need to protect the refugees from the communists. Lansdale had told them that he understood their frustration and anger, he would try to help protect the refugees, but arms—even if we could give them—were not the solution. Adding to the depressing picture were reports of massive desertion by Vietnamese troops in the North, abandoning their units to flee south or to fade away in the countryside. It was chaos. What Lansdale did not tell me was that some of his visitors were secretly helping him recruit covert agents to stay behind in northern Vietnam for intelligence and sabotage missions after the communists took over. (The operation later failed, when security was compromised and the agents were picked up by the North Vietnamese.)[10]

Circa 1934. Rural Southside, Virginia, cabin, where the author happily spent his early years. His mother is in a lawn chair to the right. (Author's collection)

Best friend, Robbie Foster, with author, celebrating the Fourth of July, 1934. Author's father got the picture published in the *Richmond Times Dispatch*. (Author's collection)

Graduation ceremony after army basic training at Indiantown Gap, Pennsylvania, June 1952.
Author in chow line with parents. (Author's collection)

Newly minted army
second lieutenant
(the author) with
paratrooper wings,
December 1952.
(Author's collection)

(Right to left) Ngo Dinh Diem, Wesley Fishel, Ed Lansdale, his aide Joe Redick, Col. Napoleon Valeriano (advising Diem's palace guards) in a secluded Cholon quarter, fall 1954. (Lansdale Collection, Hoover Institution)

October 1954. Gen. Nguyen Van Hinh (right), Emperor Bao Dai crony, Gen. Nguyen Van Xuan (center), and a Binh Xuyen warlord, Bay Vien (left), pressuring Diem (back to camera) to accept figurehead status so they can divide power. Diem refused. General Hinh's threatened coup failed. (Author's collection)

(Left to right) Nguyen Thai (of Diem's office), Lt. Nguyen Hung Vuong (army psywar), Bui Han (social services organizer), Do Trong Chu (interpreter), Capt. Nguyen Huu Man (General Hinh's press officer), and the author with President Ramon Magsaysay (center) at Malacañang Palace, Manila, October 1954. (Author's collection)

Nguyen Thai, Captain Man, and Col. Jose Banzon (left to right), with Navy lieutenant Larry Sharpe (standing) in author's Rue Paul Blanchy apartment in October 1954, finishing final report on the Philippine visit. (Author's collection)

Hanoi the morning before the communist takeover in October 1954. Note posters of Mao Tse-tung at top center, Soviet premier Georgy Malenkov to Mao's right, and Ho Chi Minh to Mao's left. (Author's collection, photo by Conein)

Vietminh soldier guarding part of the zone still under communist control near Soctrang in the Mekong Delta, November 1954. (Author's collection, photo by author)

Taking a slow boat to Long My with a mix of soldiers, civilians, and French press, November 1954. Author is at the bow, with Capt. Nick Arundel to his left. (Author's collection, photo by Colonel Banzon)

Passing a typical Vietnamese pirogue going to market on the canal leading to Long My. (Author's collection, photo by Colonel Banzon)

Traversing a wooden bridge built by the Vietnamese army to help villagers get to local market at Long My. (Author's collection, photo by Colonel Banzon)

Coming back from Long My in the heat. (Author's collection, photo by Colonel Banzon)

January 1955, Soctrang. Lt. Col. Hoang Van Duc (front right) leads a crowd to a briefing on the upcoming occupation of Camau (Operation Liberty). (Author's collection)

January 1955. The author makes a friend at the Bac Lieu District zoo, consisting of two pythons. Filipina nurse in background. (Author's collection)

February 1955. Operation Brotherhood (OB) clinic, open for patients in Camau with no running water or electricity. (Author's collection)

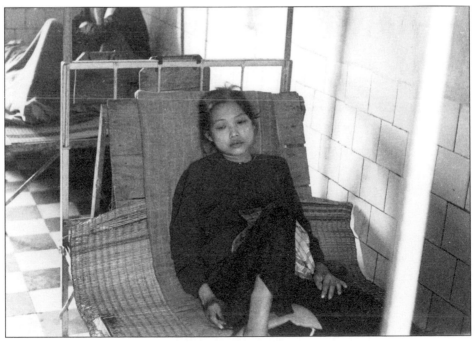

Pregnant Vietnamese woman in Camau who almost died. A caesarian by an OB surgeon, operating by flashlight, saved her and the baby. (Author's collection)

Vietminh monument inscribed "The Fatherland Records Its Thanks" in Camau Town. Operation Liberty commander, Lt. Col. Hoang Van Duc, allowed it to stand. (Author's collection, photo by author)

Vietnamese army troops about to disembark in April 1955 on the beach at Sa Huynh in central Vietnam, at the beginning of Operation Giai Phong. (Author's collection)

Vietnamese troops marching through a hamlet during Operation Giai Phong. Most villagers are welcoming, except one on far left in a Vietminh-type sun helmet, likely a stay-behind communist cadre. (Author's collection)

Col. Le Van Kim, commander of Operation Giai Phong, in his headquarters tent on the beach at Sa Huynh. (Author's collection)

Buying coconuts during Operation Giai Phong—the only sanitary source for drinking in the 110 degree heat. Fish, rice, bananas, mangos, and coconut milk made up the daily diet. (Author's collection)

April 1955. Destroyed Bong Son Bridge (left) replaced temporarily by a Vietnamese army footbridge. The need for prefabricated Bailey bridging caused Colonel Kim and the author to visit Saigon in the midst of the Binh Xuyen war. (Author's collection)

Qui Nhon's main street during Operation Giai Phong. To author's left is Lt. Col. Ton That Dinh (key player in the 1963 Diem coup), unknown officer, and Lt. Col. Vuong Van Dong, leader of the unsuccessful 1960 "paratroopers" coup against Diem. (Author's collection)

May 1955. President Diem initially in a jeep during his triumphal visit to Qui Nhon to celebrate the success of Operation Giai Phong. Colonel Kim is driving (Author's collection, photo by author)

President Diem, down from his jeep, gets closer to the crowd, whose enthusiasm generates a broad smile. Colonel Kim is behind to the left (Author's collection, photo by author)

1955. Saigon Military Mission's Dave Smith and the author at an Operation Brotherhood party in Saigon in 1955, wearing traditional Filipino barong tagalogs. Maj. Lou Conein in tie. (Author's collection)

Results of the referendum against Bao Dai in November 1955 posted on Saigon City Hall. The vote was so lopsided it appeared fixed, although the vast majority wanted Bao Dai deposed. (Author's collection)

Vietnamese Military Academy cadets marching in Saigon during National Day, October 26, 1956. The Tour d'Ivoire nightclub in the background was a favorite spot for French paratroopers in 1954. (Author's collection, photo by author)

Col. Oudone Sananikone, head of Lao Civic Action, with the author, at the Sananikone house, informal headquarters for Operation Booster Shot in 1958. (Author's collection)

1959. Lao farewell *(baci)* ceremony. Strings are tied around author's wrists as he is about to return to the United States. To upper right are Sananikone and Anne Miller, wife of the public affairs officer, Hank Miller. Stu Methven, the author's replacement, is on upper left in checkered shirt. (Author's collection)

Then he focused on me. What had I done in Korea? What had I studied at Yale, and what were my interests? I wanted to go north, to be involved in operations against the Vietminh. If the balloon went up and the North Vietnamese began to take over, he responded, we'd all be involved in paramilitary operations, but for now he had something more important for me—getting to know the "G-5" people in the Vietnamese army. G-5 was the Vietnamese army staff office responsible for psychological warfare ("psywar") and troop information. Under G-5 were a couple of specialized psywar companies that needed equipment. He wanted me to get close to the Vietnamese involved and see the situation at first hand. The Vietnamese army needed to learn how to win the trust and support of its people. This was part of G-5's mission. We should help with that.

My disappointment at not being needed up north was palpable. When I said I didn't know much about psychological warfare, he tossed me Paul Linebarger's book on the subject.[11] Did I know anything about Mao Tse-tung? I said not very much. He outlined Mao's ideas about mobilizing a rural peasant base for guerrilla warfare—the people were the water, and the guerrillas were the fish. For our side to win, Lansdale said, we had to win the support of the people, take the water away from the communist fish.[12] As for the Vietminh, their people-based strategy was very similar to Mao's.

Lansdale said he would call the Vietnamese army psywar people to set up a meeting when I felt ready. I was to make friends, see what they were doing, and figure out how to help. Confessing that my French was not really up to speed, I asked permission to take some lessons. He suggested I call Anita Lauve in the Political Section at our embassy. She was very savvy and could probably help. My education in the deceptively casual but focused Lansdale approach to nation building had begun, though I did not recognize it at the time.

Anita Lauve was in her late twenties, attractive, petite, and very pleasant. As we talked, she didn't seem to share the views about the Vietnamese of most other Americans. She provided the first favorable opinion I heard of Diem, as a Vietnamese nationalist of real stature. He had turned down the prime ministership twice before because the French refused to concede real independence. He had been arrested in 1946 by the Vietminh, who earlier had killed his elder brother, Ngo Dinh Khoi, in a purge of nationalist leaders. In a face-to-face confrontation with Ho Chi Minh in Hanoi, Ho offered him a leading position in the national government he was forming; Diem turned him down flat and fearlessly walked out. Ho let him go unharmed but dispatched a hit squad, which Diem anticipated by going into hiding in the mountains of central Vietnam.[13] Anita quoted Vietminh general Vo Nguyen Giap as saying, "There are only two real leaders in Vietnam. One is Ho Chi Minh. The other is Ngo Dinh Diem. There is no room in the country for both."[14] Anita set up French lessons for me with the daughter of a French admiral.

INITIAL CONTACTS

Three weeks after arriving, I was ready for my first contact with the Vietnamese army. Dressed in a French-style uniform of khaki shorts, knee socks, and an short-sleeved, open-neck shirt made by an Indian tailor, I drove cautiously toward Cholon, looking for Vietnamese army headquarters.

I was in a jeep just assigned to Arundel and me. The vehicle came from the Philippines, where it had been "requisitioned" from Manila car thieves by Lansdale's former deputy in the Philippines, Maj. C. T. R. "Bo" Bohannon, and painted blue to change its identity. The jeep had a canvas roof but no side curtains and was equipped with a towel to dry the seats after the late-afternoon rains. So far as I could determine it was the only jeep that particular shade of blue in Saigon and was therefore quite conspicuous, but it was my only means of transport, other than taxis or cyclos. The jeep was the first vehicle the Lansdale mission had acquired, besides a tiny 2-CV Citroën car (the "Deux Chevaux") that looked like a tin can on a baby carriage. Lansdale's arrival at a formal reception at Gia Long Palace in dress uniform in a cyclo had shocked MAAG into giving it to him, and now he drove it around town with abandon.

My search for headquarters took me down a tree-lined avenue, Boulevard Gallieni, which passed the main Saigon market and went straight to Cholon, over a mile away. Reading building numbers and dodging traffic, I came to a four-story, stucco, colonial-looking building flying the Vietnamese national flag, red stripes on a yellow background. Pulling up to an iron-grilled gate guarded by two Vietnamese soldiers, I showed my newly minted MAAG identity card, repeating several times the name of a Captain Giai, whom I was to see. After some hesitation the guards waved me through. Inside, I again showed my identity and was led up three flights of back stairs, down a corridor, and into a very tiny, crowded office.

I asked again for *"Capitaine Giai."* A stocky Vietnamese at a desk stood up and said in English that he was Giai. Suppressing a gasp of relief at not having to use my still elemental French, I introduced myself, explaining that Colonel Lansdale had sent me. I was somewhat in awe of Giai, who I knew had graduated from both the U.S. Army psywar school at Fort Bragg, North Carolina, and its French equivalent, but his smile and good English put me at ease. He explained that G-5 was also responsible for all Vietnamese army civic education of troops and public information and that it operated a medium- and shortwave radio station in Saigon. He introduced me to Lieutenant Minh, a younger and very slightly built officer, who was in charge of the radio station, and to Giai's assistant, Adjutant Pham Xuan An. (This was the first of many contacts over the years with An, who after 1975 would be revealed as a very high-level spy for North Vietnam and given the rank of lieutenant general, retired, in recognition of his services.)

Giai explained that special psywar companies, with loudspeakers and vehicles, carried out psychological warfare operations in the field. There were two such companies, one in Cholon and one still in the North. Each consisted of about a hundred officers and men who produced and distributed written propaganda, as well as educating and entertaining troops and villagers by putting on skits. Giai was awaiting orders as to what G-5's mission was to be now that the fighting had stopped. He introduced me to Capt. Hoai Duc, who spoke only French, and Lt. Nguyen Hung Vuong, whose English was excellent.[15] Duc was the commander of the psywar company located nearby, Giai explained, and asked if I would like to visit; I agreed. Their equipment was in very bad shape; Colonel Lansdale had said he would help.

Back in the courtyard, I told Duc and Vuong that I would follow their olive-green jeep. They looked at the unusual color of mine with some curiosity; all I could think to say was that it had been painted blue because Colonel Lansdale was an air force officer. In Cholon we turned into a walled compound with a few ramshackle shedlike buildings with tin roofs. Duc showed me around, apologizing for the poor conditions. Only the French had decent quarters for their units.

One shed was used as quarters for the men; the other held equipment and the disassembled pieces of a makeshift stage. The equipment consisted of dirty gasoline generators, three sets of unwieldy, French-made loudspeakers, and amplifier and microphone for each of the company's platoons. The loudspeakers could be mounted on either vehicles or boats, but they were heavy and not easy to set up. Parked in the yard were several quarter-ton trucks.

Since the war had stopped the company had been allotted only enough gas for Duc's jeep. He invited me to come back one evening to see the kind of skits they put on for the troops and the population. Vuong gave me his home telephone number in Saigon, where he lived with his parents; the compound had no telephone. He would like to meet me to explain more about the psywar company. I was still staying at the hotel, I replied, but would soon be moved to a house or an apartment, which would be convenient. I would let him know.

I drove back with mixed emotions. These officers seemed friendly, but the state of their equipment and the living conditions of their troops were deplorable, worse than anything I had seen in Korea. Back at the hotel, though, Arundel had good news. We were to room together in an apartment not far from the Hotel Majestic on Rue Paul Blanchy, which was parallel to and one street removed from Rue Catinat (the future Tu Do street, of bar-girl fame). Just as we were about to move word came that Lansdale's new house wouldn't be ready for another week; Lansdale and Redick would move into the Paul Blanchy apartment destined for us; I would move in temporarily as Lansdale's bodyguard—there were rumors the Vietminh wanted to assassinate Lansdale.

The apartment occupied the top floor of a three-story walk-up over a Vietnamese shoemaker's shop. It had a stairway with a roof on the side and a small landing and entrance door for each story. Underneath the stairway on the ground floor lived a Vietnamese couple, whose cooking sent pungent odors of *nuoc mam* wafting up the stairwell. Rooms in the apartment were arranged around an open courtyard, with the living and dining area fronting the street and two bedrooms to the rear, with window air-conditioning units. The living and dining area had ceiling fans. When I arrived, Lansdale and Redick had occupied the bedrooms. I was given a canvas cot with a mosquito net and a loaded Colt .45. When it rained I set up the cot in the living room. When the nights were clear, I slept out in the courtyard with the gun under my pillow, hoping no Vietminh would come slithering down over the roof tiles while I was asleep. Sleeping was difficult, but my bodyguard assignment gave me an invaluable chance to begin understanding what was happening and to meet other team members. There I met dashing U.S. Army major Lucien Conein.

Conein impressed me as a dangerous man, a kind of John Dillinger on our side. There was a hint of barely restrained violence about him that his alert, blue eyes under bushy eyebrows, as well as his abrupt, blustery manner and short temper, did nothing to belie. I watched in awe as he opened most of his encounters with Lansdale with "Godammit, Colonel," then saying, in effect, "You don't know shit from shinola about what is going on." This was usually followed by an equally blunt rejoinder from Lansdale about Conein failing to keep him adequately informed. Then they would get down to business.[16]

Conein could be rough as a cob or as gallant and gracious as the occasion demanded. One Sunday afternoon in 1955 he showed yet a different side, when a group of Vietnamese with children were invited over for lunch and a swim at a house we had acquired that had a pool. I was surprised to find "Lou" in the pool, lifting the children onto his shoulders and throwing them into the water, taking care never to frighten them. He was laughing, clearly enjoying it as much as they. I was struck by the direct way he related to them and by his evident pleasure. For his friends he was generous to a fault, but he had been full of ingenuity and contrariness from an early age. In high school his best friend's father had had a car that he would allow his son to drive, but no more than twenty miles a week as measured by the odometer. To evade this limitation Conein would reputedly drive around Kansas City backward.

Conein claimed to have been the first American to enter Hanoi at the end of World War II, when he parachuted in to secure the airport from the Japanese, accompanied by a single noncom. Now he wanted to be the last American to leave when the French pulled out of Hanoi in October 1954, as required by the cease-fire agreements. His contacts extended throughout the local French community and were particularly good with the Corsicans, some of whom he had met in Marseilles after the surrender of the French army in 1940. They ran many of the bars and night clubs in Saigon. He had also developed contacts in the French and Vietnamese armies and with émigré North Vietnamese noncommunist political groups, the Dai Viet and the Viet Nam Quoc Dan Dang (VNQDD). If his encounters with Lansdale often took the form of heated arguments, mainly on Conein's side, Lansdale was always careful to extract as much hard information as he could about French and Vietnamese attitudes, intentions, and actions. Conein's gruffness, offhand manner, and obvious knowledge of the local scene reinforced my feelings of inferiority as a very green second lieutenant. I envied Arundel's opportunity to work with him when they went north to Hanoi.

During that same week of guard duty at the apartment, I also met Col. Jose "Joe" Banzon of the Philippine army.[17] He was a slim, very military-looking officer who wore perpetually fresh, impeccably pressed khakis and who could fade into the background with the faculty of slipping in and out of a room without being noticed. We struck up an immediate friendship, as he took me under his wing, with Lansdale's blessing, to teach me the lessons of the Huk campaign as they might apply to Vietnam. Joe, in his unassuming way, had ingratiated himself with the Vietnamese army while not alienating the French. He knew the Vietnamese army well and had visited their units in combat. He knew about past pacification attempts, having been an observer with a combined French-Vietnamese operation in Central Vietnam called Operation Atlante. It had failed, he said, because the French insisted on visibly playing the leading role; Vietminh propaganda had accordingly pictured the Vietnamese army as nothing but French puppets. The Vietnamese could perform, but they lacked self-confidence, because the French had never given them any real responsibility.

EXPLORING SAIGON

After I had stood guard about a week, Lansdale and Redick moved out of the apartment into a larger house. Arundel and I moved in. Now we had the apartment and the blue jeep to ourselves. There was still not much to do, so I continued to explore Saigon. It was a wide-open city, but with a post-Geneva atmosphere of desperation, akin to the mood of a condemned felon about to consume his last meal. Old Asia hands likened it to Shanghai before the communist takeover in 1948.

Saigon's seamier side was centered on a large gambling casino, the Grande Monde, which closed at six in the morning; a rumored thousand opium dens; and two massive, four-story whorehouses for the French troops, each occupying an entire city block. Around the roulette wheels at the Grande Monde on any given night clustered wealthy Chinese, French rubber plantation owners with their mistresses, and some Vietnamese, betting their lives away as if it didn't matter. Numerous nightclubs and dance halls stayed open until four in the morning. One of the nightclubs, the Tour d'Ivoire, on the main boulevard between Saigon and Cholon, could be reached only by a winding staircase to a large top-floor ballroom, where a Filipino band played. The best Saigon nightclubs had Filipino bands in those days. "Le Tour," as we called it, was a favorite rallying place for French paratroopers, who took off their boots, sat on the floor drinking cognac, and banged their boot heels in time to the music or sang "para" songs when the band took a break. Taxi dancers, mainly Chinese but some Vietnamese and Lao as well, could be hired for an hour of dancing and conversation for about a dollar in black market piasters. If you stayed until closing time you didn't have to pay management to take them out. All this was an eye-opener, as it engaged my nighttime hours.

The city was in fact under the control of the Binh Xuyen, a sect of gangsters ruled by Le Van (Bay) Vien, a Vietnamese warlord who had gotten his start as a taxi driver in Saigon during the Japanese occupation but in time controlled public transportation and eventually gambling, prostitution, and opium smoking as well. He cemented his influence by inducing the French to train and pay for a five-thousand-man army that ensured wartime security of the about 120 kilometers by road between Saigon and the beach resort of Cap St. Jacques. In April 1954, Bay Vien acquired control of the National Police (his closest associate becoming the national chief of police), reportedly by bribing Emperor Bao Dai for about a million dollars. Rob McClintock, counselor in our Saigon embassy at the time, considered that transaction "comparable to the City of Chicago placing its police force in the hands of Al Capone during the latter's heyday."[18]

From the income of his gambling concession Bay Vien paid to the Vietnamese government a monthly fee, a portion of which went for Bao Dai's expenses. Across a Y-shaped iron bridge, on the south side of a branch of the Saigon River, the Arroyo Chinois, was his headquarters, where he entertained guests by feeding the tigers in his private zoo. Not having much else to do, Binh Xuyen troops cruised arrogantly around the city in mustard-colored uniforms and green berets, looking much smarter militarily than the Vietnamese army. How Diem could get control of this situation was not readily apparent.

Chapter 2
Making a Start

Lieutenant Vuong, from the psywar company, began visiting me at the apartment. He was from a well-to-do southern family and appeared too frail to be in the army. He was slight, with a concave chest, gaunt face, prominent nose, and high cheekbones, and his ears stuck out. He usually spoke so softly that I had to lean close to catch what he said. Vuong described the psywar company's situation as worse than I had been told during my visit. Two of the three portable generators didn't work, and the entire company was demoralized. Captain Duc was a good commander, but he had no resources. Duc was a former Vietminh who had rallied to the noncommunist side, leaving the Vietminh because the political commissar of his unit had insisted on using terror to intimidate villagers and had constantly pressured Duc to join the Lao Dong (Communist) Party. Now, if the South collapsed, Duc and his family would be the first to be killed by the Vietminh, as a deserter.

Vuong, for his part, as an intellectual and a university graduate, could probably immigrate to France, he said, even though he was not one of the many Vietnamese officers, civil servants, and political leaders who had dual citizenship; the emotional tug-of-war for the Vietnamese with dual citizenship would become clearer to me as time and South Vietnam's struggles went on. I began to understand that the lives of the people I was getting to know were very much at stake. From Vuong I started to get a feel for Vietnamese history and culture and for the history of the Vietminh. I was curious about Ho Chi Minh, who was reported to exert a magical appeal. Vuong took me through his history, which he knew well, telling me of his own disillusionment when it became clear that Ho was a communist first and a Vietnamese nationalist second.[1] I got the impression that Vuong regarded him as, in our terms, something akin to Benedict Arnold.

Exposure to Vuong taught me to be indirect in asking questions about nationalist leaders. If I asked Vuong directly about Diem, he usually gave an evasive answer. If I asked him instead what people thought of Diem, he would tell me that some thought Diem was too weak and that he had no popular support. Vuong, as I got to know him better, proved to be something of a pessimist, but his views about the hopelessness of the South's situation mirrored those of most of his countrymen.

"PETE" THE REVOLUTIONARY

Around this time Lansdale arranged for Arundel to meet Bui Anh Tuan, a revolutionary journalist from the North. Tuan had originally approached Lansdale for help to continue his struggle against the Vietminh. He was short and stocky with uneven buck teeth, hair combed straight back, and a wide smile. We called him "Pete," for security reasons. A member of the

VNQDD, the oldest and probably the largest Vietnamese nationalist party before World War II, he had spent time in French jails and narrowly escaped assassination by the Vietminh in 1946. Lansdale thought his writing skills could be used to fire up the otherwise discouraged noncommunist Vietnamese and that his knowledge of Vietminh propaganda could be used to fashion effective psychological warfare, to throw them off balance, maybe giving the South some breathing room.

Our first impression of Pete was that he probably felt more at home throwing bombs than wielding a pen. Nick would meet Pete late at night in our Paul Blanchy apartment. Pete's English was limited, so I sometimes sat in, as my knowledge of French was greater than Nick's. Pete would do a careful surveillance of our apartment each time before he arrived; his name was still on the Vietminh and French Sûreté blacklists. Adding to the conspiratorial air of our encounters, he always packed a gun, in the small of his back under his shirt.

One of Pete's first jobs was writing a psywar leaflet for distribution in the Delta areas not yet evacuated by the Vietminh. From intelligence sources we learned that the Vietminh planned to evacuate not just their soldiers but also young men, taking them from their parents by force if necessary, from the areas they controlled. We wanted to stimulate resistance against forcible removal and create internal difficulties, to keep the Vietminh occupied. One of our leaflets, attributed to the Vietminh Resistance Committee, reassured Vietminh evacuees suggestively that they would be kept safe below decks from "imperialist air and submarine attacks" and recommend that they take warm clothing. There was also a rumor campaign that evacuees would be sent to China as railway laborers. These leaflets, distributed by members of Captain Duc's psywar company, apparently generated popular complaints in the Vietminh areas against deportation.

Another Lansdale idea was for Pete to write inspiring opinion pieces for the local newspapers, crystallizing the noncommunist Vietnamese "cause" in order to rally the South Vietnamese and give them heart. Lansdale thought Tom Paine's *Common Sense,* which had done the same in the American Revolution, might be a good example; he procured a copy from Washington (a request that gave the bureaucrats pause, trying to figure what Lansdale was up to). Pete wrote and published several articles, but it was impossible to gauge their effect.

It became very apparent that the great, shared political cause, one that the Vietminh shrewdly appropriated for themselves, was true independence. On the extent to which the new government could assert its independence from the French would hang most of the hope for the survival of a free South Vietnam—a universal conviction among the Vietnamese whom I was getting to know.

From Pete I began to learn the tragic post–World War II history of communist betrayal within the Vietminh movement and of the assassination of Vietnam's noncommunist nationalist leadership. After the Japanese surrender in 1945, Ho Chi Minh had seized the initiative for independence from the other nationalist parties, forming a nationalist front called the Vietminh and proclaiming independence. According to Pete, when Ho Chi Minh was in Fontainebleau in 1946 to negotiate a truce the Sûreté in Vietnam made a secret deal with the communist leadership of the Vietminh. VNQDD, Dai Viet, and other nationalists under French surveillance were secretly fingered to Vietminh terror squads, who murdered them.[2] The Vietminh had already been assassinating nationalist leaders all over the country, such as Huyen Phu So, the founder of the Hoa Hao, a religious sect of over a million members in the southern Delta.

Pete himself had been late for a secret VNQDD meeting in Hanoi that was raided by Vietminh agents on a French tip. Those captured were sewn alive into weighted sacks and dumped into the Red River. General Giap had directed the assassinations. When Ho returned he disclaimed any knowledge of what had occurred, preserving his benevolent image. Ho had changed his name nine times, on each occasion after having betrayed other Vietnamese in order to eliminate them. Pete too was bitter that the French had never given the noncommunist Vietnamese true independence. He knew Diem was a nationalist, but he had little confidence that Diem could succeed. He hoped the Americans were different from the French, that we truly wanted the Vietnamese to be independent. All he had to go on was our word and the fact that we had voluntarily given the Philippines their independence.

Lansdale told him we would help him help his country but that he was never to consider he was working for us, only for his country. Any help we gave him was temporary until he was able to get a job with the new government or as a private journalist. The understanding was that if he thought something we wanted him to do would hurt his country, he was free to refuse. Lansdale had a way of drawing from the Vietnamese their political ideals and then getting them committed to living up to the beliefs they professed.

Lansdale would occasionally find a moment to illustrate some of his ideas to me in American terms. One day I told him that my college major was history. He reminded me of Tom Paine's willingness to fight for liberty everywhere: "Where liberty dwells not, there is my country."[3] Lafayette, he recalled, had come as a friend to support our revolution because he shared our ideals of independence and the rights of man; I remember his saying with a wry smile, "I wish the French remembered that about Lafayette." We should think of ourselves as friends and brothers of the Vietnamese. Our job was to help them win back their revolution from the communists. Once in frustration I asked what it was we were really trying to do. "At its heart, it's pretty simple," he said. "Our job is to find out what the Vietnamese people want and then help them get it."[4]

In Korea I had learned that Asians were not the inscrutable Orientals of American stereotype. Koreans were polite and indirect until they got to know you, and then they could be quite blunt. It was important to avoid making someone lose face, particularly in front of another Korean. Still, Koreans seemed to have little fear about voicing their political opinions; they were tough and violent with each other. The Vietnamese, I was beginning to understand, were more subtle and indirect and, by nature, much less confrontational. Nevertheless, I could feel very strong emotions running beneath their often expressionless faces. I began to watch their eyes, where emotions often showed, and to listen as much to what Vietnamese didn't say as to what they told me. They were difficult to pin down. I sensed they were captives not only of the formality and reticence of their Confucian culture but also of their insecure history, of past betrayals by one side or the other. Trust was something they gave readily only to their families and to a few close friends, most often from childhood or school. The idea of objective reality in the Western sense was often meaningless. It was one's perception of reality that mattered to them. They reached behind words to sense feelings and motivations on which to base trust; the Vietnamese could be sentimental to a fault. Their antenna were out to determine attitudes. Were the Americans they met truly interested in helping Vietnam, or in enhancing their own careers at Vietnamese expense? Over time I learned the extreme value the Vietnamese placed on personal friendship and the lengths to which they would go to protect a friend.[5]

While staying in contact with Vietnamese army psywar, I now began helping the first volunteer Filipino medical team of seven doctors and three nurses from Operation Brotherhood, which had arrived to work in the camps for refugees from the North. Operation Brotherhood was a volunteer medical assistance effort supported by the International Jaycees, led by the president of the Manila Jaycees, Oscar Arellano. The idea had been born during an earlier Filipino visit with Lansdale, sponsored by Magsaysay, who was now president of the Philippines, to see what that nation could do to help. Since none of the Filipinos spoke French, I was pressed into service as an interpreter and driver. The Filipinos were a lively, high-spirited group and, by contrast with the Vietnamese, self-confident. Their energy and devotion to the long lines of sick patients was remarkable. By their unselfish example they began inspiring Vietnamese doctors and nurses in private practice to donate their services to the refugees instead of charging the government for them. It was my first whiff of the "Magsaysay" spirit.[6]

Another Lansdale idea was the "Freedom Company," a nonprofit Filipino company under President Magsaysay's sponsorship dedicated "to preserving freedom." It was a vehicle for getting selected Filipinos involved in helping the Vietnamese. One of the first two arrivals in Saigon under Freedom Company auspices was Ponce Enriquez, the former police chief from the city of Zamboanga and an active member of the Filipino Veterans Association; he would help the Vietnamese organize a veterans association for the soldiers who were being demobilized. The other was Colonel Napoleon Valeriano, the head of Magsaysay's Presidential Guard Battalion, who helped set up and trained Diem's presidential guard. Later came Johnny Orendain, a legal expert who helped the South Vietnamese write their first constitution.

HANOI

What to do about the refugees streaming out of the provinces to Hanoi and the port of Haiphong had preoccupied Lansdale from the moment the French abruptly abandoned the Red River delta in the North. He was instrumental in persuading General O'Daniel to make a strong pitch to Washington, with Ambassador Heath's endorsement, to use Civil Air Transport (CAT) C-46 aircraft on contract, as well as the U.S. Seventh Fleet, to transport the refugees south. Diem was initially appalled at the prospect of so many refugees when he had no funds in the treasury, an army in disarray, and a practically nonfunctional government. Lansdale suggested he set up a special commission under the presidency to handle the refugees and offered, with General O'Daniel's agreement, the direct support and advisory assistance of MAAG. Now the refugees, arriving by CAT airlift and from our navy ships that began to arrive in Saigon and Cap St. Jacques, poured into temporary tent camps near Tan Son Nhut Airport.

I was anxious to see the North before it was taken over. In September Lansdale allowed me to make a brief visit to Hanoi. The CAT C-46 on which I was a passenger took off in the early morning. It was a five-hour flight. Our route north kept the coastal plain in sight for a time; then we were over a high plateau, on which few settlements or roads could be detected. Only a few Vietnamese dwelt there; most felt at home on the coastal plains, away from the mountains.

Farther north we increased our altitude to get over the Annamite chain, where rugged, jungle-covered mountains ascended close to ten thousand feet. We flew around enormous rainy-season thunderheads. The terrain below was inhospitable and looked uninhabitable. Then, abruptly, an edge of the coast appeared to the east, and the mountains dropped away to a wide plain, the Red River delta. The plane circled over Hanoi—a more compact city than Saigon, with a small lake at its center—then descended rapidly to land.

A horde of refugees, at least five hundred, waited at the airport waiting to board flights south. On the way I had befriended an attractive, French-speaking Vietnamese army nurse who had been flying the airlift for several weeks. I now asked her to accompany me in talking to one of the refugee groups squatting patiently on the tarmac in the sun. They were all villagers; no priests were around to speak for them. First, she explained to them that I was an American; then I asked what had made them give up their village. After a pause, there was an explosion of voices. The communists had warned them they would be slaughtered in the South, but they knew they could not live under the communists where they were. Their village had resisted the communists; "the communists killed my brother, my father," they said. If I had ever wondered why I was in Vietnam or what the struggle was about, this brought it down to a very human and personal level. All I could muster was, "Tell them, tell them, we will help them."

That afternoon I wandered around Hanoi, which was charming and more completely Vietnamese in character than Saigon. Practically all of the shops had Vietnamese names, with a scattering of French; there were few Chinese, in contrast to Saigon, where most of the merchants were Chinese, with a smattering of Indians. Then there was Hoan Kiem Lake (Lake of the Returned Sword), in the center of the city. A small pagodalike tower near one end marked the place where, in Vietnamese legend, a giant, golden tortoise had taken a magical sword, to give to King Le Loi, who used it to drive the Chinese out of Vietnam and then returned it to the tortoise. This was Vietnam as one could have imagined it before the French came.

It was about three weeks before the French were to leave. Some of the shops had closed, other people were packing up to go to the port of Haiphong and then south, while others said they would remain. My impression was that about half the Vietnamese intended to stay. The city seemed quiet. Except for the dirty streets, an excessive number of beggars, compared with Saigon, and some recently painted pro-Vietminh slogans on walls, it was difficult to tell that Hanoi was about to be turned over to the communists. Some of the shop owners and residents had spread out their merchandise and belongings on the sidewalks in flea-market style, desperate to sell what they could not carry with them. I had brought little money with me but could not resist a small box, the handicraft of Hanoi silversmiths, whose trade I thought might soon become a thing of the past.

I met Arundel later that night to pass on some sealed instructions that Lansdale had given me for Conein and his team. To avoid public contact, Nick came up to my room. We exchanged a few words, and he was gone. The next morning at sunrise I was at the airport. We loaded a CAT C-46 with as many refugees as could be packed onto the steel floor and into the canvas seating on both sides. I sat in the jump seat, just behind the pilots. None of the refugees, with the exception of a Vietnamese army nurse, had ever been on a plane before. Looking back, I saw a mixture of fear and determination in their eyes as we left the runway. Many became sick when we hit bumpy air over the mountains, but that look of determination never faded. They were a brave people.

FIRST VISIT TO THE PHILIPPINES

Back in Saigon from Hanoi, I heard Lansdale's ideas for extending Vietnamese government authority into the areas of South Vietnam from which, under the Geneva terms, the Vietminh were to withdraw at the same time the French were evacuating the North. The amount of Vietminh-controlled territory south of the seventeenth parallel was so extensive (about one-sixth of South Vietnam's land surface, with almost a fifth of its rural population) that if the new government failed to establish its authority and win the support of the people living there, the nation would not survive. Little formal planning or preparation had been done. It was currently being left up to Vietnamese army commanders in adjacent areas to move in their troops to ensure order, if and when they had the resources. The problem was further complicated by the refusal of General Nguyen Van Hinh, commander in chief of the armed forces, to take any orders from Diem. Much of Hinh's staff, which should have been planning to fill this vacuum, was tied up in coup plotting.

The Vietnamese army had a terrible reputation for plundering the civilian population whenever it got the chance. Given its current state of demoralization, and without training or control, it would likely alienate the very people whom the government needed to win over. It was too late to do much in the first zones to be evacuated, on October 26, but not for the next big area, Camau, scheduled for February 1955. Lansdale thought the way to get started was to send a small group of Vietnamese civilians and army officers to the Philippines to see how its army, when Magsaysay was secretary of defense, had won over the population from the Huks. This might spark the Vietnamese into generating their own approach and give them heart, seeing what the Filipinos had accomplished. It might also get staff personnel from Prime Minister Diem and General Hinh working together in a common purpose.

For the prospective trip to the Philippines we got nominations from Prime Minister Diem's office and from the army General Staff. They included a young press officer on Diem's staff, Nguyen Thai, who had been educated at Michigan State and spoke excellent English; Bui Han from the Social Action Ministry, who had successfully set up neighborhood self-governing units in Saigon through local elections; Lieutenant Vuong from army psywar; Captain Man, who was General Hinh's press officer; and a Vietnamese interpreter for Mr. Han. Vuong would interpret for Man, whose English was practically nonexistent. Lansdale somehow overcame objections from Diem and Hinh, neither of whom wanted to have anything to do with the other, to forming the group. I was designated as the escort officer.

Prior to our trip, Lansdale invited the group to his house for lunch, ostensibly to be briefed on what we might see in the Philippines, but Lansdale had something more in mind. I watched as, in a very informal and friendly way, he skillfully got the normally very reserved Vietnamese talking about themselves and what they were doing. He asked Han to explain how he had organized volunteer citizen groups to improve Saigon neighborhoods and suggested he might find similar Filipino efforts to organize barrio self-help in the Philippines. He asked Vuong about his experience in the psywar company, particularly dealing with the civilian population. By the end of the lunch the Vietnamese, who hadn't known each other before, were conversing excitedly. He had started forming from a group of individuals a team that would work together during and after their forthcoming visit to produce a report that might have practical application.

In mid-October, we flew to the Philippines, staying in the old Manila Hotel, where Douglas MacArthur had lived before World War II. The first evening I was told to expect a visit after dinner by Major Bohannon, who had been Lansdale's deputy in the Philippines and was now an informal advisor to President Magsaysay. Dressed in my army khakis, I opened the door of my room to an imperious rap, expecting to find a major in uniform. Before me, dressed in shorts, a khaki bush jacket, and sandals was a weather-beaten, very tough-looking, wiry man with sandy hair so close cropped that his head looked shaved, glaring at me through wire-rimmed glasses. The first thing he said was, "I knew they would send some goddam, green shave-tail over here to do a man's job. Son, do you know what you're supposed to be doing?" Keeping my voice even, I said, "No, sir, I was told to get instructions from you." With that he softened a bit and explained the group's proposed itinerary, gave me some pesos for incidental expenses, and told me to take further instructions from a Filipino army escort officer who would show up at 7:00 the next morning. With that he vanished.

The visit was an eye-opener for all of us. We received briefings on the successful Huk campaign and a whirlwind five-day tour looking at the civic-action and public-information operations in the countryside as well as the resettlement of Huks who had voluntarily surrendered. This was summed up in an early breakfast meeting at Malacañang Palace, where President Magsaysay expounded his "people first" philosophy of combating the communists. By that he meant that the army would devote first priority to the well-being and protection of the rural population. Toward the Huk guerrillas, the policy was "all out friendship or all out force"—giving them every chance to come in voluntarily as their popular support was sucked away, rather than be pursued relentlessly by well-trained and -led Philippine army counterguerrilla forces. The Vietnamese were astonished to see so much accomplished by other Asians on their own; they had imagined the Americans were still running the show. I was thrilled by Magsaysay, how he spoke dramatically and with absolute conviction about the need to win the support of the population. This was real democracy in action, something taken too much for granted back in the United States. Battling communism, according to Magsaysay, was a war of ideas. Democracy was the best weapon we had.[7]

The Vietnamese told me that the fact that we were not running the Philippines, the Filipinos were, demonstrated that we really did want the Vietnamese to run their own country. The enthusiasm and dedication of the Filipinos in the Magsaysay government was contagious. On our last night in Manila, returning late from an inspection trip to the provinces, Captain Man and I were amazed to see lights still on in government offices. According to our escort officer, that particular office belonged to the Department of Agriculture. Captain Man asked if there was an emergency of some kind. No, was the reply, people were working there because they wanted to, because they believed in their government. Man nodded and said to me in French that somehow that kind of spirit had to be created in Vietnam. I told him if the Filipinos could do it, the Vietnamese could. But I had my fingers crossed: it was not at all clear that anything near that level of dedication or morale could be achieved in Vietnam.

When we returned to Saigon, I suggested that one person develop a draft report for comment. Nguyen Thai was selected by consensus, and in about two weeks we had a draft that I got personally to all who had gone on the trip. I invited Captain Man to the apartment to add his own comments. Mainly, its recommendations stressed coordinated action between the civilian administration and the military and indoctrination of the army in civic action; respect for the population and responsiveness to its needs in the form of medical care, new wells and bridges, and other helpful tasks. The breach between Diem and Hinh continued through October, however, stymieing further action.

INSPECTING LONG MY IN THE MEKONG DELTA

In early November I found a note at my apartment from my Filipino friend Colonel Joe Banzon. The Vietnamese army press office was planning an inspection trip to a recently evacuated Vietminh area in the Delta; would I like to go? I went over to Joe's apartment, which was about the size of a Pullman car stateroom—a single bedroom, kitchen, and dining room combined with a bath that doubled as a darkroom where Joe developed and enlarged his own photographs. The place was spotless and orderly, which only Joe could have managed in a space that size. The trip in question was a visit to the district of Long My in Soctrang Province, some two hundred kilometers south of Saigon in the Mekong Delta. This area, evacuated by the Viet Cong on October 26, had recently been occupied by a Vietnamese army unit from the provincial capital, also called Soctrang. I checked with Lansdale, who told me what I should look for; he was particularly interested in villager attitudes toward the army and how the troops behaved with the villagers. What did the villagers need? What had they been told by the Vietminh?

Arranging transport took about a week. Most Vietnamese air force C-47s were still evacuating military units and families south. Finally, the flight was on to Soctrang Province, located along the coast of the South China Sea, north of the Camau Peninsula; Long My lay toward its southwestern edge. The sleepy capital, it was a small city of one- and two-story stucco bungalows in the French colonial style, with pleasant, tree-shaded streets crisscrossed by canals. To get to Long My we had to go mainly by a series of canals, since the road had been cut during the war by the Vietminh and not yet repaired. It would be an all-day affair. Vietnamese army lieutenant colonel Hoang Van Duc was in charge.

Shortly after dawn our inspection group drove through an edge of territory still controlled by the Vietminh; we passed a sentry post with a Vietminh soldier wearing a red-starred pith helmet standing guard. We were not stopped and went on to the intersection of two main canals where empty wooden, flat-bottomed riverboats were tied up at a makeshift wharf. Two had outboard motors, and we boarded them. Banzon, Arundel, several French journalists, and I were the only non-Vietnamese in our boat. There was a lively crowd of villagers on the canal bank, some with boats of their own, others awaiting a ride. Some of the older women clamored for rides with us; Lieutenant Colonel Duc waived a few into each boat. One carried a large wicker basket ingeniously woven in the shape of an inner tube, closed at the bottom but with a hole at the top out of which protruded the heads of ducks, trapped by their wings.

The canal went around a bend and then opened into a straight stretch that ran to the horizon. Clumps of banana, papaya, and mango trees, interspersed with coconut palms and high grass, were at eye level along the canal's banks. Occasionally there were thatched huts with people. We passed wooden sampans and pirogues loaded with papaya, jackfruit, bananas, ducks, and charcoal on their way to market. Most boats were propelled and steered by a solitary Vietnamese, often a woman, standing at the stern moving a single sweep back and forth in a figure-eight pattern. The men wore black cotton pajamas, the women had white tops. Some had the typical conical, woven straw hats, others wore headcloths against the sun.

The monotony of the canal had a mesmerizing effect as we encountered fewer and fewer boats, then none. The heat was oppressive. The boats did not move fast enough to create much of a breeze. Those of us without hats draped handkerchiefs over our heads. I was startled to feel my arm being gently stroked and discovered that the old woman with the basket was the culprit. I looked at Banzon, who laughed, "She's never seen a man with hair on his arms before," he said. The woman gave me a big toothless grin; I grinned back. I was beginning to feel at ease. Somehow, the French journalists seemed stranger to me than the Vietnamese.

After almost four hours of endless stretches of canal, a collection of huts and a single stucco building came into view. This was Long My, formerly the district capital; it had been under Vietminh control for almost five years. To get to the stucco building we had to cross a temporary wooden bridge that the army had erected over a smaller canal. A squat, dark, broad-faced Vietnamese army major named Quan was in charge. He greeted us in somewhat broken French, saying he and his troops had moved in several weeks after the Vietminh had left. Informants had told him the population was destitute, so he had brought sufficient food for his own troops. The population had barely enough food for themselves and little else. They were in rags and needed simple medicines, clothes, mosquito nets, and blankets, as the nights were becoming chilly. He needed information about the government to distribute. The Vietminh had told the population not to cooperate, that the army would steal and rape. At first the villagers had been afraid, but after seeing that the soldiers would behave, that they were disciplined and trying to help, they became quite friendly. His problem was that he didn't have much assistance to give. Could we help? He directed most of his questions to the civilian province chief, with an eye also on his immediate boss, Colonel Duc, but he kept glancing at me to make sure I took it in. I could see from the impatience in the major's eyes that the answers were evasive. I wanted to intervene, but this was a Vietnamese show.

On the way back to the boats we approached, with Major Quan, several villagers to see if they would talk. Initially they were unresponsive and tense. I could hear the Vietnamese word *Phap* (French). When the major said *My* (America), they relaxed. I asked about their needs. They repeated what the major had said, adding that they wanted a school. What had they heard about the Vietnamese government? "Nothing." How had the army treated them? I did not expect a direct answer but wanted to see their reaction. There was an immediate smile, the equivalent of "not bad." If at least one unit of the Vietnamese army could do this well without much preparation or support, I thought, there's hope.

Back in Saigon I drafted a decree to be issued by Prime Minister Diem, focusing on Long My as a pilot project for handling the upcoming army occupations of Vietminh-controlled territory.[8] Unfortunately, the threat of a coup by General Hinh against Diem interfered. Joe and I tried to arrange an air drop of mosquito nets and other badly needed supplies to Long My through the French, who at the time controlled the only C-47s available for such operations. They refused, saying it was too dangerous.

GENERAL HINH'S ATTEMPTED COUP

Back in September, my budding relationship with Captain Giai of Vietnamese army G-5 had turned sour. He was never there when I telephoned, and he wouldn't return my calls. Finally, I dropped by his office unannounced, saying I was in the area on other business. He was very formal and inscrutable, leaving me wondering if I had offended him in some way. It seemed I was failing in my first important mission. I began to doubt that I was capable of understanding or getting close to the Vietnamese. When I reported this, with some embarrassment, to Lansdale, he said it confirmed other information, that Giai was helping General Hinh plan a coup and wanted to stay away from Americans. Recently Prime Minister Diem had ordered Hinh to move some troops into areas the Vietminh were beginning to evacuate and Hinh had refused. Lansdale had talked to Diem, then Hinh. Hinh said he would take orders only from Bao Dai, who had appointed him. Afterward Lansdale went to see Defense Minister Le Ngoc Chan, only to find him in a confrontation with the head of army G-6 (irregular warfare), Lt. Col. Tran Dinh Lan, and Captain Giai. Pistols drawn, Chan had tried to arrest both. According to Chan, Hinh was using Lan, Giai, and Lieutenant Minh (in charge of the G-5 radio station) as his secret coup-planning staff, with covert assistance from French army intelligence.

The coup had to be stopped. It was widely known among the Vietnamese that Hinh was in the French as well as the Vietnamese air force and a French citizen. A Hinh takeover would only confirm colonial control of the South. To thwart the plot, Lansdale needed access to Giai and Minh, to monitor and influence their actions. He asked Washington to find American officers who might have attended our psychological warfare school with them. In about a week a list of names arrived by cable; one was Navy lieutenant Larry Sharpe, then with the Seventh Fleet. Through Adm. L. S. Sabin, Jr., the fleet commander, Lansdale learned that Sharpe not only knew Giai and Minh but had also housed them in his personal quarters at Fort Bragg. He was our man. Orders were cut for his temporary assignment to MAAG Saigon. Sharpe was to stay with me in the Paul Blanchy apartment, occupying Arundel's bedroom while the latter was up north.

General Hinh's rebellion soon broke into the open. Hinh sent Lieutenant Minh with an armored platoon to guard the Vietnamese army radio station. Minh began broadcasting anti-Diem ridicule. Lieutenant Sharpe was dropped off from Sabin's flagship by launch at Nhatrang, from where he bummed a ride to Saigon in an International Control Commission plane. With little time except to confirm Sharpe's personal relationship with Minh and Giai and give some background on the Hinh revolt, Lansdale picked him up at MAAG and drove directly to the radio station. When they arrived, the gun muzzles of the two armored cars guarding the station swiveled to greet them. Sharpe was terrified. Lansdale calmly got out and banged on the door, demanding to see Minh. A window opened above, and Minh poked his head out. He saw Sharpe and pleaded with him to go away. Sharpe and Lansdale waited, and Minh relented; inside, Minh agreed that Sharpe could act as his "technical" advisor.

Later, when Lansdale informed the embassy that Sharpe would be advising Minh, there was consternation and incomprehension. How could an American be an advisor to a radio station that was making anti-American as well as anti-Diem statements? Within a few days, though, Sharpe persuaded Minh to shift from direct attacks on Diem to challenges to improve his government, while eliminating the anti-American broadcasts entirely. Sharpe's main obstacle was a French intelligence agent, Jean Barré, who had secretly been writing most of the broadcast material. Barré, it developed, was also a "stringer" for the Agence France-Presse and United Press wire services. He would repeat in his AFP and UP dispatches items from radio broadcast scripts that he had written. His dispatches would appear in major French and American newspapers, such as the *New York Times*, under the AFP or UP byline; he would then insert quotes from the newspaper articles into the broadcasts. Barré was without peer, a one-man propaganda operation. Now, however, no longer able to hide his role because of Sharpe's presence, he was forced to leave for Cambodia, where he found better accommodation for his anti-American screed. For a time the Hinh coup stalled.[9]

Then, in early October, Bao Dai, still holding court on the French Riviera, sent a letter to Diem urging him to take General Hinh and Bay Vien into a coalition government, along with General Nguyen Van Xuan as deputy prime minister.[10] Bao Dai had appointed Diem as prime minister, and supreme power remained in the emperor's hands. Diem temporized, sending emissaries to get Bao Dai to withdraw his letter. Meanwhile, Hinh was getting impatient and seemed unstable. He once boasted to Lansdale that he had ridden his motor scooter onto the Independence Palace grounds late at night yelling insults at Diem, knowing he had little to fear from Diem's palace guard. To head Hinh off, Lansdale arranged for President Magsaysay to invite Hinh to visit the Philippines as his a personal guest, bringing his staff with him. Colonel Banzon, who had been briefed by Lansdale, took the invitation to Hinh's headquarters; Hinh replied that he really wanted to go but urgent affairs demanded he remain in Saigon. What about your staff? Banzon asked. On his way out he tipped off the staff, who had heard a very favorable report about Manila night life from Captain Man. Lansdale flew to Manila with Lan, Giai, and Minh. Hinh could not run a coup without them.

The Hinh-Diem standoff began to ease. American insistence that Diem be given a chance was finally conveyed in unequivocal terms to the French and Bao Dai. This was followed by a request from Bao Dai that Hinh visit him "temporarily" in France. After further foot-dragging, Hinh finally departed in mid-November. Gen. J. Lawton "Lightning Joe" Collins (of World War II fame) arrived as President Eisenhower's special emissary and Ambassador Heath's replacement in time to give Hinh a final push.

"PACIFICATION" PLANNING BEGINS

Here was the break we had been waiting for. Diem had by now visited Long My (taking with him the mosquito nets and blankets we had recommended after our own visit) and had come back convinced that the former Vietminh-controlled zones had to be given a high priority. The small group I had taken to the Philippines and I began analyzing previous French pacification operations in Vietnam, as a preliminary to preparing a national plan. At the same time, General O'Daniel's efforts to provide direct American training and advice to the Vietnamese army were advancing. An American- French planning staff was created to map out a joint training and advisory mission. Some of the French started developing a "pacification" approach to reoccupation, recommending mainly negative control measures to monitor the population, such as identity cards and checkpoints. To keep the occupation of the formerly Vietminh-controlled areas on track, Lansdale moved quickly, with O'Daniel's support, to put in place American-French support of the effort. We would use our influence to make it a people-winning approach. The pace was quickening.

The Vietnamese army General Staff's principal planner, Colonel Le Van Kim, was a small, wiry, intense officer who also acted as director of cabinet of the Ministry of Defense. Kim, a Buddhist born in Binh Dinh Province in central Vietnam, was one of the few Vietnamese officers who had graduated from the French Command and General Staff School. Kim chaired what was called the "pacification planning committee." He was very knowledgeable about past pacification efforts by the French and skeptical about what the Philippine experience could offer. I was told that he held French as well as Vietnamese citizenship; there was some speculation in our team that he might even be a French agent. He seemed so French, in his command of the language and in his mannerisms, that my initial impression when I met him, in connection with the pacification committee, was that he was very much under their influence. I found him quite reserved; he was obviously taken aback at my junior rank and inexperience. I let him do most of the talking, and gradually we came to appreciate each other; he saw I was there to help, not to dictate, and I saw the pride he took in the pacification role assigned to the Vietnamese army. He categorically rejected French suggestions that the army was too green and needed French advisors to succeed. Later he told me, in his wry manner, that my obvious sincerity made him more tolerant of my inexperience.

A dispute arose between the French and the Vietnamese committee members over what to call the occupation effort. "Pacification" was favored by the French and seemed okay to us, but to the Vietnamese, including Kim, it connoted past French-led failures. A more neutral phrase that translated as "national security action" was coined by the Vietnamese (it remained *pacification* in French-language documents). We divided South Vietnam into three categories: national security, transition, and civil zones. "National security" zones were under completely military control, "transition" zones would have military province chiefs with civilian deputies, while "civil" zones would be entirely under civil government. All formerly Vietminh-occupied areas were automatically classified as national security zones. The two largest Vietminh-controlled zones to be given priority attention were the Camau Peninsula, at the southern tip of Vietnam, to be evacuated in early February 1955, followed in April 1955 by the final evacuation of Vietminh Interzone Five (the provinces of Quang Ngai and Binh Dinh) in central Vietnam. Occupation emphasis was to be on army civic action, relief for the population and the rehabilitation of war-torn roads, bridges, canals, schools, and other public works. We had helped shape much of this approach.[11]

GENERAL "LIGHTNING JOE" COLLINS

In the meantime, Lansdale was having serious difficulties with General Collins. Collins, who had earned a reputation as a decisive commander during World War II, had later become army chief of staff, then the American military representative to NATO. He arrived in Saigon on November 9, 1954, with a program of action drawn up in Washington. At the first "country team" meeting that Lansdale attended, Collins laid out marching orders for strengthening the Diem government while making drastic cuts in Vietnamese army manpower. When Lansdale objected, pointing out it didn't make sense to cut the Vietnamese army until the sect forces had been integrated, and further that there was a fundamental need to generate popular support for the new government, which was not in the program, Collins told him he was out of order. He, Collins, was the personal representative of the president of the United States; as such he set the priorities, and there was no need to discuss them. Lansdale then stood up, saying, "I guess there's nobody here as the personal representative of the people of the United States. The American people would want to discuss these priorities. So, I hereby appoint myself as their representative—and we're walking out on you."[12]

Lansdale waited outside the ambassador's door, expecting to be sent home, until he was called back in. Collins expressed in fatherly tones his disappointment at Lansdale's behavior as a military man. There was only one commander, he said. In the days that followed Lansdale tried to brief Collins on the realities of Vietnam. It was apparent, however, despite his courtesy Collins was impervious to information or ideas that did not fit the preconceptions he had brought with him. Collins and General Paul Ely, the commander of French forces in Indochina, had been compatriots in World War II and at NATO. The highest priority in Collins' mind was working "harmoniously" with the French, and under this rubric he saw himself and Ely as joint proconsuls.

It turned out to be a major blind spot. Collins, with his conventional, command-oriented mindset, eerily foreshadowed a manner of dealing with the Vietnamese that was to be practiced by Gen. Maxwell Taylor in 1964 and 1965. Lansdale's willingness to defy his superiors and stake his career on a different vision made him notorious within the government bureaucracy as not always respecting the chain of command or being a "team player." This was one of the reasons why he was effective with the Vietnamese—he stood up for their best interests—but it came at a cost to him within his own government.

During the remainder of December, our planning committee worked feverishly on Vietnamese-, French-, and English-language drafts of the National Security Action decree and of an operational plan for the Camau reoccupation. Lansdale informally discussed the plan with Diem and got his approval, while simultaneously we gave formal briefings first to General O'Daniel and then to General Collins. I was never sure Collins completely understood what we were talking about, but it smelled of action, so he endorsed it enthusiastically. The French attitude was that the Vietnamese army was sure to fall on its face. They would not oppose the plan; when it failed, the Americans would learn the hard way to heed French advice.

JOSEPH ALSOP

While working on National Security Action I was occasionally asked by Lansdale to do odd jobs. One of the more interesting was helping Joseph Alsop in early December. Alsop, a highly regarded and widely read syndicated columnist in Washington, had an intimidating air despite his slight frame. He barked his observations in a quasi-English accent punctuated by a sharp "eh?" implying your assent. His brusque and inquisitorial mien was reinforced by eyes peering intensely and aggressively from behind heavy horned-rimmed glasses with round lenses framing a prominent nose. He readily probed into the slightest lack of certainty or resolution in the answers to his usually abrupt questions. Since I had been in Long My, a recently evacuated Vietminh area, he wanted to know about conditions there. Did the population still support the Vietminh? He took my answers with skepticism.

Upon arriving, Alsop asked Lansdale for help in arranging interviews, particularly with President Diem. He already had access to the French, through his contacts in Paris and Saigon. Through the contacts of Max Clos, a West German correspondent who worked for *Le Monde,* he set about arranging a clandestine meeting with the Vietminh. This involved a boat trip deep into the Camau Peninsula, into what was at the time still Vietminh-controlled territory.

I learned afterward that Alsop had informed Lansdale about his impending trip and asked for some special help—that Lansdale provide him with an "L" (lethal) tablet, in case the Vietminh tortured him. He knew too much about American Cold War plans and policies, he said, which was certainly true, and some of the French who were captured by the Vietminh during the war had been subjected to torture and extreme deprivation. Alsop's request was a hot potato. If Lansdale turned him down, Alsop might not be willing to listen to Lansdale's assessment of the situation and would probably not tell us what he learned. Lansdale punted this decision back to Washington, since headquarters had suggested that Alsop seek him out. They were horrified and replied no, under no circumstances. Lansdale believed Alsop's fears were wildly exaggerated. Nevertheless, with an air of great secrecy, he gave him what was actually a locally made sugar-coated aspirin pill in an unfamiliar shape.

Off went Alsop, pill carefully concealed, to his rendezvous with the Vietminh. It turned out that his visit had not been cleared in advance. The Vietminh threatened to detain him but then relented. Afterward, he published several columns from that visit and a meeting with Diem, in which he combined an impression of implacable Vietminh strength and confidence compared with an unfavorable impression of Diem and pessimism imbibed from his French contacts. Alsop didn't think South Vietnam would last six months; Lansdale was unable to shake him from that view.

CHRISTMAS WITH PRESIDENT MAGSAYSAY

As the year drew to a close I was about to lose my monthly parachute pay. Four annual jumps were required, and I had made only one, in Korea before going to Vietnam. I had actually sneaked another in with a Vietnamese paratroop unit and gotten a set of their wings in return, but there was no way to account for it officially. The extra $110 a month was a healthy supplement to my regular second lieutenant's pay. My only possibility was the U.S. Air Force Air-Sea Rescue Unit at Clark Air Base; Lansdale made arrangements, and I left for the Philippines just before Christmas. At Clark, I was met by the same Major Bohannon who had greeted me so imperiously at the Manila hotel in October. Back then, the severity and formality of his manner had made me feel like a junior recruit. Apparently, I had gone up a degree in his estimation, for now he gave me a thin smile and told me that when President Magsaysay had heard I was coming he had insisted I stay in the tea house at Malacañang Palace and share Christmas breakfast with the Magsaysay family. In response to my astonishment, Bohannon said simply, "You're one of Ed's people."[13]

This was my first Christmas away from home. So strong were my attachments to our family traditions that I became truly homesick for the first time since coming to Asia. Spending Christmas Eve dancing the mambo in a Manila nightclub and celebrating midnight mass with a lively and engaging Filipina did little to fill the vacuum. The next morning, Luz, Magsaysay's wife, must have sensed my loneliness, because she took special care to make me feel a part of her family. Her kindness and Magsaysay's enthusiasm were irresistible as he regaled us at breakfast with stories about his days as secretary of defense, particularly about his surprise inspection trips, sometimes accompanied by Lansdale. He had once made an unannounced visit in the early afternoon to a Constabulary unit and found no one on guard. He took a rifle from the arms rack, fired it in the air, then hid behind the door. When the commander came rushing in, still buttoning up his pants from his siesta, he yelled "Stick 'em up, you dumb bastard, you'd be dead if I were a Huk!" Soon there were no more siestas.

The day after Christmas, I was invited to see the Presidential Complaint and Action Commission at work. It was being run out of a small office in Malacañang Palace by a retired colonel and past president of the Veterans Legion, Frisco San Juan. "Johnny," as he preferred to be called, showed me the pile of telegrams received daily from citizens all over the Philippines, almost all legitimate complaints about local injustices and abuses of power. Any citizen had the right to send a complaint free of charge to the commission, which sent investigators. Government at all levels had become unresponsive and often corrupt under Quirino, the previous president. This idea had originated at one of Lansdale's coffee klatches, and Magsaysay had first applied it to correct abuses by the army when he was secretary of defense. It became a way of using presidential authority to defend the rights of the average citizen. Magsaysay often read through the telegrams himself. Sometimes, he would call Johnny in the middle of the night and ask him to drive them both by jeep to the source of the complaint. He would show up at dawn at the complainant's *nipa* hut in some remote barrio to investigate personally. These visits were done without press, but word of mouth spread like wildfire.

Johnny summed up the essence of Magsaysay by recounting an incident of his open-air inauguration as president, before more than a million Filipinos on the Luneta in Manila in December 1953. After being sworn in, Magsaysay waded into the crowd, endlessly shaking hands and hugging people. It was unbearably hot under a cloudless sky; Magsaysay, without a hat, was covered with sweat. Johnny, who was at his side, unfurled an umbrella to shield him. Magsaysay turned and said, "Johnny, how can I have an umbrella over my head when our people have none over theirs?" It was so right and so like Magsaysay, Johnny recalled, that he had wanted to slink away in shame. I wondered how many leaders we had in the United States with those instincts.

As I flew back to Saigon I was inspired by what I had seen of President Magsaysay and the Filipino democratic revolution in my earlier visit and now at Christmas. I suddenly saw more clearly what the essence not just the form of my own democratic beliefs were about. So much of what I—and most Americans—took for granted about our own democracy was vividly alive in another country. Government for, by, and of the people seemed not only an American ideal but one that could be applied elsewhere. The Magsaysay way remained an inspiration to me throughout my service in Southeast Asia and even later, in American politics. To this day, recalling that example of Magsaysay's incredible sense of dedication to the well-being of the least of his people still brings a lump to my throat. "Less in life, more in law" was his philosophy. During later visits to Manila I usually asked taxi drivers what they thought of him. Invariable their reply was, "He's our guy."[14] I became more and more convinced, as the flight back to Saigon continued, that if the Vietnamese could apply these same principles, they could make South Vietnam not only a free country but one that would endure.

Chapter 3
A Nation Begins to Rise

The prospects for the creation of a coherent, self-governing nation out of the chaos of South Vietnam were not bright as 1955 began. While the attempted coup by General Hinh against Prime Minister Diem was foiled, relations between Diem and the religious sects of the Hoa Hao and the Cao Dai and with the Binh Xuyen in Saigon were on the whole getting worse, not better.

The gambling license awarded by the previous Vietnamese government to the Binh Xuyen at Bao Dai's instruction was coming up for renewal in February. It was a major source of Binh Xuyen income, but Diem strongly resisted renewal, because of its blatant identification with corruption. The air of crisis was further exacerbated when the French cut off their subsidies for the sect's armies early in 1955. In the meantime, refugees continued to stream out of the North, now through the port of Haiphong; their reception and resettlement remained a major preoccupation of the Diem government. The Vietnamese army was beginning preparations for the occupation of the Camau Peninsula in February and later Interzone Five in central Vietnam, but it was far from ready for the job. The army had never operated in larger than battalion units; the occupation operations would require division-sized forces. Moreover, the army still had little confidence in itself, remained divided in its loyalties, and was disliked, with some exceptions, by the population.

Any government dominated by the sects and without Diem would be unable to hold South Vietnam together, given the certainty of its corrupt nature and the obviousness of French influence and control. South Vietnam was still very much up for grabs. If the Vietminh were to make a move to take control, little would stand in its way. The remaining French forces, while formidable on paper, were in no mood to resist, while the Vietnamese army appeared too weak and disorganized.

NATION-BUILDING PLAN

The National Security Action decree I had worked on so hard before Christmas was promulgated by President Diem on December 31, 1954. After the New Year, I was back into the detailed planning and mobilization for the reoccupation of Camau, which had been named Operation Liberty—Tu Do means liberty in Vietnamese—and scheduled to kick off on February 8, 1955.

My role as an informal advisor was now more complicated, because the joint American-French military training group, called the Training Relations Instruction Mission (TRIM), had finally gotten off the ground. Lansdale had been put in charge of the National Security Division within TRIM, with broad responsibilities for training and advising the Vietnamese army in its National Security Action (pacification) operations, psychological warfare, and the demobilization of veterans. I found myself serving in the National Security Division side by side with French officers, most of whom were pure intelligence types from the French Intelligence Service (SDECE) and whose main job was to keep an eye on Lansdale and the rest of us. What we were doing, though, was straightforward; we had little to hide. The Vietnamese, however, didn't want the French to know the details of their pacification plans, for fear the French would foul up their operations just to make the Vietnamese look bad. They actually gave a phony briefing on their plans for Operation Liberty to General O'Daniel when French officers were present. (I was able to tip Lansdale off in advance so he could advise O'Daniel. Later we arranged a private briefing on the real plans.)

The National Security Action program gave me a chance to work more closely with Lansdale and better understand his ideas. At the time, I thought we lacked an overall plan to help South Vietnam become a real country. I could see that "national security action" was an important part, but I was curious about what else Lansdale had in mind. When I asked Lansdale about his thinking, he took a memorandum out of his safe for me to read. It was addressed to General Collins and dated January 3, 1955.[1]

Lansdale said that it was more of a strategy than a plan. In it he listed three elements for achieving a free Vietnam: successful teamwork, strengthening the free Vietnamese, and the creation of a willingness in the bulk of the population to risk all for freedom. Better teamwork was needed among the Americans; we needed to keep the French informed of our intentions but not let them control our relations with the Vietnamese; and we should establish better personal relations with the Vietnamese, on a footing of equality. Teamwork among the Vietnamese had progressed slowly: "There is still too much partisanship, distrust, and obstructive jealousy," he wrote. As remedies he suggested more effective people-government-army cooperation, some form of government that people felt was honestly representative, and democratic political techniques among leaders. He expressed concern "about whether all our aid and efforts here will strengthen the Vietnamese or make them more dependent on us." He wanted to see the efforts geared "to the operating philosophy of helping the Vietnamese help themselves."

He dwelled on the "willingness to risk all for freedom," quoting Mao Tse-tung to the effect that guerrilla warfare could not "survive and develop once it is cut loose from the people or fails to attract the participation and cooperation of the broad masses." We should face up to the fact our side was "cut loose from the people" in too many areas, which we must now win back. The correct method of winning them back was "to attract their participation and cooperation in what free people do and cherish—not force, scare or coerce, but attract." If we took the right approach, it would be the first major step in attracting people to our side. We had to "set about convincing, and accomplishment is most convincing, the people that their own future (and that of their children and their children's children) will be more rewarding under our own system than that of communism—more rewarding politically, socially, economically and spiritually. When the hope of such a rewarding future is raised within the people, coupled with hope of its possible attainment (which includes military means to protect the attainment), then the first big cleavage between the Communists and the bulk of the population will start taking place."

Lansdale observed that a critical piece was missing in Collins's program: "giving the people a truly representative government," which must be keyed around a charter or constitution that contained a bill of rights and set forth plainly that the government was to be the people's. "Our strong point," he wrote, "is that their document [the Vietminh constitution] does not do what the constitution of a free people can—and the sooner we have such a document, the sooner we can start making this plain to the people." He stressed that "along with moving as rapidly as possible toward a Constitution, the Free Vietnamese must establish government and the benefits of government as rapidly as possible throughout Vietnam south of the 17th Parallel. This is what we have termed 'national action' of which military 'pacification' is an integral part . . . and the first means of raising hopes." Lansdale concluded with a request he be permitted to devote a major share of his time to coordinate efforts in "national security action."

After reading the memorandum I had a clearer understanding of what we were trying to do but wondered if General Collins understood it. Lansdale shrugged and said that at least Collins had approved his leading this effort. I should get back to work on my part, National Security Action, which was "damned important." What Lansdale had put down was an outline of how to help the Vietnamese build a nation.

A SOOTHSAYER'S ALMANAC FOR TET

My January days were spent at TRIM or Vietnamese army headquarters working on the planning and preparations for Operation Liberty. At night I took on a covert propaganda project, a soothsayer's almanac for the Vietnamese New Year (Tet) in February, a project that Lansdale had conceived to boost South Vietnamese morale. The Vietnamese, like most Asians, placed a great deal of stock in soothsayers. They were usually consulted about propitious days for weddings, the location and orientation of houses, business and political decisions, even the launching of combat operations. A number of Saigon soothsayers, including recent arrivals from the North, were well known and widely consulted. In the days before Tet many Vietnamese wanted to learn what was in store for the coming year.[2]

When I first tried out the almanac idea on Pete (Bui Anh Tuan), he thought it crazy; it would never work. Vietnamese soothsayers were fiercely independent, liked to work alone, and usually made their predictions in private to individuals or families, not as general divinations in newspapers, like Western astrologers. Moreover, Vietnamese astrology was mainly intuitive, although it used a person's time and date of birth as a reference point. Each practitioner consulted his own personal set of charts and books; some cast bones and read the future from the pattern. Much of the lore and technique derived from centuries of Chinese culture.

The almanac would have to be sufficiently interesting to attract broad readership but should contain optimistic predictions for the Diem government and signs of bad fortune for the Vietminh. The Diem government had improved its chances of survival from the early odds of ninety to ten against to maybe forty-sixty, but the issue of the sects remained unresolved, and there were still many fence-sitters in the army and the civilian population. This almanac might add something positive to the climate of opinion, and it would be fun to work on.

Pete quietly contacted several prominent soothsayers. At our next meeting he had a big smile on his face—the initial reaction was encouraging. For relatively modest sums enough prominent diviners were willing to participate to make the almanac attractive to readers. The southerners among them saw it as a way of more widely advertising their services to the recent arrivals from the North. One well-known astrologer from the North saw it as an introduction to potential southern customers. How then to tackle to job? Pete suggested a second round of conversations, feeling out who might be willing to slant their predictions the way we wanted.

He found two, one from the North, who would focus on the Vietminh, and another from the South, who would predict that the Diem government would prevail over its enemies. Another soothsayer came forth with a calendar of propitious dates for various personal activities, depending on the year of one's birth in the twelve-year Buddhist calendar cycle. In the process, Pete learned enough about Vietnamese divination to write an overview piece for the almanac.

The almanac we produced was an eight-page, modestly priced tabloid, with a wheel showing the twelve-year cycle, in color, on the front page. Five thousand copies hit the streets a week before Tet and promptly sold out. Five thousand more were taken north to Haiphong, and they sold out. A second printing also sold out. We recovered the entire investment of Agency funds and made a profit, which was donated to a fund set up for the refugees from the North.[3]

OPERATION LIBERTY

During mobilization for Operation Liberty (the occupation of the Camau Peninsula), under the command of Lieutenant Colonel Hoang Van Duc, various battalions were assembled in Soctrang, on the coast northeast of Camau, and in Rach Gia on the Gulf of Siam. This was the same Duc I had encountered on our early visit to Long My. He was a southerner with a good combat record but no specific experience in pacification. However, he had shown sympathy for the population's needs in Long My.

Duc intended to send the larger force south by road from Soctrang and a smaller force by boat from Rach Gia through the canal system along the west side of the peninsula, the two joining up at Camau Town. Before the operation Captain Duc's psywar company was to give the officers and troops a short civic-action course in how to behave with the population, but we were apprehensive it would not be enough.

The army units, which totaled about twelve thousand troops, had few medical supplies for the civilian population, which we knew to be in dire straits. Operation Brotherhood was willing to send in a medical team with the army, but Colonel Duc, with strong support from Diem, had decided no foreigners were to accompany the troops into Camau—which initially excluded personnel from TRIM as well. Vietnamese nationalism had come into play. From Diem on down the Vietnamese were very sensitive about having Americans out in the countryside; it would look, they thought, as though they had exchanged French for American rule. There was also the problem of how to keep the French away if the Americans were allowed to participate. We would certainly have to keep a low profile.

After much negotiation and some behind-the-scenes persuasion by Lansdale, Diem granted permission for two American officers, Lt. Col. Sam Karrick and myself, to go in civilian clothes, ostensibly as observers, to Soctrang, where Colonel Duc's headquarters was located. Karrick was a regular army officer with only conventional military experience now assigned to Lansdale's National Security Division. His main responsibility was logistics support. My mission was to assist the psywar company, to ingratiate myself with Colonel Duc so I could accompany the operation into Camau, and to wheedle his acceptance of the badly needed Operation Brotherhood medical team. Karrick looked askance at my being given so much latitude and thought I should be reporting to him. I avoided friction by spending most of my time with the Vietnamese while keeping him verbally informed. At the same time, I had a radio channel to Lansdale, if indirect and unreliable, through the Vietnamese army.

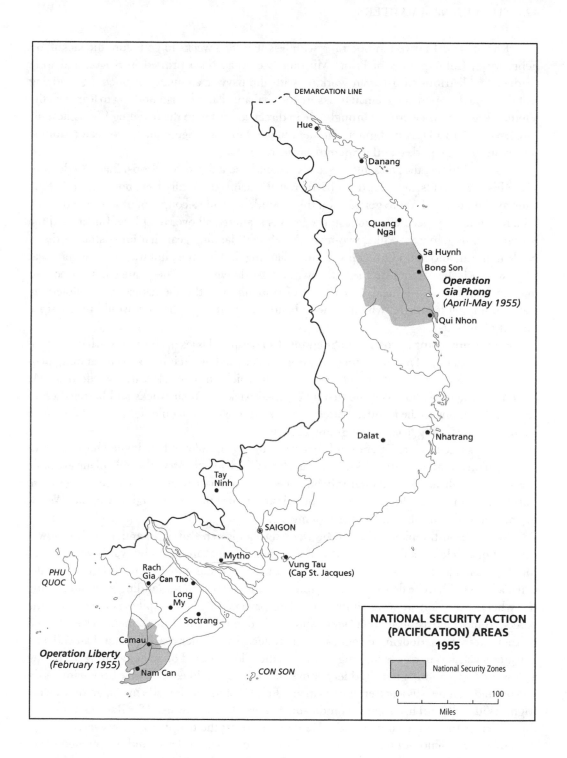

DEMARCATION LINE

Hue

Danang

Quang
Ngai

Sa Huynh

Bong Son

*Operation
Gia Phong*
(April-May 1955)

Qui Nhon

Dalat

Nhatrang

Tay
Ninh

SAIGON

Mytho

Vung Tau
(Cap St. Jacques)

PHU
QUOC

Rach
Gia

Can Tho

Long
My

Soctrang

Camau

Operation Liberty
(February 1955)

Nam Can

CON SON

**NATIONAL SECURITY ACTION
(PACIFICATION) AREAS
1955**

National Security Zones

0   100

Miles

Karrick and I arrived in Soctrang with less than two weeks to go before the kickoff on February 8. Color posters of Prime Minister Diem had been printed in Saigon and were readied for distribution. I began working with the psywar company in Soctrang readying leaflets to be dropped into Camau to assure the civilians that they had nothing to fear from the Vietnamese army. The project brought me in direct contact with the fledgling Vietnamese air force, which had a Dassault fighter-bomber fitted out for passengers and a two-seater Morane observation plane parked at the Soctrang airfield.[4]

I wanted to test the Dassault to see if we could use it for leaflet drops. Eager to demonstrate his flying skills, my pilot did a barrel roll at takeoff, about fifty feet above the end of the runway. Anxious as I was to get back on the ground, we made a couple of passes over the city. The minimum airspeed was too fast; the leaflets scattered all over the place. I next tried the Morane, an ungainly, storklike, two-man aircraft with landing gear that hung straight down while in the air and spread to each side upon landing. Behind the pilot was an observer's seat from which leaflets could be easily thrown out a side window. The plane's low speed and maneuverability made it ideal. I struck up a friendship with the Vietnamese who piloted my leaflet-dumping test flight, which came in handy later—though the man would nearly scare me out of my wits.

For the unit going by road from Soctrang, I suggested classes in courteous driving, stressing the importance of not alienating the population by killing their chickens or running people off the road. I attended one of the classes, at which an officer lectured vociferously. At the end of the class, however, the drivers climbed back into their trucks and barreled off in various directions to their units, scattering chickens, pigs, and people right and left. A single lecture was not going to change ingrained habits.

About a week before Operation Liberty was to begin, Colonel Duc invited me to accompany him on a visit to his units assembled at Rach Gia. Unfortunately, the only plane available was the Dassault, and its seats were already filled; I would have to get to Rach Gia on my own. I approached my pilot friend, who got permission to use the single-engine Morane. We left the next morning on the wildest flight of my life.

After takeoff the pilot indicated he wanted to go lower. Failing to anticipate how low, I nodded okay. He took the Morane down just above a canal about twenty yards wide. It was the dry season and the water level was low, so the cockpit was about even with the top of the canal's banks. Then he flew even lower, touching the water with the landing gear and making the wheels turn as if we were running on hard pavement. The cockpit was now below the banks, from which astonished villagers watched in open-mouthed amazement as we whizzed by their straw huts, dodging pirogues on the water. Finally, after roaring around a bend, still at water level, and narrowly missing a sampan, the pilot got tired of demonstrating his daring and went up to about a hundred feet above the dry rice paddies. Looking back with a grin he shouted that he was a better pilot than any Frenchman, which made me laugh despite my fright. With yells and hand signals I indicated that we should now head for Rach Gia at something greater than minimum altitude. He couldn't resist the temptation, however, to buzz a herd of water buffalo, scattering them and throwing off their herders, children perched sleepily on their backs. As we pulled out of the dive I pounded on his shoulder—enough! When we landed about an hour later I complimented him on his skill but indicated firmly that there were to be no wild maneuvers on the way back.

Colonel Duc had already arrived and gone into Rach Gia, so I thumbed a ride into what I found to be a pleasant, small city on the Gulf of Siam, with coconut and mango trees lining the streets. The principal industry was fishing. (After the North Vietnamese takeover of the south in 1975, the Rach Gia area would become the main jumping-off point for the thousands of "boat people" who fled oppression across dangerous seas to Thailand and Malaysia and an uncertain future.) Getting to Colonel Duc's local headquarters just as he started his briefing, I listened attentively, but I heard no answer to one question: Why were the troops going completely around the U Minh Ha area, when the Vietminh were reportedly leaving behind an active, armed unit there? The U Minh Ha was an almost impenetrable, heavily forested swamp on the western side of the Camau Peninsula. During the war against the French, the Vietminh had developed it into a safe area into which their forces could rest and reequip. Arms could be smuggled into it by sea.

Lunch was served at the customary long table at which all the visitors and local notables were seated, about forty in all. The usual delicious prawns came first, served cold with aioli, and then a variety of dishes that included small, crisp, fried rolls that resembled the traditional Vietnamese spring rolls, or *cha gio* (the second word pronounced "yo" in the South and "zo" in the North). When I inquired, Colonel Duc replied blandly that they were *"vers de coco,"* a specialty of Rach Gia. *"Vers"* was not a word I recognized, but since everyone else was biting into them with relish, I did the same. They were delicious, with a slightly sweet, nutty flavor, entirely different from *cha gio*. On returning to Soctrang that evening I found from my dictionary that *vers* were worms. I had just eaten a plate full of fried coconut borers!

After lunch, I asked Colonel Duc why he was avoiding the U Minh Ha. He wasn't sure, he said, that his units were prepared for combat if it came to that. In any case, his primary mission was occupying the populated areas of the peninsula; dealing with an armed Vietminh unit was a job for irregular forces. Then he introduced me to a civilian who had been at the lunch, Lam Quang Phong.[5] According to Phong there were about a thousand men around the U Minh Ha who had fought alongside the Vietminh but were not communists and refused to be evacuated north. He thought he could persuade them to support the new Diem government, and if so, they could help establish security by taking on any hard-core forces the Vietminh left behind. He did not know Diem personally but believed he was an honest nationalist, and that his government was the country's last chance for true independence from the French and from communist domination.

I told Phong I would get the word up to Saigon and that I hoped the government would enlist his services. Later, Phong was named as a delegate to Camau, but nothing came of his proposal about the resistance group. We had no one to shepherd the idea; too much attention had to be paid to the struggle with the sects and stay-behind operations up north. The U Minh Ha remained largely unpenetrated, and it would reemerge in the 1960s as a formidable Viet Cong base.

ENTERING CAMAU WITH OPERATION BROTHERHOOD

Back in Soctrang I got on the radio to Lansdale, using slang to explain about Phong and to let him know that Colonel Duc was still opposed to sending in an Operation Brotherhood medical team. Recent reports coming out of Camau about public health were even worse than we had imagined. The Vietnamese army units assigned for the occupation had only nurses, no doctors; in fact, there wasn't a single civilian doctor or nurse in the entire Camau Peninsula, some fifty-five hundred square miles and five hundred thousand people and the Vietnamese army had few to spare. After a brief silence, Lansdale said he thought he had a solution: he would make an inspection visit to Soctrang tomorrow, with some Operation Brotherhood personnel, for lunch. Would I advise Colonel Duc?

Duc was reluctant, but it would have been impolite to spurn such a visit. Just before noon the next day a MAAG C-47 arrived with Lansdale, two Operation Brotherhood doctors and three Filipino nurses, and Colonel Banzon. I drove over to the plane in a quarter-ton truck I had commandeered. Lansdale was in a jaunty mood that my report of Duc's reluctance did nothing to dispel—he thought Duc could be turned around. Colonel Duc greeted us very formally. At lunch Lansdale gallantly gave up his place on Duc's right to the prettiest and most vivacious of the Filipino nurses. The other two scattered among his officers, who quickly unearthed previously hidden reserves of English; I saw what was afoot and could hardly keep from laughing out loud. After lunch Duc insisted on giving the visitors a short tour of his forces and then a briefing, which I interpreted. When he described the situation in Camau, how poorly off the people were, I could see him changing his mind. Afterward he approached Lansdale, beckoning me over to interpret for him. Did Lansdale think the Filipino doctors and nurses would really be willing to go to Camau? He didn't think the Vietminh would attack, but he couldn't guarantee their safety. Lansdale listened gravely and said that he would talk to them.

Lansdale, Banzon, and I met. There was a problem. There were not enough Operation Brotherhood personnel in Vietnam to take care of the refugee camps and go to Camau as well. However, an additional team was on stand-by in Manila. Could they be mobilized in time? What about their safety? As Duc had said, we didn't know what the Vietminh might do. Banzon said he would go in with the team. I was willing to go too, but Colonel Duc still had not agreed to my presence. Lansdale, thinking he could kill two birds with one stone, told Duc the Filipinos were willing to go if Banzon and I could go with them. Banzon could be taken for a Vietnamese; I, so as not to be mistaken for a foreign military advisor, would wear civilian clothes. He could tell the population I was foreign press. Duc smiled—I was going in.

There was less than a week left before the kickoff of Operation Liberty. First, Operation Brotherhood sent four doctors and two nurses to Soctrang, borrowed from the teams with the refugees in Saigon. Two days before February 8, four new Operation Brotherhood personnel destined for Camau arrived in Soctrang. Fresh from Manila, they had spent only a few hours in Saigon en route. We now had a total of ten OB personnel. First, I helped move five doctors and three nurses to Bac Lieu, the district capital, south of Soctrang. The Camau zone still under Vietminh control began just south of Bac Lieu. One of the Filipino doctors was a highly qualified surgeon, with instruments but no anesthesia except Novocain and bottled ether. Operations would have to be done with what they had. More medicines, along with water purifiers, bottled water, U.S. Army C-rations, and electric stoves (but no generators) had arrived, by air to Soctrang and thence by road to Bac Lieu. Along with the doctors and nurses from Manila came Oscar Arellano, Operation Brotherhood's chairman; Cesar Climaco, recently appointed director for Vietnam; and Dr. Emmanuel "Manny" Ho Quang Phuoc, a Vietnamese-Chinese dentist and the sparkplug of the Saigon Jaycees who sponsored OB.

Oscar Arellano was taller, more heavy set, and with a darker complexion than the average Filipino. Voluble, easily excited, and prone to issuing peremptory commands when he felt uncertain, he had a complex about suggestions of American "superiority." I found out later that as a student in the United States he had suffered discrimination because of his brown skin. At this moment he was uneasy about going into Camau. Cesar Climaco had been the popular mayor of Zamboanga in Mindanao, where he had managed to get along well with Moslems as well as Christians. Climaco was stocky, with a broad face and infectious enthusiasm. He was action oriented, not a worrier by nature, but was completely new to Vietnam. Manny Phuoc, the dentist, was a lively, funny man who often seemed more at home with the Filipinos than with his own people. He had urged Operation Brotherhood participation in the Camau operation, sending Arellano an "SOS" in late January, but on the final decision he had deferred to Arellano.

To find out what the team might be in for, a reconnaissance party of several doctors and nurses, with Joe Banzon and an interpreter, went early the next day to Gia Rai, an intermediate town in the occupation zone, in two jeeps, flying a red cross flag and carrying a sign saying *Bac Si* (doctor). When they returned we found that they had actually gone all the way to Camau Town, finding it largely deserted. One masonry building in fair condition appeared to have been a clinic in the past, but it was filthy and had no running water or electricity. The town had no sanitary ground-water supply, and all rainwater tanks had been emptied by the Vietminh. We would have to take water out of the canals and sterilize it. The Filipinos felt confident, moreover; the few people encountered had not been unfriendly. Some, recognizing they were doctors, had approached them and asked for treatment.

As we got ready to go in with the Vietnamese troops, Arellano suddenly concluded that OB might not be accepted by the population if it accompanied the troops. He had heard the army was not very disciplined or civic-action minded. There might be incidents, and this would hurt Operation Brotherhood. The team must go in, he said, ahead of the army's main convoy scheduled to start from Soctrang early the next day. I disagreed, saying to go in without the accompanying troops could offend Colonel Duc and offered no guarantee of security. Joe Banzon supported me, but there was no holding Oscar back. Finally, in an emotional outburst that ended the argument he said, "Either we go in first or not at all." (I got to know Oscar well in the years ahead; we became great friends. But at this point he appeared recklessly stubborn and impulsive, something we could have done without.)

Lieutenant Colonel Karrick returned to Soctrang from Saigon just as I was leaving for Bac Lieu. We had agreed I would wait for him in Bac Lieu to receive any final instructions before leaving for Camau on the morning of February 8, but when he arrived in Bac Lieu I had already left. Not knowing that Oscar had insisted on starting early and feeling that I had violated orders, he returned to Saigon and protested heatedly to Lansdale. It was difficult for a regular military officer to get used to Lansdale's very informal chain of command. Eventually word got back via OB to Lansdale about what had happened. When General Collins found out that no senior TRIM advisors, only one American second lieutenant, had accompanied the operation, he objected to General O'Daniel, who replied laconically that the lieutenant was "one of Ed's people." This apparently satisfied Collins, who probably thought my lowly rank was a cover.

Had I been fully conscious of how much responsibility had been conferred on me, I would have been even more apprehensive. As it was, what worried me most, now that we were actually committed, was the safety of the Operation Brotherhood team. I was dressed as a civilian and carried only a small, Belgian-made Beretta automatic, concealed in the small of my back. Banzon was in civilian clothes and carried a concealed sidearm as well. It was not a sure bet that the Vietminh would continue to observe the Geneva Accords. The reconnaissance team had not been molested, but now we were entering the Vietminh heartland, an area that had been exclusively theirs, with the exception of limited French forays, since 1946, when I had still been in high school.

The trip began in the pitch dark before sunup and was uneventful. The Camau Peninsula was absolutely flat, with nothing showing above the horizon except clumps of coconut palms, mango trees, and other lesser palms, with banana trees and high grass in lower relief. The dirt road we followed was in severe disrepair in some areas, with deep cuts in a sawtooth pattern, made by the Vietminh. These cuts stopped vehicles but permitted bicycles and pedestrians to weave their way through. We were often forced to detour over rice paddies—fortunately dry, because the rains had stopped in October. Our progress often slowed to a dusty crawl. We went through a few dilapidated, deserted villages, then stopped at Gia Rai, where we left a doctor and a nurse with supplies. The lack of people along our route added to an apprehension that was gradually dispelled by time and fatigue as the morning wore on in the growing heat. There was not a cloud in the sky. Finally, shortly after noon, we crossed a narrow wooden bridge and pulled into the main square of Camau Town, in front of what appeared to be the old provincial administration building. There were no people to be seen. Bullet holes from French strafing pockmarked its walls and those of the surrounding ramshackle buildings. In the middle of the square the Vietminh had erected a concrete obelisk on which a star in bas relief was clearly visible. At the foot of the monument was a wreath of wilting flowers. The next day when people began to congregate, a Vietnamese army soldier accidentally dislodged the wreath. A youngster stepped forward and propped it back up without a word, and without being molested by the army.

Operation Brotherhood set up shop in the abandoned building initially identified by the scouting team. Word got out quickly, and a few patients began to appear, lining up wordlessly in the dust outside the main door. At the end of the day, the main army force finally arrived. Banzon and I convinced Arellano to apologize to Colonel Duc for OB's having gone ahead—due to his "lack of understanding of the operation." Duc accepted his excuse graciously.

The next day the OB medical team started early. A hand-painted sign saying "Doctor" and "Free Medical Clinic, All Are Welcome" in Vietnamese, with the International Jaycees logo, had been put on the building. As it became apparent that, contrary to Vietminh propaganda, the troops were Vietnamese, not French, and were not pillaging, people appeared in the town with rice and some fruit to sell. By the middle of the morning more than fifty people were in line, mainly mothers with sick children. The team treated people until dark without stopping.

At the end of the second day a young woman arrived on a makeshift stretcher. She had been two days in labor; her baby was completely blocked. She would die unless a caesarian section could be performed immediately, but we had no electric power. It was up to young Dr. Espiridon Alvarez, the only surgeon of the team. He looked at Joe Banzon and me and asked us what we thought. We said he was the doctor. With a wry smile, he said he would try using flashlights for illumination, but it was a major operation. Water was boiled over an open fire. A blanket and strips of white cloth were laid out on a wooden table. Lifted onto a wood table, the woman was immobilized by cushioned wires nailed to its side.

Alvarez explained to the patient through an interpreter what he was going to do. She assented with a weak nod. We had four flashlights. Joe Banzon, Cesar Climaco, a nurse, and I held them in one hand, waving palm fronds with the other to brush away the mosquitoes. The only anesthesia was liquid ether on a rag, periodically pushed under her nose, and Novocain, which Alvarez skillfully injected as he cut into her abdomen, layer by layer. It was slow going—first the injections, followed by a cut, followed by clamps to staunch the bleeding, then each layer of tissue peeled back, interspersed by whiffs of ether. Silence was total, except for the whine of mosquitoes and soft commands from Alvarez for bandages and fresh instruments. The woman grimaced at the pain but never cried out. Occasionally I looked beyond the table to where light reflected from curious eyes peering through open windows. After more than an hour, a baby boy suddenly appeared. Alvarez swung it up by its feet, hit its bottom; it cried, the woman smiled, we cheered. I saw Alvarez grin behind his mask. Stitching her back up was an anticlimax. Weeks afterward, the woman and her husband visited the OB team. It had been their first child. They wanted to name it, "Obi," after Operation Brotherhood.

By the third day patients were pouring in, more than three hundred each day, with every conceivable affliction. Joe Banzon and I took it upon ourselves to clean the clinic, because the doctors and nurses were so busy. By this time Joe had taken to wearing his uniform, which ensured respect from the Vietnamese soldiers assigned to assist OB, but we still could not get them to perform menial tasks, such as cleaning the floor. They would just stand around until they saw Joe, a full colonel, strip down to his undershirt, roll up his trousers and, in bare feet, start scrubbing the clinic floor, accompanied by me, a large, pale-skinned Westerner, acting as his assistant. Joe and I had a great routine. He gave me orders, to which I responded with a snappy "Yes, sir!" followed by action. Gradually the soldiers began to get the idea; when it came to helping civilians, no job was beneath their dignity. They started to pitch in—civic action at work.

Because food available on the local market was limited, I was introduced to a Vietnamese and Filipino specialty that the Filipinos called *balut*. I noticed hard-boiled eggs being sold by women vendors; the Filipinos cracked them open and ate them with great relish. They were duck eggs with embryos already formed. Overcoming my qualms I began eating them. At least they added protein to my usual diet of rice, bananas, and coconut milk.

Despite the good will generated by Operation Brotherhood, the population remained reserved toward the army. I accompanied platoons from the psywar company around the limited road network and by boat along the canals, its loudspeakers announcing, "This is the Vietnamese government of President Ngo Dinh Diem, truly independent, a new chapter in Vietnamese history. We are different from the Vietminh who left you in poverty and disease. We will help you. There is now a free clinic in Camau." The psywar people wore traditional black pajamas, which Captain Duc believed would put the villagers more at ease. At the larger hamlets, the platoon would stop and address the local people. The loudspeakers were always turned up to maximum volume, whether for speech or music. The volume of the medium seemed to be part of the message. The villagers didn't appear to mind as they listened, but there was little overt response.

While the troops in the regular units seemed well behaved and there were few reported incidents, neither was there much personal contact with the local population. Army boats and trucks ferried people to the medical clinic and distributed blankets and mosquito nets, engineers repaired roads and bridges, but little else was happening. I saw the army was handicapped by a state of mind, that "civic action" was somebody else's job, not that of the average soldier or even the average commander. From the population's reaction it seemed that just haranguing was not likely to change minds. Their attitude was reserved, essentially passive. They had been told not to cooperate by the Vietminh, who had said they would return and, the people knew, might inflict severe reprisals on those who did. It was going to take concerted, positive action to convince them to support the new government.

To break down the population's reserve, the psywar company's theatre troop began giving folk-song concerts and staging Vietnamese historical dramas, such as *Tong Tuu Don-Hung-Tin* (General Don Hung Tin), about a famous general of the Tuy Duong dynasty of the seventh to tenth centuries who loyally defended the legitimate dynasty in a civil war against his best friend.[6] The message was that Diem now represented the legitimate government of the South, though how well that message got across was not clear. The villagers clearly knew the story by heart, often anticipating the lines. Sharing cigarettes with civilians, troops scattered through the crowd. Gradually the troops and the population got more used to each other. This worked particularly well, I noticed, with units from the South; those from the North or center usually remained apart.

In one village, almost all the huts had badly faded black-and-white photographs of Ho Chi Minh pinned to the interior walls. I quietly suggested to Captain Duc that his men offer to trade, hut by hut, new color posters of President Diem for them. Substantial numbers of the Diem poster would begin to insert the new government into their minds. His men would have to be careful, though, not to push the posters onto people. Captain Duc readily agreed, and he began the next day. About half the huts took the Diem poster and handed in Ho Chi Minh. I was surprised.

As army units spread throughout the peninsula, relatively few incidents were reported—mainly domestic animals run over by reckless drivers and occasional passes being made at village girls—and no crimes. Colonel Duc was careful not to act in ways the Vietminh could exploit. Vietminh monuments such as the one in the Camau square were left standing, to be discreetly replaced at some later date. Vietminh graveyards were not touched. Gradually the population opened up. When they did, we learned that the thirty thousand Vietminh troops who evacuated to the North had made one serious mistake, at least in the short term: they had taken from the villages, by force in many cases, almost five thousand twelve-to-fourteen-year-old males. Their families were, for the most part, very unhappy. Information began to flow about the location of secret arms caches, which were found and dug up, several hundred of them, in the first two months of Operation Liberty. It seemed the Vietminh weren't putting much stock in the free elections proposed by Geneva.

ON TO NAM CAN

The smaller force coming down by boat from Rach Gia was a week late, delayed by blocked canals, which had had to be cleared by hand. Because of that Colonel Duc postponed pushing on to Nam Can, at the southern tip of Camau. This was the second-largest population center on the peninsula and a major producer of charcoal, but it could be reached only by canal. With the boats in hand, Colonel Duc organized a visit with a company-sized force and invited me to go. Colonel Duc felt it was too risky to take any Operation Brotherhood personnel. He had little intelligence on the area and no advance knowledge of the reception we were likely to receive.

Not knowing what to expect either, except it would be very hot going, I showed up in my habitual khaki shorts and a short-sleeve shirt. The trip was expected to take all day—Nam Can was at least sixty kilometers due south. Climbing into the usual wooden, flat-bottomed boat with outboard motors, we left in the early morning. Lily pads choked some of the canals and intermittently fouled propellers, which stopped the whole expedition. The scenery was completely flat and monotonous, with few huts on canal banks and no sampans. In the late afternoon we turned into the Song Cua River, where mangrove trees began lining the banks. Gradually the river widened to about five hundred yards. Dusk began to fall. What looked like a cloud of steam emerged gradually from the mangrove shores; asked about it, an officer in our boat replied laconically, "Mosquitoes." I looked down at my short-sleeved shirt and bare legs, thinking I might be eaten alive before we ever got to Nam Can. At that moment we swung around a bend. There before us, on the shore about a quarter-mile away, lay a collection of wooden buildings and huts. This had to be Nam Can. Beyond, the river continued to widen. We were less than fifteen kilometers from the open sea. Our speed increased, and it looked like we might beat the mosquito cloud that was closing the gap in clear pursuit of fresh blood—ours.

We pulled up at some rickety docks and leapt ashore just as the mosquitoes hit. It was a whining blizzard. Hand swipes in the air left a clear trail. My only defense was a handkerchief, which I waved frantically with one hand while swatting with the other. Hustled off to a local open-air café, we were seated at crude wooden tables under a thatched roof. The proprietor put smoke pots under each table and began serving tea. The smoke cut the mosquitoes but left us gasping, choking for air. How in the name of God, I wondered, do these people survive? As I began to drink my tea, a crowd gathered around the café. It was difficult to see their faces through the smoke and in the fading light. At first I was too preoccupied with breathing to notice much; then a low murmur began from the crowd. The murmur increased to a discernible growl. My companions had not noticed until I asked Colonel Duc what was going on. He turned, got up and approached the crowd, obviously asking the same question.

The response was a roar sounding, like *"Phap."* Duc yelled, *"My, my!"* (America, America). The roar died suddenly and completely. Beyond the hut there was total silence. I told Lieutenant Vuong, seated across from me, that from now on I would be speaking English and he could translate. Vuong translated that—our Vietnamese companions began to laugh, and then the crowd began to laugh. I found out later the French had repeatedly bombed the civilian population of Nam Can during the war. I thought then that Americans would never make that kind of mistake. I was wrong, as future events would show.

Our party bought soup, rice, and fish for supper at the same café. The mosquitoes continued to whine in the shadows. Colonel Duc talked with the crowd. Their greatest need was for mosquito netting; the smoke pots were their only defense. Wondering how we were going to survive the night, I learned that cots with nets were being rigged in a small godown, or warehouse, where charcoal was usually stored. At the end of the meal we made a mad dash for the godown, jumping under the mosquito netting. Sleep was practically impossible, however, not because of the few mosquitoes who got under the net but from the sound of the hungry squadrons trying to bore up through the canvas of the cot beneath. The whine was so loud it was like sleeping on a turbine.

In the morning we toured Nam Can. The people were poverty stricken and diseased; their clothes were in rags. There were numerous kilns and stockpiles of charcoal but few boats to get it to market. Still, it could become a rich area, I thought. Colonel Duc said he would ask for mosquito nets as the most urgent priority and for an Operation Brotherhood team to make periodic visits. I said I would push to get the mosquito nets air dropped as soon as possible; this would dramatize the government's concern. After a monotonous trip back we arrived after dark in Camau Town, where the mosquitoes were tame by comparison.

LESSONS LEARNED

I wanted to get back to Saigon, where I could best help the operation by pushing Colonel Duc's requests for additional boats and materials to bridge the larger canals, as well as for relief supplies and mosquito nets. While explaining this to Colonel Duc, I was conscious of the even bigger occupation operation coming up in April, in central Vietnam; I asked what he thought were some of the lessons of Operation Liberty. I set out to make him feel he could be the author rather than the victim of such a review. Many of his observations coincided with mine, particularly about better logistics, more advance intelligence, more engineers, adequate relief supplies for the population, and so on. I took them all down, asking questions to elicit additional points related to civic action. Mainly, he thought, much longer troop indoctrination was needed.

One of the actions suggested in the National Security Action directive issued by President Diem that had not worked well was a complaint and action system, a letter box into which villagers could drop complaints The purpose was to correct any abuses committed by army troops and counteract secret Vietminh harassment. Unfortunately, most units didn't understand the importance of the idea, and many villagers were illiterate. I suggested that the letter box be supplemented by interviews with villagers about their problems and needs, as well as complaints. Duc accepted the idea.

Good ideas worked best if the Vietnamese thought they were their own. Through a process of dialogue, the Vietnamese would adapt to their own culture and psychology ideas that seemed workable. Sometimes it took a while, but the results justified the effort. Lansdale worked in a way that took advantage of basic principles of human psychology and behavior that could be applied anywhere. I hoped I was getting the knack of it.

Chapter 4

A Bucket of Eels and Operation Giai Phong

The Saigon I returned to was a pot beginning to boil, a veritable basket of crabs, or a bucket of eels, as others called it. Prime Minister Diem had refused to renew the Binh Xuyen gambling concession for the Grande Monde casino. Making a deal with the Binh Xuyen was immoral and would mortgage the government's future once again to the French, who were behind the sect. Diem wouldn't bend. The French had canceled their subsidies to the sect armies. This, in addition to a desire for power, precipitated the formation of a "front" by the Hoa Hao, Cao Dai, and Binh Xuyen against Diem, nominally headed by the Cao Dai pope, Pham Cong Tac, but stage-managed by Bay Vien, the Binh Xuyen warlord, with hidden French support. While the Binh Xuyen were essentially gangsters with nationalistic elements, the Hoa Hao and the Cao Dai were genuine religious sects, each with several armies.

The Hoa Hao, named after the home village of Huynh Phu So, its founder, had about a million adherents in the southwest Delta. Inspired by a revelation in 1939, So began preaching a reformed version of Buddhism based on internal faith rather than ritual and devoted to "the mass of small people." In 1940 he was arrested by the French and committed to an insane asylum, where he converted the Vietnamese doctor in charge of his case. After his release he continued to spread the faith and started to build up a small military force, until he was assassinated by the Vietminh in 1946. After his death the Hoa Hao split into three principal factions, each with its own army, all subsidized by the French.

The Cao Dai religion was a more complicated and eclectic faith of unclear origins, having been founded either in 1919 or in 1925, depending on which adept one talked to. Using a symbol of the all-seeing eye of Buddhism, the Cao Dai; it revered Jesus and Buddha as major saints, with Joan of Arc and Victor Hugo in minor roles. It was a mixture of Confucian teachings, Taoism, and Buddhism, brought up to date and blended with Christianity, the other major Vietnamese religion. Its million and a half adherents too had split into factions, with the major branch centered in Tay Ninh and another principal faction located in the Delta province of Kien Hoa. Like the Hoa Hao, the Cao Dai had a military force, started during World War II with arms from the Japanese. After first resisting the French, it had rallied to Bao Dai and had been supported by French subsidies, with the exception of one important group, headed by General Trinh Minh Thé.

With the cutoff of French subsidies a reality and the prospect of integration into the national army foreboding a loss of power, Bay Vien had a natural basis for promoting the front and plotting a revolt. General Ba Cut, one of the Hoa Hao generals, was already openly dissident, threatening to lay siege to Saigon. Playing the role of a wild man, Ba Cut was eccentric, brave, murderous, and often shrewd. He refused to cut his hair, vowing to let it hang around his shoulders "until Vietnam was unified." Charismatic and compelling, he had persuaded some correspondents who interviewed him, such as Joe Alsop, that he would cut off Saigon unless accommodated. Known to rely heavily for advice on Major Savani, an old colonial hand still active with French army intelligence, he had rallied to the French and gone back into opposition three previous times.[1] At the same time, Bao Dai was playing an ambiguous role, keeping a foot in all camps, which had the effect of diluting Diem's authority. Elements in the army were still susceptible to Bao Dai's influence.

A critical break in the combined hostility of the sects came with General Thé's decision to support Diem by integrating his troops into the Vietnamese army. His was the most disciplined and effective fighting force of the Cao Dai. At Diem's request, Lansdale had made a secret visit to Thé in September 1954, at his Nui Ba Den (Black Lady Mountain) headquarters north of Tay Ninh. The diminutive general impressed Lansdale as a true Vietnamese patriot, nationalist, and effective grassroots guerrilla leader, a man who had fought both the French and the Vietminh with considerable success. Their one-day meeting—during which the conversation went from Lansdale to Joe Redick in English, from Redick to Thé's aide in French, and from the aide to Thé in Vietnamese, and back again—created a bond of mutual trust. Thé, like Diem, was personally incorruptible. French claims of bribery to the contrary, all he wanted was pay for his troops and help for the civilian population in Tay Ninh. Diem, who had practically no available resources, was given covert funds by Lansdale, initially to accept some refugees from the North and subsequently to pay Thé's men.[2]

On February 13, while I was still in Camau, twenty-five hundred of Thé's soldiers, who had been selected for integration into the national army, marched in Saigon in their black pajamas. The men in the outer ranks wore shoes; the inside ranks wore peasant sandals or went barefoot. According to Conein, who had seen both, Thé's troops looked remarkably like the hardened Vietminh veterans who had marched into Hanoi on foot as the French, with their panoply of armored vehicles, pulled out the previous October. It was one Saigon parade I was sorry to have missed.

The deteriorating political situation in Saigon was further complicated by the relationship between General Collins and General Ely, the French commander. Collins trusted Ely as a "man of honor," usually believing what Ely told him. General Ely did seem to be a man of honor, but he had a bitter prejudice against Diem, which his staff fed by lying to him. Added to local French distaste for Diem because of his uncompromising nationalism was the charge that the Americans had been responsible for Diem's appointment in the first place. References in the French press to Diem were universally to the "American-backed Diem," "the American marionette." The truth was the Americans had had little role in what had been Bao Dai's decision, with French acquiescence, as a last gesture of "decency" in a losing cause. At the time, American contact with Bao Dai was severely limited. Our Paris embassy did not want to offend the French by taking a more direct role in Indochina affairs. Its primary objective was to get France to join the European Defense Community. French harping about how we had appointed Diem got Secretary of State Dulles so irritated that he bluntly told General Collins, "Diem was picked not by us but by the French."[3] The French line on this, and much else that was fabricated out of their bitterness over our role in Vietnam, would unfortunately persist in many subsequent American accounts of our involvement.

Despite the uneasy situation in Saigon, I expedited support for Colonel Duc's most urgent requests, working through the same Colonel Kim I'd gotten to know earlier through our joint planning efforts. Kim arranged for an air drop of mosquito nets for Nam Can almost immediately after I explained its urgency. Colonel Duc's other requests for additional assistance received further support from Prime Minister Diem, who had made a brief trip to Camau, shortly after I returned to Saigon. I also prepared a written report about Operation Liberty, which Lansdale rushed to Diem. Saigon was such a rumor mill that most of the reports he was getting about Colonel Duc were unfavorable: Duc was conspiring with the Hoa Hao, Duc was siphoning off troop pay, and so on. Diem remained skeptical even after his trip to Camau, but he had come to trust Lansdale's judgment. I found the same malaise at the Vietnamese army General Staff, but Kim was beginning to trust me. I told him Duc was not very imaginative but that he supported civic action and was getting better at it. He was also honest, and his requests were realistic.

Many Vietnamese found it difficult to work with each other. Mutual trust was lacking, dishearteningly at times. Bad reports tended to be given more credence than good. People seemed conditioned to expect failure and double dealing. This was understandable, given the conspiratorial nature of their political history. The decades leading to the 1950s had been marked by ferment and underground political rivalry among nationalist groups, encouraged to splinter by French policies of divide and rule. In this divisive environment, Lansdale and some of his team began playing a catalyst role of honest brokers to help make things work while giving the Vietnamese the time and, they hoped, the opportunity to begin dealing more openly and frankly with each other. That the Vietnamese sometimes trusted Lansdale and his team more than each other was perhaps unusual but not astonishing. We made it clear that their best interests were our interests, which generated trust. This trust did not always pull the Vietnamese together, but it helped and later became a missing element as American participation in Vietnamese affairs grew more formal, massive, bureaucratic, and insensitive.

OPERATION GIAI PHONG

Trying to cope with sect plotting, Collins' obtuseness, and resurging French colonialism occupied practically all of Lansdale's time, so I was given free rein to help Colonel Kim and his staff plan for the upcoming occupation of Interzone Five in central Vietnam, Operation Giai Phong ("Breaking Chains"). Two army divisions were pulled together, the 31st and 32nd, with approximately twelve thousand men each from various Vietnamese army territorial battalions, some of which were already in central Vietnam.[4] Troops from central Vietnam were to be used to the extent possible, to avoid some of the difficulties encountered in communicating with the population in Camau. The divisions would be formed and located as soon as possible in temporary camps in upper Quang Ngai Province, just north of the Interzone Five boundary, so training could be started at least a month in advance of the kickoff on April 22. The paper I drafted on lessons learned from Operation Liberty was translated by Lieutenant Vuong and widely circulated as a Vietnamese document to the unit commanders who would be involved in the new operation. Kim designated a G-5 staff officer for each battalion taking part in the operation, with responsibility for troop education and indoctrination and for planning civic action and public information. "Every soldier a civic action agent," was the theme. A code of conduct was printed on pocket-sized cards and distributed to each soldier.

I developed a two-week course, "Morale Action and Psychological Warfare Field Operations," for the G-5 officers. "Morale action" was meant to convince the average soldier that service to the population was something he had a stake in, that good troop behavior was important to South Vietnam's survival as a free country. "Psychological warfare" was defined this way: "In order to win in its struggle against Communism, the government of Free Vietnam must win the support and the loyalty of its citizens down at the village level. How the government goes about this job, the means it uses, and the behavior pattern of loyalty and support that the means produce is in the largest sense psychological warfare." After revisions by Colonel Kim, the course was taught to all the G-5 officers, down to battalion level.[5]

The idea that an independent Vietnamese government existed worth fighting for—or in this case, carrying out civic action for—had to be instilled in the minds of the troops. Since most of Interzone Five had been under Vietminh rule for nine years, it seemed a daunting task. By early March, the Vietnamese were able to run the course, and before the end of April all the G-5 student officers had returned to their units, where they began giving a concentrated version to all the troops. Every soldier had to be reached. A psychological change was going on among the officer corps of the army. As French intervention became more blatant (as we'll see later), Vietnamese pride and nationalism rose, which raised army morale at all levels. Many Vietnamese politicians continued sitting on the fence, but officers with dual citizenship began renouncing loyalty to France. Colonel Kim was one of those. It was a brave act, given the uncertainties of the time. Lansdale had suggested to Diem that Kim was the most qualified to command Operation Giai Phong; in a direct meeting, Kim made it clear to Diem his loyalty was to South Vietnam. I was overjoyed when I learned Diem had agreed to appoint him.

French participation in planning Operation Giai Phong with the Vietnamese was useful, particularly when their senior logistics officers and their navy got involved, because the Vietnamese army remained dependent on the French for gasoline as well as for bridging and road reconstruction equipment. Since there were no ports along our route of advance south within Interzone Five, all equipment and materials would have to be transported using shallow-draft, World War II LSTs (landing ship, tank) with ramps capable of being lowered directly onto beaches. All the LSTs were in French hands. On the other hand, the French intelligence types serving in the National Security Division spent most of their time keeping track of me. When they learned that I was once again the only TRIM officer permitted by the Vietnamese to accompany the operation, they protested vehemently and demanded their officers be permitted too. Colonel Kim said, "There will be no foreigners." The French replied, "What do you mean no foreigners, he's a foreigner," pointing at me. Kim said, "He's no foreigner, he's our friend." The French stomped out.[6]

Lieutenant Colonel Jacques Romain-Defosses, Lansdale's deputy, had spent seventeen years in Vietnam and had great affection for the Vietnamese. He was the most positive French officer in our division. A man of sensibility, he was bothered, one could sense, by the negative atmosphere. To improve relations, he invited Americans to his home for social, get-acquainted evenings. One evening, when I was the sole American present, the situation became tense when other officers could not refrain from criticizing us for not intervening to support the French at Dien Bien Phu, for "appointing" Diem, for turning the Vietnamese against the French, for not listening to the French, who knew Vietnam best—a litany of complaints.

At first I refused to respond, in deference to my host, who tried to restrain them, but they would not stop. Everything that was going wrong and had gone wrong was our fault. Finally

I responded, "We don't pretend to know everything there is to know about Vietnam or that we are always right, but we do listen to the Vietnamese. What they want above all is true independence, which you failed to give them. Why are you still unwilling to see them be independent?" The more I talked the angrier I got. "And more than that, how can you ever justify in 1946 helping the communists hunt down and kill anticommunist Vietnamese nationalists? Tell me about that," I practically yelled. Dead silence fell. Romain-Defosses averted his eyes. Some faces were tinged with guilt, others looked at me with hatred that I had touched on something so damning.

Madame Romain-Defosses broke up the confrontation by asking me about my family. Talk switched to social and personal matters. As soon as I could with courtesy, I excused myself. Romain-Defosses went with me to the door. "I am sorry," he said with obvious sadness. "We French should not behave like that." I told him I had arrived as a Francophile and would never become a Francophobe, no matter the provocation. That was my last social contact with the French, although Romain-Defosses remained unfailingly courteous and kind at work. I found I could count on him to follow up on the logistical support the Vietnamese needed for Operation Giai Phong. In contrast to many other of his fellow officers at TRIM, he genuinely wanted, I believe, to see the Vietnamese succeed.

IN THE BINH XUYEN LINE OF FIRE

On March 29, Binh Xuyen hostility to the government broke into the open. At midnight the sect attacked the national army headquarters and the Saigon police headquarters, earlier peacefully occupied by the national army. They also began lobbing mortar shells at the presidential palace from their headquarters across the "Y" bridge, where the Saigon River split into two tributaries. I had moved from the Paul Blanchy apartment to the Rue Taberd "pool house," so named because it had a swimming pool. That night I awakened to the sound of mortar rounds exploding nearby. Unfortunately, the "pool house" was in the direct line of fire between the Binh Xuyen and the palace. Its masonry construction appeared capable of withstanding a direct hit on the roof by a "short" round, but an exposed back room downstairs contained several thousand pounds of plastic C-3 explosive, along with detonators and primacord (a high-velocity explosive in clothesline form) destined for burial as caches for possible stay-behind agents up north or in the south, should the Vietminh take over. While we were trying to decide whether we were safer in the house or the open street, the shelling ceased. The nearest round had landed about fifty yards away, in a corner of the palace grounds. The next day, all was quiet. We got sandbags for the back room.

Events leading up to the Binh Xuyen attack had begun on March 4, when the religious sects had formed their "front." In addition to the sects, the front had some support from Vietnamese political figures known to be close to Bao Dai. For about two weeks nothing much happened. Then on March 21 the front issued an ultimatum to Diem: "Reorganize your government within five days. Replace it with one that is suitable." Diem was to be kicked upstairs as honorary prime minister; the sects would run the government. While Diem offered to negotiate, the chief of national police, Lai Van Sang, refused to follow any orders from the government. Diem fired him. Sang holed up in police headquarters, refusing to leave. In order to take the national police headquarters, the army would have to cross a French-controlled corridor within Saigon. Diem asked Collins to intercede with the French, so as to permit the government to gain control over its own police force. Collins refused. Two of the Cao Dai generals, Trinh Minh Thé and Phuong, who had joined the front when it was first organized, now announced their support for the government. The Binh Xuyen evidently thought this was their best chance to move. They were surprised—the national army's smaller forces repelled the attacks. When an attempt was made to move up reinforcements for a counterattack, the French army, which still had thirty thousand troops in and around Saigon, blocked off the streets and enforced a truce.

During the truce, Howard Simpson from the USIS press office interviewed a leading Binh Xuyen at General Bay Vien's headquarters. As the official was blandly claiming the Binh Xuyen were the true nationalists, with the best interests of Vietnam at heart, a French officer emerged from the Binh Xuyen radio room with a clipboard full of papers, and a French army dispatch rider roared up on his motorcycle and rushed into the headquarters with a leather folder under his arm. When Simpson reported this obvious direct French involvement to the embassy political section, he was not believed.[7]

Lansdale went to see Collins to protest the truce. Collins told him the primary goal must be to prevent further bloodshed. Ely had said the French army must be used to enforce a truce, and Collins had agreed. The truce incensed the national army. Even though they had only six battalions to the Binh Xuyen's combined forces of eleven, they believed they could win, and so did Diem. Saigon settled into an uneasy thirty-day truce, but Vietnamese nationalist sentiment was inflamed by the blatant French interference. There was a groundswell of popular support for Diem.

Around this time, Lansdale held an emergency meeting of his immediate staff. Conein came in late and was the last to report. In a casual way, he said he had learned from some of his Corsican friends about a plot to blow up President Diem, with a bomb already planted along the route of a car trip that was scheduled to occur in a few hours. Lansdale turned pale. "Why didn't you tell me about this sooner?" "Well," Conein countered in typical fashion, "you didn't ask." Lansdale rushed off to the palace to warn Diem. Conein's contrariness drove Lansdale wild at times, but he tolerated it, because it came with the territory.

TAKING OFF FOR CENTRAL VIETNAM

In mid-April, in this uncertain atmosphere, Colonel Kim and I took off for central Vietnam to inspect the units being assembled to launch Operation Giai Phong on the 22nd. We landed at the port city of Tourane (Danang) and after inspecting the units there made our way south by jeep to the town of Quang Ngai, in the province of the same name. It took us twelve hours, so badly damaged were the roads. The northern part of Quang Ngai had been occupied by the Vietnamese army in October 1954, but almost nothing had been repaired.

Central Vietnam's narrow coastal plain was very different from the Mekong Delta. Often the coastal strip became so narrow one could see simultaneously the mountains on one side and the sea on the other. Here, every inch of available land was cultivated; the people were not strung out along canals as in the Delta but clustered in hamlets surrounded by rice fields. In the dry season, which was upon us, the days were unbearably hot in the broiling sun, relieved only by the shade of the ubiquitous coconut palms. On the coast the air would usually cool down at night, with breezes off the South China Sea. The people appeared even more poverty stricken than in Camau. There was very little room to bivouac without damaging rice fields, although a few uncultivated fields were available, so Kim had decided to assemble one division back at Tourane for transport by ship and one in Quang Ngai ready to enter by road.

Under the agreement with the International Control Commission, the occupation was to take place in three successive territorial sections (or "tranches"), from north to south. The occupation of each tranche was to take about a week. The first tranche was the southern part of Quang Ngai Province, ending at the beach of Sa Huynh, a natural harbor for landing the division from Tourane by sea for subsequent entry into Binh Dinh Province. Binh Dinh was in turn divided into two tranches. The last tranche consisted of the lower of these, from which the Vietminh were to evacuate their forces on May 16 through the port city of Qui Nhon.

Our drive to Quang Ngai and then briefly south to the current demarcation line of the Vietminh-controlled zone gave us an idea of what we were facing. There was one railroad line, on which some of the bridges were out, and one road, in bad condition. Reportedly, parts of the road in Vietminh territory had been restored and the bridges repaired by the Vietminh themselves after Geneva. Progress would be slow and difficult in any case. Some bridging material was on hand, however, and more had been promised by the French, though not yet delivered.

This time two Operation Brotherhood teams, including personnel with previous experience in Vietnam, stood by to support the operation. At Colonel Kim's insistence, the teams were not to enter until the army had located facilities for them. The initial need for medical assistance, a high priority, would be met by Vietnamese army nurses, many of whom were no longer needed for refugee relief. First Lt. Dave Smith had arrived in late December and was assigned by Lansdale to support Operation Brotherhood.[8] Unaware of Smith's arrival because of garbled messages, none of us met him at the airport. He found his way to MAAG by taxi, where he was received as part of their regular staff. He spent his first week in Saigon as the acting headquarters commandant for MAAG/Saigon until Joe Baker, our administrative officer, discovered him and got him released to Lansdale's command. In the meantime he had signed for all the furnishings and equipment in MAAG headquarters. Getting someone else at MAAG to take over the inventory consumed a lot of administrative time our small mission didn't have.

Dave began sitting in on our Giai Phong planning meetings with the Vietnamese when we discussed Operation Brotherhood support. He had the most fractured French imaginable but used it with unflappable verve. I never saw the Vietnamese more attentive than when he was speaking. They would hang on his every word, trying to figure out what he was saying. At one meeting I didn't attend, he learned that the Vietnamese had a nickname for me, *le monstre aimable,* "the amiable monster." I was pretty sure Dave, an inveterate jokester, had originated the name himself.

One of Dave's more urgent assignments was to locate the U.S. Army field hospitals, complete with operating-room equipment, that were known to have been delivered as American military assistance to the French. The French were shipping all unused American military aid back to France as fast as they could for use in Algeria, unless we could specifically locate it and request that it be kept in country. By dint of extraordinary detective work, Dave found two completely equipped field hospitals in a warehouse on the Saigon docks just as they were about to be loaded on a French ship. Only an order personally signed by General O'Daniel stopped the shipment. With this equipment we planned to set up one hospital in Quang Ngai, just outside the boundary of the zone to be occupied, and another in Qui Nhon at the end of the occupation, both to be operated by Operation Brotherhood. In the two provinces there was a population of almost one and half million people. The OB doctors and nurses would find the population in the occupied zone even worse off medically than that in Camau.

While Colonel Kim concentrated on getting his units into a final state of readiness and the logistics in place, I spent my time with the psywar companies and with the G-5 officers who had been trained in Saigon. There were now two psywar companies—one under Captain Duc that had gone into Camau and another that had recently been reorganized. The companies were busy performing "good soldier"/"bad soldier" skits for the troops to illustrate how to behave with the population. I also monitored the courses being given by the G-5 officers and found them faithfully following the course material. The troops seemed more attentive than had those whom I had accompanied into Camau. Every night the soldiers' radios were tuned to Vietnamese broadcasts from Saigon. I interpreted the Voice of America and BBC English-language news for Kim. We also heard French shortwave, which was full of quotes from sect leaders referring to "bloody Diem." I wondered how it was all going to turn out. Nationalist sentiment was running high among the troops, against the sects and against the French. But whether there was going to be a legitimate Vietnamese government to turn Interzone Five over to once it had been occupied was not clear.

OPERATION GIAI PHONG BEGINS

On the night of the April 21, word came from the commander of a French engineer company assigned as a buffer between the Vietnamese national army and the Vietminh that the Vietminh had pulled out. We could start our occupation in the morning. Kim offered me the option of going with him in his jeep or coming later, which might be less hazardous. When I asked him if he wasn't concerned the Vietminh might use my presence to say the South Vietnamese were colonial puppets, Kim laughed: "Who would believe that someone as young as you in civilian clothes could be my advisor?"

When Kim left early in the morning, I was in the back of his jeep. We were preceded by an engineer unit and followed by a convoy of the division's troops in jeeps, followed in turn by troops on foot. The convoy included a few civilian administrators who were to begin setting up government services. (Some turned out to be a nuisance, as they had few practical ideas of what to do and spent most of their time reporting rumors.) Initially, we made fair progress toward Sa Huynh, formerly a center of salt production, some sixty kilometers to the south. Our intelligence was poor, however, on the exact state of the road ahead. Kim had heard that the Vietminh had recently destroyed bridges and recut parts of the road, just to obstruct our entry. He had tried to send in an unarmed reconnaissance team before the operation began, but it had been blocked by the French buffer company. He had spoken to the French major in charge asking him about the condition of the road, but the major had arrogantly refused to give any information. So we were flying blind.

By the end of the day we had used up all of our bridging material for repair and were only at the village of Duc Pho, about twenty kilometers north of Sa Huynh. The coastal road ahead crossed several streams, some with old concrete bridges, now destroyed, and others with makeshift bamboo and wooden bridges, some of them recently wrecked by the Vietminh. A rendezvous had been arranged with French supply ships for the next morning at Sa Huynh. The ships were at sea, and we had no way of communicating with them. Given the current French state of mind, if they arrived and we were not there, they would probably return to Tourane. Kim decided to keep going, using the railroad tracks; most of its trestles were intact. Kim said he had no idea of what we might run into—maybe it would be better for me to stay and make the trip during daylight. I said no, maybe he could use me as ballast in the back of his jeep. He smiled. With help from his troops we pushed the jeeps up a steep incline and onto the railroad tracks in the last few minutes of daylight.

After eating C-rations, we started bumping across the ties, the jeeps' wheels just outside the narrow-gauge rails. It was pitch dark except for the headlights. I began to wonder if I had made the right decision as we jolted along; riding in the back seat was particularly tooth jarring. We were slowed by the need to stay on the tracks; otherwise the jeeps bounced so badly they could easily fly off. When we came to each trestle we stopped and reconnoitered on foot with a flashlight. The jeep headlights gave the illusion that the track continued, but only on foot could that be proven. The flashlights didn't reach far enough to determine the height of some of the trestles or whether all the foundations were still in place. We could hear streams but not see them. It was slow going, but we were making progress.

Finally, about three in the morning, when we thought we should be at Sa Huynh, we came to a trestle that had recently been destroyed. About fifty feet out, the track dropped off into an abyss. We would have to go down into the gulch. We slid down the embankment leading to the bridge and found a wide depression with a shallow stream, which could be forded if the jeeps could get off the railroad and back on what remained of the old road. By backing up, we found a route. We maneuvered the jeeps into the stream bed and pushed them up the other side and back onto the road, which then went over a rise. From the other side we now heard the steady beat of surf. As we coasted down the hill, we saw diked salt ponds looming in the headlights. It had to be Sa Huynh. At the bottom of the hill, we tumbled onto ponchos on the ground and slept the few remaining hours before dawn.

In the morning, across the salt ponds, we saw at first light a half-moon beach about a thousand yards long, ringed by a grove of coconut palms over glistening white sand. Steep, jagged cliffs fell shear into the sea at both ends. Behind us was the road on which we had come, ascending to a saddle between the seaside cliffs and the dramatic backdrop of a mountain ridge that curved to run north and south, parallel to the road. Just in front of us but back from the beach a small village nestled in the palms. We drove around the salt ponds to the palm grove, which was so picturesque as to seem imaginary, as if it had magically been transported from Tahiti. At the south end, large rollers came in from the South China Sea, while to the north the cliffs curved enough to provide shelter; the beach there was reasonably flat and the water much calmer than at the south end. It was ideal for the LSTs. Kim decided to set up his headquarters in a large palm grove. The coconut trees would provide shade and at the same time easy observation of the entire sweep of the beach and of any ships rounding the northern cliffs.

As the morning wore on, tents were pitched in the palms for our quarters and additional vehicles and men began to arrive. The first LST steamed in, opened its bow doors, and dropped its ramp without difficulty. Out came pierced steel planking, which was laid as a roadway across the beach. Then came troops, trucks, and various crates of supplies, but little bridging material. Kim's radios could not communicate on the ship's frequencies, so he had to walk on board through the bow to meet the captain and review the manifest. He was upset when he returned, having found almost no bridging material. The captain knew nothing about the schedule of the rest of the ships or what they might be carrying. Using my direct radio contact with MAAG in Saigon, I let them know we had arrived and that more bridging was urgently needed for our next advance south in about a week. By midday, Captain Duc and Lieutenant Vuong had arrived with the psywar company.

Sa Huynh proved a pleasant place. The dry season was at its height, without a cloud in the sky. The temperature soared during the day, particularly near the beach, where the sun was reflected off the sand. I stayed mainly in the shade of the palms for most of the day, swam and bathed in the surf in the evening. The news by shortwave radio from Saigon was not encouraging. Violent incidents—ascribed to the Binh Xuyen by Radio Saigon and the Voice of America, and to the Vietnamese army by French radio—were happening with increasing frequency. On April 25, Diem broadcast an appeal to the sects to negotiate. The appeal was refused. I could feel gloom descending on Kim and his staff. Were the sects going to win? I started to worry about the morale of the troops, which had so far been high despite the uncertain situation in Saigon.

The swath of territory now occupied by the national army extended down to a wide river near a town called Bong Son, which was slightly inland and had been the Vietminh headquarters for Interzone Five. French troops had landed south of Qui Nhon during Operation Atlante in 1953 but had never penetrated very far north. The Bong Son bridge across the river, an impressive steel structure on large concrete piers, had been blown up, I was told, during the war against the French. It appeared possible to erect a makeshift pedestrian bridge on wooden piles. In the meantime, troops and vehicles would have to be moved across the river by local ferry if we were to continue the march south.

The French major commanding the buffer force between us and the retreating Vietminh was deliberately frustrating Kim. He would not allow an advance party of Kim's engineers to cross the river to find the best location for a temporary bridge, even though the Vietminh forces had already left. He said he would open fire if Kim's engineers so much as budged across the stream. Kim asked me to send a special message to Lansdale requesting General O'Daniel's intercession with the French command. I got on the radio to TRIM, repeating Kim's words in French. Without my knowing it, those words were immediately conveyed not to Lansdale but to O'Daniel's French chief of staff, Colonel Jean Carbonel. Carbonel then complained to O'Daniel that one of Lansdale's men was inciting the Vietnamese against the French. It was as they had suspected, now they had proof. He demanded that Lansdale be removed from command. O'Daniel rejected the charge, but it was a diversion Lansdale did not need. The French were already pressing at higher levels for his removal. I knew something was wrong when I received a terse message from Lansdale asking me to come to Saigon immediately. I was reluctant to go as we were about to enter the northern part of Binh Dinh, but I had my orders. Kim thought I could do more good in Saigon at that moment by getting better French cooperation and the needed bridging materials. The problem was how to get out.

I urged Kim to return to Saigon as well, to see what was going on and to get more support for the operation, if he could get a plane to pick him up. Although he did not say so, I knew he was concerned for his family, who lived in what could become a combat zone if war broke out in the city. There was nowhere at Sa Huynh for a Morane to land, except the beach, which was tricky. Kim arranged a Morane for the next day, but it had only one passenger seat. He was willing to risk a takeoff from the beach if he was the passenger but thought it too dangerous for me, with my extra weight. Travel by road back up to Tourane would take a minimum of two days. In the meantime, we now knew, there was a French LST due that same morning that would turn around after unloading to go back to Tourane. I could board the LST, catch a military flight to Saigon from Tourane the following morning, and arrive the same day as Kim, who would fly out after supervising the initial entry of his troops into Binh Dinh Province. As soon as he arrived he was to call me at Lansdale's house. In the meantime I would set up a meeting with Lansdale and General O'Daniel.

The French LST came on schedule, but despite several tries, large swells caused by a distant storm made beaching impossible. The captain indicated by loud hailer, the only means of communication, that he was returning to Tourane. I grabbed a loud hailer from the army psywar company and told him I wanted to board the ship but got no reply. The ship backed away from the beach area and but then appeared to heave to. I persuaded a local fisherman to take me out in his sampan. While he rowed and steered from the stern I stood precariously in the bow trying to yell to the captain on the ship's bridge. The waves were so high that we would drop out of sight in a trough, only to be swept to the top of the next wave, from which I could yell a few words, and then wait for the next wave to get the reply. After an interval that seemed interminable, only the fisherman's dexterity keeping us from capsizing, the captain signaled I could come on board.

Now the problem was how to get there. The hull rose and fell above us; there was no accommodation ladder. A cargo net was lowered over the side. With great skill the fisherman maneuvered us alongside, bow into the waves and about six feet from the hull. At the crest of a wave I made a desperate leap for the net, a small bag slung over my shoulder; I managed to hang on and began to climb before the next wave came rushing by. My gyrations attracted a crowd of seamen, who applauded as I clambered over the ship's rail.

The captain was gruff at first, but he relaxed when he saw my TRIM identification card. To the crew I was, *"le fou Americain."* In Tourane, I managed to talk my way onto a Vietnamese air force C-47 to Saigon the next day by waving my TRIM card and dropping General O'Daniel's name.

Chapter 5
The Battle for Saigon

Flying to Saigon from Tourane on April 28, I was unaware of the events then transpiring in Saigon. General Collins had left for Washington on April 20, after telling Lansdale that American policy was still firmly behind Diem. However, he was really going to Washington to reverse that policy and support a new coalition government without Diem. In a series of briefings after his arrival, including a meeting with President Eisenhower on Friday, April 22, Collins recommended strongly that Diem be replaced. Eisenhower commented on congressional difficulties such a change would entail and made no final commitment, awaiting Secretary Dulles, who was away over the weekend. General Collins met with Dulles and CIA director Allen Dulles on April 25 and with Senators Mike Mansfield and William Fulbright on April 26.

Collins came away from these meetings, including the one with the president and another with Mansfield, convinced that his views had been accepted. Secretary Dulles was not fully convinced Collins was right, but he nevertheless cabled Paris and Saigon on April 27 (April 28 in Saigon), proposing a change in policy favoring the removal of Diem and his replacement by a coalition government. Only six hours later, on the same day, Dulles sent another telegram disavowing the first. Between these two telegrams, Lansdale had sent a message from Saigon recommending against any change in U.S. support for Diem.[1] While it is not clear why Lansdale sent this telegram at that time, it seems probable that he found out about the pending policy change through a back-channel communication from the CIA in Washington.

I arrived at the Saigon airport early in the afternoon of April 28 and took a taxi direct to Lansdale's house. By this time there was a thick pall of smoke over Saigon. As I approached the house, the thump of 105-mm artillery shells and the crackling of machine gun fire were heard from the Cholon side of the city. Only two people were there: Major Bohannon from the Philippines and a tall Marine lieutenant my age, John Gates. Bohannon told me Lansdale was out but expected back. He filled me in. An initial Binh Xuyen drive-by shooting at Vietnamese army officers had occurred the day before. The Binh Xuyen had started dropping mortar rounds on the presidential palace around 1:15 today. (Lansdale had visited the palace around noon to talk to Diem and returned home. Then Diem phoned Lansdale after the mortaring started to say he was calling on the army to attack.) The initial reports about the army's success were favorable, but the outcome was still uncertain.[2]

Gates had recently arrived and seemed stunned. Lou Conein had driven him from the airport into Saigon, a Gauloise cigarette hanging from one side of his mouth, in a wild ride punctuated by voluble curses in gutter French and laconic but colorful descriptions in English of the combat. When Gates reported in he was completely ignored; Lansdale and Conein

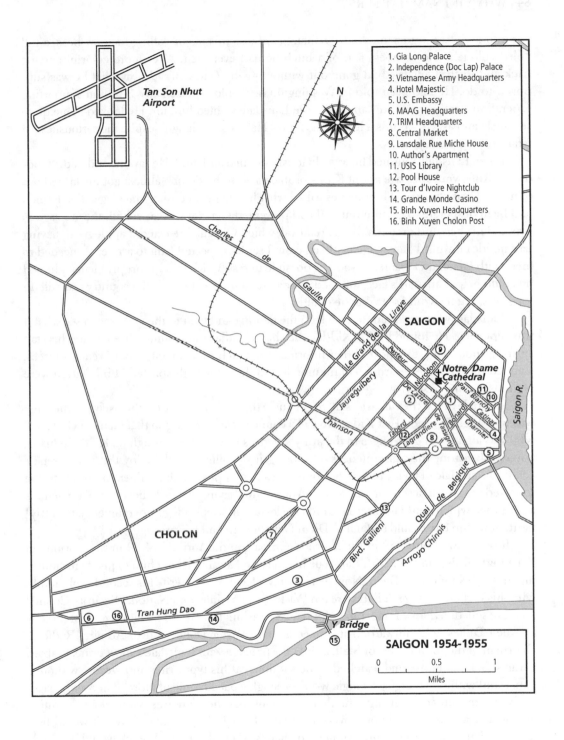

Tan Son Nhut
Airport

N

1. Gia Long Palace
2. Independence (Doc Lap) Palace
3. Vietnamese Army Headquarters
4. Hotel Majestic
5. U.S. Embassy
6. MAAG Headquarters
7. TRIM Headquarters
8. Central Market
9. Lansdale Rue Miche House
10. Author's Apartment
11. USIS Library
12. Pool House
13. Tour d'Ivoire Nightclub
14. Grande Monde Casino
15. Binh Xuyen Headquarters
16. Binh Xuyen Cholon Post

Charles

de

Gaulle

SAIGON

Le Grand de la Liraye

Pasteur

Jaureguibery

De Norodom

Notre Dame
Cathedral

Paris Blanchy

Catinat

Saigon R.

Chanson

Taberd

De Lattre de Tassigny

Lagrandiere

Bonard

Charner

CHOLON

Blvd. Gallieni

Quai de Belgique

Arroyo Chinois

Tran Hung Dao

Y Bridge

SAIGON 1954-1955

0   0.5   1

Miles

got into a violent argument. All he remembered was this major calling his new boss, a full "bird colonel," the dumbest son of a bitch he had ever seen. After more colorful cursing back and forth, Lansdale had gone out without giving Gates any idea of what he was supposed to do. He had been told in Washington he would replace Dave Smith in supporting Operation Brotherhood and anything else Lansdale wanted him for. He looked at me quite seriously and asked, "Is this a lunatic asylum?" He made me laugh despite the seriousness of what was happening.[3]

When Lansdale returned he was obviously strained and tired. He saw me and said, "Goddamit, Rufe, your message about Kim's problems with the French almost got me kicked out of here." I was stunned. Then he described what had happened to my message. The French had been desperate to get him out and had presented General O'Daniel with the message as proof of his bias and grounds for his removal, which O'Daniel rejected. I apologized, having had no idea it would have such an effect. Now, I said, I expected Kim to arrive; we needed to meet with General O'Daniel as soon as possible to resolve Kim's support problems. I hoped he could help. Lansdale's face softened. There was a war on, he said, the country was still up for grabs, but he would see what he could do.

Lansdale went out again to check on the fighting and then to the embassy to see what it was reporting. He found Randy Kidder, the chargé d'affairs in Collins' absence, and his staff arguing about what to report. Their information, which came mainly from French sources, claimed the Vietnamese army had no morale and that "the high spirited" Binh Xuyen were obviously going to win.

Lansdale urged the embassy staff to get out in the streets and see for themselves—the army was winning. He tried to get Kidder to call a country team meeting so that General O'Daniel, who was already an eyewitness to the army's aggressiveness, could weigh in. Kidder refused, apparently fearing the consequences of going against Collins. Frank Meloy, the first secretary, accused Lansdale of trying to use the country team to oppose Collins. Then the army attaché reported in and sent a separate message to Washington saying that he believed "any US actions at this time which could by inference indicate lessening support legal government current[ly] fighting within city would be fatal to Diem Government and US prestige here."[4]

It was now about 5:30 in the afternoon in Saigon on April 28 (4:30 in the morning in Washington, also on the 28th). Lansdale had received a cable asking him to justify his morning message supporting Diem. Now he had only a few hours to write his second cable amplifying his earlier message. It had to reach Washington in time for a National Security Council meeting scheduled for the morning of April 28, Washington time. The message went directly to Allen Dulles, who forwarded it immediately to Foster Dulles and to Admiral Radford, chairman of the Joint Chiefs of Staff, as was the practice with Lansdale's most critical cables. I was still at his house and watched as he sat down at his typewriter and wrote—without a pause and without changing a single word—a single-spaced cable of more than twenty pages analyzing the situation, giving a firsthand account that the army was winning and pointing out once again that a coalition government with French fingerprints all over it would be a disaster, that "any successor government to Diem's acceptable to the French would be unable to carry out the reforms essential to deny Vietnam to the Communists."[5] After that he was exhausted. Redick pushed him into bed. I drove myself over to the Rue Taberd "pool house" and bunked in.

This cable bolstered Secretary Dulles' inclination not to abandon Diem and probably helped persuade President Eisenhower to withdraw the approval he had reluctantly given to General Collins' recommendation to replace Diem. (Eisenhower was close personally to Collins and had specially picked him for the Saigon assignment.) Despite Collins' plea at the National Security Council meeting of April 28 not to waiver from replacing Diem, the consensus was to continue to support the existing South Vietnamese government, "while recognizing the composition of the government might have to be changed and keeping the situation constantly under review."[6] There was no change in support for Diem, although this was not stated directly, probably in deference to Collins, who left the next day for Saigon.

Lansdale had gone out on a limb to report the facts, risking his career. Caving into a deal with the French and the Binh Xuyen, whom the French were protecting, would have spawned a new government with no nationalist standing with its own people. By the time Collins arrived back in Saigon the Vietnamese army had driven the Binh Xuyen from the city and American policy was firmly behind Diem, despite the almost hysterical reactions of General Ely and his staff. Collins accepted the change with grace and even complimented Lansdale in a cable to Washington, saying he had "performed a highly useful service."[7]

While producing that important cable on April 28, Lansdale also called General O'Daniel at his residence. Our meeting about support for Operation Giai Phong was on for the following morning at the MAAG headquarters in Cholon. Kim met Lansdale and me at the TRIM compound on Boulevard Gallieni wearing his army uniform and driving an army staff car. A bizarre scene had just occurred in front of TRIM. A French officer carrying in his arms a young Vietnamese girl with a flesh wound in her leg had given her to Lansdale, accusing him of "killing children." Lansdale had been stunned but gave the girl to another American officer, Lt. Col. George Melvin, who took her to the TRIM dispensary. Lansdale looked at Kim and said he had better come with us; one military post we had to pass to get to MAAG was still in Binh Xuyen hands. Lansdale had rigged an American flag on the fender of his black Citroen 14 sedan, the car favored by French superior officers and often seen in French gangster movies. This particular Citroen and several others had been abandoned by the French during the final evacuation of Haiphong in the North when Conein, carrying out a classic "midnight requisition," had changed the license plates and put the cars on a U.S. Navy ship bound for Saigon. With the exception of the CD (Corps Diplomatique) license plates and the flag, we looked like part of the French general staff or French gangsters on a raid, depending on one's point of view.

The way to Cholon was littered with burned-out buildings and cars. The debris of war and a few bodies were still strewn on the sidewalks. As we entered Cholon, after taking a series of detours around the sporadic fighting, we passed the Binh Xuyen post near MAAG. We could see green berets with eyes underneath peering out over machine-gun barrels from the post's corner turrets. We had pushed Kim down on the floor so he could not be seen. Lansdale drove slowly to give time for us to be identified as official Americans. Nobody fired as we rode by, in eerie silence except for the sound of the car engine and the hum of the tires. With relief, we pulled into the MAAG compound in the next block and were ushered into General O'Daniel's office on the ground floor. We sat on a couch beneath the front windows and had just begun talking when firing broke out. First there were the guttural crumps of artillery shells landing nearby and then the rattle of machine-gun fire. Bullets were ricocheting into MAAG. Scrunching down in our seats to get as far below the window sills as possible, we carried on, yelling to each other above the swelling din.

For about fifteen minutes we shouted above the crumps, the cracks, the rattles, and the whines of ricochets hitting the walls. Then silence fell. Our hollering continued for a few seconds until we laughed at ourselves: "Sounds like they quit without much of a fight," said O'Daniel. He asked for Kim's list of needs again and said he was pleased to hear how well the operation was going, particularly how the troops were being welcomed by the population, despite the logistical problems. He promised Kim he would get the bridging even if he, O'Daniel, had to carry it up to Binh Dinh himself. He slapped us on the back, said he was proud of the national army, and returned a particularly affectionate salute to Kim.

We drove back by the same Binh Xuyen post we had passed. Green berets were strewn on the sidewalk outside. The Binh Xuyen had deserted without much of a fight, taking off their mustard-color uniforms, changing into civilian clothes, and running away—so much for their vaunted ferocity. The greed of their leadership and their identification with the French had provided little motivation to resist a fired-up Vietnamese army moved by newfound national pride. Kim asked us to stop near his house on the way back. There was still sporadic shooting in the area, and the phones were cut off; he would walk home to see how his family was faring and retrieve his car later. I got out of the car. We stood in the street for a moment to shake hands. I asked, "Do you have a gun?" He said, "No." Pulling out the same Beretta I had been carrying since Camau, I said, "Here, take this." I could see tears beginning to form in his eyes. "I am very proud to be Vietnamese," he said. I replied, "You should be." We were a curious sight, a short, slight Vietnamese colonel and a huge American lieutenant hugging each other in the middle of that debris-strewn street. Lansdale looked at me with curiosity when I got back in the car, for there were tears in my eyes too. "He's my friend," I said.

The Vietnamese had come to seem like family. Somehow the aspirations for freedom and independence I took as a given in my own country were now being lived out in another, and I had become part of their fruition. When I thought about it afterward, it seemed to me that I was in some sense reliving our own revolution in another land, where everything had initially seemed strange but was becoming increasingly familiar.

Back at Lansdale's house, people filed in and out with the latest reports on the fighting. In the late afternoon, Lansdale got an urgent call from President Diem to see him at the palace. Diem informed him there that the army had largely cleared Saigon of the Binh Xuyen, except for the area across the Arroyo Chinois, but that the troops were exhausted. At the same time he had just received a vituperative cable from Bao Dai ordering him to turn everything over to General Nguyen Van Vy, whom Bao Dai had just appointed commander in chief of Vietnamese forces and come to France. Diem had the backing of his cabinet to defy Bao Dai, but he wanted to know what Lansdale thought. Lansdale suggested he follow his conscience. At that moment they heard the Binh Xuyen broadcasting Bao Dai's cable. Diem said he would not follow Bao Dai's orders; it would be the end of any moral basis for the Vietnamese government. Lansdale returned and reported the latest turn of events to the embassy over the phone.

The next day Kim and I met again at Lansdale's house with Colonel Melvin, who had taken the wounded girl to the dispensary the day before. Melvin had replaced Sam Karrick in the National Security Division and was acting as its executive officer. Although stunned from the events of the day before, he was fired up to help. We explained in more detail how vital the bridging was. Kim then went back to Ton Son Nhut to fly up to Tourane and then into Binh Dinh.

I stayed in Saigon for a few more days, through May 3, when I learned that Trinh Minh Thé had been killed in combat against the Binh Xuyen. Lansdale was shocked. He had lost a "brother." Grief was plain in his face. We all felt the loss. Thé had been only thirty-three.

Unassuming in person, slight in physique, he would sneak into Saigon dressed in traditional black pajamas, disguised as a cyclo driver, to see Lansdale. A great attraction was his lack of an impressive family background or connections. His rise as a guerrilla commander had been rooted in his performance as an unselfish leader willing to share the sacrifices of his own people as well as in his inner fire and patriotism. These were leadership characteristics that he shared with another former guerrilla, Magsaysay. The French had tried to buy him; he could not be bought. Trinh Minh Thé was nothing like the corrupt warlord portrayed by Graham Greene in *The Quiet American*.[8]

ON TO QUI NHON

The day after Thé's death, I returned to Binh Dinh by Morane, flying into a dry rice paddy south of Bong Son, where Kim now had his headquarters. We were now almost two-thirds of the way through the troop-movement and occupation phase of the operation and were very encouraged by the population's response. Reports of how well the troops were behaving and how helpful they were being to the population were spreading ahead of them by word of mouth. The troops walked south and also west toward hamlets off the main north–south road, usually in single file, each carrying on his pack a small yellow and red national flag. We were near the height of the dry season. Temperatures rose easily to 110 degrees Fahrenheit in the sun. People were beginning to bring drinking water voluntarily to the thirsty men.

To see what was happening, Captain Duc or Lieutenant Vuong and I sometimes rode out in front and waited for a column of troops to appear, in order to see public reaction. I was struck by how more disciplined the troops looked than they had in Camau in February. They wore the same fatigues with the same floppy bush hats, but their posture and step had changed. They seemed to be proud of what they were doing. There was a sense of confidence I had not seen before. The population reacted much more warmly than in Camau. I could sometimes pick out in the crowd the obvious hard-core Vietminh cadre who had been directed to stay behind. He would watch the troops with intense, cold hatred in his eyes. Once, after I locked eyes with one, he faded quickly back into the crowd.

The population didn't seem to be following the Vietminh line. In order to sustain morale during the war, the Vietminh had made promises about educating children and providing better medical care once the fighting was over. The war had been over for almost a year, nothing had improved, and now the Vietminh were leaving. Moreover, they had persuaded the population to cut some of the roads again just before the army's entry, to "keep the corrupt French puppets from raping the people," they said. The Vietminh had clearly lied about the new national government and its army. The troops were not robbing or mistreating the population; the last-minute sabotage had only hurt the villagers. Disenchantment and resentment were further fueled by the forcible removal of young boys to the North; by the time of the final Vietminh evacuation, on May 16, the numbers had climbed to about ten thousand, twice the five thousand taken from Camau.[9] The rigidity of Vietminh tactics and propaganda made them vulnerable. Nonetheless, their preparations for the future were plain: not only were they kidnapping youth but they had ordered all single evacuees to marry local girls and get them pregnant if possible before leaving, and they had done the same in Camau.

The Vietminh had made no provisions to convert their currency into Vietnamese government piasters. That meant that when Kim's forces paid liberally in Vietnamese government piasters for labor in repairing the roads and other tasks, and for local food purchases, whatever savings the local population had in Vietminh currency rapidly became worthless.

An opportunity existed to capitalize on the population's rising irritation. Why not put out a leaflet, ostensibly from the Vietminh Interzone Five Committee, offering to exchange all Vietminh *dong* for Vietnamese government piasters? It would require careful preparation. First we had to obtain authentic Vietminh proclamations, in order to copy the paper, the writing style, and the typeface. Kim's G-2 staff were already preparing false Vietminh identification documents for agents gleaning information about Vietminh stay-behind preparations; the agents were given the additional task of collecting samples of Vietminh proclamations. Working with several samples, the psywar company soon produced an authentic-looking Vietminh proclamation stating that two days before the final evacuation, the population could exchange Vietminh *dong* for Vietnamese piasters at the rate of one for one at Vietminh headquarters in Qui Nhon. This was circulated surreptitiously by Kim's agents.

As the day for the final march to Qui Nhon approached, we had another wide river barrier to cross, the Lai Giang. Again the army would have to use ferries. While reviewing plans with me the evening before we were to enter the last and final zone, Kim suddenly told me he might not be allowed to finish the operation. When, in consternation, I asked why not, he recounted an earlier incident. The commander of one of his divisions, Ton That Dinh, had pulled a pistol and accused him of plotting with General Vy to turn over his troops to Bao Dai.[10] I was astonished. I knew that Bao Dai had sent a cable to General Vy naming him commander in chief of the armed forces. This had occurred while Kim and I had gone to Saigon and returned, but I knew the army was holding firm and was not going to follow Vy. Kim had told Dinh he had not seen Vy in Saigon and that he took orders only from the government headed by Diem. Dinh had apologized and said that there had been rumors Kim had gone to Saigon to pledge his support to Vy. I asked Kim if he wanted me to intervene through Lansdale. He said no.

The rumors against Kim would persist, however, fueled by envy and political paranoia, a hangover from the colonial era of conspiracy as a means of political survival. Unfortunately, it was being fed by agents from Diem's brothers, Nhu in Saigon and Can in Hue, who did not trust Kim. Diem seriously considered replacing Kim but consulted Lansdale, who persuaded him to resolve his doubts by sending an impartial observer to Binh Dinh, who gave him accurate reports of Kim's actions and accomplishments. This laid the matter to rest, but it was another indication of how difficult it was to get the Vietnamese to trust each other. Lansdale's advice to Collins in January seemed prophetic. An institutional basis for government had to be created soon, ideally to serve as a commonly understood and accepted set of rules within which the noncommunist Vietnamese could learn to work openly and in mutual confidence with each other. Otherwise, they would not prevail.

The next morning Kim kicked off the final stage of the operation, leading the way in his jeep, followed by units of the 31st Division on foot. I rode in a separate jeep, keeping my usual low profile. We negotiated the Lai Giang by ferry. As we climbed the south bank, army engineers were already starting work on a temporary footbridge across the river. We moved slowly, staying just ahead of the walking column. The population lined the road through the villages. There were smiles. Soldiers took the small South Vietnamese flags off their packs and gave them to children. As the march progressed and the day wore on, the heat rose. More and more villagers began bringing water out for the troops to drink. I felt like getting out of the jeep and clapping for the troops. All the months of preparation and troop indoctrination were paying off.

By early afternoon, a unit of the advance company had returned to report that all was quiet and secure in Qui Nhon but that the city was largely in ruins from French bombing during the war. The last Vietminh unit had boarded a Polish ship the day before. According to several inhabitants, an angry mob at the dock had seen them off, protesting their inability to exchange Vietminh currency as "promised." Stones had been thrown. An officer of the unit showed Kim one of the "Vietminh" leaflets promising the exchange. Kim examined it very seriously, as if he had never seen it before. "Score one for our side," I thought.

That evening we camped north of Qui Nhon, which was another day away for the main body of the troops, provided the footbridge across the Lai Giang had been completed. At midmorning word came that the engineers, working around the clock, had completed the bridge. Borrowing a jeep and driver, I went back to see. When I arrived a long line of army troops was coming toward me across the bridge but no civilians. As I made my way over the bridge, dodging around the troops, I saw a file of villagers carrying market goods in baskets on shoulder poles or standing with bicycles waiting for the ferry, just as they had been doing since the bridge had originally been destroyed. At the north end of the bridge was a soldier busily directing all the troops onto the bridge and all the civilians down to the ferry landing.

The engineer in charge was a captain, about my age. I introduced myself and told him I would tell Colonel Kim about his outstanding work on the bridge but was afraid the colonel would not be happy at something that was not true civic action. I pointed to the people still paying the ferry to cross and suggested they should be using the bridge instead. True civic action, I suggested, was letting them use the bridge even if it temporarily delayed the troops. Understanding flickered in his eyes. While I stood aside he stopped the troops, then beckoned to the file of civilians and persuaded them to follow him onto the bridge. He insisted with a smile and said something to the civilians, and the first to reach the bridge smiled back. When he came where I was standing, he said he had told them it was their bridge, the people's bridge. I told him I would tell Colonel Kim that he had built the best damn people's bridge in the shortest time I had ever seen. He grinned. Back with Kim, I told him the whole story, insisting he commend the captain. He looked at me curiously and said I was becoming "too Vietnamese."

When we finally arrived in Qui Nhon, Kim set up his headquarters in an old abandoned Catholic monastery to the south of the city near the beach. The monastery was a white, three-story, concrete building of some age, some of the roof blown off and the walls pockmarked by French air force strafing. It was surrounded by palms that kept it reasonably cool, but the sand on the dunes that hid the building from the sea was too hot to be walked on during the day.

On the second day in Qui Nhon, Kim asked me if I would accompany him on "a sentimental journey." He wondered if I would like to see where he had been born, though there might not be much left. He drove his own jeep north toward the town of Binh Dinh. Turning west on a narrow dusty road, we passed two brick-red towers, a ruined temple on a hill—remnants of the original Cham civilization, which the Vietnamese, in their historic push south had conquered in the fifteenth century. One could see the Hindu influence in the design. Eventually, we came to a ruined village, Huynh Kim, where Kim showed me the remains of his family home. Sitting beneath some palms on the rubble of a house, we ate small, green, very sweet mangoes, native only to Binh Dinh, while he talked about his life and family.

Kim's father had originally come from the North but had moved to Binh Dinh to set up a silk factory before Kim was born. When Kim was eleven, his father sent him to be educated in France. After graduation he went to work for Marcel Pagnol, the famous French movie producer and director. He became in charge of the film lab, acting in one film and assisting with the direction of others. In 1938, he was drafted into the French army for what he thought would be a year's service, graduating from French Artillery Officers School as a second lieutenant in time to fight against the Germans. After the defeat, he was put in a repatriation camp in Frejus in the south of France. In 1941 he was sent back to Vietnam, where he was reassigned to a French artillery unit at Cap St. Jacques. When the Japanese took over in 1945 he escaped imprisonment and hid in his home village. He rejoined the French when they returned after the Japanese surrender. Subsequently he went to the French General Staff College in Paris, served as deputy regional commander of the combined French and Vietnamese forces in the Highlands, and was chief of staff for Minister of Defense Phan Huy Quat in the last government before Diem.

At age forty-three he was back in his home village for the first time since 1946. His family had escaped before the Vietminh took control of Binh Dinh, but his father had stayed and died there. We looked for the grave but could not find it. Kim talked about how during his time away he had longed to be back. His early sense of being Vietnamese—of the sounds, sights, and smells of his village—had never left him. Life had seemed so simple and peaceful during his early childhood, he said, gesturing with his hands at the surrounding coconut trees. "If you close your eyes and listen to the sound of the wind moving the palm fronds, perhaps you can imagine how it was."

When we returned to Qui Nhon, I busied myself helping an initial scouting team from Operation Brotherhood locate a site for their field hospital, which was ready to be shipped from Saigon. One of their medical teams in Quang Ngai had already set up a field hospital and dispensary there that had treated more than a thousand patients a day, some coming from mountain valleys as far as a hundred kilometers away. The only building with sufficient space was the monastery, currently used as Kim's headquarters. Kim's reaction was, "When do they want us to move?" He said he would have the engineers repair one of the buildings in town for his headquarters. Operation Brotherhood was more important than his convenience.

DIEM VISITS OPERATION GIAI PHONG

Less than a week after arriving, Kim was staring in shock at a message from Diem: the president wanted to come for an inspection visit in just five days. The city was a mess, with dirt and rubble in the streets, and the primitive airfield was still being repaired. Kim was muttering to himself. How could he possibly get ready for the president's visit in five days? He worried about ensuring security and how the population might react. I reminded him how angry they seemed to be with the Vietminh and how positively they had reacted to the army. Kim decided to put radio receivers, which USIS had provided, in as many public places as possible and tune them to Radio Saigon. The news about Diem's successful defiance of Bao Dai and the French and the defeat of the Binh Xuyen would be a powerful message to those who had not already heard about it by word of mouth. His engineers and troops began an around-the-clock effort to finish repairing the dirt strip that was the airfield and to spruce up the city by whitewashing the most visible buildings, as well as constructing a reviewing stand.

President Diem's C-47 arrived in midmorning of May 26, landing without difficulty in a cloud of dust on the dirt strip. A huge crowd of Vietnamese from nearby villages and Qui Nhon, dressed in traditional black pajamas and conical hats, had gathered near the airport. Loudspeakers had announced Diem's visit for several days. For security reasons Kim had not wanted a crowd at the airport, but they had come. Soldiers were stationed to ring the crowd on the airfield side, but the people appeared friendly. When the plane rolled to a halt, Kim drove his open jeep alongside. The crowd surged against a cordon of soldiers surrounding the plane. Diem came to the door and waved. Cheers broke out. I was standing to the rear of the crowd on the hood of another jeep. Diem began coming down the ladder; the cheers became louder.

Diem got into Kim's jeep and stood up while Kim began to drive. The crowd lined both sides of the road. At one point he got out of the jeep and plunged into the crowd. There was more excited yelling. The crowd went wild; all the traditional Vietnamese restraint was gone. After a moment, from my perspective on the back of a jeep just ahead, his stocky figure disappeared from view, then reappeared in the jeep beside Kim. Kim drove Diem slowly through the crowd. I remembered the camera slung around my neck and snapped some shots. People lined the route five to ten deep. I got to the city square, where the reviewing stand had been assembled, and took a seat way in back. When Diem climbed onto the platform Kim introduced him to all of his principal officers and key Vietnamese civilians who had accompanied the operation. He waved me to come down to meet Diem. I heard my name and then Lansdale's. Diem broke into a broad smile, shook my hand warmly, and said, "Colonel Lansdale is my friend; thank you so much for what you are doing for our country." He gave a relatively brief address after some welcoming speeches by local dignitaries, then pinned decorations on Kim and the two division commanders. The acting secretary of state for defense, Tran Trung Dung, decorated others, and the ceremony was over.

In an area completely controlled by the Vietminh for nine years, Diem had received a remarkable response. This kind of reaction could not have been coerced; it was too genuine and spontaneous. I wanted to understand what lay behind the enthusiasm, randomly questioning a number of local Vietnamese through interpreters. The answers were that Diem was widely known as a nationalist leader who had never compromised with the French; now he was winning complete independence for Vietnam. They also called him honest.

THE SAIGON SCENE

Not long after Diem's visit, I returned to Saigon. Dave Smith greeted me at the airport and surprised me by pinning first lieutenant's bars on my collar, joking that he was still my superior officer—his date of rank preceded mine. The city was greatly changed from my last visit, during the war with the Binh Xuyen. The streets had been swept clean. Vietnamese army morale was sky high. Not only had the Binh Xuyen been chased out of Saigon, but the army was successfully pursuing them to the south and east, wading through the Rung Sat swamp into Binh Xuyen fire by day and resting at night by tying themselves to the mangrove branches above high tide. The French were pulling out, withdrawing from Saigon to the Cap St. Jacques area. At TRIM, the French officers assigned to the National Security Division no longer showed up at their desks. The Vietnamese newspapers were full of calls for Bao Dai's resignation. General Vy had fled to Dalat and then to France after an unsuccessful attempt to take over in Bao Dai's name. The French press was vitriolic against Diem and violently anti-American, a prejudice they would carry forward for the next twenty years until the Americans too were forced out—we were ignorant boobs with "blood on our hands." General Ely had departed for France in great anger, and General Collins had been replaced by a career ambassador, Frederick Reinhardt, a welcome change for Lansdale, who had never been able to get through to Collins.[11]

After capturing most of the Binh Xuyen and driving remnants out of the Rung Sat, negotiations began between the government and the Hoa Hao rebels, General Soai and Ba Cut. Both were asking for enormous bribes, and Ba Cut wanted to be named a general in the Vietnamese army. Their forces had holed up in a large fort at Cai Von, on the Bassac River across from Can Tho, the largest city in the Delta south of Saigon. When the Hoa Hao started bombarding Can Tho, the army routed them. At Long Xuyen, General Ngo, with the largest force of Hoa Hao, remained loyal to the government. General Duong Van Minh (known as "Big Minh"), a southerner who had led the successful campaign against the Binh Xuyen, was in charge of the government forces. Using a civic-action approach similar to the campaigns in Camau and Binh Dinh, combined with effective small-unit operations, General Minh induced the surrender of large numbers of dissidents, leaving only small groups that eventually dispersed into the Plaine des Joncs (Plain of Reeds), to the west of Saigon, and into the Seven Mountains area, near the Cambodian border.

Responding to the extremely deprived state of the population and to a request from General Ngo, Operation Brotherhood sent a medical team to Long Xuyen, which I visited. The team had set up a clinic and a small hospital at Long Kien, across the Bassac River from Long Xuyen, on Cu La Ong Chuong, a large island between the Mekong and the Bassac. After French official subsidies were cut off early in 1955, the Hoa Hao had kept all government services out of the area and had taxed the population severely to support its armies. I found the Filipino team treating a population of almost two hundred thousand Hoa Hao, some of whom were refugees from combat areas. By this time the Operation Brotherhood teams throughout Vietnam were training nurse's aides to carry on as part of the Vietnamese public health service. This team had added a sanitation engineer, who dug deep wells on the island for the first supply of uncontaminated water the villagers had ever seen.

I met General Minh briefly at his Cantho headquarters to get an idea of how the army's operations were going against the remaining resistance. He had broken his forces down into hundred-man "companies" and was running these units through a five weeks' guerrilla-type training course in which officers and men trained together without insignia. This had generated team spirit, since the officers and the men often had different backgrounds (the officers mainly coming from more educated families in the cities and the men primarily from the villages).[12]

Besides the continuing need for pacification in parts of the Delta, the government was preoccupied with two major political problems. Bao Dai was persisting in his efforts, with French support, to undercut Diem. Nationalist sentiment was rising to depose Bao Dai, who had lost what little support he might have once enjoyed. At the same time the British and the French were pressuring the United States to get Diem to agree to initiate consultations with the North on the elections contemplated under the Geneva protocol. Consultations were to start in July 1955, pointing toward a general election in July 1956. The United States feared the Vietminh might launch an attack, once the French had withdrawn, if South Vietnam refused consultations. Ambassador Reinhardt tried, but Diem refused, on the grounds that the South Vietnamese had not signed any Geneva documents—certainly true—and he did not trust either the French or the British to insist on measures by which free elections could be assured in North Vietnam. Diem prevailed. No consultations took place.[13]

The North Vietnamese protested the lack of consultations, but they were actually preoccupied with acquiring an iron grip on the North through a massive "agrarian reform" program directed at eradicating all "bourgeois elements" from rural society. They were, therefore, in no condition to attack. As in Mao's land reform campaigns in China, Vietnamese landowners with small plots were condemned to death by kangaroo courts organized by Vietminh cadre and composed of their terrorized neighbors, then executed in front of their entire villages. Thousands were killed. A favorite method was to bury victims to the neck, then trample them with water buffalo or decapitate them with buffalo-drawn plows. This persecution generated defections and additional refugees, sometimes from Vietminh military ranks, and finally open revolt in 1956 in the province of Nghe Anh, bordering the coast.[14] Ironically, this had been Ho Chi Minh's birthplace. In Saigon there was growing awareness of the horror the communists were wreaking on their own people in the North. Diem's attitude toward elections seemed justified. Lansdale felt, however, that an opportunity had been lost to put Ho Chi Minh on the defensive by proposing truly free elections. He believed it was possible to call Hanoi's bluff, but he was not a party to the formal discussions with Diem.

Chapter 6
Civic Action

When I got back to Saigon from central Vietnam, Lansdale asked me to see what could be done to support a new government program called "Civic Action." This had been an outgrowth of his meeting an unusual Vietnamese named Kieu Cong Cung, who had ideas about what the government should be doing in the countryside. Cung had been put in touch with Diem, and a crash program of putting teams in the villages was being attempted, but it was meeting difficulty. Lansdale arranged for me to see Tran Trung Dung and his assistant, Nguyen Dinh Thuan, who had offices at the presidential palace.

I first met Dung and Thuan while Dung was serving as secretary of state to the presidency and we were developing the plans for Operation Giai Phong. Thuan, a northerner and a Buddhist, had a lively sense of humor and an impish manner. We soon became friends. Dung was slight and gentle, while Thuan was stockier, blunter, and more forceful. When I explained that Lansdale wanted me to help Civic Action, Thuan was delighted. He said Kieu Cong Cung was having a hard time getting started. The army was too busy clearing out Hoa Hao rebels in the Delta to give much help. The civilian ministries didn't understand Civic Action, and the regional delegates and province chiefs thought the program was designed to undermine them. Thuan was getting a lot of calls complaining about Cung. "You'll see why when you meet him," he said, with a twinkle in his eye.

When I entered Thuan's office the following morning, he introduced me to a Vietnamese wearing the black pajamas of the typical Vietnamese villager. "This is Kieu Cong Cung," he said, "the commissioner of Civic Action." I could see why he was causing a stir in the ministries, where most functionaries still dressed in white sharkskin suits. Thuan expected some reaction to Cung's appearance. There was a flash of disappointment in his eyes when I remained impassive; then he showed a glint of amusement—I had out-Vietnamesed him. In the future he would tease me back. It was the beginning of a friendship.

Cung was a southerner, about forty-five, stocky in build, and bigger than the average Vietnamese, with a large head, brush cut, graying hair, and large, hooded eyes. He looked like a Vietnamese farmer in his black pajamas but had an air of command, lending authenticity to his reputation as a former guerrilla commander. He was very earnest in describing Civic Action. Special government teams would be sent to the villages to fill a very real gap in government administration, little changed since the inception of the semi-independent Bao Dai state. Before, in the South, Frenchmen occupied all key positions down to district chief. For a few years, Vietnamese civil servants unused to rural life had taken over. Rudimentary public services reached the province and district level but were nonexistent in the villages. Most villages had communal lands from which the village councils traditionally derived some rent, but it was not enough to meet their public-health, education, or public-works needs, and this system had been disturbed by the war. Civic Action, by working directly in the villages and meeting immediate public needs, would give the village renewed importance and fill this vacuum. The ministries were understaffed, their *functionaires* unequipped by training or background to work at that level; Civic Action teams would provide the resources they lacked. As village needs became known and public services better organized, firmer links could be fostered between the villages and rest of the government. Then Civic Action would no longer be needed. In the meantime, his teams would fill the gap instead of the Vietminh.

Cung was obviously reluctant to begin telling a stranger anything about his real problems. I suggested he take me to see the training center, near Tan Son Nhut Airport. When I explained, as we rode out to the center, what I had seen of civilian administration indifference and incompetence in Binh Dinh, he warmed up. He told me with some amusement that when he went to talk to the ministries, his dress caused consternation. I laughed and said Thuan and Dung must have gotten a few irate calls. Yes, he said, but they and the president were backing him. I said he was just what the civilian administration needed, and I wanted to help him as a friend. If I could understand his program and his problems, maybe I could explain it to other Americans and get some support.

The training center consisted of several bare-bones, wooden buildings that the trainees had constructed themselves within a fenced-in compound. Classes were in progress for several teams of young men and a few women, all dressed in black pajamas. Cung's goal was to have several teams operating in each of 150 districts of every province by 1956, before the looming elections. He realized that two weeks was too short to get much done, but the teams would return for longer stays, particularly in villages that most needed help. In the meantime, they would uncover needs for roads, bridges, wells, dikes, and other assistance, which he hoped the provincial governments would provide.

So far, Cung was short of good instructors from the various ministries; lacked funds for training, operating expenses, and equipment and materials for the teams; and was receiving little cooperation from traditionally minded provincial administrators. He had been given the piaster equivalent of only about $100,000 to get started. (This was mainly seed money from Lansdale, since there was little to be spared from the regular Vietnamese government budget.) That would soon run out. To fund the program properly he needed the equivalent of one or two million dollars, a year's costs. He had read about community development and wanted American experts to advise him. He believed propaganda was not enough; the teams must improve villagers' lives. I said I would do all I could to help and asked to see one of his teams working in a village.

We visited a team working in the Cu Chi area, to the immediate northwest of Saigon. Cu Chi, Cung explained, had been an area of communist influence since before World War II.[1] It would be a real test to see if Civic Action could make any headway there. Plying dirt tracks between rice paddies by jeep and then walking a considerable distance, we reached a village where there was a team. The provincial Civic Action coordinator accompanied us. The villagers we encountered were not particularly friendly or unfriendly either, mainly impassive. The team was constructing two buildings, with the help of the villagers: a meeting hall for the village elders and a dispensary. The team had first assembled the village council of notables and explained their mission, and the council had agreed to cooperate. Now the first phase, a self-help approach to putting up the two thatched buildings with materials supplied by the team, was almost complete.

The team was also dispensing some medicines, distributing information about the government, and taking a census. The need for wells closer to all the hamlets had arisen. The dirt trail coming in needed upgrading to a road so the villagers could more easily get their rice and fruits to market. The villagers were willing to dig the wells themselves and build the road if they could get hand tools. Scissors and thread were needed for sewing. The village youth were eager to play sports, but there was no equipment to give them. The village needed the school they were building, but the team was having difficulty locating a volunteer teacher to carry on after they left. Still, the team's morale was high, and they seemed to be striking the right note of persuading the villagers, not trying to coerce them.

Cung began to lose his formality. He told me about his life as a revolutionary commander with the Vietminh. He had been in the French army in Indochina at the beginning of World War II. When France surrendered, the "Marseillaise" had been played in the mess hall. All the Frenchmen rose to their feet with tears in their eyes. He found himself still seated, alone, suddenly realizing France was not his country. Soon afterward, he resigned from the French army and in 1945 joined the early Vietnamese resistance against the returning French. He rose through the Vietminh ranks to brigadier.

Raised as a Buddhist, Cung was an agnostic but didn't believe in communism and consistently refused to join the Lao Dong Party. There was a party purge in the South against the Vietminh commander Nguyen Binh. Cung was reassigned to the North, near the Chinese border, where he commanded a unit fighting the French, but he was closely watched by his unit's political commissar. Friends within the party warned him that he might be arrested at any time. In late 1952, he and his wife, carrying their two small children and false papers, fled at night on foot. They walked all the way from the Chinese border to the Mekong Delta, evading the French army and the Vietminh. It took months. After arriving safely in the South, he dropped out of sight, as just another farmer in a small village, where his wife's relatives protected him. He had known Diem as a nationalist only by reputation, but when he saw Diem's courage in taking on the sects and the French, he came out of self-imposed obscurity to volunteer his services. He had heard that Lansdale, whom he first contacted, was a way to reach Diem.[2]

I talked about help for Civic Action with other American agencies. USIS was cooperative, agreeing to loan movie projectors to the teams as well as train projectionists. I tried our economic aid mission, the U.S. Operations Mission (USOM). The answer I got was that Civic Action didn't fit into their programs with the government ministries. As for education, whether to retain the French *lycée* system had to be dealt with first; in health, the provinces lacked hospitals, there was a great shortage of doctors, a school of medicine was needed; home economic skills should be taught through the secondary schools system; sports was not development; it was wasteful to give tools to villagers who didn't know how to use them— roads should be built by public works engineers; village medical kits, which USOM already had in stock, should only be dispensed by personnel trained by the Ministry of Health; and so on. What Vietnam really needed, they said, was a better trained civil service beginning at the top and gradually working to the bottom. There was a vacuum out there, I said, and the Vietminh would fill it if our side didn't. That was political, they said. Their business was economic development.

Leaving USOM was like stepping off the moon. The USOM divisions I spoke to saw themselves as separate entities: Health, Education, Public Administration, Public Works, Public Safety and Agriculture, each working with its counterpart Vietnamese ministry at the Saigon level. Everything was centralized, from the top down. Not only did they appear incapable of understanding the bottom up idea of village development but they seemed to perceive it as a threat to their own programs. Afterward, only the Public Health Division agreed that the Vietnamese Ministry of Health, after training Civic Action personnel, could distribute USOM's village medical kits through them.

Considerably discouraged, I reported to Lansdale, who wanted me to work up a detailed budget with Cung. In the meantime he would urge Diem to squeeze more material support from the army and the ministries. We would try USOM again. If they thought this was a Lansdale scheme to flood the villages with secret agents supported by economic aid funds, he would try to disabuse them. Anticipating the worst, I suggested we get supplemental funds from the CIA, or have USOM funds disbursed through CIA, to save time and complications. But Lansdale had already received strong indications from headquarters that the modest amount of funding he had gotten as seed money would soon be cut off. This was not normal CIA business.

CAR BOMBS

John Gates (now known as "Demi") used his excellent French to make friends with a number of French officers in TRIM. He was being harassed, however, by a particular French intelligence officer in our National Security Division, Major René Goussault. Goussault kept questioning Demi, "Who are you really working for, certainly the CIA?" Finally, in desperation, he told Goussault, "The CIA is just a cover." Word of this got back to Lansdale, who called him in. Apprehensively, Demi explained that he had just blurted it out because he couldn't think of anything else. For a moment Lansdale looked at him hard, then said "Brilliant!" and started laughing. Goussault's harassment stopped, but it had been minor compared with other French actions that started not long after I returned from central Vietnam.

I awoke around two in the morning in my old apartment on Rue Paul Blanchy. There was an explosion in the direction of the USIS Library, about two blocks up the street. The plate glass of the main library window had been completely shattered, with shards in the street and among the shredded books inside. Shortly thereafter cars belonging to Americans, including the personal car of Anita Lauve, who had been so helpful to me when I first arrived, were blown up at random. Members of Lansdale's team got a mimeographed note in their mailboxes from a purported "Front for National Unity and against American Domination." The "front" claimed to represent all patriotic Vietnamese. Americans were to stop meddling in Vietnamese affairs and leave immediately; otherwise their safety could not be assured.

I was now driving the Citroen "Deux Chevaux" tin can that Lansdale had once used. It was a delightful car for Saigon—if a street was blocked by traffic, I could drive it on the sidewalk. But it was certainly vulnerable. Every morning I checked it carefully for bombs. During the Binh Xuyen war, Lansdale had been shot at once, and unknown assassins had killed a Frenchman staying in the house across from his, an apparent case of mistaken identity. Through Conein's sources we learned that associates of Colonel Carbonel, the chief of staff of TRIM, were involved in the bombings. Lansdale called a meeting. This business has gone far enough, he said, and it would be taken care of.

That evening when I dropped by the pool house, as I often did to keep in touch with other team members, everyone was out except Conein, who was in the kitchen alone. Spread out on the enameled kitchen table in front of him were bars of C-3 plastic explosive, orange-colored primacord, a roll of fuse, a box of caps, and rolls of friction tape. Conein was muttering a string of curses, alternating in French and English—"*salauds, espèces de con,* bastards, goddam sons of bitches, assholes"—while cutting chunks of C-3, wrapping them with primacord and friction tape, crimping caps onto cut portions of fuse, then taping the fuses with caps to the primacord wrapped around the C-3. In astonishment, I asked what he was doing. "None of your goddam business; what the hell does it look like?" was the reply. I asked if I could help. He gave me a kitchen knife and asked me to cut up the rest of the C-3 into five-inch lengths and tape primacord to the sections, just like the others. Not another word was exchanged. We worked in silence broken only by a continuing string of colorful cursing, until I finished, when I asked if he was sure he didn't need me. Conein glowered, "No goddamit, you didn't see any of this, get out of here." I left.

After midnight Conein, taking his fiancée, Elyette Brochot, with him without telling her his purpose, started driving his car through the Saigon streets. She was given the bombs, cradling them in her lap. Conein went first to Colonel Carbonel's house, then to the houses of the other ringleaders. Elyette passed him the bombs we had made. He lit the fuses with his cigarette lighter, and tossed them over the walls and into the yards of each residence. The final one went into the yard of the French ambassador. There were complaints to the American embassy the next day about Lansdale's "threatening remarks" to Carbonel. The French had no more to say, however, when it was learned on that same evening that a group of French junior officers had been caught in a jeep by the Vietnamese police with explosives and a list of American targets. Bombing the Americans stopped cold.[3] It was hard to believe the French could have gone so far. A year before, I had arrived in Vietnam considering myself a francophile, but the way the French had treated the Vietnamese, even more than their hysterical behavior toward us, had changed my thinking. France, French culture, and at least half of the French people retained a certain attraction, but it would be some time before I would completely recapture my earlier feelings.

FINAL TRIP TO CENTRAL VIETNAM

Before leaving Vietnam, I took one last trip to see Colonel Kim in Qui Nhon, accompanied by my old friend Lieutenant Vuong, of Vietnamese army psywar. This time we began in Hue, the old capital, which I had never visited. My Vietnam experience would not be complete, Vuong said, until I spent a night in Hue in a sampan on the Perfume River. We flew into Hue in the afternoon and toured the old citadel of the Imperial City. It was still oppressively hot during the day, but the air on the river had begun to cool at dusk as we located a sampan and Vuong haggled over the price. Two Vietnamese girls in *ao dai*s manned the sampan, rowing us up and down the river, taking turns at cooking, serving, and singing plaintive melodies, while strumming a traditional Vietnamese lute. Our sampan was lit by a single lantern, which swayed with the current and the evening breeze. Vuong spoke softly of Vietnamese emperors and legends, how more than one emperor was known to have sneaked out to the sampans incognito to escape the boredom and routine of the royal court. Passing an evening on the Perfume River in a sampan with singsong girls was a practice centuries old. The air after dark on the river did seem sweet, with an indefinable, perhaps imagined, perfume. Other sampan lanterns winkled fitfully like fireflies, while the slight tones of voices and lutes could be heard until the splashes of cast anchors halted the sounds, the lanterns went out, and the river fell quiet, broken occasionally by faint peals of feminine laughter.

The next morning we started on the long ride south in a jeep. South of Tourane, because of the improved road the trip to Quang Ngai, which had once taken twelve hours, now took only five. South of Quang Ngai new bridges existed over most ravines. The road cuts had been filled and the surface graded and graveled. It was still rough, but it was passable. The village of Sa Huynh had changed; there were now more fisherman and nets. The beach was still as beautiful. We pushed on to Bong Son and then to Qui Nhon, finding similar road improvements, and arrived at dusk at Kim's headquarters. It was a warm reunion. During a festive dinner with Kim I couldn't resist asking, "Where's my fish and rice?" Back in April and May we had subsisted largely on just that, washed down by fresh coconut milk and leavened by bananas and those small, green mangos when we got to Binh Dinh.

The following day we toured Qui Nhon and the surrounding area. The army had improved the side roads, built dikes against seawater intrusion, repaired irrigation canals, dug wells, and helped patch up buildings in Qui Nhon, which now had a thriving market and newly opened shops. Villagers had volunteered the location of more than a hundred arms caches left behind by the Vietminh. The Vietminh stay-behind network had threatened to even the score with "collaborators" when they again took over, but it was not working. Not only were the villagers giving information on arms caches, they were also fingering Vietminh agents. Kim's main problem remained the slowness and incompetence of the civil administration.

We visited one Civic Action team. They were doing good work, Kim said, but it would be better if they were composed entirely of central Vietnamese. Team members from the North had difficulty communicating; the dialect and even some customs differed. Also, he had only four teams, while at least ten of his districts needed to be covered. No official announcement had been made, but the civil administration and the Civic Action teams were preparing for a referendum on Bao Dai. Demonstrations denouncing Bao Dai had been organized. The Vietminh were still in a state of shock about it, Kim said. Their morale was low. They were in a dilemma: they opposed Diem but couldn't support Bao Dai. They would probably boycott the referendum, but the boycott would not be effective. Popular sentiment was overwhelming against Bao Dai. Diem was even more popular than when he had visited in May. The cement between the army and the population had indeed begun to bind.

It was moving to see come true what had only been a dream at the beginning, the non-communist Vietnamese claiming their independence and beginning to win popular support in their own right. The metamorphosis in Binh Dinh was like watching bamboo shoots grow—change was visible. I saw a vast difference from when we had first come in May. The typical wariness in villager eyes was vanishing. As we stood together on the tarmac at the Qui Nhon airport—there was now Air Vietnam DC-3 commercial service—saying goodbye, I could no longer evade Kim's question about whether I would come back. He knew that my two years of obligatory army service after graduation from OCS was ending in November. He said his country needed me; I understood them. It was hard to suppress my emotions; all I could do was mumble that I was seriously thinking about coming back. Later on the plane I wondered to Vuong how his country and his people had come to mean so much to me. "Maybe you were born Vietnamese in a previous incarnation," he joked. He made me laugh; Vuong always joked when our conversations touched on the personal. Momentarily, though, turning surprisingly serious, he said, "You wear your heart where we Vietnamese can see it."

WINDING DOWN

By mid-September most of the French advisors in TRIM had left Vietnam, and they were not being replaced. While TRIM was not immediately disbanded, the Americans within it began taking over the functions of training and advising the Vietnamese army. The National Security Division continued to operate, becoming directly responsible for training and advising the Vietnamese army in intelligence operations, psychological warfare, and troop information. Colonel Melvin and I began developing a permanent G-5 organization for the army, with psywar, troop education, and civic-action staff responsibilities at all levels down to battalion, as part of General O'Daniel's overall reorganization plan for the army. Wanting to ensure that the army never returned to its old ways of ignoring or preying on the civilian population, we began preparing a course in military civic action, troop education, and psychological warfare. I worked out the organizational details with Nguyen Dinh Thuan, who was taking more and more responsibility at the Ministry of Defense. The course would stress the civic-action role of the army, partnership with government civilians in an atmosphere of mutual understanding and respect, and the importance of the army's remaining above partisan politics.

For part of the curriculum, we needed American instructors with psychological warfare experience who spoke French. Through the office of Commander in Chief, Pacific (CINC-PAC), we were pleasantly surprised to learn there were three soldiers in the U.S. Army's psywar company in Hawaii who spoke French. We got them assigned on temporary duty to MAAG/Saigon. When I met the contingent at the Saigon airport, one of the first to descend to the tarmac was, to my astonishment, a Yale classmate, Pfc. Edward Auchincloss. He recalls squinting in the noonday sun at this officer who looked vaguely familiar but was dressed in unfamiliar shorts and a short-sleeve shirt. He saluted. Then we realized we knew each other. This unusual encounter became a standing joke between us, eventually maturing into a deep friendship.

The group from Hawaii also contained Pfc. Peder Konz, a brilliant Swiss lawyer with a doctorate who had somehow been drafted into the U.S. Army, and Pvt. Chris Bird, a Harvard graduate with a genius-level IQ who had been drafted after being fired by the CIA for trying without success to recruit, "cold turkey," a member of the Soviet embassy in Tokyo, and Gil Grosvenor (son of the *National Geographic*'s founder). He didn't speak French but lent administrative support. Heading the group was a huge, fat army captain who had no French and knew little about psychological warfare. (We later arranged for his recall, on the grounds that his company needed its commanding officer back in Hawaii.) When I tried to fit him, Konz, Bird, and myself into my little Citroen for the drive to MAAG headquarters, the undercarriage sank to the pavement; the car wouldn't move.

Melvin and I spent a week briefing our three American lecturers about the Vietnamese experience in Camau and Binh Dinh. We stressed the Vietnamese officer's typical lack of exposure to psywar and civic-action concepts in their training under the French. As a guide, I gave the trainers the short course I had prepared earlier for all the Vietnamese G-5 officers involved in Operation Giai Phong. The fact that the American trainers were enlisted men but would be training Vietnamese officers was a problem. We told the Vietnamese that their lack of rank was a disguise: they were actually high-ranking psychological warfare experts under cover. They were an unusual but highly effective group, teaching part of the course in a series of locations over the next several months.

The CIA wanted me to continue with them as a civilian when my army commitment ended, and Lansdale wanted me to return to Saigon. Briefly, I thought about continuing in the military, particularly after some long talks with Colonel Kim during Operation Giai Phong. I had acquired a genuine respect for the best of our military, and there was much I admired about their devotion to duty and sense of honor. Kim felt strongly that the U.S. Army needed officers with my unconventional experience. But I could see the downside of military routine at some post stateside or, worse, at the Pentagon. Taking up the CIA's offer had greater attraction, so long as the possibility of doing useful but nonbureaucratic work in political action remained open. I did not feel particularly compatible with the more "professional" intelligence types whom I had met in the regular CIA station in Saigon. The informal, "amateur" atmosphere that characterized the Lansdale team appealed to me. I would miss the referendum on Bao Dai set for October 24, but there was no doubt in my mind how it would come out.[4] Even among Bao Dai's formerly staunch supporters, some of whom I knew, no one had a good word to say for him, so thoroughly had he become self-identified as a French stooge.

Chapter 7

South Vietnam Stabilizes— Laos Up for Grabs

Prospects for South Vietnam had greatly brightened as 1956 began. The Vietnamese army occupations of Camau and central Vietnam had established a beneficial government presence in those formerly Vietminh-controlled areas. The army had overcome the sect rebellions and had achieved a unity and pride in itself that had been completely lacking one year before. French military forces were finally leaving South Vietnam after more than a century of occupation. Bao Dai was no longer indirectly controlling the Vietnamese government from the French Riviera. Close to a million refugees from the North had been successfully resettled. Above all, President Diem could rightfully claim that he, as a Vietnamese nationalist, had freed all of Vietnam from French domination, something Ho Chi Minh had not accomplished. The opportunity now existed to create a political cause in the South that could challenge the North in what was likely to be a continuing struggle for the allegiance of the Vietnamese people.

Unfortunately, the need for the new government to generate a political cause for the South beyond independence and to cement a positive relationship with the rural population would become obscured. The image of Diem's sudden rise to power had a mesmerizing effect. American complacency set in and was further complicated by poor understanding and political judgment. A routine and conventional bureaucratic approach began to prevail. Our embassy and information service, economic aid mission, military advisory group, and the CIA became increasingly preoccupied with their standard bureaucratic responsibilities, as if South Vietnam were a developed country with a firm tradition of government. The military challenge from the North was assumed to be the threat of an overt invasion, à la Korea, across the seventeenth parallel, resulting in the reorganization of the Vietnamese army to fight a conventional war; internal security was conceived as primarily a police function. The Saigon Military Mission, with its different view, while still influential, would be increasingly sidelined. Would the gains of 1954 and 1955 be consolidated into something that would last and could successfully oppose the communists when they began to reactivate their subversive struggle to control the South?

As 1955 faded into 1956, I was in Washington becoming a civilian case officer in the CIA's clandestine service, a process that took longer than expected. Lansdale returned to Washington in January for dental work. While there he made sure I personally saw everyone, from Frank Wisner, the head of CIA's operational arm, on down, but it did not speed up the processing.

When we met a few days before he left for Saigon, Lansdale had said he had something to tell me in confidence that might affect my desire to return. A decision had been made that the development of a secret political party called the Can Lao, for Diem, was to be given covert support through his brother, Nhu. He thought it was a grave mistake; it would only generate mistrust and drive the other political parties and groups underground, compounding the air of distrust that already existed. The resemblance to communist organizational methods was too close for the idea to be anything but ultimately divisive. He had fought it but lost; the "so-called political experts," as he described them, who didn't understand Vietnam, had won. Building a lasting political base for the South Vietnamese would be much tougher. Also, he told me, a firm decision had been made by the Department of Defense to remake the Vietnamese army into a conventional force to stop an open invasion across the border, when in fact the more dangerous threat was renewed guerrilla warfare. Somehow we would have to ensure that civic action didn't get lost. He was telling me all this to warn me—I might not want to go back. I said I was going back if he was. He said wryly, "I'll be there."

More details from Lansdale about what happened over the Can Lao would emerge. The initial decision had been made, incredibly, without consulting Lansdale. He had protested to Ambassador Reinhardt and to CIA headquarters by cable but had gotten nowhere. At an angry meeting with Allen Dulles and Foster Dulles in Washington, he failed to change their minds. All the political experts were unanimous, they told him: Diem must have his own political party, which was to be the "Movement for National Revolution." Because of communist subversion, however, the party must be tightly controlled, and the Can Lao would be the mechanism. If there were abuses, they could be corrected. Lansdale's concept of a democratic political system with Diem playing a nonpartisan political role of "father of his country" was too "visionary and idealistic." Helping with political organization was now the regular CIA station's responsibility; he should disengage from guiding political parties in Vietnam. He then requested reassignment to the Philippines, but both Dulles brothers insisted he remain in Vietnam for another year. He could focus on preparations for the plebiscite proposed by Geneva and help the Vietnamese develop a new constitution.[1]

The regular Saigon CIA station had won a bureaucratic victory. Jealousy had been rampant since the arrival of the separate Saigon Military Mission in 1954, and an agreement dividing responsibilities and contacts had been worked out with great difficulty. Nhu was their contact. This was their opportunity to play a major role. How the director of CIA, Allen Dulles, could have committed such an error of judgment—in not involving Lansdale in the decision, when he had previously reposed so much trust in Lansdale's political judgment in the Philippines as well as in Vietnam and knew Lansdale was Diem's closest advisor—defied reason. That Reinhardt and the embassy political section would support the idea, however, was understandable. It seemed logical and conformed to conventional political wisdom, if one ignored the fractious political culture of Vietnam and the revolutionary milieu in which it functioned. In bureaucratic terms, reducing Lansdale's influence would enhance that of the embassy, an added attraction. I was beginning to get a whiff of how out of touch with reality our government establishment could be and how agency infighting could cripple the effectiveness of policy on the ground, where it counted. I didn't like it but thought Lansdale could overcome it. His inability thereafter, however, to persuade Washington and Diem to pursue a more open and democratic approach would prove his greatest failure.

HOME IN SAIGON

When I arrived back in Saigon in February 1956, I was greeted by Demi Gates and Dick Mellor, a navy lieutenant who had arrived in the fall of 1955. A house with three bedrooms had been rented for us. It was practically next door to that of Nguyen Dinh Thuan, a rising star in the Diem government.

I had worked with Nguyen Dinh Thuan the previous year on psywar organization, training the army, and Civic Action; we had become close personal friends. Our friendship had been further cemented by a stopover in Paris on my way home; there a Vietnamese delegation including Thuan was negotiating a military agreement with the French and designated me their "advisor." Now I was being invited to his home on a regular basis and getting to know his wife and two small children. After I returned, the first thing I did was to visit him with a gift, an electric train, for his young son. Thuan and I sat on the floor putting it together while he brought me up to date on what was going on. Radical changes were under way in the American Military Assistance Advisory Group. Thuan wanted to know about the new American commander, known as "Hanging Sam," and how to deal with him. I said I would find out.

"HANGING SAM" WILLIAMS

The MAAG, to which I was assigned, had undergone a considerable change. General O'Daniel, whom most of us venerated, had left, his place taken by Gen. Samuel Williams, known as "Hanging Sam" for having imposed the death penalty on a rapist under his command. My task was to ensure that G-5 was included in the new table of organization of the Vietnamese army that was being developed. General O'Daniel's plans for the army to retain some light divisions, with a dual mission that would include internal security, had been scrapped at Washington's insistence. The army was to be cut loose from protecting and helping the population, a role toward which we had, with considerable success, been guiding it. The critical job of internal security was to be turned over to the yet-untrained Civil Guard, which then existed mainly on paper. It was to function as a rural police force under the Ministry of Interior.

General Williams' Korea experience, where the guerrillas had been North Korean irregular units operating in the South, influenced his thinking about such warfare in South Vietnam. Because the North Korean irregulars operated without a base of support in the population, they were easy to identify, isolate, and eliminate by regular military force. In any case, he had his orders, which were to create a regular army force capable of repelling or at least slowing down an overt invasion until U.S. and presumably other Western forces, under the South-East Asia Treaty Organization (SEATO), could intervene. The possibility of guerrilla warfare was not in the picture.

Dealing with General Williams was a challenge. Lansdale's group, with the exception of Lansdale, gave him a wide berth. Those still in uniform came to work every day in clean, starched khakis, while civilians like myself wore coat and tie. The boss of anyone caught arriving after 7:45 in the morning was subject to a personal chewing-out by Hanging Sam, whose angry tones were often heard ringing across the headquarters courtyard. When Lansdale took me in to see him, he glared at me as Lansdale explained I had just doffed my uniform to return to Vietnam as a civilian and that I had probably spent more time in the field with the Vietnamese army than anyone on his staff. His expression softened. "Maybe you can teach my officers something," he said. "None of them seems to know a damn thing about the Vietnamese army." Lansdale explained I would be helping with troop information and psychological warfare, then attempted to describe the role of G-5. Williams cut him off with an impatient gesture, said he was glad to have me, then said to Lansdale, "Maybe he'll add something to that band of gypsies you've got working for you."

Mainly Williams ignored us until later in March, at the time of the brief "mango rains," when he saw Lieutenant Colonel Quereau of Lansdale's staff unfurl an umbrella as he walked from his jeep to the building. The phone rang, I picked it up, identified myself, and listened as a voice said, "This is General Williams, tell your boss to get his ass over here on the double." Lansdale went. Quereau had just come in the office; none of us had seen him in the courtyard, so we had no idea of what it was about. Williams' voice roared out of his office window: "What kind of candy-assed, sissified bunch have you got in that outfit of yours. No damn officer of mine is going to be seen parading around MAAG under an umbrella." On it went for about five minutes. We looked at Quereau with the umbrella still under his arm and started laughing. Even Lansdale couldn't keep a straight face when he returned. He said, "Look you guys, just be a little more careful." We took pains to arrive on time, or sufficiently late to seem to have gone to the Ministry of Defense or somewhere else first, and without umbrellas, rain or shine.

Part of the problem at MAAG was the annual turnover rate of American officers. None of Williams' new officers seemed to understand much about G-5 or why it was needed. George Melvin, who had extended his tour, was invaluable as a regular army officer in helping make our case. I quickly struck up a friendship with Col. John Finn, Williams' chief of staff, who was very perceptive. I helped him become Williams' main contact with Nguyen Dinh Thuan. Thuan used me to convey sensitive background indirectly to Finn, material that Finn could use but was not obliged to report directly to General Williams, as he would have been if Thuan had given him the same information directly. Finn, in turn, was able to help us preserve the G-5 staff structure, at least on paper, as part of the Vietnamese army's reorganization. It would, however, later fall into neglect.

BACK WITH CIVIC ACTION

I renewed my visits to Kieu Cong Cung at Civic Action to check on progress and try to get a formal economic assistance program approved by USOM. The financial support Cung was getting from the government continued to be inadequate, and he was behind in putting teams in the field. Moreover, some teams had been diverted to support the anti–Bao Dai referendum and would shortly again be diverted to help organize the upcoming Constituent Assembly elections. With the army removed from its territorial mission, Civic Action could no longer count on the logistical support it had previously enjoyed. Lansdale had persuaded the Agency to continue some interim support, but it was now definitely running out. "Intelligence" was the Agency's real job, according to headquarters, not "economic aid." According to an interagency "understanding" in Washington, USOM was to take over. Cung's teams needed community development training and materiel support for self-help projects in the villages if they were to have a more lasting impact. They also needed a larger piaster budget, which meant using some "U.S. counterpart" funds, with USOM's concurrence.

Cung and I wrote a list of a year's worth of tools, equipment, and supplies for the teams to use for self-help projects, as well as a training and operational budget, in piasters. Most of the funding and materials would have to come through American aid; the Vietnamese government treasury was bare, as usual. We discussed the budget with Thuan, who got President Diem's blessing. Cung, not wanting to ask the Americans for support himself, asked me to make the presentation for him. I finally coaxed him into appearing with me and speaking briefly; I would present the details.

At the briefing for Leland Barrows, head of USOM, Lansdale gave a summary of the creation and accomplishments of Civic Action to date. Cung reviewed the approach and work methods of the teams. He finished his exposition by stating that he would very much like to have American advice in community development, as well as aid. I pointed out that since the army was now being withdrawn from its territorial security role, the need for Civic Action was even greater. I commended Cung for a valiant effort conducted on a shoestring, emphasized this was a bare-bones program, and then described the budget and commodity support requirements. Silence ensued.

Why was Civic Action still needed, Barrows asked? Hadn't reestablishing government in the provinces been concluded, and couldn't Civic Action's functions now be taken over by the regular civil service? Moreover, wouldn't it be more appropriate to train the existing civilian service? Through no fault of Civic Action, I said, a gaping hole remained at the village level, one that the Vietminh would fill if the government didn't. Training the civil service would take years. Most of the existing officials had attitudes left over from the French-dominated era; besides, they were mainly city boys, with little understanding of the rural population. It would take time to change their mentality, time the government didn't have.

Barrows thought the major focus of economic development should be on industrialization. There was a labor surplus in the cities. South Vietnam needed to develop locally produced substitutes for some of its imports, to cure its severe foreign-exchange problems. It had traditionally produced a rice surplus. Land reform and agricultural credit would take care of any problems in the rural areas. Community development, while worthwhile, was a secondary consideration. What the Vietnamese civil service needed was professional training. If communist-inspired violence arose it would be up to the army, the Civil Guard, and the village-level Self-Defense Corps to handle it.

At the end, sensing he had been negative, Barrows said he would think about it. But I could see that actual conditions in the Vietnamese countryside were beyond his experience and therefore his understanding. He could not imagine the disorganization and poor attitude of most of the existing "civil service," the isolation of the average rice farmer from any useful contact with the new government, nor could he comprehend the need to continue cementing a positive relationship with the rural population started through national security action and civic action.

Afterward, Cung asked me anxiously what I thought. I reminded him that the USOM chief had promised to think about it. Lansdale thought the best we could do was to continue to press USOM for support through Ambassador Reinhardt, which he did. Finally, after considerable pressure from Reinhardt, a modest agreement was signed in June that USOM would provide Cung only limited commodity support (mainly sewing equipment, village health kits, and tools). It would take until February of the following year for the first aid shipment to arrive.[2]

POLITICAL AND SECURITY CONCERNS
Through my housemate, Dick Mellor, I kept tabs on the constitutional process. An old Lansdale friend and constitutional lawyer, Johnny Orendain, had come over from the Philippines

under Freedom Company auspices to assist in the drafting of a Vietnamese constitution. A Constituent Assembly was to be elected on March 4 to consider and adopt one. This was, as Lansdale had said in his January 1955 memorandum to General Collins, the "critical missing piece, giving the people a truly representative government." But problems had developed with Diem over the initial draft, particularly about the provision for an independent judiciary. Diem felt communist subversion was such a danger that he needed to be able to act by decree, without reference to the legislature or judicial review. Lansdale had spent hours explaining the "checks and balances" concept of the U.S. Constitution, how it had worked in practice in the Philippines under circumstances of subversion and insurrection similar to what Diem might encounter in Vietnam. Diem was still not convinced. The draft that went to the Assembly would not have an independent judiciary in it.

Despite bureaucratic restrictions on our freedom to work with political parties, Lansdale managed to encourage independent candidates for the March elections. Most politicians from the established parties that had their base mainly in the North, such as the Dai Viet and the VNQDD, refused to participate. In the South, the Hoa Hao and the Cao Dai put up candidates, many of whom won. When the election results were counted, candidates of the Movement for National Revolution and independents in open support of Diem had won eighty-four of the 123 seats. About 85 to 90 percent of the electorate participated, despite Vietminh propaganda to boycott the election. Diem had a comfortable majority, but the Assembly members insisted on writing the constitution themselves, not rubber-stamping the draft Diem had prepared. Orendain went to work directly with the Assembly's drafting committee. Again the issue of an independent judiciary came up. Lansdale's feeling was that Diem could be persuaded if the United States took a strong stand, but he was not able to convince Ambassador Reinhardt. The prevailing American view was of the constitution as primarily a device to "legalize" and consolidate Diem's power, not a popular basis for participation in government. Everything would now depend on how Diem implemented the constitution. It lacked adequate checks and balances that might have obliged him to lead more democratically.

I took a trip back down to Long Xuyen and Camau in the southern Delta, wanting to take the pulse of progress. With peace restored and signs of prosperity emerging, the general situation seemed encouraging, but there were danger signals. An excellent village chief in Camau who had been particularly helpful to Operation Brotherhood had been murdered. The unofficial word was that the Vietminh were responsible. The province chief told me that some members of a Civic Action team had just been killed in another area, near the U Minh Ha. Local officials expressed concern about the army territorial forces being pulled out. The newly formed Civil Guard, functioning more as a police force and sometimes used for personal security by the province chiefs, appeared insufficient in number and training; it was still equipped with bolt-operated French rifles and pistols. Its men lounged around the provincial capitals, looking even sloppier than the Vietnamese army had in 1954. Some village Self-Defense Corps units existed, but they were unpaid volunteers. They were completely untrained and had only an occasional pistol, shotgun, or ancient French rifle, with practically no ammunition.

I saw Thuan at home, and he asked for my views. I said I thought the withdrawal of army territorial units for training and their reformation into permanent divisions should be delayed until the Civil Guard and Self-Defense Corps were really ready to take over. Thuan said the Americans were insisting on the reorganization of the army as rapidly as possible. The only plan the United States had for coming to Vietnam's defense depended on the South Vietnamese first stopping the North's forces north of Tourane (Danang) in central Vietnam. Since the war against the French, the North Vietnamese had created a number of heavily equipped divisions whose only purpose could be such an invasion. What were the South Vietnamese to do? I didn't have an answer. I just knew that the Civil Guard and the Self-Defense Corps were not ready to take over security in the countryside.

We continued to believe the main threat lay in a revived Vietminh guerrilla movement in the South, but General Williams had his orders from Washington. Lansdale had no sway with the senior military in the Pentagon when it came to changing traditional concepts of army organization and conventional warfare. There was not much to be done, except to try to speed up the development of an effective Civil Guard and the Self-Defense Corps. Lansdale had suggested that this could best be done with Filipino participation, taking advantage of the Philippine Constabulary's experience, but he had gotten nowhere. Barrows insisted that the Civil Guard was an arm of civilian government, and he was not interested in the experience of the Philippine Constabulary, which had paramilitary as well as standard police functions. There was a contract between the Vietnamese government and Michigan State University for Civil Guard advice and training; USOM was not initially happy over its secondary role but valiantly defended the arrangement against any outside influence.[3] Reinhardt was not disposed to intervene.

Colonel Kim was now back at the General Staff. Operation Giai Phong had been declared complete at the end of 1955, with the area turned over entirely to civilian control. He was sorry he could not have continued another six months. The army units that remained still enjoyed good relations with the population, so security was ensured, but more time was needed to consolidate popular support and to identify and arrest any hard-core Vietminh who actively threatened the population. He confessed worry about the army's reorganization and conventional training. The General Staff was slow in coming up with plans (a common American complaint) because they were not sure how to meet both demands, to defend the seventeenth parallel against an overt invasion and to ensure internal security. I told him we shared his concerns but that it seemed impossible to change overall policy.

The conversion of the army into regular, U.S.-style heavy divisions completely ignored the critical role the troops had played in establishing and maintaining local security and in closing the gap between the rural population and the government. No strong civilian presence had yet been established. The bureaucratic hardening of the arteries within various American agencies as they all went their separate ways, combined with Vietnamese institutional weaknesses, was to plague the future.

CAN LAO TENTACLES

In early May I contracted a severe case of infectious hepatitis and was evacuated to the military hospital at Clark Field in the Philippines, where I stayed for almost two months. Demi Gates took over most of my liaison work with Civic Action. When I returned to Saigon in late June, Thuan immediately invited me for dinner, saying he had a lot to tell me. Only limited progress was being made, he told me, in organizing and training the Village Self-Defense Corps. The lack of adequate training and equipment for the Civil Guard also worried him. Army reorganization was in full swing. But what he really wanted to say was most confidential. First, what did I know about the Can Lao? I said I had heard something but had few facts. He began tracing its history. Initially founded abroad as the Vietnamese Labor Party by

Diem's brother Nhu and five others, he explained, it had been taken over by Nhu, who had made it a secret political organization to penetrate and control the loyalty of the Movement for National Revolution, Diem's political party, as well as the government civil service, and now it was extending itself into the army.

Nhu had decided, Thuan said, to begin organizing secret Can Lao cells at various army command levels. Generals were not being recruited; most would not be informed of the cells. Dissension within the army would inevitably arise if those in the party were favored for promotion. The first target, instead, was the G-5 organization. Making G-5 officers into political commissars, I asked? Thuan nodded. I wanted to know how Nhu's doctrine of "personalism" squared with the creation of a secret political organization copying the communists. (Personalism stressed humanism and the dignity of the individual versus Lenin's all-powerful state, but it was a vague, highly intellectual doctrine.) Thuan shrugged. He did not believe Diem was fully aware of what Nhu was trying to do, but it was clear Nhu wanted to use the Can Lao to control the army and ensure its loyalty. It was understood that I would protect Thuan as a source.

I saw Lansdale immediately. We were under restraints about what we could do about the Can Lao, but this had to be stopped; Lansdale said he had been told by Diem that the Can Lao would be a political organization outside the army. Lansdale felt Nhu was proceeding without keeping either the CIA station or Diem fully informed; Nhu would present Diem a fait accompli, the "ensured" loyalty of the army. First, Lansdale would talk with General Williams, without revealing my source. Then we would see how to proceed. He would go to Diem himself, if necessary, but if he could get Williams to raise it with Diem, that would be best. Diem respected and liked Williams, and there was an understanding between them that the army was not to be involved in partisan politics. Diem would be ashamed not to order the Can Lao stopped.

General Williams' initial reaction was negative. He had been assured by Diem that the army would not be involved in partisan politics, and he believed him. Lansdale said Diem had given him the same assurance and that he had never known Diem to go back on his word when it had been given to someone he trusted. But he then explained Nhu's political thinking, suggesting that Diem might not be aware of what Nhu was doing. Williams said he had his own sources. He would check. He understood the sensitivities, but he didn't want to make a fool of himself with Diem if he was wrong.

We never learned how or whether General Williams got any corroboration, but in a few days he called in Lansdale to say that he was convinced our report was, unfortunately, true. He would take it up with Diem. As his next regular meeting with Diem ended, Williams asked everyone else to leave and spoke privately to the president in English. He was sorry to inform the president about a situation involving partisan politics in the army that was contrary to the assurances the president had given him, and of which he was sure that he (Diem) had not been informed. Describing the Can Lao plan, he gave his opinion that this would divide the army, not ensure a strong and unified defense force. Diem appeared shocked, pondered for a moment, and assured General Williams that if it was true he would stop it. Afterward, Thuan told me the plan had been dropped. I wondered out loud how long that would last. "As long as Nhu thinks the Americans might find out," he said. I wondered who would be in a position to find out and do something about it after Lansdale left. The answer, unfortunately, turned out to be no one.[4]

FIRE AND SHADOW

A group of Vietnamese nationalists, mainly Dai Viet, who had been unable to persuade their compatriots to get involved in the elections now had the idea of making South Vietnam's first feature motion picture. They were willing to put up their own money to finance the production but needed the government's agreement to buy copies of the film, to recover at least part of their investment. They also needed Vietnamese army cooperation in shooting it. Lansdale wanted me to help. The producer was Bui Diem, whom I had first met at Lansdale's Rue Miche house in 1954 and had seen casually a few times thereafter. Our association on this movie cemented a lifelong friendship. He had a sense of fairness and objectivity about events and his fellow Vietnamese that was rare among Vietnamese politicians. I liked him immediately and felt I could trust him.[5]

The move script was based on the true story of a Vietminh captain who had fled to the South after his parents, small landowners, were convicted by a communist land-reform court in their home village and brutally killed. His fiancé, whose father was the communist cadre leading the trial, had fled with him, love and horror overcoming her traditional family loyalties. The film was called (in Vietnamese) *We Want to Live,* renamed *Fire and Shadow* for international distribution. It would have drama, a love story, and suspense (would the lovers escape?), and it would show what life was like under the communists. The main actor and the actress, Mai Tram, who was quite beautiful, had limited stage experience. Others were novices. Extras would be recruited from northern refugees to play the villager roles, including that of the Vietminh captain's parents. Bui Diem would learn his producer's role on the job.

When I saw Thuan about Ministry of Defense support, he kidded me about wanting to get him in political trouble. The president had a very poor opinion of the Dai Viet, going back to the time General Collins had tried to force Quat (the Dai Viet leader) onto Diem as minister of defense. Thuan claimed that Quat had later tried to get Bao Dai's support for himself as Diem's replacement. I said Quat was not involved, that the film was a way to keep the Dai Viet occupied outside of politics. The film would cost about a million and a half piasters (about forty thousand dollars)—no small sum in those days. Bui Diem would raise the whole amount privately, with the investment to be recovered from copies sold to the Ministry of Defense and from commercial theaters and from distribution in the Philippines. The ministry would have free distribution rights through army psywar and Civic Action, after a commercial first run. It was a low-risk proposition; the ministry would only be committed to buy copies when the film was finished.

Thuan got President Diem's approval, provided Lansdale supported the project and kept a close watch. Bui Diem, puffing imperturbably on his ever-present pipe, presided over the operation. I ran interference through Thuan in arranging army logistical support. The filming proceeded without incident, taking place mainly in a refugee village on the South Vietnamese coast that looked authentically like North Vietnam. When the film was finished, a gala premiere was arranged at the largest movie theater in Saigon. Secretary of State for Defense Tran Trung Dung and Thuan were to be the guests of honor. I had seen the first edited copy of the film. It was powerful and moving, particularly the land-reform trial condemning the hero's parents to death, and it had a crowd-pleasing shark attack, taken from an old foreign film, spliced into the escape sequence.

But on the morning of the premiere, Bui Diem startled me by rushing agitatedly into my apartment. Nhu had found out about the premiere and had told Dung and Thuan not to attend and to cancel the contract, because the Dai Viet was involved. Bui Diem burst into angry tears—he had tried so hard to do something for his country. He was beside himself, and I became deeply angry myself. I knew he and others had already spent more than their budget; now they stood to lose most of that. I suggested he postpone the premiere. I would talk to Thuan.

I called Thuan at his home and said I had to see him as soon as possible. We met at his house that evening. It was a stormy scene. He said Nhu had raised hell with the president and that the president had reluctantly agreed. I said I'd seen the film, and it was good. Never mind the premiere, what about buying the copies? Did he tell Nhu there was a signed contract? He had, but Nhu had said the Dai Viet had gotten it under false pretenses. It was a plot to raise money for its political activities against Diem. I told Thuan that was wrong and he knew it; the Dai Viet weren't going to make any money off the film, even selling copies to the ministry. Now they were going to lose their shirts after being encouraged to go ahead. Thuan suggested that Lansdale intervene; he could do nothing. I said a lot of American support, including thousands of dollars of raw film stock, had already been donated.

Thuan and I remained close friends, as it was not really his fault, but we were unable to turn the palace around on honoring its agreement. Lansdale felt he had too much political capital already tied up in trying to persuade Diem on important political and constitutional issues. He raised the case but didn't press it. We did arrange for the Ministry of Information to purchase some sixteen-millimeter copies, but it was of little help. The film was popular commercially, but Vietnamese movie houses were limited in audience size and the price they could charge for admission. It took Bui Diem years to pay off his debt. The incident exhibited Nhu's tendency to political paranoia, which would serve his brother the president poorly in the years ahead.

PHASING OUT

Continuing to follow civic action and developments in the army, I began introducing Ogden "Oggie" Williams to my contacts. Oggie had arrived to replace Joe Redick; he was to stay on after the Lansdale team left at the end of 1956. Williams had been in the army air force at the end of World War II, subsequently worked in New York as a lawyer, and then had been asked by an old family friend to come down to Washington to be interviewed for "something exciting," which turned out to be the CIA. He could have continued as a lawyer—it would have been good work, riding the subway every day, getting one month's vacation in the summer, making a lot of money, and in the end, dying. He decided to try something new. His decision spoke for a lot of us.[6]

Initially assigned to intelligence work in Germany, he had returned to a boring desk assignment in Washington. When Lansdale requested a replacement for Redick, whose time was up, Oggie, whose French was good, jumped at the chance. Vietnam was new to him, but he was eager to learn and did not have that condescending manner toward Asians too typical of Agency types whose main experience was in Europe. (I could never quite figure out if colonialist attitudes had unconsciously been absorbed by some from their European exposure or if it was a heritage from "yellow peril" attitudes of our American past—maybe both.)

Williams' icebreaking appearance as Lansdale's interpreter at the presidential palace came at a formal dinner at which one course was served with a side dish of *nuoc mam* sauce with red rings of very hot local pepper. One of the peppers scorched his mouth, so he surreptitiously removed the remaining rings from the dish with his finger. Later, when the party repaired to a drawing room and he was seated between President Diem and Lansdale, he was given a cigar. Smoke got in his eye, which he unconsciously rubbed with the same finger he had used to remove the pepper. Tears began flowing uncontrollably. Diem noticing his distress, put his arm around him consolingly and said he shouldn't be so sad that his chief was leaving. Feeling sheepish, in time he got his tears under control. Afterward he was struck by Diem's kindness.

Williams would stay behind after Lansdale left, as the last remnant of the original Saigon Military Mission. At first the regular CIA station ignored him, but they soon learned it was through his friendship with key Vietnamese officials who were his contacts that they could find out what was really going on inside the presidential palace or at the Ministry of Defense. The station's own idea of how to get inside political information, Williams later said, was to recruit somebody from the palace housekeeping staff to collect trash from the wastebaskets, which could then be surreptitiously analyzed. That was "hard" information. When that didn't work they had to ask Williams for help. In most cases, he would just ask openly and get the answers.

In early October 1956, my father wrote me, concerned that Diem was becoming a dictator, citing the views of a Vietnamese whose letter had been published in the *Washington Post*. The characterization of Diem was wrong, I replied. Despite some reports of Vietminh assassinations in the countryside, growing adverse reactions of some political groups, such as the Dai Viet, to being excluded from an active political role, and reports of Can Lao activities (it was often difficult in Saigon to separate rumor from fact), the political climate seemed reasonably healthy. There were opposition delegates in the Assembly and some opposition press. But the accusations could prove right if the United States did not stand firm for some of its principles. I went on to say that one of the few Americans (an obvious reference to Lansdale) willing to stand up for those principles and translate them into something meaningful was leaving shortly. Too many of our people, I added, felt that any means was sufficient to the anticommunist end; we only defeated ourselves in the long run with that type of thinking. I was not enthusiastic about the constitution that had been adopted but remained optimistic about South Vietnam's future.[7]

It had taken some time to resume a full work pace after returning from my illness in the Philippines that summer. By the time I resumed my contact with Kieu Cong Cung, I learned that Diem had just abolished the traditional village councils in July and henceforth would appoint the village chiefs himself. Cung said he favored it as a temporary measure; too many chiefs were corrupt holdovers from the French or were controlled by the sects or the communists. I didn't pursue it further, because, he said, elections were planned in about a year for new councils. Unfortunately, they were never held again under Diem.[8] This was something Lansdale neglected, and in retrospect it may have been my fault, as I was the main person keeping up with what was happening in the provinces.

There was still much to be done politically at the national and local levels, but the official American view was that the Saigon Military Mission had served its primary purpose as a catalyst for the Vietnamese in the earlier, more desperate days. It was time for the regular American agencies to take over.

The challenge of the earliest days had faded. Lansdale's mission was ending, even though the job was not finished. The Vietnamese government, and particularly Diem, continued to need good political advice, but this had become the regular job of the embassy and the CIA station, which were equipped by neither outlook nor experience for this task. Unfortunately, no one on the American side in a leadership role enjoyed either the confidence and trust of the Vietnamese (and thus the influence with them) that Lansdale possessed or had any depth of understanding of the basic political and security challenges the Vietnamese still faced.[9] A chasm would begin to develop between the Americans and the Vietnamese, which would become critical in what would follow.

WHAT NEXT?

I was wondering what to do next. It would be hard to go into routine CIA work, particularly back in Washington. I wanted to stay in what was loosely called "political action." It was mainly overt nation building—work that had gone to the CIA by default, since it was not being done by any other government agency. Yet if you took an overview of the typical underdeveloped country under threat of communist subversion or rebellion, it was the most essential kind of work; it went to the heart of what a country's people and government had to do together to prevail. The Magsaysay experience, and its embodiment in the Filipinos' unselfish service in Vietnam, as well as the "people first" approach we had helped to introduce, had fired my imagination and enthusiasm. I saw it as an extension of American democratic principles and beliefs. Where else would I believe so strongly in what I was doing? I knew it would be hard to work for anyone else, after Lansdale's unconventional imagination, democratic principles, empathy for other peoples, and singular views. I had done more than I originally thought possible in Vietnam. My encounters with the Agency bureaucracy back in Washington had not impressed me favorably. My father wanted me to join him in his engineering business, or I could go back to law school or into some other private endeavor. Lansdale, however, urged me to stay with the Agency. He thought it needed younger people with my attitude and experience.

This was running through my mind when Lansdale told me he had been asked by headquarters if I would be interested in going to Laos to start a civic action program there. I was now the "expert," Lansdale said with a smile. Was he going? He said that unfortunately he had now become too well known, too controversial. They wouldn't even let him back in the Philippines. Frank Wisner, head of the covert side of the Agency, was expected out shortly and wanted to talk to me about it.

Things were going well in Vietnam, Wisner told me. Laos now had top priority. If the North Vietnamese, working through the communist-controlled Pathet Lao, were able to subvert and control the Lao government, they would achieve an end run around South Vietnam and could provide direct support to dissidents in Thailand. The Thai government was weak and divided, a prime target for subversion. If that were to happen, the Southeast Asian dominoes would really begin to fall. Negotiations were under way in Laos to incorporate the Pathet Lao into the Lao government and to hold elections with Pathet Lao participation. In the meantime, subversion at the village level by the Pathet Lao had increased, not ceased. The Royal Lao government, headed by Crown Prince Souvanna Phouma, had practically no presence outside Vientiane, the capital. Would I go there to develop a civic action program similar to the one in Vietnam? Saying I would give it serious consideration, I arranged an exploratory weekend trip to Vientiane. After discussions with Milt Clark, our Vientiane station chief, and General Ouane Ratikoun, the Lao army chief of staff, I came back with sufficient optimism to accept the assignment.

LAST IMPRESSIONS OF VIETNAM

The Republic of South Vietnam's first anniversary was coming up on October 26, the day the newly adopted Vietnamese constitution would go into effect and the new National Assembly was to open. The previously elected Constituent Assembly, which had adopted the constitution, had converted itself into the country's first legislature. On September 27 the French flag would finally be lowered over all their installations except the embassy. South Vietnam was now completely independent. Ceremonies were to be held at the palace and the old Opera House, the home of the new National Assembly. The whole city was hung with banners. Lansdale team members sat in the stands for an afternoon parade down former Boulevard Gallieni (renamed Tran Hung Dao), between Saigon and Cholon, the street I had traveled looking for Captain Giai back in August 1954.

Three Vietnamese army divisions and the military academy cadets from Dalat took part. The soldiers appeared full of pride, manifesting a vibrant, self-confident spirit that had been so sadly lacking in 1954. A squadron of U.S. Navy jets flew overhead, and warships from five nations were anchored off the Saigon waterfront. As day turned into evening after the ceremonies and the parade, I wandered around the streets for hours, savoring the happiness of the large Vietnamese crowds with their families. They seemed wreathed in smiles. There was the smell of freedom in the air, I thought. I basked in the warmth of it and felt proud that our small, unobtrusive team had contributed in some measure to their happiness. While my second tour in Vietnam had not turned out to be as intense or exciting as the first, I still felt a considerable sense of accomplishment.

The glow of that evening stayed with me on the trip home in November and pushed away for a time my concerns about what might ensue after Lansdale left. The Diem government's antidemocratic tendencies, as manifested in the Can Lao, with its disdain for other preexisting political parties and religious sects and its secretive communist-like approach, bothered me. Would the ideals imbedded in the new Vietnamese constitution be implemented in a way that would create a counter-ideology to communism and serve as the political base of resistance to its revival in the South? I was certain the South Vietnamese and the Diem government would be tested by the Vietminh, but I could not foresee the future, certainly not the future that was to transpire. Even now, over fifty years later, thoughts of that day fire up my spirit, despite all the tragedy and final loss that was to ensue.

Back in Washington over the 1956 Christmas holidays, awaiting reassignment to Laos, I took stock. Mainly, I had learned that the way to be effective with Asians was through friendship and mutual trust. I had never asked someone to do something for us that he was not willing to do for his own country. Any financial help given was to help that person help his country, never for him personally. They did not work directly for us; we were brothers working for a common cause. Any influence I might have should be used constructively, not to seek advantage for its own sake or some narrow bureaucratic goal. This earned me the right to point out when an Asian friend deviated from his own goals and principles. Friendship and objectivity would be maintained; I would never go "native," in the sense of confusing my personal interests with those of the people with whom I worked. This was a hard but necessary standard to live by.

I knew about the bitter experience of Lawrence of Arabia, who had supported the Arab revolt for independence against the Turks, only to see it subverted by his own government's colonial ambitions. But we Americans believed in independence and self-government. I had no reservations about supporting real Lao independence, which I knew meant freedom from

North Vietnamese and Pathet Lao subversion and pressure. The French, while hanging on to influence in Cambodia, seemed to have abdicated their colonial ambitions in Laos. This, I thought, would leave me free to seek out and work with Lao who sincerely wanted to help their own country. Also, I was dedicated to democracy as the best way to defeat communism. This was an ethos formed in Vietnam and supported by what I understood of the Magsaysay revolution in the Philippines. I would try to put it to work in Laos.

Trying to save Laos from a communist takeover seemed almost as important as what we had just lived through in Vietnam. Given Cambodian "neutrality," the institutional and political weakness of Thailand, and the insurgency already raging in Malaya, the road seemed wide open for communism to outflank South Vietnam into the rest of Southeast Asia. The "domino theory" was valid, given the prevailing circumstances.[10] I was motivated to go but had no experience in Laos and would find it very different from Vietnam.

ON TO LAOS

The three years I spent in Laos with the CIA from February 1957 through most of 1959, with six months in Washington as the Lao desk officer, amounted to a learning experience. Under a fairly transparent official cover as an economic aid mission (USOM) employee in Laos, my main assignment was to help the Royal Lao government reach out to the villages through a civic action program similar to the one in South Vietnam.

While a third larger in territory than South Vietnam, Laos was populated by only two million people, about half of whom were ethnic Lao, living in the lowlands close to the Mekong River, while the rest, more than twenty different tribal groupings, lived mainly in the mountains. Landlocked, Laos lay athwart the route by which communist North Vietnam was already attempting to extend its influence and operations into the rest of Southeast Asia. The immediate threat came from an indigenous movement, the communist-controlled Pathet Lao. From base areas near the North Vietnamese frontier they were gradually extending their influence into the rest of Laos, while a pocket of expatriate Vietnamese in northeastern Thailand were supporting subversion in that country.

The Royal Lao government's king had largely ceremonial powers. A parliamentary system existed, with a prime minister, Souvanna Phouma, who was also a crown prince. Souvanna's half-brother, Crown Prince Souphanavong, headed the Pathet Lao. Throughout 1957 negotiations went on between Souvanna and Souphanavong to bring the Pathet Lao into the government, integrate their armed forces into the Lao army, and hold supplementary elections for the Lao General Assembly, with Pathet Lao participation. The dispatch of civic action teams to the villages would, it was hoped, create a link with the Lao government and thus forestall a Pathet Lao election landslide.

But civic action did not proceed as planned. Originally, the teams were to consist mainly of Lao army soldiers, who had at least a limited education and some basic skills. General Ouane, whom I had met during my brief trip to Vientiane the previous year, appointed one of his ablest officers, Lieutenant Colonel Oudone Sananikone, to head it up. But Souvanna Phouma dragged his feet and, when he established civic action, forbade army participation; the teams had to be civilian. This created a recruitment problem, as few civilians were available with the requisite primary education and skills. While the Agency provided financial support, USOM was to provide commodities such as tools, village medical kits, and construction materials for the teams to use. USOM's negative attitudes toward the Lao and toward any cooperation with the "spooks," as we of the CIA were called behind our backs, further hampered progress.[11] Nevertheless, Oudone was able to field twelve trained teams by the end of 1957. Unfortunately, by that time an agreement had been signed with the Pathet Lao. They now had two posts in the government and supplementary assembly elections were scheduled for May 1958.

Earlier in the year, I had taken Oudone to Saigon to see Vietnamese civic action. The ground had been laid for this during a stop in Saigon on my way out from Washington. While Oudone went to villages to see the Vietnamese version in operation, I got called to the palace to see President Diem. President Magsaysay had just died in a plane crash, and I was in a state of shock—a light had gone out, not just for the Philippines but for the rest of Asia. Diem was also in shock. He had been about to make a state visit to the Philippines; he had wanted to tell Magsaysay personally, he said, how much he and the Vietnamese people appreciated Filipino help when they really needed it. Now Magsaysay was gone. We sat in silence for a moment. He recalled seeing me in Qui Nhon, and his face brightened. He asked about Colonel Lansdale (now deputy of the Office of Special Operations under the secretary of defense in the Pentagon). Then he began to ask about Laos. He was worried, he said, about the Lao caving in to communist pressure. I described the Lao leadership, saying the older ones seemed self-indulgent and indifferent, while the younger leaders were the future but had little current influence. Still, I believed, there was enough resistance in the National Assembly to forestall any outright surrender. If and when an agreement was reached, elections would be key. We hoped Lao civic action would link the government to the villages and help pro-government candidates in the elections. Diem said he had already ordered Cung to provide training assistance and any other help needed. He shook my hand warmly as I left.[12]

With little time left before the elections, two ideas emerged about how to influence the outcome. One was to launch a crash village-aid program, using mainly air drops of construction materials and tools followed up on the ground by Lao army and civic action teams to help the villagers build new schools or repair old ones.[13] The other was to persuade pro-government candidates to coalesce, with only one running for each open seat. I was put in operational charge of the crash aid program, which was called "Booster Shot." After delays in getting Washington approval, less than a month remained to assemble materials, such as sheet roofing and cement, along with tools, and air drop these materials to about a thousand villages, but it got done. Some of the roofing bundles came loose, sending sheets spinning like large snowflakes through the air and then slicing into the ground, while errant cement bags burst, dusting the landside. Close calls were recorded, but fortunately no one was killed. Leaflets were dropped attributing the aid to the Royal Lao government. Nothing on this scale had ever happened before in Laos, certainly never as fast. It was an example of how to get aid to remote villages quickly.

Unfortunately, Booster Shot had little effect on the elections. The pro-government candidates refused to put up a unified slate, and most of those who ran failed to establish a connection in villagers' minds between their candidacies and the aid.[14] There were seventy-five pro-government candidates for the twenty-one available seats, while the Pathet Lao and a small party of leftist allies put up only twenty-four. The Pathet Lao won thirteen seats. This shocked the noncommunist Lao, particularly the younger Lao leaders in the civil service and the army, who now lost all respect for the older generation, whose corruption, selfishness, and insouciance had brought about defeat. Ironically, however, Booster Shot had an unanticipated effect on Lao attitudes, convincing them for the first time that the Americans were serious and could actually deliver. Unfortunately, for the next year and a half no effective follow-up rural aid program was developed, nor was any practical training and advice given to the Lao army, as the United States could still not decide how to set up an effective military aid mission.

After a stint in Washington as CIA Laos desk officer in the latter part of 1958, I decided to leave the Agency. I was told I had a bright career ahead, my efficiency reports were good, and I had even been awarded the Intelligence Medal of Merit for my service in Vietnam.[15] I saw little future in the Agency, however, for the kind of nation building that had fully engaged me in South Vietnam and to a lesser degree in Laos. I loved the operational freedom afforded by the Agency in the field, but not the bureaucracy in Washington, and I was not attracted to pure intelligence work. Also, a new chief of operations for the Far East, transferred from Europe, turned me off. He wanted to evaluate case officers by the number of agents they recruited. Supposedly, for effective political action you had to have agents directly under your control. Some in the Agency were obsessed with "controlling" the people they dealt with. My own experience had been the opposite. I enjoyed supporting leaders who were too independent and proud to be controlled by anyone. They were the future of their countries. Also, my belief that democracy was the only enduring answer to communism, long before the idea had any currency in the Agency or in Washington, got me classified as naïve by the prevailing practitioners of realpolitik.

Perhaps the last straw was a younger case office who sought my views about Asians. When I told him Asians had very sensitive antenna out to determine Westerner attitudes, that he should establish relationships based on mutual trust and respect, he said I was naïve. He was going to recruit agents to work directly for the Agency, deceiving them if necessary and controlling them by persuasion, along with fear that he might blow their cover. He was much smarter than any Asian; I was a boy scout. We almost came to blows. If this was the mindset of the people the Agency was fielding, I thought, it was not the place for me.

My experience with rural development in Laos would stand me in good stead, as would the friendships I had developed with some Americans whom I would see more of later. Among them was Bert Fraleigh, who had come from Taiwan to get more effective rural development going but was largely frustrated in Laos; Stu Methven, who replaced me there; and Henry Hecksher, who had become my station chief toward the end of 1957.[16] I also learned in Laos how thoroughly the communists indoctrinated their soldiers and cadre with hateful images of their noncommunist countrymen, as "running dogs of the Americans."[17] The same communist approach was already being used to undermine the South Vietnamese government.

During the years of my involvement, Laos lurched in slow motion from one political crisis to another, always beneath the shadow of direct threats from the North Vietnamese. With a split General Assembly, Laos veered from Prime Minister Souvanna Phouma's neutralism, under which the Pathet Lao were gaining the upper hand, to a more openly anticommunist stand by Phoui Sananikone. The younger Lao formed a pressure group, the Committee for the Defense of the National Interests, which pushed against corruption fostered by our aid program, and promoted Lao independence.[18] They harbored doubts about Souvanna's true beliefs, although he expressed anticommunist sentiments after the elections.[19] U.S. policy veered back and forth, trying to support a stronger stand by the Lao while placating French and British concerns about not undermining the Geneva Accords. Through it all, except for Booster Shot, American economic assistance remained astonishingly ineffective.

Inherent in my support for Lao independence was an unspoken commitment that the United States would intervene if North Vietnam invaded. The Lao were a decent, peaceful people who deserved to have a free country, but I knew they would never be able to face the North Vietnamese alone. I had pangs of conscience about leaving but thought that if the North Vietnamese were to invade, surely the United States would come to its defense. I was to be badly disappointed. The North Vietnamese began setting up posts inside the Lao border at the end of 1959, nibbling away at Lao territory to cover the route of the future Ho Chi Minh Trail, without significant reaction by the world community, including the United States.

Part II
SOUTH VIETNAM AT RISK
1960–63

Prologue

B y the 1960 U.S. presidential election, the situation in Vietnam had deteriorated badly
since Lansdale left at the end of 1956. The American mission became divided after the
arrival of Ambassador Elbridge Durbrow in 1957. On one side was the ambassador
and the USOM director, who became very negative about President Diem, while General
Williams at MAAG maintained a good relationship with him. The Agency devoted itself
mainly to building up the regime's intelligence service through Diem's brother, Ngo Dinh
Nhu, and to working with the Special Police to ferret out suspected communists, overlooking the adverse political implications of this narrow focus. After initially supporting it, the
Agency cut off the Can Lao. Nhu began raising funds for the Can Lao by granting economic
monopolies and siphoning off proceeds from the National Lottery, actions that damaged the
regime's reputation because of the appearance of personal corruption.

At least part of Diem's conflict with the embassy was inherent in how he viewed his problems. He was rightly concerned about subversion in the countryside and saw a democratic
political system as open to exploitation by the communists and their followers—hence the
justification for the Can Lao as a means to ensure loyalty and assert secret control. Ambassador Durbrow, who correctly analyzed the Can Lao as part of the regime's political problems,
was surprised to learn the United States had been involved in supporting it in the first place.[1]
USOM focused primarily on the urban areas and on developing light industry to reduce the
need for imports, aimed at lowering the aid burden by lessening the need for counterpart
funds. Organizing, training, and equipping the Vietnamese Civil Guard was judged a civilian
endeavor, assigned under contract to Michigan State University and supported by USOM
funds.

The main experience of the Michigan State advisory team was in American big-city
police work, but the Civil Guard was supposed to take over the rural security role previously
assigned to the Vietnamese army (now converted into regular divisions to defend against an
overt invasion by the North). The Michigan State effort was so ineffective that Diem wanted
the Civil Guard to be trained and equipped by MAAG. General Williams supported Diem;
Durbrow and the USOM director were opposed. The quarrel dragged on for several years,
and the Civil Guard languished, leaving a security vacuum in the countryside, just as we had
feared in 1956.

The Diem government had launched a negative campaign of anticommunist denunciation and was imprisoning former, as well as continuing, Vietminh supporters.[2] While eliminating much of the Vietminh political infrastructure, it also alienated the people, particularly
in the Delta, who had supported the Vietminh but were not communists and might have
been persuaded to support the noncommunist cause. The assertion of secret political con-

trol through the Can Lao had the divisive effect Lansdale had predicted. Fear of communist subversion overcame the need for a more open political system; more open democracy came to be viewed as a danger rather than an asset. Without an independent judiciary in the constitution, there were insufficient checks and balances. Diem's tendencies toward isolation and autocracy were reinforced by events and intensified by the influence of his family, particularly his brother Nhu.

In 1960 the "paratrooper coup" occurred, preceded by an overt campaign by Ambassador Durbrow to pressure Diem into broadening his government. While the objective was laudable, Durbrow's tactics were counterproductive. Frustrated that his political advice was not being followed, he organized a campaign among other members of the diplomatic corps to bring Diem around. This became widely known and inadvertently contributed to the impression that the Americans no longer supported Diem. During the coup, when Durbrow refused to give Diem clear public support, Diem concluded that he supported the coup. This was reinforced when one of the Agency's case officers was identified as being with the coup forces and had to be hurriedly flown out of the country.[3]

The coup collapsed, but it would leave deep psychological damage beneath the surface. Diem no longer trusted the local Americans, except General McGarr, who had replaced Williams as head of MAAG. Relations between Durbrow and Diem became uncivil, though Durbrow reported that they continued to have meaningful conversations.[4] Nhu had been skeptical all along about American intentions. The coup further isolated Diem from a number of key Vietnamese civilians and army officers who had been his supporters. Nhu, with his paranoid cast of mind, concluded that many of them had secretly supported the coup. His influence over Diem increased enormously as Diem became less sure about whom he could trust. Prominent army officers who had not supported the coup but who Nhu thought were secretly sympathetic, such as General Minh and General Kim, were marginalized. Opposition politicians were arrested and locked up. Loyalty rather than competence began to be stressed from the center out. The position of Vo Van Hai, the president's private secretary, was damaged, though he was not part of the plot, because he had tried to arrange a compromise with the coup leaders to keep Diem in power but send Nhu and Madame Nhu into exile.

In 1958, the North Vietnamese Politburo began to reconstitute local guerrilla groups in areas of South Vietnam where the Communist Party had been traditionally strong. The term used by the Vietnamese government for the guerillas, "Viet Cong" (Vietnamese communists), came into general use. Viet Cong agents intensified their assassination of local officials. Viet Cong cadres, including some of the youths who had been forcibly evacuated to the North in 1954 and 1955, were infiltrated down the Lao side of the border area back into South Vietnam. By 1960, isolated assassinations had grown into an armed insurgency; the National Liberation Front was proclaimed. Carefully controlled from within by secret Lao Dong (communist) members, it presented a nationalist face of southerners rebelling against the "American-dominated" Diem government and calling for reunification with the North. The Vietnamese government and army were increasingly unable to cope, in a period coinciding with the Eisenhower administration's end and marked by paralysis at the State Department (due in some measure to a leadership vacuum caused by John Foster Dulles's illness and death in May 1959). From 1958 on, Diem repeatedly asked through various channels that Lansdale be sent to assess the security situation.[5] Such visits were repeatedly blocked by Durbrow, backed up by the State Department. At one point, to buttress his opposition, Durbrow would say, "Lansdale is no expert [on] anti-guerrilla activities."[6]

In January 1961, the new Kennedy administration inherited not only an immediate crisis in Laos but also an unanticipated one in Vietnam. During the transition Eisenhower had reportedly talked to Kennedy at length about Laos but said little about Vietnam. In the meantime, the security situation in South Vietnam became so palpably critical that Ambassador Durbrow could no longer block a visit to Saigon by Lansdale, who had been promoted to brigadier general in 1960 and was by now the acting chief of the Office of Special Operations under the secretary of defense in Washington. His visit to South Vietnam on January 2–14, 1961, resulted in a report to the departing secretary of defense, Thomas Gates. An incoming Kennedy advisor, Walter Rostow, read the report and a companion memorandum about a successful counter-guerrilla community called Binh Hung and found both so compelling he insisted Kennedy read them. Kennedy became very excited, asked Rostow for books on guerrilla warfare, and telephoned Lansdale directly, asking him to publish the companion memo. (This would appear in the May 1961, edition of the *Saturday Evening Post* under the title "The Report the President Wanted Published.")

On January 28, 1961, Lansdale was called to a full-blown meeting on Vietnam with key senior personnel from the president's staff and the State and Defense departments at the White House. Kennedy had a copy of Lansdale's report in front of him and asked for his views.

Kennedy listened approvingly, then asked if Secretary of State Dean Rusk had informed Lansdale that he (Kennedy) wanted him to go to Vietnam as the new ambassador. Lansdale had not; taken aback by the suddenness of it, he hesitated, telling Kennedy he was really a military officer not a diplomat. What Lansdale had recommended was an unconventional advisory setup in Vietnam with the right kind of Americans being assigned, in particular a new ambassador, and a special advisor for political operations, both of whom could "influence Asians through understanding them sympathetically"; were "knowledgeable about the Mao Tse Tung tactics now employed to capture Vietnam" and were "dedicated to feasible and practical democratic means to defeat these Communist tactics." Lansdale wanted "an extra-bureaucratic uninhibited advisory system consciously built on shared U.S.-Vietnamese goals (validated by shared experience) and based on mutual trust and admiration."[7]

Kennedy persisted with the ambassadorial idea, and Lansdale communicated through Rostow his willingness to serve, but the idea fell victim to Lansdale's prior wars with State over Vietnam policy. In fact, Secretary Rusk, a veteran of the Foreign Service, threatened to resign if Lansdale was appointed, so vehement were the objections of his closest Foreign Service advisors.[8] As a result, Kennedy's offer never materialized, and Lansdale was eventually sidetracked. The decision was made to rely exclusively on the regular government bureaucracy to help South Vietnam. Each agency would pursue the bureaucratic, top-down, formalistic approach it knew best. The close-in advisory effort Lansdale recommended was ignored.

President Kennedy was convinced he had to draw the line in Vietnam. South Vietnam would become the test case for defeating Nikita Khrushchev's vociferously proclaimed doctrine of "wars of national liberation." The means would be counterinsurgency. The original concept, which Lansdale had been instrumental in creating within the Pentagon as an essentially unconventional approach to defeating wars of national liberation, was now proclaimed as administration doctrine. Neither the new secretary of defense, Robert McNamara, nor the regular military brass understood Lansdale's emphasis on a people-first approach to defeating insurgency or the use of irregular counterinsurgency forces and tactics. In their minds it became a traditional military assistance program, delivering military materiel to the Vietnamese army and placing American advisors with regular Vietnamese units to conduct conventional warfare, with the new tactic of using helicopters for improved mobility.

Lansdale had earlier tried to brief Secretary McNamara about the nature of the enemy and the war. Already aware of McNamara's mindset, Lansdale decided to get his attention by dramatizing his presentation with such primitive Viet Cong weapons as handmade pistols and knives, old French rifles, and bamboo pungi sticks. These he laid out on McNamara's desk; the enemy in Vietnam, he explained, used them. Many were barefoot or wore sandals and tattered black pajamas, but they were winning. "It doesn't take weapons and uniforms and lots of food to win. It takes ideas and ideals." McNamara let him go on for about ten minutes and then, during a pause, asked if that was all.[9] He would call on Lansdale very little afterward, except for the exchange over the "x factor," mentioned in the preface of this book. McNamara's thinking encompassed only tangibles; to Lansdale, intangibles were the key.

Before he was taken out of the picture, Lansdale had one last chance to influence Vietnam policy. President Kennedy wanted him to be a member of the Maxwell Taylor/Walt Rostow mission dispatched in October 1961 to develop a program to support the Vietnamese. Lansdale quickly found out that he was not to be included in the formal high-level meetings with the Vietnamese, that General Taylor thought of him only as "an idea man." Nevertheless, Lansdale was called directly from the Saigon airport to the palace for a personal meeting with Diem and Nhu. They wanted to know if they could trust the Kennedy administration. Neutralizing Laos had so alarmed them that Diem had requested American troops be sent to Vietnam, figuring that this would so engage the United States as to preclude a "neutralist" solution for his own nation. By subtle suggestion Lansdale turned Diem around on his request for troops, which he didn't really need.[10] Afterward Lansdale briefed Taylor, who didn't seem to understand much of what he was being told. Lansdale was still excluded from subsequent high-level meetings, and Taylor made it clear he didn't want his political advice, asking him instead him to develop a plan for electronic surveillance of the borders with the North and with Laos and Cambodia. Lansdale protested that this wasn't his expertise, but Taylor insisted. (Lansdale farmed out the task to the local military advisory staff, who quickly figured out it would cost several billion dollars, which sank the idea. Incredibly, a similar project was revived by McNamara about five years later, with negligible results.)

Lansdale had an entirely different idea of how to jump-start counterinsurgency on a popular basis—that is, by arming existing natural resistance groups such as the Hoa Hao, the Cao Dai, the Catholics, and the indigenous tribes on the High Plateau. He reasoned that this would build a popular base for counterinsurgency. If it were done carefully, he thought, he could get Diem's agreement; one consequence would be to oblige Diem to reach out for political support to groups who had been ignored and even repressed. His ideas never got a hearing.[11]

Out of this mission came the creation of a higher-level military command, the Military Advisory Command Vietnam (MACV), over the existing Military Advisory Assistance Group (MAAG), and the assignment of American military advisors to all regular Vietnamese army units, battalion size and above, and to the Vietnamese province chiefs who were also military sector commanders. American-flown helicopters were introduced to improve Vietnamese army mobility, and American-flown aircraft were provided for close air support. Also proposed was the introduction of U.S. troops on an ostensible humanitarian-relief mission, and the bombing of North Vietnam as a last resort. The latter two recommendations were rejected by Kennedy. The only unconventional aspects approved were the assignment of U.S. Special Forces units to work with the indigenous tribesmen, initially under CIA supervision, and CIA semicovert support for other irregular forces.

The last line of a cable to Washington describing Taylor's final visit with President Diem noted Diem's desire for "Lansdale's services here in Vietnam." Written in the margin of that cable in the National Archives are the words, "No, No, NO!" in an unidentified hand.[12]

At the end of General Taylor's briefing at the White House about his mission, President Kennedy pulled Lansdale aside and asked him to take charge of a secret operation to get rid of Fidel Castro; the plan, called Mongoose, was supervised by the president's brother Robert. Doomed from the start by the push for immediate results, the operation was to be a failure, for which Lansdale got at least part of the blame. It was started without prior consultation with John McCone, who had been appointed the new CIA director and under whom all such activities should have normally fallen. But the Kennedy White House did not trust the CIA to be in charge.

On December 6, 1961, just before his move to State, Walt Rostow wrote in his last memorandum to Kennedy that Lansdale was "a unique national asset in the Saigon setting; and I cannot believe that anything he may be able to do in his present assignment could match his value in South East Asia."[13] Rostow was not always right, but on this his foresight was twenty-twenty. Rostow would later write that the failure to send Lansdale at that time to Vietnam "lay deep in the American military and the civil bureaucracy. The American ambassador and the ranking General in Saigon—and the departments backing them in Washington—did not want another American that close to Diem."[14]

Chapter 8
Return to Vietnam

My transition from the Agency after 1959 to the business world was not easy. It was a complete change not only in my line of work but also in the operating environment. I went to work for Airways Engineering, a consulting firm specializing in airport planning and design started by my father and a few others at the end of World War II. It was a profession about which I knew little. The closest I had come was taking drafting lessons one summer while in college and working part-time as an assistant to one of the firm's draftsmen. The change appealed to me because of the prospect of foreign travel and the chance to become involved in Latin America, a region I was unfamiliar with.

In early 1960, I met by chance in El Salvador the person who would really change my life. Barbara Hubner, a Chilean, lived in Georgetown, less than a block away from my parents' apartment. (In the summer they stayed mainly at Gravel Hill.) A resident of the United States since 1956, Barbara was in 1960 the first interpreter to be hired by the newly created Interamerican Development Bank, whose first organizational meeting was in San Salvador. I was there studying the expansion of the Ilopango International Airport to accept jets. My client, Roberto Parker, the Salvadoran minister of public works, introduced us at a reception given by the bank. Otherwise, we would never have met, since we lived and worked in such different circles.

I was surprised to learn that we both had read and admired a 1959 book by Max Ways, *Beyond Survival*. Its thesis that American foreign policy should be based on our democratic ideals had appealed to my deepest beliefs. Barbara was an immigrant to the United States— "by choice" as she put it—in large measure because of what she believed America stood for. She had been working previously as an escort interpreter for the State Department, shepherding Spanish-speaking visitors all over the United States. What she saw and heard supported her convictions. The common chord struck by *Beyond Survival* was an added attraction, an amazing accident of fate that we shared our fundamental beliefs.

After a whirlwind courtship, we were married at the end of May. By the fall of 1961 we had bought a house in what was then mainly rural McLean, in northern Virginia, and already had a son, Rufus. A daughter, Anne, was on the way, to be born slightly less than a year after Rufus. I had settled into my job at Airways but still followed events in Laos and Vietnam as closely as possible. It was difficult to let go. I had been too deeply involved.

At the time I was neither a Democrat nor a Republican, but I supported Kennedy in the 1960 election, because of his strong anticommunist stance combined with the feeling he represented a new beginning in American foreign policy. I knew from occasional contact with Lansdale during 1960 that things were not going well in Vietnam. I also stayed in informal contact with Stu Methven in Laos and followed with pessimism the continuing success of the

North Vietnamese incursion into Laos without a significant reaction from our government or the international community. The Eisenhower administration was slow to wake up to the rising insurgency in Vietnam, where it was pretty much business as usual.

I spent the early months of 1961 monitoring the Kennedy administration's decision to revive neutralism in Laos and writing angry letters to the editors of the *Washington Post* and the *New York Times,* some of which got published. The efforts many of us had made to help the Lao sustain their independence had failed. Lao cohesion, always vulnerable, had fallen apart. A curious mixture of American ineptitude and disarray, combined with Lao institutional fragility and disunity under intense North Vietnamese political and military pressure, all in an atmosphere of divided international support, was doing the country in. The neutralization of Laos would turn out to be a strategic disaster for Vietnam, as it provided protection to the North Vietnamese for the Ho Chi Minh Trail, located mainly on Lao territory. Any future invasion of that part of Laos by us or the South Vietnamese would be a breach of international law, while the North Vietnamese could violate Lao sovereignty at will. Our much later semicovert efforts at bombing the trail and providing CIA support to the Hmong (Meo) tribesmen harassing the North Vietnamese were insufficient to choke off the flow of supplies and men going south.

The new doctrine of counterinsurgency interested me, and in April 1962 the RAND Corporation invited me to participate in a five-day symposium about it. In addition to General Lansdale, there were Lieutenant Colonel Bohannon, Colonel Valeriano from the Philippines, Colonel Wendell Fertig (a leading guerrilla commander in the Philippines against the Japanese), and Lt. Col. Sam Wilson, a member of Merrill's Marauders during World War II and now Lansdale's executive officer in the Pentagon. Other participants came from Great Britain, Australia, and France (Lieutenant Colonel Galula of the marines, whose pacification operations had been successful against great odds in Algeria). I talked mainly about civic action and troop behavior, but it was a great learning experience, covering the full gamut of successful counterinsurgency policies and practices.[1] Later I wished that many senior American officers and civilians had had the same opportunity.

A CALL FROM AID

Toward the end of May 1962, I was in my business office in Washington when I got a call from Rutherford Poats. He identified himself as the deputy for far eastern affairs of the U.S. Agency for International Development (USAID). Could I come talk to him? It was about Vietnam, he said, without elaborating. Maybe, I thought, they need some advice about how to deal with the Vietnamese government.

When I saw Poats the next day, he came straight to the point. I had been recommended to his immediate boss, Seymour Janow, as someone who knew a lot about Vietnam and counterinsurgency. I had followed in a general way what was happening in Vietnam through the newspapers. I knew Lansdale had been out there, that he was deeply worried about the situation, and I had read his article in the *Saturday Evening Post* about Father Hoa. I understood the basics of counterinsurgency, my understanding heightened by participation in the RAND symposium.

To my complete surprise, Poats asked me to go out to South Vietnam as a consultant for AID to survey the insurgency situation and recommend a counterinsurgency program. AID was under pressure to come up with something but was nonplussed about how to proceed. He took me to see Janow, a pleasant, reserved man who had been part of the postwar remaking of Japan under General MacArthur. He and Poats admitted to knowing little about South Vietnam and even less about counterinsurgency. Developing a civilian economic and social component to the counterinsurgency effort in Vietnam, Janow said, was a very high priority, not only for AID but for the administration. He practically pleaded with me to accept the assignment. It would only be temporary, not more than a month. I had to consult my wife, I said, and my father, for whom I worked, before I could answer.

It turned out that Lansdale had been asked to recommend people who knew South Vietnam and something about counterinsurgency and had mentioned me. He hadn't thought much would come of it, so he hadn't informed me. My wife was all for my taking it on. She knew how strongly I felt about my country and the Vietnamese. Lansdale said he thought I was the only one who could come up with something that might be effective. I was not so sure. It looked like a real challenge.

But the appeal was very strong. Kennedy's inaugural call to arms—"Ask not what your country can do for you, ask what you can do for your country"—had struck a deep chord. Notwithstanding my newfound life as a husband and a father, my old convictions resurfaced that freedom was indivisible, that life for the Vietnamese people free of communism was not just their cause but an American cause. And there was the attraction of a dip back into "national security" work, which had been my life for seven years in the 1950s. I decided to do it, but I dreaded what I knew would be a head-on clash with my father, not just because he needed me but because he had a long-standing visceral reaction against what he saw as American over-involvement in Asia.

His opposition was immediate, vehement, and bitter. I would be deserting the business and leaving undone many active projects and proposals. He was certain I would become so involved again that it wouldn't be temporary. Without my having mentioned him, my father said, "That godammed Lansdale, he must be behind this." To little avail, I said it was only a month at most, that I could hardly turn down a request like this to serve my country. He raged on. I let it go for a day. The next day, he said he supposed my mind was made up. I said it was something I felt I had to do. He hated it but wouldn't stand in my way. "Only for a month," he said.

I told Poats I was willing to go but had a few conditions. I needed unrestricted access to any Vietnamese or Americans I wanted to talk to, the complete cooperation of the Saigon AID mission, and the dispatch of Bert Fraleigh from Taiwan to join me in the assignment. From my Laos exposure I knew Bert had an essential knowledge of AID and its programs in the field, which I did not. He also had a "can-do" attitude, without a bureaucratic mindset. Bert, I soon found, had a reputation as a nonconformist in AID headquarters, but Poats went along without hesitation.

In Laos I had learned about Bert's Taiwan experience in rural development and public works, helping to resettle Chiang Kai-shek's unschooled veterans. In contrast with most of the AID personnel I had known there, he was direct, full of enthusiasm, down to earth, and obviously knew how to work with Asians. Educated as a civil engineer, he had served in the navy in World War II and subsequently worked for the United Nations Relief and Rehabilitation Agency (UNRAA) in Shanghai. There he switched to the American Economic Cooperation Administration (ECA) mission, where he evacuated thirty-two shiploads of economic aid supplies to Taiwan in a period of six weeks before the city fell to the communists, for which he received ECA's highest award. He remained in China to run a private firm after the communists took over in May 1948. Under house arrest for over a year and harshly interrogated, he was finally allowed to leave in 1950, one of the last Americans to get out. In 1952, he joined the economic aid mission on Taiwan. Bert was honored in 1957 as one of ten outstanding young (under forty) men in federal service. He was just the partner I needed.

I didn't know in advance what I would recommend, but I advised Poats it would probably cut across traditional bureaucratic lines. He didn't object. The paperwork, including my security clearance, got done in record time. By the third week in June I was on a flight to Saigon to meet Fraleigh, survey the state of counterinsurgency, and develop a program.

BACK IN VIETNAM

Three years had passed since I last visited Saigon, from Laos. Its streets were still more familiar to me than those of Washington. Not much on the surface had changed, although the Vietnamese appeared more prosperous. There were more cars, motorcycles, and scooters. The tree-lined boulevards were much the same, and the cyclos and the cyclo drivers still fixtures. There were more Americans in uniform, as the military advisory buildup was well under way. The late afternoon thunderclouds and the evening downpours of the rainy season were just beginning. Bert Fraleigh and I lodged together in a small, two-bedroom apartment furnished with cots, window air conditioners, a mini-kitchen, and a bathroom with a hand-held shower.

Our first meeting was with Bill Fippen, the deputy director of the AID mission (USOM/ Saigon). He was in temporary charge, awaiting the assignment of a new director. Fippen had been one of the American commissioners of the Joint Commission for Rural Reconstruction on Taiwan, where he and Bert had known each other. The mission was completely open to us. There was none of the dog-in-the-manger attitude at the top we had encountered in Laos. Bert investigated the mission to find out what its programs were and what the Vietnamese government was doing in economic and social development. He also tackled the daunting problem of how to ship development supplies out to the rural areas. I looked into the Vietnamese government's approach to counterinsurgency from the top down and visited the provinces, while talking to our military, the embassy, the CIA station, and USIS to see what they had under way and how USOM might fit in. An important issue was how to spend a special USAID ten-million-dollar counterpart fund in Vietnamese piasters, created specifically to support counterinsurgency.

On our first day Fippen called together all the division chiefs in USOM. He introduced us, explained our mission, and asked all to cooperate. I explained, and Bert elaborated on, how we intended to work. At the time, the mission numbered some 110 American employees, but only three Americans were permanently stationed outside of Saigon.

In Washington I had asked that Nguyen Dinh Thuan, now secretary of state for defense, be notified I was coming. As soon as I arrived there was a message from Thuan, making him the first Vietnamese I saw. It was a warm and emotional reunion. We had kept in touch over the intervening years. He kidded me about no longer being the bachelor he had known back when we had run around Paris together at the end of 1955.[2] Some of his impishness remained, although he had obviously aged. He had a heart condition, and his doctor advised him to slow down, but there was more to do than ever. I asked if this meant he was working hard, "like Paris." This made him laugh, but I could see lines of strain in his face. Despite becoming the most influential official in the government after Diem and Nhu, he was as direct and unpretentious as before. The old relationship of mutual frankness rapidly reemerged.

I explained that I needed to know what the Vietnamese were doing. He told me about the

Strategic Hamlet Program. Now the focus of the government's counterinsurgency efforts, the program sought to provide the rural population with security at the level of the smallest community, the hamlet—agglomerations of houses within traditional Vietnamese villages. In central Vietnam and some parts of the South, hamlets consisted of dwellings that were naturally and historically grouped together. In some areas of the Mekong Delta houses were strung out along canals, so the program there involved regrouping the population into hamlets that were being constructed. "Strategic hamlets" were to be surrounded by moats and barbed wire to keep the Viet Cong out, and hamlet militias were being recruited and trained to defend against incursions. Hamlets were intended to be largely self-governing; elections were being held for chiefs and councils.

The hamlet program's main theoretician and driving force was the president's brother, Ngo Dinh Nhu, who chaired the Strategic Hamlet Central Committee, an intragovernmental body supervising the program. The committee's chief of staff was a Vietnamese army colonel, Hoang Van Lac. Lac, Thuan said, was very level headed and competent. Thuan suggested I see Lac next, then President Diem and Nhu. I thought, however, that I should postpone seeing Diem and Nhu until I had a better grip on what was going on in the provinces. Thuan put a plane at my direct disposal—I needed to just let him know where I wanted to go.

Where did the struggle stand, I asked? Progress was being made, he said, but not as much as the government was claiming. There was still a lot to do. I asked about the current state of relations with the Americans. He said things had much improved on a personal basis with our new ambassador, Frederick (Fritz) Nolting. Though Nolting's commitment was trusted, there was deep concern the United States might try to neutralize Vietnam. The Kennedy policy of neutralizing Laos, based on trusting the Russians, was particularly troubling and had caused doubt about American intentions. I said, I hoped not about mine. He laughed and said not with old friends. He was as I remembered and would become a key figure in vetting ideas and getting Vietnamese approvals.

The next few days were consumed by a stream of meetings, seeing Vietnamese friends and officials, and calling on U.S. officials at the operating level. I wanted to stay away from top Americans, such as our ambassador, until I could make on-the-ground inspections and talk to different Vietnamese and to some of my old Agency friends now in Saigon—Stuart Methven, who had replaced me in Laos, and Lou Conein from the early days in Vietnam.

Methven and Conein were supporting local paramilitary groups that provided security in areas such as the High Plateau, where U.S. Special Forces, units under Methven's eye, were working with the Montagnards (indigenous tribes of Indonesian stock who lived only in the highlands and practiced slash-and-burn agriculture.) Conein was assigned as an advisor to the minister of interior, Bui Van Luong, who had been the commissioner for refugees back in 1954–55. Typically, Conein had established a good rapport with Luong despite his being a civilian *functionnaire* and not one of his Vietnamese army drinking buddies. Conein had grown to like Luong but had little patience for his long-winded speeches to local notables and villagers during inspection trips. After suffering in silence during too many visits, an exasperated Lou slipped Luong a note: "Declaration of Independence—500 words, Gettysburg Address—200 words, keep it short." Lou told me, "It didn't do a damn bit of good."

Using 1955 Saigon Military Mission files on National Security Action as a guide, and with the government's approval Lou developed a pacification pilot project for Phu Yen Province in central Vietnam, about halfway up the coast between Saigon and Hue. He persuaded the military commander of the Second Region to assign a Vietnamese army regiment permanently to Phu Yen to help the province chief defend against larger Viet Cong units while the Strategic Hamlet Program was started in the more secure areas. Its basic concept was first to secure and hold the inner areas, close to the provincial capital, by creating strategic hamlets, training hamlet militia for self-defense, and setting up hamlet chiefs and councils. This was the "yellow zone." When the yellow zone was secured, the army and Civil Guard would extend their operations farther out into the "red," or insecure zone, and new hamlets would be created. Lou called it "secure and hold." He had financed the beginning of the project with CIA funds and with some contributions from the Vietnamese government. With the exception of continuing CIA support for local Catholic militia and for Montagnard irregulars, Lou wanted USOM to take over the project. Economic and social development was urgently needed.

I saw Bill Trueheart, the second in command in our embassy and chairman of the Provincial Rehabilitation Committee. Made up of working-level representatives of all the American agencies involved in counterinsurgency at the provincial level, the committee was designed to coordinate support for the Vietnamese. Trueheart told me how badly AID's active participation was needed. USOM had nobody in the provinces. He offered any help the embassy could give. I asked about documents actually describing the Strategic Hamlet Program. There was a lot of anecdotal information from conversations with the Vietnamese, but there were no official documents in English. I found that curious. Here we were supposedly supporting a program when we didn't know much about the thinking behind it. Trueheart wanted me to see Col. Carl Schaad, the officer at MAAG in charge of supporting the hamlet program.

I found Schaad in the same old building that had earlier served as MAAG headquarters where I worked in 1956. He was the main staff officer in MAAG for support of counterinsurgency in the provinces. The chain of command was complicated because of the presence of the Military Assistance Command Vietnam (MACV), which had been placed over MAAG and made responsible for direct American support to Vietnamese army military operations by helicopters and attack aircraft. MAAG had assigned military sector advisors with small supporting staffs to all provinces to work with the province chiefs. Each province was also designated a military sector. The MAAG sector advisors were advising on local security operations, learning as they went. As the only Americans in most provinces, they were being drawn into civilian activities, such as refugee relief and hamlet development, for which they had no supporting resources.

Schaad, a U.S. Army colonel with World War II combat service, was about eight years older than I and completely unpretentious, sincere, and open. His first words were, "Boy, oh boy, am I glad to see you." We got along instantly, a friendship that was to endure long after we had left Vietnam. Schaad was dedicated. He would do whatever he could to support the Vietnamese and work together with other Americans. Our encounter was heartening.

COLONEL HOANG VAN LAC

Colonel Lac was the permanent commissioner (chief of staff) for the Interministerial Committee for Strategic Hamlets. He was taller than the average Vietnamese and had a calm, reflective, and self-effacing manner and a slightly pockmarked face. Born in North Vietnam, he was two years older than I. We had first met in Binh Dinh, where he had been a regimental commander during Operation Giai Phong in 1955. He lucidly and straightforwardly described how the insurgency had grown, how it functioned, and how he thought the hamlets could counter it.

The insurgency had started up seriously in 1958–59, beginning mainly in the centers of rebellion against the French before World War II, which became bases of Vietminh resistance during the Indochina War. Although the Vietnamese government had made inroads in many of these areas, it had failed to follow up with significant improvements in villager lives. The Vietminh, now the Viet Cong, had gone underground to resuscitate guerrilla activity. They had started with the assassination of local government officials to create a political vacuum, focusing on the good ones, precisely because they were effective, and on the incompetent, the crooked, and abusive, in order to curry local favor. Geographically, Viet Cong operations had radiated out from these base areas. The main sources of initial support were families with Viet Cong relatives; most had longtime connections to the Vietminh. That family network had been reinforced by the reinfiltration of Viet Cong cadre who had been evacuated north in 1954 and 1955. In addition to older cadre there were the youths who had been forcibly taken north in 1955, then intensely indoctrinated and sent back. Finally, there were Viet Cong families created by last-minute marriages with the evacuating troops during the same period. These extended families not only directly supported guerrillas but also served as informers, to keep the rest of the population under control. Counteracting this web of family influence was difficult. (The strength of family loyalty in Vietnamese culture, I already knew, usually surpassed that of practically all other bonds, and I was not surprised to hear that the Viet Cong used it pragmatically. It was, after all, what they had planned before and during their evacuations north in 1954 and 1955.)

When I asked Lac for more details about the Strategic Hamlet Program, he handed me a twenty-five-page mimeographed document in Vietnamese. It described the philosophy of the program and how it was supposed to function. I got a USOM translator to produce an English text in twenty-four hours and made copies for Bert, myself, and Trueheart at the embassy. Apparently, it was the first time that anybody at a senior level on the American side had seen it.

I asked about the relationship of the Strategic Hamlet Program to an early 1962 effort, Operation Sunrise. That had grown, Lac said, out of initial recommendations from the British advisor, Sir Robert Thompson, copying a tactic that had been used in the Malayan insurgency of forcibly moving villagers into new villages to deny the insurgents a source of supplies and popular support. The insurgents in Malaya had been practically all Chinese, as were the villagers supporting them, so moving them into what were essentially concentration camps did not adversely affect the Malay majority. In most of Vietnam, however, there was no such differentiation. Operation Sunrise had been started north of Saigon in the Ben Cat District in Binh Duong Province, a longtime hotbed of communist activity. Several hamlets had been created on the edge of the district by moving villagers out of the communist-controlled areas. The operation had been poorly prepared, the families had not been adequately compensated, and the government was unable to provide adequate security. As a consequence, the hamlets remained under Viet Cong influence, if not outright control.

Instead, the Strategic Hamlet Program's emphasis, Lac said, had to be on winning the support of the population and on providing security at the same time. Ideally, it should have started with the organization of hamlets in the more secure areas, where the population was basically friendly toward the government, and then worked outward gradually into the areas controlled by the Viet Cong. This was not the case in all provinces. Funds were short for such essential activities as compensation for relocation and training hamlet militia; self-defense was critical. I told Lac I wanted to see the combined Vietnamese-army/provincial-government strategic hamlet operation in Phu Yen. He agreed and suggested Vinh Binh Province in the Delta as an additional example. He also suggested I visit Quang Ngai in central Vietnam, as a bad example. Lac seemed judicious in his opinions and extremely knowledgeable. I got the instant impression, which I didn't with every Vietnamese, that his opinions were free of personal bias.

INSPECTING THE PROVINCES

Lou Conein took me to Phu Yen, in central Vietnam, in a twin-engine Piper Comanche at his disposal. Knowing how formally the Vietnamese treated outside visitors, I had asked Thuan to tell the province chief that this was not a ceremonial but a working visit. Landing at the provincial capital, Tuy Hoa, we were greeted by the province chief, Major Dong, and his MAAG advisor, Major Cronia. First came the mandatory briefing at provincial headquarters. With maps and charts (one thing the Vietnamese military had really learned from their American counterparts was how to do military briefings), Major Dong told his story. In early 1962, when he had taken over, security had been so bad that most of his security forces were confined to Tuy Hoa City. The province would have been lost in a few months if he hadn't received outside help. This crisis had sparked the joint military-civilian approach called "clear and hold." An area was initially "cleared" of active Viet Cong units and security established; then strategic hamlets were organized, the "hold" phase. Launched in the first week in May, by mid-June the operation had established about ninety strategic hamlets, spread over most of the coastal plain. Not all hamlets were complete or entirely secure. Consolidation was continuing and needed more support.

We visited Phuoc Khanh, where the hamlet militia had killed one Viet Cong and wounded others the night before. For several nights a small party of Viet Cong had tried to break through the bamboo fence around the hamlet. The militia had no firearms but had scared them off by beating gongs, shouting, and throwing rocks and homemade spears. Realizing that the Viet Cong would return, the district chief had come up with four shotguns and one hand grenade. The next night the Viet Cong had come again, this time in three parties on different sides of the hamlet. As soon as the militiamen heard them, they split into three groups and moved to the break-in points. Two groups fired their shotguns and scared the smaller parties off. The third group, confronting the largest VC party, waited until the fence was partially broken down before they fired and threw their single grenade. One VC was killed outright; bloodstains on the ground indicated two more had been wounded.

The province chief had brought six American carbines provided by Conein for the hamlet militia. I presented one to the person who had tossed the grenade. He was a little guy, less than five feet tall, obviously very proud. The success was a shot in the arm. I was seeing something I knew mattered, popular resistance. Major Cronia said visiting this hamlet several months before had required an armored car and a truckload of soldiers. We had come this time in a couple of jeeps with only a few armed guards, which were needed mainly to protect the visitor—me.

Major Dong had at first experienced difficulties with a powerful Catholic priest in the province. He had found the priest running things from behind the scenes through three incompetent district chiefs. Dong had objected directly to President Diem, who, over the priest's protests, backed Dong. The three district chiefs were relieved, and the priest received word through the Catholic hierarchy to confine himself to his religious responsibilities. It was evidence that the Diem government was capable of addressing local abuses of power and influence, but also that its ability to do so depended on action by Diem himself.

I learned from Dong about a major stumbling block to effective action at the provincial level, the government's pre-audit fiscal rules governing the use of Vietnamese government funds. To purchase local materials and supplies, province chiefs had to solicit three bids, send the bids to Saigon, and wait, usually more than a month, for approval. By the time approval came prices had often changed, the supplies were no longer available, or the same funds were more urgently needed for some other activity. Designed to control corruption, the system only encouraged it. Honest but conscientious province chiefs falsified documents to get things done, while the dishonest did the same for private gain. Funds that should have paid for hamlet construction materials, rice for relocated families, and other needs had accumulated without being spent. When Conein had contributed funds for this pilot project, a joint provincial committee had been set up at his request to approve program expenditures. The committee, consisting of the province chief, Conein, and the MAAG sector advisor approved all expenditures in writing. I could see that something similar was needed if USOM funds were to be effective in all the provinces. The pre-audit system had to be bypassed by decentralizing spending authority. Perhaps the joint sign-off procedure in Phu Yen could be used as a model.

Returning to Saigon, I discussed the joint provincial committee idea with Bert. He thought it sounded like a decentralized version of the Joint Commission for Rural Reconstruction (JCRR) in Taiwan where American economic aid had been given directly to a commission of three Chinese and two American representatives to support rural development. By simple majority vote the commission responded instantly to rural needs without having to seek funds from the top, through hidebound central government ministries. This has been key to supporting an agricultural revolution there.[3] Now we had a chance to do something similar in Vietnam.

Vinh Binh was a Delta coastal province about a hundred kilometers by road and ferry south of Saigon. It was here that the Vietminh had carried out their last combat action against the French the day before I first arrived in Saigon in August 1954. Memories of Soctrang and Camau in 1955 came to mind as we traversed the absolutely flat terrain, laced by canals. The provincial population of about three hundred thousand was almost a third Khmer (Cambodian). The province chief, Major Thao, a modest, dark-skinned officer, looked of Khmer origin. He had taken over Vinh Binh in September the year before. Starting the hamlet program before the official announcement date, he had organized an estimated 315 hamlets by the time I got there.

The first hamlet we saw was ethnic Vietnamese, formed entirely of relocated families. About forty young men were filling in ground for a new marketplace. In the second hamlet, to which houses had been added, about twenty Vietnamese youth were constructing hamlet defenses. Major Thao approached them in a low-key, smiling, informal way. They smiled in turn, responding without hesitation. There was no sullenness in their eyes.

Next we saw a Khmer hamlet. The hamlet militia had been alerted and was lined up for inspection, showing pride and spirit. They mustered their weapons, five old French rifles and a large assortment of machetes. All were clean. The hamlet chief said the militia had recently defeated a Viet Cong attack, killing two. This was confirmed by the sector advisor, Major Rawn. When Major Thao took over the province, he had found about two hundred Khmer in jail as suspected Viet Cong. He freed them, called them together, and said he was sure they didn't support the Viet Cong. He asked for their help in defending their own hamlets against the Viet Cong. This and other actions such as distributing badly needed school supplies to their Buddhist priests had won them over. The initial success of a few Khmer hamlets, he said, helped convince other communities, Vietnamese as well as Khmer, to join the program.

Lunch was at the province chief's house, a two-story white-walled, red-roofed bungalow typical of the Delta provinces built for the French during the colonial period. The lunch of prawns served cold with aioli sauce, with mocha cake, hadn't changed since 1954, prompting in me a wave of nostalgia. During lunch, Major Rawn said that what I had seen was typical. When he first arrived almost six months before, he and the province chief had needed two Civil Guard companies as escorts. Now, he visited most hamlets with no escort at all.

From Rawn I learned that MAAG sector advisor assignments were limited to one year. Rotation was mandatory, with no extension possible, even if requested. Because Thao was so amenable and communicative, Rawn had quickly established a good relationship. Other sector advisors he had talked to had needed six to eight months to get to know the province chief and the province. By that time they were about to leave. Although sector advisors were probably the most useful military advisors in Vietnam, this assignment received no special attention on one's service record and did not contribute to chances of promotion.[4] Nor could our military personnel assignment system be changed—one of many anomalies in the American military setup in Vietnam.

HOW THE VIET CONG WORKED

Major Thao provided invaluable insight into how the Viet Cong (VC) operated. Relying on relatives in their base areas, the VC used a several-step process to spread their influence to neutral hamlets. Initially they would send in agitators to exploit grievances against the government. One was the land situation. While land reform had been carried out to some extent, there were still absentee landlords collecting rent. The VC assured the inhabitants that "as rightful owners of the land" they would no longer have to pay rent. Also, playing to nationalist sentiment, they claimed the "invading" Americans had taken over from the French and were running the government; Vietnamese officials were just puppets. They offered to protect the hamlet youth from being drafted for military service. Initially, the VC collected no taxes, which changed when a hamlet was under their control. Next, threats were made against local officials, scaring them off if possible or, if that didn't work, killing them. This created a political vacuum; the next step was recruitment of a Viet Cong cell. Once established the cell would inform on anyone cooperating with the government. The price of such cooperation was sometimes assassination, not just of the individual but of his entire family.

These tactics were ruthless, a combination of attraction and fear, the carrot and the club. While most villagers wanted to be left alone by both sides, they did want more economic prosperity and better lives for their children. The only way to combat the VC successfully was to provide security, redress grievances, and convince the villagers by deeds that the government was genuinely interested in their welfare, would help them prosper, and could offer a better future.[5]

Major Thao needed arms and ammunition for the hamlet militia, barbed wire for defenses, radio communications and pyrotechnics for signaling, construction equipment and money to build roads and bridges into Viet Cong-controlled areas, medical kits for the hamlets, and funds for economic development. He had spent every last cent of his allocated funds, sometimes not following the pre-audit rules. (After I reported his needs back to Thuan, Interior Minister Luong and Counselor Nhu, Diem's brother, visited Vinh Binh to provide additional support for Major Thao.)

To see what Lac had cited as a bad example, I went back to central Vietnam, to Quang Ngai, where I had been in 1955. The province chief was a civilian *functionnaire* who claimed to have formed about two hundred hamlets. The hamlet defenses looked good but on close inspection proved to be poorly planned. The hamlet militia lacked weapons and training. Elements of two regular Viet Cong regiments in the province were opposed by seven army battalions and sixteen Civil Guard companies. The Civil Guard was mainly tied down in static duty guarding the railroad and roads, while for its part the army was not patrolling at night. Viet Cong incidents in this province alone accounted for about 90 percent of the total in the entire corps area from Quang Ngai up to the border with North Vietnam. Of Quang Ngai's estimated hundred thousand families, about twenty thousand were believed to have Viet Cong relatives. The Viet Cong had intimidated many hamlets, tearing down fences and distributing propaganda at night, clearly indicating who was in control.

The province's grim reality was pictured when a Vietnamese officer visiting a hamlet asked an old man how he liked it. He didn't like it all, he said. Was it because he favored the Viet Cong? No, he was against the Viet Cong. He was not bothered by working on the hamlet fortifications, either. What really bothered him was he was now in more danger than ever from the Viet Cong. Before the defenses had been put up he could flee the hamlet when the Viet Cong came at night. Now the Viet Cong controlled all the hamlet gates. What about secret exits?, the officer asked. The old man said sadly that the Viet Cong controlled those too.

The population's misery was further aggravated by extreme poverty, self-evident in the run-down huts and patched clothes. There were too many people for too little land in the narrow coastal strip to make a living out of just growing rice. The previous year the rice harvest had been largely decimated by rats. Since then, with American aid, rat poison had been used to kill over two million vermin; maybe the next harvest, about to be planted, would be good, but something new was needed. The province chief begged for help, "anything the Americans could give, food, money, anything"; he seemed bewildered by the challenge. Drastic agricultural improvements were needed, but security had to be established first. A clear-and-hold operation similar to Phu Yen was being planned according to General Don, the I Corps commander.

I finished my inspections by visiting Tay Ninh, heartland of the Cao Dai religion and Tuyen Duc, a mountain province with Montagnard refugees. As we approached Tay Ninh City, Nui Ba Den (Black Lady Mountain) rose dramatically in the background, an isolated cone some three thousand feet above the flat plain. The mountain had been Trinh Minh Thé's guerrilla stronghold in 1954 and 1955 but was now largely controlled by the VC. How had that happened?

The new province chief, Major Nhuan, was Cao Dai. He told me the province had suffered under past officials who were not Cao Dai. Nhuan had, with President Diem's support, replaced all the district and village chiefs with capable Cao Dai. This approach was winning back some support, but there was still a lot of resentment to overcome. So far only twenty-four strategic hamlets had been completed. The Viet Cong, infiltrating down through Laos and Cambodia and supported by some Cao Dai dissidents, had established a strong base in the northern part of the province, known as "Zone D," where it joined Cambodia. That area, along with adjacent territory on the Cambodian side, was already functioning as an important Viet Cong headquarters.[6]

A side effect of the hamlet program in Tay Ninh was the exposure of dishonest local officials. Residents of the newly established hamlets had complained about such illegal activities as a manioc monopoly. The accused had tried to appeal to the palace, but President Diem had backed Major Nhuan. If the government allowed more Cao Dai self-rule and rearmed some of General The's old veterans, Nhuan thought, the Viet Cong could be defeated, at least in the populated part of the province. While leaving, I went by the Cao Dai temple and looked again at its interior, ornate with representations of its pantheon of saints, not only Buddha but Jesus Christ, Lao Tse, Confucius, Sun Yat-sen, and Victor Hugo, as well as Trang Trinh, the movement's founder. I also paid a sentimental visit to the tomb of Trinh Minh Thé and thought about the influence he might have wielded had he lived.

I flew to the mountain province of Tuyen Duc, whose capital, Dalat, had been originally established by the French as a dry-season escape from the Saigon heat. The Dalat area was the principal source of fresh produce sold in the Saigon market. Before the insurgency, the province had contained only a few Montagnards. Now there were a least ten thousand Montagnard refugees, mainly from the more remote mountain areas of adjacent highland provinces. Some had fled from the VC bringing household belongings, food, and even livestock, others with almost nothing. At several Montagnard encampments I saw women and children subsisting on a few roots and vegetables.[7]

To meet the crisis a relief program had been worked out, with President Diem's approval, to distribute rice. The province chief, Major Bich, showed me a warehouse full of rice. The interior minister had told him not to distribute any until he got the order, and no order had been issued. He had used up all the resources at his command as well as supplies from relief organizations such as CARE. Could I help get the rice released?

Back in Saigon I saw Thuan right away. The Strategic Hamlet Program seemed on the right track, but there were inconsistencies in how it was being carried out. Security support from the army was uneven. More funding was needed, but it had to be decentralized to be effective. The pre-audit requirement was crippling the program. I described how the joint provincial committee worked in Phu Yen. Thuan understood the problem and said he supported that approach but that final approval depended on President Diem. I also told him about the rice distribution holdup. He promised to arrange a meeting with the president very soon. I should take up with him directly what I had learned.

PRESIDENT DIEM

Shortly thereafter I got a call to come to the palace from Vo Van Hai, the president's personal secretary. Hai greeted me warmly and said the president would be very happy to see me. Did I bring any news from General Lansdale? Was there any possibility that he might come out to help?

President Diem was much the same as I had last seen him in 1957, except there were more lines in his face and more streaks of gray in his hair. He was short and stocky, with a large head and a bland and impassive face; his eyes exuded nervous energy while, chain-smoking cigarette after cigarette, he spoke rapidly in French.

He greeted me with a warm, very friendly smile, almost—I sensed—as if I were a lost son. I felt some initial apprehension, knowing how badly relations had deteriorated under our previous ambassador. He instantly remembered not only our last meeting in 1957, when I came down to get help for Lao civic action, but also seeing me in Qui Nhon in 1955. He was not nearly as distant and reserved as others had described. When I gave him a brief personal note from Lansdale his face lit up. Did I know if Lansdale had any plans for coming out? Could I suggest this to Ambassador Nolting? I said I would try.

I was there, I said, to study reorganizing our economic aid mission and its programs to support counterinsurgency and had seen, as he knew, the Strategic Hamlet Program in operation in five provinces. He asked for my observations. I summarized what I had seen: it seemed to be working well in some provinces, particularly Phu Yen and Vinh Binh, and not so well in others, such as Quang Ngai and Tay Ninh. He asked if I thought the province chief in Quang Ngai was capable. I regretted to tell him I didn't think the man could handle the job. He nodded as if that confirmed his own impressions.

I had thought a lot, I said, about how we could most effectively use the special piaster fund, ten million dollars' worth, set aside for counterinsurgency. The government's pre-audit financial rules for expenditures by the province chiefs was crippling timely support for the hamlet program. I would like to use the special fund in direct support of the hamlet program by extending the joint provincial committee concept from Phu Yen to all provinces. Agreements would be drawn up with the provinces, following guidelines approved in Saigon by Counselor Nhu's Interminsterial Committee. After that, it would be up to the provincial joint committees to authorize actual expenditures. We would put USOM provincial representatives in each of the provinces to participate. Diem considered for a moment and then nodded his head. I took it for approval. I also managed to sandwich in Bert's request that Bui Van Loc be authorized to handle getting supplies out to the provinces. He agreed.

I suggested that more use be made of Trinh Minh Thé's veterans in Tay Ninh. Diem launched into a long monologue about how relations with the Cao Dai had evolved, at the end of which he agreed that Thé's veterans needed to used. I said I had been to Tuyen Duc to see the Montagnard refugees; he replied that he had recently approved distributing rice and other relief supplies to the refugees and then talked about the Montagnards, beginning with his experience going back to the days when they had hid him from the Vietminh. About an hour was consumed as he described the twenty-six Montagnard tribes and their locations, which he pointed out on a wall map. When he paused toward the end, I broke in to tell him the rice was not being distributed. His eyes widened with surprise and asked me to repeat what I had said. When I did, he called in Vo Van Hai and immediately dictated telegrams to be sent to all the highland province chiefs telling them to begin distribution immediately. Then he telephoned Major Bich directly and told him emphatically to start distribution right away. (Vo Van Hai told me later that Diem had roundly chewed out the interior minister, Bui Van Luong, for the holdup.)

Diem gave me his thinking about the Strategic Hamlet Program. Its importance went beyond hamlet self-defense. The hamlets were "a means to institute basic democracy in Vietnam. The government intends to give back to each hamlets the right of self-government with its own charter and system of community law." The concept would "realize the ideals of the constitution on a local scale which the people can understand. The strategic hamlet is a state of mind." Later we would use that phrase publicly to characterize the program. I took it to mean that the real battle was for the hearts and minds of the population. (At the time "hearts and minds" was not the trite expression it would later become.) Diem then detailed the security situation in each of the thirty plus provinces. His grasp of detail was amazing.

At the very end, he paused for a moment, looked directly at me, and said, "I hope you will return to help us." I was taken aback. I had been too busy to give it much thought, although the question was certainly in the back of my mind. I said I had to talk to my wife and to my father, both of whom depended on me. I couldn't make any promises; I would do my best. He said, "We need you." All I could say was that I understood.

The meeting consumed about four hours. Remembering our 1957 meeting, I had gone lightly on the traditionally served tea, to avoid a bathroom crisis. Left behind was an ashtray full of cigarette butts, evidence of his chain-smoking through several packs. In later meetings with him after my return as an AID employee, he would display the same impressive intellect and encyclopedic knowledge of every province and of practically every province chief and his family. If I said I had met a particular province chief, he would say something like, "Oh yes, his grandfather was so and so, his father was so and so. His family of good character originally came from Hue [or wherever] but moved to Mytho in 1930," and so on.

Diem's monologues were undoubtedly mind-numbing for many American officials. For some of the unprepared, drinking too much tea added to their agony. He thought, rightly in many cases, that most Americans didn't know much about Vietnam and had even less understanding. I was younger, more patient, and knew something about his country and his personality, so I let him go on until he got through whatever was on his mind while I waited for an opening to bring up what I wanted. He listened to my views with attention and responded to my suggestions. I framed my observations and suggestions in ways that presented a course of action that made sense in Vietnamese terms. I usually talked out my ideas ahead of time with Thuan, and sometimes Vo Van Hai, to see how best to present them. As always, I was careful never to ascribe implied criticism of government actions to any of my Vietnamese contacts, but to my own observations.

I left that meeting feeling that some of the old trust earned by Lansdale may have been passed on. My observations had been taken at face value. I was concerned, however, by the over-concentration of authority in his government at the center and by the gaps in effective communication between top and bottom. Why had the province chiefs needed further confirmation before distributing rice to the Montagnards, who were so clearly in dire need? I decided to give Nolting a verbal report on this meeting but not write it up—I didn't know how Nolting would react to the request for Lansdale. (Later, when I became fully official, I would carefully document all my meetings with Diem, except the last in late October 1963.)

On my way out, Vo Van Hai took me aside asking if "the boss" had said anything about Lansdale. I told him Diem wanted me to ask Ambassador Nolting to bring Lansdale out to help. I would do my best not only to pass on Diem's request but to explain how Lansdale could be helpful. The president, Hai said, urgently needed to widen his circle of advisors, and only Lansdale could help him with that. The president needed balanced advice. Nhu had isolated the president and cut off his contact with too many Vietnamese whose support was needed. Hai said Nolting had good relations with the president but didn't understand the Vietnamese political situation well enough to be helpful with Diem's more sensitive problems. Also, Nolting's relationship with the president was necessarily too formal to talk about personally sensitive matters, such as the president's family.

I checked in with some of my old friends, General Le Van Kim and Bui Diem, who were on the outs with Diem and his brother Nhu, in particular. They confirmed Hai's views about Diem's isolation. Kim was extremely unhappy at being sidelined. He was highly critical of the way the war was being fought, without a sustained focus on population security and of the fact that some of the best officers in the army were not being used; also, he was convinced that the hamlet program was not working in the Delta, despite what I may have seen in Vinh Binh. Don't be fooled, he said. While Bui Diem was more philosophical by nature, he criticized the exclusion of other national political leaders from political participation, which boosted the National Liberation Front. Particularly harmful was the influence over Diem of Ngo Dinh

Nhu and his wife, Madame Nhu. I also asked Secretary Thuan informally if he thought Diem had become too isolated from many of his former supporters. He grimaced slightly, giving me a clue to his meaning without putting it into words.

COUNSELOR NGO DINH NHU

Thuan set up my appointment with Ngo Dinh Nhu, the president's younger brother. I had never before met him. Although there was a resemblance in his facial features and oversized head to Diem, his frame was slight. He appeared more philosophical and less intense, smoking a pipe instead of cigarettes. While Diem's more inscrutable stolidity obscured a warmer personality underneath, Nhu seemed something of a cold fish. After initial greetings, which were quite cordial, I told him I wanted to learn about the Strategic Hamlet Program. He had thought it a "pipe dream," he said, until the past four months. He made constant trips to the provinces without ceremony, spending hours in meetings with hamlet teams and chiefs, as well as with village, district, and province chiefs. The experience had been tiring but exhilarating, because he had been able to test out his theories through actual experience.

Strategic hamlets, he now thought, were the means to defeat both the communists and underdevelopment. "In time of war," he said, "people think you must suppress democracy to win. To the contrary we shall use the war against communism . . . to introduce democracy and we shall use democracy to win the war. This is the strategic concept." Free elections of the hamlet chief and hamlet council by secret ballot were key. When I asked him if he thought the government should offer a surrender program to the Viet Cong, he agreed. He also thought there should be local commando teams, operating like guerrillas against the Viet Cong. He was impressed by what he had recently seen of the Montagnard teams trained by our Special Forces.

Nhu seemed more rational and down to earth than I expected. I had been leery, based on what I knew indirectly about his suspicious nature and predilection for political distrust (his reaction against the 1956 movie *Fire and Shadow* being a case in point), but he showed none of that. I was more circumspect in my comments with Nhu than with the president. I did not bring up the joint provincial committee idea; Thuan had indicated it was the president who would make that decision. While Nhu seemed the driving force ideologically behind the program, its administration seemed more Diem's concern, particularly involving American aid. In general, I felt surer about dealing with the president than I did his brother, whom I did not really know. I was aware the CIA station took a proprietary view of its relationship with Nhu, so I wrote up the meeting, making sure the CIA chief of station, John Richardson, received a copy.[8]

By the time of the meeting with Nhu, Bert Fraleigh and I had fleshed out our ideas for what we initially called the "Office of Rural Affairs and Counterinsurgency," to be headed by an assistant director of USOM, with provincial representatives in the field. From my inspections and talks with Colonel Lac, I had pretty clearly in mind the specific activities to be financed by the special piaster fund. Bert had wide-ranging ideas for provincial economic development and had already worked out, with Loc's help, how we would get supplies out to the provinces. We talked over our ideas with Fippen, who was enthusiastic. I had squeezed in a meeting with Thuan at his house to get confirmation that the joint provincial committee idea was acceptable to Diem. When I related my discussion with Diem and his reaction, Thuan said it sounded like a yes to him. He said, however, "Don't put it to the president formally in writing, just go ahead and do it." I was now ready to talk to our ambassador, Fritz Nolting.

AMBASSADOR NOLTING

Nolting was a former professor and career diplomat whose prior experience had been exclusively in Europe. This assignment was his first in Asia. There had been another candidate for the ambassadorship, Kenneth Young, who had wound up going to Bangkok instead. This was unfortunate. Young knew Vietnam, understood Diem's political vulnerabilities, and was among the very few in the State Department who liked and admired Lansdale, appreciated his capabilities, and would have been comfortable having him in Vietnam.

Tall, handsome, and courtly, Nolting had a courteous manner that reflected his Virginia upbringing. Since I was from Virginia too, we had something in common. He was willing to listen and was encouraged by what I reported from my visits and by our ideas about setting up a special office in USOM and stationing representatives in the provinces. He was particularly interested in my observations about Diem and Nhu. His questions made it clear that his primary concern was his good relationship with Diem and keeping the situation in South Vietnam on an even keel. There was an appealing, elemental decency and openness about the man. He expressed some doubt, however, about our proposal to set up joint committees in all the provinces; that it might have Diem's approval surprised him. I reassured him by explaining I had checked back with Thuan, who had urged me to ahead and set the program up that way.

I didn't know quite how to relay Diem's request for Lansdale. It was typical of the Vietnamese to use go-betweens for sensitive requests—if they got turned down, there was no direct loss of face. I told Nolting I supposed Diem had relayed his request through me because he saw me as "an old friend" from the early days. I suggested that Lansdale's special rapport with Diem might offer him an informal channel to give Diem advice he might otherwise not accept. He was noncommittal but not upset. (Years later, Nolting would recall that Diem had admired Lansdale, that "on occasion he [Diem] would say, 'I wish I could have a conversation with Colonel Lansdale on this subject,' on one subject or another."[9] That was Diem's way of asking for Lansdale without offending Nolting, but I never knew if Nolting caught on.)

Nolting's lack of jealousy or reserve at my having seen Diem and Nhu was encouraging. He asked me to consider coming back to run the program—if I came back, I could count on his full support. I gave him the same answer I had given Diem. I left the embassy gratified at Nolting's support but concerned he seemed to think everything could be handled adequately from the top down through the friendly but formal relationship he had developed with president Diem. I wondered whether the time would come when we needed to influence Diem to do something he, and particularly Nhu, might not like.

I had one last opportunity to see Diem and talk to Thuan on an inspection trip to Kien Phong Province, west of Saigon in the Plain of Reeds area, a Vietminh redoubt during the war against the French. Diem had resettled refugees from the North and some poorer farmers from the center there by draining part of the swamp and constructing land development centers. Now there were about sixty thousand people in these centers. I was interested in how the president interacted with the villagers. At each center, congregations awaited our arrival, arranged in the traditional array of notables, younger men, women, and children. Ceremonies were held and local speeches were read, in the traditional formal style.

The president spoke extemporaneously. On leaving each congregation, Diem stopped to ask questions at random about local conditions and problems. With Thuan interpreting, I could follow most of what was said. After one exchange, which was very much man to man, with a young fisherman asking for credit to finance fishing boats, the president turned to the official party and said wryly, "The newspapers call me paternalistic, but you can see how the people answer me." The fisherman had shown little meekness or hesitancy. The president, however, lacked any flair for dramatizing his concern about the population's welfare. This did not come naturally to most Vietnamese, given their cultural penchant for public formality. At the end of the trip, Thuan took me aside and asked, "You will come back, won't you?" I repeated what I said to President Diem and Nolting.

FINAL RECOMMENDATIONS

Because Bert Fraleigh and I were confident that our recommendations would be accepted, we began setting up the proposed new organization within USOM, deciding the basic activities to be supported from the ten-million-dollar piaster fund, spelling out how it was to be staffed and run and even preparing a fiscal year 1963 budget. Bert had developed an incredible range of ways to use existing but underutilized development resources and programs, as well as thinking up new ones. Fippen approved our proposed USOM reorganization, creating the semi-autonomous position of "assistant director for counterinsurgency and rural affairs," with area and provincial representatives, a deputy, a small headquarters administrative and support staff, and a logistics office. (Later the counterinsurgency part of the title would be dropped, to make it more palatable with the general image of AID.)

All Rural Affairs personnel had to be volunteers, and provincial representatives were to live simply, and on the local economy. Specialized technicians would be pulled in as support from the traditional technical divisions. "Much," we said, "would depend on the dedication, tact, imagination and common sense of the provincial representatives. They must make the image of American efficiency and quick response a reality. The counterinsurgency organization must be staffed by personnel who are primarily doers—people with enthusiasm, energy, imagination and initiative. This calls for an organization . . . capable of running . . . around the clock . . . and for personnel who are both willing and able to stand the pace."[10] The bar was set high. A traditional economic aid organization, it was not.

As our stay drew to a close, my operational bias toward getting our counterinsurgency proposals approved and into operation boxed in my future. The requests for me to return and run it were hard to turn down; renewing my dedication to the Vietnamese cause had a deep appeal. I felt Bert and I could make a difference. He was willing to come back as my deputy. I had faith that he could implement the expansive development programs he had visualized. What we were proposing was a significant part of what was missing in an across-the-board counterinsurgency approach. It seemed possible that something with a democratic ethos based on self-defense, self-help, and self-government could be built from the hamlet level up, if President Diem meant what he said. As a step on the path to self-governance and a precondition for self-help project assistance, the proposed elections for hamlet chief and council would have to be held. We would insert our provincial representatives into the bloodstream of the Vietnamese government, as catalysts to help make things work. As nonpartisan participants we could help channel Vietnamese efforts in constructive ways, working with them not as superiors but as equals and partners.

I could not see myself playing Lansdale, but maybe a way would open to get Lansdale back, to help Diem widen his base of political support and change the regime's overly authoritarian nature before anything could go too wrong. Meanwhile, if I came back I would operate with the Vietnamese in the Lansdale manner, informally and as a committed friend. I had no illusions, however, that we could win this struggle for the South Vietnamese; only they could.

Our conventional military approach concerned me. With the exception of Phu Yen, Vietnamese army units were not assigned to protect the hamlet population and were bound too much to roads and daylight, and to killing VC, to be effective. Much of the earlier spirit of civic action had been lost when the army had been organized into regular divisions with little positive contact with the civilian population. Troops were confusing the ordinary population with the VC in some areas, and indiscriminate firepower as well as bad troop behavior were helping recruit VC. A military civic action program had been approved but not implemented; army division commanders were now vested with responsibility for supporting the strategic hamlets, but it was not clear how that would work. My report on the trip mentioned this only in passing, as it was obviously controversial. I thought this situation could be corrected by making population security the main objective of most of the army. Phu Yen seemed a good model of how to do that.

By selling the Rural Affairs program, I became bound up with it. Despite my reservations about the military side and despite the Diem government's shortcomings, this was the good fight for the sake of the Vietnamese people, one I could not miss. I wondered, of course, how Barbara would react, but she had supported my going out in the first place. Confronting my father was going to be vastly more difficult. I did not look forward to it.

I wrote my final report back in Washington.[11] It summarized what I had learned, described whom I had talked to, including Diem and Nhu, and detailed how the USOM Office of Rural Affairs and Counterinsurgency would work, what programs should be supported, and how volunteers to work in the provinces were needed. Political and military concerns, which would have made the document controversial, were omitted. It was a "can do" document of how the Strategic Hamlet Program, if properly supported and implemented, could overcome the insurgency. In retrospect it was too optimistic, but I believed firmly at the time that the South Vietnamese could defeat the insurgency with the right effort and the right American support.

MEETING SECRETARY MCNAMARA

On the way home, I hitched a ride on a special plane from Saigon that took Ambassador Nolting, the MACV commander (General Harkins), and other key local Americans to a meeting at CINCPAC with Secretary of Defense McNamara on July 23. This was my first exposure to McNamara. I had heard he was a numbers man, that he had come to dominate the uniformed military by his ability to pose questions based on facts and figures faster than they could respond. There would be an opportunity, I was told, to brief him on our program.

The McNamara briefing started early in the morning and focused exclusively on the status of the Military Aid Program (MAP). Pentagon briefers presented slide after slide giving the status of practically every last bullet in the supply pipeline. McNamara asked detailed questions, displaying an encyclopedic command of the facts. When he got near the end, he said, "Stop—slide 319 does not agree with slide 5." So they put slide 5 back up, and sure enough, the two didn't agree.[12] It was an impressive performance, an exhibition of incredible capacity to absorb and remember facts and figures. Practically all the available briefing time had been consumed, however, by this demonstration of the secretary's brilliance; he could have gotten the same information in Washington. These secretary of defense conferences in Honolulu became known derisively as "McNamara's Band Concerts."

After general presentations by Harkins and Nolting, the Strategic Hamlet Program was discussed. Following Nolting, I pointed out that hamlets that demonstrated a will to resist the Viet Cong became targets and that not all were equipped with adequate arms. McNamara wanted to know what arms they had; I said only old French rifles and some shotguns and grenades. McNamara responded that we shouldn't let a shortage of arms keep us from properly arming the villagers—we should requisition carbines, if that would do the job. I said hamlet elections were important. He seemed puzzled about how hamlet elections related to security; I replied that they gave the population a political stake in the future. I wasn't sure he understood the idea. I would not meet him again until we had a head-on confrontation at the White House in September 1963.

DECIDING TO RETURN

When I told Barbara I wanted to go back for at least for a year to get the program started and reevaluate from there, she didn't hesitate to give me her complete support. Never mind, she said, that we would be taking our two very small children to Saigon, a place so distant that in her native Chile people speaking of going to the ends of the earth called it "Cochin China."

Before I told my father, I wanted to be sure that AID Washington was actually going to approve the program. I was pulled out of the office constantly for meetings at AID, then the State Department, and finally with Mike Forrestal, the National Security Council assistant covering Vietnam at the White House. He was blunt. He said President Kennedy knew about the program I was proposing, supported it, and personally wanted me to go back to run it. Pressure had been building from AID to make a firm commitment. This stunned me. I took a deep breath, knowing how difficult it would be with my father, and said yes.

My father stared at me without a word as I explained that I had been personally asked by the White House to take the job. I would commit for only a year. He suddenly looked ill, said he didn't want to talk about it, and left the office. We didn't discuss it again. Not until several years later would Barbara tell me that the next day, when she was alone at home with our children, my mother had come to persuade her to talk me out of going. If I went, did Barbara and the children intend to go with me? Yes, of course, was Barbara's answer. My mother said my father would disinherit us if we went. Barbara replied simply, "I will go where my husband goes." My mother left, distraught. My father was a man who honored loyalty and courage; he probably, if perversely, admired Barbara for that.

I went downtown to see Janow and Poats to confirm my acceptance. They immediately made an office available and introduced me to Walter "Stoney" Stoneman, the person who would head AID's Washington support office for Vietnam. Stoney, a taciturn veteran of the economic aid program, was eager to help. He was originally from Oklahoma, spoke with a drawl, favored wide-brimmed western hats, and was deceptively mild mannered. I would find out how solid he was as time went by. He was supportive and helpful from the start.

Stoney told me that AID was prepared to offer me the rank of Foreign Reserve Officer (FSR) 2, the second-highest field rank in AID. I wasn't much interested in rank, as I thought my effectiveness would mainly depend on my influence with the Vietnamese, but I called Bert Fraleigh for advice—he knew how things worked in AID. Bert said I should accept only the highest rank. Maybe it wouldn't make any difference to the Vietnamese, but American officials were very rank conscious. I had to hold out for the top, FSR-1. I went back to Stoney and said I had been advised by Bert that it had to be FSR-1 or nothing, and that I believed his advice was valid. After some hand-wringing that went up the AID chain of command, Stoney said he would fight for it. He did, and the battle for rank, which I found personally distasteful, was over.

EARLY RECRUITING

While waiting on the paperwork, I divided my time between the Airways Engineering office and AID. I started recruiting personnel. The main criteria were evidence of high motivation and a manifest capacity to understand and work with Asians. Experience in Vietnam or a similar country was a plus. No punches were pulled about working conditions. The provincial representative would be living on the local economy, and the work was likely to be dangerous.

I began rounding up people I knew from my earlier Saigon and Laos days. Bert started digging for interested volunteers on Taiwan. Hank Miller, my old friend from Laos, helped me contact four people who had been in Laos, three of whom I had known, although not well. Lansdale suggested George Melvin from our TRIM days in Vietnam.

I contacted Lieutenant Colonel "Bo" Bohannon from earlier Saigon days, now retired in the Philippines, to help with a surrender program. His book *Counter Guerrilla Operations,* co-authored with Colonel Napoleon Valeriano, had just been published and would, I thought, establish his bona fides with MAAG and MACV, whose tactics I wanted to influence. He could also help recruit experienced Filipino technical help as we needed it.

I badly wanted someone who could help develop a relationship with the Vietnamese Buddhists and get them involved. Contacting Catholic communities, who were readily identifiable and had, for the most part, already organized their own self-defense, was easy; I had good contact with the Cao Dai; and it would be easy to develop relations with the Hoa Hao—but we had no particular access to the Buddhists. Stoney sold me on an American Buddhist, Richard Gard, who knew the Vietnamese Buddhists, but my attempt to get him cleared was unsuccessful.[13] I later wished I had pressed harder, but at that point I didn't have the time. It would turn out to be a consequential omission.

Finally my official appointment came through, and I was sworn in. Barbara was advised by the AID medical staff not to feed our children anything off the local market in Vietnam. Fortunately, Dorothy Whipple, our pediatrician, had visited the country. She pooh-poohed that advice and recommended "lots of *nuoc mam,* which is full of calcium and iron." Barbara's mother and some friends drove us to the Baltimore-Washington Airport to see us off. My parents didn't show; it was too painful for them. When I had said goodbye to my father at the office for the last time and we turned away from each other, there had been tears in our eyes.

Chapter 9
Starting Rural Affairs

Barbara and I were met at the Saigon airport on September 25 by Bill and Margaret Trigg and Bert Fraleigh. Bill handled housing for the mission. Putting us up at their house while the final repairs were finished on ours, they could not have been more gracious. Despite the revolution we were carrying out within the mission, most of the administrative people were genuinely supportive. Arriving about a week ahead, Bert had already set up our office in the main USOM building, located around the block from a tall Buddhist pagoda called Xa Loi, later the center of the Buddhist rebellion.

We had hoped to recruit a significant number of volunteers from within USOM. After Bert arrived, Fippen had called a personnel meeting in the mission parking lot, spoken enthusiastically about Rural Affairs, and asked for volunteers. There were only four: Sid Glazer, who had acted as the secretary of the initial USOM counterinsurgency committee; Tom Luche, originally with International Volunteer Services (IVS) but now in the mission's Program Office; John Perry, from the comptroller's office; and Dick Evans, from Public Administration. Perry, at sixty-five, was our oldest volunteer, having briefly served in the infantry in World War I, then jumped into France with the OSS during World War II. He had been a field investigator for the controllers division of the Marshall Plan. After a job with a French machine tool company, he had returned to government service with USOM, in Djakarta and then in Saigon. He took charge as one of four area representatives. At first he appeared too old for the job, but joining Rural Affairs seemed to rejuvenate him. He was soft spoken and mild in manner, but there was steely determination underneath.

Tom Luche had been frustrated by the unwillingness of the USOM staff to become more involved with the Vietnamese. He saw Rural Affairs as a chance "to get close and personal with the Vietnamese and to have a more positive influence on them." It was also a concept "on the wings of the Kennedy Administration when an electric charge began flowing through the American administration, a sense that much was possible if we really got into it."[1] Tom spoke Vietnamese and wanted very much to be part of this show. He had accompanied me on the inspection trip to Quang Ngai Province in June, during my initial survey. Dick Evans wanted to help the Montagnards, which became his initial assignment, while Sid Glazer worked in our headquarters.

Soon after arriving, I was shown Joe Alsop's syndicated column in the September 24 issue of the *Washington Post.* I had not spoken to Alsop, but he had obviously seen my report. It quoted me as saying that every province in Vietnam could be like Vinh Binh if we tried hard enough and that for that reason I "had reluctantly agreed to abandon an extremely prosperous family business . . . to go out to Saigon with wife and children . . . to take charge of our Foreign Aid Mission's support for the Vietnamese in the Strategic Hamlets. . . . If Phillips'

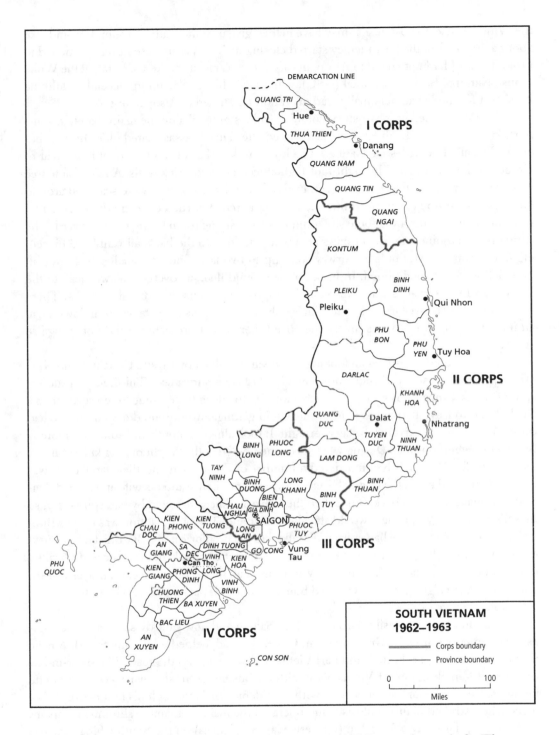

DEMARCATION LINE

QUANG TRI

Hue•

I CORPS

THUA THIEN

Danang•

QUANG NAM

QUANG TIN

QUANG NGAI

KONTUM

BINH DINH

PLEIKU

Qui Nhon•

Pleiku•

PHU BON

PHU YEN

Tuy Hoa•

DARLAC

II CORPS

KHANH HOA

QUANG DUC

Dalat•

Nhatrang•

TUYEN DUC

NINH THUAN

BINH LONG

PHUOC LONG

LAM DONG

TAY NINH

BINH DUONG

LONG KHANH

BINH THUAN

BIEN HOA

BINH TUY

HAU NGHIA

GIA DINH

Saigon

KIEN PHONG

KIEN TUONG

LONG AN

PHUOC TUY

CHAU DOC

III CORPS

AN GIANG

SA DEC

DINH TUONG

GO CONG

Vung Tau•

VINH

KIEN HOA

PHU QUOC

KIEN GIANG

PHONG DINH

•Can Tho

LONG

VINH BINH

CHUONG THIEN

BA XUYEN

BAC LIEU

AN XUYEN

IV CORPS

CON SON

**SOUTH VIETNAM
1962–1963**

———— Corps boundary
———— Province boundary

0   100
Miles

program works this war may just possibly come to an end." I reacted negatively. The story exaggerated my role and could look like horn-blowing at Vietnamese expense. I had intended to return to Saigon quietly and go to work unobtrusively, letting the Vietnamese take the credit for any successes.

Bert Fraleigh saw it differently. He was delighted: I had a line to the top—now the bureaucracy wouldn't dare fool with the program. Alsop was known to have close connections with the White House. On balance, it may have helped give us some running room. It would take about a year before the bureaucracy started closing in. The Vietnamese never mentioned it. I told Thuan I had not talked to Alsop, in case it ever came up. Mike Forrestal, of the White House National Security Council (NSC), when I saw him in Saigon in December, told me President Kennedy had personally read my report and talked to Alsop about it.

USOM assigned us a two-story, colonial, white stucco villa on the main road to the airport; known as "Ngo Dinh Khoi" street, named after Diem's assassinated older brother but originally called "Charles De Gaulle." The house was set back from the street in the rear of a spacious lot surrounded by eight-foot-high stucco-covered brick walls. A large flame tree was near the wall fronting on the street. Fruit trees and small bushes were scattered around the edges of an open lawn in front. There was an arched portico over the driveway, and a side entrance led from a vestibule straight into a large sitting room facing the front yard. The sitting room adjoined an open dining area with windows to the back, all ventilated by ceiling fans. From the vestibule a stairway went up to two large and one smaller bedroom, all of which were air conditioned. In back on the ground floor, a covered walkway lead to the kitchen and the servant's quarters, a single story-set of rooms including two baths. There was an old, unused well in back. The villa's only drawback was its distance from downtown, an inconvenience for servants unless they lived there and a problem we did not recognize at first.

Barbara settled in and began looking for servants, helped by Elyette Conein, Lou's wife. We acquired a houseboy, Dung; a housemaid, Thi Hai; a nursemaid, Thi Ba; and a succession of cooks. Since I was gone from early morning to late in the evening, often seven days a week, I had to leave Barbara to fend for herself in getting our household organized. We had difficulty getting the servants to stay overnight. It took almost a month and some questioning by Elyette to find out why. During what was remembered as the "night of long knives" in the late 1940s, the Vietminh had murdered a number of Frenchmen and their families. It was believed they had killed the original French owner of our house and his wife and stuffed their bodies down the well in back. Since then the house had been haunted by bad spirits (pi), so no self-respecting Vietnamese would stay there the night. The only solution was to get a Buddhist priest to exorcise the bad spirits. We talked to the head priest of a Buddhist temple next door, who was willing to perform the ceremony. Without being asked, I volunteered a healthy contribution to the temple. The next day, in front of all the servants, incense, prayer wheels, and chants from a group of yellow-robed bonzes sent the pi packing, after which the servants were able to move in.

I was amazed how easily Barbara took to Saigon and how quickly she made Vietnamese and American friends. Growing up in Chile, she said, helped a lot. One friend, Amelie Cecillon, who was part French and part Vietnamese, lived across the road. The sister-in-law of Nguyen Van Buu, one of Vietnam's wealthiest businessmen, she managed his cigarette factories. Buu had a family connection with President Diem's through his first marriage to a niece who had died of tuberculosis.[2] Buu operated the main Vietnamese shipping company, had a shrimp farm near Vung Tau (formerly Cap St. Jacques) on the South China Sea, and deployed two private armies—one in the cinnamon area of central Vietnam and one along the road to Vung Tau from Bien Hoa, north of Saigon. Reportedly, he had been (and was possibly still) the source for some of the financing for Nhu's secret party, the Can Lao. We met Amelie and then Buu through Bernie Yoh. Bernie, originally from Shanghai, was an American citizen and a dedicated Catholic. So far as I could figure out, he was on a wide-ranging mission against communism for the church. Bernie had looked me up with a note from Lansdale. He would become another contact and long-term friend.[3]

CRANKING UP RURAL AFFAIRS

Bert and I developed a draft "Provincial Rehabilitation Agreement" to be negotiated with every province chief to cover USOM support for the Strategic Hamlet Program. Each agreement was to be approved in draft by Colonel Lac's office and by the U.S. Provincial Rehabilitation Committee, then executed by the province chief and me. The form of the agreement and the items to be covered by its budget had to be discussed with Lac, and Lac had to show it to Nhu. The agreements were to cover an initial period of six months, which was how long we figured it would take to assess what worked and what did not. Getting the agreement format approved by the Vietnamese only took a day. Lac then started scheduling meetings for us with province chiefs—some in Saigon, some in the field—to explain the program.

In addition to specific activities related to hamlet construction, protection, and development, the agreements provided for a miscellaneous fund to be used for any reasonably related purpose, at the discretion of the provincial committee. Never before had funds been given to the provinces with such flexibility. One unanticipated use that came up almost immediately was compensation for the families of hamlet militiamen, hamlet chiefs, and hamlet committeemen killed by the VC. The initial budget for a substantial province like Kien Hoa in the Delta amounted to only about $150,000 in piasters, covering some 120 new hamlets, eight combat hamlets, and thirty-eight existing hamlets. As activities progressed, agreements were amended to shift funds back and forth between activities.

A handful of the first Rural Affairs volunteers from outside Vietnam began to arrive in October. We were gathering a dedicated nucleus, but those we had been able to recruit so far were insufficient to cover all the provinces. Bert thought some of the young volunteers from the IVS might be persuaded to join us.[4] In their early twenties, they were recent college graduates, mainly from agricultural colleges. Most had been in Vietnam for more than a year, spoke Vietnamese, and were already working in rural areas. Recalling the responsibility Lansdale had thrust on me at twenty-five, I was taken by the idea. Don Luce, then the local head of IVS, got approval from his headquarters for Bert to talk to ten prospects who had expressed an interest. (Luce would later become a prominent antiwar protestor.) Bert recruited eight as new provincial reps. Although their IVS pay was only about a tenth that of the average American on the regular USOM staff, they were as a group immeasurably more motivated. Bert called them our "young tigers."

One of the first provincial rep recruits to arrive in Saigon was Bob Burns, a crusty, funny, eccentric Irishman with a Boston accent. A former U.S. Army captain with psywar experience, he had helped USIS in Laos. Bob was unorthodox and couldn't stand bureaucracy, but he was all heart, a ball of fire. I knew the Vietnamese would take to him. I sent him to Phu Yen almost as soon as he arrived; the MAAG sector advisor I had met there in June seemed relaxed enough not to be offended by his sense of humor. Later, if you had a development idea, Phu Yen was the province where you could try it out. Burns could usually persuade the province chief to try anything that made sense. If I felt down in the mouth, all I had to do was spend a day in Phu Yen to become rejuvenated, seeing progress and laughing at Bob's antics. Bob soon acquired an extremely able Vietnamese assistant, Lam Quang, one of the many we hired to support our provincial reps.[5]

Some volunteers emerged in unorthodox ways. Coming down the stairs at USOM on my way to Colonel Lac's office, I was stopped by a slightly younger, lean, intense man with close-cropped hair and wire-rimmed glasses. He wanted to find Rufus Phillips. When I told him I was, he said, "I'm Dave Hudson, I want to volunteer." I asked what he was doing now. Dave said he was a stringer for NBC. He'd heard about our outfit and wanted to join up. Any guy who was that motivated sounded good to me. Offhandedly, I asked where he might like to be assigned. He replied, "Give me the toughest province you've got." I said, "How about Camau?" "Okay" was the answer. That was it. As soon as his clearance came through he went to Camau. His willingness to take on difficult challenges and face risks was typical of most who joined us.

Another volunteer, who contacted us from Laos, was Earl Young. He was a captain in the Army Reserve, having enlisted out of high school in 1948 and been discharged just as the Korea War began. After two years of college, he had been commissioned through the Reserve Officer Training Corps and spent nine months as a rifle platoon leader in Korea, then returning to finish college. Staying in the active reserve, he went through airborne and ranger courses at Fort Benning, passed the Civil Service exam, and crunched numbers at Air Force headquarters and then at the Bureau of the Budget in Washington. Frustrated, he responded to an ad in the *Washington Post* and joined Air America in Laos. He was there, rigging relief supplies and directing air drops, when he heard we were looking for volunteers. He flew down to Saigon at his own expense to volunteer. We tried to put him on contract while his clearance came through, but even that required Washington approval, so I asked him to help temporarily for free. He agreed. The issue of liability in case he got hurt or sick ruffled the feathers of USOM's legal section, but we waved their objections off.

We had no single document that explained the job of a provincial rep, so Earl's first job was helping pull one together. The *Provincial Representatives Guide*—or "the bible," as we jokingly called it—was an eclectic combination of exhortation and instruction, explaining the Strategic Hamlet Program, listing the proposed provincial development programs and existing USOM technical programs, and describing what an across-the-board counterinsurgency program was about. As background it also included an essay, "Democratic Development in Vietnam," by President Diem; a Lansdale talk, "Lessons Learned from the Philippines," and his description of "The Insurgent Battlefield"; and "Report on South Vietnam," by Roger Hilsman, then the director of Intelligence and Research at the Department of State. The manual made it clear that "political, economic and social progress in a community depends upon having physical protection from the communists" and that our assistance "must be closely coordinated with military security actions." The provincial reps were told they had "the most important job in Vietnam." The hamlet program's purpose was "to give the Vietnamese people something worth risking their lives to defend," and the provincial reps were "to help the Vietnamese make their aspirations for a better life come true." While appealing to idealism, the guide also provided pragmatic instruction on what to do and how to do it.[6]

By December, we had assigned about eighteen representatives to the provinces, one representative to each of the four corps areas, and recruited a skeleton headquarters staff, which we intended to keep small. As they grew into their jobs, most provincial reps were extremely effective, covering an incredible range of tasks and actions, and learning as they went.[7] They were the most dedicated bunch I had ever seen in government or elsewhere. As could be expected from such a diverse group, the level of skills varied, but an unselfish desire to help the Vietnamese overcame most personal shortcomings. There was no small measure of the Peace Corps spirit about Rural Affairs, but it was tempered with a realistic perception that this was a deadly struggle. None were killed or captured by the VC during my tenure, but several had close escapes. Later, one provincial rep was captured and never seen again; two others were captured and remained prisoners until 1973, enduring unspeakable conditions. Another was so severely wounded by a mine that he spent most of a year hospitalized.

TRAN NGOC CHAU

The first province chief I talked to about Rural Affairs support was Lieutenant Colonel Tran Ngoc Chau, from Kien Hoa. That province was probably, with the exception of Camau, the toughest in the Delta, with a long history of communist activity going back before World War II. I knew little about Chau except that he had replaced Major Pham Ngoc Thao, who had been written up in several Joe Alsop columns earlier as a worthy combatant against the Viet Cong. I had no idea what to expect.

Chau was of medium height and stocky, with a broad face and an upright military bearing. He impressed me as a proud but sensitive Vietnamese nationalist, somewhat prickly in nature. After Lac introduced us, and before I could say much, Chau declared that he wanted us to know he didn't need any help in his province. He seemed to think we intended to take over his program and tell him what to do. I assured him that was not our intention. We just wanted to know what his program was so we could support it. That broke the ice. The more he talked, the more attentive I became. He talked about respecting the feelings of the population, about the need to correct government faults and mistakes, and, above all, to earn the population's loyalty. He did not build hamlets for the numbers. He declared that no hamlet was complete until it had developed a will to resist the Viet Cong and its security was assured.

He was preaching to the choir. I got excited explaining how the provincial agreements covered all the conventional hamlet activities as well as hamlet economic and social development. His eyes began to light up when I described the proposed miscellaneous fund to cover unprogrammed expenses important to the success of the program. I explained how the joint provincial committee would work and how careful we would be about whom we sent to his province to work with him. At the end he invited me to come down to see what he was doing.

My initial visit to Kien Hoa was the first chance for an extended conversation with Chau. He had mentioned at our first meeting two innovative ideas he had developed: census-grievance and counter-terror teams. The census-grievance teams conducted a survey within each hamlet, recording grievances against the government and concurrently collecting intelligence about the Viet Cong. They asked three basic questions: Have there been recent problems in your hamlet? Who caused the problems? What would you like the government to do to help you? Because all residents were interviewed individually, information about the VC could not be traced back to any one family or individual. Chau then acted on legitimate grievances. Dishonest or oppressive local officials were removed. When VC sympathizers, mainly families with VC relatives, were identified they were not punished but rather became the focus of government persuasion to induce their relatives who were combatants to change sides. Hardcore VC cadre and fighters who could not be persuaded were targeted by the counter-terror teams. These teams, organized in small squads, were often made up of former VC. They operated unconventionally in black pajamas, usually at night, ambushing the Viet Cong's patrols and raiding its hideouts, capturing VC if possible but killing them if necessary. He monitored these teams carefully to see that they did not commit abuses.

Chau's bent was to earn the population's support by ensuring people were treated fairly and justly. Leadership had not been conferred on him because he was a military officer or the appointed province chief; it had been earned. He had updated Confucian precepts of fairness and justice in public administration and embedded them into his own practices. It was thrilling to find an authentic Vietnamese approach with principles similar to Magsaysay's way of defeating the Huks. Chau's special teams were beyond our purview, so I contacted Stuart Methven to see if quiet Agency support could be arranged. I introduced him to Chau. This began American support for those two operations, which gradually spread, with Stu's involvement, to other provinces.

Later the counter-terror teams, renamed "provincial reconnaissance teams," became the heart of the Phoenix Program. While Phoenix was undoubtedly effective in eliminating hard-core VC in the late 1960s and early 1970s, too much of the necessary close supervision and control that Chau had exercised was lost. Incidents of indiscriminate killing, while relatively few, made the program a cause celèbre for the antiwar movement at home, seeming proof of the war's immoral basis. (However, the program, whatever its faults, was regarded as highly effective by the VC and the North Vietnamese.)[8] The census-grievance approach changed as well, eventually becoming more of a conventional intelligence-gathering operation, losing the important complaint and action emphasis except where province chiefs were wise enough to continue it.

Colonel Chau and I became friends over the months that followed. Unlike most officers in the Vietnamese army, he had been a Vietminh guerrilla. Disillusioned with communist control, he defected in 1949 and enrolled in the first class of the newly created National Military Academy, under Bao Dai's government. There Nguyen Van Thieu (later President Thieu) was his classmate and close family friend. Chau became a battalion commander in the Vietnamese national army and saw action fighting the Vietminh. At the end of the war in 1954, he became the first Vietnamese commandant of the Cadet Corps (previously all commandants had been French) at the Military Academy. Afterward, President Diem assigned him to study the effectiveness of the Civil Guard and the Self-Defense Corps. His inspections in the provinces gave him a firsthand view of the rising VC insurgency. When he saw how young some of the VC were and what sacrifices they made, he began to reflect on the importance of motivation to success. He had extracted a number of lessons from that experience and was now applying them in Kien Hoa.[9]

JOHN O'DONNELL

When John O'Donnell arrived in early October I was not initially impressed. He was tall and gangly, with red hair and a freckled complexion that showed his native Hawaiian heritage. He had grown up working summers with Asians in the sugar cane fields in Hawaii. Graduating from Stanford, he had served in the army and been assigned temporarily to USIS in Laos. Now he was about to turn twenty-seven but looked eighteen, even younger than most of our IVS recruits. He appeared so young I wondered how the Vietnamese would react, as they tended to venerate age. After meeting Colonel Chau, though, I wanted to send somebody with sensitivity and intelligence to his province. John probably ranked high on the empathy scale, but I wasn't sure how he would be received.

John went with me on an initial visit to the four closest Delta provinces south of Saigon. We drove to them, spending a day in each, to work out the details of the provincial agreements. I kept Kien Hoa for last. The trip was an opportunity to talk to John, for him to learn firsthand about the program and for me to judge him. His appearance proved deceptive. While remaining in the background, he came up with acute observations from each of our stops and was able to tune into Vietnamese frequencies. He was easy with the Vietnamese, and they responded. After a day-long discussion and inspection in Kien Hoa, we spent the night at Colonel Chau's house. In the morning I took Colonel Chau aside and asked his impressions of John. Very observant, he said, but very young. He was older than he appeared, I said. He had impressed me very favorably, and I wanted to appoint him as the provincial representative to Kien Hoa. John would be able to understand what Chau was trying to do. Chau's eyes widened skeptically, but he said okay. Initially John had to cover four Delta provinces, but he concentrated on Kien Hoa.

Later Chau would tell me his real reaction. Here I was, proposing to send him this freckle-faced kid who didn't look older than eighteen. He had said to himself something like, "I don't need any babies down in this province; I've got enough problems." Afterward Chau told me that John had been such an understanding listener and so reliable that after several months he came to depend on him as much as any other single person in his province.

POPULATION CONTROL AND THE SURRENDER PROGRAM

The first meeting of the Provincial Rehabilitation Committee, chaired by Bill Trueheart in October, produced a surprise. Frank Walton, former deputy chief of the Los Angeles Police Department and now head of USOM's Public Safety Division, not a regular member of the committee, presented a massive "population control" program for the strategic hamlets. Ten policemen would be put on the national payroll in every hamlet. They would man checkpoints and restrict population movement. It had been worked out, he claimed, with the British advisory mission and was very similar to what had been done in Malaya. Walton's idea centered on keeping the VC out by policing the hamlets, making population control the primary means of defeating the insurgency.

At the end of Walton's presentation, Trueheart asked for comments. While not rejecting the need for reasonable population control measures, I said the proposal was a diversion from the main effort to win the support of the rural population, not alienate it. There was no way a national police force could be put into the hamlets without creating abuses of power. It contravened the whole idea of hamlet self-defense and hamlet self-government. In Vietnam there was no British tradition of respect for citizen rights, as in Malaya. Moreover, the Vietnamese government hardly had the capacity to carry out the Strategic Hamlet Program, much less implement another national program of such dimensions. Why not give some police training to the hamlet militia? That ended the meeting.[10]

Afterward, Trueheart was puzzled by my reaction. Washington had a strong interest in population control. I made it clear this was not a case of bureaucratic jealousy—I couldn't care less about that. What mattered was that we had a core strategy for counterinsurgency, one built on giving priority to population security and winning the people. Since Washington seemed bent on supporting some kind of population control program, maybe the thing to do was to appoint a subcommittee to study the idea and come up with something practical. Trueheart agreed.

Getting a surrender program started was another story. I had discussed the need for one with Secretary of Defense Thuan during my initial visit to Saigon in June. It had been talked about by the British advisor, Sir Robert Thompson, and on the American side as well, but no one had figured out how to get it off the ground with the Vietnamese. It might be modeled, I thought, on the successful Economic Development Corps (EDCOR) program in the Philippines, but modified to fit Vietnamese circumstances. (EDCOR had been a program to resettle landless communist Huk surrenderees in new settlements far removed from their operational bases, providing agricultural extension services and credit to ensure a productive new start.) Thuan had been intrigued. Now I proposed to bring in Colonel Bohannon to help.

By November I had Bo under contract, and when he arrived in Saigon I set up an immediate appointment with Thuan. Bo had arrived in his usual Philippine attire, sandals and a khaki bush jacket with matching shorts. This was what he always wore in Manila, even when he used to go through the back door of Malacañang Palace to see President Magsaysay. I could see it was going to be out of place in Thuan's office but figured he would be amused. The meeting went off splendidly; Bo sketched out some ideas, Thuan agreed to appoint somebody to work with him, and we left. A few days later I would have to field a complaint by the new USOM director, Joe Brent, about Bo's appearance.[11]

The surrender program, which the Vietnamese called *Chieu Hoi*, or "open arms," took some time to work out. The appeal was based upon a call to return to the true "nationalist" cause. The returnees were to be housed in special camps and given orientation and some practical training in agriculture and other skills. They would then be settled, with some assistance, back in their home communities, if they could do so safely and the community agreed. Those for whom resettlement back home was not practical would be helped to relocate to another province away from any danger of retaliation. There they would be given land and agricultural credit to make a new start. After a lot of fine-tuning, the program was announced in January 1963 and began to be organized, although the detailed presidential decree was not published until April. The Chieu Hoi program would continue after the coup against Diem and all the regime changes thereafter, and it would eventually produce an estimated two hundred thousand returnees.[12]

ACCELERATING RURAL AFFAIRS

Through Colonel Schaad, I met General Timmes, the head of MAAG, who was quite receptive to the idea of appointing sector advisors as provincial representatives until we could man all the provinces with our own staff. This was followed by a meeting with General Harkins, which was my first opportunity to talk to him face to face. He was skeptical at first, seeing the assignments as diversions from sector advisor "military duties." When I explained how it tied in with the Strategic Hamlet Program, gave the sector advisor some resources to work with, and would only be temporary, he agreed. Still, although Harkins talked about supporting the hamlet program, he gave the impression that what went on in the provinces was not really very important. He was completely spit and polish, immaculately dressed in pressed khakis with all his ribbons, but with none of the "soldier's soldier" appearance or demeanor of a Gen. O'Daniel. He was affable, but there was a detached quality about him, giving the impression he was modeling himself on Gen. Douglas MacArthur.

While getting strategic hamlet financial support under way it was equally important to get down to the provinces materials the hamlet population could use. In provinces with larger capitals, such as Mytho and Can Tho, rice, cement, and sheet-metal roofing could be purchased on the local market. In many other provinces, these supplies had to be shipped from Saigon. To get things moving, Rural Affairs set up a small logistics unit, with only three Americans. Bui Van Loc's office arranged for the same commercial truckers and barge operators he was using to deliver Catholic Relief supplies. Using commercial transport on a bid basis bypassed the question of whether tolls had be paid to the VC to get supplies through territory that might be under their control, which the government tolerated in order to get relief supplies into some areas.[13] Loc's practical approach soon proved so effective that Rural Affairs took over the shipment of barbed wire for hamlet defenses from MAAG, whose logistics system of working through the Vietnamese army was bogged down in delays. MAAG handed over some forty thousand tons of barbed wire piled up on the docks. This was in addition to more than 140,000 tons of USOM supplies: mainly cement and other construction materials, fertilizer, and Public Law 480 (the U.S. Food for Peace Program) foodstuffs. All this was moved out to the provinces in our first six months of full operation.

In the meantime, Bert Fraleigh was starting up agricultural programs in the provinces to be tied in with the hamlets. Matt Drosdoff, head of the USOM Agriculture Division, insisted that only his division was authorized to contact the Vietnamese Ministry of Rural Affairs (Agriculture) and that Bert's idea for an accelerated pig raising, along with some his other "wild" ideas, were too radical to work in Vietnam. The farmers, he thought, were not capable of learning to raise pigs differently, or the ministry of supporting such radical new practices. Persuasion with Drosdoff failed, so I set up an end run by having Defense Secretary Thuan arrange for the Agricultural Extension Service director, Ton That Trinh, to contact Bert directly. Trinh, who was full of energy, action oriented, and not the traditional Vietnamese *functionnaire,* was one of the younger administrators Diem had recruited. He and Bert took to each other immediately and began working together to develop a series of agricultural extension projects, the most prominent of which was the pig program.

Pigs have an iconic status in the Vietnamese diet. The program proposed a complete change to the Vietnamese centuries-old system of raising pigs by introducing an improved, much faster growing breed of pig and by making radical changes in pig-raising practices. These particular pigs were of American origin; they had been adapted to Vietnam at a USOM-supported agricultural extension station in the Delta and were being raised by local farmers. Weaned pigs could be purchased from these farmers. The radical changes in traditional practices involved protecting the pigs against disease by vaccination, feeding them surplus PL 480 corn and later locally raised sweet potatoes, and raising them in concrete pens that kept them clean and healthy. All support was to be extended as a loan, except the cement donated to build the pens, which also served to collect pig waste to be drained into a pit where fermentation converted it to fertilizer for the fields. Instead of over a year needed to raise a small, swaybacked Vietnamese pig (which would eventually became prized pets in the United States), these much larger pigs would grow to market size in six months. Harvey Neese, an IVS livestock specialist who had transferred to Rural Affairs, went to work directly in the field with Vietnamese technicians, becoming "Mr. Pig" to the Vietnamese. Would it work? No one knew for sure.

A pilot program was launched in Phu Yen in December 1962 with six hundred pigs, two sows, and a boar each for two hundred families. The poorest farmers were selected to test the program. If they were successful, those better off would become confident enough to try. Everything seemed fine initially, but in January we got an anxious call from Bob Burns: too many pigs were dying, almost a third of the original six hundred. Neese, with his Vietnamese agricultural counterpart, Nguyen Qui Dinh, began to investigate. They discovered that when the pigs were trucked up from the Delta, a three-day trip, the drivers constantly hosed them down to keep them clean. Still wet when the temperature dropped at night, they were catching pneumonia. Antibiotics, along with greater care during the transport of replacements, solved the problem. By February 1963, losses had been cut to practically zero. The program had been tested; it was time to start an expansion.

However, nothing held more promise over the longer run than accelerating the use of new crops and improved practices to increase radically farmers' cash income. If successful this would provide a significant contrast with what the VC could achieve in areas controlled by them. It could lift many farmers out of abject poverty, judging by a similar agricultural revolution that had brought rural prosperity to Taiwan. Taiwanese technicians, such as Leonard Chang and Tommy Chu, were convinced this would work in Vietnam, telling us that the average Vietnamese farmer was smarter than his Taiwan counterpart and just as motivated if given a chance.

The pig program, while also revolutionary, could not be spread as quickly or widely as the introduction of faster-growing and more productive varieties of rice and improved fruit and vegetable seeds, or of such new crops as soy beans, whose harvest value per hectare was much higher than that of rice. All of this could be done on a loan basis to the individual farmer, once an initial investment was made to get the process started. An initial step was made in 1963, with the wide distribution of improved rice seed and fertilizer. Nationally, this would produce the first surplus rice for export since the insurgency began.

Hamlet schools and hamlet self-help projects were two other major programs. Education was almost as revered in Vietnam as one's ancestors. Each hamlet was offered materials to construct an elementary school on a self-help basis. Rural Affairs supplied the cement, sheet roofing, and tools, while the villagers supplied the labor. Teachers came from literate local volunteers, who were subsequently trained and paid by the province, while books came from the Education Ministry. By the summer of 1963, 850 hamlet schools had been constructed and supplied with teachers and books. Schools leveled by Viet Cong hamlet raids were usually rebuilt by the inhabitants as soon as security was restored. In one hamlet, the Viet Cong destroyed a school three times, and three times the inhabitants rebuilt it. Hamlet self-help projects, selected by the elected hamlet council, consisted of improvements other than schools, such as access roads, small bridges, and communal fish ponds (particularly popular in the Delta). By the summer of 1963, over a thousand of these projects were complete or under way.

VIETNAMESE FARMER'S STORY

Leonard Chang told a story about one very poor Vietnamese farmer near Hue in central Vietnam, an episode that explained the impact of new agricultural practices better than statistics. Leonard had run across this farmer in the early morning standing with his five children huddled in front of their hut, a primitive mud-walled structure with a poorly thatched roof and a single room. When he told the farmer who he was, he was invited in. The farmer went to the back of the hut and started talking to a pile of straw from which, to Leonard's surprise, a voice emerged. It was the farmer's wife, who had been covered by straw because they had no blankets. She was cold and nursing a newborn baby. The farmer asked Leonard if he and the Vietnamese technicians with him could help. He wanted to bid for the loan of some communal land for his rice crop but was not sure he could make enough money to pay the rent. With Leonard's assurance, the farmer bid for and won the right to farm one-fourth of a hectare (about a half acre). Instead of rice, Leonard made sure he received improved vegetable seeds on credit, particularly cauliflower and eggplant, which were in good demand in Hue, as well as insecticide and technical advice.

When the farmer's crop was ready for harvest Leonard returned and asked him how much he expected to make. His family, he said, had not seen a thousand piasters for three generations; he would be happy if he could make just that. When Leonard told him what the crop was really worth, about forty-five thousand piasters, the farmer was completely overcome. What would he do with the money? First, he said, he would buy his wife a kilo of pork; she hadn't eaten meat in over a year. Then, looking at the rags of his children and his hut, he said, "Many, many things." Subsequently, Leonard found the farmer had improved his house, clothed his children and his wife, and was going to bid for even more land next time, so he could eventually buy some of his own. This was the potential waiting to be unlocked for many poor farmers in the hamlets. Bert Fraleigh would see this clearer than most of us, and he never gave up on it.

ANOTHER ENCOUNTER WITH NGO DINH NHU

In early December, Ngo Dinh Nhu asked to see me. Our meeting, in Nhu's office at the palace, was curious. Unlike President Diem, Nhu never asked a question. Our meeting was all Nhu, talking in rapid-fire French expounding his theories of guerrilla and counter-guerrilla warfare (his terms). Some of his ideas were practical—such as counter-guerrillas adopting guerrilla tactics against the guerrillas and that defenses had to be mobile, not static. Shifting from the practical to the theoretical, he veered off into what he called "a new theory of counter-guerrilla warfare." There were three interdependent levels of self-sufficiency, to be added to three degrees of personal vigilance, to equal "Personalism," an existential philosophy that he propounded, feeling that the Vietnamese people instinctively understood and would be motivated by it. I was baffled by his combination of wooly-headedness with some fairly good insights.

In his wandering discourse, Nhu had one thing right: you could not provide security through static defenses alone. He spoke about small counter-guerrilla forces operating in Viet Cong-controlled areas in the same way the Viet Cong operated, but that aspect of his thinking never got across to MACV. As for the Vietnamese army, while some of the more intelligent senior officers probably agreed with Nhu about such tactics, most of them didn't like or trust him. I was struck by the dichotomy between the highly theoretical, professorial Nhu and the practical Nhu, talking from firsthand observations. It was obvious he now considered himself not just an expert but the single reigning expert in Vietnam on counterinsurgency.[14]

PHU BON

A newly created province north of Dalat combining portions of Pleiku, Darlac, and Binh Dinh Provinces, Phu Bon needed help in resettling an estimated eleven thousand Montagnard refugees. Its capital, Hau Bon, formerly known as Cheo Reo, had been the site in early 1954 of a Vietminh ambush that almost wiped out a French *groupe mobile* (a reinforced battalion). A few Vietnamese troops, a small MAAG advisory team, and a twelve-man U.S. Special Forces "A" Team, along with the refuges in desperate condition, now occupied the place. Conditions were dire, because relief supplies had to be delivered mainly by air. Living conditions were certain to be primitive. I looked for a volunteer for provincial rep. Earl Young, because of his military background and experience with indigenous tribes in Laos, seemed a likely candidate. He wanted to take a look before committing, and so did I.

We landed at Hau Bon in a helio-courier, a short-field-takeoff-and-landing aircraft, on a dirt strip reinforced by pierced steel planking. The town, just a road juncture with few permanent buildings, was in a flat valley surrounded on several sides by mountains. After the obligatory briefing in an abandoned local schoolhouse, now the headquarters of province chief Major Chi, we were shown the MAAG advisory team's area. The team's living quarters consisted of a squad-sized tent for the major, two captains, and a sergeant.

The sector advisor, Major Will, offered to lend Earl a smaller tent for his quarters and office, complete with a gasoline lantern. He could use the team's standard slit-trench latrine. Bathing was nearby in the Song Ba River, with one man on guard for crocodiles. He could eat with the MAAG team, whose food consisted mainly of produce, meat, and some game from the local market, supplemented by C-rations and prepared by an indigenous cook. At the end of our visit I asked Earl if he was still enthusiastic. He was, so we returned to Saigon to pack up his gear.

From Earl's later periodic visits to Saigon, I gleaned how things were going. Shelter was being constructed for the eleven thousand refugees, but most were in deplorable health. Only one small, French-style infirmary existed in the province, staffed by two Vietnamese Catholic nuns and by a mainly absentee Vietnamese doctor. The Montagnards were afflicted by malaria, trachoma, snake bites, and wounds from tiger attacks as well as buffalo gorings. Earl was helped immensely by the active support of USOM's Public Health Division (in contrast to Agriculture), particularly by Doctor Emmanuel Voulgaropoulos, or "Dr. V," as he was called. Dr. V had been a volunteer in Dr. Dooley's medical clinic in Laos and loved nothing more than to be out in the field. He had come to Phu Bon to survey the situation. Seeing the dire need, he returned to Saigon and came back promptly with a supply of prepackaged village medical kits, a MERCK manual, a full medical bag, and an official Vietnamese license authorizing Earl to practice medicine, for legal protection if he was challenged. While examining patients, Dr. V showed Earl how to recognize and treat the most common diseases. Nobody thought this was particularly unusual; it was just what was expected of our provincial reps. Earl's only complaint was about being denied part of the standard nine dollars per diem for the field because his tent was considered "government furnished quarters" by the USOM Finance Office.

FORRESTAL AND HILSMAN VISIT

As the year was ending, I had to spend time with two important visitors from Washington, Mike Forrestal and Roger Hilsman, the deputy assistant secretary for far eastern affairs at the State Department. Forrestal was thoughtful and seemed a good listener without preconceived ideas, but he deferred to Hilsman on counterinsurgency. Hilsman emanated an air of certainty based on his limited experience with guerrillas in Burma during World War II and on his reading about the British experience in Malaya. I took both to Kien Hoa Province to meet Colonel Chau and see how successful the Strategic Hamlet Program could be when correctly pursued. Hilsman was impressed by Chau but wanted to know why there was so much variance in effectiveness from province to province, and he questioned the lack of population-control measures similar to those set up by the British in Malaya. He was also concerned about the various civilian irregular defense units (CIDGs), who had been armed: the Montagnards, the Catholic militias, Nguyen Van Buu's "shrimp and cinnamon soldiers," Father Hoa forces in Camau, and the irregular defense units sponsored by the president's brother Ngo Dinh Can in central Vietnam. He liked the irregular quality of their operations but criticized the lack of nationwide organization.

I explained the inherent barriers to a standardized top-down effort in Vietnam—the varying situation and leadership competence across provinces and regions and the different religious, ethnic, political, and economic groups involved. A lot of the militia were effective precisely because they were locally based. Implementing a comprehensive national plan was not feasible at this time. We were working with what we had, intending to develop a more effective approach from the bottom up while also helping the Vietnamese government function better from the top down. When I read his report, it was clear he had not understood why the Vietnamese were not more like us. He still wanted extensive population-control measures, including a national police force in the hamlets. The one thing he had right, however, was his criticism of conventional military operations. It was my first extended contact with the "made in Washington" thinking of some of our policy makers. Hilsman, I decided, was not a good listener unless what he heard matched his preconceived views.[15]

TAKING A BREAK

Every day there were a hundred things to attend to, mainly ensuring our provincial reps were able to work productively with their particular province chiefs and that the funds were getting out to the provinces (often flown out in suitcases of cash, as Vietnam had no effective banking system except in the larger provincial cities), dealing with the rest of the U.S. mission, keeping Lac and Secretary of Defense Thuan informed, and making sure President Diem was kept abreast and Nhu not alienated. A large part of my job was smoothing out communications between our Americans and their Vietnamese counterparts. The Vietnamese were particularly sensitive to perceived slights, which were usually inadvertent. Then there were the visitors from Washington. I had very little time for my family except at breakfast. As the end of the year arrived, Barbara and I decided we needed to get away.

Right after the New Year, even though the temperature had turned cooler in Saigon we decided to take a few days off in Dalat, about four thousand feet above sea level and an hour's flight north from Saigon. Dalat, built by the French in the late nineteenth century as a hill town for relief from Saigon's sweltering heat, had continued as a vacation spot for foreigners and the Vietnamese. I told Vo Van Hai casually that we planned to go. He had mentioned this to the president, who insisted we stay in the presidential guesthouse. I tried to beg off, but it wasn't possible.

We were met at the Dalat airport in the late afternoon by the president's local staff. The day was still sunny, but cooler than I expected. We were whisked off to the guesthouse, which was an imposing colonial villa built by some past French governor general. The place was like a tomb, without heating and with an inside temperature of around 50 degrees Fahrenheit. The curtains were completely drawn. All the furniture was covered to keep off the dust. When we opened the closets, swarms of mosquitoes flew out. Despite our misgivings we stayed the night, ensuring that we and the children were under blankets and secure behind mosquito netting. In the morning the house was even colder. Our ten-month-old daughter Anne was crying. Obviously we couldn't stay there.

After much hand-wringing we extricated ourselves and found a room at the old main hotel that overlooked a lake. Even so, by that evening Anne had come down with a high fever. By luck we ran into an old friend, Dr. Ho Quang "Manny" Phuoc. Manny, a dentist, found a local doctor who diagnosed a severe ear infection. We flew back to Saigon the next day, abruptly ending our first break. I asked Vo Van Hai to thank President Diem, explaining that we had been able to stay only one night because of our daughter's sickness.

Chapter 10
An Uneven Path

As 1963 began, there were more than twelve thousand American military in Vietnam, mainly as advisors to the sectors (provinces), battalions, regiments, divisions, and the four corps headquarters of the Vietnamese army. In contrast, USOM Rural Affairs had about twenty-five people out in the provinces. The sheer number of American military advisors and their wide distribution throughout the country were the cause of unease, not just in the presidential palace but to the Vietnamese as a whole, for the boost it gave to VC propaganda that the Americans had replaced the French. These sensitivities were not well understood by the American side.

The Strategic Hamlet Program had thrown the VC off balance. They had not yet developed an effective response. On the other hand, there was a great deal of unevenness in pacification from province to province. The hamlet program was better in central Vietnam than in the Delta, where it was overextended in a number of provinces. While the Operation Sunrise approach of first diving into VC-dominated territory had been abandoned in favor of working outward from the more secure areas, there was still a carryover from Sunrise in some provinces where leapfrogging had left too many hamlets exposed. Having been pressed to implement the program rapidly, most province chiefs were reluctant to provide Saigon with an honest assessment of where the program actually stood. Colonel Chau in Kien Hoa was an exception.

In a number of Delta provinces resettlement had not been handled well. Too much uncompensated labor had been used to build new hamlets. Some families had been moved too far from their rice fields. Too many hamlets had been declared complete when they were still insecure, and too many province chiefs were playing a numbers game with Saigon, claiming progress where it didn't exist. Yet in at least two Delta provinces, Kien Hoa and Vinh Binh, progress was steady and sound. In Kien Hoa, despite historical Communist Party entrenchment, Colonel Chau was gradually winning support. This was evidence the program could work in the Delta.

In central Vietnam, progress was being made in most provinces. At least two coastal provinces, Phan Thiet and Phan Rang, were almost entirely pacified. Clear-and-hold operations similar to Phu Yen had been launched in two of the most difficult provinces, Binh Dinh and Quang Ngai, supported by regiments of the 25th Infantry Division, ably led by Col. Lu Lan.[1] Through reinfiltration down the Ho Chi Minh Trail, substantial Viet Cong forces had reemerged in Binh Dinh and Quang Ngai, supported by VC family networks created in 1955 by last-minute marriages to local girls or linked to the youth forcibly taken north at that time. Pacification in this area would be tough going.

Economic development was starting. Bert Fraleigh's enthusiasm and freewheeling style, while annoying some of the mission bureaucracy, was just what was needed. He had a unique talent for getting things done. With the pig corn program back on track in Phu Yen, Bert and Trinh in the Ministry of Rural Affairs set an incredible goal of reaching five thousand families with fifteen thousand pigs during 1963, mainly in the poorer areas of the center. Diem gave it his full backing. USOM's Agricultural Division had tried to persuade the mission director, Brent, to withdraw support—"It can't be done; it's certain to fail," they said—but Bert prevailed. In the meantime the hamlet self-help program, the hamlet school program, the drilling of wells in water-short hamlets, the introduction of windmills to pump water for irrigation to get two annual rice crops, the introduction of improved seeds and new varieties of vegetables, and the distribution of fertilizer to improve crop yields were beginning to get under way.

There were lots of holes in the hamlet program, but the basic idea of village self-defense was sound. Those closest to it were convinced its faults could be corrected over time. There were reasons to feel optimistic about the year ahead.

THE BATTLE OF AP BAC

A sour note intruded at the very beginning of 1963: the battle of Ap Bac. On the edge of one of the communist sanctuaries southwest of Saigon, the Plain of Reeds, a Viet Cong battalion had repelled the assault of a much larger Vietnamese army force that had been using armored personnel carriers and had been supported by American-piloted helicopters. It was a major defeat for the Vietnamese army, as reported by Neil Sheehan of United Press International and American advisors on the scene, particularly Lt. Col. John Paul Vann, our advisor to the Vietnamese army's 7th Division. Editors back in the United States began concluding the Vietnamese were losing the war, while the Saigon English-language newspaper *Times of Vietnam,* the unofficial organ of the government, proclaimed it a victory.[2] American helicopters supporting the Vietnamese had been shot down, and three Americans had been killed.

Vann was angry about what he considered the cowardice and incompetence of the commander of the Vietnamese army IV Corps, General Huyen Van Cao, and had sounded off to Sheehan and other reporters. Cao happened to be a favorite of Diem's, because he had faithfully served as chief of his Presidential Guard during the war against the Binh Xuyen in 1955. Vann was also upset by his differences with the upper levels of MACV, particularly General Harkins, over the way the Vietnamese, with our advice, were fighting the war. Later he would tell me and others that if he "had his 'druthers" he would have armed the Vietnamese army with long knives, obliging them to get close enough to see the enemy they were trying to kill. Vann understood the need for local civilian support and thought large-unit sweeps counterproductive, because they alienated civilians and got few if any VC. Vann had requested a hearing with General Harkins about tactics but was turned down.[3]

From our point of view, Ap Bac had little effect on what we saw as "the real war," the war for the rural population's support. The main problem with Ap Bac was its characterization as evidence that the entire Vietnamese army was incompetent and lacked the will to fight and that everything was all Diem's fault. Diem's natural sensitivity about Vietnamese army casualties was elevated into a press consensus that unit commanders were under standing orders from him to avoid casualties at all costs.[4] Editors back home took the battle as evidence we were losing the war.

A contributing factor to the "Ap Bac effect" was the growing dislike by much of the American press for Diem personally, as well as for his government. This had come to a head initially with the government's expulsion of Francois Sully, a *Newsweek* correspondent who was French and a personal friend of many younger American correspondents who vehemently objected to the American embassy's pro-Diem stance. (Sully had written an article criticizing Diem's family that had been taken as a personal insult.) The government stood its ground.

The Vietnamese didn't know how to deal with the foreign press. To admit openly that Vietnamese officers had been less than decisive or courageous was an unacceptable public loss of face. As it became clear that some American advisors were the sources of criticism, questions began to arise, particularly in the minds of Diem and Nhu, about the whole military advisory effort. But it was not just Diem and Nhu. Colonel Chau in Kien Hoa, who thought highly of Vann personally, told John O'Donnell that Vann should not have aired his concerns with outsiders but locked himself in a room with General Cao, with neither coming out until their differences had been settled. That was the Vietnamese way. Rural Affairs had less than one person per province in the field and deliberately kept a low profile, but American military advisors in uniform in the provinces and with regular army units were highly conspicuous. Their visibility reinforced Viet Cong propaganda that the South Vietnamese were American puppets. The VC constantly referred to Diem as "My-Diem" (American Diem). Diem's concern about this would come to a head in April and cause a significant diversion of Rural Affairs attention.

THE PROVINCE CHIEFS

The Vietnamese province chiefs were the key actors in carrying out the hamlet program. All were army officers. Most were majors, with some lieutenant colonels and a few full colonels. They fell into four groups. There were the truly outstanding, such as Colonel Chau in Kien Hoa. I put the province chief of Phu Yen, Lieutenant Colonel Oai; the province chief of Vinh Binh, Major Thao; and Major Bich, the province chief of Tuyen Duc (Dalat), who dealt with the Montagnards, in that category—although Chau occupied a special niche. As a group, rather than looking to Saigon constantly for direction, they were more focused on the people's well-being. They shared a genuine concern and respect for the rural population and an instinctive understanding that this was more a political than military struggle. Then there were the more run-of-the-mill province chiefs who understood the hamlet program's emphasis on winning the population's support but remained circumscribed by their own military training and background. They tended to rely on Saigon rather than drawing inspiration from the local population. Nevertheless, many got caught up in the program and proved capable of learning and improving. They were the majority. A third category, in the minority, were those whose overriding concern was how they were viewed from Saigon and whose attention was focused on numbers of hamlets created rather than on whether the hamlets genuinely supported the government. They did not object to or impede the economic and social development programs we were supporting, but they were largely passive about these aspects.

The remaining category consisted of the genuinely dishonest, purely militaristic, and even despotic, such as I would soon encounter in Vinh Long Province, where the province chief would prove to be in a class by himself. Sometimes, though, what appeared to be dishonesty turned out to have an underlying reason. In one case, the MAAG sector advisor in Dinh Tuong Province, west of Long An, was tipped off that two hundred sacks of cement had been diverted to the Vietnamese 7th Division from a Rural Affairs shipment. It turned out the division had supplied the trucks to transport the cement, and the province chief had agreed to give the division some sacks as compensation. The two hundred sacks were not for sale but were to be used for division fortifications. Nevertheless, the cement was returned from the division the next day after our provincial rep asked about it. In general, there was often a logical explanation for odd or even suspicious Vietnamese behavior, but you had to dig to find it. Vietnamese actions had their own logic, which was not always the same as ours.

The province chief of Kien Tuong, Major Nhut, was a different case. He had just awarded bids for local materials, such as clothing, tools, and rice, without the concurrence of John O'Donnell, who was covering Kien Tuong at the time. Instead of showing the bids to John, Nhut had hastily accepted them, for each commodity, from four different bidders. When John compared the bids with average retail prices in the local market, collusion was obvious. Nhut dismissed his objections. I preferred to let Colonel Lac handle such problems, but this had already gone too far. I told Lac, who agreed that the province chief, in addition to possibly being corrupt, had clearly violated the joint provincial committee agreement, so he had no objections to our meeting him and called to set it up. The bidders had been requested to be there. When we confronted the province chief and the bidders with written evidence of local market prices, the bidders agreed on the spot, after obvious embarrassment and lots of arm waving, to lower their prices. The province chief was reassigned, after some time passed for face saving.[5]

THE RURAL POPULATION

My impressions of the rural population came from direct observation going back to 1955 and from Vietnamese who were best at working with villagers. Those who did not deal respectfully with the rice farmers or fishermen tended to think of them as isolated, ignorant, and largely indifferent to the world beyond their hamlets or villages. The traditional culture of ancestor worship and self-government by local consensus did tie the average villager more to his immediate local environment than to more the abstract and distant entities and concepts of nation and government. The villagers were often referred to as peasants, which had a pejorative ring in English. Vietnamese leaders I knew who had worked with the rural population on an intimate basis had a different impression, whether out of perceptiveness, instinct, or guerrilla experience against the French.

The average villager was much more aware than he let on. One way of avoiding trouble from either the VC or the government was to act dumb. They were expert at dissembling as a means of survival. Beneath the surface they shared a common sense of nationhood and were intensely opposed to real or perceived foreign domination. One had only to look at how effectively the VC appealed to this part of their nature by conflating the American presence with French colonialism. The common history of the Vietnamese and of their heroes, who had resisted Chinese domination and unified the nation, were known by word of mouth to the literate and illiterate alike. In 1955, the largely illiterate and isolated population of Camau had responded enthusiastically to that shared heritage when army psywar companies staged historical dramas. They knew all the stories by heart.

Some Americans viewed villagers as mainly wanting to be left alone to till their rice fields and follow the path of their ancestors, or as willing to follow whoever was strongest. Many villagers did have a "plague on both your houses" view of the VC and the government, but this stemmed mainly from being forced to do things unrelated to, or even against, their own welfare, whether it was being resettled without assistance by the government or paying arbitrary taxes to the VC. At the same time, a sense of elemental justice existed, enhanced by a shared

Confucian heritage. That same heritage carried over into a love of education, reflected in how they cherished their schools. As for democracy, while they may have had little appreciation of national elections per se, they understood the difference between arbitrary and responsive government behavior at their level. To the extent that elections brought about changes in leadership attitudes, they had no difficulty in making the connection. They knew when they were being consulted, when their opinions were being taken into account, and when that resulted in positive change. The average villager clearly discerned in the most basic sense the difference between democratic practices and autocracy, and he would support the former if given a decent chance. All this gave me faith in the beneficial effect of hamlet elections, no matter how guided they were in the beginning, and ultimately in building democracy on a national scale.

THE LONG WALLS

In March, I got a terse message from Rob Warne, now the provincial rep for Vinh Binh and Vinh Long. The Vinh Long province chief, Lieutenant Colonel Le Van Phuoc, was building long walls between the hamlets using corvée (forced) labor. Could I come down to take a look?

Rob had arrived in December, having just finished a two-year stint in the army. He seemed almost too serious but was extremely well motivated and had a deep sense of public service. His father had been an outstanding official in the early Point Four Program. Rob had agreed to take over Vinh Long and Vinh Binh provinces from John O'Donnell, initially leaving his wife and small child in Saigon. For safety reasons, and also for the lack of even minimal housing in most provinces, practically all of our wives lived in Saigon. Rob and his wife Suzy, however, wanted very much to live on the local economy. I was initially leery about it, but after seeing how secure Vinh Binh was, they prevailed. Moving in February to the provincial capital of Phu Vinh, they shared a bungalow with a Vietnamese couple on the main street across from province headquarters. Suzy adapted readily to the simple lifestyle—even primitive, by American standards—of a Delta province and began teaching English classes at the local high school.

Colonel Lac had warned me before leaving for Vinh Long that Phuoc was a favorite of Ngo Dinh Nhu and of his brother, Archbishop Thuc. Arriving by plane early in the morning, I was met by Rob, the MAAG sector advisor, Major Ring, and Colonel Phuoc. Phuoc was taller than the average Vietnamese, with a self-assured air verging on arrogance. He had set up a tour of all five districts of his province.

The first district chief briefed us on plans to build a single wall some thirty kilometers (eighteen miles) in length, following the main highway to the largest city in the Delta, Can Tho, and separating the highway from the district's interior. All of the population was to be moved from the interior to new houses between the wall and the highway. We saw an already constructed part of the wall eight kilometers long paralleling the highway and running across rice paddies, not contiguous to any existing hamlets. The typical wall was a steep pyramid of packed earth, about six feet high, dug from the adjacent rice paddies and topped by four strands of barbed wire. On one side there was a moat of varying depth, from which the mud for the wall had been excavated.

In another district about two hundred villagers labored on a wall running straight across the rice paddies; it would be twelve kilometers in length when finished. One of the workers, when asked how long he had been working on it, said fifteen days without stop. Given the current rate of progress, its completion would take another forty days of forced labor. Hostility lurked behind his obvious sullenness.

"How are these walls going to keep the VC out?" I asked. "The main purpose," Phouc responded, "is controlling the civilian population to keep them from moving freely across the rice fields. When people are forced to use the roads, checkpoints will be set up to control their movements. I will evacuate the population from the interior out to the lines of communication (the roads and rivers) and then control them between walls while creating a free-fire zone in the interior." Phuoc boasted he had over six thousand farmers working on the walls. He had little or no popular support for what he was doing, but he thought this would come later—"Organization and control come first." Once a hamlet was under his control, families with VC relatives were given three months to call them back. If a family's relatives didn't return, he took away its land and gave it to the hamlet committee, the income from which was then used to pay hamlet officials and the hamlet militia. He claimed the work parties we saw were all volunteers, but these were certainly not volunteers.

I was appalled—this was bizarre. I looked for an indication that Phuoc might change his thinking based on our questions and obvious dismay. There was none. In an aside, Major Ring told me he agreed with my reactions and had tried to influence Phuoc, as had Rob, without success. Unexpectedly, I had a test case on my hands. Could mistakes be corrected in how the hamlet program was being carried out even if a well connected province chief was involved?

My report to the mission director, Brent, recommended that we suspend further aid to Vinh Long but not circulate the report until we saw what the response was on the Vietnamese side.[6] I hand-carried a confidential copy to Colonel Lac, saying I was holding it in abeyance. Lac briefed Nhu, who promptly convened a meeting of the Interministerial Committee on Strategic Hamlets, summoning Colonel Phuoc to appear. Lac knew his man; he had the Vietnamese air force take aerial photographs of the province beforehand. At the meeting, Phuoc denied he was building long walls between the hamlets, only around the hamlets. He claimed I had insulted him. Lac fanned out the aerial photographs on the conference table; Nhu asked Phuoc for an explanation. There was none. Phuoc was verbally reprimanded on the spot and ordered to stop building the walls. A decree was promptly issued forbidding all province chiefs from building long walls between hamlets. Afterward, Rob reported that all long-wall building in Vinh Long had stopped and that Phuoc had delegated the hamlet program to his deputy, who was much easier to work with. It took several months for Phuoc to be transferred to Saigon to avoid widespread embarrassment up the governmental chain of command.

Nhu spoke to Diem about the incident and later mentioned it to Ambassador Nolting as an example of how the Americans should advise the Vietnamese. Vo Van Hai told me Diem had gained a lot of confidence in us from the way we had handled it "in the family." We were becoming accepted as a partner in what the government was doing in the countryside. It was evidence that Diem and even Nhu—certainly in his rational moments—were susceptible to informed American advice, but revelations of mistakes had to be handled subtly. It was disturbing that a province chief like Phuoc could have gotten as far as he did with such a harebrained scheme. Either Phuoc was phenomenally self-confident or had sold somebody a bill of goods.[7]

A WELCOME VISIT
As mentioned, a time-consuming and not always productive aspect of the job was catering to

visitors from Washington, who had to be briefed and shown around. A few were really useful and therefore welcome. Walter Stoneman, the director of the Office of Vietnam Affairs in AID/Washington, was one of those. Stoney had taken us pretty much on faith and was unstinting in his support. We needed to show him what we were doing, particularly to explain why we had sometimes to bypass the Vietnamese ministries and sometimes the AID mission divisions to get aid out to the provinces. The inside sniping in Washington had begun, mainly from some of the AID technical departments, reflecting similar discontent within some USOM/Saigon divisions.

We took Stoney on a flying tour, first to Phu Yen Province, where he got a vivid view of provincial operations, saw the pig program in full swing, and witnessed how some recent Montagnard refugees were being resettled. We went to Kien Hoa to see a successful hamlet program in the Delta, to Long An to illustrate the problems with resettlement, and then to Camau, at Stoney's specific request, to see the operation of Father Hoa commanding a fortified village enclave, Binh Hung (the subject of Lansdale's article in the *Saturday Evening Post* back in 1961). MAAG put an eight-seat DeHaviland Otter aircraft at our disposal.

To get to Father Hoa, we had first to fly to Camau City in the Otter, then from there by helicopter about twenty kilometers north to his fortified village. Most of the Camau Peninsula was controlled by the VC, but not the Binh Hung complex, which had been expanded to include eleven local villages surrounding the original outpost established some five years before. We helicoptered into Binh Hung without incident. This was my first visit. Father Hoa needed help with a bridge over a canal he was building as he extended his secure zone. He showed us a new school built with the cement and sheet roofing we had been able to ship to him earlier.

A month before Father Hoa had received some fresh recruits, and they had just seen their first combat action. He said they were former "cowboys" (the Vietnamese term for juvenile delinquents) of Chinese origin from the slums of Cholon. Fraleigh, who spoke Chinese, and I wandered into a thatched hut where some of the "cowboys" were talking about their first combat. "How do you like Binh Hung," Fraleigh asked? "Very much," they replied. "But wouldn't you prefer to be back in Saigon?" "No, if we don't defeat the communists, they will take over Saigon with our homes and our families." Their spirit was a real tribute to Father Hoa's leadership. His fighters were mainly Chinese-Vietnamese but included some pure Vietnamese. Many were not Catholic. After lunch we flew back to Camau City, where we picked up some additional passengers for the ride back to Saigon.

It was late afternoon when we took off. The Otter lifted off for several hundred feet then took a sudden nose-dive toward the ground. The pilot leveled out at the last second as we pancaked into high grass outside the airport, crossing an irrigation canal, ripping off the landing gear, and coming to a stop with the wings still attached. Nobody was hurt, except for a few bumps. It all happened so fast that no one except the pilot had had a chance to react. The blade of an army helicopter parked beside of the runway had clipped an aileron as we took off, obliging the pilot to set it down before we spun into the ground. As we walked out of the grass toward the airfield's security zone, I could see Stoney had taken it like a trooper. I was lucky, he joked, not to have lost my Washington support. Later I sent him a piece of the plane and some VC weapons, which he displayed in his office in Washington.

I didn't get home until late at night and didn't want to alarm Barbara about the crash, figuring I would tell her the next morning, but I had to leave for an early breakfast meeting before she woke up. Later, she went to a morning coffee given by Mrs. Brent, the mission director's wife, where one of the AID wives was highly indignant that her husband had nearly been killed in a plane crash the day before. She wanted him to resign and return with her to the United States immediately. Barbara asked, "What plane crash?" The woman was incredulous. "The one with your husband, didn't you know?" Without blanching and in an even tone, Barbara said I had arrived too late and left too early to tell her, but she supposed if it had really been dangerous I would have said something. She had noticed a splinter of painted wood on her night table in the morning, which she now supposed was part of the plane. She was certain to hear all about it when she saw me at lunch. Silence ensued.

By the end of his visit, Stoney had acquired complete confidence in what Rural Affairs was trying to do and became an even more stalwart defender back in Washington. I was confident enough in him to talk about ideas I had, which I thought he could help with, about going beyond the Rural Affairs program.[8]

THE SELF-INFLICTED FUNDING CRISIS

After the first fiscal year of the Strategic Hamlet Program, a discussion with AID/Washington had begun about funding for the next fiscal year, beginning in July 1963, when most of the original ten million dollars would run out. Initially we were asked for our opinion and had requested a simple replenishment of the special fund, calculating we needed about eight million dollars for another year. Then we heard no more about it. The Vietnamese government was facing a general funding shortage, particularly in providing support for the Self-Defense Corps. We assumed Washington wouldn't interfere with success and that common sense would prevail, since these funds were so essential to the entire counterinsurgency effort. We were wrong.

On April 30, about a month after the "long walls" affair, I was abruptly told by Director Brent that Ambassador Nolting had abandoned the joint provincial committees because of objections from President Diem. Brent showed me a Nolting cable to Washington dated four days earlier in which he had agreed that beginning in July the Strategic Hamlet Program would be funded by the Vietnamese government and that spending at the province level would no longer require a sign-off by our provincial reps. The cable said, "We are not interested in vetoing expenditures, the existing procedure was originally introduced at GVN [government of Vietnam] request as a check on local officials." Nolting claimed in the same cable that Diem would not accept joint control of such expenditures in the provinces even if U.S. funds were involved.[9] I was dumbfounded. How had this happened? Nolting's take was wrong. The provincial committees had been created to facilitate spending, not veto it. Whatever point Diem was making, it didn't have anything to do with Rural Affairs. Negotiations had been going on with the government for over a month without us being informed or consulted. "Who decided it, and why weren't we consulted?" I demanded. Brent said, "Ambassador Nolting recommended it, and Washington agreed." "If this goes through," I said, "I will have no alternative except to resign." Agitatedly, Brent replied, "There's nothing I can do. Talk to the ambassador."

Nothing our own staff or the Vietnamese ever did was to make me so angry. How could I even face our people, who were risking their lives and working their backsides off to make the effort a success? For a moment I thought back to Lansdale's experience in 1955, when key policy decisions were made about the Can Lao without his advice, largely undercutting his political efforts. It was hard to stomach the ham-handed and essentially ignorant way next year's funding had been handled.

That day I wrote Brent a memorandum to be sent to Ambassador Nolting protesting the decision. "We are now being asked," I said, "to give up essential US participation in counter-insurgency operations directed at winning the population. Yet it is precisely this participation and the funding system that has supported and made it possible. Based on intimate contact with many Vietnamese, including Nhu and the president, most are not yet psychologically prepared to make a decentralized, post-audit system work; the Ministries are even less prepared to accept it." The proposed changes would seriously jeopardize the success of the Strategic Hamlet Program, and if it failed "the war will be lost."[10] As backup I submitted a separate memo based on an evaluation of the hamlet program by our regional reps. "After six month's field experience (for Rural Affairs), it is clear the strategic hamlet concept is excellent but its implementation is seriously handicapped. Across the board there is great difficulty in grasping the idea of the strategic hamlet as 'a state of mind.' Conditioned by years of experience with the French and having no experience with democratic methods of leadership, many feel unable to carry out the program without using methods sure to alienate the population. The task at heart requires a psychological revolution in the way the Vietnamese Government and its officials operate."[11]

After Nolting had gotten both memos, we met. I asked if he realized what eliminating the provincial joint committees meant: "They are making the Strategic Hamlet Program work." "But that is what the Vietnamese want," he said. "They are complaining about American advisors being too intrusive." "Not about us," I said. "Diem is complaining about American military advisors criticizing the Vietnamese directly to the American press. The way we handled the Vinh long-walls issue was a vote of confidence. I think you are wrong, Mr. Ambassador. Did Diem or Nhu specifically complain about us?" He admitted they did not. "Why didn't you consult us and let us explain directly to Diem and Nhu the need to continue the committees? *We* don't need the provincial committees; the *Vietnamese* need the provincial committees." He responded dismissively, "Nothing can be done now; there are larger policy issues involved." "Larger than winning war," I asked? There the conversation ended before it got completely out of control. I left abruptly, without saying another word. Afterwards I saw earlier Nolting telegrams to State saying that Diem had complained about the actions of civilian as well as military advisors. I was certain Diem had not been referring to Rural Affairs.

Our staff heard through the grapevine and quickly congregated in Saigon. "You should go straight to the White House, never mind the bureaucrats," was the advice. I sent an urgent letter to Janow, the assistant AID administrator for the Far East asking permission to return to Washington immediately. I wanted personal assurances that if the proposed arrangements did not work out, AID/Washington would provide the necessary funds by some means. None of us here were "summer soldiers or sunshine patriots," nor did we "hesitate to fight an uphill battle." We would, "therefore, do our utmost to make the proposed system work. Should, however, we be asked to discharge our duties under impossible circumstances, I shall have no choice but to resign."[12]

After cooling off, I saw clearly that we were boxed in by Washington's refusal to put up U.S. funds and by Nolting's assumption that even if American funds were provided Diem would no longer permit us to sign off on disbursing it. My resignation would have no practical effect. We had to find a way around the new agreement. I talked to Lac, who wanted me to see Nhu as soon as possible to clear the air. Maybe a modus vivendi could be found.

How had this happened? I asked Secretary Thuan. Throwing up his hands he said, "Sometimes it's impossible to communicate between the Americans and Diem. The president has just had it up to here," he said, pointing to the top of his head, "with the publicized criticism by some American military advisors [Vann and Ap Bac] and above all with the unfavorable report by Senator Mansfield." (Mansfield, with a small party, had made a brief visit in January, never talking to us.) "Mansfield is an old friend," Thuan said, "who has turned unfairly against the president." All this had impelled Diem to make a stand for Vietnamese sovereignty and against too much American interference. "It isn't you, and it isn't Rural Affairs," Thuan said. Thuan agreed, however, that the program would bog down in traditional Vietnamese bureaucracy unless we could keep the provincial committees functioning. "You have to see Nhu and the president."

A few days later, on May 7, I met with Nhu in his office at the palace. Nhu greeted me cordially but started criticizing how the Strategic Hamlet Program was being carried out in the western zone of the Delta, where "only about twenty percent of the hamlets had any value." He had argued with the president about pursuing too many major objectives at the same time in the Delta. The province chiefs were given insufficient support, which resulted in either financial irregularities or "work for show purposes." This gave me an opening. "Faced with indifference and even hostility from much of the population," I said, "I see officials reacting in two ways. Some use persuasion to generate a spirit of confidence and then use this spirit as the basis for constructing hamlets, while others, not understanding the hamlet is 'a state of mind,' try to create them by command. This produces the illusory hamlets you mentioned." Nhu nodded in agreement.

"The province chiefs," he said, "are too extravagant in using [American] funds; the bidding procedures which follow American rules invite collusion by the bidders." "The bidding requirements," I said, "actually stem from a ruling by the Interministerial Committee that American, as well as Vietnamese, disbursements have to follow Vietnamese government bidding rules. We originally proposed a simpler method of getting quotations from several suppliers simultaneously thus preventing collusion." That gave him pause.

I was glad he had raised the funding issue. "Perhaps, Mr. Counselor, the government has the impression the joint committees were set up as a control device, but this was not the reason; it was to facilitate expenditures. Even when you personally sent government money to the provinces, very little got spent. Perhaps the government also thinks we put representatives in the provinces to control the government and somehow they have been undermining the government. Nothing is further from the truth. We have been doing the opposite, strengthening the government by providing the means to reach the population. Perhaps the government thinks what we have been doing is wrong. I would like to know what the government thinks. The effectiveness of our assistance depends on the morale and spirit of the people who administer it. Most are volunteers like myself who came to Vietnam without *arrière pensées* (hidden agendas) and with an open heart to help."

This was the first time I had ever given such a speech to either Nhu or Diem. I had no idea how he would respond. Nhu thought for a moment and said, "I welcome your frankness and appreciate your help, particularly in the provinces. You mustn't think we don't understand or appreciate what you are trying to do. There are just too many Americans in Vietnam. Needed are less Americans in general but more who are . . . true ambassadors for their country. We mainly ask discretion in how the advisory role is handled; if you see something wrong you should report it to the government to take corrective action. Problems exist but they should be kept in the family. I appreciate how you've handled problems and am not referring to your people, but to others who aired their complaints directly to journalists, or tried to undercut their superiors. I would like a better common understanding. This is necessary for the success of the whole effort. I will study what can be done." The meeting spoke for itself. I wrote it up without comment, sending it to Brent with copies for Nolting, Trueheart, and Richardson (the CIA station chief).[13]

When I told Colonel Lac what had happened, he thought of arranging a meeting of all our provincial and regional reps and key staff directly with Nhu, to clear the air completely. I said it was a great idea. Lac said he would suggest it.

The issue remained on dead center until I saw President Diem three weeks later, on May 27. After the usual greetings and personal inquiries, I began: "I think it would be useful, Mr. President, if I explained the functions of the USOM provincial representatives. They are volunteers, all of good will and their sole purpose is to help and reinforce the government at the provincial level. Perhaps the government has the impression our representatives are trying to control its operations. I have heard you may feel the sovereignty of certain province chiefs is being questioned. We have not had difficulties with province chiefs who are true nationalists but with those who are unsure of themselves or not doing well and want to hide this from the government. Please give me your opinion, Mr. President. Do you believe our provincial reps are carrying out their jobs correctly? Are they helping?"

"We appreciate," Diem said, "the work you are doing. Criticism was not directed at your people but at certain military advisors." He brought up accusations made by Colonel Phuoc against Major Ring in Vinh Long; by Major Nhut, the Kien Tuong province chief, against Major Poston; and by General Cao against Vann. I said I only knew about two cases personally, the complaints of Colonel Phuoc and Major Nhut, and neither had told him the truth. "Colonel Phuoc had ordered the long walls, and Major Nhut was dishonest. The behavior of the sector advisors in those two provinces has been to my knowledge, Mr. President, of the highest order. I can only conclude Colonel Phuoc and Major Nhut were shifting the blame for their own shortcomings." He replied, "Often I have difficulty finding out what is happening in the provinces, and I do not believe everything I am told by any means." I said, "We have recently prepared an evaluation of the hamlet program on a province by province basis and wonder if you may be interested in seeing it." He said he would very much like to read it. I promised a copy.[14]

The conversation ended with the president saying he appreciated my frank opinions and would like me to keep in close touch with his minister of interior, Bui Van Luong.[15] It struck me that what Nhu and Diem had said directly contradicted Nolting as to whether their objections applied to Rural Affairs.

The Rural Affairs meeting with Counselor Nhu was held at the presidential palace on May 30. All of the provincial reps (by this time there were twenty-six), the four regional reps, Bert Fraleigh, Colonel Bohannon, Tom Luche (our program officer), Kitty Hay (women's affairs), and Jeanne Wright (public health) were there. This was the first and only time Nhu ever met with a group of Americans from the working level. We were seated at a long table, with Nhu at the head. He began by saying that since the government had accepted more direct American involvement after the Taylor mission in 1961, Vietnam's situation had improved. "Some people now criticize the government," he said, "for continuing the U.S. presence throughout the country." People had more time to criticize, now that the situation was better; some people were even thinking about preparing for future elections. But officials who misbehaved did not like outside observers. "What about the American side," he asked? Bert said we were all enthusiastic about the effort the government was making in the provinces and hoped for continued close liaison and government emphasis on hamlet development.

"The government wants to improve liaison," Nhu said. "You should report frankly what is not going well but should do this discreetly." Bob Burns asked, "Will the already established simplified funding system continue to be used by the government?" After saying that "a good method has been settled on," Nhu talked about funding amounts and corruption. I asked Nhu to clarify his response—Burns had referred to funding procedures, not amounts. "Our experience," I said, "is that complicated paper procedures encourage rather than prevent corruption." Nhu replied, "Yes, procedures should be quite simple with the condition publicity is widespread so the sums received . . . are widely known." He wanted Rural Affairs to help with that.

The meeting went on for about three hours, covering a wide range of subjects about problems with the hamlets.[16] While Nhu never answered Burns' question directly, he seemed to be saying that the existing provincial committees could continue to operate as before even if the funds were Vietnamese. The meeting ended on a warm note as he shook everybody's hand and thanked us for what we were doing.[17] Colonel Lac told me afterward that Nhu now seemed to trust us much more and approved of what we were doing and how we were doing it. I thought we now had an opportunity through further dialogue and persuasion to change how the hamlet program was being implemented and to modify the autocratic leadership attitudes and arbitrary actions of some government officials toward the civilian population.[18]

The provincial committee sign-off on expenditures including Vietnamese government funds continued as before. While not claiming outright victory, I wrote Janow that no instructions had been issued by the government and that we were certain we could make things work. In fact, no new instructions were ever issued, even after Nhu became convinced I was no longer the government's friend. It had all taken much too much time and energy and could have been avoided. Still, a more cooperative and understanding bond had been forged. The experience was also a lesson in the tenuousness of top-level communication and understanding between us and the Vietnamese, a symptom of worse to come.

POPULATION SECURITY, THE VIETNAMESE ARMY, AND MACV

In many provinces the lack of effective backup military support for the hamlets made permanent security difficult if not impossible. When properly armed and at least minimally trained, the hamlet militia could resist small-scale, local VC incursions. The village-level Self-Defense Corps (SDC) was the next line of defense, but it was often poorly trained and underarmed, at a time when more and more VC were armed with AK-47s smuggled in from Cambodia, via the port at Sihanoukville, or down the Ho Chi Minh Trail. While most MAAG sector advisors understood the importance of the SDC, at higher levels its needs received little attention. At the next highest level, the Civil Guard was mainly employed in static duty, guarding bridges and provincial and district headquarters.

With few exceptions, mainly in central Vietnam, Vietnamese army divisions were kept intact and had designated areas of responsibility covering several provinces. These units were habitually deployed in battalion-sized or larger sweeps looking for regular VC forces, based on intelligence usually twenty-four hours old. Sometimes regular VC units would be trapped, but for the most part they evaded the sweeps, fading back into their base areas. While MAAG sector advisors were clearly tied in with the strategic hamlets, MACV headquarters and the corps and division advisory levels were not, and with few exceptions they were more interested in conventional military operations. There was an overreliance on airpower and indiscriminate interdiction shelling, too often striking civilians but hitting few Viet Cong. There was little understanding that the war could be fought more effectively by protecting the population, and little appreciation, particularly at the top, of its unconventional aspects.

Though General Harkins issued an order in February 1963 explaining the importance of "clear and hold" operations and support for the Strategic Hamlet Program, declaring that it was "absolutely essential" that Vietnamese army resources be applied to this effort, the main emphasis at division and corps remained on large-unit sweeps.[19] Most of these operations were ineffective and not worth the side effect of driving more recruits to the Viet Cong. A MAAG "lessons learned" report of June 1962 had condemned sweep operations as "indicative of poor intelligence," recommending that they "should be avoided." This was obviously being ignored, as was another recommendation that "participating troops and commanders must be "Civic Action minded." Troop abuses continued. It was hard to figure out why the top levels of MACV remained so impervious to their own firsthand, field-based recommendations.

To question military tactics openly would have brought Rural Affairs into direct conflict with General Harkins on a subject on which we civilians were thought not qualified to speak. A further complication was Ambassador Nolting's endorsement in April of increased air interdiction, arguing it had few unfavorable side effects.[20] Typically, Rural Affairs had not been included in any discussions, although we were better informed about the actual side effects than others except the sector advisors, who also believed that air and artillery interdiction was much too loosely controlled.

We had hoped the assignment of Brig. Gen. Richard Stilwell to MACV as J-3 (Operations) in April would change the emphasis. Bohannon had known Stilwell during the campaign against the Huks in the Philippines, when Stilwell had served as acting director for Far East operations of OPC, the covert operations arm of the nascent CIA, and had been well aware of the Huk campaign. I found Stilwell pleasant, down to earth, easy to talk to, and straightforward.

We began giving Stilwell verbal reports about harmful Vietnamese army actions. He listened, but little happened. Later we sent written memos. One dealt with abuses of the civilian population by soldiers in Pleiku, Binh Dinh, and Phu Yen provinces.[21] A program to encourage civic action by the army had been announced by MACV but had never got off the ground. The old G-5 organization that I had help set up for the Vietnamese army back in 1955 still existed but was not effective, despite the appointment of a Vietnamese general to head it up. Most of the American advisors had no experience with this aspect of warfare. Few at the senior level seemed to think it important.

Stilwell was reading our memos and reports; he said he had warned some of the American advisors about improper Vietnamese army troop behavior. But we saw few results from our verbal or written warnings. I explained how back in 1955 the Vietnamese had taken two much less disciplined and untrained army divisions and, after three weeks of intensive indoctrination, had been able to occupy an area previously controlled by the Vietminh for nine years without a single civilian/soldier incident. Comprehensive civic-action indoctrination was again needed. Stilwell seemed to agree, but the idea received no priority within MACV. There were also other problems with army operations in the Delta. Some regular Army of the Republic of Vietnam (ARVN) units were not aggressively going after the Viet Cong when they had the chance, and many of their operations were ineffective. (This latter view had been first reflected in a detailed report sent to General Harkins not long after the battle of Ap Bac by the IV Corps advisor, Col. Daniel Boone Porter. His report had never been acknowledged). I described the situation in a two-page memo to Stilwell on July 30.[22]

In our first systematic attempt to change things, we focused on the largely indiscriminate use of firepower by our planes and helicopters when fired upon even from friendly villages, as well as on bombing and shelling of suspected VC locations when they included villages with civilians. I had hoped to bring it up with Secretary of Defense Thuan and with Ambassador Nolting rather than confront the American military establishment directly, but the Buddhist crisis intervened. We were unable to get the paper to Nolting before he left on home leave. By the time he returned word was out he was being replaced, but we gave it to him anyway, assuming he would pass it on his successor. We gave an informal copy to Stilwell, not wanting him to feel we were going behind his back.

The memo addressed a major error in our military tactics, by emphasizing that winning the support of the people was the only way to defeat the insurgency. What that meant "was [that] . . . so long as actions taken in the war contribute to winning the people, they contribute to winning the war. When they do not contribute to winning the people, they contribute to losing the war." A mistaken view, all too prevalent in practice, was that "those who do not support the government, or are not in government-controlled areas, must suffer for this (after all, war is hell). . . . [A]fter suffering enough they will either blame the VC or will come over to government controlled areas to escape the bombs, shells, . . . their lot when the VC are around."

Consistent with American principles, we argued, there were two reasons why the United States should neither countenance nor support such actions. First, "No one should be punished for actions beyond his control or forced on him by fear of his life . . . [and] when punishment is possibly unjust, as well as excessive, it is certain to create hatred for those that inflict it." Second, we should, therefore, "absolutely prohibit any attacks by U.S. aircraft or pilots on . . . targets where the absence of women and children cannot be positively determined." This meant "inhibiting them from attacks on houses or villages. So called 'Free Fire Zones,' which could be shelled or bombed indiscriminately, should be eliminated." The memo concluded, "This war is not an isolated phenomenon. The actions that we take, or support, here in Vietnam, must be viewed in that context, and as they may be made to appear long after our major involvement here has ended."[23]

The latter was more prophetic than I could have ever imagined at the time. Unfortunately, nothing ever came of this memo. These same thoughtless tactics would be intensified during the later American direct-intervention phase of the war, under Gen. William Westmoreland, alienating not only many Vietnamese but the American public as well.

Chapter 11
The Buddhist Crisis

This crisis, beginning as an incident in the ancient imperial capital of Hue in central Vietnam, developed into a full-blown political uprising that no one had foreseen. I had been warned by Vo Van Hai that Diem's support was weaker, even within his own government, than most Americans realized, but I never thought the Buddhists would become the unraveling agent.[1] While the aging patriarch Thich Tinh Khiet was recognized as the preeminent Buddhist in the country, the Buddhists were not well organized nationally, like the Catholic Church. We, and most Vietnamese I knew, were blind-sided by events. For the first several weeks I did not think it was a critical problem.

On May 8, Buddha's birthday, a crowd of about three thousand assembled in front of the government radio station in Hue to protest a government decision the previous day forbidding the public flying of Buddhist flags as part of the celebrations. This was in accord with a government decree issued in 1958 limiting the display of religious flags to homes and places of worship on religious holidays. Loosely observed in the past, it had been ignored completely by the Catholics during their own religious holidays. Although the demonstration was peaceful, the province chief ordered a Civil Guard unit and some army troops to disband the crowd. A grenade exploded, killing four children and one woman. The crowd panicked and was apparently fired on by the Civil Guard; tear gas was thrown. Some people were trampled, others were run over by one of the armored cars on the scene. Altogether eight civilians were killed and about fifteen wounded.

The next day, an orderly crowd of about five to six thousand Buddhists met at the main pagoda in Hue. A manifesto demanded that the government's order against the flying of Buddhist flags be rescinded; that Buddhists be allowed to enjoy a special regime like that afforded to the Catholics under a decree of Emperor Bao Dai, still in effect; that the government stop any arrests of Buddhist followers; that Buddhist bonzes and the faithful be allowed freedom to preach and observe their religion; and that families of the victims of the riot be compensated and the instigators of the killings punished. The manifesto stated that the five signatory bonzes were prepared to make sacrifices until their demands were realized. The province chief addressed the crowd, expressing regret and declaring that the government was ready to guarantee payments to victims' families. He was reportedly cheered, and the order concerning the flags was blamed on Bao Dai. The American consul in Hue, John Helble, thought the crisis might be nearing an end.

After an unsatisfactory meeting with a government representative, however, the Buddhist leaders took their demands directly to President Diem in Saigon. Diem reportedly responded to the first demand by saying he supported the intent of the 1958 decree, which was to subordinate all religious flags to the national flag. He promised to investigate giving the Buddhists the same land-ownership rights as the Catholic Church, whose privileges had been protected by Bao Dai's decree. Diem said suspending the practice of arrests could be exploited by subversive elements. Buddhists' rights to worship and propagate their creed, Diem said, were guaranteed by the constitution; any suppression of it should be reported to the authorities. To the fifth and last point of the manifesto, he promised financial aid to the affected families. While technically correct, these were impolitic answers.

Behind the scenes, Diem's brother, Bishop Thuc, was insisting on a hard line from the beginning, as was Nhu, while the role of Ngo Dinh Can, the political power in central Vietnam, seemed ambiguous. Nolting discussed the problem directly with Diem on May 18, urging that an independent investigative commission be established as a face-saving way out. At that meeting he learned that Diem believed the Buddhist leaders had provoked the incident and that the grenade deaths had been caused by the VC or other dissidents, not by the government.[2]

THE CRISIS WORSENS

Incomprehensibly, Ambassador Nolting left Saigon for home leave on May 23. I was thunderstruck when I learned about it from Bill Trueheart, and I expressed unease. Bill said Nolting was very tired, had long postponed his leave, and thought the crisis was on the way to resolution. But as Nolting later said, he "could not have made a worse mistake."[3]

After I saw President Diem about the funding crisis on May 27, I had asked Vo Van Hai about the Buddhists. He hoped that it could be resolved. He thought the Buddhists were reasonable if handled correctly but that Nhu and Thuc were pressing Diem to take a hard line. He had been urging a soft approach, to no avail. Then he said in words I would never forget, "If one hundred people came to Diem and called something white and Nhu called it black, Diem would believe Nhu." I looked at him incredulously and asked if he really meant that. He did. I began to think we were in for real trouble. We had no one on the inside of Diem's decision making.

After an initial period of calm, tensions between the Buddhists and the government began to rise despite a government communiqué on May 29 affirming freedom of religion. Adding to government irritation, the Buddhists were beginning to make their case internationally. David Halberstam published a story in the *New York Times* on May 15 saying Diem had called the Buddhists "damn fools" for asking for religious freedom when it was guaranteed by the constitution. Diem took this as a personal insult. Meanwhile Buddhist monks in Hue, including Thich Tri Quang, went on a hunger strike, and on the first of June large crowds of Buddhists assembled at the main pagoda in that city to protest, though they dispersed peacefully. Protests continued despite the government's communiqué and despite the replacement of the government's regional delegate as well as the Thua Thien (Hue) province chief and his deputy. On June 3, martial law was declared in Hue after tear gas dispersed various demonstrations, causing some nonlethal casualties—the tear gas used was an older French variety with a blistering effect.

Finally, on June 4, a commission was appointed by President Diem to find an overall solution. Diem dispatched Colonel Chau, the province chief of Kien Hoa, to Danang to relieve the mayor, whose ineptness was causing problems. Chau was a Buddhist in good standing and with personal connections to Buddhist leaders in central Vietnam. When he asked Diem for instructions, he was told to do what he thought was right. (According to Chau's later accounts, he was able not only to negotiate a settlement with the Buddhists in Danang and its surrounding province but to assist in creating an overall accord by influencing the central Vietnam Buddhist association. He would blame Diem's brothers, Bishop Thuc and Nhu, for sabotaging the process.)

An accord was reached in private discussions between Secretary of Defense Nguyen Dinh Thuan, representing President Diem and Thich Tien Minh, head of the central Vietnam Buddhist association. Minh went back to central Vietnam and was expected to return in a few days accompanied by the patriarch, Thich Tien Khiet, to meet with Diem, after which the accord would be published. On June 8, Madame Nhu's Women's Solidarity Movement issued a statement castigating the Buddhists. This delayed any announcement of the accord, although Diem apparently had never approved or known about the statement beforehand. Then on June 11, a Buddhist bonze burned himself to death in Saigon, an act captured in a photograph that received worldwide circulation. The USIS chief, John Mecklin, characterized it as having "a shock effect of incalculable value to the Buddhist cause," as becoming "a symbol of the state of things in Vietnam."[4] Despite the burning, less than a week later the Interministerial Committee and the Buddhist delegation issued a joint communiqué that addressed the original five Buddhist demands. The government agreed to form a committee to examine Buddhist complaints and another committee to determine who was responsible for the incidents of May 8 and to punish those responsible. An informal two-week truce went into effect to demonstrate good faith on both sides. Beneath the surface, however, positions had hardened.

On June 11, Roger Hilsman, now the assistant secretary of state for the Far East, instructed Trueheart to tell Diem the United States would publicly disassociate itself from his government unless it "fully and unequivocally meet[s] Buddhist demands."[5] Trueheart gave Diem a paraphrase of this cable the next day, with the threat in it. (When President Kennedy found out, he ordered that no further threats were to be made and no formal statement issued without his approval.)[6] Then there was a leak in Washington to the *New York Times* that the American government had warned Diem it would publicly condemn his treatment of the Buddhists unless he addressed their grievances. This caused a storm at the palace, which was not about to show it was responding to such overt American pressure. Nevertheless, the joint communiqué was released on June 16.

Hilsman again cabled Trueheart on June 19, expressing displeasure over the joint communiqué and recommending a "hard hitting" demarche to Diem with a series of points, including the resurrection of an old demand for "broadening" his government. Trueheart met with Diem on June 22 and gave him a paper simply conveying Hilsman's instructions. Its tone was one of command, as to not only what Diem should do but how he should do it. which was personally insulting.[7] Earlier the same week, Trueheart had also informed Diem that Nolting was being replaced by Ambassador Henry Cabot Lodge Jr. Afterward, Thuan said Diem thought a new American policy must be in place to force him to do Washington's bidding or unseat him. Diem had said, "They can send ten Lodges, but I will not permit myself or my country to be humiliated, not if they train their artillery on this palace."[8] The distrust and enmity of the Durbrow days had returned in full force. The State Department, mainly Hilsman and W. Averell Harriman, undersecretary of state for political affairs, thought they could move Diem by directly threatening him. Anyone who knew him, however, would understand that it would simply cause him to dig in. For Diem it was a matter of national pride and personal honor. He had refused to take orders from the French; he would refuse to take them from the Americans.

ANOTHER APPEAL FOR LANSDALE

Concern over the downward political spiral provoked me to send Trueheart a memorandum on July 5 urging that General Lansdale be asked to come on "immediate temporary assignment . . . as an official personal advisor to Diem." I had not gotten anywhere previously with Nolting on the same subject, but now communication was almost nonexistent between us and Diem. "There is no other American," I said, "regardless of position or rank, who can evoke the same response from the president or in whom he has any comparable degree of confidence. Our attempts to influence the situation through normal channels seem unsuccessful. General Lansdale, as many of us can attest, has repeatedly demonstrated his ability to cause President Diem to act in accordance with high U.S. policy, when all other appeals . . . were unavailing. I most emphatically recommended his immediate assignment."[9]

In view of Nolting's imminent return, Trueheart didn't think he could act on the recommendation himself. I sent an informal copy by courier to Lansdale in Washington to alert him: "I realize this is unsolicited by you and you may not approve, but it is the only thing I can think of to get us out of the mess we are now in." Trueheart agreed that I could show it to John Mecklin who, in turn, wrote a favorable covering memo for Nolting, who saw it the day after he returned. Mecklin defined the problem as "very nearly narrowed to Diem's individual personality traits, to the need to persuade him at a basic, human level to break out of the neurotic straight jacket in which he seems increasingly to be wrapping himself, and be reasonable. If any man outside the Ngo Dinh family, much less a foreigner, can achieve this, it must be done on a relatively unofficial advisory basis."[10]

It boiled down, as much did in Vietnam, to personal relationships and an understanding of the Vietnamese and of how things worked in that context. Diem had painted himself into a corner and needed effectual help in getting out, particularly in the face of advice from Nhu. The beating he was taking from the United States only served to harden his opinions. Outrage over his treatment by the American press was clouding his vision. Mecklin sent a copy of his and my memo to General Stilwell, who told me he agreed. I had couched my recommendation in insider terms of accomplishing "high U.S. policy," but I really thought it was a chance for something positive to emerge from the complete standoff between us and Diem. Our best interests and those of the Vietnamese were essentially the same.

I saw Secretary Thuan on July 9. He asked how serious I thought the Buddhist crisis was. Very serious, I said, and asked his opinion, "friend to friend and off the record." (It was tacitly understood I would be telling the ambassador about it but no one else.) The president was "completely a prisoner of his own family," Thuan declared, emphasizing the word "completely." No member of the family was giving Diem an even partially true picture. The Nhus, and particularly Bishop Thuc, had such an inflated view of their own importance that they had no idea of how they were hurting the president. The bishop was "medieval in his outlook. The Nhus, particular Mrs. Nhu, have gone out of their minds. Nhu has no conception of reality. The one danger in the present situation not to be dismissed is that Nhu might attempt his own 'coup,' swathed as he is in delusions of grandeur. Several people have tried to tell the president the truth but he is completely deaf to any talk about his family's actions."

Thuan concluded, "The president is going to let the family ruin him; nobody can do anything to prevent it. If this continues the government is doomed unless some miracle occurs, the only question is when. If there is an overthrow it will be chaos, the end of Vietnam." I asked, "What can be done?" "The most useful thing would be to bring General Lansdale back, but the time is not yet ripe." "How do you determine when the time is ripe?"

He thought for a moment and said, "Perhaps Lansdale should be asked to come out immediately." He would discuss this with Ambassador Nolting, who was due back shortly and who, he was sure, would understand and not take it personally.

Nolting returned to Saigon on July 11. My memo to him about Thuan included the words, "Even if events might have passed the stage at which the President could be saved, of which I am not entirely convinced [a bow toward Trueheart, who told me he had absolutely given up on Diem] General Lansdale's presence would still be of the utmost value in helping to put together a new government." I suggested Lansdale be assigned as a personal assistant to the ambassador, working directly for him. Nolting seemed at last favorable to the idea.[11]

Mecklin later told me that a request for Lansdale had been forwarded to Washington. Although no such message appears in the official record, it was quoted in a memorandum to Hilsman from Paul Kattenburg, director of the Vietnam Working Group in Washington, after a lunch with Lansdale at which he volunteered to go to Saigon. Kattenburg suggested Hilsman speak positively with former senator Henry Cabot Lodge (who would become the new ambassador) about it.[12] It is not known whether the message was ever passed on to Lodge. Lansdale would later say that during the Buddhist crisis he had tried several times, unsuccessfully, to talk to Hilsman. Given that Lansdale felt strongly that a coup against Diem had to be avoided, Hilsman may not have wanted to listen. Yet another request for Lansdale vanished into the Washington ether.

LAST EFFORTS

On July 18, President Diem broadcast a conciliatory message directing the Interministerial Committee to cooperate closely with the Buddhist delegation in settling all complaints. All government personnel were ordered to contribute actively to its implementation. As a next step, the Interministerial Committee proposed a joint government-Buddhist commission to investigate Buddhist claims. Although there were a few disturbances, relative calm ensued; the barricades around the pagodas were lifted in Saigon and Hue, and arrested Buddhists began to be released.

The next day, unrelated to the Buddhist affair, I saw President Diem to give him our June progress report on the Strategic Hamlet Program. I told him I had just been to Phu Yen, Quang Tri, and Thua Tien, where the Strategic Hamlet Program was continuing to make progress. Pigs had been distributed even to the most remote hamlets. He beamed at that, the only time he smiled during the entire meeting, except when he greeted me and said goodbye. I said that the population certainly appeared pleased but that I was concerned that many of the farmers I had seen were wearing small pieces of saffron cloth (the color of Buddhist robes). He didn't respond. I gave him the promised report, which he indicated he would carefully read.

Then, as if he had been reading my mind, he said, "So much depends on the province chief in carrying out the hamlet program." He launched into a detailed discussion of several province chiefs, their shortcomings and problems, and then talked about how difficult it was to find good ones: "Civilians tend to be too afraid or regulation bound while the military are often too inflexible with the population, directing instead of persuading." He had recently replaced three province chiefs, whom he named. (The three he had replaced *should* have been replaced, from what we knew about them.)

Abruptly, he changed the mood and began a bitter denunciation of the American press. He could not understand why Vietnam had to be humiliated, particularly when it was one of the true friends the United States had in Asia; correspondents didn't treat Burma, Indonesia, or Cambodia that way. He asked, parenthetically, why he was now being referred to only as "Roman Catholic President Diem," no longer just "President Diem."

I nodded sympathetically. The cultural divide between the American press and Diem seemed unbridgeable; both had become radioactive. When I thought about it afterward I was not sure any other Vietnamese government would have fared much better with the American press. Its inclination to focus on what the Americans were doing and then, mainly, on Vietnamese shortcomings, actual and perceived, not only treaded on the nationalistic sensitivities of the Vietnamese but was the antithesis of their cultural code of politeness, indirectness, and public restraint.

Diem went on to a lengthy lecture on the Buddhist problem in general, with the conclusion that Buddhism had very little political support and much of that communist inspired. "Buddhist actions are the ultimate in ingratitude. Under my government more Buddhist temples have been built than in the previous twenty or thirty years and this government has been the first to contribute to the construction of Buddhist temples." (The latter was true, I thought, but now irrelevant.)

This was followed by a blow-by-blow account of the Buddhist affair. To sum it up: the government had been right and the Buddhists wrong from the beginning. The VC, not the Civil Guard or the army, had set off the plastic charges during the incident in Hue. I said, "No matter what is true, Mr. President, from the information I have it appears that over 95 percent of the population in Thua Thien and Quang Tri provinces believes the government was at fault." (This was an estimate I had gotten from our provincial reps during my recent visit.) "That might have been true right after the incident," he said, "but this is no longer the case. I strongly object to a conciliatory attitude toward the Buddhists while they are systematically trying to subvert the government. The government's weak position has been forced on it. The current situation is comparable to the attempted 1960 'paratrooper coup' when Ambassador Durbrow's representations lowered the prestige of the government and almost resulted in its overthrow." (This was evidence of the lingering bitterness over how Durbrow's actions were seen as favoring the 1960 coup, a perception the State Department had adamantly refused to acknowledge.)

I asked the president, "Do you feel you always get the truth from your own people?" He replied, "I do not believe everything I am told and I have my own private sources of information. The Buddhist claim that the government is carrying out mass arrests is only a provocation." "This may be so," I said, "but there are specific incidents of Buddhists being arrested with no apparent cause. A Buddhist monk who left the American embassy was trailed by several policemen who tried to arrest him, so he fled back into the embassy for sanctuary. It created a very bad impression."

Emerging from his depressed mood he asked if I knew what Lansdale was doing. He was still in the Pentagon, I said. "Do you think the ambassador might have any objections to Lansdale's coming out to Vietnam again if it could be arranged?" "I discussed it with Nolting," I said. "He seems favorable to the idea." "What do you think General Harkin's reaction might be?" "I don't know," I replied, "but I don't think he would object, because Lansdale, if he came, would not be concerned with military affairs."

I reported the meeting to Ambassador Nolting, commenting that Diem was convinced that he was being kept informed accurately (which he was not) and in the minutest detail (which he seemed to be). He felt that his sincere efforts to satisfy just claims were being willfully disregarded by enemies manipulating the Buddhists, misinterpreted by Western newsmen because of animosity against him, and that their distortions were given too much credence by the American government. Negative stories in the *Times of Vietnam* seemed an accurate reflection of his views. "Despite his obvious friendliness throughout the conversation toward me personally," I said, "it was most depressing to find him with his mind so closed, and so convinced he was being unfairly treated."[13] Diem's heart was clearly not in his conciliatory public statement of the day before. If anything was to come of it, something had to give soon on both sides.

At our meeting on July 9, Thuan had asked if I could talk to General Van Thanh Cao about the Buddhist crisis. Cao was involved in mediating with the Buddhists; as a Cao Dai, he was considered reasonably neutral by both sides. Curiously, I had gotten a call from Cao around the same time asking for me. When I saw Cao, he had just come from an informal meeting of most of the Vietnamese army generals with Ngo Dinh Nhu. Nhu had discussed the Buddhist problem very frankly, admitted the government had made mistakes and soliciting the cooperation of the generals in overcoming the crisis. Nhu had characterized Ngo Dinh Can's handling of the situation in Hue as "stupid" and had criticized Bishop Thuc. Cao believed Nhu had concluded the government's situation was desperate and that it had to change tactics. What Nhu had to say, Cao thought, was generally well received.[14] Afterward we discussed ideas on handling the Buddhists. I knew Cao was not accepted as a "member of the club" by the other generals and that accordingly his opinions were based on overt reactions he observed. Other sources agreed on the substance of the meeting but ranged in reaction from downright hostility to receptivity. It was clear Nhu was trying to co-opt the generals. According to General Kim, Nhu had even said he would not blame the generals if they were thinking of a coup; he would be with them.

In another meeting with Thuan on 20 July, I told him what Diem had said to me about the Buddhists. He replied that Diem had been forced to make his reconciliation statement and that indeed his heart wasn't in it. General Cao was to be named as the secretary of the proposed joint government-Buddhist investigative commission, if it got off the ground. Had we, Cao and I, come up with any ideas on how to get the commission going? As an immediate move, I suggested that a permanent secretary be named for the existing Interministerial Committee and that the committee begins its own independent investigation without waiting for the joint commission. The permanent secretary should have his own staff, office, and an airplane at his disposal. Buddhists and newsmen could be invited to join him on trips to investigate Buddhist complaints. It was a way to get the whole matter out in the open to show good faith. Cao was willing to serve as the permanent secretary. Thuan asked for something in writing, which I subsequently got to him before the end of July.[15] Thuan told me later that he discussed it with the president but that Nhu's idea of a crackdown killed it.

Without much hope, and as a final shot in the dark, I drafted a letter, at Vo Van Hai's suggestion, for Diem to ask President Kennedy for Lansdale directly.[16] Later Hai told me Diem had almost sent the letter, but Nhu was against it. Except for this last salvage attempt, I kept Nolting verbally informed of what I was doing. I remember him expressing discouragement at the cryptic and tepid public support from Washington for Diem's July 18 conciliatory statement. George Ball (under secretary of state for economic affairs), Harriman, and Hilsman were not interested in supporting Nolting. In fact, Harriman had angrily suggested to Hilsman on August 1 that he be recalled "at once."[17] The official policy was wait and see, which had the effect of supporting the Buddhists, whose objective by this time was clearly the Diem government's overthrow.

I was intensely frustrated by my inability to change the course of events. It was perhaps too much to expect, from a second-ranking position in the AID mission with no real authority, but the need was so tangible that I had to try.

RUNNING RURAL AFFAIRS

While intervening where I could in the Buddhist crisis, I remained busy with Rural Affairs, getting out to the provinces as often as I could. One trip to central Vietnam was particularly memorable. Using an Air America plane, capable of short-field takeoffs and landing, on informal loan from Lou Conein, I stopped in Phu Yen, where Burns took me to see a new combat hamlet on the edge of the pacified zone. Besides Burns' Vietnamese bodyguards (assigned by the province chief, over Burns' objections, and whom he humorously nicknamed Matthew, Mark, Luke, and John), we were accompanied by the province chief and a few provincial Civil Guard troops. Approaching the hamlet we received scattered shots from a distant tree line. The next thing I knew I was in a roadside ditch with Burns on top of me. "For God's sake, Bob," I yelled, "get off of me and shoot somebody!" He looked at me and said, "I don't want to lose my source of funding." Nobody was hit. The rest of the visit went without incident. It was the only time I was fired at, except for some routine VC potshots at helicopters and planes.

After Tuy Hoa, I flew to the northernmost South Vietnamese provinces, Thua Thien and Quang Tri, to inspect some of the more remote strategic hamlets off the main coastal highway. We landed in rice paddies, still dry because the rains had not yet come, where we were met by small provincial delegations. At one remote hamlet in Thua Thien, nestled against the mountains, I was greeted by an elderly hamlet chief; he was tall and gaunt, with a wispy goatee, wearing a long, black formal gown, and a fierce look. I explained that I was there to find out his economic needs. He looked at me for a moment and said, "Never mind our economic needs, what we really need are guns. All we have are a few French rifles and old shotguns. The VC are better armed." I tried turning the discussion back to economic development, but he would have none of it, repeating emphatically, "Guns, more guns, better guns." I gave in, saying, "Okay, we will help you." I had no direct source of arms but thought Lou Conein might. When I got back to Saigon I went directly to Lou's house and told him about the old guy, whose image I could not get out of my mind. I needed Lou's help to honor my promise. After a spate of swearing about being nothing but a "goddam arms merchant"—"Don't expect me to go around arming hamlet militia"—Lou said he would get the old guy some carbines, which he did.

Meeting the old man and seeing the fire in his eyes was an elemental reminder of why we were there. It was a feeling shared by most of us who worked directly with the Vietnamese in the provinces and hamlets. We felt duty bound to honor their will to resist.

In May and June, six new provincial reps arrived, including two newly minted Foreign Service officers, Vladimir Lehovich and Richard Holbrooke, the first to serve with Rural Affairs. Not knowing what to expect, they arrived at the Saigon airport in coats and ties, which Ralph Boynton, our administrative officer, told them to take off. "Rural Affairs," he declared was, "a shirt-sleeves outfit, a can-do operation." Holbrooke was somewhat brash and outspoken but obviously very bright. Lehovich was quieter, seemed more thoughtful, and spoke excellent French (his father and mother had been White Russian émigrés to the United States). Both had taken six months of Vietnamese language training in Washington, but were not yet fluent. I thought the action orientation of Rural Affairs would be great experience for the Foreign Service and took a special interest in these first two. As a way of getting their feet wet I initially assigned them as assistants to two of our area reps.

I learned that Bob Friedman, assigned to Ba Xuyen (Soctrang) in the southern Delta, was completely at odds with Lieutenant Colonel Chieu, the province chief. Chieu, withdrawn and remote, kept Friedman at arm's length and seemed uninterested in anything except the mechanical hamlet-building part of the program. I visited Chieu to see if I could patch up the situation, but I came away annoyed with his attitude. Usually I could get through the characteristic Vietnamese reserve of province chiefs to make a human connection, but not with him. I was determined to pull Friedman out, but the province was too important to leave unattended. Holbrooke volunteered for the job, and I decided to send him. He was only twenty-two, much younger than Friedman, but I figured his youth and his brashness would be advantages. It was also a way of sending a message to Chieu. Holbrooke did well despite Chieu, and so did Lehovich who would later take over a province in the Delta.

Around this time Rural Affairs was visited by two State Department inspectors from Washington who wanted to perform an end-use audit of our program in one of the provinces. It was obviously important that they get an accurate view. Where best to send them? Phu Yen had the most advanced and widely varied development and agricultural programs, but Burns' no-nonsense personality and unconventional take on things was a risk. I wasn't certain how the inspectors would react. Still, I thought, progress there might speak for itself.[18] I had been struck the last time I had visited not by the statistics of progress, however impressive, but by the population's high morale.

When the inspectors returned after three days in Phu Yen, they had a story to tell. On their first day, after a morning briefing, a visit to a nearby hamlet, and lunch, Burns had taken them to a combat hamlet on the edge of the secure zone, where the pig program was already in full swing. The hamlet's pig pens were so constructed that all of their waste was washed into two large pits to ferment until it was ready to be spread on the fields as fertilizer. The pits were now full, and one needed to be emptied, in which the waste had cooked enough to be spread as fertilizer. Little had been done about it except by one Vietnamese, who was already shoveling.

"Who's that?" the inspectors asked. "The province chief," Burns replied. "You guys have to help us; we've got to get this done before dark or the VC might get us." With that, Burns took extra shovels from the back of his jeep, gave one to each of the inspectors, took one for himself, jumped into the pit, and began shoveling. The inspectors had little choice but to take off their ties and coats and join in. They described this to me with great enthusiasm, saying it was "the first time we ever saw American aid personnel and their counterparts getting their hands dirty really doing something for rural people." They went on to talk about the other hamlets visited, the schools and self-help projects they had seen, but what really excited them was shoveling out that pit. It sounded like an epiphany. I wanted to laugh out loud. Who else but Burns could make a couple of crusty, straight-laced inspectors from Washington happy shoveling pig shit in their street clothes?

My own future with Rural Affairs was becoming uncertain, however. I was now too deeply involved to want to leave, but I had been hearing from my mother that my father was ill, without any details. Then I got a letter from him saying he was better but reminding me of my promise, the anniversary of which was September 25. He needed me to take over the family business. I had been so occupied between Rural Affairs and the Buddhist crisis that I had not given it much thought, but now I was faced with a decision. I didn't want to go back, but I had to talk to him. While Rural Affairs had made great progress and could very well have carried on without me in more normal circumstances, the fragility of the Diem government made my personal relationships with key Vietnamese an important consideration. I wrote Stoneman explaining my dilemma and suggesting I come back to Washington to talk about my future. Stoneman agreed that I should return, leaving the timing up to me.

THE RAID ON THE PAGODAS

By August 15, as Ambassador Nolting was preparing to leave, to be replaced by Henry Cabot Lodge, conciliation was still not working. The government didn't trust the Buddhists, and vice versa. Though Nhu had told Nolting he supported a conciliatory line, in fact he was working behind the scenes to undermine it and clearly had the upper hand with Diem. Nhu was also maneuvering the Vietnamese army into supporting a confrontation. Madame Nhu told CBS-TV in an interview that aired on August 1 that all the Buddhists had done was "barbecue a bonze with imported gasoline." This was repeated in the international press and was followed by a Reuters dispatch on August 3 saying Nhu was threatening to crush the Buddhists at the Xa Loi Pagoda (the center of Buddhist agitation in Saigon and the base of the main agitator, Thich Tri Quang). A showdown was in the offing, but Diem, according to Nolting, had promised not to take violent action. He had, at Nolting's urging, given an interview to Marguerite Higgins of the *New York Herald Tribune;* her article, published on August 15, the day Nolting left, quoted Diem as saying, "The policy of utmost reconciliation is irreversible."

A brief and deceptive calm seemed to come over Saigon. Although the Buddhists continued to agitate, self-immolations occurred in the provinces, and one girl in Saigon reportedly chopped off her own hand in protest, previously arrested Buddhists were being released. On August 20, however, a critical meeting took place at the presidential palace. Vietnamese army generals, apparently alarmed by what appeared to be government indecisiveness, met with President Diem and Counselor Nhu to urge martial law, with the intent of peacefully returning the monks who had assembled in Saigon back to their home provinces and keeping them there.

I was awakened early in the morning of August 21 by our houseboy, Dung; someone was at our gate with a message for me. It was Director Brent's driver; the note said that Brent had been told by the Marine guard at USOM headquarters that the streets were barricaded around the Xa Loi Pagoda, access to the USOM building was blocked, and the streets were full of soldiers and police. Brent's home telephone line had been cut, as had those of all top U.S. civilian officials. My telephone was still working, so I called Bert Fraleigh at home to advise the other Rural Affairs personnel who were in Saigon to stay home.

My USOM car was always parked in our carport overnight, so when my driver, Binh, showed up about at eight for my usual drive to USOM, I told him to take me instead to the embassy, as fast as he could. As we exited our driveway, I noticed policemen guarding the entrance to the Buddhist temple next door. At the embassy, there was some confusion, but the word was that the government had declared martial law in the middle of the night and early in the morning had raided the pagodas where supposed agitators were hiding. The main objective in Saigon was Xa Loi, where a large number of monks had been arrested. Some had been hurt. Two monks had escaped and were holed up in the USOM building, where they were requesting asylum. No Americans had been informed in advance, and no one at that point understood what was going on. I briefly saw Trueheart, who was shaking his head and saying,

"Now the fat's really in the fire." The pagoda raids sent shock waves through the local American mission, and also through Washington, where it was seen as a complete breach of Diem's promise of reconciliation to Nolting. The conclusion drawn was that Diem and Nhu had decided to present Ambassador Lodge with a fait accompli. The Vietnamese started pressing the USOM mission to disgorge the two monks who had taken refuge there; Trueheart stalled for time. I went back home to await further developments.

Word about the raids would reach Ambassador Lodge by phone from Washington on August 21 after he had gone to bed in Tokyo, where he had stopped en route to Saigon. Lodge detested long flights and had contemplated a leisurely trip to Vietnam via Hong Kong, but now he would fly by American military plane direct to Saigon, arriving late in the evening of the twenty-second. The best aircraft the military could find was a prop-driven Lockheed Constellation, which took nine hours to make the trip. In Saigon, we were all waiting for the American shoe to drop. Ambassador Nolting was in Honolulu, on his way home. When he heard about the raids he was so shocked that he sent a personal telegram to President Diem: "This is the first time that you've ever gone back on your word to me."

Long after, Nolting would see Nguyen Dinh Thuan in Paris. Thuan told him he had taken the telegram to Diem. Diem had shaken his head when he read it, saying, "He doesn't know what the provocation was."[19] I would later hear from various sources that the supposed provocation constituted reports by Nhu that the Buddhists were stockpiling arms inside Xa Loi, which was untrue.

Chapter 12
Ambassador Lodge Intervenes

I did not know Lodge or his people, but the day following his arrival I received an early morning telephone call from one of Lodge's aides, Frederick "Freddy" Flott asking if he and Lt. Col. John Michael "Mike" Dunn, Lodge's other assistant, could come to see me urgently—he repeated "urgently." I suggested they come for lunch.

Flott and Dunn were an odd pair. Flott was a career Foreign Service officer, part of the "Eastern Establishment," and a friend of Lodge's son, George. George had asked Flott to consider going with Lodge as his personal assistant. Lodge was leery of trusting the regular Foreign Service and was looking for someone who would be personally loyal, along with having good connections within and outside the service. Flott's fluent French was an added attraction. Flott had a pleasant but vague diplomatic manner about him, a seemingly dilettant-ish air. His demeanor was a contrast to the intensity of Dunn, a streetwise, black haired, blue-eyed Irish-American with a sharp sense of humor and considerable charm. He was a regular army officer on detached service with Lodge, dressed as a civilian. Lodge had served as a reserve major general in the Pentagon, where Dunn had been assigned to assist him. Dunn impressed me as more of a tough political "pol" than a typical army officer. From the start, it was apparent he was the go-to guy for Lodge. Dunn would serve as Lodge's principal source of political intelligence, his gatekeeper and administrative enforcer, and his hatchet man when necessary.

According to Dunn, Lansdale had described me to Lodge as one of the few Americans in Saigon really close to the Vietnamese. "Lodge wants to know," he said, "what the hell is going on?" How had the raid on the pagodas come about, who was involved, who was responsible, and what did the army and other key civilian leaders think? I sketched out the Vietnamese I knew well. Dunn asked me to contact the most knowledgeable and influential. "Has Lodge talked to the CIA station?" I asked. He said yes, but Lodge wanted to hear from me. Dunn gave off a fleeting whiff of distrust at my reference to the station. I said I would do whatever I could to help. Dunn asked me to write up any meetings as "Eyes Only" memos for Lodge, classify them "Secret" or higher, and deliver them only to him, Dunn; he would get them to Lodge.

This was the beginning of a more intimate involvement with Ambassador Lodge than I had reckoned on, but I welcomed it as a chance to affect how we dealt with the crisis and the Vietnamese. The entire counterinsurgency effort against the Viet Cong, everything we were trying to do through Rural Affairs, depended on the Vietnamese government's being able to surmount this crisis. I knew in my gut that it had reached a nearly untenable stage. Whatever I learned, I assured Dunn, would be presented accurately, recounting exactly what the Vietnamese told me, pulling no punches. He said that was what Lodge wanted. Immediately,

I called General Kim's home and spoke to his wife, Gaby, saying I would like to see Kim as soon as possible. Soon after, Gaby called back, inviting me out to their house that evening. I also called Defense Secretary Nguyen Dinh Thuan at his office and was invited to his house for breakfast early the next day.

General Kim was extremely upset with Ngo Dinh Nhu and the raid on the pagodas. He said bitterly that the army was now "acting as Nhu's puppet"; Nhu had tricked it into establishing martial law. "The army knew nothing of the plans to raid Xa Loi and the other pagodas. This was carried out by Colonel Tung's Special Forces and the Combat Police on Nhu's orders." Kim said that 1,426 monks and laymen had been arrested and that the explosives and arms found in the pagodas had been planted. Nhu was now in direct control.

According to Kim, Nhu had deliberately split the army command between General Tran Van Don, General Ton That Dinh, and Colonel Tung. While Don nominally commanded everything outside of Saigon, the corps commanders had de facto control of the forces in their areas, while Dinh now commanded the regular troops in Saigon, including the 5th Division north of the capital, and Tung had separate command over the Special Forces, which were mostly in Saigon. General Don did not enjoy much natural support among the officer corps, but most of the generals and other senior officers could be expected to rally around him.

Kim said, "The key question is where does the U.S. stand? If the U.S. takes a clear stand against the Nhus and in support of army action to remove them from the government, the army, with the exception of Colonel Tung, will unite in support of such an action and would be able to carry it out." Even though he personally did not like him, Kim said, "retaining the president would be preferable providing all Ngo family influence could be permanently and effectively eradicated." He and seven other generals had been obliged to sign an oath of loyalty to President Diem, pledging full support of government actions against the Buddhists. The United States must not be fooled: the vast majority did not approve repressing the Buddhists in this manner but had to sign or expose themselves to individual elimination by Nhu.[1]

The next morning I had breakfast with Thuan. Never had I seen him so distressed. First, he asked, "What do you think of Lodge?" I hadn't met him yet, I replied, but was in close contact with his two aides. "I have decided not to resign yet," Thuan said. "I am sticking with the president for three reasons: my personal feelings of loyalty, the safety of my family, who are all in Saigon, and the fact that the president at his own volition sent Madame Nhu a letter ordering her to make no public statements and give no press conferences."

It would be difficult to split the Nhus from Diem, but Thuan felt strongly the United States should attempt this. "I see no alternative to Diem as the leader of Vietnam. The Americans have to lead and be firm, otherwise chaos will ensue. Under no circumstances should you acquiesce in what the Nhus have done. Nhu is in a dangerously triumphant mood, believing he is in full control, and is contemptuous of the Americans. He has successfully tricked the army by dividing it into three commands while hiding his plans for raiding the pagodas. Nhu, however, has very little support in the army. The army will turn against him if it knows the U.S. will not support a government with the Nhus in control. The U.S. must not be afraid of leaving the door open to the communists by withdrawing support from the government so long as it contains the Nhus." The United States, Thuan reiterated, had to be firm. If it was, the army would respond.[2]

I wrote up both meetings rapidly, classified the memos "Secret, Most Sensitive," stamped them "Eyes Only," and hand-carried them to Dunn at the embassy. I figured Lodge would read them and call me in for a talk. Afterward I learned that my meeting with Thuan had been converted in its entirety into a cable and sent with "Operational Immediate" precedence to Washington on August 24, about an hour after I had delivered it. This was followed by another cable transmitting the full text of my meeting with Kim. Hilsman would later cite my meeting with Thuan in his book *To Move a Nation* as "perhaps the most convincing judgment of all" about Vietnamese dissatisfaction with Nhu's campaign against the Buddhists.[3] I had no idea that it would serve as part of his rationale for the controversial cable from Washington that followed.

On the same day, Lodge sent another cable to Washington describing a meeting of Lou Conein with General Don confirming what General Kim had told me. These three cables were followed on the same day by another message from Lodge saying that a "suggestion had been made that all the U.S. needed to do was encourage the generals that it would be happy to see Diem and/or Nhus go, and deed would be done." I never knew who made this suggestion. I told Dunn verbally that something had to be done, I thought, to get the Nhus out of the country. Lodge's cable expressed caution, saying the "situation is not so simple." It went on, "Action on our part in these circumstances would seem to be a shot in the dark. Situation does not call for that, in my judgment, and I believe we should bide our time, continuing to watch situation closely."[4]

GREEN LIGHT FOR A COUP

The green light to the Vietnamese generals for a coup came in an ambiguous and subsequently contentious cable from Washington to Lodge, drafted by Assistant Secretary of State Roger Hilsman and sent over the weekend, on August 24. At the time, most high-level officials of the Kennedy administration were on vacation. President Kennedy was at Hyannis Port. In a memo to the president requesting his approval for the cable, Mike Forrestal, of the NSC, acknowledged that Lodge had recommended a "wait and see" position on what to do about the pagoda raids but that Harriman, Hilsman, Forrestal, and Ball at this point recommended taking action "now," as indicated by the proposed cable. The cable put forth two seemingly contradictory proposals for action. Lodge was instructed that "Diem must be given a chance to rid himself of Nhu and his coterie" and to offer Diem a "reasonable opportunity to remove [the] Nhus"; on the other hand, "You may also tell appropriate military commanders we will give them direct support in any interim period of breakdown of [the] central government mechanism." General Taylor and Secretary McNamara would vehemently object that the cable had never been cleared with them. As events were to show, its implications had not been thought through. General Taylor felt the message was insufficiently explicit, did not give Diem an adequate chance to do what was wanted, and reflected "the well-known compulsion of Hilsman and Forrestal to depose Diem." In his autobiography, *Swords and Plowshares,* Taylor would call it an "end run."[5]

Lodge's response on August 25 chose to ignore the language giving Diem a chance, stating that the "chances of Diem meeting our demands [are] virtually nil" and proposing instead that "we go straight to [the] Generals with our demands, without informing Diem," telling them that "we [are] prepared to have Diem without Nhus but it is in effect up to them whether to keep him." (What caused Lodge to change his mind from the hesitation of his previous cautionary message never became clear.) Lodge went on to request that his previous instructions be modified along these lines, saying General Harkins concurred.[6] An immediate cable came back from Acting Secretary of State George Ball agreeing with Lodge.[7] Whether the cable was formally cleared by Kennedy is also not clear. General Harkins, who came under some pressure from General Taylor in Washington not to support a coup, was to claim later that he had not clearly understood the original cable of the twenty-fourth, that he had thought Washington had already made up its mind in favor of a coup and was asking him to follow orders.

FIRING UP A LIGHTNING COUP

I was completely in the dark at the time. I was called to the embassy by Mike Dunn on August 26 and found Lou Conein in his office waiting for me. Dunn told us that Washington—he implied the president—had ordered Lodge to encourage the generals to mount a lightning coup. When I asked what about Diem, he said the generals were to be told it was up to them whether Diem stayed or not. I was appalled at the lack of significance attached to Diem. This was not what Thuan wanted, nor was it what General Don wanted, according to Conein. Dunn said the instructions were unambiguous. The principal message-bearer to the generals was to be Conein; I was to help him in any way I could.

Lou asked if I was willing to vouch for him personally with General Kim as someone Kim could trust. Kim was probably the best person to arrange for him to talk to General Minh.[8] Faced with going along with what appeared to be a clear set of orders from President Kennedy, however uncomfortable they made me, or taking myself out of any further chance to influence events, I agreed to help Conein. Dunn ushered me in to meet Lodge (Conein had already met him). Lodge was very cordial. He got up from behind his desk, shook my hand and said cryptically, "I'm counting on you." Dunn ushered me out.

After the meeting I called Kim's wife at home and arranged to come to his house that night. I said I was bringing a friend I wanted Kim to meet. Conein and I drove out near Kim's house, on the side of the officer's golf course close to the Tan Son Nhut Airport, parking some distance away. Kim came to the door. We met in a side room. I told Kim that Lou was a personal friend whose trustworthiness I could absolutely vouch for and that he had an important message from Ambassador Lodge. Then I left the room and waited for Lou on Kim's veranda overlooking the golf course. Lou's only comment, as we drove back to town, was that he appreciated my help, that Kim appeared to have taken his words at face value and would vouch for Lou with General Minh.[9]

Shortly thereafter I had my first chance to talk to Lodge. I was invited over to his house for lunch. Only Mike Dunn was present. Lodge was a tall, handsome man with an impressive air of patrician self-confidence. It was clear he felt in command of the situation. From what I had gathered from Trueheart and others, Lodge was very formal and peremptory in his dealings with the agency heads. He had very quickly established himself as the absolute boss, moving offices, changing titles, and issuing commands. The brass plate on his office door no longer read "Ambassador" but rather "Mr. Lodge." With me, perhaps because I was younger, he was informal and very friendly, inquiring about my wife, whom he had heard was a most charming young woman from Chile, and about our two children. Lansdale, whom he admired, had given him a very good report on me. He was relying on me to keep him accurately informed.

During lunch, Lodge veered into stories, with himself as the main subject. He said his close contact with Eisenhower at the end of the war in Europe had convinced him not only that Eisenhower would make a great president but that he could be persuaded to run as a Republican. When Eisenhower became the president of Columbia University, Lodge had convinced him to run and was thereafter instrumental in ensuring his nomination and managing his campaign. The implication was he thought dealing with the Vietnamese was going to be political child's play compared with what he had done in American politics. There was no direct mention of the coup. He did say he would appreciate any advice I might have on dealing with the Vietnamese—he found them difficult to understand, with their superstitions and reliance on soothsayers. I got the feeling he considered the Vietnamese primitive and not worthy of much respect, although he did not say that in so many words. He asked a few casual questions about the strategic hamlets. The lunch, I sensed, was mainly a charm offensive to impress me and ensure my support and loyalty. I had expected to be asked some searching questions about Diem and Nhu or about the generals and their capabilities, but I was not. I concluded he already thought he knew as much about the Vietnamese as he needed to know, and that he much preferred to talk about himself. With him it sometimes seemed that the "Cabots talk to the Lodges, and the Lodges talk only to God," to paraphrase an old doggerel about the Boston Brahmins.[10]

As a matter of strict need-to-know, which had been drilled into me during my Agency days before I ever got to AID, I told no one about the coup plotting, including Barbara, except Bohannon, on whose clandestine experience I could rely. The only other person in USOM who was aware of some of what I was going on was my secretary, Marguerite Webber, who had a Top Secret clearance. (She typed up all my memos, squirreling away copies in the office combination safe. She was invariably willing to type from my handwriting at all hours, put my handwritten memos in the burn bag, and keep what she did absolutely secret. Her help was invaluable.)

Anxiety hovered over the last days of August. The heat and humidity of the rainy season added to the simmering tension. The suspense was tangible. Would the generals actually organize and start a coup? Would Nhu attempt his own coup? According to the station there were other coups being planned—by Dr. Tran Kim Tuyen, former director of SEPES, the Vietnamese CIA, and separately by Colonel Pham Ngoc Thao with some of the younger Vietnamese officers.

On August 26, Lodge had his first formal meeting with President Diem. Lodge lectured Diem on American politics and the importance of placating American public opinion and the Congress, while Diem justified his actions toward the Buddhists and defended his family. Diem asked for discipline in American actions in Saigon and an end to "diverse activities interfering in Vietnamese affairs." He had just arrived, Lodge replied, and naturally could not know everything that was going on, but he would look into it.

The next day, Lodge met with Ngo Dinh Nhu for an hour. Nhu complained about a Voice of America Broadcast condemning the pagoda raids shortly after they happened. Lodge said he sympathized with U.S. government efforts, emphasizing that we did not support Madame Nhu's inflammatory comments. Nhu expressed the hope that there would be no more statements out of Washington; Lodge hoped there would be no more inflammatory speeches out of Vietnam. Lodge's take on Nhu was that he was ruthless and not wholly rational by our standards, that he was interested above all in the survival of himself and family. While the meeting was superficially cordial, Nhu had certainly not made a favorable impression on Lodge.[11]

"Situation here has reached a point of no return. Saigon is armed camp. Ngo family has dug in for a last ditch battle. It is our considered opinion that general officers cannot retreat now," was CIA chief of station Richardson's melodramatic cable to Washington on August 28.[12] The same day, Tad Szulc reported in the *New York Times*, "Some officials in Washington believe the only solution for the Vietnam crisis was to remove Nhu, or Nhu and Diem if the two brothers were inseparable, by a military coup." This kind of loose-cannon talk from somebody high up in Washington annoyed Lodge, as it brought American support for a coup out in the open, further alerting Nhu and adding to the tension.

On August 30, Nhu met again with the generals. He claimed that the CIA would like to see him out of the way. Local CIA personnel were doing their utmost, he charged, to alienate people from supporting the government, and a mobilization existed aimed at overthrowing the Vietnamese government, supported by secret U.S. government elements. He also said, however, that Ambassador Lodge was now getting a better picture of the situation. "We can manage him," Nhu said, referring to Lodge. "He will fully agree with our concepts and actions."[13] According to one source, he gave the impression the United States would shortly confirm this. It was a warning to the generals.

I learned Kim wanted to see me, this time at his mother-in-law's house, down a small side street inside the city, rather than out at the golf course. Nhu's warnings to the generals were making overt communication between us dangerous for him. I cleared the meeting with Dunn before going. When I arrived, I was surprised to find my old friend Bui Diem there. I had seen Bui Diem earlier in the month informally; we had discussed the Buddhist crisis. I knew he and Kim were close friends, but I had not known that Kim was consulting him politically. Kim first took me aside, asking for reassurance that Conein's dealings with General Minh had had the ambassador's blessing. I assured him they did. Kim said Minh needed help in planning the operation. Conein should contact General Khiem, who was helping Minh.

While making it clear Bui Diem was not involved in coup plotting, Kim said he had asked Bui Diem for political advice. He wanted to assure Lodge that the generals were not considering a military dictatorship. We talked about how a future government might be organized. I suggested that Diem be retained as chief of state, because of his standing as a Vietnamese nationalist, to preserve the constitution as much as possible and to give legality and continuity to any new government. We talked about Vice President Tho taking over day-to-day government functions, at least temporarily; Kim seemed to favor that, but I sensed by his silence that Bui Diem did not. Kim wanted to know if keeping Diem was Lodge's idea. I said, no, it was mine. I was sure Lodge would not object. Kim asked me to work informally with Bui Diem in developing a political platform for a new government should that transpire.[14]

Bui Diem and I met shortly thereafter at his apartment, where he described a basic political program that Kim had generally agreed to. The main points were: a policy of national reconciliation between Catholics and Buddhists, as well as between honest leaders who supported the regime and honest leaders who opposed it; continuation of the war against the VC, including an improved Strategic Hamlet Program; reform of the army and the civil administration; no military dictatorship; and a provisional mixed government of civilians and military, with elections within a year. "What about retaining Diem as chief of state?" I asked. If it wasn't possible, Bui Diem volunteered, under no circumstances should he be harmed. A revolutionary committee of civilians and military should take charge until a provisional government was formed. The military should renounce all political ambitions. He had told Kim his fellow civilian nationalists would never accept a military dictatorship and neither would the Americans.[15]

When I reported back to Lodge, he was not interested in the generals' political plans—he wanted to know if the generals were actually getting on with the coup. I did not tell him about the discussion about retaining President Diem, sensing he would think that out of line. I was unaware at the time that Lodge had completely written off Diem. This was the gist of a cable he had sent to Washington on August 29: "We are launched on a course from which there is no respectable turning back: the overthrow of the Diem government. . . . [T]here is no possibility, in my view, that the war can be won under a Diem administration, still less that Diem or any member of the family can govern the country in a way to gain the support of the people who count, i.e., the educated class in and out of government service, civil and military—not to mention the American people."[16]

In a meeting at the White House on August 29, with President Kennedy participating, the split continued between General Taylor and Secretary McNamara (who urged caution and a return to the policy of pressing Diem to replace Nhu) on one hand, and the State Department, strongly supporting the coup, on the other. After the meeting, but on the same day, President Kennedy sent Lodge a Top Secret "Eyes Only" message reminding Lodge, with an air of anxiety, of the president's constitutional responsibilities and stating, "Until the very moment of the go signal for the operation by the generals, I must reserve a contingent right to change course and reverse previous instructions." Lodge replied that of course he would respect the president's right to change course but pointed out that to be successful, "this operation must be essentially a Vietnamese affair with a momentum of its own. Should this happen you may not be able to control it, i.e., the 'go signal' may be given by the generals."[17] The message from President Kennedy was startling confirmation that Washington had little realistic idea of how things actually worked in Saigon, holding that we should be in direct control of the generals and at the same time that we should be equally able to deny any responsibility.

THE LIGHTNING COUP EVAPORATES

General Harkins tried to meet General Khiem to convey the message that he supported the coup, but Khiem had been putting him off. When Harkins finally met Khiem, on the morning of August 31, he was told that General Minh had called off all coup planning. The generals did not have sufficient forces under their command, compared to those controlled by the president. Also, Khiem said, Minh and others could not put too much stock in Conein's word as representing the position of the United States, since he was in a low Agency post; it would take someone like the ambassador or Harkins to give them complete confidence. When this got back to Conein he was furious, figuring that Harkins had made it up in order to give himself a more influential role.

Lodge, not having much confidence in Harkins, was frantic to find out exactly what had happened, so I was pressed into service again. I saw General Kim alone at the same house in town, this time taking some additional precautions to be sure I was not being surveilled. I never thought I was in any particular danger but found it ironic that suddenly I was more involved in covert activity as an AID employee, with Lodge acting as my station chief, than I had been during most of my career in the CIA.

The coup had indeed been called off, Kim said. Clearly anticipating an attempt, Nhu had put Tung's Special Forces on full alert, and those units were in a position to prevent any coup from succeeding. Was Kim aware, I asked, that Harkins had seen General Khiem that same morning, that Khiem had told Harkins all planning had ceased, and that perhaps the best solution was for Nhu to become prime minister, in exchange for more authority for the army? Kim was vehement that Khiem had not spoken for the rest of the generals. Under no circumstances was Nhu acceptable. He did not know why Khiem had made such statements. He would check immediately with General Minh, whom he would try to bring to a meeting that evening with Colonel Conein and me to confirm that Khiem was not speaking for him. I agreed to the meeting but pointed out that Lodge now seemed convinced the generals lacked the will for a coup and that it might be necessary to continue supporting the present administration, which meant the Nhus. (Lodge had instructed me to say this). The best way of clarifying the situation was for Minh to speak to Harkins. Kim's response was that Minh, if he spoke to anyone at that level, would only speak to Lodge: "We don't trust Harkins." (I kept this out of my written report to Lodge, but I told Dunn.) Kim and I agreed to meet again at eight that evening.

Conein and I saw Dunn at Lodge's residence, where Lodge was dressing for dinner. Dunn disappeared briefly to talk to Lodge and came back saying that a meeting with Lodge was not advisable but that I should see Kim, accompanied by Conein. At his mother's house, Kim was even more concerned about security; he asked Lou to stand guard by a window where he could see if anyone was coming. Minh could not come but had asked Kim to explain why the coup had been called off. Because of Nhu's knowledge of the generals' intentions and his putting Tung's forces on alert, he declared, it was not possible to do anything at the moment without courting disaster. This did not mean that planning was discontinued or that Minh was not determined to go ahead. Under no circumstances was Nhu acceptable. Minh was sorry the Americans believed the generals lacked the will. "They did not, but at the moment they lacked the means." The Americans had given so much support to Nhu in the past that it was impossible to organize a counteraction in a few days. As far as most Vietnamese officers saw, the United States still supported the present government. Words to the contrary had been said, but there were no actions to back up the words. As a result the whole operation rested upon his own word and that of a few others. That was not enough for immediate action. Minh said he understood why it was not feasible to talk with the ambassador, but he did not wish to speak to General Harkins.

After relating Minh's views, Kim said he was confident if the United States indicated disapproval of the Nhus they would be overthrown, but this would take time. The most important thing we could do now was to clamp on tight security to protect those who opposed the Nhus and to indicate by actions as well as words that the United States did not support the Nhus. (A full account of this meeting was cabled to Washington.)[18]

Lodge was deeply disappointed in the outcome, likening his attempts to encourage the generals to "pushing spaghetti on a plate." I was not surprised, though. A coup could not be ordered up like a dish from the kitchen, even if some of the generals had been talking about it among themselves for some time (General Don had first indicated to Conein back in July that there was discontent in the army over the handling of the Buddhists). The stand-down of the coup gave us time to make a decent try at getting the Nhus out of the country and at retaining Diem without a coup. I began to think about how that might be done. The key, I thought, was to get Lansdale to Saigon as Lodge's assistant. I sensed from my contact with Lou Conein that Lodge might be receptive to a renewed effort to separate Nhu from Diem, the first coup attempt having failed.

On September 2, the *Times of Vietnam* published a front-page article headlined, "CIA Financing Planned Coup d'Etat" with a subtitle, "Planned for August 28; Falls Flat, Stillborn."[19] The article said, "CIA agents in the Political Section of the U.S. embassy, the Public Safety Division of USOM and the G-2 Section of MAAG, with the assistance of well-paid military attaches from three other embassies, had prepared a detailed plan for the overthrow of the Vietnamese government. The CIA plan, it is said, had the blessing of high officials in the 'distressed' State Department. The whole diplomatic corps is aware of the plan. Lodge is expected to fire the responsible 'adventurers.'" This item almost certainly originated with Nhu, although Madame Nhu would take credit for it. American involvement was now clearly out of the bag, even if there was confusion, deliberate or otherwise, about who had been involved.

After the story appeared, I saw Vo Van Hai to get an idea of where Nhu might be going with this. Hai wanted me to warn the American "secret service," as he put it, that Nhu would make a major effort at incrimination; the article was only the beginning. The attack would probably focus on USIS as a cover mechanism for the "secret service." The papal delegate, Salvatore Asta, and the Italian ambassador were endeavoring to persuade Nhu to leave Vietnam. Hai did not believe Nhu would honestly agree to leave, or that the president would agree to his leaving, unless someone who had the president's confidence replaced him. The only suitable person was Luyen, the president's youngest brother, currently the ambassador in London, who had the respect and liking of the army, along with the flexibility to deal with the situation and to rally good people around Diem. Hai thought it would be difficult, however, to persuade Luyen to come; only Lansdale might be able to do that.[20]

President Kennedy, interviewed by Walter Cronkite of CBS on September 2, said that he did not believe the war could be won unless the Vietnamese government made a greater effort to win popular support. "We can help them . . . but they have to win it." Asked whether he thought the Vietnamese government still had time to regain the support of its people, Kennedy said, "With changes in policy and perhaps with personnel I think it can. If it doesn't make those changes, I would think . . . the chances of winning . . . would not be very good."[21] The interview was aimed at the domestic American audience and at the regime in Saigon as well. It contained a message for Diem—to get rid of the Nhus—but as events turned out, Nhu would read it differently. It was an illustration of the difficulty of sending the Vietnamese messages through a public forum and expecting them to be understood.

This was confirmed by what I learned the next day from my 1954–55 army psywar friend Nguyen Hung Vuong, now a press stringer. I had called him "a reliable Vietnamese journalist" in my memo to Lodge. Vuong's source was Colonel Huong, the president's chief of staff. According to Huong, Nhu had told him the dangerous period was over—he (Nhu) was extremely happy and confident. President Kennedy's TV statement meant that the United States had backed down. The opposition had neither troops nor guts. The United States was concerned only about the military situation. So long as he (Nhu) could show progress militarily, the United States would back him.[22] This was confirmed by his air of self-confidence when he saw Lodge in the evening of September 2 and dangled the prospect of retiring to Dalat "after lifting martial law and the removal of certain U.S. agents . . . promoting a coup against [the] family." He could not leave the country, however, because of his contacts with the VC, who were "extremely discouraged and ready to give up."[23] Lodge was not convinced that he really intended to retire voluntarily, and when I heard about it from Mike Dunn, neither was I.

To confuse the picture further, General Charles DeGaulle was inserting French influence into the crisis. Through the French ambassador, Nhu was in contact with the Polish member of the International Control Commission, Mieczyslaw Maneli, who had in turn been talking to the North Vietnamese. The impression given, which Nhu made little attempt to hide, was that if the United States pressed the regime too hard, a negotiated settlement with the North might be possible. I viewed the implied threat with skepticism and told Dunn that Nhu was attempting to bluff us. I could not see how even a minimal level of trust could exist between the Ngo family and the North Vietnamese communists, given the assassination of Diem's older brother Ngo Dinh Khoi in 1945. However, another Vietnamese with excellent access to the palace at the time believed the contacts were very serious and even that an attempt had been made to arrange a secret meeting in India between Diem and Ho Chi Minh.[24] A separate settlement was something Washington worried about. According to some of the generals supporting the coup, it was a motivating factor—how serious was difficult to judge, because it was also a convenient excuse.

General Harkins and the station chief, John Richardson, were in favor of business as usual. I believed that would be seen on all sides as American acquiescence in Nhu's power grab, with disastrous effects on the morale of key Vietnamese in the struggle against the VC. This was reinforced by something Colonel Lac, the key official for the hamlet program, told me. I described Lac to Lodge as an "honest, level-headed, patriotic officer, without personal political ambitions"; he had never made political comments to me before. Now he said the Strategic Hamlet Program had greatly slowed over the past three months because of the Buddhist problem and deteriorating relations with the Americans. He had told Interior Minister Bui Van Luong and Secretary of Defense Thuan that the program was failing in the Delta, with the exception of portions of Kien Hoa, Kien Tuong, and An Giang provinces. Lac absolutely deplored the articles in the *Times of Vietnam* and the attitudes of some officials toward the Americans. "In my opinion," Lac said, "the Nhus would not last twenty-four hours if the Americans made it clear they would not tolerate what was being said about them. Any action by Nhu which was seen as turning the country over to the communists, such as negotiations with the DRV [the Democratic Republic of Vietnam, i.e., North Vietnam] or actions forcing the Americans out, would provoke an almost universal reaction from the officer corps of the army."[25]

The next day I saw Vo Van Hai again. He was highly emotional. Nhu not only wrote all of Diem's speeches, Hai said, but his answers to press inquiries as well, while being careful to respect Diem's conviction that he himself, and not Nhu, was actually making the decisions. Hai thought extreme pressure on Diem by Lodge might make him relinquish Nhu, but he was not optimistic. The American ambassador's discretion in public pronouncements was a good tactic, but at the same time, he should make his true position clear so as not to discourage Nhu's opponents. Hai went on to say—and this absolutely shocked me—that he favored a change in the government now even if it meant losing the president. "Do you really mean that?" I asked. He just nodded gloomily; he had given up. The government, he said, had completely lost the confidence of the people. Any subsequent government must not be a military dictatorship. The Americans should be firm on that point.[26]

What Lac and Hai had to say about Nhu's attitude, Diem's isolation, and the air of discontent within the officer corps and civilian administration was alarming. Combined with what I was hearing from Secretary Thuan, it was truly depressing. These were not palace intriguers or coup plotters but responsible officials who had staked their entire careers on trying to help Diem.

The Nhus and their entourage had an aura of increasing zaniness. I had been called at six in the morning by Denis Warner, an Australian correspondent whom I knew through Colonel Ted Serong, head of the Australian training mission. Warner said he was taking a morning flight to Singapore and had something important to tell me; could I meet him at seven at Givral, a popular coffee shop on Tu Do Street across from the National Assembly building? After ordering coffee, Warner said he had had a four-hour conversation with Tran Van

Khiem, Madame Nhu's brother, on August 31. The Americans, Khiem had said, were weak and would do nothing. The main problem was Ngo Dinh Nhu, "the greatest evil in Vietnam!" Nhu had to be eliminated, so they (Khiem and his sister Madame Nhu) could run the government. Khiem said he was now building up his own secret police, with money from his sister and the help of Lieutenant Colonel Phuoc (the "long walls" province chief from Vinh Long). They would take over security in Saigon once martial law had been lifted. Khiem had then scribbled on a piece of paper his "secret" list of Americans to be assassinated. He had showed Warner the list but would not let him keep it.

According to Warner, John Richardson was the first name on it, followed by an undecipherable name from USOM, then John Mecklin and Lou Conein. Warner had told Khiem that any direct action against Americans would bring the U.S. Marines into Saigon. There were no troops in the world more ferocious, and it would take them no more than three hours to wipe out every Vietnamese soldier in the city. This threat had completely deflated Khiem. Madame Nhu had given an interview to the German newspaper *Der Spiegel* in which she had accused the Americans of conspiring with the communists to overthrow the government, using the Buddhists. The government was ready to negotiate with the North Vietnamese at any time, and a number of Americans would be assassinated if any coup was attempted. Further, in response to a question he had submitted to President Diem about responsibility for the Buddhist affair, Warner had received a claim that there was evidence of a conspiracy involving the communists and the Americans. Warner was concerned Diem might actually think this. We could expect further blasts from Madame Nhu through the *Times of Vietnam*. However, he thought, if we kept our nerve and demonstrated our guts and principles, the Nhus were certain to collapse.[27] Warner and I agreed that Khiem was nuts, but I told him I would report this to Lodge anyway.

My memo to Dunn caused quite a stir. While making it clear that I put little stock in Khiem's ability to do real harm, it was an indication of the bizarreness of the situation at the palace. It seemed Nhu and Madame Nhu, and now Madame Nhu's brother, were hatching Byzantine plots to discredit the Americans, while we seemed to be drifting without a plan. I had two thoughts: first, our policies toward the Nhus needed definition, direction, and a psychological boost; second, this was an opportunity to sell Lodge on the idea that Lansdale would have the know-how and contacts to deal with the situation before it spun completely out of control.

I prepared a memorandum, classified it Top Secret, and gave it to Dunn for Lodge. "We are facing a crisis of confidence with the Vietnamese," I said, "because of our apparent vacillation over the Nhus." We should, I argued, quietly demonstrate our determination not to deal with those directly responsible for repressing the Buddhists, by refusing to support the proposed takeover of hamlet militia training by the Vietnamese Special Forces as long as Colonel Tung was in command. The next step was to resume direct U.S. funding of the Montagnard civilian defense irregulars rather than going through Colonel Tung. I recommended that General Lansdale be brought in to manage the campaign against the Nhus. His arrival, I said, would be a dramatic demonstration of U.S. good intentions and faith, and it would throw the Nhus off balance. Dunn later returned my memo, saying Lodge had read it but did not want it kept at the embassy.[28] I squirreled it away in our safe at USOM. No immediate action was taken it, but it planted two ideas that emerged later. One was that we should no longer support certain key Vietnamese who were directly connected with Nhu and the raid on the pagodas; the other was to call for Lansdale.

Having failed to get Lansdale out to help Diem surmount the Buddhist crisis before the raid on the pagodas, my last hope was to get Diem out of the morass before a coup succeeded, now that the initial attempt had failed. Lansdale was the only one who had a prayer of being able to assuage Diem's pride, come up with an honorable exit for the Nhus, and at the same time give Diem confidence that he had an official American he could work with and trust. The scheme suggested by Vo Van Hai of bringing in Luyen to replace Nhu came to mind. Nothing was going to be achieved by continuing to pressure Diem at the diplomatic level; for Diem to give up Nhu under such direct foreign pressure was too much of a sacrifice of dignity, sense of nationalism, and traditional Vietnamese duty to family. It would be, in his terms, dishonorable.

I had an indirect sense from Conein that Lodge had already given up on separating Nhu from Diem, so I hid my complete views from Lodge to avoid being cut out of his confidence. It made me uncomfortable. I don't think Dunn picked up on my state of mind initially, but years later he would describe Conein and me as having had our own agendas.[29] He was right in my case.

There is evidence that Diem may have earlier considered sending Nhu out of the country. In June, during a visit by Lieutenant Colonel Chau to Saigon for consultations before being sent to Danang, Diem had asked him what he thought about dismissing Nhu and sending him and his wife abroad for a time. Chau told the president, "It would be wrong for him to dismiss Nhu for his own personal gain, but if dismissal was in the best interest of the country, then it would be a wise and correct decision." Diem's response was that "perhaps Nhu could be reassigned to some official position outside the country." "Diem seemed to understand that Nhu was causing him harm," Chau felt, "but he was afraid if he sent Nhu abroad, the Vietnamese people would think the Americans had made him do it."[30] Later Diem did send Bishop Thuc and Madame Nhu out of the country. At the very end he concluded he had to compromise, but it was too late.

PREPARING TO RETURN TO WASHINGTON

In response to increasingly urgent messages that my father had cancer, I had booked a Pan American flight home for September 8. Earlier, I had been told I might be asked while in Washington to speak to the Special Group for Counterinsurgency, of which Robert Kennedy was a member. To prepare for this possibility, a meeting of our provincial and regional reps had put the final touches on our second nationwide report on the Strategic Hamlet Program; I wanted to take it with me. The report's gist was, "The Strategic Hamlet Program has continued to make steady and reasonably sure progress in all Corps Areas except the Delta. There the program has suffered serious reverses in many provinces, is in effect at a standstill in others and moving ahead slowly in only a few. . . . Despite the gains in Central Vietnam, government handling of the Buddhist problem has undoubtedly turned the population against it and while the hamlets may continue to defend themselves locally against the Viet Cong a dangerous vacuum in acceptable leadership has been created at the central and possibly provincial government levels."[31] Finally, the report acknowledged that the program was progressing at a slower rate than during the previous six months, because of overextension and unsound planning and execution; nevertheless, it estimated, the program's ills could be overcome by persistent, intelligent effort. To ignore them, however, would endanger the entire counterinsurgency effort. The report was widely distributed at the time, including at MACV, but few if any there would read it.[32]

The day before my departure turned out to be extremely busy. It started with an urgent early-morning call to see Mike Dunn at the embassy. A cable had just come in saying Washington had decided "to make an intensive effort to obtain at first hand attitudes toward the GVN [government of Vietnam] held by wide spectrum of [the] populace." Major General Krulak from Defense and Joseph Mendenhall from State were arriving early in the morning the next day to assist in polling opinion; they would do so in as short a time as possible, only two days. Their efforts were to be paralleled by those of John Mecklin and myself, polling our people in the field. The same cable stated it was possible that "Mecklin and perhaps Phillips would be asked to return with Krulak and Mendenhall for a personal report."[33] A separate cable had a list of questions involving attitudes toward the top government and military leadership, the VC, and the war. The basic question was whether the crisis had eroded the Vietnamese government's and army's will to fight.

I doubted the value of such a quick survey. I knew Krulak only by his reputation as a skillful bureaucratic infighter who worked his way into McNamara's confidence and cut out Lansdale in the process. Mendenhall I knew as a determined enemy of Diem from his days in Saigon with Ambassador Durbrow. In an internal State Department memo written back in 1962 he had argued that the only solution in Vietnam was to get rid of Diem and Nhu, and he had recommended U.S. support for a coup by the Vietnamese military.[34] I told Dunn I would stick with my original schedule, which had me leaving by Pan Am the afternoon of the eighth. I had already surveyed our personnel in the provinces and would follow up on that. I was particularly concerned about the Delta, from where I had recently gotten some disquieting news.

Earlier in the week, Earl Young, who was now in Long An as provincial rep, called to tell me bad things were happening there. I knew security had been deteriorating, but this sounded like an emergency. After seeing Dunn, I had driven to the town of Tan An, the provincial capital, about forty kilometers south of Saigon. There I met Earl and the sector advisor, Major Fields. I learned that in addition to what I already knew about a number of hamlets being penetrated by the VC in June and July, an additional sixty hamlets had been overrun during August. The VC had forced the inhabitants to take the roofs off their houses and cut up the barbed-wire defenses, effectively destroying the hamlet. Earl had recently flown with Major Fields over many of these hamlets; most now appeared abandoned. The extent of destruction was appalling. Calls to nearby Vietnamese army units for security reinforcement had been ignored. The troops were confined to quarters, an indication that coup fears were restricting operations. According to the sector advisor, his previous pessimistic monthly reports sent up the MACV chain of command through the corps advisor's office in Can Tho were also being ignored.

When I got back to Saigon, at the suggestion of regional rep Ralph Harwood, I attended an afternoon briefing at Vietnamese army 5th Division headquarters north of Saigon. It was about a military operation just conducted in the "Iron Triangle," to the north of Saigon between the Saigon River on the west and Road 13 on the east, north of Bien Hoa, a VC stronghold since the communists had organized the Michelin Rubber plantation workers back in the 1930s. Before the briefing started I talked to several American captains who had been advisors on the operation. They told me nothing had been achieved; no VC had even been encountered.

Colonel Miller, the 5th Division advisor, was the briefer. The operation had been an incursion, mainly by Vietnamese armored personnel carriers and troops, into the Iron Triangle. Miller called it a victory, claiming the VC had been completely driven out.. None of the senior officers present challenged this assertion. I was incredulous and could not help approaching Miller after the brass had left. How could he call it a victory, I asked, when according to his own advisors no VC had been encountered? "We drove them out," he said. I asked if the Vietnamese troops were going to stay. He said no. I asked, "What do you think is going to happen after our side leaves?" He was nonplussed. In fact the VC had simply gone underground, in their tunnels, until the operation was over; it was an illustration of how some senior MACV advisors allowed themselves to be deluded. I didn't share the MACV headquarters view about the utility of such sweeps, but wouldn't learn the extent of the difference in perceptions until I arrived in Washington.

Returning to my office after the briefing, I sent Colonel Lac a memo I had written several days before urging that new hamlet construction be stopped, particularly in the Delta, and that efforts be focused on consolidating existing hamlets.[35] Long An had heightened the need. Consolidation was as much Lac's idea as mine, but he had been unable to get Nhu to act. He thought Nhu had now acquired sufficient confidence in us that my memo might be persuasive. The irony did not escape me of Nhu's finally accepting us and giving weight to our opinions about the hamlets, at a time when, at Lodge's direction, I was secretly trying to get Nhu out of the way. I wondered what good might have been accomplished had Nhu's draconian approach to the Buddhists not prevailed.

I also found a note at my office from Secretary Thuan, who wanted to see me. Then I learned that Joe Alsop had just arrived in town and urgently wanted to talk to me as well, so my wife and I invited him for a short, early dinner at our house, before I saw Thuan. Only Bohannon, whom he knew from the early days in Vietnam, and Barbara were present. Joe had not changed from the feisty figure I remembered from 1954, full of panache, still barking question-like statements. I gave a pessimistic view of Nhu's influence and the discord it was provoking not just with the Americans, which he already knew, but among leading Vietnamese as well. I urged him to interview Nhu to make his own assessment. I told him I had to return to Washington temporarily because of my father. Who are you going to see in Washington, he asked? I wasn't sure. He scrawled a note, enclosed it in an envelope on which he wrote "Mike Forrestal," and said, "See he gets it." I got the impression that Alsop might have been asked by the White House to come out, but he never said so.

During the ten days he spent in Vietnam, Alsop visited Kien Hoa and wrote a column about a particular hamlet that had fought off the VC—an example, he suggested, of the Vietnamese will to resist at the village level, a story not being reported by the resident press corps. He would also interview Nhu and Diem, then write a highly critical column claiming that "Nhu had lost touch with the real world" and that Diem "had lost his ability to see events or problems in their true proportions, no doubt because his natural tendency to be suspicious has been daily played upon by his brother." It concluded, "There are likely to be changes here." When he returned to Washington he briefed Kennedy that Diem had lost his ability to govern. (Years later he would write of this period that "Nhu had gone stark raving mad," but he would regret his conclusions about Diem, feeling his columns may have influenced the course of events that led to the coup.)[36]

After the Alsop dinner, I got to Thuan's about 9:30 that night. We talked briefly about my return to Washington. I told him about the situation in Long An and urged he get security support. Throwing up his hands, he said he could do nothing. Usually Thuan had a mordant sense of humor; now he was obviously desperate, literally wringing his hands. He felt completely useless. Nhu was accusing him of having been bought by the Americans and would certainly kill him if he tried to resign. Nevertheless, he would like to resign, and he wanted to know if we could get him out of country. I said I would get a request to Lodge, though I was leaving the next day. Nhu was in effective control of the country, he said: "Nhu is the only one the president trusts. Normally at meetings, Nhu speaks for the president, and the president gives assent; on other occasions the president simply repeats what Nhu has told him to say." Thuan thought Nhu and the president were both completely unrealistic about the progress of the war. Each had asked Thuan how long he thought the country could last without U.S. assistance. He had replied, six months, if nonmilitary aid were cut; collapse would be almost immediate if military aid were cut.

Thuan continued. Colonel Lac had recently told him that the government would lose the war by 1965 if the present situation continued and that it was already losing the war in the Delta. Thuan said several generals (he wouldn't say who) had contacted him seeking his views about a coup; he had not responded, for fear they were provocateurs directed by Nhu. In any case, he had little faith in the generals. The current state of the government was exemplified by the minister of national economy, who had recently visited him carrying a detective novel under his arm, saying "All we, or anybody else, can do in the office is to read these. We are waiting." I asked what he thought the Americans should do. He said we should cut off aid; that would cause everyone to realize we meant business about the Nhus.

I scrawled the conversation in longhand after I got home and asked Bohannon in the morning to get Marguerite Webber to type it so the transcript could be taken to Lodge. I appended an observation that Thuan was deeply disturbed, convinced the situation could be resolved only by the Americans, and felt helpless to do anything. Lodge sent Trueheart to see Thuan the day I left. He confirmed my conversation; Thuan had repeated his lack of confidence in the generals and indicated considerable concern for his personal safety, saying he was on Tran Van Khiem's assassination list. At the same time Nhu was claiming he had the backing of Ambassador Lodge, that "Lodge wanted him (Nhu) to be his political advisor." The accounts of my and Trueheart's meetings with Thuan were combined in a single cable to Washington.[37]

On the morning of the eighth, before leaving, I saw Lodge briefly to tell him I was more convinced than ever that he needed someone like Lansdale to coordinate an effort against the Nhus. It was like a political campaign at home: the campaign needed a campaign manager. He seemed to agree and said anything I might do to help with that would be welcome.

ARRIVING IN WASHINGTON

My commercial Pan Am flight arrived in Washington, by way of Los Angeles, around five in the afternoon the next day, September 9. After two days in Vietnam, Krulak and Mendenhall left Saigon late that day, flew nonstop to Anchorage and then on to Washington, arriving early in the morning of the tenth. Mecklin accompanied them on the special air force plane, provided by Secretary McNamara, that had brought them out. It had been a very tense flight during which Krulak didn't speak to Mendenhall and strenuously objected to Mecklin's bringing back USIS film of the riots and student arrests in Saigon.

On my own way home I had had some time to reflect. Diem's government under Nhu's domination had been spinning out of control since the Buddhist affair began in May. Diem's most loyal and longest-term supporters were at a loss and had initially thought the solution was somehow to get the Nhus out of the country. Some now thought that was impossible, although I had not given up. A few supported a coup, others clearly did not. In the army, preexisting sentiment against Nhu had hardened against Diem as well, as Nhu seemed to have practically taken over from Diem, issuing orders in his place. Certainly, Lodge's support for a coup had emboldened the generals, but U.S. policy was not entirely clear to most Vietnamese outside of the general's inner circle, and even there doubts existed. None of our economic aid had been cut. While no details had emerged, Nhu was reportedly plotting a countercoup to take over the government, even to push Diem aside, while eliminating most of the generals in the process. Apparently there was at least one other coup being plotted as well, maybe two.

The uncertain atmosphere was being fanned not only by crazies like Madame Nhu's brother but also by the declarations and demeanor of General Ton That Dinh, whom Nhu had put in charge of the Saigon Military District. Dinh was erratic and unstable, given to ferocious statements about how he intended to deal with the government's "enemies." He had designated Conein as his personal contact with the American embassy, installing in Conein's house a special red telephone, a direct line to his headquarters. He periodically called Conein on the red phone to say he was coming over, then roared up Conein's narrow street with a motorcycle escort, swaggered into the house, sat down at the bar surrounded by armed guards, and asked for Scotch. He and Conein would banter back and forth, and then he would go roaring off again. At this point Dinh was not involved in the generals' coup plotting and was unaware that Conein was. It was opéra bouffe, but he had the guns. Later Dinh would change sides.

If the situation had its comic aspects, the apparent American vacillation in the face of provocations being printed almost daily in the *Times of Vietnam* seemed to encourage the Nhus' excesses. The crisis was adversely affecting the counterinsurgency campaign, particularly in the Delta. The situation in central Vietnam, with villagers wearing bits of saffron cloth symbolic of their support for the Buddhists, was disquieting. If Lodge could get Lansdale to help, I believed, it was still possible to come up with a face-saving way to separate Nhu from Diem and avoid a coup. In the meantime, however, we needed to make it plain the United States did not acquiesce in Nhu's actions. Richardson seemed to think Nhu was essential to the war effort and wanted to retain the relationship, because he, Richardson, could influence Nhu. That was a delusion, I thought. Whether I would have the chance to present any ideas and how I might do so if I got it was unclear. Maybe the Special Group for Counterinsurgency in Washington would offer a chance, particularly if Robert Kennedy was in attendance. That was a possible way to reach the top.

I called my mother from the airport when I got in. She had received an urgent call from a Mr. Hilsman. Would I please go directly to the State Department from the airport before going home? I took a cab to State and was ushered up to Hilsman's office, where I was greeted by Hilsman and Mike Forrestal. Both began asking me intensive questions.

I summarized our latest strategic hamlet progress report, particularly about the Delta. Then I related the recent destruction by the VC of a number of hamlets in Long An. I recounted my most recent conversations with various Vietnamese, such as Colonel Lac and Vo Van Hai, in addition to Thuan, which they already knew about. Forrestal asked if I thought it still possible to separate the Nhus from Diem. I said it was possible but difficult, given that Diem had been put into a corner in which he felt honor bound to defend his family. It became clear as the meeting concluded that the information I had been providing to Lodge about Vietnamese attitudes had had a greater impact in Washington than I could have imagined. They told me a meeting was set for the next day at 10:30 AM at the White House for the president to hear from Krulak and Mendenhall. They wanted me to come with them. There might be a chance for me to speak; they weren't sure.

Before leaving I gave Alsop's sealed note to Forrestal, explaining that Alsop had been at my house the evening before I left. I was unaware of the note's contents. I discovered many years later it said, referring to me, "He knows more about this show and judges it better than anyone I know. I think he ought to see Mac and Averell personally but you will know more about this." ("Mac" referred to McGeorge Bundy and "Averell" to Averell Harriman. The note, when I first saw a copy in 2005, had scribbles on the back including, "You should ask Phillips to report," in what seems to an archivist at the John F. Kennedy Library in Boston to be the president's hand. Apparently, on going back to the White House that evening or early the next morning, Forrestal had shown Alsop's note to him.)[38]

I did not talk about involving Lansdale to Hilsman or Forrestal. I knew Lansdale was controversial, particularly with State. I was not sure how these two men felt. If I had a chance to speak directly to the president, I thought, I would raise it. In Saigon, I had a vague notion of the policy divisions in Washington, gleaned indirectly from Mike Dunn, but no idea of their intensity. Neither Forrestal nor Hilsman tried to influence what I might say.

When I finally got home, my father was already asleep. My mother told me his cancer was beyond cure; I would see this, and we could talk about it the next day when I got back from my meetings. It had been a long series of flights and then the meeting at State; she pushed me off to bed, handing me an alarm clock. My father was still asleep when I left the next morning.

I arrived at Hilsman's office around eight. I read a just-received cable from General Harkins contradicting much of what Thuan had said to me. Harkins, after reporting some of Thuan's pessimistic remarks—such as, "Even he has been accused of being in the U.S. pay," and "things were going so well and then everything seemed to disintegrate"—stated that he had told Thuan he "did not believe things were really as bad as he thought." Harkins recounted how he visited the corps and divisions in the past ten days, finding that "though there was a slight diminution of the military effort because of martial law and elections, things were getting back to normal and the war was still being carried to the VC." Harkins went on to say that Thuan "agreed that he [Thuan] was out of touch and not up to date." Harkins had visited units in central Vietnam that same day, and "all knew what was going on in Saigon but all agreed it had no effect on them." Harkins concluded, "Thuan gave no indication he was thinking of or wanted to quit and leave the country."[39]

I knew Thuan personally, Harkins didn't. Harkins had never established anything but a very formal relationship with the Vietnamese, precluding frank exchanges of views. He was so fond of his own optimistic opinions that, out of politeness and in deference to his position, no Vietnamese ever contradicted him. He was blind to his limitations, and so were his superiors. General Taylor had said to Secretary of State Dean Rusk earlier in August of a Harkins meeting with General Don that it reflected "a private exchange between two old friends."[40] In fact, however, Don was no friend of Harkins. Harkins had complained earlier in the year to President Diem that Don was "not aggressive enough" as the I Corps commander; Diem had reassigned Don to army headquarters, and Don undoubtedly knew through the grapevine what Harkins had said. When the Vietnamese told Harkins what he wanted to hear, Taylor thought these were their true thoughts—an illusion difficult to dispel.

Lodge finally had a meeting with President Diem the day after I left Saigon, after repeated requests from Rusk, with President Kennedy's backing. At this, his first formal meeting with Diem since presenting his credentials, Lodge told him bluntly, "Nhu should go away, not returning at least until [the] end of December—after the [congressional] appropriations have been voted." Diem was aghast and objected vigorously. Lodge persisted, saying he hoped very much that "there would be changes in personnel and in policy . . . to make continued support of the war possible." Lodge was polite, but the message was insulting. Diem's reaction would only harden Lodge's initial thinking that to get rid of Nhu, Diem had to go too. Lodge's approach thereafter was, as he put it, "silence." To most Washington policy makers this initial attempt by Lodge was definitive evidence that Nhu could never be separated from Diem. I came to hear about this gradually, during my next several weeks in Washington, but I did not know what Lodge had said when I went to the White House the next morning.

Chapter 13
Meeting President Kennedy

A bout 9:45 on September 10, Hilsman and I walked over to the White House and got to the cabinet room about 10:15. Forrestal was already there; he advised me to speak only if requested. Others began filing in. I recognized Dean Rusk, Secretary McNamara, and Gen. Maxwell Taylor, all of whom took a seat on one side of the long table that dominated the room. McNamara and Rusk left open a seat between them that I assumed was for the president. Just behind the president's chair was McGeorge Bundy, Kennedy's national security advisor. Also there were Director Bell from AID, Edward R. Murrow from USIA, and John McCone, Director of Central Intelligence. I was seated in the back row of chairs, away from the table, along with John Mecklin. Hilsman and Forrestal were in front of us, while Krulak and Mendenhall were seated at the table across from McNamara and Rusk. Robert Kennedy did not arrive at all.[1] Promptly at 10:30 President Kennedy walked in, flashed a smile, and sat down. It was my first chance to see him up close. He exuded self-confidence and charisma as he nodded at Krulak and said, "Please proceed."

Krulak spoke first, explaining with an air of optimism that he had visited all four of the corps regions, meeting American military advisors in each, as well as lower-ranking officers and noncoms on advisory teams. In each corps area, a representative group had been assembled for him to interview, some eighty-seven Americans in all. He claimed to have also talked to twenty-seven Vietnamese officers, as well as to General Harkins and his staff. He had found that the shooting war was still going ahead at an impressive pace. It had been adversely affected by the crisis, but the impact was not great. Most Vietnamese officers viewed the Buddhist issue with detachment. There was some dissatisfaction among the officers, but it was focused more on Nhu than on Diem. Nhu's departure would be hailed, but few would extend their necks to bring it about. The war against the VC would be won if current American programs were pursued, whatever the defects of the regime.

All this was presented with an air of absolute certainty. None of it reflected the actual situation in the Delta. Krulak seemed utterly convinced he had accurately divined the thinking of the Vietnamese officers he had talked to, not realizing that they would never reveal their true thoughts to a high-ranking American whom they did not know personally, certainly never openly in front of other Vietnamese officers.

Then Mendenhall spoke. He had been to Hue and Danang, as well as Saigon, and had spoken to Vietnamese whom he had known before, both in and outside the government. In Saigon he had found a virtual breakdown in civil government and a pervasive atmosphere of hate. "The war against the Viet Cong had become secondary to the war against the regime," he said. He had found a similar atmosphere of hate in Hue and Danang. The Viet Cong had made recent advances in two provinces in the center, where Buddhist agitation had extended into the countryside, and there were reports of villagers in one province opting for the VC. Students in Hue and Saigon were talking about the VC as an alternative to the regime. His conclusion was that the war against the VC could not be won if Nhu remained in Vietnam. (I thought I heard him say Diem too, not just Nhu.) The picture painted by Mendenhall was dire in the extreme. South Vietnam was literally falling apart.

"The two of you did visit the same country, didn't you?" President Kennedy asked, so different were the two presentations. This provoked a laugh and then a stunned silence. Neither had it right. Mendenhall had painted an exaggerated picture of imminent collapse. Krulak was equally as far off the mark. When no one commented, Hilsman spoke up, saying this was the difference between a military and a political point of view. Krulak suggested that the difference was that Mendenhall was reporting on urban attitudes, while he himself was reporting on "national attitudes." The clear implication was that in going to the countryside, he, Krulak, had gone where the real war was, while Mendenhall had only visited the cities. Nolting pitched in, reminding Mendenhall that in 1961 he had made the same prediction of government paralysis and consequent defeat by the Viet Cong, which had not happened. McGeorge Bundy pointed out dryly that in 1961 we had overcome paralysis by strengthening the government's effort against the Viet Cong; how could we strengthen a government that was causing its own paralysis?

Neither Krulak or Mendenhall had communicated the complexities of South Vietnam. Nor had they captured the nature of the insurgency—mainly a political struggle for the loyalty and support of the rural population. This was the other war, the real war. I was particularly upset at Krulak's report because I had just been in Long An Province, in the Delta. To generate the will to resist the Viet Cong and to win the population's support, the hamlets had to provide security as well as improve the population's well-being. Most hamlets could defend themselves against local Viet Cong squad- and platoon-sized attacks, but not against main-force assaults. That was the Vietnamese army's job, and it was not being done, particularly in most of the Delta, and certainly not in Long An. Tangible improvements in schools, wells, and crops were happening, but these alone were not enough.

Politically, I understood the thinking of many key Vietnamese who were not "palace intriguers" but Diem supporters who had become disillusioned over Nhu. Because of Lodge, and at his request, I had become involved with the coup conspirators and given them assurances of American support. What I knew, however, of Vietnam had convinced me that though Nhu had to go, Diem had to be saved. It was still possible, but this seemed the last chance.

Suddenly, I heard Forrestal's voice: "Mr. President, we have with us Rufus Phillips, who is in charge of the Rural Affairs program in South Vietnam, as you know. I think you ought to hear his views." Kennedy nodded, "Yes, by all means." I was ushered to a chair at the table, and Kennedy gave me a warm smile, which encouraged me. Whirling through my mind were two thoughts: "I owe him the truth as I see it," and a question—"How can I tell him what I know about South Vietnam in a few minutes?"

"Mr. President," I began, "I have known South Vietnam since 1954 and have close personal relationships with many Vietnamese in and out of the government and know President Diem and his brother Ngo Dinh Nhu. The problem is Nhu. He has lost the respect of the majority of the civilian and military leadership, who would change the government if they saw an alternative. The opinions of the Buddhist leadership, which are violently anti-Diem, are not representative, but there is a general crisis of confidence in the regime, shared by civilian and army leaders alike." At this point, McNamara started shaking his head sideways, a gesture he continued throughout my presentation.

I went on to say that our own military advisors were not an accurate source of political information. They were under a directive not to talk politics with their Vietnamese counterparts, and the Vietnamese knew it. It was only with old American friends that they would discuss such matters. General Krulak interjected at this point that the advisors were not good on politics or palace intrigue, but were good on whether the war was being won or not, and they said the war was going well.

I continued, "I have spoken with many Vietnamese political and military leaders, such as Secretary of Defense Nguyen Dinh Thuan, President Diem's secretary, Vo Van Hai, General Le Van Kim of the General Staff, and Colonel Hoang Van Lac, who heads the Strategic Hamlet Program. Thuan, the most powerful man in the Diem government after Diem and Nhu, thinks Nhu must leave the country or there will be chaos. He says security is deteriorating; the government is now losing the war in the Delta. Most Vietnamese would like to see Diem remain, but they are unalterably opposed to the Nhus. Thuan feels America must act to show it does not support Nhu. We cannot continue to ignore Nhu's actions at the cost of losing Vietnamese respect and support."

The president said he recalled making a number of public statements condemning Vietnamese government actions. I said we had criticized the government before, but what the Vietnamese were looking for was concrete action illustrating the U.S. position. "What is needed," I stated, "is a campaign to isolate Nhu and get him out of the country. The campaign needs a campaign manager. Most Vietnamese would like to see Diem remain but are unalterably opposed to the Nhus. We cannot win the war if the Nhus remain. This is the opinion of Secretary Thuan, Colonel Lac, head of the Strategic Hamlet Program, and many others. We need a person to guide and direct a program to isolate the Nhus and to convince the government and the people that the U.S. will not support a government with Nhu in it. That man is General Lansdale. Ambassador Lodge agrees that Lansdale should come back. If it doesn't work, no one would be more qualified to help put together a new government. I recommend you send him there as soon as possible." The president took notes while I spoke. When I finished, he said, "Mr. Phillips, I want to thank you for your remarks, particularly for your recommendation concerning General Lansdale." He indicated I should remain at the table.

The president then asked for my specific recommendations for dealing with Nhu. I suggested we cut off CIA aid to Colonel Tung's Special Forces, which had raided the pagodas, and that USIS stop producing films laudatory of Nhu. We should make it clear that Nhu was the target of our actions. This would isolate him and produce a psychological squeeze for his removal. President Kennedy asked, "What about the possibility that Nhu's response would be to withdraw funds from the war and the field to Saigon, charging that the U.S. was causing them to lose the war?" I said the army would not stand for this. "If worse came to worse, we could take our piasters out to the provinces in suitcases. We started supporting the Strategic Hamlet Program that way; we could finish it that way."

"What do you think of the military situation?" the president asked. "I am sorry to have to tell you, Mr. President," I replied, "but we are not winning the war, particularly in the Delta. The first, second, and third corps areas are okay, but the war effort in the fourth corps, the Delta area south of Saigon, is beginning to go to pieces. I was just in Long An Province, where within the past few weeks the Viet Cong destroyed sixty strategic hamlets, forcing the inhabitants to cut the barbed-wire defenses and take the roofs off their houses. ARVN troops, who were supposed to be defending the hamlets, were confined to quarters for fear they might be used for a coup." Hilsman asked if security had started deteriorating in the Delta before August 20 (the cataclysmic day of the raid on the Buddhist pagodas). I said it had.

Krulak interjected, "Mr. Phillips is putting his views over those of General Harkins, and as between Mr. Phillips and General Harkins, I would take General Harkins's assessment. The fourth corps is the most difficult, but we hope to drive the Viet Cong into this area to compress them so they can be destroyed. The war is not being lost militarily." My God, I thought to myself, Krulak must have gone to the moon—but the moment was too serious to laugh at the absurdity of a Viet Cong "human cattle drive" into the Delta!

Secretary Rusk asked if I could explain the totally different stories coming from my last meeting with Secretary Thuan and Harkins' meeting with Thuan the following day. I said Thuan had been frank with me, because we were friends, but he didn't know General Harkins personally and would say what he thought the general wanted to hear. Rusk then asked what I thought of Colonel Thompson's (the British senior advisor in Saigon) idea that the Viet Cong might be turning to the cities. I said I didn't think so—there was too much activity in the Delta. "The strategic hamlets are not being adequately protected, they are being over-run. Furthermore, this is not a military, but a political war. It is a war for men's minds more than a war against the Viet Cong, and it's being lost."

John Mecklin, the USIS director in Saigon, spoke next. He said he shared my views and the recommendation about Lansdale, though he felt I hadn't gone far enough. He thought we should directly deploy American forces in South Vietnam to support the war effort. At this point the meeting broke into an uproar, General Taylor vehemently saying, "No, no, under no circumstances!" I was stunned by Mecklin's proposal. I could not figure out where he got the idea. It diverted attention from the real problem, which was dealing realistically with the Nhus. McCone, in his turn, argued the Vietnamese military could work with Nhu and that the situation was not as ominous as reported. Harriman said the situation was obviously coming apart and that we could not continue with Diem.

There was no consensus. The complete split in the Kennedy administration and some of the anger and bitterness it was provoking was patently clear. The president said he was disturbed at the tendency in both Washington and Saigon to fight our internal battles in the newspapers. He quoted some recent stories reflecting the differences between the State and Defense departments; he wanted such disputes fought out at this table, not indirectly. He asked the group to meet again the next day.[2] As I left the meeting, the director of AID, David Bell, put his arm around my shoulders and said, "Thanks for telling it as you see it."

Outside the White House, it had begun to rain. I slipped on the pavement and cut a deep gash in my shin but didn't feel it—I was numb. The sharp divisions, bureaucratic rivalries, and towering egos of the top officials in that room had stunned me. They all seemed so sure of themselves. The president was the only one who seemed genuinely interested in what was really going on in Vietnam. Despite the confusion and lack of understanding, however, I was encouraged. I had seen Krulak's ignorance as well as Mendenhall's narrowly focused views masquerading as fact, but Kennedy had taken notes only when I had spoken. Maybe he would cut through the bureaucracy and act decisively despite McNamara's clear opposition to what I had said. At the same time, I would have preferred to make a more direct pitch about the need to save Diem, and for Lansdale as the means, but I thought my approach had been the only way of finessing Lodge's apparent conflation of Diem with Nhu, an error I now knew was clearly shared by Hilsman and Harriman. This might be a turning point. My mind was in turmoil as I returned to my parents' apartment.

When I got home it was just after noon; my father was up and about to eat lunch. I hadn't seen him for almost a year. He was much paler and thinner than I remembered. He seemed normal but, tragically, could not speak complete sentences, only disjointed words and sounds. He understood what mother and I were saying, but he could not respond. He reacted with a smile to my presence, obviously glad to see me. All the bitterness of our parting almost a year before had gone from his eyes. I told him how much I had missed him, which brought tears to his eyes. It was hard not to break down. Afterward, my mother explained. The cancer, which had begun in his lungs, had now spread to his brain. The doctor had told her the end was near, maybe a month away. There was nothing that could be done. I asked myself, if I had known this when I made the decision to go to Vietnam, would I have still gone?

A POSSIBLE TURNING POINT

That same afternoon, I got a call from Hilsman. Could I come back to the State Department for a 5:45 follow-up meeting? I did, and this time Robert Kennedy was present. Trying to develop a unified front after the earlier contentious meeting, McGeorge Bundy declared that U.S. policy was as the president had defined it in his interview with Cronkite. Robert Kennedy thought we should now concentrate on specifics, not discuss differences of view. McNamara said we ought to go back to where we had been three weeks ago (before the so-called Hilsman cable). Harriman strongly disagreed: Diem had created a situation in which we could not back him. Hilsman talked about forcing Diem to change policies. McCone doubted that alternative leadership existed in Vietnam. General Taylor thought we should continue to work with Diem and not think about using U.S. troops.[3] The protocol was that I was to speak only if asked, so I sat in acutely frustrated silence, watching the policy ping-pong match between Harriman and McNamara, with others playing supporting roles. Firsthand views from the field had become superfluous. This was a policy battle, in which realism was not relevant. I was disappointed at Robert Kennedy's absence from the first meeting and fantasized that if he had heard what I had said to his brother then, he might have asked for my thoughts now. It was not to be.

That evening I called Lansdale at home. He said that I had really stirred things up in the Pentagon. I related my clash with Krulak, my recommendation to the president that he be sent out there, and the president's favorable reaction. There was still an opportunity to get Nhu out of the country, I urged, but only he could do it. He said he would go if asked. I said I was going to the country with my father and mother and would touch base when I got back.

The next day, the eleventh, a Top Secret assessment from Lodge came in. I did not see it at the time, but it was quite pessimistic about the results if our posture remained one of "wait and see." The future leadership of Vietnam might lose heart and, more importantly, individuals the regime viewed as threats might be systematically eliminated. Lodge claimed that the situation was "worsening rapidly." The time had come for the United States to use what effective sanctions it could to bring about the fall of the regime. He wanted cuts in economic aid, to force a drastic change in the government.[4]

I went to AID to see Stoneman, who wanted to know about my father. He was likely to die, I said, within a month; I had no alternative except to come back to Washington with my family for a leave of absence from Saigon. My first responsibility was to my mother, to see that she was okay financially and otherwise. She, my sister, and I were the majority owners of Airways Engineering. I would have to see what shape it was in, whether it could be run effectively with existing personnel, putting one of them in charge, or whether I would have to take it over and possibly sell it. As a consulting engineering business, it was dependent on personalities as much as on technical skills. I would be back to Saigon at the end of another week to wrap things up and make arrangements for my family to leave and for someone to take over temporarily. I felt very bad about leaving Rural Affairs, even temporarily, but had little choice. Stoneman said he fully understood; arrangements would be made on any schedule I might suggest. He hoped I would continue as a consultant to AID/Washington, helping to recruit additional personnel and advising on requests for support from Saigon while I was sorting out my affairs, and that I would find a way to return. I said I would do my best.

We discussed the status of things in Vietnam, my meeting at the White House, which he had heard about, and what was happening with the Strategic Hamlet Program and Rural Affairs out in Vietnam. We broke for lunch at the cafeteria and then resumed in the afternoon. There was a lot to talk about.

The next day, the twelfth, I talked again to Stoneman at AID, where I got a call from Hilsman saying he wanted me to attend another meeting at the White House, at six in the evening. Could I come by his office an hour before to see something? It turned out to be a cable from Harkins to Krulak that had just come in. Harkins claimed because the communists had seen they were losing the military battle they had seized on a new approach, "the religious one." He called the revolt of the bonzes and subsequently schoolchildren as "another well organized covertly led Communist trick."[5] I told Hilsman it sounded like Nhu had given Harkins some of the opium Nhu was rumored to smoke. I had no idea where he might have gotten such an idea. Undoubtedly there were VC sympathizers among the Buddhists and the students, but any idea that the VC had engineered the whole protest movement was absurd. Harkins' cable gave no source, just his personal opinion. He had a way of giving offhand personal opinions with little to back them up; in June, for instance, Bill Trueheart had shown me a misleading letter from Harkins to Diem predicting victory over the VC by the end of the year. Such opinions were a disservice to Diem, giving him an unrealistic view of the war. Later, after the setback to the hamlet program in Long An, Harkins gave an interview to UPI, as reported in the *Times of Vietnam* of September 23, 1963, declaring, "I can categorically say we are winning the war in the Delta."[6]

At the meeting on September 12 all the principals were present who had been at my first White House meeting, except the president, plus this time Robert Kennedy. General Taylor presided over the meeting, with his steely persona, but contributed little to the discussion.[7] A CIA summary of all the messages that had come in recently was circulated and read. McGeorge Bundy began by reading the Harkins cable claiming that the communists had deeply infiltrated the Buddhists and the students. There was silence. I thought I detected some embarrassment on Krulak's part. Taylor was impassive. (I later learned he had been primarily responsible for Harkins' appointment, which would account for his consistently giving him the benefit of the doubt.) McCone said the Agency had little specific information on that. McNamara said he would query Harkins to determine the factual background.

It was decided to postpone any response to Lodge's tough cable of the eleventh, to tell him only that it was still being studied. Various ideas were brought up, including having President Kennedy send a letter to Diem. McNamara characterized the Defense Department viewpoint as one of objectives and actions, not personalities. "What the hell is he talking about?" I wondered. The problem was how to deal with Diem and his brother; it was about human beings, not esoteric objectives, as McNamara seemed to think. Discussing "objectives and actions" in this context was not only meaningless but useless. Again I was left fuming in silence. I wanted to get up and yell that nobody in the room understood a damn thing about Vietnam. In rural Virginia parlance, I felt about as useful "as the hind tits on a boar hog."

After this inconclusive meeting, Ambassador Nolting and I crossed paths. He had been surprised by what I had said at the first meeting at the White House and thought my opinions that we were losing the war unwarranted. I didn't think I had gone that far. He said, "You just ruined it." I replied, "No, you ruined it by not getting Lansdale out there when it would have done some good."[8] We glared at each other for a moment. He had clearly not understood that I wanted to save Diem but also to tell the truth about Vietnamese reality. Afterward I felt a sense of regret. He had tried mightily to do the right thing, yet he had not understood his personal limitations or those imposed by the formality of his position.

As I walked back to State, I told Hilsman that I was flattered at having been included in these meetings but found them mainly esoteric exercises to which I could contribute little unless asked—and I was not being asked. I needed to get out of town over the weekend with my father and to do that I wanted to be excused from any more such meetings.

The next day I drove my father and mother down to Gravel Hill, our family place in Charlotte County, a four-and-a-half-hour trip. It was too early in September for the leaves to show color. We got there in the afternoon; the old house, with its Greek Revival double portico in front, was just as I had last seen it. I mixed my mother and father their usual bourbon highballs before dinner. My mother cooked a simple meal. The next day we wandered around the place. My father could walk, but his balance was off, so he hung onto my arm and pointed where he wanted to go. He took me down past the old barn and back into the grove to a stand of two tall poplars and pointed to an open area at the base of the trees. I knew from my mother that this was where he wanted to be buried.

That evening we sat out on the terrace, watching the sunset. It was his favorite place. There was a touch of fall coolness in the air, which was clear enough to see the outline of the Blue Ridge Mountains, about fifty miles to the west. We sipped our drinks. I told him how much I had missed him. With his hand he gave me a gentle signal that I was not to worry about it. I could not understand anything he said, but I could read in his eyes a wistful happiness that I was there and regret that this might be the last time he would enjoy his favorite view. He took it all in, the open grove of trees going down to the barn, the pasture to the side with the mountains beyond, and the golden, fading light. We stayed there until almost dark, went in to eat and then to bed. The next day I walked all over the place wondering about the future, my father, and what was happening with my request about Lansdale. The following day we came back to Washington. My father had an appointment to see his doctor; I had to check on the continuing crisis in Saigon.

That Sunday evening I wrote Barbara in Saigon saying that I was okay but that I had to stay another week because of my father and some unfinished business with AID. I wrote to Bohannon, giving the gist of what I had said during my meeting with President Kennedy at the White House and saying I was staying an extra week to help my father and to work for "a right decision" in Washington. I got a letter from Barbara posted on the ninth reporting that Madame Nhu had finally left for her overseas trip to Yugoslavia, where, it was rumored, she was going to cut a deal to form a neutralist bloc with Tito. The other rumor was that she had left with all the money in the Vietnamese treasury. The Saigon rumor mill, as usual, was working overtime. More significant was news that on the day I left Saigon, the government had arrested a large number of students at the Pedagogical Institute. Many had parents in the government and in the army, which would contribute further to the malaise. Later, just before

I returned to Saigon, I got a letter from Bohannon telling me that the word at MACV was I had told the president that "60 percent of the hamlets" had been destroyed in Long An (Krulak, I later learned, had cabled this right after the meeting with the president). I also learned that Minister of Interior Bui Van Luong was reportedly annoyed at me; he had heard I was talking against Colonel Tung in Washington. That gave me pause. How had that leaked to the Vietnamese?[9]

During my remaining time in Washington, I shuttled back and forth between State, the AID/Vietnam office, and Airways Engineering, and I met with my father's doctor. There was no specific news about my request for Lansdale: Forrestal was evasive, Kattenburg was not optimistic. I spoke to Lansdale several times. He was not optimistic either. He had tried for some time to get ideas through about how to induce Nhu to leave. In late August he had floated an idea at a breakfast in Washington with Averell Harriman and John Kenneth Galbraith, then our ambassador to India. A way to separate Nhu from Diem might be to create an academic position for Nhu at Harvard. "Kick him upstairs," Lansdale suggested. "Tell him he's an intellectual." Such an appeal to Nhu's intellectual pretensions would allow him to lecture to his heart's content and would get him out of Vietnam. "Once he's away," Lansdale added, "Diem will be a very different person." Harriman liked the suggestion, but Galbraith was incensed: "We don't do that at Harvard!"[10] Apparently, nation saving was not academically responsible.

When I saw my father's doctor, he confirmed my father had another month at most. When I explained that I had to go back to Vietnam to make arrangements for my family's return, he said I could expect to hear at any time that my father was in his last days.

At AID, before leaving for Saigon, I told Stoney about the latest word on my father's condition; that this would definitely require me to come back soon with my family and to take the time needed to decide what to do with the business. He reiterated that a leave of absence would be arranged, in the hope that I would later resume my post. The only note of levity from this headquarters visit was the reaction of incredulity when I told some of the administrators that the provincial committees were still in operation, controlling the spending of Vietnamese funds. They had assumed that the formal agreement signed between Nolting and Thuan had eliminated the committees. I tried to explain how in working with the Vietnamese, personal relationships and trust sometimes trumped formal agreements. Heads shook—it didn't fit into conventional American notions of how governments should operate.

STORM IN SAIGON

During the ten days I spent in Washington, I didn't realize what a storm I had stirred up in Saigon by taking on Krulak and McNamara in front of the president. MACV had turned itself upside down to prove I was a liar about the "60 percent" of hamlets in Long An that Krulak had said I had reported destroyed. Major Fields, the Long An sector advisor had been called to Saigon, relieved, and reprimanded. At a dinner given by the Truehearts, General Harkins had been unable to restrain his fury and had said openly to Trueheart and his wife, Phoebe, that he was "going to get that goddammed Rufus Phillips." Phoebe had replied sweetly, "But, General, he doesn't work for you." Her soft southern accent must have lent her words a special note. General Stilwell had asked Bert Fraleigh to refute what I was reported to have said; Bert refused, saying he didn't know what I had said but that our September report on the hamlet program, of which Stilwell had a copy, pointed out that the VC were overrunning hamlets in Long An.[11] Such was the overreaction that for a brief period the sector advisors were ordered not to talk to the USOM provincial reps. Bert's impression of Stilwell was that he was just holding to the "party line."

I found out when I got back that I was now out of favor with some in the CIA station as well. At another reception while I was away, Richardson, the station chief, had approached Barbara and asked whether it was true that she had sat in on my lunch with Dunn and Flott back in August when Lodge first arrived. When she said yes, Richardson told her, in an intimidating way, that she should not have been present when secrets were being discussed. She said it had been just an informal get-acquainted lunch, at which, so far as she could remember, I was asked to try to find out what was going on—the raid on the pagodas had just occurred. That was all she knew.

Barbara's encounter with Richardson had been followed a few days later by a personal visit by a junior case officer's wife whom we had known back in Washington. She had tried to pump Barbara about what she knew about the Vietnamese Special Forces and other "secret" projects. Barbara told her she knew nothing, which was true. What exactly lay behind this attempt was hard to say. I never got to ask Richardson directly. Even before I had left for Washington in early September there had been a split among Agency personnel on what to do about Nhu. After initially supporting Lodge's attempt to generate a quick coup, Richardson had decided that a workable accommodation could be reached in which Nhu would remain in the government. I knew from Conein, who did not see eye to eye with Richardson, that others in the station, including Richardson's deputy, Dave Smith, did not agree with him either. The division of opinion within the station had been picked up by the American press and highlighted in the *Times of Vietnam* on September 19 under the headline, "Pardon CIA, Your Split is Showing."[12] The story reported that the "CIA in Vietnam has split wide open into pro-coup and anti-coup factions."

Nhu could sound sweetly reasonable when talking with key Americans, but that was not how he sounded to senior officials within his own government. With the exception of a few Nhu partisans, such as Colonel Tung, most thought Nhu had become an unhinged, self-destructive force capable of sinking the government and the war against the VC with it. I got the feeling from Conein that Richardson thought his own personal relationship with Nhu was a two-way street. In the superheated atmosphere of Saigon in those days, given what I had heard from the Vietnamese whose opinions I valued, it was hard to understand how that could be so.

A TURNING POINT LOST

For a time the idea of sending Lansdale back to Saigon remained in play. Lodge pursued it aggressively, sending a Top Secret, "Eyes Only" personal letter to Secretary Rusk on September 13, asking that Rusk show it to President Kennedy. "For maximum security, I am typing it myself and am sending it to you by messenger," he said. "What I ask is that General Lansdale be sent over here at once to take charge, under my supervision, of all U.S. relationships with a change of government here. To function efficiently he must have a staff, and I therefore ask that he be put in charge of the CAS [CIA] station in the embassy, relieving the present incumbent, Mr. John Richardson." There were "grace words" about this being no reflection on Richardson himself, who was "a devoted, intelligent, and patriotic American." His request was made "not because I have anything but praise for Mr. Richardson, but because of my belief that we need a new face and that General Lansdale has outstanding qualifications."[13] Apparently, Lodge thought that by appealing directly to the president he could cause the decision to be made at the very top, without interference. Of course, the "Eyes Only" restriction was not observed. The news got around very quickly that Lodge was attempting an end run around the CIA to replace Richardson with someone he wanted.

In a telephone conversation with Rusk on September 17, the CIA director, McCone, stated that he had "no confidence at all" in Lansdale and "could assume no responsibility for the operation." McCone claimed that "this whole thing was built up by him [Lansdale] through Rufus Phillips," that "Lodge does not know this fellow." Rusk said "Lansdale denied this," but he called the point "fairly incidental" and went on to say, "If [the] Lansdale thing is not appealing to McCone and McNamara[,] . . . it is a small part of it."[14]

Lodge had tried to kill two birds with one stone: get rid of Richardson and get a manager for his efforts to change the Diem government. I had sold Lodge on the former with the idea of Lansdale acting as his personal assistant, not as a replacement for Richardson. Had I known what Lodge had in mind I would have recommended against it, precisely because of the bureaucratic objections it was certain to generate. In no way had I cooked this up with Lansdale in advance. During my time in Washington, I tried through William Colby (director of the far east for the CIA) to get a meeting with McCone but was completely unsuccessful, for reasons that eventually became obvious. Based on apparent suspicions within the CIA station, it is possible that someone relayed the idea to McCone that I was responsible for the notion of Lansdale as station chief.

In retrospect, it appears that McCone may have also been bitter about Lansdale's connection with the ill-fated Operation Mongoose, whose purpose was to eliminate Castro. Operation Mongoose had been initially run out of the White House at Bobby Kennedy's direction and without McCone being fully briefed, which was not Lansdale's fault. McCone also seemed to have had his own emissary in mind, Colby, to talk to Nhu and Diem. That idea never went anywhere, most likely because Lodge would not agree. While Colby had been close to Nhu, he had had no personal relationship with Diem that would have allowed him to act as a trusted advisor. From Lodge's point of view, there was already one station chief whose views differed from his. It would have made no sense to accept another CIA man whose loyalty was to CIA headquarters, not to him.

Then there was Secretary McNamara. I remembered that National Security Council meeting when McNamara had shaken his head so vigorously when I had made my recommendation to the president. In addition, Taylor had "flatly refused to have Lansdale in Vietnam";[15] Rusk would have been lukewarm at best, because he had opposed President Kennedy's initial intent to appoint Lansdale as ambassador in 1961. Poor judgment, bureaucratic prejudice, and personal hubris would prevail at the top of the administration, with American and Vietnamese best interests taking a back seat. Any opportunity to change direction on the ground was thus lost. With the dispute between Defense and State remaining unresolved, Lodge had an open field to continue fanning a coup against Diem.

Lodge expressed his disappointment about losing Lansdale in a letter dated September 24 informing Rusk of the turn-down by McCone. Lodge said, "It is really a pity. Had my request been granted, I believe the coup might have been pulled off." He went on to characterize the personnel he had as "persons trained in the old way, who are widely (and however unjustly) believed to be in touch with those who we are trying to replace and who, without ever meaning to be disloyal, do in fact neither understand nor approve of current United States policy."[16] "Persons" primarily referred to Richardson, who remained a player so long as he stayed on as station chief. General Harkins had been largely sidelined by

Lodge. While Lodge doubtlessly saw Lansdale's role as confined to bringing off the coup, whether he would have been able to restrict Lansdale to that never got tested. Lansdale had a way of jumping the fences if he thought a particular policy didn't make sense, and he was a master at generating events, creating "running room," and changing the established ball-game. Diem would have requested a personal meeting with Lansdale as soon as he arrived. It would have been difficult, if not impossible, for Lodge to have prevented it, particularly if Kennedy had sent Lansdale out with the specific purpose of making a final effort to separate Nhu from Diem.

As I was getting ready to return to Vietnam, Forrestal asked for my reaction to Mecklin's proposal to introduce U.S. forces into Vietnam. While, I said, the eventual use of U.S. troops to protect American dependents during a coup should not be ruled out, it would be a mistake to use them to fight the VC. (Mecklin had suggested this possibility.) Forrestal forwarded this in a memo to McGeorge Bundy, commenting that he thought my "judgments of Vietnam-ese reactions were as good as any we have," that I was "the only reporter we have with first hand–long term knowledge of this situation both in Saigon and in the field."[17] When many years later I saw what Forrestal said, I wondered why he and Hilsman made such narrow use of my views.

As it was, my opinions, seemingly valued in some quarters, were never enough to break through the logjam in Washington. The factional dispute acquired a life of its own without much relevance to the real issues in Vietnam. Used as it was by the State and NSC faction to undercut Defense and the CIA, my attempt to advance a positive way to keep Diem, exile Nhu, and pull the Vietnamese together had been lost. The simplistic belief that the war was unwinnable unless Diem were removed was irreconcilable with the other, equally simplistic belief that the war was being won by Diem and Nhu and no changes were needed. Both were wrong, but somebody had to get to the president on a sustained basis to explain why, and I was too junior in rank, without access.

President Kennedy decided to resolve the differences by sending the most senior pos-sible mission to Vietnam to resolve the differences. It was to be headed by Secretary McNa-mara and General Taylor. They were to get to the bottom of what had become by now a public dispute, being played out in the newspapers, between the two factions. I could see that the mission's purpose was mainly one of domestic politics. I didn't see how it would result in anything positive on the ground.

LANSDALE'S LAST CHANCE?

It is possible that when Lodge's request for Lansdale was being considered, President Ken-nedy wanted to confirm whether Lansdale was still willing to go back. There is an uncon-firmed story that Kennedy asked him that personally. If so, I would never hear about it directly from Lansdale. It may have been too painful for him, since I had made such an effort, directly to the president, to get him back. According to Daniel Ellsberg, Lansdale revealed the inci-dent in a late-night drinking session in Saigon after he finally got out there, as an assistant to Ambassador Lodge, in 1965.[18] Some time in late September or early October 1963, appar-ently, Lansdale was ordered up to Secretary McNamara's office and told to accompany him to the White House. Once there he was ushered into the Oval Office to meet the president, with only McNamara present. President Kennedy said he wanted him to go to Vietnam to try to influence Diem to send Nhu out of the country, "but if that didn't work out, or I changed my mind and decided that we had to get rid of Diem himself, would you be able to go along with that?" Lansdale had replied, sadly, "No, Mr. President, I couldn't do that. Diem is my friend."

According to Lansdale, as Ellsberg told the story, the president seemed to understand his response and didn't say anything unfriendly or express disappointment, but the discussion was over.

In the limousine on the way back, the secretary was furious. He said, "You don't talk to the president of the United States that way. When he asks you to do something, you don't tell him you won't do it." Given the circumstances, Lansdale probably felt a firm decision had already been made to support a coup and that he would have been boxed into that without being allowed a decent chance to separate Diem from Nhu. Lansdale told Ellsberg that McNamara never spoke to him again. Lansdale would be ordered to retire by the end of October. As an old friend of Lansdale's, Albert Ravenholt, who had known him in the Philippines, told me, one of Ed's unique qualities was his ability to say no to anything he believed wrong, no matter who was asking it.[19]

Chapter 14
The Overthrow of Diem

On my return to Saigon I was greeted by Fraleigh and Bohannon. I told them about my father's condition and that I would soon have to take a leave of absence. They informed me that MACV was trying to clear in advance what our provincial reps might say in any briefings for Secretary McNamara or General Taylor. Fraleigh had objected. No matter how what I had said in Washington was interpreted by MACV, I said under no circumstances should we agree to any precooked briefings. I had had a chance to talk to Bill Bundy, the assistant secretary of defense, while I was in Washington. Bill had been very interested in the June and September Rural Affairs reports on the Strategic Hamlet Program, so I had gotten copies to him before I left for Saigon. Bill was going to be part of the McNamara-Taylor mission and had said he would get our reports in front of McNamara and insist he read them on the way out.

The day after I arrived, I attended a staff meeting at MACV chaired by General Stilwell to discuss the schedule for McNamara and Taylor. Stilwell couldn't resist criticizing me for voicing my opinions in Washington about military matters, about which I was not qualified to comment. It wasn't worthwhile contradicting him publicly, so I just took it, shaking my head. I could see he was going through the motions. After that we got down to business. Our folks were going to get their crack at McNamara and at Taylor too. That's what mattered. I would stay in the background, since I had obviously become the focus of controversy. Let McNamara and Taylor learn on their own. Our guys could take care of themselves. I intended to make sure they understood that their sole obligation was to the truth as they saw it.

VIETNAMESE POLICE SURVEILLANCE

I noticed when I got back that the policeman who usually stood guard outside the front gate of our house had been changed. I took this as clear evidence I was now under surveillance by Nhu's minions. Nhu had his plants at MACV among the Vietnamese employees; they had undoubtedly overheard some of the furious conversations about what I had said in Washington. Combining that with what Conein had heard from Minister Luong about my bad-mouthing Colonel Tung, I decided to take some precautions for Barbara and the children's safety. I contacted Lee Picar, the head of Eastern Construction Company's office in Saigon, to see if he could help.

The next day two Filipinos showed up at the house, Procula Mojica and Amador Maik. I remembered "Proc" from 1955, when he had served as personal bodyguard for Lansdale. Proc had been a scout for Bohannon's guerrilla group against the Japanese in World War II. Bohannon claimed he had once tested Proc's skills by standing in the middle of a rice field during the dry season to see if he could sneak up without being detected; the first hint of Proc's presence had been when Bo felt an arm around his neck. By day, Proc and Maik were teaching Vietnamese army mechanics how to maintain their vehicles, but they would be available in shifts to guard our house at night. I borrowed two M-16 automatic rifles with ammunition from Conein. The weapons were to be kept out of sight during the day.

Barbara took the security presence with equanimity, but it caused an embarrassing moment. At an afternoon tea in the downstairs sitting room for some of the Rural Affairs wives (Barbara periodically got them together so they could share their daily concerns), one of them moved a rattan chair by lifting it off the floor. Lying underneath on the ceramic tiles was one of the M-16s. This produced audible "eeks" and intakes of breath. Barbara tried to treat it nonchalantly, saying it must have been misplaced; I was keeping it for some Vietnamese. She picked it up and put it back under the chair. It broke up the tea, however. That night I told Proc he needed to find a better hiding place.

A DESPERATE PROPOSAL TO KIDNAP NHU

Nguyen Van Buu, the businessman close to Diem with private defense forces, had become more than a casual acquaintance through a project I arranged to give social-welfare and health training to Vietnamese nurses who were part of his irregular forces guarding his shrimp farms and the highway from Bien Hoa to Vung Tau. As the Buddhist crisis grew, he became more candid in his thoughts. He told me he had tried from the beginning to persuade Diem to be conciliatory, but without effect. The main obstacle was Nhu. Behind his usually stolid exterior, Buu became even more agitated after the raid on the pagodas. After my return from Washington he approached me with a desperate proposition.

This time Buu asked me directly if the Americans could not do something to get Nhu away from the president. I said we had tried, but unsuccessfully so far, without revealing details. He had a plan to get Nhu out of the country that required American help. He would take all the risks, but he needed an unmarked, special short-field airplane to fly Nhu out of the country. Over a weekend, he would indulge Nhu in one of his passions, tiger hunting. The hunt would be set up in a cinnamon forest in central Vietnam, within the area controlled by his troops. He had arranged such hunts in the past and was certain Nhu would accept. He would kidnap Nhu on the spot and keep him unharmed until the plane arrived to fly him directly to Bangkok. There he would hire a private jet to fly Nhu to Paris. Once Nhu was out of the country, he believed, the United States could somehow, in collusion with the foreign ministry and despite Diem's objections, prevent his return. Buu would explain it all personally to Diem.

I was amazed at his willingness to stick his neck out for such a risky proposition. Buu was a sober and very practical person, so his anguish had to be extreme. I agreed to present the plan to Lodge, who was skeptical but intrigued. I was sure Buu could pull off the kidnapping and get Nhu to France, but then what? How could a return be prevented if Diem was president and still wanted him back? I was pretty sure Buu would not be able to carry the day by explaining he had done it in the president's best interests. It would be seen as a shameful act—the president was a very traditional Vietnamese. I had to tell Lodge that I didn't see how it could work. When I saw Buu, disappointment mingled with understanding. I thanked him, saying it showed his loyalty to Diem. I tried to offer hope that somehow Diem would come around to separating himself from Nhu.[1]

THE MCNAMARA-TAYLOR MISSION

When the McNamara-Taylor mission ("circus," as some called it) arrived, the only member I saw was Bill Bundy. He had spent time on the way out with McNamara, who had read our hamlet reports avidly. Bill made sure our regional and provincial reps were able to present their views to McNamara and Taylor in an unrestricted fashion. With some satisfaction, I later learned that Taylor received from Earl Long and the new sector advisor the same information about the destruction of Long An's strategic hamlets as I had related to President Kennedy. I would receive a note from Bundy saying McNamara had "read no document more carefully than he did your field representatives' province summaries on the way out, and thereafter he took it and reread it before each of the field trips and used it as a basis for many of his questions." "Furthermore," Bundy said, "your idea of bringing in the field representatives on Monday and Tuesday was certainly excellent[;] . . . the raw responses they provided were read by us and are being summarized here." Bundy went on to say that "what we saw in Vietnam certainly underscored our tremendous admiration for the job you all are doing."[2] It was a nice note. I passed it around Rural Affairs. McNamara's own final conclusion was, however, that much more statistical data and narrative detail was needed in the military sector advisor's monthly reports. New Pentagon orders soon came down requiring a much more complicated and detailed progress report, causing inordinate amounts of additional time to be spent in report writing rather than advising.

Whatever McNamara and Taylor might say in their report to the president, they had received concrete evidence that we were not winning the war in the Delta and that the war effort was suffering because of the political crisis. Needless to say, I never received any personal acknowledgment that I had been right. My bucking of the Defense establishment probably cost me influence in the long run, but I never regretted trying to get the truth to the top.

One of the ironies was that during the McNamara-Taylor visit, Secretary Thuan really unloaded on McNamara confirming my earlier reporting. Thuan told him, "To save his country we [the United States] must put pressure on Diem to force him to stop the repressive measures and force Nhu to leave. Otherwise a coup will occur and this will be disastrous. Don't believe what you see on the surface; the people are angry. In the bottom of their hearts many officers have . . . turned against the government. People hate Madame Nhu. . . . If Nhu tried to succeed his brother, there will be war. . . . [M]any of the cabinet members . . . are fed up. They want to resign[;] . . . if they do they are lost. Many cannot afford to leave the country and those who don't will be put in jail."[3] It was one of the few cases of a Vietnamese official speaking so frankly to so high-level an American official whom he didn't know personally. It was a measure of the desperation felt by many Vietnamese loyal to Diem but not to Nhu.

The visit's only comic relief came when General Taylor played tennis with General Minh, expecting somehow that Minh was going to discuss his plans for the coup. Minh had been burned once before by being overly frank with General Taylor. This time Minh never said a word except vague generalities about improving military operations against the VC. Afterward, Taylor expressed great frustration.

The visit culminated in an important meeting with Diem. McNamara and Taylor, accompanied by Lodge, raised directly the need for Diem to make changes to accommodate the American point of view. Diem stuck by his guns, insisting the Americans were mistaken. He wouldn't budge. I was not surprised; in a way, I admired him for his guts. Here were two of the highest possible emissaries of the Kennedy administration, obviously representing President Kennedy as well as the Pentagon, telling him he had to change his government. As future events would show, Diem was not the only Vietnamese leader who, out of national and personal pride, refused to accept direct American orders. Diem might change his mind, but not in an immediate and direct reaction to that kind of confrontational pressure.

To avoid inflaming congressional and press opinion, the official report issued by McNamara and Taylor after their visit reflected very little of the reality they had encountered, except for acknowledging some adverse effects from the political crisis. There was even a recommendation to reduce the advisory effort by a thousand men by the end of the year, apparently designed to convey optimism to the American public about the war. How the Vietnamese could make any sense of this was hard to understand, except to conclude that the Americans were just as guilty as the French of speaking out of both sides of the mouth.

As I got the inside story from Mike Dunn and others, I felt validated to a degree—but to what useful end? Diem and the United States were more firmly on collision courses than ever. Any chance to get Lansdale had evaporated; the odds had never been great, but it had been worth a try. In any case, it seemed to me, to Bohannon and to Conein, that it was now too late for Lansdale to do anything except be present at the current government's funeral. It was clear the widespread disaffection among the Vietnamese, combined with Nhu's irrational domination of his brother and the government, could not continue much longer. The train was already well down the track. A wreck, in the form of a coup, either by Nhu or by the generals, with consequences that no one could foresee, seemed inevitable. It was particularly agonizing for me, having witnessed the optimism surrounding the birth of an independent South Vietnam in 1955. I had returned in 1962 with renewed hope to help the Diem government win the war against the VC. Now all that was at risk, with no logical conclusion in sight except for the government's violent overthrow, with great uncertainty to follow, a considerable leap into the unknown. But I knew the generals meant well for the country and that Bui Diem and his civilian friends could provide commonsense political advice. I was certain that a violent takeover by Nhu would be worse. The knowledge that I soon needed to return for a leave of absence to put my father's affairs in order was an added burden.

ANOTHER *TIMES OF VIETNAM* STORY

On October 7, the *Times of Vietnam* published a front-page story headlined, "Saigon CIA Chief Recalled on Eve of Congressional Inquiry." The article speculated that Ambassador Lodge might be behind the recall, "but the CIA Chief's purge confirms earlier reports of the deepening rift within the U.S. Agencies in Saigon between elements favoring an antigovernment coup d'etat and others favoring continued cooperation directed toward winning the war . . . against the Viet Cong. . . . Simultaneously there were contradicting reports to the effect that the number two CIA man, widely believed to have been responsible for the assumed purge of Richardson, may himself be preparing his suitcases for retirement. The number two man is reported to be Rufus Phillips, chief of the Rural Affairs section of USOM, the section that controls the Strategic Hamlet Aid funds. Another man on the way out is reported to be John Mecklin, chief of USIS. Phillips and Mecklin flew to Washington several days after the planned coup d'état was revealed on September 2, but returned to Vietnam about ten days later."[4]

On the same day of the *Times of Vietnam* article, I received a cable from Stoneman at AID saying, "Your father in critical condition . . . not expected live beyond a few more hours. Your mother asks you come soonest." As I made arrangements to leave for Washington the next day, I wrote President Diem an angry letter, labeling it "Private" and "Personal." I was sending him the attached article, I said, "which has deeply shocked me. . . . Friends had informed me upon my return that scurrilous rumors and lies were being circulated about me but I hardly expected that they would be believed. In view of my deep personal attachment to your country. . . . I find this gross calumny particularly hard to bear. Even more so because it seeks to exploit the occasion of my father's impending death to imply that I am being recalled for other reasons. For your eyes only, I am enclosing the latest in a series of cables which speaks more eloquently than I of the true nature of my personal situation." I concluded, "I am sure, Mr. President, that such an article would have never been printed had you known of it in advance and it is in a spirit of continued, personal friendship for you and your country that I wish to ask that the *Times of Vietnam* print a retraction." (My letter did not mention that I would be taking a leave of absence of uncertain duration from Vietnam because of my father's death.)[5] I did not get a response until the end of October.

The atmosphere within the American community in Saigon had grown increasingly unhealthy, driven by fundamental disputes about U.S. policy. It had affected me when I was accused by someone of holding "press conferences."[6] Then, on October 2, a story had broken in the *Washington Daily News* with the headline, "The CIA Mess in South Vietnam— Arrogant CIA Disobeys Orders," under the byline of Richard Scarnes, whom I had never met or even heard of. The article completely blew Richardson's State Department cover, identifying him as the CIA station chief and claiming he had twice refused to carry out explicit orders from Ambassador Lodge. It denounced the CIA performance as "a dismal chronicle of bureaucratic arrogance, obstinate disregard of orders and unrestrained thirst for power." It had reverberated in the American press, and it was that which forced Richardson's recall.

Initially I wondered if a dissident inside the CIA station had talked. Details about Agency support for Colonel Tung and the Special Forces had leaked earlier to the press. For Agency employees, however, this would have been a violation beyond the pale of their oath of office. The Agency people I knew were uniformly angry at Starnes' story, regardless of any policy disagreement with Richardson. I soon concluded that only Lodge was ruthless enough for such a hatchet job. Shortly after Lodge arrived in Saigon he had told the USIS chief, Mecklin, whose responsibility was press relations, that henceforth the press was his own private domain. "The leak," he said, "is the prerogative of the Ambassador. It is one of my weapons for doing this job."[7] Lodge had every motive to get rid of Richardson—symbolically, because he was evidence to the generals the United States still supported Nhu, and practically, because he did not trust him, although Richardson had faithfully followed his orders in August to crank up the coup. When that failed to come off, it was logical for Lodge to assume that CIA director's McCone's continuing reservations about the coup stemmed to some degree from Richardson, who had his own secure line of communications back to Washington that Lodge could not monitor.

BURYING MY FATHER

I had been scheduled to accompany Barbara and the children back to Washington on October 10 to be there before my father died. Now I had to go immediately, on October 8, leaving them to follow. I got to Washington on October 9 and to the hospital that night before my father died, though I was able only to see him unconscious, in a final coma. I sat with him for a while thinking about the past and then went home. He died early in the morning. The day after, Barbara and the children arrived. A memorial service was held at a funeral home. The following day I drove down with my mother, followed by the hearse, to Gravel Hill, where we buried him, as he had requested, in a simple pine box. Besides my mother, my sister Lucretia, and myself (Barbara was too exhausted to make the trip), only the Mortons, who worked on the place, were at the gravesite beneath the two tall poplars he had pointed out to me back in September. I read a few verses from the Bible before the coffin was lowered into the freshly dug grave. We went back to the old antebellum house on the hill. I returned to Washington that evening to help Barbara and the children get settled in our house in McLean.

I was torn. I felt under a personal obligation to see the Saigon crisis through, however it might come out. I owed it to our people in Rural Affairs and to the Vietnamese. I couldn't affect the outcome of a probable coup, but maybe I could affect the aftermath. Airways Engineering was in a holding pattern. My mother could spare me another month. Barbara understood, and I knew she could take care of herself without me. She was seven and half months pregnant with our third child, but we had arranged to bring our *amah,* Nguyen Thi Thao (Thi Ba), to help her with the children. Barbara's closest friend, Ana Maria Pages, was ready to stay at the house as well. Arranging all this took about a week before I could return to Saigon. By this time the coup seemed inevitable and unstoppable, a matter of a few weeks, but I felt I had to be there, at least for a while, to assist with what was going to be, at minimum, a wrenching transition for any new Vietnamese government and for Rural Affairs.

BACK AGAIN IN SAIGON

The atmosphere in Saigon was very tense and strained when I got back in the middle of October. The whole city seemed as taut as a piano wire. Lodge was upset over rumors that the embassy was about to be attacked and that he was going to be assassinated. Conein wasn't saying much, except to attribute the rumors to an unwise attempt by Nhu at psywar. At one point Conein complained without elaborating, "That stupid Harkins almost blew it." I found out later that Harkins had told General Don at a British embassy party on October 22 that it was the wrong time to stage a coup, because the war against the Viet Cong was progressing well.[8] This had caused a large hiccup, because Don wondered if this indicated the White House was still supporting Diem and Nhu. Lodge instructed Conein to reassure Don that Harkins was not speaking for Lodge or expressing U.S. policy. Harkins tried to explain it away as a misinterpretation, but it provided Lodge with the excuse to cut him out of things altogether. From Washington's perspective, it appeared that the White House was being dragged into the coup picture.

I was glad to be out of any involvement in the simmering coup and to have some time to reinvolve myself in Rural Affairs in the days I had left. By this time all forty-one provinces were covered with USOM employees as provincial representatives, except three where we still depended on deputized MAAG sector advisors. Six of our provincial reps were from International Volunteer Services, generally doing excellent jobs. Provincial development operations were in full swing in a number of provinces, mainly in central Vietnam. For the first time it looked like Vietnam, despite the political crisis, would have enough rice to export, due to our distribution of improved rice seed and fertilizer on credit. We were going to reach the target of distributing pigs to some five thousand hamlet families. The irony was that here we were, finally in a position to go full bore with provincial development in support of the strategic hamlets, just as the government was failing and the hamlet program was in trouble in most of the Delta. It was very emotional to be leaving without a definite sense of when or if I might come back. I could not help be affected by the intense devotion of our volunteers. I could only tell them I would make every effort to return.

I busied myself with some of the administrative changes that had to be made, appointing Bert Fraleigh as acting chief—presuming that I might be able to come back early in the coming year. To relieve the grimness of Saigon, I managed to make a final sentimental visit to Phu Yen to investigate a complaint about Bob Burns, lodged by the new MAAG sector advisor with the II Corps advisory headquarters. The new MAAG advisor, in contrast with his predecessor, was so uptight that he had converted his detachment's housing compound into an armed fortress, ringed with barbed wire, even though the area was perfectly safe. Bob, who sometimes ate with the advisory detachment, had gotten tired of hearing the advisor boast that his compound could never be penetrated by the VC.

Bob with his assistant, Lam Quang, and two American Special Forces noncoms had driven a small truck in the middle of the night onto the beach side of the compound. Taking wire cutters to the security fencing, they then pulled down a section of it using the truck. Entering the compound surreptitiously, they had planted "VC" homemade bombs under the sector advisors' barracks, with fuses partially burned to indicate a misfire. When he discovered the break-in and the bombs, the sector advisor was initially alarmed, then outraged when he saw he was being laughed at. Suspecting Bob, he lodged a general complaint with II Corps headquarters that the local USOM rep was not cooperative. In the meantime, Bob had been basking in compliments from most of the MAAG advisory detachment. When I got back to Saigon I phoned the II Corps senior advisor and told him I hadn't found anything serious except that the sector advisor had badly embarrassed himself; I didn't think he really wanted to know the details. The complaint died there. It was my only comic relief.

SEEING PRESIDENT DIEM THE LAST TIME

Vo Van Hai called me about a week after I got back. President Diem wanted to respond to my letter personally; he could see me on October 30. It had apparently disturbed him; he had mentioned it to Lodge during a dinner in Dalat on October 29, saying he realized the *Times of Vietnam* "had been a little bit inaccurate concerning the departure of Rufus Phillips which he understood was due to the fact that his father was sick."[9] Lodge confirmed that but was puzzled why Diem raised it. I did not know about this conversation when I came to the palace that morning and was ushered right in to see the president. I wondered what to expect, but he was friendly. After inquiring about my father and saying he was truly sorry to hear about his death and that I had to return to the United States, which he had learned from Vo Van Hai, he said he wished to apologize for the story published in the *Times of Vietnam*. He had known nothing about it beforehand. I thanked him. He inquired about General Lansdale: had I seen him, how was he? I said I had been busy with my father's funeral but had talked to Lansdale on the phone, and he was well. I regretted to tell him that despite all my efforts to get General Lansdale out to Vietnam to help him, particularly during my previous visit home, I had not been successful. He reacted with a sigh.

There was none of the agitation I had seen in him during the height of the Buddhist crisis. He seemed philosophical about whatever fate might bring. We sat in silence for a moment while he looked down and puffed on his ever-present cigarette. There was no more to say, I thought. Then he looked up directly at me and asked softly, "Do you think there will be a coup?" I looked him in the eye. I couldn't lie to him, "I am afraid so, Mr. President."[10] I felt like crying and wanted to take him aside out of the room, which I thought might be bugged, to tell him, "For God's sake talk to Lodge to reach some agreement." Then I thought I couldn't do that; I had already said more probably than I should have. Further words might endanger the lives of Conein and the generals, because of how Nhu might react.

Reading the emotion in my face, he tried to comfort me without words by putting his hand on my arm. He stood up, took my hand, said again he was sorry to hear about my father, that he hoped after I had settled my family affairs, I would come back, then goodbye—*au revoir* not *adieu,* but I had the feeling it might be the last time I saw him. I passed by Vo Van Hai's office. We looked at each other sadly and could say nothing. Hai's despair was particularly acute because of his long and close personal relationship with Diem. We shared each other's thoughts of a decent and brave man, brought to this point by pride and stubbornness, but mainly by his own family—which he had not so much used as been used by.

Around this time, anxiety at the top in Washington about the coup was reaching epic proportions. Great unease was being expressed over White House identification with the coup in case it failed (a result of Don's interpretation of the meaning of Harkin's seeming recommendation against a coup and of Conein's denial to Don that Harkins represented U.S. policy). The issues were deniability and the reliability of Conein as the sole go-between with the generals. In a meeting on October 25 at the White House, McCone, Conein's ultimate boss, had worried that Conein was "overt"—that is, that everyone knew he was CIA. McNamara complained, "We're just like a bunch of amateurs. We're dealing through a press-minded ambassador and an unstable Frenchman," meaning Conein. Bobby Kennedy wanted to cut off all contact between the embassy and the coup plotters, but that was clearly not possible. Finally, the president concluded that the United States had no choice, Conein was the only working link. A cable was sent advising Lodge to supervise Conein closely and not let the embassy become too intimately identified with the coup.[11]

During the last week in October events moved toward a climax. Early on Monday, October 28, Lodge went to the Saigon airport for a flight to Dalat, where he had been invited by President Diem for a ceremony, staying in the same guesthouse where Barbara and I had spent an uncomfortable night back in January. At the airport he had a brief encounter with General Don, prearranged by Conein. Don had one question: Was Conein authorized to speak for Lodge? Lodge said yes, he was. Don said the coup had to remain purely a Vietnamese affair. Lodge agreed but wanted to know when it would take place. Don was not yet ready to say.[12] Lodge's declaration that Conein was authorized to speak for him was the unequivocal endorsement the generals had been looking for.

In Dalat Lodge would spend the day and evening with Diem and finally get to know him better, though there was still no meeting of the minds. At one point, for instance, Diem said, *Je ne vais pas servir* (in effect, I am not willing to be a servant), but Lodge didn't understand, thinking he must have meant *ceder* (to cede). The difference was important, particularly since in the same conversation Diem had expressed concern over the cutting of financial aid, admitting that he couldn't continue to govern without it.[13] Returning to Saigon on Friday, November 1, Lodge had to accompany Adm. Harry D. Felt, Commander in Chief, Pacific, to a morning meeting with President Diem at the palace. At the end of the meeting, Diem took Lodge aside and told him, "Please tell President Kennedy that I am a good and a frank ally, that I would rather be frank and settle questions now than talk about them after we have lost everything. Tell President Kennedy that I take all his suggestions very seriously and wish to carry them out, but it is a question of timing."[14] Lodge would later characterize Diem as saying in effect, "Tell us what you want, and we'll do it." Whether by design or oversight, however, the cable describing Diem's plea was labeled "Priority," which downgraded its importance and it arrived in Washington well after the coup had begun. Later when I learned about it, I saw it as tragic evidence that something could have been worked out with Diem to get Nhu abroad and that the coup could have been avoided.

THE COUP

On November 1, I had an early phone call from Thuan inviting me for breakfast. He told me President Diem had asked his personal opinion about the suspension of American aid. Thuan had painted a gloomy picture, and the minister of economy had given, with his prompting, the same opinion. The president apparently realized the seriousness of the situation but was not admitting it; he was still talking about "self-sufficiency." Everybody in the government was marking time, waiting for a resolution of the conflict with the Americans. He had emphasized to the president that he must discuss these matters with Lodge. As an indication of how security was deteriorating, he said, the Long Thanh rubber plantation in Bien Hoa Province just north of Saigon had shut down, and production had dropped at the Terre Rouge and Michelin plantations as well. This was due to increasing VC harassment—kidnappings and assassinations—according to the plantation managers. I wrote up the conversation that morning for Lodge, dropped it by the embassy, and then went to General Stilwell's for lunch.[15]

The lunch at Stilwell's was a convivial gathering, despite a sense of suspended animation hanging over us and the rest of Saigon, uncertainty whether or when a coup might occur. Along with Stilwell and his wife Alice, Bill and Phoebe Trueheart and Mike Dunn were there. Whatever bitterness Stilwell may have felt at my report to the president in Washington had disappeared. At about 1:45, the phone rang inside the house. Stilwell went to get it and came back with vivid excitement on his face. He had received a direct call, in the clear, from General Don at Vietnamese army headquarters: the coup by the generals had begun. (Our breakfast meeting that fateful day was to be the last time I would see Thuan. After the coup started, he called the embassy to ask someone to inform the generals that he wanted to surrender. No one at the embassy would speak to him, afraid to acknowledge we even knew there was a coup going on. He probably also called my house, but I was not there. The morning after the coup he turned himself in at army headquarters, was held for a few days, and then was allowed to leave for Paris, where he had already sent his family.)

Earlier in October, shortly after I had gotten back from Washington, Lou Conein had invited me for dinner at his house. He had told me the coup might take place within the next several weeks. He had made arrangements for an American Special Forces "A-team" to guard his house and, if anything went wrong, to cover the evacuation of his wife Elyette and their three children. He would be with the coup leaders. Could I stay at his house and look after Elyette and the children, if and when the coup occurred? That was where I went from Stilwell's luncheon and where I would stay until the next morning. I reported in to the American captain in charge of the twelve-man A-team, explaining I had military and paramilitary training, could handle an M-16, was under his command, and had a personal obligation to look after the family.

From Conein's house we could hear intermittent sounds of gunfire during the afternoon and evening. About four in the morning, a tremendous racket of firing, including heavy weapons and what sounded like tank cannons, broke out from the direction of the presidential palace and lasted for over an hour. Then there was silence. While the Special Forces guards remained awake, I caught a few hours sleep before dawn, when we expected word. About 7:30 in the morning Lou showed up at the house to shower, change his clothes, and eat. He had been at the Vietnamese Armed Forces General Headquarters, from which the coup had been run, since the previous afternoon. He had just reported in to the embassy, then come straight home.

The coup had been successful. Diem and Nhu had surrendered at a church in Cholon and were going to be picked up and taken to General Headquarters, to be held there until an

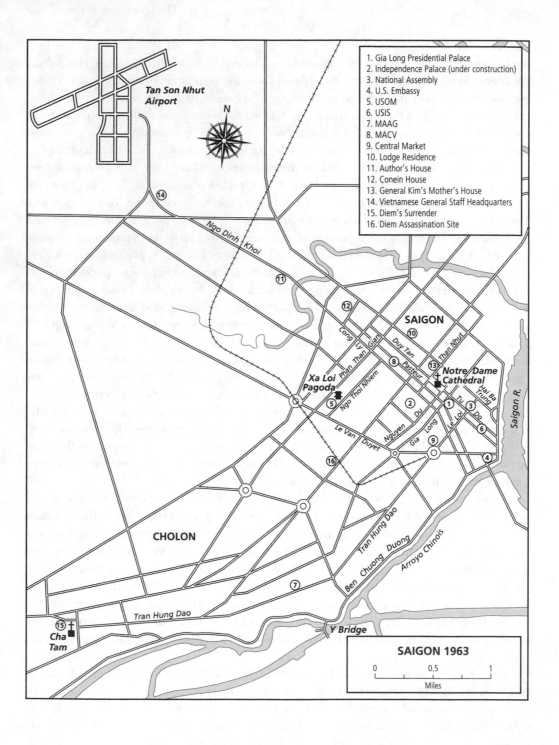

1. Gia Long Presidential Palace
2. Independence Palace (under construction)
3. National Assembly
4. U.S. Embassy
5. USOM
6. USIS
7. MAAG
8. MACV
9. Central Market
10. Lodge Residence
11. Author's House
12. Conein House
13. General Kim's Mother's House
14. Vietnamese General Staff Headquarters
15. Diem's Surrender
16. Diem Assassination Site

Tan Son Nhut Airport

N

Ngo Dinh Khoi

SAIGON

Cong Ly
Phan Than Gian
Duy Tan
Than Nhut
Pasteur
Xa Loi Pagoda
Ngo Thoi Nhiem
Nguyen Du
Gia Long
Le Loi
Le Van Duyet
Notre Dame Cathedral
Hai Ba Trung
Tu Do

Saigon R.

CHOLON

Tran Hung Dao
Ben Chuong Duong
Arroyo Chinois

Tran Hung Dao

Cha Tam

Y Bridge

SAIGON 1963

0   0.5   1

Miles

American plane could take them into exile. That was all he could tell me. Then he left to go back out to General Headquarters to make sure about the arrangements for holding Diem and Nhu until the plane arrived, which would be some time. I felt a combination of sadness and relief that the coup was over. I was particularly happy that Diem had not been hurt. I waited for Lou to return with final word that everything was okay.

Lou came back to the house about eleven in the morning, but his face was ashen. He looked sick. The "goddam bastards," he said. "They killed Diem; they murdered him and Nhu." He was in a towering rage. I was deeply angry too but mainly sick at heart. For the first time in Vietnam since the death of President Magsaysay, I was overwhelmed by grief. "Why, how?" I asked. "I thought the understanding was they were to put Diem and Nhu on a plane and fly them out of the country. What happened?" Lou said that had been the understanding but something had gone wrong during the transfer of Diem and Nhu to General Headquarters. They had surrendered peacefully but had been murdered in the back of the armored personnel carrier sent to pick them up. All of the generals denied having ordered it, and some thought they should call it a suicide. Conein had told them that was the stupidest thing he had ever heard—Diem and Nhu had been Catholics, nobody would believe they had committed suicide. Conein had refused to look at the bodies, did not want to be a witness. Lou was beside himself, and so was I. I should have known, I suppose, that it might go wrong, but I had believed there had been a commitment by the generals to send Diem into exile unharmed. The man had been literally the father of South Vietnam—not the best father, but the man without whom there would not have been an independent South Vietnam.

The details about who was responsible for the deaths would not come out for some time. The most authoritative version, based on a number of accounts, is that General Minh, acting on his own, had given the order to his bodyguard, Captain Nhung, to commit the murder, and that he had given it either out of personal rage at Diem or fear that he and his family might succeed in returning from exile, or a combination of the two. According to some reports, General Mai Huu Xuan, in command of the detail that went to fetch Diem and Nhu, had been complicit in the scheme.[16]

In Washington, President Kennedy was holding a meeting in the White House with his principal Vietnam advisors when the news came. General Taylor would say afterwards that "Kennedy leaped to his feet and rushed from the room with a look of shock and dismay on his face that I had never seen before. He had always insisted that Diem must never suffer more than exile and had been led to believe or had persuaded himself that a change in government could be carried out without bloodshed."[17] Arthur Schlesinger would write that he saw the president "soon after he heard that Diem and Nhu were dead" and he was "somber and shaken," looking more depressed than he had since the Bay of Pigs invasion. On November 4, President Kennedy dictated into a tape recorder a private memo that would not be released until 1998:

> I feel we must bear a good deal of responsibility for it beginning with our cable of early August in which we suggested the coup. In my judgment that wire was badly drafted, it should never been sent on a Saturday. I should not have given my consent to it without a round table conference in which McNamara and Taylor could have presented their views. I was shocked by the death of Diem and Nhu. I'd met Diem with Justice Douglas many years ago. He was [an] extraordinary character and while he became increasingly difficult in the last months nevertheless over a ten year

period he held his country together to maintain its independence under very adverse conditions. The way he was killed made it particularly abhorrent. The question now [is] whether the generals can stay together and build a stable government or whether Saigon will begin to turn on [*sic*] public opinion in Saigon, the intellectuals, students, etcetera, will turn on this government as oppressive and undemocratic in the not too distant future.[18]

President Kennedy was more prescient about the possible consequences than many of his advisors. The memo is particularly poignant because of an interruption, captured on the recording, by his son "John John," who came into the room and began a child's conversation with his father. "Why do the leaves fall?" asks the president. "Because it's fall," replies John John.

THE IMMEDIATE AFTERMATH
After leaving Conein's, I went back to my house, where I got a call from Oggie Williams. Would I care to try to walk with him into the presidential palace to see what had happened? I was initially reluctant but finally agreed to meet him in the early afternoon near the palace. We walked together through the gates. There were still soldiers around and inside the palace, ostensibly guarding against looting and keeping a crowd of gawking civilians out. The outside of the building was riddled with bullet holes. Others from the embassy and some correspondents were already there. Oggie and I walked up to a Vietnamese officer standing at the main entrance, asked if we could go in, and showed some identification as American government employees. He waved us by.

We went up the stairs and past Vo Van Hai's office to the sitting room where Diem and I had sat only two days before. The sofa and the stuffed armchairs showed bullet holes, but the coffee table in front was intact. There was an ashtray with cigarette butts still in it. The sight hit me in the pit of my stomach—visions of our last meeting passed before my eyes. I couldn't avoid feeling that I should have done something, somehow, to save him from being killed. As we left the palace, Oggie was upbeat, talking about a new beginning, but I felt infinitely sad, deeper in the dumps than I ever felt before in Vietnam.

Late that afternoon I went down to the embassy to see Lodge. He had briefly toured Saigon on his way to the embassy that morning and had been cheered by crowds of Saigon residents, for whom the oppression of the final months of the regime had finally been lifted. Lodge was in a self-congratulatory mood, and so was Dunn. They had pulled it off. The Diem government was no more. It was a new day, Dunn said, "A new beginning." Again, I didn't share the mood. The circumstances of Diem's death cast a pall.

There was, however, something that could be done to honor the contribution he had made to South Vietnam's creation and to assuage some of the grief and resentment I knew most Catholics, as well as many others, would be feeling over the manner of his death. The imputation of suicide was not tenable, and the deaths could not be explained away as accidental. I admired Lodge's steadfastness but wondered if he had thought about Vietnamese perceptions. I told him that I thought they presented a real problem, not just for us but even more for any future Vietnamese government. There will be great distress, I warned him, among Catholics and even among military supporters of the coup who had held Diem in high regard and who had backed his overthrow only as a last resort in the belief that he would not be harmed. "There will be bitterness beneath the surface which we cannot see," I said. "It may provoke acts of revenge later, undermining the new government. I strongly believe the generals ought to give Diem a state funeral as the first president of South Vietnam, despite his failings. Most Vietnamese understand, even if they disliked Diem, that above all others he was responsible for creating the republic. A decent funeral would help overcome some of the bitterness which is sure to follow."

Lodge looked at me incredulously. He thought for a moment and said the situation reminded him of what had happened to him when he had been defeated by Jack Kennedy for reelection to the Senate from Massachusetts. "Until that moment," he said, "everybody knew who I was but afterwards nobody even knew my name, or seemed to care." He made a sweeping gesture with his hand and said, "This is how it will be with Diem." I could not help replying, "But Mr. Ambassador, Vietnam is not Massachusetts." He gave me a frosty look. I had offered the thought with only the best interests of Vietnam and the United States in mind, I assured him, and hoped he would think it over. To Lodge the Vietnamese were not quite real, a set of enigmatic figures to be dealt with arbitrarily. He had been sent out by Kennedy to resolve the crisis. He had resolved it with a clean sweep. Now the generals could win the war. The reality was not so simple, however, and it had been further complicated by the dishonorable circumstances of Diem's death after he and Nhu had surrendered. I would never hear Lodge refer to Diem again, even in passing.

Long afterward, Lodge would claim to have felt affection and sympathy for Diem and to have wanted to make sure he was unharmed. However, there is no evidence in the record that this concern was ever specifically transmitted to the generals as a necessary condition for American support for the coup. (Admittedly, when at one time there was talk about assassinating Nhu, the Americans had discouraged that.) Lodge and Dunn would claim they had been prepared to pick up Diem and Nhu in Lodge's ambassadorial car to give them asylum at the embassy if there had been the opportunity. But I saw no sign of regret by Lodge over Diem's death when I recommended a respectable funeral. I talked to Dunn about it and got the same cold reaction. Diem was passé.

Chapter 15
The New Regime

After Diem's murder, I was initially reluctant to deal with the generals, although Kim was my friend and I knew and liked "Big Minh." Despite my personal distress, however, I had to do what I could to influence the new government in a positive direction during my few remaining weeks. There had been a lot of discussion by Bui Diem and other civilians about what to do politically, but I was certain the plans had not completely jelled. I didn't want to contact the generals directly or interfere unnecessarily with their initial efforts to get a new government organized, but I wanted a hearing before any firm decisions were made, particularly about the hamlet program and Rural Affairs support. I wanted to bring Kim up to date on what Rural Affairs had been doing and how the provincial committees worked and also to advance some ideas about how the Strategic Hamlet Program's defects could be overcome. I knew he and General Minh shared a deep prejudice against it; I feared they might throw the baby out with the bathwater.

The impulse of many of the generals was to dismantle everything that might have the stamp of the previous regime. This impulse might be restrained if I could show it was not necessary in all cases and would actually hurt the war effort. By offering the generals advice, particularly Kim and Minh, I might be invading Lodge's prerogatives or those of the CIA station, but I felt I had to go ahead. It was impossible to separate politics from what had to be done to pacify the countryside and defeat the VC. The war was, after all, as I had called it at the White House, mainly political. My remaining time in Vietnam was limited to three weeks at the outside. I felt duty bound to get my point of view across, particularly to Kim, who was the real thinker among the generals.

I got in touch with Bui Diem the day after the coup asking him to let Kim know that though I didn't want to interfere I would appreciate his seeing me as soon as it was convenient. Two days after the coup, I got a call that Kim wanted to see me at General Staff headquarters. We talked about my personal plans. He had heard from Bui Diem about my upcoming departure and about my father's death. (He had met my father during a visit to Washington in late 1959 after attending the U.S. Army's Command and General Staff School at Fort Riley. I was back from Laos at the time and had invited him to dinner at my parent's home.) After expressing his condolences, he asked if I represented Ambassador Lodge. I said no, I was there as a personal friend only. He asked me to come back at 12:45 the same day; General Minh wanted to see me. When I returned, however, Minh's aide said he was not there. It was best to return home and await a call.

The following day Kim invited me for lunch at his house, where we talked briefly. He said he anticipated discussing the security situation in the provinces with me as soon as possible. Dr. Quat (the titular head of the Dai Viet party) had refused to accept the post of minister of health. This was regrettable, but the important thing was to form the government and get it recognized. There were many objections to Vice President Tho as prime minister, but General Minh felt an obligation to him, and Tho knew about the economy, which needed to be stabilized as soon as possible. Objections had also been raised to other members of the former government, but, Kim felt, the people would judge this government on what it did, not who was in it. The most important thing was to get on with the main task of reforming the army and getting it and the civilian administration working together in harmony so that the war could be won. I said I knew from previous conversations he didn't think much of the Strategic Hamlet Program but that I believed it could be fixed and shouldn't be just thrown out. He nodded. At least I had an opening.

It didn't take long for word that I was in touch with the generals to get to Lodge. The same afternoon Dunn told me Lodge was disturbed to hear that I had sought out the generals, given them political advice, and that they were unhappy about it. I reminded Dunn that I had informed him earlier by phone about my initial contact with General Kim and that my second meeting with Kim had been reported verbally to Trueheart the same day. No political advice had been solicited, nor had I rendered any.[1] I said a number of the generals were opposed in principle to almost anything the previous regime had done; I wanted to ensure that the basics of the hamlet program and the provincial committees were preserved. Dunn agreed and said he would get Lodge's authorization for me to pursue this with the generals, since I had the contacts and this was not the ambassador's or Conein's area of expertise. The next day Dunn said Lodge understood the need to get the ruling Military Committee (composed of the leading generals who had carried out the coup) to deal with the Strategic Hamlet Program but that I should confine my advice to counterinsurgency. This was all the charter I needed. I would interpret "counterinsurgency" as liberally as the circumstances warranted.

By November 5, the generals had announced a provisional government with General Minh as president and former vice president Tho as prime minister and minister of economy and finance; Generals Don and Dinh in charge of Defense and Interior (renamed Security), respectively; General Oai as minister of information; two other important ministries, Foreign Affairs and Justice, headed by civilians; and a number of civilian secretaries of state, including a few holdovers from the Diem government. A representative advisory council (the Council of Notables) was to be appointed. The provisional government would rule for three to five months until elections could be held.

The Military Committee and the newly formed government quickly became embroiled in endless meetings about command and policy. General Minh, although the titular head, was not assuming a leadership role. Kim, to whom the role of political planning had fallen, was occupied with it all day and most of the night. He kept passing word through Bui Diem that he was too busy to see me—if I had something I wanted to communicate, please send him a memo.

Conein told me that the former minister of the interior, Bui Van Luong, was slated to take over the Strategic Hamlet Office, which was to be converted into a commissariat and possibly placed under the Ministry of Rural Affairs, while Colonel Lac would be relieved and transferred to the Ministry of Defense. I wanted, if at all possible, to salvage the hamlet program and also Lac, the one officer with intimate knowledge of the program and its problems. I had little confidence in Luong. He knew the program, but he was essentially a bureaucrat and a yes-man.

Lac had been summoned in front of the Military Committee, including Prime Minister Tho, to explain and defend the hamlet program. There was a lot of hostility and not much understanding. General Kim had even asked, in a sarcastic tone, "What the shit is a strategic hamlet?" Tho and General Minh had been friendlier, Minh asking him what should be done to replace the program. Lac said that if the program was to be changed or replaced now, the idea should be thoroughly discussed. Until a replacement could be developed, the main thing was not to let the communists take advantage of the situation and mobilize the people to destroy the hamlets. At the end of his briefing he asked to be authorized to study English and go to the United States for additional training. The meeting ended without a decision.[2]

Lac asked me not to interfere on his behalf, which put me in a quandary. In knowledge and capability, he *was* the program. I decided to intervene and wrote Kim a memo. Having worked so closely with the program for over a year, it said, I was in a unique position to give him frank and reasonably accurate opinions about it and the people involved. "First, the only person with major responsibilities involved in the program at the central level who did a competent job was Colonel Lac. He was trustworthy, honest and truthful despite the difficulties of having to serve as a buffer between Nhu and the Americans." He was the only person who would tell Nhu the truth, and above all, "he understood and tried to apply the concept that Strategic Hamlets were valid only if they existed as something the people wanted and would defend." (My normal rule was not to recommend one Vietnamese to another, because it usually backfired, but this was an emergency and seemed worth the risk.) I also suggested that an interministerial "Special Committee for Victory" be formed, with Minh at its head. This would provide needed authority and give the new government a coordinating body equivalent to the American Interagency Committee, while also giving General Minh direct supervision over the main government elements needed to pacify the countryside.[3]

Prime Minister Tho sent a request to Lodge to meet with me about the Strategic Hamlet Program, and Lodge agreed. General Kim asked for a meeting at seven the next morning for breakfast, before I saw Tho. He wanted me, I learned, to talk to the prime minister about creating a high-level coordinating committee for pacification within the government. He said, "The generals are in favor of such an idea but are not sure how the prime minister will react since General Minh will head that committee. The Military Committee is very sensitive to any feeling by the civilian government or the Americans that they are trying to set up a military dictatorship. They are firmly against any such dictatorship. On the other hand, certain aspects of the effort have to be taken into firm hands if the war is to be won."

The Military Committee was very concerned about Harkins. They believed that "Harkins was prepared to level charges of military dictatorship at them at any time." Harkins had not only been against the coup but "was personally against the committee, particularly General Minh." Kim warned me, "We are not winning the war and we must reorganize the army and make many other changes if we are to win. Harkins is opposed to changes because he has told so many lies, which he now cannot now retract, about how the war was being won. We tried to tell him many times what the true situation was but he would never listen." I said if this was how the committee truly felt it should try to work this out with Ambassador Lodge and not just tell me. Kim understood.

Kim described the situation inside the military as he saw it. "President Diem deliberately split the various military forces and divided the chain of command." That needed to be corrected by establishing a single chain of command. A territorial organization should be set up to reverse the current top-heavy organization at the corps level. In comparison just a single officer existed at the district level, where the people were. He drew a pyramid on a sheet of paper and turned it upside down it to illustrate his point. He wanted to see a military-civil team working together in the provinces, with civilian province chiefs replacing the existing military officers as soon as capable civilians could be found. I said maybe some of the military province chiefs could be indoctrinated now on how to improve their dealings with the population. He agreed.

"The Military Committee is proceeding cautiously," Kim said. "They want to be sure they were doing the right thing and not offending the civilians. Some people want to see General Minh take credit for the revolution in order to build himself up as a national leader right away, but the people know it was not just Minh but the committee who made the revolution. The Vietnamese people are more mature and democratic in their political judgment than most people realize. A leader cannot be forced on them, he must emerge naturally. Vietnam needs a popular leader and popular enthusiasm is essential to winning the war, but it would be an error to create a leader artificially."

I told Lodge that I had recommended to Kim that the Military Committee take up any problems they had about Harkins directly with Lodge and not involve me.[4] On the same day a story by Halberstam appeared in the *New York Times* reporting the negative feelings of the Military Committee's leaders toward Harkins. The assumption in Washington was that it may have leaked from the American side, and if so, probably from Lodge; however, Halberstam also had good Vietnamese sources.

I met Prime Minister Tho over at the presidential palace. Although it had been cleaned up, the walls still had bullet holes. Tho, whom I had only seen occasionally at ceremonies while Diem was in office, was very friendly and forthcoming. He said he had been told by people in the Strategic Hamlet Program and by the generals that I was the American to talk to. He wanted my frank views, and he would give me his. "If there was one thing I reproach in the Americans," he said, "it is that they are too diplomatic, they seem to be unable to say what they mean. Only by a frank exchange of views can we work together successfully." I said I would tell him what I thought.

He reminisced for a moment, recalling the early days of the Binh Xuyen, the Hoa Hao, and the Cao Dai, and how he, Colonel Lansdale, and Big Minh had worked together for President Diem on those problems. Afterward he had remained the president's chief advisor until 1959, when, he said, he was pushed aside by Ngo Dinh Nhu. He had tried to tell Diem that his policies were losing the support of the population in the Delta, but Diem had called him and Minh "defeatists" and pushed them farther aside.

It was difficult for the Americans to understand what had happened in the Delta and how the support of the population had been lost, but they must understand it now. "Citing statistics," he said, "one has only to mention that the VC are greater in number now than two years before, yet supposedly around twenty thousand have been killed. Beyond that … people have told me why they were turning to the VC. In my home province of An Giang, the government, through forced labor, as much as a hundred days per person, built the hamlets and many other public works, such as roads and canals. This cost most people at least a thousand piasters in cash to pay for substitute labor, or in losses because they could not farm or pursue other trades. The VC only collected fifty to a hundred piasters per person in taxes. Naturally the people supported the VC. Many people came to me and broke down in tears over the situation. When I reported this to President Diem, he said he was shown long lists of signatures on petitions from people who had 'volunteered' their labor. I told Diem the documents were fake. Diem then talked about his trips to the provinces and how he was always welcomed. I tried to tell him it was a 'mise-en-scène' by the province chiefs, but he wouldn't listen."

The policy of the previous administration had been one of divide-and-rule against the major religious groups. The results were "disastrous." He and Minh had begged Diem to arm these groups, particularly the Hoa Hao, because they were so firmly anticommunist. Diem had been on the point of agreeing "when Nhu persuaded him he could not trust us [Minh and Tho] or the Hoa Hao." (It was interesting that Tho and Minh's thinking paralleled the recommendation made by General Lansdale to arm local Hoa Hao and Cao Dai forces when he came out with the Taylor-Rostow mission in 1961).

"American aid had been rapid and efficient but not always intelligent. Above all we need . . . firm support for what is right. The Americans should stand up for their own democratic principles and must always insist that what we do helps and not harms our own people." "We must find a way to lift up the burden placed on our people and . . . pay them for their work." I told him I agreed completely with the principles he espoused, which we had tried to promote.

The main ideas he and General Minh had for the Delta were to "correct the abuses of the past government . . . and . . . do everything to lift up the morale of the people; train . . . and arm the Hoa Hao and Cao Dai population in the Delta. . . . their mission will be mainly local security; to concentrate on the economic and social development of the hamlets already built; organize a special effort in the Camau Peninsula to disrupt VC bases; build more hamlets and move some which are poorly placed but this will be done very selectively and the people will be paid for their work and, finally, form a high-level directing and coordinating committee within the government for the overall pacification effort." I was happy that an idea I had originally suggested to Kim had come full circle.

I agreed the government should concentrate initially on consolidating existing hamlets and giving them adequate security and the economic and social benefits that had been promised, while there should be no more unpaid labor for constructing hamlets. USOM would do everything it could to help build morale and win the population's support in the Delta.[5] I knew that Tho's critique did not apply uniformly throughout the Delta, but it was sufficiently on target there was little sense in arguing about the details. The program would be salvaged but modified along the lines Rural Affairs had long wanted. The new government obviously wanted to work with us. Recruitment of the Hoa Hao and the Cao Dai was long overdue. I was only sorry, I said, that I might not be around to work with him, explaining why I had to return. "Please come back," he said; I replied that I would try. The new government was obviously open to cooperation and advice in which I could play a key role, which made me feel bad to be leaving. They were headed in the right direction. Would we be willing to provide the right kind of support and advice?

After seeing Tho, I learned that Colonel Lac would be kept on. Without saying anything to Lac about what I had said to Kim, I told him how happy I was. Later he would say he thought I had influenced the decision and was sorry he did not thank me at the time. He had nothing to thank me for: I had done it for Vietnam and for Rural Affairs and for him. I felt better about the possibility of a workable transition in which the best of the hamlet program could be salvaged and improved. But I shared Lac's concern: What forces would be defending the hamlets while the Military Committee continued sorting out promotions and changes in commanders, and province chiefs?

Time was closing in. No pronouncements of public policy were coming from the new government or the Military Committee, and General Minh, who had real standing with the population, was still not asserting leadership. The proposed advisory council was slow in being formed, while wholesale changes were being made in the appointment of province chiefs. The U.S. side lacked direction and coordination. Lodge was still operating out of his vest pocket, keeping all contact with the new leaders to himself, except for the limited opening I had been granted. Bohannon was convinced that our "hands-off approach" was not working, so he wrote his own memo for Lodge, bluntly entitled, "The Increasing Ineffectiveness of the United States in Vietnam."[6] Its main thesis was that we had failed to give clear and useful guidance to the Vietnamese before the coup and were still failing to do so. His principal recommendation was to assign full-time advisors, knowledgeable in Asian revolutionary politics, to key leaders and to set up an operations coordinating group within the U.S. mission. Lodge did not react at the time, but later the idea of advisors would emerge in the form of a "brain trust."

I finally saw General Minh, at his request on November 18, only four days before leaving. He was the same modest person he had always been, almost six feet tall and husky with a gap-toothed smile and a frank, direct manner. Speaking in a very personal way, he said he now found himself playing a role he had never wanted, as the chief instrument of a coup he had always wished to avoid. He reminded me of a conversation at Kim's house over eight months before, when he had said the Diem government was in a steep nose-dive, that it was doubtful it could be pulled out in time.[7] He didn't know the answer yet; the new government had inherited a truly formidable task, beyond what any outsider could realize.

He had always been in favor of the basic concept of the Strategic Hamlet Program, but it had been misapplied and exploited for personal political gain by Nhu. It was necessary to fulfill its implied promises to the population and to consolidate existing hamlets. At the same time, in areas of the Delta where mass relocation had occurred the people should be given a choice of returning to their original homes or of staying in the strategic hamlets. Central Vietnam was best suited for the program, but its model should not have been applied indiscriminately in the Delta. "It is important," Minh said, "to fit the strategic hamlets into an overall concept of pacification and to understand that pacification, not spectacular combat actions against the VC, are the main mission of the military. . . . The VC aren't afraid of actions involving large units, but are afraid of small combat and civic action operations to disrupt and destroy their support organization. The way to break up their organization is to win the support of the population by working with them and gaining their confidence."

Minh reiterated what Kim had said earlier about reorganizing the army. Units should be assigned to definite areas and given pacification missions for extended periods. Highly mobile small-unit operations would be emphasized, as would decentralization to subordinate echelons, allowing them to operate without constant reference to higher authority. (Ironically, General Minh's practical approach to combating the Viet Cong, which Lansdale had urged back in 1961, would have to wait until the latter half of 1968, when Gen. Creighton Abrams began focusing our military advice and support on pacification at the local level.)

Minh launched into a wide-ranging discussion of corruption. Province and district chiefs had been selling Military Aid Program barbed wire to the population. The new government intended to punish the most flagrant cases. I suggested that if he could make an example of a relative of an official in the new government, that would be even more impressive. (I had heard that at least one relative of a member of the Military Committee was trying to take over Buu's ships.) He paused but got the point.

Minh went on to say the Americans had no idea of how widespread corruption had been under the previous government. I didn't try to dispute him, though I knew the Vietnamese tendency to attribute corruption to people they didn't like. (While the story about the barbed wire was a new one, I thought that if it was really widespread we would have heard about it, but I couldn't show him in one meeting that some Americans were better informed than he thought.) Minh cited other examples. General Don had been approached by a group of Chinese who wanted to continue monopolizing the Camau charcoal trade; they had offered fifty million piasters to the army and twenty million to Don personally. (I thought this was probably one of the ways Nhu had raised money for the Can Lao and for his intelligence operations.) The only way to correct this, Minh said, was to reorient officials in the provinces and carry out not only announced but unannounced inspections. I said he needed to get out into the provinces himself, to set an example; he assured me that he intended to make field inspections. "Changing the attitudes of most government officials towards the population is perhaps the most important task the government has to accomplish," he said. Reminding me how well he understood the rural population, he said, "One thing a lot of people have never realized is that the average peasant is very intelligent. He knows when he is being robbed and he knows the difference between good and bad government." I couldn't have agreed more.

In my memo to Lodge about the conversation I excluded most of my responses to Minh, not wanting to be perceived as having given advice beyond my "authorized" purview. I commented that nothing in General Minh's personal manner had changed since he had become chief of state, that he was "still as unpretentious and candid as in the past. "Further, "He obviously has no illusions about the difficulties or that the main task of leadership falls on him. He is still the only top Vietnamese leader . . . who projects the personal warmth and sympathy required to stir popular enthusiasm in Vietnam. The man has the necessary elements of a popular leader in his character but he will have to be pushed into assuming this role because he is essentially a humble man."[8] I had left my meeting with Minh wondering who was going to give him the push he needed and the personal advice he would listen to. Certainly not Lodge, from his Olympian heights.

I saw Kim again before I left. It was hard to say goodbye. I felt I was deserting in a time of need, and he didn't make it easy. It seemed that the door was even more open for me to advise the new government than of old. I said I would do everything I could to return. I thanked him for retaining Lac, assuring him he would not regret it. I asked what, if anything, could be done about retaining at least a few of the good province chiefs, putting in a particular word for sending Tran Ngoc Chau back to Kien Hoa Province. It was out of his hands, he said; those decisions were being made by the new corps commanders, in coordination with the Military Committee; his responsibility was mainly political planning. He again expressed concern about Harkins. I told him Lodge was aware of the problem.[9]

In my final days Lodge was busy getting ready for another McNamara status-of-the-war meeting in Honolulu, to begin on November 20. I got to see him only briefly. He said he wanted very much for me to return; I gave him the same answer I had given everyone else. Mike Dunn and I talked. I told him the new government, and particularly General Minh, needed advice from Americans they felt they could trust. Minh needed encouragement to assume a more active leadership role. Dunn said Lodge felt strongly he, Lodge, was the one to give Minh political advice. I said sure, in the overall sense, but Minh also needed a more informal, day-to-day advisor who could offer suggestions on how things could be done in practical ways acceptable to the Vietnamese. He said, "You mean, somebody like Lansdale." I said, "Exactly." Kim and Minh were right about reorganizing the army, focusing it on protecting and helping the civilian population. The real obstacle to change was General Harkins. Dunn said Lodge understood the Harkins problem and would address it when he went to Washington to see President Kennedy after the upcoming Honolulu conference with McNamara.

I saw Vo Van Hai, briefly at his house, to say goodbye. He was in tears about the killing of Diem. He had stayed quietly at home after the coup and had not been disturbed. Bui Diem and others were well aware of his honesty and of everything he had done to moderate the previous regime and counteract Nhu's influence. I said goodbye to Bui Diem, who was busy trying to organize the Council of Notables. It could serve as a transitional institution, he said, to provide support and constructive criticism for the new government until elections could be held for a constituent assembly to write a new constitution. A new democratic base had to be laid to develop the common political cause needed to defeat the VC. He wondered if somehow Lansdale could be gotten back to help with political advice to the new government. I didn't know but thought it might be easier now—Lansdale had retired from the U.S. Air Force at the end of October and was no longer under McNamara or, therefore, subject to his outright veto. I would do what I could in Washington to support Bui Diem's ideas about the need for democratic reform and for elections.

The most emotional goodbye was to Rural Affairs. For over a year we had been a highly motivated team, run more by inspiration than by top-down direction. Everybody was treated as an equal; we were all on a first-name basis. I was comforted by how strong an organization it had become and believed it would run well without me, at least until I could get back. Our regional representatives had the knowledge and contacts to support the provincial reps, and most of the provincial reps now knew their provinces and understood how things worked in Vietnam. The necessary commodities, such as cement and fertilizer, were either in place or arriving, and a resumption of the commercial import program would provide local currency to be distributed to the provinces, where the provincial committees would continue to function.

Whether Rural Affairs would have a functioning Vietnamese government to work with, at the top as well as in the provinces, and whether the necessary military actions to protect the hamlets would be taken were the questions. The reported widespread replacement of province chiefs was not a good omen, since the VC had been attacking the hamlets in weak areas since the beginning of summer. Good province and district chiefs were being swept out with the bad, and some incompetents were hanging on because of personal connections. Some of the accusations of corruption were based on personal prejudices and envy. Many of the local irregular defense units that did not have close connections with existing or new army commanders were being disarmed. This included the civilian irregulars organized in central Vietnam under Diem's brother, Can, many of which had been quite effective in bolstering hamlet security. Some of the Catholic militias were being disarmed. Buu's cinnamon and shrimp soldiers had been disarmed. Even some of the hamlet militia had had their arms taken away. Minh and Tho were headed in the right direction, but actions by others were undermining the hamlet program where it had been solid and not reinforcing it where it was weak.

THE WAY HOME

I took off from Saigon on November 21 thinking about what might be done. I had credibility with some of the key players in Washington. The idea of trying to get a small, informal team of experienced advisors to work closely with key leaders such as Minh, Tho, and Kim had already been broached with Bui Diem and with Mike Dunn. Dunn seemed to understand the practical limitations of what Lodge could do alone. Lodge saw himself as the supreme political advisor, but he had neither the relationships, knowledge, nor the patience to work in a way the situation demanded, in daily intimacy with the Vietnamese, serving as a catalyst and good-faith communicator, helping to pull them together. His role as ambassador was necessarily a very formal one. To the Vietnamese he was a proconsul, who by the nature of his position could intimidate but not persuade.

I had been frustrated for more than a year by insensitive American political thinking and guidance, and I was not willing to go through it again. I was willing to sell the consulting firm somehow, return to Vietnam, and take over Rural Affairs, but only if I could get Lansdale back to pull the political side together, making it fundamentally an undertaking of, by, and for the Vietnamese people. He could influence our own military, too. General Minh, as the new leader, desperately needed both reassurance and political advice. He would have to be nudged and nursed into necessary action. If it were done subtly, with the American hand remaining in the background, I was certain he would welcome it.

I returned west on Pan American One, stopping off in Pakistan, where I had been asked by Airways Engineering to see the firm's representative. Arriving in Karachi the evening of November 22 and checking at my hotel, I went straight to bed. Washington is about nine hours behind Karachi, so it was about eleven in the morning there. The next morning, coming down to breakfast, I noticed a teletype machine in the hotel lobby spouting news tape. I wandered idly over. A long roll of paper coming directly off the machine had accumulated in coils on the floor. The tape contained sporadic sentences with intermittent words, some partial, others mangled, followed by blanks, then by more blanks. I saw "President Kennedy," then missing words, then "Dallas," then more blanks and a period. Then came a lot of blank space and mangled words, then the word "dead." No, it couldn't be. I tore through the rest of the rolls of paper, working my way back from the lead sheet piled on the floor. The details were not clear, but the gist was unmistakable. The word "assassinated" appeared; there were more references to Kennedy and Dallas.

I sat down in the nearest chair and bowed my head. I was not accustomed to prayer, but in my mind I was saying, "Please God, tell me it isn't so." I went to the main desk to see if they knew anything. One of the clerks said he had heard over the radio that Kennedy had been assassinated in Texas. He was so sorry. Here I was, stuck in Karachi, waiting for the next flight out. Not knowing the circumstances, I wondered if it was part of a Soviet attack on the United States. I saw the firm's Pakistani contact for a few minutes, asking him to send the firm a letter about what was going on; I was too distraught to focus. I worried about my family and called Barbara from Karachi before going to the airport. She said Lyndon Johnson had been sworn in the same day, I shouldn't worry. I couldn't sleep on the flight. First my father had died, then Diem, and now President Kennedy, who had lit a fire in so many of us, all within two months—it was all I could think about.

I arrived at Dulles Airport two days after the assassination. The next day, Barbara and I climbed to the attic of the four-story building occupied by Airways Engineering on 18th Street. From there we could see down Connecticut Avenue and across the intersection with M Street and Rhode Island Avenue, to St. Matthew's Cathedral, where the funeral mass for the president was to be held. The sight of the horse-drawn caisson with the casket coming up Connecticut Avenue, followed by the walking crowd of dignitaries with Mrs. Kennedy, Charles DeGaulle towering in the front row, was something we would never forget. It seemed so unreal that Kennedy had died.

After a few days I began to check in with Airways Engineering, with Walter Stoneman's Vietnam office at AID, and with the Vietnam Working Group at State. I was now on indefinite leave without pay but still officially an AID employee. A medical exam discovered that my liver function was below normal; maybe I had never fully recovered from the 1956 hepatitis. Between Christmas and New Year the doctors punched three times with a large biopsy needle but somehow couldn't connect with my liver. I refused additional tries and went home from the hospital. Three weeks rest was prescribed, but it was hard to do. I was to take another liver function test in January (that test would show normal function—the first result would prove to have been an error). My energy began to recover. I managed to stay informed. Bohannon and I corresponded back and forth, which kept me in touch with events in Saigon.

Lodge had arrived in Washington from the Honolulu conference just at the time of Kennedy's assassination. In his presentation in Honolulu he had been optimistic about the new leadership but doubted the wisdom of democratization or early elections. He believed, he said, that "in Vietnam the technique of changing governments by violent means is not yet ready to be displaced in favor of changing governments by election."[10] Neither he nor the top American leadership at the meeting seemed to draw the obvious conclusion that if Lodge was right, the new government about which Lodge was so optimistic rested on shaky ground.

Lodge saw President Johnson in Washington on November 24, just forty-eight hours after his swearing-in on the plane coming back from Dallas. McNamara had sent Johnson a brief memorandum saying one of the major problems in Vietnam was the "need for teamwork," that "particularly Ambassador Lodge and General Harkins [should] work in close harmony and with full consultation back and forth."[11] He cited recent news stories about Harkins being out of favor with the new regime as evidence of interagency backbiting. At his meeting with Johnson, Lodge was again optimistic and hopeful, giving the president the impression that we were on the road to victory. McCone's assessment, however, was skeptical, not optimistic. The difference left Johnson particularly concerned about dissension within the American official community. He said bluntly that Lodge was in total charge and that he wanted no more divisions of opinion, no more bickering: "Any person who did not conform to policy should be removed." Also, he didn't want so much emphasis placed on "so-called social reforms," which he thought were efforts to transform a country in our image. "It was too much," he said, "to expect young and underdeveloped countries to establish peace and order against well-trained and disciplined guerrillas, to create modern democratic political institutions and to organize strong economies at the same time. We could assist them with all three jobs but the main objective at present was to help them resist those using force against them." He said he "thought the Vietnamese . . . knew far better than we . . . what sort of nation they wanted to build."[12]

In a note appended to the minutes of this meeting, McCone commented that this was a significant change in tone from Kennedy, that Johnson had little tolerance for "do-gooders." He interpreted this as less emphasis on our supporting Vietnamese efforts to win popular support versus simply fighting the war. Kennedy had had, I thought, a better understanding of Vietnamese nationalism and aspirations, despite the blindness of some of his own bureaucracy to these issues. Inability to appreciate the link between democratic measures to gain popular support and purely military efforts to win the war was a fault line that would plague our Vietnam efforts in the years ahead.

Lodge had his first one-on-one meeting with General Minh, back in Saigon, on November 30. Minh said he wanted a U.S. team to work with, as a "brain trust."[13] If Nhu had kept the Americans at arm's length, the new government had nothing to hide. On December 2, I told Ambassador Lodge in a letter that I had spoken to Lansdale, who was "free and willing, in his retired status, to come out to Vietnam on a space-available basis." I suggested, "The quickest and easiest way to clear existing obstacles, which are less formidable than when General Lansdale was on active duty, would be through a personal communication from you to President Johnson. I believe Governor Harriman could be counted on to assist. I have not discussed this proposal with anyone except General Lansdale." I was forwarding "these thoughts to you, not from any desire to interfere in this matter but from deep conviction, born of long personal contact with the Vietnamese on whom Vietnam now depends, that Lansdale's help is most urgently needed if they are to succeed."[14] The "brain trust" was an opening. The opportunity had finally arrived for Lansdale, I thought.

McNamara, sensing President Johnson's need for somebody he could rely on, began taking over the leading role on Vietnam policy. This was a fateful move but not unreasonable at the time, given the passivity of Rusk at State and Johnson's tenuous confidence in Lodge. At Johnson's direction, McNamara scheduled a visit to Vietnam on December 19, coming around from a NATO meeting in Europe. In Saigon, one of the first things he saw was a report on Long An Province, where the situation had gotten even worse since my report to President Kennedy in September. The 219 hamlets reported complete in September had now been reduced to about forty-five in the entire province. The army, the Civil Guard, and the Self-Defense Corps seemed frozen in place, unable to provide protection against VC assaults. The hamlet militia, armed with old shotguns, pistols, and few ancient French rifles, were outnumbered and outgunned.

On December 20 McNamara met with Generals Minh, Don, and Kim and Prime Minister Tho in Saigon. McCone and Lodge attended, with Lodge acting as interpreter. The meeting was vintage McNamara, the secretary applying his technique of rapid-fire, demanding questions of the kind that he had used to cow the American military. This peremptory and accusatory approach was by its very nature personally offensive to the Vietnamese, who, nevertheless, tried to answer as best they could. According to Bui Diem, who got it from Kim afterward, "The generals bit their tongues in rage."[15]

McNamara's first words after perfunctory introductions were, "Okay, which one of you here is the boss?" After a considerable pause, General Minh replied that General Don was in immediate command of the army. McNamara, clearly not satisfied, said that Don was also minister of defense. In regard to Long An and other critical provinces, McNamara said he was familiar with the way things were at the bottom of the social structure, and it was obvious that there was no strong hand in charge. He demanded to know who was chief of state. Taken aback at McNamara's arrogance, Minh said he was. If any stronger or abler man could be found, Minh said, he would step aside in his favor: "I am not Naguib, and there is no Nasser." (This was a reference to Muhammad Naguib and Gamal Abdel Nasser, who together had staged a military coup in Egypt in 1952, but Nasser had soon shoved Naguib aside.) McNamara brought up the need for General Minh to make speeches giving the people hope for the future. Minh said he wanted to introduce television to Vietnam so he could use it as a way of rallying the people. The generals tried to point out, however, that things were different in Vietnam—the Vietnamese "were difficult," and too many speeches would make the generals look like dictators. The best way to accomplish things and solve problems was without talking too much. (The generals meant that the population treated most speeches as propaganda, having been harangued for so long by the VC and previous governments.)[16]

McNamara would cite his meeting with the generals as a first step in pushing the leadership to do the right thing, not realizing that on a personal level he had had the opposite effect.

His assessment of the new government when he returned was harsh. The military leadership was preoccupied with politics and largely distracted from prosecuting the war. The civilian element of the government was of marginal quality. Provincial officials were unsure of themselves. The chain of authority was still preoccupied with its survival; orders were unrealistic. The most critical situation was in the Delta. McNamara admitted the situation had been deteriorating in the countryside "to a far greater extent than we realized," but he blamed this on "our undue dependence on distorted Vietnamese reporting."[17]

If the secretary's overall assessment was reasonably accurate, the last point was simply untrue, and his recommended actions were wrong. Except for the recommendation that Minh give speeches, the focus was all on process, not on helping the Vietnamese address the underlying need for governmental stability, unity, and a changed military approach as prerequisites to effective action. He wanted to make everything secondary to fighting the war, to signal to the VC that the United States and the Vietnamese were resolute about reversing its post-coup successes. This was to be accomplished by high-level exhortation of the Vietnamese military leadership. He proposed assigning more American advisors, to be increased from nine to twenty-three in Long An, an additional 360 American military advisory personnel in the Delta as a whole, sending Americans down to the district level.[18] McNamara seemed unaware that while the new government wanted close, informal advice at the top, it was against giving Americans greater visibility in the provinces, which would fuel VC propaganda. McNamara assumed that inserting more Americans at the operational level improved Vietnamese performance and that overall success could be achieved through occasional formal, high-level meetings telling the new government what to do. Also stressed was President Johnson's preoccupation with unity and "coordination" within the local American bureaucracy.

At the end of December, President Johnson sent General Minh, through Lodge, a message pledging a "renewed partnership with your government and people in your brave struggle for freedom." Accompanying it were instructions to Lodge to stress a set of eleven points designed to follow up McNamara's visit to Saigon eleven days earlier. One of the points was new, to "accept with pleasure General Minh's invitation to set up an American brain trust to work with his government. . . . [W]e are prepared to furnish any personnel needed for this purpose." Lodge delivered Johnson's message and the eleven points to Minh on New Year's Day.[19]

Bill Jorden, a special assistant of Harriman whom I had gotten to know during earlier visits to Vietnam, spent a week in Saigon, returning on December 20. Jorden had worked for the *New York Times* before joining the Kennedy administration and had a nonbureaucratic outlook unmarked by past internecine struggles over Vietnam policy. On his return he showed me a memo he had prepared. In it he described the Saigon situation as critical. "The raking over the coals of the past," he said, "has become a national pastime and has helped to freeze most of the machinery of government. . . . As a result, most individuals are . . . unwilling to make decisions or to take action on anything but routine matters. The most desperate need is for clear, forceful and imaginative leadership." It was "no time for traditional approaches or routine solutions." Jorden proposed the creation of a small advisory team of

perhaps six to eight men, who know the Vietnam scene, have a real appreciation of the problems, totally devoted to the cause of preserving the country's independence, and who have demonstrated skills in working with the Vietnamese. They should be individuals who through past contacts have developed ties of trust and confidence with the Vietnamese . . . assigned on a man-for-man basis to work with the leading figures in the present government. One man should act as team director and coordinator and the entire operation should be under close supervision of the ambassador.

He recommended for the team Lansdale, Conein, myself, Joe Mendenhall, and Jim Kent (who was in Defense and the only person I didn't know) as the kind of persons to be selected. "The final choice should be the ambassador's with the team leader, preferably Ed Lansdale, having a voice in the selection. Lansdale knows as much about Vietnam, about this kind of political action and about the key figures in Saigon as almost any living American. In this critical situation, bureaucratic rivalries and jealousies must be forgotten. Ed can do a job that desperately needs doing."[20] Jorden's memo, which he said had Lodge's approval and Harriman's support, was the clearest expression I had yet seen of why the brain trust with Lansdale was needed and what it could do. The year 1964 began with some hope that we might find useful ways to help the Vietnamese make a new start. I was mentally preparing to sell the business somehow and go out there again.

Part III
HOPE AND FRUSTRATION
1964–1968

Prologue

Despite the depression among old Vietnam hands stemming from the assassination of Diem and Kennedy's death, 1964 began with some hope that a way could be found to give the Vietnamese practical as well as useful help. Would our approach be dominated by high-level thinking that the solution in Vietnam boiled down to better American interagency coordination and exhortation of the Vietnamese to get on with the war? Would we fall into the trap of thinking that the political solution was simply to find a leader we could back who would start issuing commands that all Vietnamese would willingly obey, or if that failed, to win the war ourselves and give the country back to the Vietnamese?

The political situation within Vietnam was almost a throwback to the disorder of the early days of 1954 and 1955, when a small group of Americans had helped the Vietnamese pull themselves together, largely on an informal basis. But that small group had had backing then, all the way to the top in Washington. This time there were large American military and civilian bureaucracies engaged whose leaders, on the basis of their past accomplishments, were absolutely confident they knew what to do and how to do it. A critical question was: Would our efforts include helping the South Vietnamese start developing democracy as a political cause worth rallying around and fighting for, or would a façade do? Several possible turning points would emerge in the years ahead: the initial post-coup government headed by General Big Minh, the subsequent coup by General Nguyen Khanh, the Phan Huy Quat–led civilian government, and finally the Thieu-Ky transition to elected government. What would be made of these moments?

Unfortunately, there was little understanding then of the need for a compelling political cause for our side, despite the example of an enemy whose every action served its political cause. The idea of America fostering democracy abroad, now enshrined in the National Endowment for Democracy, was far in the future, as was the emphasis on human rights. The prevailing mindset of American leadership was process oriented and mechanical rather than political and ideological. Would regime stability be seen as an end in itself, or would we understand that we were in the midst of an ongoing Vietnamese revolution that required a different approach if we were to affect its outcome beneficially?

It would become clear that Diem's death had left a political and security vacuum in South Vietnam. Would we support the South Vietnamese to fill that vacuum by helping them unite around a workable approach to elected government, or would we, out of frustration and impatience, try to fill it ourselves, first by bombing North Vietnam, in part as a morale booster for the South Vietnamese, and soon thereafter by the insertion of American troops directly into the struggle against the Viet Cong? Would the conflict become mainly an American war of attrition against an enemy who was prepared to suffer unlimited casualties so long as the

Politburo in Hanoi survived, or would counterinsurgency, properly conceived and executed by the Vietnamese, with American backup, be pursued as the primary course? Would winning the support of the rural population continue to be ignored and further impeded by counterproductive military tactics of indiscriminate firepower? Would the means employed remain consistent with our goal of preserving the independence of South Vietnam? Would we take to heart the axiom that the war was "not an isolated phenomenon," that our actions had to "be viewed in that context, and as they may be made to appear long after our major involvement here has ended?"[1] Could the way our actions played out be explained to the American people in terms they would understand and support, or would it appear that we were carrying on our backs a people who seemed not to care enough about their own future to fight for it?

Hope would be raised for a political approach by the return of Lansdale as an assistant to Ambassador Lodge in the summer of 1965. Lansdale had posed a question in the title of an October 1964 article in *Foreign Affairs:* "Viet Nam: Do We Understand Revolution?" What would be the answer? What would become of the flickering moments of hope and opportunity along the way that we Americans, together with the Vietnamese, might get it right before we lost the American people's support?

Chapter 16
Events Go Wrong

As 1964 began, there was little action from the new Vietnamese government. The door kept revolving for province and even district chiefs, making it almost impossible to mount a consistent campaign of consolidating and protecting the good hamlets in the provinces. The VC were intensifying their campaign against the hamlets, many of which were left undefended as army units remained static in the absence of definitive orders from Saigon and because of changes in command. Bohannon had written me that the Military Committee sought to govern by committee but did "not know how to make a committee achieve even the limited effectiveness of which it is capable. Its members seem to be indulging in a good deal of self-justification and vindictiveness, and apparently, efforts at self protection."[1] Subsequently, he wrote that *New Yorker* writer Bob Shaplen was "full of dark misgivings about a counter-coup by the young officers."[2] (Shaplen's information came mainly from his stringers, my old friends Nguyen Hung Vuong and Pham Xuan An, who were unusually well informed.)

Lodge responded with a personal note around Christmas to my December 2, 1963, letter recommending that he ask for Lansdale. He had made several moves concerning my recommendation, "but none had been successful." Then I got a letter from Mike Dunn saying he didn't have much for me on my "favorite project. The matter in which you are interested has been discussed with people there at very high levels with as yet inconclusive results. I and the ambassador hope your health and other personal considerations will permit you to consider again assuming an active role in Saigon."[3] This was disappointing. Unless Lodge was sending unrecorded letters to President Johnson, which was doubtful, it seemed clear the president was not engaged on this issue. McNamara seemed more and more to be taking over as his chief advisor on Vietnam. Knowing of the secretary's dislike for Lansdale, I could only speculate that he remained opposed. McNamara would not have understood or liked an informal, unconventional approach.

On January 10, Lodge met with Generals Minh, Don, and Kim, Prime Minister Tho, and Foreign Minister Tran Van Lam. The meeting responded to Johnson's end-of-December eleven-points cable. Lodge opened up with a series of rhetorical questions, followed by prescriptions. "How is it the VC guerrillas put up such a tough and relentless fight without helicopters?" Then, answering his own question: "Obviously because they believe in something; the communists have conveyed to these men a clear picture of a program which they think will make life better. We have not. They are also well organized politically; we are not." This was followed by a series of questions, with answers as to what should be done. The Vietnamese replied that they were aware of what needed to be done and were beginning to do it.[4] Some of their answers made sense; others didn't and seemed instinctively prejudiced against whatever the Diem government had done. What the generals and Tho most strongly objected to, however, was placing American advisors down at the district level. It would feed VC propaganda.

This meeting like others with Lodge, provided no opportunity for real dialogue. There was no follow-up from the American side, no informal sitting down with the Vietnamese and coming to a consensus about action that made sense in Vietnamese terms. A step-by-step process was needed to wring order out of increasing anarchy. One Lansdale "coffee klatch" would have been worth more than all of Lodge's formal meetings with the new leadership. The Council of Notables, as a positive channel for civilian political energies and grievances, was moving ahead, aided by Bui Diem as deputy chairman, but it attracted no American attention or support.

I remained involved, often visiting the Vietnam offices at AID and State, and I got to see a draft State proposal to Lodge to implement the "brain trust" idea. Three key advisors would be assigned, a senior Foreign Service officer from State to work with Minh and Tho on broad program implementation, a ranking AID official to work with GVN on counterinsurgency, and economic officials and a high-ranking military officer provided by MACV to work with Ministry of Defense and joint General Staff officials. The advisors would have American assistants (Vietnamese-speaking if possible) and maintain offices in Vietnamese government buildings close to the officials they would advise.[5] The word was that I was the main candidate for the AID position. I had misgivings and tried unsuccessfully to insert a broader view of the "brain trust" into the cable. "What we are facing in Vietnam," I said, "is a leadership vacuum which needs to be filled by inspired leadership imbued with democratic principles." General Minh had the potential to become a national leader, but given his hesitant character it would require a "full-time, day-to-day effort to advise, coax and lead" him into such a role. "Otherwise the existing vacuum will be filled by somebody, but it may be filled too late or by the wrong man." Needed most was "the service of an American with proven political action experience capable of molding General Minh into a national leader." The Vietnamese leadership that was needed to win could only be developed by "an essentially unconventional U.S. political advisor effort."[6]

On January 14, Lodge responded negatively to the "brain trust," claiming that the Vietnamese government refused to treat the idea "as a businesslike proposal." He doubted the government "would like the idea of high powered Americans on an 'opposite number' basis in adjacent offices all through the government." Such a scheme had a "colonial" touch. Instead, he recommended continuing on a purely advisory, friendly basis through existing channels. "Through my frequent meetings with the generals and our other close contacts at all levels, we can bring our weight to bear."[7]

Soon after, Lou Conein arrived in Washington to accept a medal from the Agency for his actions during the November 1 coup. He told me that Lodge wanted an informal kitchen cabinet to follow up with the Vietnamese on his, Lodge's, political ideas. He particularly did not want Washington or MACV appointing personnel whose first loyalty would be to their agencies, not to him. He still wanted Lansdale and had asked Lou to push the idea of Lansdale as the head of an informal team of advisors to the Vietnamese but working directly for him. Lou would later claim he saw practically everyone who mattered in Washington and talked up Lansdale widely as the only person who could lead the team. He thought most had been receptive.

I still had not given up hope, having heard Lodge might be called back to Washington for another meeting with President Johnson in late January or early February. Then, on January 30, General Nguyen Khanh struck, taking over from the first Military Committee in a bloodless coup that quickly became known among the Vietnamese as the "Harkins coup." The knowledge that the generals leading the November 1 coup didn't like or trust Harkins, and vice versa, was widely known. While General Harkins officially denied any foreknowledge, Khanh's American military advisor, Col. Jasper Wilson, had received information several days before that Khanh was about to stage a coup to forestall what he claimed was a pro-French plot by General Mai Huu Xuan, the national chief of police. Years later, when asked in an interview if he had known Khanh was going to take over, Harkins admitted, "Yes he told me. I told them back in Washington it was coming up. I got this word. And they didn't do anything about it." Circumstantially, it seems unlikely that Harkins did not also inform Lodge in advance. When asked in the same interview if Khanh had been a change for the better, Harkins replied, "Yes I did [think so]. Because one man was running things then, and he was strong enough to make decisions."[8]

Lodge's initial reaction to Washington characterized Khanh as a "cool, clear-headed, realistic planner; has good record; is tough, ruthless, farsighted." Khanh had shrewdly passed the word through Colonel Wilson that he would "rely heavily on Lodge for political assistance." Lodge's personal reaction to the demise of the Minh-Tho government was, "Good riddance."[9] It was in actuality a setback, an indication of the fragility of any regime in Saigon without a claim to legitimacy. I had met Khanh and thought he was one of the better corps commanders, but, unlike General Minh, he was an unknown quantity politically with no significant civilian or military base of support.

Khanh's first act was to arrest the key generals in the Military Committee and send them under guard into exile, initially near Danang, then to Dalat, except for General Minh, who was allowed to stay in Saigon. Khanh named himself chairman of the Military Committee, replacing Minh. The previous government was dissolved. The Council of Notables was allowed to linger on for several months, then dissolved. While some civilian ministers were appointed by Khanh, Vietnam was now governed in essence by a one-man military dictatorship. Khanh wanted to keep Minh as titular chief of state, to show some continuity, but Minh refused to play an active role while his friends were under house arrest. Conein, who would be assigned as Khanh's informal aide when he returned from Washington, thought Khanh's move had been motivated mainly by ambition, but also by anger at the assassination of Diem. Khanh immediately arrested Minh's personal bodyguard, Captain Nhung, who had actually shot Diem and Nhu; soon thereafter he was found in his cell hanged on his own shoelaces. The ostensible reason for the coup, as proclaimed by Khanh, was to save the country from "neutralism." The leaders of the original Military Committee had supposedly been cooperating in a French scheme to neutralize Vietnam, a preposterous claim. Although repeatedly promised by Khanh, no evidence was ever produced to sustain the charge.

Washington took Lodge's initial favorable reports at face value. Lodge was told to tell Khanh that it was essential "he and his government demonstrate to the people of South Vietnam, the people of the United States and the people of the world their unity and strength. To do so the tempo of South Vietnamese military operations much be stepped up immediately and visibly so."[10] Lodge told Khanh bluntly that "he would rise or fall, as far as American public opinion was concerned, on the results which he obtained in the effort against the Viet

Cong. Nothing could be more fatal to U.S. confidence than another six weeks of interregnum, or a period . . . devoted to fumbling around and to so-called 'reorganization.'" Wanted was "not rhetoric but concrete results in the provinces," where the situation was critical. Khanh "agreed emphatically with all of this," according to Lodge.

Khanh asked Lodge's advice on forming "a government of national union"; Lodge replied that he didn't know enough to give him specific advice. Khanh also asked Lodge who to name as prime minister to replace Tho; Lodge said he would let him know if he had any ideas.[11] Unlike the previous generals, Khanh had figured out how to handle Lodge by flattering him and agreeing with his recommendations, regardless of their practicality. Khanh threatened to take action against the French for their supposed support of a neutralist plot. This caused heartburn in Washington where State repeatedly attempted through Ambassador Charles E. Bohlen in Paris to get DeGaulle to modify his neutralist stance. Though this was a red herring, Khanh would prove shrewd and clever in dealing with the Americans. How he would deal with his own people was the question, though, and little American thought was given to it.

At a press conference in Washington on February 1, President Johnson read a public letter to General Khanh saying he was "glad to know that we see eye to eye on the necessity of stepping up the pace of military operations against the Viet Cong."[12] The day before President Johnson's announcement, he had received a cable giving Lodge's assessment of Khanh. Lodge had characterized the junta of the first coup as comparable to "those who manage election campaigns in the U.S. but who are not the same as those who occupy important posts after the election is won. . . . Similarly the group that ended the Diem regime and cleaned out much of its dry rot has rendered a service and now a new man has the job of winning the war. In this country it rarely occurs to anyone that an election is an efficient or appropriate way to get anything accomplished. The traditional way . . . is by well planned, well thought out use of force. What General Khanh has done does not appear to have shocked the Vietnamese." Lodge had heard "expressions of admiration for the smoothness of the technique" (citing his houseboy and cook as sources!). The real question was, "Is Khanh able?" Lodge concluded that he was, that he had "a lot of drive" and was "not tolerating any delay." Lodge cited Gen. William Westmoreland as being "in Can Tho yesterday morning and reports that none of the officers there feel any lack of a definite policy or definite directive from the top."[13] When I heard about Lodge's comments, I told Bill Jorden it was foolishness; Lodge was clueless about the Vietnamese.

Toward the end of February, during a trip to Tay Ninh, Lodge gave another glowing impression of General Khanh. Khanh told Lodge he had moved the timing of the trip forward a day, because the French "have put 100,000 piasters into Tay Ninh to assassinate me." Lodge apparently believed this. According to Conein, it was a fairy tale dreamed up by Khanh to bolster his campaign against French meddling, the main rationale for his coup. Watching Khanh address the assembled crowd, Lodge concluded, "I continue to be favorably impressed by him. He is invariably good humored, intelligent, unruffled and quickly comprehending. He is really very much more able than the Minh Don Kim group and, of course, he is so far above Diem and Nhu that there is no comparison."[14] The reality was that Khanh spoke very good English, was superb at putting on appearances, flattering key Americans, and blaming his troubles on other Vietnamese.

Shortly after the Khanh coup, I began maneuvering to get back to Vietnam on a temporary trip to see what was happening with Rural Affairs and the hamlet program. Also, I desperately wanted one last chance to talk to Lodge about Lansdale. I was ready to tell Lodge that I would commit myself to coming back as head of Rural Affairs or in whatever other capacity he might want me if he would bring out Lansdale. Mike Forrestal was all for my going and had written a note to Lodge suggesting it. However, Lodge failed to respond, and William Sullivan, who had just taken over a newly created Vietnam interagency coordination committee, found bureaucratic reasons against it. Whatever was to be done had to be decided jointly among all the agencies.

My chances of bringing any influence to bear on what was happening in Vietnam were running out. Bohannon's contract with AID was up at the end of February and could not be renewed. Bo had volunteered to stay on for a dollar a year, but that option no longer existed under current rules. My informal channel to Dunn and Lodge was about to disappear with Bo. It seemed clear that Lodge wanted the status quo, with himself as the prime political advisor, playing the lone wolf with Khanh.

Out of frustration, around the middle of February I sent a personal letter for Lodge through Bohannon, asking him to show it informally to Dunn before he delivered it to Lodge. Bo was to take it back if Dunn felt Lodge would react negatively. The letter set forth my appraisal of the politics of Lodge's standing with the president—that his being a potential Republican presidential candidate gave him such leverage that the president dared not refuse him any support he wanted, which meant that if he insisted directly on Lansdale, he would get him. Also, I said I had definitely decided not to come back unless Lansdale did. Rather than discussing it with Dunn in advance, Bohannon who had become fed up with inaction, gave it to Dunn in a sealed envelope to give to Lodge directly. The letter treaded on Lodge's towering ego and was much too impertinent for him, even if my assessment was accurate. Afterward Lodge said angrily that if that was the kind of political action I wanted, I should get into that field; Rural Affairs was not the place for me. Having clearly offended Lodge, Dunn said I should wait for the next ambassador.[15]

As I heard about Lodge's reaction, another McNamara-Taylor mission to Vietnam was being organized for early March. It was to include McCone, Sullivan, Forrestal, and AID director Bell, as well as a supporting cast including Colby from the CIA and Stoneman from AID, among others. The mission was to determine how best to support General Khanh and to create, under Lodge, a new operations directorate for interagency coordination. The operations directorate supposedly involved me, as the proposed deputy, with the top position to be selected by Lodge. I was told that this had been cleared with McNamara. I told Stoneman about my letter to Lodge, explaining that I was probably no longer persona grata. Stoneman and Director Bell were, nevertheless, willing to fight to get me sent back in a meaningful role. I tried but failed to get myself included as a subordinate member of the mission.

At Mike Forrestal's suggestion I wrote, "A Political Plan and Pacification Approach for Vietnam," which he circulated to Sullivan's Vietnam Coordinating Committee and the proposed mission to Saigon. Mainly needed, I said, was "a political plan of action to create tangible evidence of an idea on our side worth fighting for which the Vietnamese would adopt as their own. That idea was democracy, steps toward which would create a climate of growing unity and ensure a people oriented approach toward winning over the rural population." These were not just my ideas but were themes picked up from many Vietnamese and confirmed by own on-the-ground experience. It was my first attempt at conceiving an across-the-board approach; it had no perceptible impact.[16]

As the mission prepared to leave for Saigon, Lodge had convinced President Johnson that Khanh was the man we needed. Johnson, in a burst of enthusiasm, instructed McNamara and Taylor to "make Khanh 'our boy'" and to proclaim "the fact to all and sundry." He wanted "to see Khanh in the newspapers with McNamara and Taylor holding up his arms."[17]

The McNamara-Taylor mission got to Vietnam on March 8. One full day was devoted to touring the countryside with General Khanh. When I saw the photographs of McNamara with Khanh in the newspapers, McNamara holding up one arm, Khanh's hand in his, and Taylor in full uniform clutching the other, I cringed. Presuming that Khanh, given intelligent advice and support, might have had a chance to succeed, at least as an interim leader, this was close to a kiss of death, for two reasons. In the eyes of noncommunist Vietnamese, we were stuffing Khanh down their throats. To the VC it was a godsend, visible proof that Khanh was an American puppet. The National Liberation Front's president, Nguyen Huu Tho, reportedly later claimed that "the greatest gift for us was when McNamara came and toured the countryside, holding up Nguyen Khanh's hand and shouting, 'this is our man.' This saved our propaganda cadres a great deal of effort."[18]

To the assembled Vietnamese crowds, it would have seemed absurd, particularly McNamara crying out in his midwestern accent, *"Vietnam Muon Nam"* (Vietnam ten thousand years), the Vietnamese way of saying "long live Vietnam." As McNamara pronounced it, the phrase came out as, at best, "Vietnam wants to lie down," or at worst, "Ruptured duck wants to lie down."[19] The top Americans on the tour and President Johnson at home were seemingly oblivious to its real effect. McNamara would later excuse his actions, saying they had been ordered by the president, but that didn't account for his lack of common sense in failing to tell the president that there were better ways to protect Khanh against another coup than publicly making him look like an American stooge.

A counter note to the administration's embrace of General Khanh was sounded by Brig. Gen. W. W. Strong, an old friend of General Minh's. He reported Minh's concern over the fate of the generals under house arrest and its effect on the army. The charges of neutralism and plotting with the French were "absolutely false. Many officers . . . were bitter and frustrated about it. The four generals must be freed and reintegrated into the army or the war will not be carried through vigorously because so many officers . . . will not have their hearts in it." Minh would do "everything in his power to support Khanh," but he wanted Lodge to force Khanh to reintegrate the generals. He would "give his personal guarantee that the four will bury the hatchet in the interests of the country." Minh was willing to "do everything possible to reunify the army for the government. Only I (Minh) have the possibility of doing that."[20] There was no indication that Lodge, McNamara, or Taylor, in their optimism, took Minh's warnings into account.

The McNamara-Taylor mission proposal for an operations directorate was not acceptable to Lodge, but it was decided to send a permanent replacement for me as head of Rural Affairs, an idea that I supported. There were two candidates: Col. Sam Wilson, who had been on Lansdale's staff in the Pentagon, and George Tanham from RAND, a counterinsurgency expert. The decision was to send Tanham as the assistant director and Sam as his deputy. Concerned about where this left Bert Fraleigh, I suggested that a practical solution was to give Tanham two deputies: Sam could focus on counterinsurgency and Bert on provincial development, which was his natural bent. This would have worked, had it not been for the arrival of James Killen as mission director.

SENATOR HUBERT HUMPHREY

Some of us who had worked for Lansdale during the 1954–56 period began meeting on an informal basis to consider what should be done in Vietnam now. In late February, Bert Fraleigh made a trip to Washington that launched the group, principally Lansdale and me, on a new path of trying to influence Vietnam policy through Senator Hubert Humphrey of Minnesota. Humphrey had first come across Fraleigh in 1959 in Taiwan, where Bert was a recognized expert on Chinese refugee resettlement and the use of surplus food under the Food for Peace Program, of which Humphrey had been the main sponsor in the Senate. At their first meeting, Fraleigh expected "a perfunctory handshake and a few minutes of pleasantries. Instead he [Humphrey] was intensely interested in the poor people in Asia and how American could really reach them." Fraleigh described Humphrey as having "a lot of farm boy and common horse sense and human feel in him."[21] In the years that followed Fraleigh had kept in touch. Now, when he got to AID headquarters, there was a note asking him to call Humphrey's office. That same afternoon a meeting was arranged, and he was able to describe intimately and directly the situation in Saigon and to talk about Lansdale and me.

Meeting Humphrey was to encounter a human dynamo, brimming with energy and obvious intelligence but also human interest and curiosity. Despite his reputation as a talker, what struck me instantly was his willingness to listen and his ability to understand what we were talking about. He was the first and last high-level official I would ever encounter in the U.S. government who took the time to listen to a detailed explanation of what Vietnam and the war was about and how it had to be fought, and who walked away with a good understanding of what he had been told.

Humphrey had an instinctive feel for the unconventional people-based, political nature of the war, the "x factor" that McNamara failed to comprehend. He believed our aid had a political impact and that we should try to promote not the form of U.S. democracy but the substance of it. He had no difficulty in understanding why the Vietnamese would tell people like Fraleigh and me things they wouldn't tell more distant and official Americans, or how one could work behind the scenes as a friend to help the Vietnamese get things done. In contrast to other high-level officials I had talked to ad nauseam, he had an intuitive feel for political common sense, often lacking in the U.S. effort, and an appreciation of the people-first approach we advocated. When we explained how the VC penetrated and took control with absolute ruthlessness at the village level in Vietnam, he understood. It reminded him of his own experience fighting communist attempts to take control of the Farmer-Labor Party in Minnesota. There was nothing wooly-headed about his views, nor was his anticommunism exaggerated. All this was a part of Humphrey's philosophy. It was what drew us to him and him to us.

Lansdale did most of the talking at our first meeting, but I had a chance to explain how the underlying idea of American democracy, that government depends on the will of the governed, could be translated onto the ground in Vietnam. The farmers in the countryside understood instinctively the difference between a government that was arrogant, in which everything went from the top down, and a government that worked with and for them. They understood the differences in local officials in the way they reflected these attitudes. The top-down approach to governance had to be up-ended in order to win over the population at the bottom, and winning popular support at the bottom would, in turn, inspire the right kind of leadership at the top. If consistently applied over time this would make the countryside, and hence South Vietnam, largely impervious to Viet Cong influence. Humphrey understood.

232

People were his bottom line. Meeting Humphrey was as exciting as my first encounter with President Magsaysay in 1954. I came away inspired and renewed. To quote one of his close associates, "When you were involved with Humphrey it really made you feel good."[22]

I developed a friendship with Humphrey's administrative assistant, Bill Connell, who had the same practical understanding of what we were talking about. Bill was a couple of years older than I, having served in the navy at the end of World War II. He was a speechwriter for the University of Minnesota's president when Humphrey first hired him in 1955 as press secretary and as his "Minnesota man" for constituent affairs. Now, as administrative assistant, he had the most direct access to the senator. If I couldn't see Humphrey, whose calendar was always overcrowded, I could usually get to see Bill.

It was becoming clear that Lodge would not remain much longer, as pressure built for him to involve himself directly in Republican politics back home. On March 11, while remaining in Saigon, Lodge had won the 1964 New Hampshire presidential primary with a write-in vote. His candidacy died in the Oregon primary of May 14, after which he gave his delegates to Nelson Rockefeller, but there was still a chance to block Barry Goldwater's nomination if he went back. The administration's need to find a replacement for Lodge gave us an opportunity. Humphrey, because of his closeness to Johnson when he had been speaker and his influential role on the Foreign Affairs Committee, had a direct channel to the president. Ideally this would offer us a path around most of the bureaucracy that was unreceptive at best to our ideas about how to fight the war.

As winter gave way to spring in 1964, little was being done in the provinces in Vietnam to stop the VC. Khanh, despite his promises to Lodge, continued to make changes in command. TheStrategic Hamlet Program had been renamed the "New Rural Life Program," and my old friend Colonel Lac was the leading staff person, but there was still no clear chain of command down to the provinces. The Vietnamese army corps commanders now had more say, and they constantly interfered. Province chiefs were still being changed, and those in charge were reluctant to act or to spend already allocated money. There was no consistent follow-through on the American side. MACV's focus remained on the purely military aspects of counterinsurgency, not on population security. General Harkins was still in charge, although he now had a new, more vigorous deputy, Gen. William Westmoreland. With Lodge increasingly preoccupied by Republican politics, Khanh focused on balancing the political and military forces critical to his political survival.

HOWARD SIMPSON

Ironically, the old "brain trust" idea had been revived by Lodge with Khanh, and an American, Howard Simpson, was being posted as press advisor to Khanh. Simpson was an old Vietnam hand, having been with USIS during the French period, when I first arrived in 1954, and was returning to Saigon for the first time since 1955. His counterpart was Colonel Pham Ngoc Thao, whom Khanh had installed in the palace nominally to handle the press but mainly to keep an eye on him. Thao was an adroit "agent provocateur" and operator whom Simpson found would mysteriously disappear from time to time. (Eventually he was killed by the South Vietnamese, who became convinced he was working for the other side. After the fall of Saigon to the communists in 1975, he was given a "hero's" recognition in their graveyard on the outskirts of Saigon.)[23]

On his way to Saigon, Simpson attended one of McNamara s flying-circus conferences in Honolulu and found himself in a time warp in which he imagined General Taylor as General

Henri Navarre and General Westmoreland as General René Cogny, who had constituted the French high command back in 1953. He sensed "a great, possibly dangerous gap between what was going on in the air conditioned conference room and what I had known as the on-the-ground reality of Vietnam No Vietnamese government could possibly be so acquiescent . . . to . . . the recommendations being discussed. Didn't these people realize that when a Vietnamese . . . agrees readily with outside advice you're likely to be in trouble? Hadn't we yet learned that the Vietnamese willing to argue his case with his American counterpart had a potential greater than the eager yes men we found easier to deal with? Even worse, the Vietnamese were being cast as the little men who weren't there."[24] His sizing up of the detached and unrealistic quality of top American thinking about the Vietnamese was right on target. Simpson's tour would turn out to be an adventure of coups and counter-coups, with some comic moments in between, but of insufficient relevance to Vietnamese reality that was not his fault.

SENATOR HUMPHREY INTERVENES

As Lodge was about to give up his post as ambassador, Senator Humphrey intervened with President Johnson to change the approach in South Vietnam. On June 8 he wrote to Johnson proposing that Lansdale and I be sent back to Saigon. He prefaced his memo with a declaration that there was

> a clear and positive alternative to either pulling out of South-East Asia, or of launching what is essentially a Korea-type conventional war. . . . Attached to this Memorandum is a detailed proposal, "Concept for Victory," which I strongly urge you personally read. It was prepared by a small group of men who have impressed me with their brilliance, their patriotism and their tough, sophisticated approach to the task of winning a U.S. victory in Vietnam. They are veterans of campaigns where we gave the communists memorable lickings. They have written about what they themselves would be prepared to go out and do.[25]

"Concept for Victory" had been written mainly by Lansdale, with contributions from Bohannon and me. It was a political plan for the Vietnamese that had to be sold to them as their own idea by the right people, but—if carried out—could develop the Vietnamese leadership and political cause needed to win. While he had not specified it in the plan, Lansdale thought if he got out there he could convince Khanh to become a national hero by leading the transition back to elected government, while renouncing any personal ambitions to become president, in order to convince others of his sincerity. To the uninitiated it would sound Pollyanna-ish, but I thought Lansdale could pull it off. He could be that persuasive with the Vietnamese.

Humphrey sketched out for Johnson the general situation. "The restoration of security in South Vietnam and the neighboring states is not something than can wholly be accomplished in a short period (probably requiring a commitment of 8 to 10 years before the total job is done)," but "marked progress can be shown in a year."[26] The military situation had been grimly and accurately described, supported by a May 8 report, "The Situation in Long An Province," by Earl Long, still the Rural Affairs provincial rep there. Politically and psychologically, the situation was equally grim.

The Vietnamese people were "not so much antigovernment as indifferent. "The government was "uncertain, the leadership divided and mistrustful of each other." The U.S. advisors were overconscious of the sovereignty issue, with little rapport with Vietnamese leaders and "neither the understanding nor ability to insist upon political/psychological emphasis in the war. The Vietnamese government has promulgated no goals that are believed and has begun no action programs that would give the people something to be for and there was no effective program of troop indoctrination in sharp contrast . . . with the Viet Cong."

The most urgent tasks were "stabilizing the Vietnamese leadership and giving some hope to which the Vietnamese people can rally." This hope could evolve, provided the Vietnamese government announced "a sweeping program of economic and social reform," characterized its role as that of "caretaker," and came up with "a practical program for establishing a new Constitution, for eventual national elections and a return to civilian government." The key was "not to increase the number of U.S. personnel . . . in Vietnam but to restructure the command and control organization. This could be done by sending in a seasoned team of men who have demonstrated their ability to defeat Asian insurgents." The rural development program being run "by only about 40 dedicated and motivated men" was an example. "Direct U.S. military action against North Vietnam," U.S. assumption of command roles, and the participation in combat of U.S. troop units were "unnecessary and undesirable." Humphrey concluded by recommending that "at least two individuals, Lansdale and Phillips," be called in by the president "to discuss the possibility of organizing such a team." Appended to Humphrey's memo was a description of Lansdale's credentials and service.[27]

Nothing came of Humphrey's recommendation. Johnson never talked to Lansdale. He gave Humphrey's memo to his special assistant, Douglass S. Cater, who sent a memo back to him suggesting that Humphrey's proposals be considered. Johnson wrote back, saying "Doug, This good—carefully comb Humphrey for all ideas and then forward to appropriate officials."[28] Humphrey's memo was also read by Johnson's military aide, Maj. Gen. Chester V. Clifton, Jr., who saw "nothing new or nothing contrary to what we are already doing." The first priority for our advisors was "stabilizing the insurgency and protecting their own lives[;] . . . civic action . . . will have to come later or be performed by a separate group of people." Clifton went on to say, "Fine as these men are, they have the reputation of using the 'lone wolf' approach rather than being men who can participate as part of a team effort. I do not recommend that you inject Lansdale-Phillips into the action at this time."[29] "Lone wolf" was just the term to raise Johnson's hackles, since it was precisely what had made senior people in Washington uneasy about Lodge. Humphrey's memo coincided with Johnson's decision to replace Lodge with General Taylor as ambassador, and Taylor, for his part, had a negative appreciation of Lansdale. The Vietnamese political situation would not be addressed. It would continue to deteriorate.

Chapter 17
General Taylor Replaces Lodge

O n June 23 President Johnson announced Gen. Maxwell Taylor as his new ambassador to Vietnam. Taylor had been reluctant to take the job but had been persuaded by a combination of McNamara and the president. He was a soldier, and this was a call to duty. It was, however, a deep disappointment for all who looked for real change. Taylor had previously exhibited only the most conventional approach to Vietnam, looking on it mainly as a military and geopolitical problem. Although he had a reputation as an intellectual, at heart he was a very traditional and often rigid military thinker, imbued with the formal hierarchy of command and wanting always to be in control. Once when he was praised for an apparently extemporaneous, forty-minute speech without notes, his reply was, "I never do anything impromptu."[1] As ambassador he would exhibit an extreme inability to understand or adapt to the constantly shifting dynamics of the Vietnamese side of the war. He was a big-picture man whose vision was unable to focus on the nuances of Vietnamese politics, which constantly surprised him. He had long thought part of the answer to the VC insurgency was to bomb its ultimate source, North Vietnam. As security and political conditions continued to disintegrate in the South, the option of attacking the North became even more attractive to him.

JAMES KILLEN

In late June 1964, a change in AID mission directors in Saigon finally took place. The new director was James Killen, a former labor organizer who had been mission director in Pakistan and Korea. I sensed some anxiety from Walter Stoneman about Killen's adaptability to Vietnam when he asked me to brief the new director in early July. A large man with a tough look about him, Killen was an impassive audience. I gave him a detailed rundown on Rural Affairs; why its somewhat unconventional structure and procedures were now more essential than ever because of the chaotic nature of the Vietnamese government. I stressed how important the people we had in the field were in terms of their unselfish commitment and how well the Vietnamese responded to them.

I urged Killen to "shatter precedent" by going outside of Saigon to see for himself before making any judgments. "Do what most high-level visitors don't do, which is to stay overnight so you can talk to local Vietnamese officials and American advisors informally to get a feel for what is really going on. Exceedingly few, if any, high-level American officials," I continued, "have ever had the time, and in some cases the inclination, to stay longer and probe deeper. That is probably why . . . our advisory effort has all too often reflected an inadequate appreciation of the situation. . . . The Vietnamese will simply not let down their hair and tell their problems to four-star generals and under-secretaries of state." At the end of my talk he asked for my views in writing, which I got to him.[2] He gave the impression of listening carefully but was entirely noncommittal, asked no questions, and departed abruptly, without a handshake.

Not long after his arrival in Saigon in mid-July, Killen not only ignored what I had said but set out with considerable determination to do the opposite. He downgraded Rural Affairs, renaming it "Provincial Operations" and changed policy on a whole series of matters affecting counterinsurgency. George Tanham had arrived in July to head up what had been Rural Affairs, with Sam Wilson as deputy. Killen refused to talk to either Bert Fraleigh or Len Maynard, who had been an area rep since 1962 and had previously been in charge of Rural Affairs, when Fraleigh was out with hepatitis in early 1964, about the history or the status of Rural Affairs and its programs. He also refused to listen to Tanham, the new head of Rural Affairs. He just started issuing orders. Despite the deterioration in Vietnamese government effectiveness, Rural Affairs was still functioning in most provinces. The province chiefs could be persuaded to sign off on expenditures, provided they had joint committee support. Killen decided to disband the provincial sign-off committees, saying they were an affront to Vietnamese sovereignty and against standard AID procedures.[3] He claimed Rural Affairs was a crash effort to give away AID commodities with the intention of bribing the rural population for support. Many of the special programs undertaken by Rural Affairs should either be terminated (well drilling, for example, which he called a "boondoggle") or turned over to the traditional USOM technical divisions and worked through the ministries.

In a bizarre move, Killen brought out the famous Greek city planner Doxiadis to see how the aid program might improve security around Saigon. Doxiadis recommended the construction of a major beltway circling the city. The project involved several major new bridges over branches of the Saigon River, costing millions and producing an especially attractive target for sabotage. Presumably the VC would be kept at bay by circling vehicular patrols. The proposal rose like a hot air balloon, remained in the air longer than it deserved, and then collapsed under the weight of its irrelevance.

Killen stayed in Saigon and never went to the field except for a few quick day-trips. He claimed he could not leave his invalid wife overnight. Killen so frustrated Tanham that he quit after only three months on the job. Tanham knew both General Taylor and the deputy ambassador, U. Alexis Johnson, but when he told them Killen was wrecking the program and undermining pacification, they did nothing. Killen did not stop with changing the program. He determined to get rid of most of the original Rural Affairs provincial representatives; he had brought with him his own inspectors. They were sicced on the provincial reps, accusing some of being homosexuals and others of falsifying expense accounts or of colluding with Vietnamese officials for their own account, forcing many to resign or transfer out.

Malicious and stupid charges would dog some of the provincial reps who were regular AID employees for more than a year thereafter. By 1966, John O'Donnell was with AID in Peru. There he was chased down by a security investigator who claimed he had been lax in administering AID funds in Vietnam. The evidence was his acceptance of free meals from the Kien Hoa province chief. Responding angrily, he said of course he had frequently had lunch and dinner with the province chief. It had been the only time available to discuss the counterinsurgency program. He never got an official answer back from AID.[4] (O'Donnell's service was so outstanding in Peru that the Peruvian government, despite its anti-American orientation at the time, gave him official recognition for his agricultural work—and only him, in the entire American mission.)

I would not get wind of what Killen was up to until early September 1964, when I got a letter from Bert Fraleigh.[5] I protested to Stoneman. He confessed to similar reservations but said there was little he or anyone else in AID/Washington could do. Only a bad report from someone like General Taylor would have any effect. Taylor had formed what he called the Mission Council, consisting of all agency heads, to coordinate U.S. policy and operations. Coordination, instead of being effected at the operating level, as practiced by the Trueheart Committee in 1962 and 1963, was now carried out at the very top by agency heads, who had no firsthand understanding of what was happening in the countryside or with the Vietnamese. This top-down approach meant that what Taylor knew about USOM Provincial Operations was what Killen told him. Why Taylor didn't listen to Tanham was never clear to Tanham.

By this time I was really tied down at Airways Engineering, making repeated trips to Saudi Arabia pursuing an opportunity for us to get an airport project there. Nevertheless, when in Washington I continued pressing Stoneman about Killen. Stoneman said it wouldn't do any good if I went to Bell; complaints had already been made to Bell, and no action had been taken. AID was a weak organization centrally, which left the operation of their overseas missions up to the local director unless gross misfeasance or malfeasance could be shown. Fraleigh had asked me to go to Senator Humphrey's office with the problem, but they were tied up in the presidential campaign. I volunteered to go to Saigon without pay for a brief trip to review the situation but was told that it would have to be approved by the mission in Saigon, a possibility so unlikely it was not worth trying.

In December 1964 I reached the limit of my leave-without-pay status and was officially discharged. The director of AID, David Bell, unexpectedly sent me a letter saying that I had mounted "an unparalleled operation which introduced many of the economic and social measures desperately needed to balance the over-all U.S.-Vietnamese counter-insurgency effort. The fact that political turmoil and military setbacks later caused some severe reverses does not discredit your work. . . . Economic and social action alone could not win the struggle without a measure of political stability and security."[6] I was sure Stoneman had a hand in it, for which I expressed appreciation, but I found it deeply ironic that Killen, at the same time, was getting away with wrecking the program for which I was being commended. It made me so angry that had I been in Saigon I probably would have worked behind the scenes to generate Vietnamese demonstrations against Killen to get him out of there.[7]

THE VUNG TAU CHARTER

By August 1964 Khanh had dissolved the Council of Notables, but he had not been able to get General Minh to give his government any public blessing, though Minh remained nominally chief of state. Khanh thought U.S. bombing in reaction to the Tonkin Gulf incident had strengthened his hand to seek solutions to his political problems. In July he finally convened a special tribunal to try the Dalat generals, which found them guilty only of "lax morality, insufficient qualifications for command and lack of a clear political concept."[8] The verdict was ridiculous (the lax morality charge was aimed at General Don, a renowned Lothario). The generals were suspended from any command functions; they were told they would be assigned to the prime minister's office, but months passed before they were allowed to return to Saigon. This further embittered General Minh, increasing Khanh's uneasiness. The Catholics who might have supported Khanh at the beginning were angry over the execution of Diem's brother Ngo Dinh Can. Khanh was at odds with his deputy prime minister, Nguyen

Ton Hoan, a southern Dai Viet, whom he had appointed. He had been quietly urged by the American embassy to put his government on a more legal basis and to clear up the division of power between a nonfunctioning chief of state, the office of prime minister, and himself as head of the Military Committee. Beleaguered by rising discontent from all directions and spooked by the specter of Big Minh looking over his shoulder, Khanh convinced himself that the solution was a new constitution, with himself as president.

Lou Conein was the first to know a new constitution was in the works. While at General Staff headquarters in July, Lou came across a Vietnamese army major whom he knew casually. The major was busy at a desk with a great pile of books on it. Asked what he was doing, the major said he was writing a constitution for General Khanh. He showed Lou various reference books on the American constitution, the French constitution, and a copy of the first South Vietnamese constitution. As for his experience in writing such documents, he shrugged and said, "None"; he had just been assigned the job by Khanh. Lou thought this odd and reported it back to the Saigon station but was never asked to follow up.[9]

Later, at a meeting with Ambassador Taylor in Vung Tau, Khanh discussed his proposed new constitution. In a cable to Washington, Taylor said he told Khanh the embassy found it brusque in language and felt that "its present form would raise criticism in the U.S. and the world press. We stressed to him," Taylor said, "that internal problems of acceptance in Vietnam were his own affair, and we could only offer observations on the objective issue of international reactions." This was followed by comments that the preamble was not clear, that the bill of rights was unnecessarily abstract, and that a careful public relations campaign to prepare for the constitution's proclamation would be necessary. Khanh expressed "general agreement that these matters should be dealt with" but stressed the urgency with which action had to be taken, "inside of two days, five days at most." The next day he was going to meet with the Military Committee. He promised a draft proclamation for further embassy review.[10]

The evening before the Military Committee was to meet, without embassy guidance, Conein, who had accompanied Khanh to Vung Tau, tried to argue him out of the project, saying he was overreacting to General Minh. Lou sat in on most of the Military Committee meeting the next day as the only American present. It was clear that Khanh's claim of American support carried the day. By saying Vietnamese acceptance of the charter was entirely Khanh's affair, Taylor had given Khanh a green light, which he took as official American approval.

The following day, Khanh returned to Saigon and proclaimed the new constitution, popularly known as the "Vung Tau Charter," with himself as president. (He deliberately used a different Vietnamese word for president than Ngo Dinh Diem had, but the meaning was the same.) There was no time, he would later claim to our embassy, for his proclamation to be reviewed. In less than a week, the Buddhists and the students were in the streets protesting. Khanh tried to mollify them with little success. (By the end of August, Khanh would be forced to rescind the constitution.) Through Conein, he asked General Taylor to issue an official statement of support for the new constitution and for him personally. Taylor was appalled at the opposition already arising and refused to make any statement. Taylor told Conein to tell Khanh he had never approved the constitution; the demonstrations were Khanh's fault. When Lou gave Khanh Taylor's response, Khanh flew into a rage. By this time Lou had become the main informal channel of communication between Taylor and Khanh, and now the relationship between them, never an easy one (Taylor was not an easy man), began to unravel. Lou was in the middle, faithfully reporting to Taylor what Khanh had to say, and vice versa, as the temperature of the exchanges began to rise.

Like much of what was happening in Saigon, if the results had not been ultimately so serious, Vietnamese politics and American involvement therein would have had all the character of a farce. Despite his intellectual ability, it was increasingly apparent that General Taylor did not understand the Vietnamese or what was going on. His reserve, formality, and conventional nature made him a poor diplomat as well. He could not understand how what seemed self-evident to him—the need for the Vietnamese to unify in the face of an aggressive communist enemy—was not also self-evident to them. The more he lectured the Vietnamese about what to do, the more they seemed to do the opposite.

TAYLOR FIRES CONEIN

Relations between Taylor and Khanh deteriorated so badly that Lou Conein, trying to be an honest reporter of what they had to say to each other, became the object of Taylor's wrath. Forced to rescind the Vung Tau Charter, an action he attributed to a failure of American support, Khanh had retreated to Dalat in early September. There he was set off by a Voice of America broadcast saying he was in a depressed state. He demanded that Lou fly to Dalat immediately. When Lou arrived Khanh went into a tirade against Taylor; he wanted Lou to go back to Taylor and report exactly what he, Khanh, was saying about him, including a number of vulgar insults (*espèce de con,* among others). Conein took it all down, word for word, on a sheet of paper. Was he doubly sure he wanted all this transmitted literally, Lou asked? Khanh insisted.

Lou flew back to Saigon and waited while Taylor and Deputy Ambassador Alexis Johnson finished a tennis game. When he had read his notes Taylor asked him angrily, "Are you sure you understand French?" Then Taylor took off in an embassy plane to confront Khanh. He couldn't land in Dalat due to bad weather; when Taylor finally did get to see Khanh the next day, Khanh had calmed down and was thoroughly polite. In the meantime, Khanh's brother had tipped off journalist Beverly Deepe of the *New York Herald Tribune* about his brother's anger at Taylor. When Deepe's story was put on the wires, Taylor got a copy. He summoned Conein and, without reference to Deepe, told him he no longer wanted him in touch with Khanh; Conein had thirty days to leave the country.

After seeing Taylor, Lou took a call from Sam Wilson of USOM Provincial Operations. Sam had heard that General Duc, the Vietnamese army commander of IV Corps, was about to start a coup against Khanh. Could Lou do anything about it? Since Lou knew Duc personally (the same Duc who had commanded the 1955 occupation of Camau), he telephoned him and read him the riot act, warning him not to start a coup. Duc promised to call it off. When Taylor heard about it, instead of congratulating Lou for having stopped a coup, he gave him only forty-eight hours to leave the country, for assuming he had any such authority. On September 13, the day after Lou arrived in Hong Kong to pick up his family (American families had earlier been evacuated from Saigon), General Duc marched on Saigon and launched his coup.[11]

The coup had its comic aspects. Some of Duc's units got all the way into Saigon with their American advisors, who had been told they were going to Saigon to preserve law and order. An American captain advising a Vietnamese ranger unit went into the presidential palace, where he ran across Howard Simpson in his press advisory office. He learned from Simpson to his complete surprise that he was participating in an anti-government coup; Simpson suggested they walk out of there, since the word was the palace was about to be bombed by the Vietnamese air force. Fortunately, no bombing occurred, and Duc and his fellow coup leader,

General Phat, were talked into standing down without bloodshed. I heard all about it when Lou got back to Washington. If the American mission had been flying semiblind politically with regard to Khanh while Lou was there, it was now almost totally blind. I had to laugh to keep from crying.

By October 1964 it had become apparent that the Johnson/Humphrey ticket was going to win by a large margin. I sent a memo to Bill Connell asking him to warn Humphrey that we were in for trouble in Vietnam. I cited Taylor's kicking Conein out, leaving himself completely blind, and the destruction being wrought within USOM by Killen. Divisions among the South Vietnamese remained "deep and unresolved," while the United States was "providing no meaningful backing or assistance to meet Vietnamese political needs because our representative [meaning Taylor] does not have the skill or inclination." Recognizing how tired the vice president–elect was going to be after the campaign, I urged that he turn his attention to Vietnam immediately. Humphrey was, I said, "the only man I have spoken to . . . [who] grasped the essentials of that situation and what the U.S. needs to do." I urged the vice president go to Vietnam after the election to make an on-the-spot assessment for President Johnson; "After the inauguration might be too late. He must do this *not* Secretary McNamara if any meaningful changes are to be made. Revolutionary changes have to be made in the structure and thrust of our efforts. . . . Those . . . so far assigned the responsibility have such a vested interest in past and present policy . . . they cannot be expected to generate the changes required. Thus the sole hope . . . rests with you and your boss."[12] This was not flattery. At this point those with an intimate feel for Vietnam were near their wit's end over American ineptness and lack of communication with the Vietnamese. Connell would later tell me that Humphrey did ask Johnson to send him to Vietnam, but Johnson turned him down.

BERT FRALEIGH RECALLED

Killen thought he could force Fraleigh to quit by ignoring him, but Bert refused to take the bait. In a head-on clash during a presentation by Fraleigh, Killen exploded, "Stop, I've heard enough about your corrupt half-baked projects!" Bert replied that he knew nothing of Killen's allegations, but was simply presenting the facts about the well-drilling program. It was delivering water to people who needed it. Killen jumped to his feet, swore, and said he was "going to clean it all up. The first thing I'm going to do . . . is appoint regional directors who have been former AID mission directors who will report directly to me. Every provincial rep will have to be . . . at least 36 years old and an experienced AID professional. I will set these people up in the field with decent offices and houses where everybody will respect the way they live." Fraleigh could not resist responding, "By your standards Bobby Kennedy would not have qualified when he was appointed attorney general." Killen stomped out and shortly thereafter arranged for AID/Washington to recall Fraleigh for consultation.[13]

When Fraleigh arrived in San Francisco, in December 1964, he was given a note asking him to go directly to Humphrey's Senate office when he got to Washington. The first thing Humphrey said was, "Don't tell me about Killen. I already know about that wild man and we're taking care of him."[14] On February 6, an article appeared in the *San Francisco Chronicle* headlined, "Feud within U.S. Viet Aid Mission," stating, "A ranking official of the United Sates Overseas Mission (USOM) here was relieved after he expressed his view on Vietnam policy directly to Vice President Humphrey." A companion story by Charles Mohr appeared in the *New York Times* a month later under the headline, "Controversy over Chief Disrupts U.S. Aid Mission in Vietnam." The story confirmed that Killen had gotten rid of a number

June 1962. Inspection trip to Phu Yen Province. Author presents a carbine to a militiaman who has just successfully defended his hamlet against the Vietcong. The province chief, Major Dong, laughs at the size difference. (Author's collection)

Author inspecting strategic hamlet defenses with the Quang Ngai Province chief (dark suit) in June 1962. MAAG sector advisor (back to camera) and Tom Luche of USOM look on. (Author's collection)

Hamlet children in Quang Ngai, one of the poorest provinces in Vietnam and a hotbed of Vietcong activity. (Author's collection)

Vinh Binh Province chief, Major Thao, with his staff and the author during an inspection visit to the Delta, June 1962. (Author's collection)

Hamlet militia of Khmer (Cambodian) origin in Vinh Binh, June 1962. Note that armaments consist only of old French rifles and machetes. (Author's collection)

June 1962. Montagnard refugees fleeing the Vietcong resettle in Darlac Province. Lieutenant Colonel Conein and the author look on. (Author's collection)

November 1962. Inspecting strategic hamlet operations in Kien Hoa. Province chief Lt. Col. Tran Ngoc Chau leads the way, followed by the author and the Rural Affairs regional rep, Ralph Harwood. (Author's collection)

December 1962. Washington visitors in Vinh Binh Province, (left to right) Michael Forrestal (National Security Council), Roger Hilsman (State Department), province chief, William Trueheart (embassy DCM), regional delegate, author, Colonel Hoang Van Lac, and Colonel Schaad (MAAG). (Author's collection)

Provincial rep Earl Young practicing medicine, treating a Montagnard in
Phu Bon Province, January 1963. (Courtesy Earl Young)

Earl Young's office and living quarters in Phu Bon, January 1963. Three dollars was deducted
from his daily living allowance because his quarters were "government furnished." (Courtesy
Earl Young)

Author with children, Rufus and Anne, and the family dog, Hai Yen. Front yard of their house on the road to Tan Son Nhut Airport, February 1963 (Author's collection, photo by General Le Van Kim)

Barbara, author's wife, with daughter Anne in the same front yard during a Sunday visit by the Kims, February 1963. (Author's collection, photo by General Le Van Kim)

January 1963. Strategic hamlet elementary school under construction. USOM provided the materials, while the inhabitants contributed labor. More than a thousand were built in the first year of the program. (Author's collection)

Homemade strategic hamlet defenses of sharpened bamboo in Phu Yen Province, before the arrival of barbed wire for reinforcing. (Author's collection)

March 1963. Long-wall construction in Vinh Long Province in the Delta. Author and the provincial rep, Rob Warne, look on, appalled. On the basis of the author's report, President Diem's brother, Ngo Dinh Nhu, stopped the construction. (Author's collection)

April 1963. Minister of Interior Bui Van Luong visits Montagnard hamlet in Phu Yen Province. Lieutenant Colonel Conein (upper left) and Col. George Morton (upper right), new commander of U.S. Army Special Forces, look on. (Author's collection)

May 1963. Diem's brother, Nhu, meets with entire Rural Affairs staff about the American role in the hamlet program. Nhu at head of table with author, his deputy, Bert Fraleigh and regional reps, John Perry and George Melvin, to Nhu's right. (Author's collection)

June 1963. Visiting a strategic hamlet self-help irrigation project with Taiwanese agricultural technician Leonard Chang and a Vietnamese farmer. (Author's collection)

May 1963. Diem visits An Giang Province, where the province chief exaggerated numbers of completed strategic hamlets, having alienated local inhabitants by overzealous relocation. (Author's collection)

From right to left, provincial reps Dick Holbrooke and John O'Donnell confer with a MAAG sector advisor on security and development in Kien Hoa Province. (Courtesy Sharon O'Donnell)

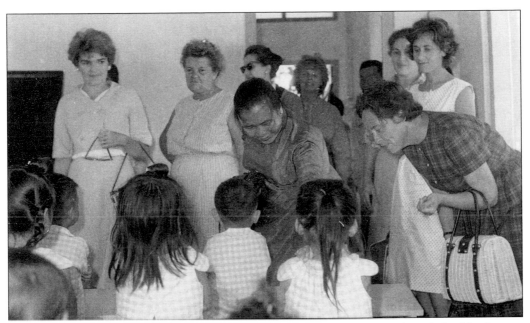

September 1963. Author's wife, Barbara (on left), visiting Vietnamese war orphans helped by the local American Women's Association. Mrs. Brent, wife of the USOM/Saigon director, is to Barbara's left. (Author's collection)

Secretary of Defense Robert McNamara and Gen. Maxwell Taylor confer with President Kennedy after a National Security Council meeting, fall 1963. (U.S. Naval Institute files)

Vietnamese army ranger troops, against a backdrop of bullet holes in the Gia Long presidential palace facade, morning after the November 1, 1963, coup against Diem. (Author's collection)

Diem's palace guard after surrendering to ranger troops, morning of November 2. (Author's collection)

Secretary of Defense McNamara raising self-proclaimed leader Gen. Nguyen Khanh's hand, yelling "Vietnam ten thousand years!" in fractured Vietnamese that nobody could understand—reinforcing Khanh's image as an American puppet. March 1964. (U.S. Naval Institute files, JFK Library)

March 1964. Ambassador Henry Cabot Lodge and McNamara with Khanh shaking Vietnamese hands. Lodge mistakenly assumed Khanh was just what was needed to win the war. (U.S. Naval Institute files, JFK Library)

September 1965. General Lansdale facing Prime Minister Nguyen Cao Ky with General Khanh, head of pacification, on left during a typical evening songfest at Lansdale's villa. (Courtesy Ambassador Bui Diem)

September 1965. Typical evening discussion of pacification at Lansdale's villa. To right of author are General Ky's advisor Bui Diem, Gen. Hoang Van Lac, and Lieutenant Colonel Bohannon, and to the immediate left agricultural director, Ton That Trinh. (Author's collection)

John Paul Vann of USOM provincial operations, later a senior official in CORDS, striking a skeptical pose in 1967. Vann died tragically in a helicopter crash in 1972. (Courtesy Oggie Williams)

1967. Author and Bert Fraleigh (seated at far end) go by boat to visit experimental soybean growers in An Giang Province. (Courtesy Calvin Mehlert)

Lansdale with author at South Vietnamese embassy ceremony in Washington in fall 1968, recognizing the author's service to Vietnam. (Author's collection)

May 2002. Pham Xuan An, former North Vietnamese super spy, with author at the Majestic Hotel, where author first lodged in August 1954. (Author's collection)

of Rural Affairs personnel and had "jeopardized the rural aid program on which much of the hope of pacifying the countryside depends."

Despite the adverse publicity, Killen was able to weather the storm, in part because he reversed field, now favoring decentralization of the aid effort to the provinces. Deputy Ambassador Johnson told Bill Bundy he "totally supported Jim Killen," that Killen was "generally doing a fine job." The damage had already been done.[15] It proved impossible, however, to revive the provincial committee sign-off process. Provincial development continued to be stymied by the lack of funds. In the bureaucratization of provincial operations, part of the focus of concern shifted inevitably toward the creature comforts of the new regional directors and more senior provincial representatives. While individual provincial reps continued to do excellent work in some provinces, the unconventional nature of Rural Affairs was lost. So was much of the accompanying high morale, motivation, and indispensable knowledge of local conditions and the personal relationships so necessary to helping the Vietnamese succeed.

OPPOSING BOMBING THE NORTH

Throughout 1964, pressure built within the administration for more direct American intervention in Vietnam. After the initial retaliatory air raids in July against North Vietnam for reported torpedo boat attacks on our destroyers in the Gulf of Tonkin, McNamara and the Joint Chiefs of Staff began pressing for a sustained bombing campaign against the North to boost South Vietnamese morale and persuade the North to back off from supporting the insurgency. This had been strongly supported by General Taylor for some time. Since Johnson did not want the war to become a campaign issue, no final decision was taken prior to the November election.

After the election, I became involved, because of my misgivings, in the internal administration debate about bombing the North. I knew a similar unease was felt by Vice President–elect Humphrey, who asked me for my views. Bohannon and I collaborated on a paper, "United States Policy Options in Vietnam," dated November 25, 1964, which was circulated under my name to the civilian policy makers within the administration and directly to Humphrey. It described four general courses of action for the United States: "punitive/interdictory bombardment of installations in North Vietnam; limited ground force intervention and commitment of US (and perhaps SEATO) troops in selected areas; negotiation for a ceasefire, followed by US withdrawal from a position of dominance and responsibility in Vietnam and Southeast Asia; and, positive, politically-oriented action for the development of a free, stable, democratic Vietnam and Southeast Asia."[16]

The proponents of bombing the North were insisting that it was the cheapest, most antiseptic, and dramatic way to shore up the South and "force the North Vietnamese to call off the war . . . at least temporarily, thus buying time for the formation of a strong Government in the South." My paper questioned whether bombing was "capable of inducing the collapse of the North Vietnamese regime. A strengthening of popular support for the regime seems more likely because the North Vietnamese are not dependent economically or politically on these installations but upon the Communist Party, their army, and ultimately the population." In the South it would raise hopes for an easy victory, as had the Gulf of Tonkin bombing raids, which had "created just illusions . . . subsequently shattered leaving South Vietnamese morale even lower."[17]

I argued that intervention by ground forces was not practical and that negotiation for a cease-fire should be rejected as dishonorable. (The paper did not consider massive intervention by U.S. troops in the South, so far out of the realm of rationality did it seem at that point.) The paper concluded with an argument for a politically oriented approach, rejecting the notion that it is now "too late [for that], that the political situation has deteriorated so badly in South Vietnam that drastic action *now* is essential, if total collapse is to be avoided." South Vietnam, I pointed out, had been in an even more demoralized and disorganized state in 1954 but had survived. The major difficulty of a political approach was that

> since its essential ingredients are intangibles, the determination and will of patriots, the excitation and constructive use of human emotions and abilities, it can no more be set forth in Pentagon style briefing charts supported by statistics than could the basis for the success of our own Revolution. For the President of the United States to decide to put his blue chips on a small group of people of lesser rank, with necessary and pertinent experience . . . and back them to the hilt, is not uncommon, historically [a reference to the Philippines and early Vietnam]. It is such a departure from what has become the standard US approach to it problems overseas that it may be too much to hope for. The resulting changes would constitute almost a quiet revolution in themselves but they are certainly less hazardous and ultimately less painful than the alternatives.[18]

Vice President–elect Humphrey read it personally and told me that it reinforced his own convictions. Though Bill Jorden helped me get the paper fairly widely distributed within the second level of the administration (Bill Bundy phoned me about receiving it), it would have no practical effect. When I talked to Forrestal and Bundy personally, they listened sympathetically but told me a policy consensus had already been reached and could not be changed.

At the same time Lansdale went public. In an article for the December 1964 issue of the influential establishment quarterly *Foreign Affairs*, "Vietnam: A Test of American Understanding of Revolution," Lansdale explained that we were dealing with a country in the midst of a revolution; we had to identify with that revolution and work to guide it toward democratic ends as a means of defeating a communist insurgency. He quoted Vietnamese political leader Dan Van Sung as saying,

> By emphasizing anti-Communism rather than positive revolutionary goals and from lack of a better adaptation to the local situation, the US has reduced its anti-Communist efforts in Vietnam to the maintenance of an administrative machine and of an army. . . . The way out, to our mind, is not by an abandonment but, on the contrary, by going deep into every local revolutionary problem and helping solve them using principles of justice and freedom, and perhaps in fusing them with the revolutionary spirit of 1776.[19]

Lansdale pointed out the obvious need, as helpers for the Vietnamese, for Americans who understood the revolutionary nature of the situation in which they were working and who were known and trusted. He described some of the political actions the Vietnamese might undertake with quiet American support, repeating some of the ideas from his "Concept for Victory" paper, which had formed the basis for Humphrey's original recommendation to Johnson that he and I be sent back to Vietnam. While Lansdale's article was noted by some of the intelligentsia, the minds of the president and his inner circle remained impervious.

Toward the end of 1964, Joe Alsop wrote increasingly aggressive pieces urging the administration to confront the North Vietnamese directly; otherwise the war was lost. Recalling the credence he had given my views, I invited him and Bo to our house in McLean for a talk about U.S. policy. Joe arrived in his usual jaunty style. One of the first things he did was to inspect the bookcase in the living room, probably to render judgment on the level of my reading—he was a self-admitted intellectual snob. After Alsop had accepted coffee and settled in a chair, Bo and I offered our arguments. We understood how frustrated he might feel by the South Vietnamese failure to defeat the communists in the South, but bombing the North, we were convinced, would only divert us and the Vietnamese from counterinsurgency in the South. Bombing would rally the people in the North around the regime and generate more volunteers to go South. Surely he didn't think the dedicated communists in the North were going to give in. For the bombing to be effective we would have to invade North Vietnam, and we were not going to do that, for fear of the Chinese. In the meantime, the South Vietnamese would be likely to slack off, expecting us to win the war. We talked also about Lansdale's article in *Foreign Affairs*.

Alsop rejected all our arguments; neither of us made a dent. If the bombing was intense enough, the North Vietnamese would have to bow to U.S. pressure. The Russians would be impressed and would use their influence to get the North Vietnamese to pull back. Given the weakness in Saigon, Alsop maintained, the pure application of American power was the only way to go; it would show we were "standing firm," buck up South Vietnamese morale, and make the North back off. It was a disappointing meeting. Alsop had renewed his old love affair with pure American military power as the only way to respond to the communists and had forgotten what he had once known about communist toughness and perseverance in pursuing a "people's war."

Around this time, Humphrey's office got in touch with *Pageant* magazine, which asked me to write an article about Vietnam. *Pageant* was similar in appearance to the *Reader's Digest* but more liberal and controversial. I agreed and submitted a manuscript—under a pseudonym, "Paul Roberts," since I was still actively involved with government policy makers and didn't want to harm my access. The article, "A Program for Winning the War in Vietnam," was finished in December but hit the newsstands only in late March, too late to have even a minimal effect (the bombing had already started).[20] Still, it was satisfying to put on public record, even under a pseudonym, what I had been saying in government circles. In the piece I tried to popularize a new approach, saying,

> The only effective help . . . in Vietnam is that which strengthens the spirit and assists the Vietnamese people to unite behind a common cause. Such help is not to be given by top-heavy bureaucratic organizations, nor by conventional military officers, diplomats or administrators, such as we now have in Saigon. Where would we be today had the French made a condition of their aid during our Revolution the establishment at Valley Forge of a mini-Versailles to advise General Washington? We must send to Vietnam instead, volunteers who command the trust and confidence of the Vietnamese and who can work with them on a more informal basis as compatriots, not as "officials." These men must feel at home with the Vietnamese revolution, as Paine, Lafayette and Pulaski felt at home with ours.[21]

I quoted from a speech given by Father Hoa in September in Manila when he was awarded the Magsaysay Prize for "his extraordinary valor in defense of freedom, strengthening among a beleaguered people the resolution to resist tyranny." He had said:

> Why are we not winning in Vietnam? My answer is simple: the misplacement of the order of importance. The Magsaysay way is winning the people first, winning the war second . . . in Vietnam today the order is reversed. Weapons are important. Fighting is necessary to protect the people from being physically harmed by the communists. But arms are useful only for defensive purposes. Our offense must rely solely on winning the people, because as soon as the people understand what communism means, and as soon as they have faith in our ability to protect them, and as soon as they have confidence in our integrity, the battle is won.[22]

GENERAL TAYLOR OUT OF HIS ELEMENT

While we tried unsuccessfully to influence Washington policy, General Taylor was having a direct confrontation in Saigon with the younger generals, now the driving force within the Military Committee. After the failure of Khanh's Vung Tau Charter, and with American urging, a twenty-member High National Council had been formed (a smaller version of the earlier Council of Notables). An older southern nationalist with Cao Dai affiliations, Pham Khac Suu, was named its chairman and the chief of state. The Military Committee and Khanh wanted to retire some of the senior generals, but Suu, as chief of state, refused to approve. In response, the Military Committee forcibly took most of the council, under guard, off to Pleiku, on the High Plateau. Taylor was outraged. He had warned the leading generals at a dinner at General Westmoreland's house not to upset the status quo.

Taylor summoned four of the generals, including Nguyen Cao Ky and Nguyen Van Thieu, to the American embassy (Khanh refused to show up). He lectured them like schoolboys, demanding, "Do all of you understand English?" Then he declared that the Americans were "tired of coups" and that he had "wasted his words" at Westmoreland's dinner.[23] The generals found his manner personally insulting and complained bitterly to Khanh afterward about being affronted and humiliated. Vietnamese sovereignty had been violated. Khanh called up Taylor to complain; Taylor threatened him with a loss of U.S. support. Khanh recorded the conversation and threatened to play it over the airwaves and to have Taylor declared persona non grata. Deputy Ambassador Johnson intervened with strong words from Washington, and Khanh backed down. By this time it was clear to the younger generals, having got over their anger at Taylor, that Khanh no longer enjoyed American support; they began maneuvering to get him out.

It was finally becoming apparent to higher levels in Washington that Taylor was out of his element. President Johnson cabled Taylor on December 30, 1964, saying, "I still do not feel that we are making the all-out effort of political persuasion which is called for. In particular, I wonder whether we are making full use of the kind of Americans who have shown a knack for this kind of communication in the past. I do not want to pick out any particular individual because I do not know these men first hand. But I do think that we ought to be ready to make full use of the specialized skills of men who are skillful with the Vietnamese, even if they are not the easiest men to handle in a country team." LBJ elaborated about having "the most sensitive, persistent and attentive Americans we can find in touch with the Vietnamese."[24] (Only Lansdale fit this description.)

Responding to Johnson's message on January 6, 1965, Taylor deflected his offer of help by picturing the state of Vietnamese political and military disintegration as so bleak that no American could effectively influence the outcome. The basic factors at play were "chronic factionalism, civilian-military suspicion and distrust, absence of national spirit and motivation, lack of cohesion in the social structure and lack of experience in the conduct of government." These were "historical factors . . . susceptible to change only over the long run. Perhaps other Americans might marginally influence them more effectively but generally speaking we Americans are not going to change them in any fundamental way in any measurable time."[25] (Few Vietnamese, though granting the accuracy of the ailments described by Taylor, really believed these handicaps could not be overcome with honest leadership and a consistent approach toward building democracy.)[26] In the same message, Taylor pressed his case for bombing the North in order to bolster the South politically.

Taylor's myopia about his mission's closeness to and understanding of the Vietnamese was to be reflected in his autobiography, *Swords and Plowshares:* "There was not a country in the world in which the United States had closer communication with the government and the people. In Saigon we had over fifty embassy officers for this purpose and in the provinces hundreds of civilians and military officers in daily contact with their Vietnamese counterparts."[27] He was measuring the quantity, not the quality, of communication and understanding, particularly at the top. Many at lower levels knew a great deal about Vietnamese realities, but their knowledge hardly ever penetrated the highest levels. Taylor's assertion was the diplomatic equivalent of McNamara's way of measuring counterinsurgency effectiveness.

When Taylor's cable was received, a meeting occurred between the president and his closest advisors, a discussion recorded by McGeorge Bundy in fragmentary notes that he entitled, "Max to Stay?" McNamara read to Johnson an account of Taylor's meeting with the generals, to which Johnson said something like, "Don't you think that effect of withdrawing Taylor? Whatever pretense." Dean Rusk responded, "He could well be used up politically—that happens. Mistake to return him—but you could put him in CIA." Earlier, in response to Rusk's saying, "We can't fail to make every effort to change the situation on the scene," McNamara had mentioned Lansdale as having "some ideas, better contact with Vietnamese. Conein contact w/ Khanh lost—lack effective contact w/ students. Lack effective relations w/ Buddhists." Near the meeting's end the notes have Johnson saying, "Great feeling for Taylor in tough position."[28] Later, in early March 1965, Bundy in a memo to the president would say, "McNamara and I, if the decision were ours to make, would bring Taylor back and put Alex Johnson in charge. . . . Max has been gallant, determined and honorable to a fault, but he has been rigid, remote and sometimes abrupt."[29] However, the memo recommended no immediate action. Taylor would not be replaced until June, the end of the one-year period he had originally agreed to serve.

For a time in early 1965, General Khanh managed to hang on to power with his fingernails. He was finally forced out in February, by the combination of yet another attempted coup and the loss of support from younger generals now heading the Military Committee. Before leaving on a "good-will tour" as nominal ambassador at large, Khanh, with Military Committee support, appointed the veteran civilian politician Phan Huy Quat as prime minister. Quat persuaded his longtime associate, and my old friend, Bui Diem to join him as chief of cabinet. Quat, a northern Dai Viet, was the most able and experienced of the available civilians. Although he lacked a firm political base with the military, various southern political factions, or with the Catholics or Buddhists, all of whom had become increasingly active, his government had potential as a turning point toward elected governance, because it had, at last, a civilian at the top who understood how important that goal was and had dedicated himself to it.[30]

It was extremely frustrating to hear about Quat's difficulties in the weeks that followed (Bob Shaplen was a particularly good source of information), but there were no Americans on the scene with the relationships or skills to help knit the Vietnamese together. Shaplen tried to introduce influential Vietnamese political thinkers, such as Dan Van Sung, to our embassy staff, but little meaningful contact was established.[31] (Sung, despite several tries, would apparently never achieve a sustained dialog with any embassy official.) In this vacuum, with little understanding and no meaningful political contact, American pronouncements about Vietnamese unity were empty.

THE EXCLUSION OF HUMPHREY

Frustrated by his failure to make a dent verbally against the proposed bombing campaign, Humphrey sent the president on February 15, 1965, a formal memo opposing it. He used mainly political arguments about American public opinion and congressional backing that he thought would strike the right note with Johnson.[32] Instead, the memo angered Johnson, who told Humphrey, "We do not need all these memos. . . . I don't think you should have them lying around your office."[33] Soon thereafter, when asked for his opinion by Johnson in a National Security Council meeting, Humphrey spoke out very forcefully against the bombing campaign. Johnson got the impression that Humphrey had been talking about his views outside the immediate administration circle, which was not true. He got so angry he cut Humphrey out of any further high-level discussions about Vietnam for a year. He stopped having formal NSC meetings on the subject, convening as a substitute a smaller executive committee of Bundy (head of the NSC staff), McNamara, and Rusk, sometimes with their aides.

Humphrey's action was viewed by some of his staff as a foolish mistake, a contravention of his pledge of loyalty to Johnson. Not so, according to Bill Moyers of Johnson's staff, who thought Humphrey fully justified in speaking out within the highest inner circle of the administration, that it was not a breach but a principled reaffirmation of his loyalty to tell Johnson what he honestly thought.[34] As it was, countervailing opinion against a purely military approach was left in the hands of Undersecretary George Ball, who, although eloquent, was considered a special pleader, since he had been opposed to helping the South Vietnamese since the beginning of the Kennedy administration.

Humphrey's exclusion from top Vietnam policy meetings made our influence even more tenuous. Nevertheless, we kept trying other channels. Senator Thomas Dodd of Connecticut, close to Humphrey and a strong voice on the Foreign Relations Committee, wrote the president on February 23 suggesting that "the most serious weakness handicapping our effort in Vietnam has been the lack of adequate liaison with the leaders of various sectors of the Vietnamese community." While expressing "the greatest admiration for General Taylor," Dodd pointed out it was "simply impossible for any man, no matter how gifted, to plunge into a new situation in a foreign country and overnight establish a rapport with and win the confidence of scores of contending military officers and the leaders of at least a dozen contending political factions." Dodd recommended that "a special liaison group . . . be dispatched to Saigon immediately" to help the embassy "establish the broadest and most effective liaison with army leaders, Buddhists, intellectuals and political leaders."[35]

Johnson replied that he was grateful for Dodd's informative letter, adding, "I am thoroughly familiar with the problems that you outline and some of the suggested solutions have been explored by my advisors in detail."[36] Chester Cooper of the NSC staff commented archly to McGeorge Bundy that "based on our recent trip . . . the embassy was not as badly equipped to handle key personalities as I had thought. Nor am I now convinced this is the critical task before us. It may well be that Lansdale could be more effectively used than he is at present—either here or in Saigon. But Lansdale is one thing—a platoon of Lansdales is another."[37] It was yet another futile exercise at overcoming Washington misconceptions about how important it was to understand the Vietnamese.

ESCALATION

By this time, all other considerations within the embassy in Saigon and the administration in Washington had been pushed aside by the bombing campaign against the North, "Rolling Thunder." McGeorge Bundy, Johnson's national security advisor and a staunch bombing supporter, had been on his first trip to Saigon when, on February 7, the VC attacked an airfield in the highland province of Pleiku at which American helicopters were parked and advisors housed. Some ten aircraft were destroyed, eight Americans killed, and 126 wounded. Washington had resisted reacting to previous VC attacks on Americans, such as the bombing of the Brinks Hotel officer billet in Saigon on Christmas Eve, but it saw the Pleiku attack as clear justification for retaliation. Bundy, with Taylor's and Westmoreland's strong endorsement, recommended an immediate response, and the bombing had begun.

This was done without adequate explanation to the American public and with little advance consultation with the Quat government in Saigon. No leaflets were dropped in the North attempting to justify the bombing. Ambassador Taylor had strongly opposed the direct intervention of American troops. Now he would find that bombing the North, which he had long supported, led inexorably to the need to protect bomber bases on Vietnamese soil with American troops, and then, once the troops were on the ground, to the expansion of their mission to active combat.

In the meantime, as later described by former ambassador Bui Diem in *In the Jaws of History*, the Vietnamese were largely in the dark about what the Americans intended. First, two battalions of marines landed in Danang in March, with practically no advance notice to the Vietnamese. This was followed by a request in early April for Prime Minister Quat to approve twenty thousand additional support troops, expanding their operational perimeter to fifty kilometers and making the marines available for emergency use at Vietnamese request. The Vietnamese thought the Americans must have some plan that they were not revealing. Bui Diem saw little indication that "American decision makers understood our perspective or that we understood American intentions."[38] One American official maker called it a break point.

On April 24, Ambassador Taylor asked Quat to agree to a further increase in American troops, to eighty-two thousand, and the introduction of some 7,250 third-country troops. (Taylor had been on the losing end of battles over the introduction of American troops, and this was a supposed compromise.) Their mission was still defined as the protection of coastal enclaves. Despite Quat's and Bui Diem's reservations, the Vietnamese generals were generally in favor, feeling it would give them breathing space to induct and train more men for their own forces. A surprising number of civilian politicians, because they were worried about the depth of American commitment, were also in favor. Quat gave his approval with regret, apprehension, and reluctance: direct deployment of substantial American forces on the ground was going to look too much like a second coming of the French. It would undercut the perceived independence of the nationalists and give further motivation to the VC.

To give the administration its due, there was real fear the Vietnamese government and army were on the point of collapse, that the VC backed by North Vietnamese regulars were in a position to cut the country in two in central Vietnam, and that therefore we had to intervene, not only by bombing but with American troops on the ground. General Taylor, as I've mentioned, did not think direct troop intervention was either desirable or necessary, and I thought at the time that fears of imminent collapse or of the country's being cut in two were overblown. Nevertheless, these fears would play a main role in fateful discussions in Washington between Johnson and his advisors about what to do in Vietnam.

President Johnson had initially been reluctant to make any commitment of American troops larger than the previous upper limit of about a hundred thousand, but by July he had been confronted by a request from McNamara, supported by Westmoreland and the Joint Chiefs, to double the ante. He had been fearful a major move on Vietnam would endanger his Great Society domestic initiative, which he desperately wanted to focus public attention on. At the same time, he was deeply afraid of losing Vietnam and thought its loss would be a fateful blow, for which he would be blamed, just as the loss of China had been blamed on Truman. A crucial internal debate over escalation would enfold in late July, based mainly on a July 20 memorandum from McNamara to the president presenting a stark picture of political and military deterioration in South Vietnam.

McNamara's message was clear. Only the introduction of around a hundred thousand additional American troops and a mission change to aggressive operations would prevent an internal South Vietnamese collapse and a Viet Cong victory. There were three alternatives: cut our losses and withdraw, which would humiliate the United States and be "very damaging to our future effectiveness on the world scene"; continue largely as we were, eventually reaching the same result as the first option; or radically increasing troops and changing their mission. Increased bombing of the North, intensified engagement of the North in negotiations, and calling up of reserves were also recommended. Johnson would approve the additional troops but avoided calling up reserves or introducing budget increases, which would have, he believed, alarmed Congress and the public, at the expense of his domestic programs.

The way Johnson and McNamara handled this publicly, not being frank about where the troop commitment was heading, would lead the public and the Congress to believe they had been deliberately deceived. The failure to call up the reserves meant that 50 percent of the 1st Air Cavalry Division would be deployed to Vietnam without air-mobile training, because so many of its men's enlistments were up. All this so upset Gen. Harold Jackson, army chief of staff, that after retiring he spoke of the day. "I was ready to go over to the Oval Office and give my four stars to the President and tell him. . . 'I resign, and will hold a press conference after I walk out of your door.'" Regretting his decision, he said, "I made the typical mistake of believing I could do more for the country and the Army if I stayed in than if I got out. I am now going to my grave with that lapse of moral courage on my back"[39] Although by staying in he was able to support General Abrams in changing the way the war would be fought, this apparently did not comfort him.

Chapter 18

The Lansdale Mission

By July 1965, Taylor's one-year assignment to Saigon was up, and he was glad to be out. It had been a trying time. He had not succeeded on the Vietnamese political front, nor had he been able to head off a direct commitment of American troops to combat. Facing the need for a replacement, President Johnson decided, primarily for political cover with the Republicans, to call once again on Henry Cabot Lodge. Lodge agreed mainly out of genuine patriotism, but he also felt he understood how to get things done in Vietnam.

My reaction was negative. If Lodge continued to operate the way he had during his initial stint, we were in for another period of political failure. Then, to my surprise, at the urging of the vice president and under some pressure from Senator Dodd, Lodge invited Lansdale to lunch in Washington on July 27, coincidentally at the same time as the internal debate within the administration about troop escalation was finally resolved. Lodge said the president wanted Lansdale to go to Vietnam. Lodge indicated he would like him to consider coming out as the head of the CIA station, which Lansdale declined as not feasible because of CIA opposition. Lodge then asked him to become his personal assistant to work on "pacification." He would, so long as "pacification" was broadly defined, Lansdale responded, to which Lodge nodded assent. Lodge said Lansdale could assemble a supporting team of his own choosing.[1]

This looked like the opportunity that Lansdale had been waiting for. Lodge had given him an expansive charter designating him the ambassador's "executive agent, responsible for getting an effective political-social program moving in Vietnam . . . for . . . tactfully and persuasively braiding together the separate economic, social, information, military and other programs as necessary to its success . . . without altering the existing U.S. military command." Lansdale was authorized "to act in an advisory capacity to Vietnamese and American personnel at all echelons necessary to achieve the major aims of having the people adhere to the government."[2]

I told Lansdale that Lodge had an inflated ego about his own political sagacity and a very superficial understanding of Vietnam, along with authoritarian notions about how the Vietnamese should do things. I wasn't sure his political philosophy was compatible with Lansdale's ideas of a democratic revolution. Lansdale asked whether Lodge would listen to advice about dealing with the Vietnamese; I was not certain. Lansdale wondered if Lodge would understand enough to give him the backing he needed to operate in a situation increasingly dominated by large American bureaucracies. He thought our side could win if he could only refocus the thinking of Lodge and the president. To that end, he wrote a memo for Lodge pointing out the political nature of the war and expressing concern about the impact of U.S. forces.[3]

"The enemy," Lansdale wrote, "sees his every act as a political act and uses psychological, military and socio-economic weapons to gain his goals. Our side has broken this rule over and over again." To get a counterinsurgency program going we had to start "obeying and applying the prime rule of war in Vietnam," which was political. "It is the basis upon which the war . . . will be won or lost. The psychological, military, and socio-economic programs are its instruments, not ends in themselves. Political bankruptcy in Vietnam and the direct use of U.S. combat forces complicate your task vastly." U.S. commanders tasked to attack a suspected enemy position are "going to clobber it first by bombing or artillery to cut his own U.S. casualties to a minimum; casualties of Vietnamese noncombatants" are "secondary. . . . [S]omething brand new, perhaps of considerable difference from anything previous will have to be worked out in Vietnam to put the war on the essential political footing."[4]

Lansdale's memo was passed on to President Johnson by McGeorge Bundy with the shallow, almost frivolous observation that "Lansdale appears quite ready to take over MACV—and yet he's not all wrong. Can we afford some creative tension?"[5] ("Creative tension" was likely the opposite of what Johnson wished, given his proclivity to want everybody on board with official policy.)

On balance, Lansdale said, he had to answer the call; it was his last chance, no matter how tenuous, to have any effect on how the war was going to turn out, and he felt a deep bond of affection for the Vietnamese. He had great misgivings over the introduction of American troops; it was bound to undercut the independent standing of the South Vietnamese leadership with its own people, but maybe that effect could be mitigated. He knew it was a risky proposition, but he would give it everything he had. Clearly though, Lodge's backing and willingness to give him running room for his informal and unconventional approach to the Vietnamese would be key.[6]

He asked me to help by coming out as part of his team. Unfortunately, I had become too deeply involved in Airways Engineering, dealing with the Saudis over our design for the new Jeddah International Airport, a project subject to changes often arbitrarily dictated from the top. I was the only one who could deal with that. Consequently, selling the firm without me was not an option. Over time I would build a management team, but nothing like it was yet in place. The best I could do was go out for almost a month at the beginning to help Lansdale get started. I was willing to act as a backstop in Washington and thereafter to make periodic visits to Saigon as often as I could. In my Washington backstopping I would deal mainly with the deputy assistant secretary of state for Far Eastern affairs, Leonard Unger, who was also chairman of the Vietnam Coordinating Committee at State.

Members of Lansdale's original 1954–56 team who volunteered to go back included Lou Conein, Joe Baker (who had been Lansdale's administrative officer), Joe Redick, and Napoleon Valeriano (now a U.S. citizen), all detailed from the CIA. Also from the original team were Bohannon (on contract to AID), Sam Karrick (detailed from the Pentagon), George Melvin (transferred, at his request, from AID/Vientiane), and myself as a consultant to AID. Most of these old associates were skeptical about the chances for success and no longer owed their careers to Lansdale, yet they rallied 'round. Other team members were new, the most notable being Daniel Ellsberg, the future source of the *Pentagon Papers*.[7] How the team was going to operate was not clear, but it seemed, on the surface, that Lodge wanted us and was prepared to grant Lansdale a charter giving him room to work on the pacification and political side of the war. There were also promises of an operating budget.

While everyone in Washington was completely cooperative in helping with the transfer or hiring of personnel, the attitudes in Saigon of various agency heads would become revealed over time as more like that of the proverbial dog in the manger. In contrast to the 1963 period, five power centers had greatly expanded within the Saigon American establishment. By mid-1965 USOM, under its new director, Charles Mann, had practically as many personnel in one regional mission, in the city of Can Tho in the Delta, as there had been in the national mission in 1963. USIS, under Barry Zorthian, had become JUSPAO (Joint U.S. Public Affairs Office), with a vastly expanded organization. The embassy political section, under Philip Habib, now had numerous provincial reporters (mainly information gatherers) outside of Saigon, as well as an expanded Saigon staff. The CIA station had personnel scattered throughout the provinces supporting Vietnamese counter-terror, political action, and census-grievance teams and other intelligence operations. The MACV staff had ballooned, converting its headquarters into "Pentagon East," while simultaneously launching offensive operations and managing the deployment of American troops and their logistical support, by now pouring in on a significant scale. The operating mantra seemed to be the more staff, the more effective the effort.

The attitudes of the heads of these agencies to the coming Lansdale intrusion was epitomized by the reaction of the Saigon CIA station chief, Gordon Jorgensen, when he first heard about Lansdale's appointment from a journalist friend, Keyes Beech. According to Beech, he and Jorgensen were having a drink when he asked Jorgensen, "What do you think of Ed Lansdale coming back out here?" Jorgensen, Beech said, "damn near dropped his martini. He didn't know." Beech rubbed it in by saying, "Well, I thought you knew everything[;] . . . you have these immense intelligence resources at your command." Jorgensen said, "You know, I used to work for that broken-field runner." Beech said he could see "what was going through his mind right away. He was throwing up the barricades to protect his turf, and that's what everyone was doing out there at the time. There was a great deal of empire-building or turf-building."[8] Sure enough, not very long after the team arrived in Saigon Jorgensen would tell his staff, "Don't give Lansdale any running room."[9] This attitude would not surface openly for several months after Lansdale's arrival, although there were hints in the air, and was not apparent to me during my initial visit.

The publicity surrounding Lansdale's arrival would also create more of a problem than was apparent at the time. He was branded as a mysterious miracle worker who would instantly bring order out of chaos on the Vietnamese side. The *Washington Post* noted on August 26 that he had some of the characteristics of Lawrence of Arabia, that like Lawrence, "Lansdale has inspired admiration, ridicule and above all, controversy." His "unorthodox manner may incur the opposition of certain American officers." The *Post* went on to quote an unnamed official's comment, "If he doesn't perform a miracle, his friends will be disappointed and his enemies delighted." Beverly Deepe, in an article in the Paris *Herald Tribune* of August 25, "Our Mystery Man in Saigon," speculated that he was considered suspect by various elements of the American bureaucracy for his unconventional traits and also by the Vietnamese bureaucrats, "because they think he's looking for a new Magsaysay and they don't know who that is." She predicted, "The real enemy is now the Communists—but that will be the least of his worries. He has a lot of other problems to solve before he gets a clean shot at the enemy." Deepe was prophetic. The unreasonable expectations that were created and the jealousies that were exacerbated were to prove no help to his mission.

The Vietnamese political scene too had changed considerably since the beginning of 1965. After the collapse of the Quat government in June, the Military Directorate (previously the Military Committee) had once again taken over, this time dominated by the younger generals, the "Young Turks." A "war cabinet" was formed with General Thieu as chief of state and General Ky as prime minister. Thieu was withdrawn, cautious, and colorless, while Ky was impulsive, outgoing, and colorful, if not flamboyant. They were rivals from the start, with little trust in each other, but Ky at least had a predilection for action, and he soon started seeking Bui Diem's political advice, despite his closeness to Quat. The new government was shaky and untested, but there were prospects for a fresh start in developing popular support, provided the demands for participation and influence by various political and religious groups could be met and internal military restiveness quieted.

I arrived in Saigon on September 5, six days after Lansdale and most of the team, which became known as the Saigon Liaison Office (SLO). Team activities quickly began to center in a large, two-story villa rented for Lansdale at 164 Cong Ly Street. It had space on the ground floor for a reception room, a dining room, and rooms that could be used for offices. The second story had an expansive sitting room with a black-and-white, checkered terrazzo floor, surrounded by six bedrooms that provided sleeping quarters for Lansdale and team members, plus guests. The villa came to be called "the monastery"; the rule was, no women visitors at night. Lansdale promptly hung in a prominent location an official photograph of Vice President Humphrey, whom he called the team's "patron saint." The villa made it easy to meet with Vietnamese visitors informally, without being tied up at the crowded embassy with endless coordination meetings, which grew exponentially with the ballooning of the U.S. mission.

Back in Vietnam, it was nice to be dealing directly with real people and a live situation rather than producing memos in Washington and talking oneself blue in the face without discernable effect. I felt immediately at home with the surroundings and with the Vietnamese, although I found Saigon considerably changed by the influx of American soldiers. There was no doubt that our direct military presence had blunted the possibility of any VC-precipitated Vietnamese military collapse, yet what I saw made me wonder at the cost.

The impact was indeed conspicuous. Hotels and apartments had been taken over as officer quarters, while countless new bars catering to GIs had sprung up along Tu Do Street. American cars and jeeps were causing frustrating traffic jams, while hundreds of gasoline generators added an irritating hum to the noise level. The American presence was not only highly visible but verged on the overwhelming. The American troops, which by the time I got there numbered over a hundred thousand and rapidly growing more numerous, were allowed to spend as much of their pay as they wanted on the local economy. Initially troop pay was in dollars, then in military scrip, which really didn't make any difference because of the scrip black market. Someone estimated that American military support and troop expenditures on the Vietnamese local economy, in the twelve months from August 1965 to August 1966, amounted to the entire Vietnamese government national budget for the same period. It was on a scale hard to imagine in terms of the Vietnam I had known, and it was having a visibly adverse impact on the economy and society, undermining Vietnamese cultural pride and sense of self-worth.

Toward the end of my stay, I drove north from Saigon to Bien Hoa to take a look at the American army's 1st Division, whose arrival I had heard about and was by then almost complete. Stretched out on both sides of the highway between the Saigon Bridge and Bien Hoa, for most of its twenty-kilometer length, was the division's logistics support (for our forces, the relation of support to frontline troops was about seven to one). This was an army fit to confront Soviet divisions in Europe, completely off the charts in comparison with the organization and scale of the Viet Cong.

My days in Saigon were a blur of activity as I tried to grasp what had essentially changed and what had not. My job was to initiate key contacts and take political soundings for Lansdale as quickly as possible, helping identify main problem areas and scoping out the pacification situation. The day of my arrival I saw my old friend Bui Diem at his apartment, to get a quick reading. He was now an advisor to Prime Minister Ky.

Bui Diem was the same thoughtful person I remembered, puffing on his ever-present pipe and giving a balanced view of events and personalities. We stayed up until 1:30 in the morning in a tour d'horizon, The publicity surrounding the return of Lansdale had aroused the generals' suspicion that "dirty tricks" would be worked to install a civilian government. Taylor's handling of the generals had made them very sensitive. The lack of mutual trust and confidence between Vietnamese and Americans was a problem that had to be repaired before anything else constructive could be done. He would go to work on it, but his position was delicate, as he was known as a friend of Lansdale.

I suggested that Bui Diem arrange an informal meeting between Lansdale and Ky. He said okay, but he thought Ky would be afraid Lodge would object. I told him (with considerable confidence at the time) that things were different now. Bui Diem was convinced that Ky was sincere and honest. He had good reactions, listened to advice, had become less impulsive, and had grown on the job; this was why he (Bui Diem) had decided to stay on as his advisor. During a recent Military Directorate meeting the generals had discussed how to handle Lodge and Lansdale. Several favored a cagey approach, but Ky had come out strongly for sincerity. If the generals thought they could be trickier than the Americans, he had warned, they were foolish. The best attitude was sincerity and mutual trust. Ky also attacked corruption, saying the government could not win the war or the people if corruption continued. The problem was mainly with wives and relatives at the top; if people at the top did it, everyone would feel free to do it. The guy Ky was really aiming at was General Co, the chief of staff, who the next day issued a general order that relatives must be prevented from engaging in corruption. (I would later hear that Co's wife had gambled away fifteen million piasters of charity funds to which she had access and had desperately tried to raid other army funds to replace the loss. Much of the corruption problem did in fact involve wives and families, although it would not have occurred had each head of household put his foot down. One Vietnamese even suggested the drastic solution of banishing all the wives to Dalat and having all the generals in Saigon eat at a common mess.)[10]

Bui Diem talked about other hopeful signs of Ky's leadership—his willingness to admit mistakes, for example. After setting overly draconian curfew hours, he had softened them and had admitted his mistake publicly. Ky was very interested in pacification and in helping "the poor people," about whom he spoke with genuine feeling. He was concerned about the plight of the peasants while the rich got richer. He was particularly interested in agricultural development, schools, and land reform. Ky's main handicaps were his playboy past and his youth.

The biggest underlying problem, Bui Diem thought, was the increasing breakdown of Vietnamese leadership into cliques and groups. New divisions had been added to all the old ones I had known before. There was a phobia about the Can Lao, which was why so many people remained in jail, like businessman Nguyen Van Buu. Another problem was how to make use of "good guys" on the sidelines, such as General Le Van Kim. The obstacles were often old grudges, some of them mistaken.

When we parted, it was past curfew time. All I had to get me through any street patrols was Bui Diem's calling card with a note to identify me, but I was not stopped. I left Bui Diem encouraged by his role as an advisor to Ky with also a relationship, and some credibility, with Thieu. (His position as an advisor and go-between earned him the nickname in American circles of "McGeorge Diem.")[11] My report to Lansdale was that Ky seemed to have leadership potential.

Next I saw General Van Thanh Cao, the Cao Dai leader with whom I had tried to head off the Buddhist crisis during President Diem's time. When it had first been known that Lansdale was coming back, Cao said, General Thi, the I Corps commander in central Vietnam, had flown to Saigon to ask General Thieu as chief of state to prevent it—Lansdale was "dangerous." Thieu had told Thi he could not stop Lansdale without embarrassing Lodge. Cao had followed the newspaper reaction to Lansdale's return closely. The Catholic papers were happy, the Buddhist papers were saying nothing. The general reaction was that the Cao Dai, the Hoa Hao, and particularly the Catholics were happy, while the generals and the Buddhists were apprehensive. Cao wanted Lansdale to meet with the Cao Dai church hierarchy, but first with leading laymen, some of whom were now feuding with each other. The Cao Dai were in the best position to mediate between the Catholics and the Buddhists and were willing to do so.[12]

Within a few days Lansdale would develop a good working relationship with Minister Nguyen Tat Ung, newly in charge of pacification, whose vigor and openness appeared promising. (Unfortunately, Ung would die in an Air Vietnam plane crash on September 16, setting back Vietnamese and American efforts.) Lodge had clearly designated Lansdale to take the lead on pacification, appointing him as chairman of a reactivated Mission Liaison Group, composed of representatives of the key American agencies. This appointment afforded him a coordinating mechanism but consumed inordinate amounts of time trying to put across a workable concept of pacification and mediating bureaucratic differences. Lansdale also started informal evening meetings at his villa with key Vietnamese and Americans to exchange pacification ideas. The technique was typical of him; this was how he had worked effectively before in the Philippines and in Vietnam, getting everybody reading off the same page. I attended two such meetings before I left and thought they were a promising start.

A TRIP TO THE DELTA

I alternated between seeing various Vietnamese leaders and trying to get a handle on pacification. Aided by the good relations I had established with USOM in Laos in 1963, when Charles Mann was the director there, I went to see him as the new director of AID/Saigon. He seemed happy to see me and wanted my firsthand observations of the mission's field operations. This resulted in a trip to the Delta, with several objectives: to take a look at the current state of pacification, including USOM's field operations; to check in with the Hoa Hao in An Giang Province; and to see my old friend Tran Ngoc Chau, who had been assigned back to Kien Hoa Province as its chief in 1964. I knew Chau would give me his unvarnished views.

The head of the USOM regional mission in Can Tho and the two USOM provincial representatives I met complained about program inflexibility and about the joint provincial committees having been dissolved, a continuing hangover from Killen. USOM was still providing commodity support, and that helped its advisory role but not enough. The provincial reps also complained about having to respond to a bifurcated chain of command, from the USOM regional mission in Can Tho and also from the Provincial Operations assistant director in Saigon. Still, it was encouraging that security in An Giang Province, where I met with Hoa Hao leaders, had improved to the extent that I could drive throughout the province day and night without armed guards.

I went back up to My Tho and over by ferry to Kien Hoa, to spend the night with Lieutenant Colonel Tran Ngoc Chau, once again the province chief. Chau had been struggling for over a year to bring provincial security back to where he had left it in June 1963. After dinner at his house, we talked for almost eight hours, until early morning. The ceiling fans moving the languid air and the chirping crickets outside reminded me of my many visits during 1962 and 1963. Chau walked me through all the disappointing things that had happened after the coup against Diem until his return to Kien Hoa. He was as painfully honest as ever. I was as open with him as I knew he was with me.

"Vietnam is now in a state of anarchy," Chau said. "Fewer people are willing to commit themselves." The only person he trusted among the generals was Thieu, an old personal friend. Many Vietnamese feared the Americans were just trying to make the VC negotiate by using air power against them, and it was wrecking the countryside. This was particularly true of religious leaders, whose temples and churches were being destroyed. Without the air strikes we might lose the war militarily, but with them we were losing politically. Neutralist sentiment was increasing, and it was difficult to reproach his friends who took that attitude. "The present government is very inexperienced, and the generals are full of complexes. Too many educated Vietnamese believe the United States has installed the government and put Ky in as a puppet it can control."

The government had made three major mistakes: a renewed attack on the "ghost of the Can Lao," resulting in twelve capable officers being relieved; the army pay raise, which wrecked the morale of the Popular Defense force and of village and hamlet leaders, because their pay was now less than that of an army private; and the draft, which was destroying provincial civil government by taking its men into the armed forces. (This was to me another example of something that looked good on paper but when translated into practice in Vietnam had adverse consequences.)

If he were asked by Ambassador Lodge what the Americans should do, Chau said he would recommend: "First win the . . . confidence of the generals, second set up an informal joint staff for pacifying the country, and third select some experimental provinces where the province chiefs would be given a completely free hand, but working with American advisors in joint committees." Chau was an intensely proud Vietnamese nationalist, for whom sovereignty had always been a touchy issue, yet now he recommended a joint approach: keeping the country free was more important than preserving the technicalities of sovereignty. "Too many Vietnamese who refuse to work openly and honestly with the Americans do so because they have some dishonesty to hide."

In addition to security, what the people in the provinces wanted most, Chau said, was good behavior and decent treatment by the government, care for war widows and orphans, care and compensation for war victims, care for war refugees, a sincere open-arms (Chieu Hoi) policy toward the VC, and more education and training for young people. If the government wasn't able to take care of its own people adequately, they would expect nothing from the government. The current system was too inflexible to meet these needs. Solving the immediate problems created by the war should have priority. As for pacification, in addition to adequate security forces the key to success was popular local participation in government. He was working on his own land-reform program, settling land issues by consensus, with village administrative committee participation. He wanted to be able to form his own people's self-defense force in the hamlets (a paid version of the old hamlet militia) and to hold elections for village advisory councils.

The only effective American assistance he had received during the past year had come from "Jorgensen's people" (the CIA station). They had supported the census-grievance and counter-terror teams, which were helping maintain the status quo. The security situation was about as bad as it had been when he first arrived in Kien Hoa in 1962, but he now had a solid base of political support, an experienced staff, and a tested program. He was sure he could pacify the province in two years if given a free hand.[13]

Chau said General Thieu had discussed with Westmoreland about assigning a regular Vietnamese army unit to support Chau in Kien Hoa, and Westmoreland, curious to see what Chau was doing, had gone there. He had briefed General Westmoreland and his staff for about two hours on his pacification efforts. At the briefing's end, Westmoreland took Chau aside privately and asked for suggestions on the war. Chau said priority should be placed on security at the village level and that pacification should be the primary objective of the Vietnamese military and paramilitary forces, with the Self-Defense Corps acting as a frontline force, supported by the Civil Guard and backed up by the Vietnamese army, broken down into mobile brigades assigned on a territorial basis so as to respond quickly. The Vietnamese divisions were too heavy and clumsy. American troops should be stationed strategically to defend the seventeenth parallel and to cut off the Ho Chi Minh Trail, with Vietnamese Special Forces being used to harass the North Vietnamese on the trail itself. Westmoreland listened without comment. At the end he got up politely, saying he had to go; his staff would be in contact. There was no follow-up. Chau was left puzzled and frustrated.[14]

Near the end of our long discussion, Chau began to ask direct questions. What were the Americans up to? The wholesale introduction of American troops would inevitably result in the Americanization of the war unless our military presence was only temporary and was limited mainly to the northern periphery of the country, while the advisory effort focused on support and training for local defense forces, on provincial development, and on the reorganization, retraining, and reequipment of the Vietnamese army for counter-guerrilla warfare. Instead, we were introducing whole American divisions to do the fighting ourselves. We would be imitating the French. Were we going to continue bombing and shelling the civilian population? Did we really believe bombing the North would result in their abandoning the insurgency? "What is your strategy? What is the American plan for winning the war?"

I owed Chau an honest answer. "I'm sorry," I replied, but "we don't have a plan that makes any sense to me. The main reason Lansdale has come back, I said, is to try to make sense out of what we are doing here. He will try to help the Vietnamese get a political plan going based on reform and democracy to provide the political cause for the Vietnamese, not the Americans, to win the war. I didn't know if this would succeed. A lot depends on how much support Lodge gives Lansdale and how we are going to fight the war. That's all I can tell you. Too much time has passed and I've become so involved in my business I cannot come out full time. I will come when I can and will back up the team in Washington. In the meantime I will make sure you are introduced to Lansdale."[15] I reported all this to Lansdale in memos before I left, except for the discussion about American policy and Chau's meeting with Westmoreland, which I described verbally, because it was too sensitive to put down on paper.

Lansdale brought Dan Ellsberg out because he had credibility with McNamara and, being young and bright, presumably had an open mind. Lansdale thought Dan could get to know and like the Vietnamese. I hoped he could pick up the work I might have done on pacification while enhancing the team's credibility with the rest of the American bureaucracy through his high-level policy connections. I had a chance to brief Dan in general but didn't have time to introduce him to any Vietnamese directly. Subsequently, he would meet Chau through John Paul Vann and strike up an enduring friendship. Chau was badly treated by General Thieu later in 1970, and I believe this influenced Dan's conclusion that Vietnamese political reform was hopeless and the war as well, a conclusion that was to be part of his motivation for giving the Pentagon Papers to the *New York Times* in March 1971.

I touched base with another friend, Colonel Hoang Van Lac, now the principal staff person for Rural Construction (the latest iteration of the original Strategic Hamlet Program). He was upset by the destruction wrought on Rural Affairs by Killen. While he did not directly criticize the existing USOM Office for Provincial Operations, it was obvious that Lac missed the way things had operated before. Doing away with the joint provincial advisory committees had been a mistake. He was particularly happy with his close relationship with Mark Huss, who had become the principal liaison with Lac for USOM.[16] I found Mark living in the house that Barbara and I had occupied three years before; our houseboy, Duong, was still there. Through Duong I inquired about Thi Ba, the *amah* who had come with us to the United States and was now back in Saigon. She was doing well, he said. With the money saved in the United States she had acquired a fleet of sixteen cyclos that she leased out to independent drivers. I asked him to locate her; I very much wanted to see her.

The isolation of much of the American bureaucracy was highlighted by the behavior of the embassy's economic section, which claimed that the American influx was having little inflationary effect. Team members were informally hearing the contrary, but the embassy seemed content with the statistics it got from the Vietnamese government. Mike Deutch of our team decided to try to get the facts. He had the latest official list from the embassy of local market prices for various everyday commodities. We were together in the Cong Ly villa when Thi Ba showed up to see me. After hugs, photos of our children, which brought tears to her eyes, and questions about our family, I introduced her to Deutch, who asked if she knew about local prices in the market. She had just been there that morning, buying food. (Like most Vietnamese she had an extended family to look after.)

Deutch found his official list and with my help started asking about the market prices of a kilo of rice, of sugar, of pork, of fresh fish, and so on. Thi Ba reeled off the current prices for each, on average about 20 percent higher than those on the official list. Deutch immediately went to the embassy and insisted that a cable go out to Washington with the new data. After much insistence, a cable was actually sent to Washington, with the data sourced to "Rufe Phillips' family *amah*."[17] This story provoked a laugh from the team, but, thinking about it later, I became sure it had caused considerable resentment against SLO. This was to be compounded as the divergence between some of the official reporting and what the Vietnamese were telling Lansdale and his team became increasingly apparent.

After my visit to the Delta, I briefed Mann at USOM in response to his "expressed interest in my firsthand observations." He was attentive but noncommittal. I gave him a written memo that opened bluntly, "From what I have seen in the provinces so far, USOM operations are not at present sufficiently effective to make any significant contribution to winning the war here." The problem was organizational and procedural. Organizationally, the dual chain of command to the provincial reps from the USOM Office of Provincial Operations and from the USOM director through the regional directors caused delay and confusion. The regional directors should be called "regional coordinators" and be taken out of the chain of command. Money and policy should flow directly from the central Provincial Operations office to the provinces.

Further, my memo argued, the joint provincial coordinating committees should be reestablished as soon as possible. With the aim of flexibility and quick reaction, the "former miscellaneous fund" should also be reestablished, using purchased piasters if necessary. His assistant director for provincial operations understood counterinsurgency; his current crop of regional directors did not. "If the Assistant Director for Provincial Operations is put back into business as your field commander, I believe the essential qualities of vitality and dynamism can be restored to USOM's operations in the provinces. You have good people, what they need are the mission and the means."[18]

Mann held my memo very close to his vest and never showed it to Sam Wilson, the head of Provincial Operations, when he got back from leave. Back in Washington, I got a query sent by Unger to Lansdale about reestablishing the provincial sign-off committees. I called Lansdale by phone urging him to follow up (he had a copy of my memo to Mann). Lansdale discovered that Lodge's nose was out of joint, because he thought he should have been queried first. Lansdale also sensed that Mann's bureaucratic instincts were against giving so much authority to one of his subordinates, so he, Lansdale, backed away from actively pushing it, which made me extremely unhappy.[19] A strong push for reconstituting the provincial committees, combined with another special fund of U.S. piasters, might, I thought, have gotten pacification moving in the provinces, where it mattered. This was a tactical mistake by Lansdale, since it could have made short-term pacification progress visible in some provinces, such as Kien Hoa. Instead of addressing Lodge's obsession with immediate pacification results, Lansdale focused on getting a common concept for pacification accepted.

COLLECTING FINAL IMPRESSIONS

Before leaving I had more meetings with Vietnamese ranging from the director of police to the governor of Saigon, to key personnel in the ministries of Information and Agriculture, to religious leaders, dispossessed former Can Lao, President Diem's former secretary Vo Van Hai, and then Bui Diem two more times. I found the most irreconcilable obstacle to South Vietnamese unity to be the religious-cum-political split between the Buddhists and the Catholics, exacerbated by the turmoil of so many coups and governments after Diem's overthrow. This did not show up adequately in the official reporting to Washington.

Near the end of my stay I saw Bui Diem several times at his apartment, once for an informal dinner including old friends, General Le Van Kim and his wife Gaby. Kim's retirement had not, I found, reduced the liveliness of his mind. After dinner Bui Diem took me aside with Kim. We talked about the religious split. Bui Diem called it "the major obstacle to South Vietnamese unification." The differences were "deep and bitter." The problem revolved, on the Buddhist side, around Thich Tri Quang, who had three unshakable beliefs: "He despises all French, hates and mistrusts all Catholics and sees plots and conspiracies behind everything. He is a Buddhist Ngo Dinh Nhu." On the Catholic side was Father Quynh. Each was surrounded by troublemakers.

Bui Diem had reluctantly concluded that the Vietnamese were not solving their problems by themselves; General Lansdale could help as a catalyst in bringing the Buddhists and Catholics together. When General Thieu had talked about this with Lansdale he had been appealing for Lansdale's help. Then Bui Diem asked me to pass along the desire by General Ky to work very closely with Lansdale on pacification. He urged Lansdale to draw up an outline political plan for Ky, who tended to be noncommittal at first when new ideas were presented but then grasped them quickly and took them up as his own.[20]

As the evening drew to a close, I could not help thinking about the waste of Kim's talents. He had not only been the most brilliant staff officer in the Vietnamese army but understood military civic action to its core. More than that, he had been cameraman, then assistant director, to one of the most brilliant French filmmakers, Marcel Pagnol. He had all the talent needed to make educational and inspirational films for the army and even for wider Vietnamese civilian audiences, yet he was unable to contribute. I would try to help.[21]

I told Lansdale that all the Vietnamese I had talked to said religion was a very delicate issue but that "most hope we can help do something about it." I added, "My own feeling is that we must do something about it." I recommended he take up a Cao Dai proposal to meet their religious leaders in Tay Ninh toward the end of October, and attempt to unify the Cao Dai laity after that.[22] This wasn't even on Lansdale's plate of Lodge-assigned responsibilities, nor was it any kind of official American priority. Afterward Lansdale talked to Lodge, but Lodge refused to give Lansdale a free hand, saying it was "a delicate problem" and insisting instead that he concentrate solely on pacification. Lansdale would initiate religious contacts notwithstanding, but he would never receive any backing from Lodge until the question of religious unity became wrapped up in avoiding an election boycott by religious groups, mainly the Buddhists, in 1966.

Most Vietnamese and Americans at the top had an inadequate understanding of pacification. The clearer perceptions were at lower levels on both sides. It was going to be an enormous educational exercise to get a people-oriented approach accepted and implemented from the top down. It had to begin with Prime Minister Ky and whoever was designated to take over from Minister Ung, but it also had to be pushed down to the regular army commanders and to all the province and district chiefs. An important start would be for Ky to issue a clear concept.

The late Minister Ung had proposed pacification concentrate initially on experimental or priority provinces, which I thought was the right approach. Small successes could help dispel the widespread apathy and discouragement that characterized the attitude of many GVN officials and ARVN officers toward pacification. Maximum authority and flexibility had to be given to the provincial level while strengthening local government and taking care of government dependents and war victims (Colonel Chau had this just right). To get around the anarchy and political confusion within the central government, a special war emergency fund should be created, with flexible procedures.[23] This was a pretty radical approach, although no more radical than the special 1962–63 ten million dollar fund in piasters. I hoped Lansdale could sell it to Lodge without becoming bogged down in interagency conflicts. I was sure it could be sold to the Vietnamese, given time and persistence. My earlier days of just going to President Diem after preparing the way through Secretary of Defense Thuan were gone.

I left Saigon after three intensive weeks overoptimistic as to how effective Lansdale was going to be in the midst of so much bureaucracy. The Vietnamese were clearly open to sensitive American advice, but Vietnamese religious and political divisiveness was a grave matter.

It would take an extraordinary and unconventional effort to help them pull themselves out of the morass. If Lodge gave Lansdale a broad enough charter and then backed him up, he could begin to help shape Vietnamese politics and pacification in a positive direction. Lodge had been very friendly and supportive during the meetings where I had been present, including an informal get-together with Lansdale's team at the villa. Lansdale's initial meetings with Thieu and Kim had gone well, and both wanted to seek his advice.

A MEETING WITH VICE PRESIDENT HUMPHREY

Back in Washington, I immediately checked in with Bill Connell, who shortly thereafter arranged for me to fly up to New York with Vice President Humphrey, who was to address the United Nations. On the way back I got an hour of his undivided attention in which to brief him. I was hopeful, based on Lansdale's initial good relations with Lodge and his ability to establish close personal relationships with the key Vietnamese. "The main obstacles of Vietnamese sensitivity and U.S. bureaucracy were slowly being overcome. (I was right about the first; dead wrong about the second.) I thought if we could help the top three Vietnamese generals—Thieu, Ky, and Thi—pull together, that stability could be achieved.

"Do you think Lansdale can pull it off?" Humphrey asked. I said, "Yes, with some time and a little luck despite all the difficulties." Humphrey inquired what he could do to help. I replied, "Give Ed the time. There is so much deterioration and anarchy in South Vietnam. The creation of a common cause will take time. Negotiations with the other side any time soon would be disastrous." Humphrey said he was trying to put that across to the president. I said solutions to the problems of corruption, religious division, and the lack of a moral basis for the war could be found only with time and patience. At one point Humphrey invited senators Moss and Bayh, who were along, to hear my explanation of how actions that looked good in the United States could undermine the South Vietnamese. I cited a recent example of American press coverage that was all about how *we*, not the Vietnamese, were going to resettle refugees.[24]

Thereafter, while attending to Airways Engineering out of necessity, I was in constant contact with Lansdale by letter (sent via the State Department pouch) and by telephone (over the Pentagon's system—a particular number allowed direct dialing to Lansdale's phone at the villa in Saigon). I found Deputy Assistant Secretary of State Leonard Unger, the chairman of the Interagency Vietnam Coordinating Committee, to be supportive. So were Bill Bundy, the assistant secretary for the Far East, Bill Jorden at State, and Stoneman at AID, to whom I gave similar reports. I had no access, however, to a solid phalanx of senior advisors at the top with a different focus; led by McNamara, they were directly advising President Johnson. Johnson's concerns, heavily influenced by this phalanx, were mainly military or focused on pacification as a mechanical process designed to produce immediate positive results. This limited any influence Unger, Bundy, or Jorden might have had, even if they had been disposed to dissent. Humphrey was gradually coming back into President Johnson's good graces but was still on the outside of top policy making, so the good I could do there was limited.

In his December letters, Lansdale continued to sound optimistic. He had submitted a proposal through Lodge for some funding for SLO to support various Vietnamese actions on a relatively small scale. (The concept harkened back to the original Saigon Military Mission in 1954, which had spent relatively small amounts of money from CIA coffers while leveraging funds from other U.S. agencies and the Vietnamese government.) He had received a charter from Lodge to contact religious groups, so long as the groups approached him and he stuck to talking about pacification. He intended to interpret that liberally. Ky had asked him to help with religious and political unity. He was getting some backwash from Habib and the political section but said he could understand it to an extent—because Habib had a deputy ambassador, he didn't expect to have to do a lot of work normally his, and then there was "this unconventional gang who have muscled in on his political scene." He didn't see how he and Habib could team up "unless he understands that we are giving constructive political advice to guys we treat as friends—and who don't look upon us as information gatherers, as they do Habib and Jorgy [the CIA station chief, Jorgensen]."[25]

Lansdale had submitted a paper to Lodge, which Lodge, in turn, had issued to the various mission heads, clarifying SLO's role as the principal mission coordinator and contact point with the Vietnamese government for pacification. He was optimistic that this would overcome some of the bureaucratic resistance he was already experiencing, and he was hopeful he could get at least a modest "slush" fund to help with his operations. The Vietnamese had selected priority areas for pacification. Lansdale had designated specific SLO team members to specific regions for follow-up. On December 22, Lansdale left for Washington on leave and for a conference on pacification that had been set up for early January. After he left, USOM (Mann) and JUSPAO (Zorthian) countered with proposals restricting Lansdale's reach. MACV also had objections. Bureaucratic resistance to the anomaly of his mission would be much stiffer and more effective than he realized. He was about to have much of the ground cut out from under him.

Chapter 19
Triumph of the Bureaucrats

Aid administrator David Bell made a trip to Saigon, arriving January 1, 1966, and returning to Washington on the fifth. He reported directly to President Johnson that the number-one problem was rural pacification and that he was disturbed the United States had no one in charge of it. He revealed that there was a "tentative conclusion [agreed to by Westmoreland, Mann, and Lodge] to place responsibility on [Deputy] Ambassador [William] Porter, give him a small staff and integrate the overall program." According to condensed meeting notes, he was asked by the president, "What about Lansdale?" Bell replied, "Has good effect on VN side—divisive effect on American community. His personality is the reason. . . . Key question is whether he is worth the cost. Lansdale however is rated valuable above his cost."[1] During his trip Bell had not asked a single Vietnamese about Lansdale; his opinions were based on what various agency heads had to say. The stress was on bureaucratic harmony. Unfortunately, Lansdale was not in Saigon to present his own point of view.

The conference on pacification that Lansdale had come back for was held over two days in early January at Airlie House, outside of Washington near Warrenton, Virginia. Ambassador Lodge and all the key agency heads, Mann, Jorgensen, and Zorthian, as well as Habib and Lansdale and MACV staff, came from Saigon. Deputy Assistant Secretary Unger cochaired the meeting with Deputy Ambassador Porter. Senior representatives from CIA, State, AID and the Pentagon also attended. Unger opened the meeting by stating that the United States was well positioned to encourage the Vietnamese to take a "revolutionary role." "What we do on our own," he said, "is not important unless it is keyed into the Vietnamese effort," sounding a bit like Lansdale. But then he focused exclusively on the need for coordination and rationalization of all the U.S. programs and activities with what the Vietnamese were doing. There were "conflicts over resources and manpower" and "no clear priorities."[2]

The next day the meeting morphed into an interagency power struggle over pacification, with State and AID arguing for civilian control and the Pentagon saying it should fall under Westmoreland. The ground was shifting from under Lansdale. None of the proposed interagency organization charts being circulated put SLO in the chain of command below Lodge and Porter. I circulated a handwritten note saying we didn't understand that pacification had to be part of a larger political effort to capture the Vietnamese revolution for our side. "You cannot separate a decision about what kind of organization we should have in Vietnam to run pacification from . . . *who* is to lead this organization and *who* is to integrate our pacification efforts with a political plan and a political effort."[3] The meeting was an exercise in bureaucratic self-absorption.[4] Behind-the-scenes maneuvering was going on between Lodge, the White House, State, and Defense on how to improve coordination.

The conditions in which Lansdale could play the role he had originally hoped for were rapidly fading. Lodge would be revealed as backing him much less than Lansdale had had reason to expect. In contrast with his 1963–64 tour, Lodge, though preserving his prerogatives as the ultimate political advisor to Thieu and Ky, was no longer acting as the prime exponent of across-the-board American policy with the Vietnamese. Although he privately deplored his lack of influence over Westmoreland, he didn't resist the increasing military dominance with any conviction. He did not interfere with how the various agencies or even his own political section conducted themselves unless they were clearly treading on his prerogatives. There was also another factor—that he did not work very hard. (John Roche, who came out from the White House in 1966 to help with the proposed new Vietnamese constitution, complained to President Johnson about Lodge's laziness. Lodge, he said, worked only five or six hours a day and was off on vacation when the Vietnamese constituent assembly elections were only ten days away.)[5]

To keep his own position supreme, Lodge was not above playing divide-and-rule. In the process he relied increasingly on Philip Habib, head of the embassy political section, whose normal duties of political reporting and of giving Lodge political advice conflicted with what Lansdale did best, political action. Habib was an extremely able diplomat with high ambitions, and Lodge was responsible for his efficiency reports. Habib tried to stake out political contacts with high-level Vietnamese as his exclusive preserve while playing to Lodge's ego and limiting to his staff American political contacts with the Vietnamese. As an inside man, he gained Lodge's confidence and circumscribed Lansdale's political operations as much as he could. Barry Zorthian would describe Habib as part of the "conventional standard machine structured to carry out State Department missions. He [Habib] regarded Lansdale as an unprogrammed, loose cannon, a maverick upsetting things without acceptance or commitment to Washington direction."[6]

Lodge combined too little understanding of pacification in a Vietnamese context with a fixation on making American, rather than Vietnamese, concepts work. A prime example was his obsession with an operation called "Hop Tac," the literal translation of which was "cooperation." Started in 1964, it had shown no discernable progress, but General Westmoreland had made optimistic claims about it, thus canonizing the idea. This program—"Rings of Steel," as it was sarcastically called by some—was designed to improve security in the Saigon region. Civilian and military pacification efforts were to be focused in a series of concentric rings, beginning with the most secure areas and working outward. It applied the "oil spot" theory—like spilled oil, security would spread gradually outward. This was how pacification had worked best in the Strategic Hamlet Program, when it was tailored to the location of VC strongholds, which were seldom distributed in even geographic patterns. In the case of Saigon, however, there were traditional VC base areas close in, such as Cu Chi, home of the infamous tunnels. Spreading pacification outward from Saigon in neat, concentric rings was impossible. The Vietnamese regarded Hop Tac as an American idea and despite repeated promises never put any consistent effort into it. Lodge continued making it a priority and was incapable of understanding why Lansdale couldn't rally the Vietnamese behind it.

Lansdale developed with Prime Minister Ky a close personal relationship that he used to promote a people-first direction for pacification, introducing ideas on how to gain popular support for the government by starting a process that would lead toward legitimacy. Frustrated Buddhist and Catholic leaders were coming to him informally as a channel for influencing the government in favor of elections. Lansdale worked quietly with Bui Diem behind the scenes. Together they were persuasive with Ky. Lodge was initially skeptical about the need for elections for a Constituent Assembly, but then the idea got backing from the Johnson administration, primarily for appearances—the American public was getting increasingly restive about the war. Lodge viewed the Assembly as mainly a public-relations exercise to give the Vietnamese government a patina of international legitimacy. On their part, Lansdale and many Vietnamese saw it as the way to spark a genuine, national democratic cause to rally the noncommunist population.

The Honolulu Conference that opened on February 6, 1966, was regarded as a chance to highlight the nonmilitary side of the war to the American public. President Johnson and a panoply of senior American officials from Washington and Saigon, including Lansdale, were in attendance, along with Vietnamese chief of state, General Thieu, and Prime Minister Ky, accompanied by such key aides as Bui Diem. Getting Ky committed to a program of social reform and to the development of democratic government had taken several months of behind-the-scenes collaboration between Bui Diem and Lansdale. They had provided Ky with a stream of concepts and phrases that he used in his speeches. Ky was much more open to suggestion than Thieu, but Bui Diem managed to mediate between the two, to get Thieu's acquiescence to what Ky was saying. (To give Thieu credit, he had also expressed a desire directly to Lansdale to find a path back to elected government, though he favored a more restrictive process than Ky.) Ky's opening speech at the Honolulu Conference was a perfect opportunity to commit himself to social and economic reforms and a return to elected government. This led to a joint declaration signed by Johnson, Thieu, and Ky committing the Vietnamese "to formulate a democratic constitution in the months ahead, to take it to the Vietnamese people for discussion and modification, to seek its ratification by secret ballot and finally to create, on the basis of elections, a representative government."[7] Its language would resonate with the Vietnamese, even if it was viewed cynically by most of the American press.

Lansdale, in a letter to me at the time, felt a tangible sense of accomplishment, as he had worked hard for that commitment. Vice President Humphrey visited Saigon just after the Honolulu Conference and met with the team at Lansdale's villa, boosting its morale and status in Vietnamese eyes. Humphrey, uninformed about the proposed appointment of Porter to coordinate pacification, heard nothing but praise about what Lansdale was doing, conveying the sense that SLO was playing a useful role. Lansdale's absence from Saigon from December 22 to January 19 would, however, prove to have been critical.

THE PORTER APPOINTMENT

On February 17, Ambassador Lodge announced that he was naming Porter as chief coordinator for pacification. Lodge was persuaded that this would produce immediate pacification improvement. President Johnson subsequently claimed he had ordered Lodge to make the change. Whoever was responsible, it ignored the reality that quick results were inherently impossible, no matter whom the Americans put in charge. Too much Vietnamese confusion and disunity had to be overcome first. It was easy for Lodge to fault Lansdale for not pulling a rabbit out of a hat and to conclude it was time to try somebody else. Conventional thinking held that Porter, as deputy ambassador, would give the position more weight and hence would be more effective—a confusion of position and rank with influence. This was not how things worked in Vietnam. In Washington, as an additional measure, Robert Komer of the NSC staff was named special assistant to President Johnson, with authority to supervise administration support for pacification.

Ambassador Porter defined his new position of mission coordinator as that of an administrator, an overseer of civilian agencies, not as an agent of change, of influencing the Vietnamese to make pacification effective. MACV would remain separate, not under Porter's direction, yet security support was needed from the Vietnamese army if pacification was going to work. While General Westmoreland paid lip service to pacification, he was completely involved in deploying American troops in large "search and destroy" operations. Porter, then, was miscast in the job. American coordination was needed, but the greater need was for effective Vietnamese action. Had Lansdale been put in charge, with somebody like Sam Wilson, who was by this time mission coordinator, as his deputy, it would have made sense. Lansdale could have run interference on the Vietnamese side while his deputy coordinated, or at least tried to coordinate, the increasingly large and competing American bureaucracies.

The lack of a unified concept, among either Americans or Vietnamese, of how pacification should be carried out remained a significant obstacle. For some it was mainly population control, a matter of the use of police forces, identity cards, and checkpoints. Lansdale's focus was on protecting the population and winning its support, emphasizing localized counter-guerrilla operations. It was a replay of the struggle over a coherent approach that had gone on in 1962 and 1963, when the people-first orientation of Rural Affairs had pretty much prevailed, except for MACV and the Vietnamese army's predilection for large-unit sweeps and uncontrolled firepower. Now the old argument was back but with much larger agencies, each believing its particular view was key.

The Vietnamese army was still not operating at less than battalion strength mainly during daylight, and it had few practical ties to pacification. This disconnect with the population also encouraged poor army troop behavior toward civilians, further undermining government support. At the same time, American military forces were fighting more and more independently of the Vietnamese and going after regular VC units in "search and destroy" operations. The massive use of firepower against suspected VC targets, including villages, was the antithesis of pacification. Most of the problems Colonel Chau had described to me in 1965 remained unresolved. Lansdale, raising his voice on the American side and quietly trying to influence the Vietnamese, was sometimes heard but he was insufficiently heeded. Lodge had neither the perception nor the understanding to separate out a coherent concept, no matter how much Lansdale tried to educate him. Lodge's devotion to population and resources control as the main answer was the opposite of Lansdale's approach. The shallowness of his thinking remained a constant problem.

One thing made me smile about Porter's appointment. Reportedly someone had suggested me to Porter as his deputy. Supposedly Porter had said, "He's too close to the Vietnamese." I repeated the story to friends like Bill Connell as something of a badge of honor. In truth, it was a sad commentary on the inverted order of things within the American hierarchy in Saigon. The main problem, in truth, was not coordinating the Americans; it was helping the Vietnamese. Despite the demotion, Lansdale would manage to keep a partial hand on pacification, because the Vietnamese preferred to talk to him. When Porter told General Thanh, who had become the rural construction minister, not to deal with Lansdale any more, because he was no longer in the chain of command, Thang told him, "Lansdale is my friend and I am going to see him any goddam time I feel like it and tell him any goddam thing I want. If he gives me any advice, I'm going to welcome it."[8] This did not endear Thang or Lansdale to Porter, but Porter learned with some diplomatic grace to live with it and actually got along relatively well with Lansdale, in contrast to Habib and Zorthian.

Lansdale had mixed feelings about Porter taking over the formal coordination role, since it consumed inordinate amounts of time and had little to do with what the Vietnamese were doing. However, it could only be perceived as a diminution of his own role. His influence with the Vietnamese was tied not only to personal relationships but also to his ability to influence American policy and support. This diminution was exacerbated by the interpretation of the move by the American press as a Lansdale demotion.

Shortly after the Porter appointment, on February 24, 1966, Stanley Karnow published a story in the *Washington Post* headlined, "Failure to Produce Viet Miracles Puts Gen. Lansdale on the Defensive." It said, "His adversaries, who are numerous within the U.S. mission, contend that Lansdale and his eleven-man team have failed to make the slightest impact on the Vietnam situation. They support this view by pointing out that in a major reorganization this last week, Lansdale was bypassed and authority for overall nonmilitary programs was vested in Deputy Ambassador William Porter, a career diplomat." Karnow defined the problem as a changed set of circumstances since Lansdale's previous assignments: "The U.S. mission had proliferated into a huge bureaucratic machine," and "without the authority or finances of a U.S. agency under his command, he lacked real weight." The article ended by quoting "a seasoned American official here" as saying, "The Lansdale group has not been able to meet the requirements of the present Vietnam situation. We are up against a superb Communist organization that must be uprooted by a better organization. This simply cannot be done by a few men of goodwill."

The assumption that uprooting the VC was just a question of Americans willing a better organization, presumably South Vietnamese, was supercilious and arrogant. Karnow's sources clearly intended to put Lansdale down. Although many Vietnamese would continue to consult Lansdale via the back door, without informing their official American counterparts, the apparent demotion had an effect. Some Vietnamese sardonically ascribed the attempt to cut Lansdale down to too much American exposure to Vietnam—it sounded like something the Vietnamese usually did to each other. Karnow's story made me intensely angry, but I was in Washington where I could do little except explain to sympathetic listeners that the bureaucrats appeared to have gotten the upper hand. It was a sorry piece of work. Lodge, for his part, far from cushioning the blow, did nothing to soften it. He had found a scapegoat for the lack of tangible pacification results. All this hurt, and it was particularly discouraging to many of the team members, although Lansdale would soldier on.

Sam Wilson later described an example of prevailing bureaucratic small-mindedness. As Lodge's mission coordinator he kept the minutes of the Mission Council meetings. When Porter was appointed pacification coordinator, Lansdale was taken off the council, but Sam always showed him a copy of his draft minutes to keep him informed. When Habib found out, he got Lodge to order Sam to stop.[9] The SLO team got very upset with this kind of put-down and wanted Ed to precipitate an open confrontation. In a June 1966 letter to Mike Deutch in Washington, Lansdale asked, "How does a guy go about getting policy folks to understand the nature of the problem they are trying to solve?" He had been asked repeatedly to act in ways that would generate a "head-on clash" of views. The only clash capable of being made was "on something awfully simple and so kindergartenish that even a win has little long-term meaning." My having "taken on McNamara in front of President Kennedy," he said, had been "a moment of truth that had no lasting effect at all among US policy folks." He thought it senseless to throw himself or the team in the path of the "big juggernaut the US had built just to have a spectacle of a big spla-a-a-t, which would be us."[10] As frustrated as I got over the way Lansdale was being treated, I could not refute his argument.

CHANGED CIRCUMSTANCES

Lansdale's difficulties made me reflect about the changes from the time he had been so effective in the earlier Vietnam days. The inability to make his influence fully felt during this Saigon tour stemmed from four primary factors. Most important was the lack of personal backing from Ambassador Lodge, backstopped from the top in Washington, which would have given Lansdale operating authority and room to act as the principal American contact with key Vietnamese leaders on politics and pacification. Lansdale characterized SLO as having "quasi-support in many places but not a staunch friend who can 'do,' in supporting us, anyplace." He saw his "support in Washington and Saigon as a series of melting ice floes" on which SLO had to "keep slipping from one to the other" to stay afloat.[11] Effective backing carried with it the capability to override or go around bureaucratic parochialism when necessary. Lodge was too detached and unknowing, still acting as political queen bee but not providing effective leadership. Lansdale had enjoyed enough backing from Ambassador Heath in 1954 to give him a foothold from which he could not be dislodged by our subsequent ambassador, General Collins, whose divorce from Vietnamese reality almost lost South Vietnam in 1955. He had also had the Dulles brothers in Washington firmly behind him during that period.

Another significant impediment was the outsized, bureaucratized nature of the American agencies in Vietnam and their turf-protective focus. Each agency had independent access to its mother ship in Washington, where performance was judged on "results" as defined by the Washington–Saigon nexus, unrelated to the Vietnamese themselves. Inordinate time was wasted in interagency squabbling or in program self-justification unconnected to results on the ground. There was little breathing room in which to operate in an across-the-board manner that had been essential to Lansdale's earlier successes. Bureaucratic resistance during the 1954–55 period, and there had been some, had been either dodged or overcome.

A third factor was the demand from Washington for instant or nearly instant pacification results. In 1965, I pleaded with Humphrey to use his influence to give the Vietnamese time to achieve effective political unity, cure the underlying atmosphere of mistrust that undermined everything, and get effective pacification going. I gave the same message to my contacts at the White House (Bill Jorden) and at State (Ambassador Unger and Bill Bundy). Because he had opposed bombing North Vietnam, Humphrey was still in Siberia with the president—how far removed from the action he was, I did not fully realize at the time. My second-level contacts had influence only at the margins. In Johnson's view, there was no time: the war had to be won very soon, the Vietnamese government stabilized now, and American troops withdrawn as soon as possible thereafter. Genuine progress in Vietnam was never susceptible to that kind of time frame, but nobody had the guts or the understanding to buck the consensus and say so to the president or to level with the Congress and the public about it. President Johnson's need for results now, unless modified by a principled stand by Lodge, would have made Lansdale's mission extremely difficult even with better support. Johnson's expectations were summed up by his later comment to columnist Drew Pearson: "I sent Lansdale over there but nothing happened."[12]

A fourth factor was more personal. Lansdale's way of operating, his personal and informal approach to working with the Vietnamese, was in stark contrast to American formality at the top. He and others of his staff acted as catalysts and go-betweens to get the factionalized Vietnamese talking to each other and working together. Advance approval could not be required for every step. His informal ways gave him room to put his political imagination to work in generating effective ideas that the Vietnamese could internalize and carry out as their own, but his manner of working grated on American bureaucratic sensibilities. His ability to get close to the Vietnamese and be heeded when others were unable to achieve a comparable degree of access and influence or were unable with such skill to anticipate Vietnamese actions generated jealousy, an additional motivation to cut him down.[13] Jealousy had also been present during the 1954–55 period, but there had been no one powerful enough then to hinder him significantly because of it. Added to this was Lansdale's palpable aversion to meaningless "official" doctrine, formalistic bureaucrats, and blatant careerists, a distaste that he had difficulty hiding. Always patient with the Vietnamese, he had little tolerance for Americans' shortcomings and at times could not resist needling those he considered enemies.[14] Lansdale and the bureaucratic establishment were oil and water.

A further hindrance, more in the background, was the view, popularized by some of the press (but not restricted to them—it would bleed into the work of some historians), that Lansdale was a naïf trying to impose a carbon copy of American democracy on a Vietnamese culture that neither understood nor was receptive to it.[15] Viewed from the inside, however, there was nothing naïve about the way Lansdale operated. While he might explain to outsiders a set of goals that sounded simplistic, he was in fact wily, practical, and completely realistic about how to help the Vietnamese get useful things done. When he talked about American ideals and principles it was to provide a positive framework that average Americans could understand as a guide for their actions, as a set of signposts they could relate to. Also, he deeply believed that we had to stay true to our own principles, understanding that letting the end justifying the means inevitably undermined American public support.

Finally, Asia was particularly his element; he bonded easily and quickly with the people there even when speaking through an interpreter. Joe Redick, from the early Saigon days, who had seen him in operation up close more than anyone else, marveled at his ability not to be taken in, to persuade even the scoundrels he sometimes had to deal with to engage in positive acts. He understood that they all wanted to be seen as patriots.

Chapter 20
Refusing to Give Up

After the Porter appointment, despite his behind-the-scenes success in orienting General Ky, Lansdale's relations with Lodge became severely strained. By early April 1966 Lodge had issued instructions prohibiting SLO members from contacting Vietnamese leaders. Lansdale promptly put a memo under his nose proposing that SLO be disbanded. Lodge backed off, removing restrictions on the team but later requiring prior coordination with himself, Habib, or Porter. Lansdale refused to give up and would work around these restrictions by indirectly generating requests from the Vietnamese side to meet with him, which Lodge could hardly refuse. Having helped work Ky around to the idea of an elected Constituent Assembly, he proposed to Lodge that he (Lansdale) help the Vietnamese form "groupings of political parties and factions so that strong national coalitions will emerge that transcend sectarian and sectional affiliations" as part of the upcoming Constituent Assembly election process. This was "one more service yet to be performed." Finally, "When it has been performed SLO should be disbanded."[1]

Lodge responded patronizingly that he wanted "the U.S. to get the full benefit of the talents, experience, special relationships and special position of your good self and your associates." That is, Lodge said, "You will to the greatest degree possible be present, to listen, to report." He hoped Lansdale would "make recommendations" on "forming groupings of political parties and factions," but he directed that "specific policies should be carried out subject to check with me, after whatever consultation . . . may be necessary . . . with Washington and the GVN."[2] It defined Lodge's attitude: don't do anything without asking him first.

Lansdale's main purpose was to give the elections credibility with the Vietnamese by ensuring that they were clean and honest. Forming political groupings, while important, was only a smoke screen for what he intended to do. He laid this out in a letter in early May, during a visit to Washington in which he recounted being told by Bill Connell and Robert Komer, now Johnson's principal staff assistant on Vietnam, that he was expected "to be bolder." Lansdale had replied okay, he would get bold, "but if or when I get chopped down for it, I'm then blowing the whistle on the poor work of the U.S. in VN. This alarmed them," Lansdale said.

> They asked me to please stick and take it. I didn't tell them that I'm really going to stick to going around left flank, as we have been doing the past 3 weeks in Vietnam. I have the word out in VN circles—and as I see people, I just report what they tell me, and what they plan to do next. I leave out my advice to them. I stick strictly to U.S. policy guidelines but I don't want to be spending most of my time explaining every last move to Lodge and Habib in kindergarten terms they would understand.[3]

This was now the first of July, and the Constituent Assembly elections were scheduled for September 11. I arrived in Saigon on August 11 and stayed for almost thirty days. One of Lansdale's first actions, working through Bui Diem, was to have Prime Minister Ky invite him for a discussion about the elections, which allowed him to suggest informally that General Thang be given the responsibility for managing the process. Lansdale's already close relationship with Thang made it possible for Thang to seek Lansdale's advice. Porter, saddled with primary responsibility for pacification, did not want to become involved in the elections. Habib, who had the official American responsibility, would have crossed lines with Porter had he attempted to become a direct advisor to Thang. This left the door open for Lansdale, who moved into play.

My primary task became helping to diffuse attempts to boycott the elections or undermine the honesty and openness of the process. I met various Hoa Hao factions and some of the Cao Dai I had known to urge them to participate and to unite behind a slate of candidates. I necessarily swore to the good faith of the United States in backing honest elections. In so doing, I started crossing my fingers when I learned that Lodge apparently didn't care whether they were free or not, only how they might be viewed in the American press. He had defined his attitude with considerable irritation during a staff discussion at the embassy about the importance of free elections, declaring, "I've spent most of my life rigging elections. There is a limit to how naïve or hypocritical we can afford to be out here."[4]

"PEACE AND PROSPERITY" VILLAGE

I also found myself inadvertently sticking my nose into pacification when my old friend Pham Xuan An came by the Cong Ly villa to see me, having heard via the grapevine I was in town. His usual sidekick, Vuong, was not with him, tied up on a family matter. He told me something had happened the day before at a village called An Phu (Peace and Prosperity), only three miles from the edge of Saigon-Cholon, which he thought I should see.

We went there in his green, beat-up, four-horsepower Renault sedan.[5] Eventually leaving the main paved road, we bumped over a dusty path on the top of ricefield dikes to Hamlet One of An Phu. There I found survivors of a VC attack still holed up in a small fort and women weeping over the dead. The day before, a VC company of about a hundred men had infiltrated the hamlet at two in the morning and, shortly after daylight, ambushed the Popular Forces and the Combat Youth (hamlet militia). Twelve Popular Forces and Combat Youth, including the PF commander, had been killed in the ambush. Eighteen had been wounded, the rest captured. Two of the captives, the deputy PF commander and the head of the Combat Youth, had been executed by the VC on the spot.

Asked why they did not give any warning, the hamlet families said they had been forced to evacuate or hide in bunkers under their houses while the PF and Combat Youth slept in the small fort. No civilians had been hurt, and no civilian property had been damaged. Artillery support had been requested by radio when the attack began, but only two hours later, long after the VC had left, did even a spotter plane appear. Later in the day, about eight hours after the attack, a Regional Forces company finally got to the hamlet. (It was sent about twenty kilometers across the rice paddies from Tan An, the capital of adjacent Long An Province, rather than from nearby Cholon.) Despite the presence of the Regional Forces, the VC the same evening visited the homes of all the families with killed or wounded to express their sympathy and to say they had had no choice, that the local forces were tools of the Americans.

With An's help I talked to a number of the residents, including the village chief's mother. She refused to let her son come to see her; she preferred to live out her old age alone but in peace. I learned from another resident that the VC were currently operating a checkpoint between Hamlet One and Hamlet Two every day after five in the afternoon. When asked what he feared most, another resident listed artillery, bombs, GVN troops, and the VC, in that order. Recently, the Vietnamese army had shelled one of the hamlets, killing three civilians.

In my memo to Lansdale, after describing the massacre and its aftermath, I gave a brief history of the village. During Diem's time and into the middle of 1964 it had been considered one of the most secure and pro-government villages in Gia Dinh Province. At that time VC forces within a two-district area surrounding the village consisted of only one mobile company. Now, in the single district where the village was located there was a regular VC battalion and another in the process of formation, in addition to the usual local guerrillas. In a village in which almost no families had supported the VC there were now fifty-eight VC families, twenty-nine of which lived in Hamlet One. All of the families in the village were paying the VC a regular tax of 10 percent of their annual rice crop.[6]

Ironically, Hamlet One was carried on Vietnamese government charts as having met all six criteria for a pacified hamlet, and its PF platoon had been considered one of the best in the district. I was struck by how thoroughly our side had lost the political struggle for the people in this village and by how long it had taken for armed relief to get there after the attack. It was a complete hole in the defenses of Saigon, and it was due in large part to the fact that the jurisdiction of the Vietnamese army and Regional Force units responsible for the defense of Saigon–Cholon had been confined to the city limits. This was just the area that should have been pacified and protected by Hop Tac, the ill-fated pacification operation so favored by Ambassador Lodge and General Westmoreland.

Lansdale promptly gave a copy of my memo to General Westmoreland, who was incredulous. He ordered Brig. Gen. Fritz Freund to go with me to determine the facts. I called An, who said he was willing to take both of us. The next morning, Freund showed up at the Cong Ly villa in civvies, with a Colt automatic .45 stuck under his shirt and belt in back. We waited for An, who finally appeared in a taxi because his car had broken down. There was nothing to do except take the taxi. It was the typical Saigon cab of the time, a twin of An's Renault. We squeezed ourselves into it with difficulty, because Freund was even larger than I was. Bumping over the same dirt road as before, we found the village. After interviewing the survivors and getting the same story, Freund wrote his own memo to Westmoreland, confirming everything I had said. Using USOM contacts, I was able to get some medical help and economic assistance for the village.

Nevertheless, no action would be taken before the 1968 Tet Offensive to extend the Saigon security perimeter out to a more rational distance from the city or to redress the problem of VC control of the An Phu area. During a later 1968 visit to Saigon, I was almost certain, although I could not confirm it at the time, that the same area had been used by the VC to marshal forces for the Tet and mini-Tet offensives, as well as for rocket attacks on the city.[7] The unresponsiveness of Westmoreland's muscle-bound command was amazing. Ironically, when I got back to Washington from my 1966 visit I learned that a copy of my An Phu memo had apparently reached Komer, who told me he had forwarded it to President Johnson. Like other unfavorable news that didn't fit Washington's preconceptions, it simply disappeared into the rarified ether at the top.

I would not see An again until 2002, during my only postwar visit to Saigon. We talked for a long time at his house and then over dinner at the recently renovated Majestic Hotel. Several years before, An had been openly recognized by the communist government as having been the top spy for the North and promoted to lieutenant general in retirement. I asked why he had taken me to that village. An said what had happened to those people was terrible and that he just thought I should see it. I pointed out he had exposed a significant defect in the government's defenses around Saigon to someone who was duty bound to report it to the American high command, which could then be expected to take corrective action. He acknowledged my logic but maintained it was the human tragedy that motivated him. Of course, actions like this could be seen as enhancing his cover as someone on our side; still, it risked calling attention to himself, as an action beyond his ostensible role as a journalist. Maybe his motivation had been what he said it was, mixed with some idea of showing at least one American whom he regarded as a friend the reality of what was happening. Strange for a spy, but he was no ordinary spy, in that he retained a deep affection for America and had many close personal American friends, whom he genuinely cherished. He maintained within himself widely contradictory values, particularly in supporting a cause whose success spawned so much cruelty and suffering. When I saw him in 2002, he was deeply disillusioned and embittered by what had happened after the North took over in 1975.[8]

OTHER PACIFICATION ASPECTS

I also investigated pacification in the Delta by touring Vinh Long Province (the location of the "long walls" problem with Colonel Phuoc in 1963) with John Paul Vann. The province's security showed a surprising degree of improvement. Dan Ellsberg had regaled me in Saigon with tales of Vann roaring through VC-controlled territory in the middle of the night. In contrast, this trip was not a white-knuckled affair. The areas we went through were peaceful during the day and mainly so at night as well. I had known Vann in 1962 and 1963 and was well aware of his effectiveness but found him too ready to assume the Americans had to run the show if anything was to get done. I understood his impatience but thought the emphasis had to be on getting the Vietnamese to run their own affairs, with us standing behind, pushing as necessary but not getting in front. During our ride, Vann gave me an earful about Westmoreland's preoccupation with big-unit operations against the VC and the lack of effective Vietnamese army support of pacification. Chau and Vann, who were close friends, thought pretty much alike about pacification. In Chau's case, Vann recognized and respected the need for the Vietnamese to be out front and in charge.[9]

I also accompanied Bert Fraleigh down to the Hoa Hao–dominated province of An Giang, in the southwest Delta, where he was sponsoring an agricultural experiment introducing new crops, particularly soybeans and "sugar baby" watermelons. He had put together a team of Taiwan agricultural technicians led by the familiar Leonard Chang, along with Vietnamese extension-service technicians under the local supervision of Cal Mehlert, of USOM Provincial Operations. In typical Fraleigh style, instead of a more modest experimental approach in a few villages, the soybean project had been undertaken with average farmers in all thirty-two villages of the province. The results were dramatic. The already harvested crop brought farmers five to ten times as much cash as rice planted on the same amount of space would have. Vegetables and watermelons could be grown in the off-season. Excitement was visible on the faces of about a hundred farmers from one village who had assembled voluntarily to learn how they could do it too.

With support from Saigon to expand, the program could become self-financing through agricultural loans. The average farmer's income could be doubled in less than two years. Land reform was needed—some 80 percent of the farmers were tenants—but with credit and improved incomes, a land buy-out seemed possible. With increasing political influence in the hands of the farmers, next year's village elections would have more political meaning. With follow-through, this could be carried out not only in An Giang but also in secure areas in other Delta provinces.[10] It would form part of Lansdale's proposals to seize the initiative from the VC in 1967.

I checked on how Colonel Chau's talents were being put to use. He had been moved up to the Ministry of Revolutionary Development in Saigon and been made responsible for the training of the political action teams, renamed "Revolutionary Development Teams," at the CIA-supported training center in Vung Tau. The center had been run by a Vietnamese directly on the station's payroll. Chau, with Thang's backing, had attempted to "Vietnamize" the operation, since they believed its known Agency control was propaganda fodder for the VC. Chau, who had been on very friendly terms with various Agency personnel in the past, came to believe an attempt was being made to buy his loyalty by offering to supplement his pay. Chau's response was, "I am not here to work as a CIA agent but as a friend." This devolved into a quarrel with the station. Chau openly requested that the training center be supported by USOM, not by the station. The dispute could have been resolved by putting agency personnel under USOM cover to support the operation, but it became an American bureaucratic tug-of-war, another example of the Agency's obsession with control.

By the time I saw him, Chau had resigned as the center's director and was in an anomalous position in the ministry. One of Chau's problems, I thought, was he was bright and talented but had never played inside army politics to get himself promoted, while others of lesser merit who were now his superiors had. They were at a loss as to how to deal with him. His uncompromising ethics were something of an affront, although he did not consciously try to make them so.[11]

CORRUPTION

Colonel Hoang Van Lac gave me an earful about the side effects of the large-scale American troop intervention. The inflation of the previous year had only accelerated. The allowances granted lower-ranking Vietnamese army officers in the Saigon region were completely insufficient to sustain their families. To make ends meet, officers were doffing their uniforms in the evening and using their personal motor scooters as taxis for GIs looking for a good time in city bars. This was degrading to Vietnamese dignity. Corruption was rampant among the families of some of the generals, corroding army morale.

The disappearance of American goods into the Vietnamese black market was a scandal. The post exchange (PX) had received thousands of cans of hairspray that had promptly disappeared to keep in place countless Vietnamese female bouffant hairdos, giving the American PX commander the nickname "Captain Hairspray." I had heard about the hairspray and also about boxes of American detergent used by numerous Vietnamese laundries that had sprung up to serve American troops. Lac said that was not the half of it. Also being siphoned off were televisions, refrigerators, radios, washing machines, dryers, and other appliances. Off the road to Bien Hoa north of Saigon there was a fenced-in yard where many of the black market appliances were being stored. He could show me where it was. I wrote a memo about this to Lansdale, spelling out the underlying American connection; he forwarded it to Ambassador Lodge and to General Westmoreland.[12]

I found confirmation of Lac's observations about the effects of corruption when I saw retired general Le Van Kim, now running a restaurant to make ends meet. Many of his former subordinates still kept in touch. A captain had recently come to Kim for advice. One of the captain's junior officers had told him that his family was unable to live off his present salary and that that left him with two choices: he could engage in corruption or take a second job. He realized that both were wrong, but at least the latter would preserve his honor as a soldier. Would the captain morally authorize him to do so? Now the captain wanted Kim's opinion. Kim could only say yes to the second job. The army, Kim feared, was morally disintegrating under the strain of economic, social, and political pressures. The rise of prices was having a terrible impact, particularly on the junior offices and noncoms. If all shared equally the situation would be different, but the extent of corruption at the top was already widely known lower down.[13]

When I got back to Washington, I asked Lansdale by phone about any action resulting from my corruption memo. "Nothing significant," he said. When I checked about a year later, during my next visit, I heard the black market depot had been moved but was still in operation and that corruption in general had gotten worse. Goods were continuing to flow out of the back door of the PX without ever hitting the sales floor. I found it amazing that the issue was never directly addressed by General Westmoreland or Lodge. How could this be allowed to continue, when Americans and Vietnamese were dying in combat? How did we expect the Vietnamese to be honest when Americans were either fomenting or allowing such corruption and our highest officials appeared unconcerned? It was hard to take and hard to blame the Vietnamese.

THE BUDDHIST BOYCOTT OF THE ELECTIONS

A looming threat to the Constituent Assembly elections was a boycott advocated by the Buddhist movement and by the Citizens Religious Front they had formed with Cao Dai and Hoa Hao participation. The Buddhist leadership, particularly Thich Tri Quang, was deeply angry at Ky and at the Americans for supporting the use of force in putting down their rebellion in central Vietnam. (Buddhist-led riots had even resulted in the burning of the USIS library in Hue.) Thich Tri Quang was now in Saigon on a hunger strike, reportedly determined to die in some spectacular manner in order to disrupt the elections.

This situation grew out of an earlier power struggle between Prime Minister Ky and General Thi, commander of I Corps in central Vietnam, who was supported by the Buddhists led by Tri Quang. There were personal differences between Thi and Ky, which crystallized over the handling of Buddhist agitation against Ky for his backsliding on a promise of elections for a constituent assembly. Lansdale had visited General Thi back in early March with Lou Conein, who knew Thi well. Lansdale discovered what he thought was the basis for common ground between Thi and Ky and a political solution to the growing disaffection of the Buddhists. Lodge believed that early elections were too dangerous and advised Ky not to give in on this issue. Ky then fired General Thi as I Corps commander. Thi submitted his resignation but returned to central Vietnam, where he became the focus of Buddhist resistance to Ky.

The embassy found itself supporting Ky willy-nilly as the conflict escalated. Among the Americans, supposed Viet Cong influence with the Buddhists was hyped. (A National Liberation Front leader would reveal after the war that the NLF had had very little influence with the Buddhists.) As a showdown seemed imminent, Lansdale got Lodge's agreement to try to bring about a personal meeting between Ky and Thi (they had once been friends). Lansdale saw Ky at his house and persuaded him to meet with Thi alone in neutral place. When Lansdale reported back to Lodge he found Lodge and Westmoreland had already decided that the way to deal with the Buddhists and Thi was by military force.[14] With American backing, Ky sent Vietnamese marines and tanks from Saigon to attack the Buddhists in Hue, where they were supported by some local army units. Civilian and military casualties resulted. American forces were directly involved in blocking local army units from going to the defense of the Buddhists. It was ham-handed, open intervention.[15] It might have been avoided had Lansdale been allowed to mediate between Thi and Ky.[16]

Tri Quang was now starving himself in protest against the forthcoming elections. Lodge was concerned about the impact his death would have on press perceptions of the elections. Tri Quang absolutely refused to see any Americans—several embassy political section attempts to visit him had been rejected—so Lodge had no up-to-date information about his state of health or intentions. Lodge asked Lansdale if he could find out anything. At that moment an old friend from Operation Brotherhood days, Dr. Immanuel "Manny" Ho Quang Phuoc, casually visited the SLO villa.[17] Manny, although Catholic, had many Buddhist friends, so I asked if he had any connections with Tri Quang. Manny told me Dr. Nguyen Duy Tai, who owned the clinic that treated Tri Quang, was a good friend of Tri Quang's, and so was an old, blind, Buddhist priest who threw bones and told fortunes. Manny thought he could get Tri Quang to invite me to see him, but first I had to have lunch with Dr. Tai and meet the priest.

After a friendly lunch the following day with Dr. Tai, Manny took me to the blind priest, who felt my face, threw some bones on the floor of his temple, felt them, and said I was a good man; he would advise Tri Quang to see me. The next day I received a verbal invitation from Tri Quang, through Manny. I talked to Lodge to see if he would authorize it. Phil Habib, as head of the political section, was called in and had to admit that Tri Quang just wouldn't see him or anybody else from the embassy, except possibly Lodge himself, which would give it too much importance. Lodge okayed the visit, saying he understood Tri Quang's need to save face (after the defeat of his movement) and would like to help him, but the removal of Ky and Thieu, which Tri Quang had been publicly demanding as a precondition for no longer opposing the elections, was impossible.

I found Tri Quang at Dr. Tai's clinic, lying on single cot covered by a blanket and wearing a sweater. He was emaciated and otherworldly but very alert. It was the first time we had met. His thick lips were prominent, unusual for a Vietnamese. He sat up to shake hands, then asked permission to recline during the conversation. He occasionally sipped from a bottle that I learned contained sugar water. I conveyed Lodge's personal regards. He said he knew who I was. I asked about his health. He said he was very tired. For a moment, we talked about Manny Phuoc and Operation Brotherhood, which he remembered fondly as caring for the sick in central Vietnam.

Tri Quang made these points: Vietnam needed the Americans; there was no one else to turn to. As a Buddhist monk, he should be against war but he was "in favor of this war because he was against communism." He was "pro-American, not anti-America," and against neutralism. Nevertheless, American policy was turning the Vietnamese against the Americans. Thieu and Ky had killed "thousands of Vietnamese and sent hundreds to prison." If the present government was replaced by a provisional one to hold assembly elections, he would withdraw from politics and devote himself to unifying the Buddhists spiritually and religiously. He did not wish to die, but he was willing to and was going to if the Americans did not change their policy.

I wanted to know what constructive purpose would be served by his dying. Evading the question, he said it was not important, a hundred others would take his place, and the struggle would go on. "In my opinion," I said, "your people need you to lead them into unity with other religions. This will help give Vietnam the moral force it needs to defeat communism. There is so much disunity it is difficult to see how any constitution can be made to work and any government can be both strong and just." He listened but returned to his theme that nothing good could be accomplished so long as Thieu and Ky remained in charge.

I suggested that "for the best interests of the Vietnamese people, not for the Americans," he urge his followers to participate in the elections. He was willing to modify his stand, he said, and give all-out backing by the Buddhists and the Religious Citizens Front for the elections if the Americans would just remove Thieu and Ky. Their removal was not practical even if it were desirable, I replied. He said that if the Americans continued to back Thieu and Ky to install a "Park Chung Hee government" (referring to the general who had taken over in South Korea), the people would hate the government and the Americans. I insisted this was not what we wanted; we wanted to help the Vietnamese start constructing a government that they had elected themselves and could support. He insisted we were imposing Thieu and Ky: otherwise why did the Voice of American keep praising them? "I have sent a personal letter to President Johnson about this. I will publish it only after I am dead." Dramatically, he showed me a book on his night table; it was, he said, his last testament, to be published only after his death.

The conversation lasted over three hours. When it ended, Tri Quang asked me to give Lodge his personal regards and got up to walk me to the door. He seemed depressed and nervous because of his fast but not near death. Dr. Tai told me privately that Tri Quang was a very proud man who felt deeply humiliated and therefore had to state his position in extreme terms.

I told Lodge that Tri Quang seemed too strong physically to die in the near future unless he willed it. It was important to keep a line open to him; this would help keep him from doing something drastic prior to the elections. The government should stop harassing him and avoid open threats, as they might have the opposite effect. (Tri Quang claimed that General Loan, the national police chief, had threatened him with assassination.) Offers of American financial assistance to the Buddhists should not be made, as that would be misinterpreted.[18] Lansdale was told afterward by other Vietnamese that the visit had helped influence Tri Quang, but that was difficult to judge. At least, he never committed suicide.

Keeping in touch with Hoang Van Lac, I learned there was a serious problem with an anti-election boycott decree General Thang had ordered him to draft. It was too harsh, Lac thought, and would be misinterpreted as government tampering with the elections, since there were already laws on the books dealing with such illegal activities as preventing citizens from voting. A final decision, Lac said, was likely to be taken soon. Lansdale immediately got in touch with Thang to talk about election rules while contriving, without revealing the source, to bring up the threatened Buddhist boycott and how Thang planned to handle it. Thang revealed the harsh terms of the decree that Prime Minister Ky had directed him to draft. It was another example of a Vietnamese tendency, particularly by the military, to think first of an authoritarian solution to a political problem. Lansdale suggested the best approach was, rather, to publicize VC opposition to the elections, which was real, thus associating the idea of a boycott with the VC. This was done and seemed to have an indirect effect on the Buddhists and the religious front, as they failed to carry out an active boycott.

ELECTION RESULTS

Participation in the elections, two days after I left, was much more enthusiastic, free, and open than in any election ever held before in Vietnam. The turnout was over five million voters. Some 542 candidates had run for 117 seats. Political groupings were beginning to talk to each other. Many Vietnamese expressed optimism. At last they were on the road out of the political wilderness that had consumed the previous two years. Many who had been initially doubtful, even cynical, about the process said its honesty and freedom from official fraud had given them a second wind.

In an after-action report I gave to Bill Jorden, with copies to Vice President Humphrey and to Bill Bundy, I cited a number of SLO accomplishments.[19] Perhaps the most important was getting Ky fully committed to free elections. Lansdale had done this by suggesting to Ky that he would appear in the history books as the father of the first truly free election in Vietnam's history. Then he had passed on some thoughts on what Ky might say to province chiefs at an upcoming elections seminar, as they were key to managing the elections in the provinces. At the seminar, Ky made an impassioned appeal for free and honest elections. One of the province chiefs said afterward that he had expected the usual cynical instructions but came away convinced the government truly wanted honest elections, and he was going to do his best to conduct them that way.

Besides successful backdoor contacts with the Cao Dai, Hoa Hao, and the religious front to drop their opposition to the elections, Lansdale had suggested to Ky that cadets from the Dalat Military Academy, the Thu Duc Officer's School, and the NCO School act as poll watchers. Some four thousand were actually deployed at the polls on election day, using Vietnamese air force aircraft for transport, while MACV substituted American aircraft in support of Vietnamese military operations. A reported VC attempt to sequester potential voters' ID cards was thwarted by a last-minute secret order that voters would be allowed to vote even if they could show only their voter's card (the official requirement was to show both). A Vietnamese-run election center, open to the public, was established at SLO's suggestion, with a display board on which election returns were continuously tabulated. Lansdale prevailed on key government figures to allow a free press for all candidates, even if sensitive issues, such as corruption, had been raised. In a bizarre twist, only three days before the election Ky asked Lansdale's advice on how to forestall a coup he said was being planned by General Thieu and General Co (a Thieu supporter). Lansdale, while doubting this was a real threat, persuaded Ky to calm down and make subtle moves that would render such a coup impossible. The whole operation showed what Lansdale could do when given operating room, though he never got the recognition he deserved. Other moves he and the team made were either too complex to be readily explained or appeared trivial unless seen in the context of a still very fluid political situation.

After my return, I also saw Bob Komer, the president's special assistant. He had seen my report and had unusually effusive praise for Lansdale. He followed this by sending Lansdale a personal note calling him "the only guy who understands what is going on." The note went on, "I learned more from one page of your stuff than ten of regular reporting. Everyone here from the top down has been immensely pleased with elections. Few probably realize how much your constructive backstairs advice on how to play by the rules must have helped." He was concerned about Lansdale's morale, hoped he would stay on, and wanted to know his current thinking "privately."[20] I believed Komer was sincere, but within the muddy Washington fishbowl he had a bigger fish to fry: the issue of which agency, Defense or State, was to be responsible for pacification.

The elections would have generated more popular enthusiasm and greater unity had Lansdale been given an even freer hand, but I was encouraged. The next phase would be working with the new assembly to get a constitution written and adopted and to get the next elections organized with decent candidates for what appeared likely to be a bicameral legislature (senate and national assembly) and to elect a president and vice president. In this, however, Lansdale was likely to be much more circumscribed. Lodge wanted to disband SLO after the elections and send Lansdale home, but there was reluctance in Washington to support such a move. While McNamara would disparage Lansdale as being full of hot air, the feeling was that sending him home unless he voluntarily resigned his post would be embarrassing and would court bad publicity from Lansdale supporters like Bill Lederer (author of *The Ugly American*), who had ready access to influential publications like the *Reader's Digest*.

DEPUTY AMBASSADOR PORTER GETS THE BLAME

By the end of 1966, the failure of pacification to achieve more tangible results was being blamed on Porter. Typically, Lodge was not defending him. When the initial Porter appointment failed to produce very much, a new attempt was made at better coordination by forming the Office of Civil Operations (OCO). This combined all of the American civilian elements outside of Saigon in one organization. The individual agencies, however, still exerted independent supervisory control and continued to respond individually to their Washington headquarters. The effort was still divorced from Vietnamese reality. There was an enormous amount of backbiting going on within the U.S. mission, according to Lansdale, with "the civilian vs. military aspects . . . getting ludicrous. Everyone is trying to gain brownie points at the expense of the other guy."[21]

I found it morally repulsive that a year was being wasted over bureaucratic squabbles in Saigon about pacification while American soldiers were dying upcountry. If you lingered around the Saigon airport you could see the body bags being unloaded.

At the end of November in Washington I ran into Dick Holbrooke, who was now working for Komer. Dick pleaded with me to pass the word to Lansdale to, please, help Porter; the atmosphere within the mission was really bad, and Dick blamed Lodge for it. "What about the political side?" I asked. He admitted it was being lost in the shuffle.[22] At this point nobody could help Porter. It was ironic to see Porter being put in the same beleaguered position that Lansdale had occupied a year before. An immense power struggle was going on in Washington over who was to control pacification. McNamara was winning out against State and AID. Komer swung over to support McNamara, who was coming out with Johnson's instructions to sell the change to Lodge. By May 1967, President Johnson would authorize the transfer of OCO, along with the resources in the field of the various agencies, to MACV under a new pacification directorate called the Office of Civil Operations and Revolutionary Development Support (CORDS). Komer would be sent out to take charge of CORDS. There had been no effective effort since 1963 to coordinate U.S. pacification support.

In November 1966, Lansdale produced a paper called "The Battleground in 1967," which was widely circulated and even forwarded to President Johnson, with a note by Rostow saying it was "Ed Lansdale at his best—worth reading." Whether Johnson read it is not known. Lansdale's definition of the battleground had little to do with Westmoreland's big-unit war of attrition; Lansdale knew that was not going to stop the North Vietnamese. For him the battleground was still the South Vietnamese population on the land. Lansdale thought we had a chance to build on the Constituent Assembly elections and the local elections proposed for 1967 to take the political initiative away from the Viet Cong. He talked about how weak the political foundation was, particularly in the villages where the communists were strong. We had to help the Vietnamese build that base from the ground up, replacing paternalism by fostering participation by the population in its own affairs. The elections proposed for March through May of 1967 in five thousand hamlets and eight hundred villages were an opportunity. Provisions for local self-governance should be included in the new constitution and public hearings held around the country to discuss the constitution. We should focus on raising individual farmer's incomes radically, through dramatic improvements in farm production (soybeans) and by creating marketing co-ops and agrarian credit unions, which we could do by expanding existing programs to their full potential.

The Vietnamese should give recognition to the already self-sustaining hard-core hamlets on our side, giving them priority for self-government, self-defense and self-help. Local initiative in pacification and development should be encouraged by accepting proposals from groups such as the Hoa Hao to secure specific areas. We should extend farmer's unions in the countryside while encouraging the growth of political parties in the cities. The national government could donate houses as office space for political parties—there was now no place for such meetings, except in the formal chambers of the national assembly. Family loyalties still predominated—to wit, a slogan like "Family, Home, and Country" had to be amputated to "Family and Home" to be meaningful. To install a true sense of citizenship, civics should be taught in every possible venue. A national oath should be adopted for officials as the basis for an ethic of service, something that had been effective in orienting other countries' armies in defense of a national cause. He anticipated the VC would make a special effort to establish secret control within the cities; hence, it was necessary to put a single capable Vietnamese in charge of each city to counteract that (an uncanny anticipation of the VC attempt to take over the cities in the 1968 Tet Offensive).

On the other hand, a powerful corrosive existed—the people's belief that the government and the army were "riddled" with corruption. The contrast with the enemy was stark. They might be savage in their actions, but they demonstrated a personal discipline and honesty. "They, too, are Vietnamese." To be effective, counteraction had to start at the top. The United States had a decisive voice because of its heavy input of financial support. We should use it. Finally, "command" improvement was needed within the Vietnamese government and the U.S. mission. The top man on each side needed to be capable of taking coordinated action to tell a responsible official to do something and get it done. This required operational staffs and an operational control center on both sides, "not super ministers or cabinets and mission councils."[23]

It was a trenchant blueprint for action, one of the best he had written. By this time, however, I was not optimistic the United States would find it possible to implement something like this. It would take an unusual degree of understanding from the very top down, not just a reorganization of the American side of pacification while continuing to reach for the illusory goals of military victory and a weakened enemy forced into negotiations.

I took up with Ambassador Unger (SLO's primary point of support in Washington) a paper on "Future Plans," which Lansdale had put in front of Lodge. It was clear-cut: either give the political ball entirely to traditional U.S. institutions or give him a political charter. He did not have one now and could not effectively help the Vietnamese put together a political plan or construct a political base to win. I told Unger how limited Lansdale's charter was, explaining, as I had before, why the traditional institutional way of giving advice was not working and would not work. The right kind of political input, I said, was "more important than hundreds of thousands of U.S. troops. Surely, a few administrative and bureaucratic interests and prerogatives can be temporarily given up and some institutional rules can be modified."[24] It was useless. Unger was sympathetic but unwilling to buck the status quo.

Toward the end of 1966, I thought that if the Vietnamese political process and American public support for the war could survive long enough, perhaps sanity could eventually be restored when it became clear that General Westmoreland's making the war an American military exercise was not winning it. It was already clear that bombing the North, instead of forcing the communists to quit, had on the contrary unified its population behind the regime, sending thousands of willing soldiers down the Ho Chi Minh Trail eager to sacrifice themselves to defeat the "American invaders." It still might be possible to give the South Vietnamese useful and less overwhelmingly obvious advice and support, to get down to the real task, winning the war by winning the people. In the meantime, despite the drag on South Vietnamese nationalist credentials caused by the overwhelming American presence, maybe a unifying Vietnamese political cause could be progressively built based on democratic principles. Lansdale was determined, marginalized as he was, to continue that struggle. The real question was what would happen to American public opinion. The administration kept raising troop levels while claiming we were winning and without explaining what kind of war was being fought or how long it would really take. A disconnect existed not only between the Americans and the Vietnamese but between the administration and the American people.

By early 1967 many of the original Lansdale team members had left, some because they had become too controversial, others because there was too little for them to do.[25] Remaining were Sam Karrick, as executive officer and liaison with the political section; Joe Redick, as Lansdale's personal assistant; and Dave Hudson. Others, such as Cal Mehlert (a Foreign Service officer with USOM Provincial Operations) and Charlie Sweet (originally from IVS, who had organized students to do community work in Saigon), would be assigned to help Lansdale. Some of the longer-serving provincial hands from various agencies, and Mark Huss, would drop in to brief Lansdale on problems that he would then raise in Mission Council meetings.

The constant struggle against American misperceptions about the Vietnamese and of what was really going on was taking its toll on Lansdale personally. He was staying up too late, often regaling visitors with reminiscences about earlier and better days.[26] From time to time an important event on the Vietnamese side would rejuvenate him. Such was the case with the upcoming presidential, senatorial, and National Assembly elections in the fall.

BUNKER REPLACES LODGE

In April 1967, Lodge was replaced by Ellsworth Bunker, a tall, cool, distinguished diplomat with experience under difficult circumstances in the Dominican Republic during the 1965 uprising. His Vietnamese nickname was "The Ice Box." Bunker asked Lansdale to stay on as his personal advisor to help him understand and work with the Vietnamese, and Lansdale agreed. Lansdale thought he could still help give the national elections meaning for the Vietnamese, beyond the mechanics. My friend, Lieutenant Colonel Tran Ngoc Chau, was going to run for the National Assembly from Kien Hoa. He had wanted to run earlier for the Constituent Assembly but had been denied permission to leave the army. Also, Conein's friend and General Kim's brother-in-law, retired general Tran Van Don, was going to run for the Senate. Lansdale had stayed out of the dispute between Thieu and Ky about who was to run for president, an argument that was resolved in Thieu's favor because he was better at behind-the-scenes organizing within the military than Ky, and also because he was subtly favored by the our embassy, since he appeared more stable. He was also a lot less dynamic, but the official American bent was for stability above all.

I got out to Saigon for a few days in July at Lansdale's request, flying in on an embassy plane from Bangkok. He was worried that Washington's guidance to Bunker was so focused on military operations and pacification that little attention was given to the upcoming elections for president, the Senate, and the National Assembly. During my brief stay, a number of Vietnamese military officers as well as civilian leaders told me that these elections were probably the last chance to develop a real political cause in the form of honest, representative government. For that to have a chance, the elections themselves had to be free and honest. The prospects for elections to the Senate and the National Assembly were good, but not for the presidential elections. The problem stemmed as usual from the generals, many of whom were determined to hold onto power and enhance their positions. They had imposed the Thieu-Ky marriage, and they were in a position to give the province chiefs orders to turn out the vote for that ticket. If that happened there would be no evidence of obvious fraud, but everyone would know it had been a phony election.

The alternative was for the United States to push for practical steps to ensure that the elections were reasonably free and honest. In a memo to Bill Connell for Humphrey, I suggested three steps: giving the elections immediate and top-priority U.S. attention; getting the government, the Constituent Assembly, and the candidates to agree on the designation of an election coordinator (General Thang would make a good choice); and, if at all possible, persuading Thieu and Ky to resign their government positions, turning the government temporarily over to the deputy prime minister. Retired general Tran Van Don told me that move alone would likely "make the elections at least 50 percent honest, which is all we hope for."[27] Not much came of it, except Thang was once again named election coordinator.

BOB COATE

When I was back in the United States after my brief July trip, Bill Connell asked me to meet a fellow named Bob Coate. Humphrey intended to have Coate visit South Vietnam in early September as an election observer. He was currently chairman of the Democratic Party of northern California. Not knowing what to expect, we met at my business office after lunch for what I figured would be no more than an hour or two. At six in the evening we were still talking. I had expected to meet a stereotypical party pol; an image of Jim Farley, who had run the Democratic Party for Franklin Roosevelt, had come to mind. Instead, Coate was one of the most remarkably open, bright, droll, and direct personalities I would ever encounter. He was about five years my senior—tall, slim, almost skinny, outgoing, with a lively sense of humor. He characterized his World War II experience as having run as an infantryman "all the way from Normandy to Germany without stopping while getting shot only once."[28] Afterward, he had graduated from Stanford on the GI Bill and gravitated to investment counseling, which gave him time for politics, his first love. We hit if off instantly. "Tell me what makes the Vietnamese tick," was his opening question. We went on from there.

Coate was an absolute believer in Humphrey's basic honesty and decency but had a lot of skeptical questions about the war. I would be a skeptic too, I said, if all I knew about it was what the administration was doing and saying. I felt sorry for the vice president, forced to defend administration policy when he believed that the war was mainly a political one, not military. We talked about the noncommunist Vietnamese and their aspirations, about helping them build democracy as a cause worth fighting for. In all honesty, I said, he should understand that not only were there inherent Vietnamese handicaps but that the entire, massive American presence was a handicap.

Coate had organized courses on political campaigning for prospective candidates in California, which gave me an idea. How would he like to be part of the election process, not just an observer? If we could organize a class and round up some candidates, would he be willing to teach a simplified course on how to be a candidate, adapted to Vietnamese circumstances? Without blinking, he said, "Sure." I reached Lansdale through the Pentagon phone, and he was enthusiastic. Since Coate was the vice president's representative, it seemed unlikely Bunker would object. Lansdale said it would be fun, and he hadn't been having enough of that lately.

Arriving in Saigon a week ahead of Coate, I helped set up an informal classroom on the second floor of Lansdale's villa, with chairs, a blackboard, and an easel. When Coate got there and had called on Bunker with Humphrey's letter of introduction, we arranged an informal meeting with Tran Ngoc Chau. Coate, completely at ease, solicited Chau's ideas on what would have meaning to Vietnamese voters. The seminar he put on was amazing. An American with no previous exposure to Vietnam but with enormous practical political experience, he had adapted himself almost instantly to an entirely different culture and audience. There were more than ten prospective candidates, including Chau, in the seminar; their enthusiastic participation said it all. Quietly, by word of mouth, Lansdale had issued invitations to practically all of the major factions to send at least one candidate, so it would not seem we were playing favorites.

Afterward, because I had told President Thieu's brother Kieu about Coate, Bob got a call from the palace saying Thieu wanted to see him.[29] Thieu was so taken with Bob's practical political experience that he wanted him to stay as his advisor on making his government more popular with the Vietnamese people. Bob said he had to go back to the United States but would be happy to come back when he could find the time. After their initial meeting Thieu would often ask Bunker about Coate, saying how much he would like to talk to him again. Lansdale told Coate the United States needed him more in Vietnam than in California. Coate couldn't do that, but he would make several visits to Saigon over the coming years at his own expense, attempting to help Thieu. At one point he even arranged for political consultant Joe Napolitan to present a proposal for improving the Vietnamese government's image in the United States. The informal, ad hoc nature of Coate's role fit right in with Lansdale's way of operating. Anybody who could help Thieu become a better leader was welcome. To give Bunker his due, he too encouraged Coate.

THE 1967 VIETNAMESE ELECTIONS

The election results for the Vietnamese presidency on September 3 alarmed the embassy and Thieu. Trung Dinh Dzu, a civilian candidate with a shifty past running on a peace platform, had won 17 percent of the vote to Thieu's lowly 35 percent. Vice President Ky, having reluctantly accepted second fiddle on the ticket, had been responsible for organizing the vote. He said afterward he had seen no reason to rig it in Thieu's favor so he had issued no instructions to the province chiefs. The balloting, then, was relatively free, but this was not how it was reported in the American press, which had become increasingly cynical. The results not being the strong endorsement Thieu had expected, he promptly arrested Dzu on illicit currency transaction charges and put some of Dzu's followers in jail. They were released following intercession by the embassy, but the damage to Thieu's image had been done. It would remain to be seen how Thieu would handle himself over the longer run. Lansdale hoped he would take some positive lessons from his poor election showing and begin to open up to other politicians and to the people in general.

Subsequently, Tran Ngoc Chau was elected in October to the National Assembly from Kien Hoa with 42 percent of the vote among seventeen candidates, most of whom were native to the area, which he was not. It was a tremendous tribute to his service as province chief. He was sure to provide leadership in the National Assembly, but he could be bullheaded at times; I wondered how Thieu would deal with him. General Don had been elected to the Senate by the largest vote of any single senator. Both Chau and Don would begin to form political alliances within their respective legislatures.

While I was in Saigon, rumors began circulating within MACV that Westmoreland was considering a possible run for the presidency back home in 1968. He had been on the cover of *Time* at the beginning of the year as the magazine's choice for "Man of the Year." Optimistic statements were being made publicly, that we were winning the war. I could find no such optimism on the part of the Vietnamese or the Americans who were in close touch with the situation. Granted, the North Vietnamese had been given a bloody nose in battle after battle, suffering tremendous casualties, but by unleashing our own American forces we had helped to create several million civilian refugees from the rural areas, where the Viet Cong still maintained a very strong infrastructure.

The Americans had finally got their pacification act together, by forming CORDS and putting Bob Komer in charge. He was effective in a bureaucratic context as an organizer, coordinator, and pusher for action on the American side. However, he was hyperkinetic, too full of bombast and arrogance to be successful with the Vietnamese.[30] The "Blowtorch," as Komer was known, had gotten a charter from Westmoreland to pull the American military advisors as well as practically all the civilians in the provinces under his supervision and had pushed hard to get pacification moving. There was still, however, little coordination between pacification and what the American forces were doing. Vietnamese forces were still not picking up the slack, and local security remained neglected. Only when Komer was replaced in 1969 by his deputy, Bill Colby, whose low-key approach to the Vietnamese worked, would pacification begin to succeed.

One source of public optimism was numbers. VC body counts particularly, were considered evidence that we were winning. This obscured the deeper reality of the VC's political-military control over substantial swaths of the countryside and its willingness to expend human resources to the absolute limit. By the end of 1967 there were over five hundred thousand American troops in Vietnam; that year we had lost about eight thousand Americans killed, after losing seven thousand the year before. Our limits, if one viewed American public opinion clearly, were already in sight. Nonetheless, Westmoreland came to the United States in November and proclaimed at the National Press Club, "The ranks of the Viet Cong are thinning steadily. . . . I am absolutely certain that whereas in 1965 the enemy was winning, today he is certainly losing. We have reached an important point when the end begins to come into view."[31] It would only contribute to the inflation of a balloon doomed to be punctured. President Johnson's continued confidence in Westmoreland was a triumph of faith over experience; Westmoreland had personally told the president back in 1966 the war would be over by the summer of 1967.[32] The start made by the Vietnamese in establishing an elected, constitutional government was hopeful but American detachment from reality persisted.

The image remains indelible in my mind of Lansdale returning from one of the Saigon weekly Mission Council meetings with all the chiefs of mission; he was now attending them at Bunker's request. He greeted me, shook his head in frustration, and said, "I don't know what country they were talking about at that meeting, but it sure as hell wasn't Vietnam."

THE TET OFFENSIVE

The chaotic year of 1968 would open with a bang. Several hours after midnight Saigon time on January 31, the first day of Tet, the Vietnamese new year, the VC launched a nationwide offensive against the cities and towns. The American public was treated to television images of our embassy under siege in the middle of Saigon. The ancient city of Hue fell into the hands of the VC; it was taken back only after three weeks of intensive fighting, resulting in widespread destruction and the deaths of 216 Americans and 384 South Vietnamese soldiers. A photograph of the South Vietnamese national police chief, General Nguyen Ngoc Loan, shooting with his pistol at close range a VC (who had just assassinated a police officer and his child) was on the front pages of every American newspaper and on TV as well. After all the claims by General Westmoreland and the Johnson administration that we were winning the war, this offensive became a tipping point for American public opinion. For many influential opinion makers it was the turning point as well. The most respected American TV commentator, "Uncle" Walter Cronkite, began to question the war openly, saying it was "more certain than ever that the bloody experience of Vietnam is to end in a stalemate."

In Saigon, Lansdale's villa on Cong Ly had not been attacked. But the Filipino Eastern Construction Company compound had been, and several of its personnel were missing, never to be found. Among them was an old friend, Nestor Cortez, a member of the original Freedom Company contingent back in 1955 working with the newly formed Vietnam Veterans Association. Ambassador Bunker would take temporary refuge at Lansdale's villa, accompanied by Marine guards, because his own residence was difficult to defend.

The VC, and the North Vietnamese who ordered it, had planned the Tet Offensive as a decisive campaign, in which the penetration of Saigon and other cities was to spark a general uprising of the population. This, they thought, would force the South Vietnamese government into a coalition with the National Liberation Front, push the Americans out, and open the door for a complete communist takeover. Instead, the tide of battle turned pretty quickly against the VC, as the South Vietnamese with American help retook control of Saigon and then of Hue (the latter accomplished mainly by U.S. Marines). In Hue, the VC had gone door to door with a blacklist, rounding up over three thousand civilians, mainly Catholics, Buddhists, and nationalist political party members, whom they shot on the spot and interred in hastily dug graves. Given a foretaste of what could be expected if the VC took over, noncommunist Vietnamese resistance firmed up. The VC lost thousands of their best fighters in this and a series of lesser offensives during the remainder of the year. The southern VC leadership viewed the campaign as a huge setback.

However, and as documented by *Washington Post* correspondent Peter Braestrup in his book *Big Story,* American press and TV reporting was consistently negative and even inaccurate, characterizing the offensive as a significant American-Vietnamese defeat. Horrendous setback for the VC though it actually was, it energized the antiwar movement in the United States more than any other single development in the war. I watched the television news at home and could feel its unsettling impact. Then came Lyndon Johnson's stunning decision, announced on March 31, not to run for a second full term as president; the assassination of Martin Luther King on April 4 and the riots afterward; then, two months later, Robert Kennedy's assassination, on June 5. It was a deeply divisive and distressing time. The Democratic Party was completely split about the war, with then unknown but probable adverse consequences.

Vice President Humphrey was in a difficult spot. Johnson had used him as one of the chief public defenders of the war, to the detriment of his own credibility, given his serious misgivings about the wisdom of the policies he was obliged to defend. It was an uncomfortable position to be in, but resigning was not an option to Humphrey. No vice president except John Calhoun in the nineteenth century had ever resigned in opposition to his own administration, and that had been over the deep and clear-cut constitutional issue of the extension of slavery, which Calhoun had favored.

Chapter 21
Change Comes Late

By early spring 1968, Lansdale had made a firm decision, with Bunker's agreement, to return home in June. Before he left, I traveled to Saigon for one last visit, which I thought might be useful to Vice President Humphrey. I could stay for only five days, but it was long enough to get a pretty good picture. I arrived on June 8; Lansdale would leave for good on June 15.

Lansdale had found Ambassador Bunker a much different person from Lodge. Bunker was honest and straightforward in dealing with his subordinates. He had finesse, though not enough personal knowledge of the Vietnamese or an adequate concept of how the war should be fought. He was playing a mediator role, which was not responsive to Thieu's need to learn presidential leadership. Bunker's conversations with Thieu were still too bland and generalized, and he didn't "call" Thieu when he knew Thieu was conning him. He was using Lansdale as an invaluable resource about the Vietnamese character and mentality, giving credence to Lansdale's often contrary and unorthodox views, but somehow those views were not reflected in positive political actions. He was playing a one-man political game, mainly with President Thieu, instead of using Lansdale for this purpose.[1] Lansdale in turn was deeply tired from his losing battle for operational room and top-level backing to do what he knew how to do—which was to move the Vietnamese in a positive political direction and help develop leadership at the top.

Afterward I told Humphrey that Bunker could have hung on to Ed had Bunker been willing to use him for meaningful political action, but considering him just a listening post was a mistake. "Knowledge must be wedded with power if we Americans are ever to be truly helpful in Vietnam." Still, Bunker expressed sincere regret at Ed's leaving. "Maybe privately Bunker understands better than he is letting on," I said, "but in the cables coming back and in conversation it is still too much 'Alice in Wonderland.'"[2]

By mid-1968 corruption had become a major issue with the Vietnamese. Moreover, Bill Lederer, author of *The Ugly American,* had just published *Our Own Worst Enemy,* highlighting Vietnamese corruption and calling into question whether Vietnam was worth defending. Bunker's formality with President Thieu failed to deal with this issue; how Bunker in fact approached corruption was described by Bui Diem after he became ambassador to Washington. During a visit to Saigon, Bunker gave Bui Diem a dossier of twenty-three files documenting corruption by some of Thieu's key associates and supporters, asking Diem to take it up with Thieu. Diem, on whom Thieu relied as ambassador, was nevertheless not his confidant. To have taken this up with Thieu would have severely undercut his own effectiveness, so he politely explained why it would likely backfire if he handled it. He urged Bunker to have a frank discussion with Thieu about it instead; no such a discussion ever occurred. Diem found

Bunker's "manner of intervening . . . altogether too dignified and polite to be effective."[3] (Corruption continued to fester, undermining Thieu's leadership not only in Vietnamese eyes but with the American public, which saw him largely as a corrupt dictator.)

My last visit started with Charlie Sweet, a former IVS advisor assigned to help Lansdale, who took me on a tour of Saigon's District Eight, on the south side of the Arroyo Chinois branch of the Saigon River (the location of Binh Xuyen headquarters during the 1955 war for Saigon). Vice President Humphrey had toured this same district with Sweet during his 1967 visit. District Eight had been under VC influence and covert control in 1966, when Charlie had started working with a student group to help the inhabitants improve their slumlike living conditions. So successful had the effort been in turning the district around that by the time of the Tet Offensive, the population was strongly against the VC and had kept them out.

Nevertheless, during a second offensive, called "mini-Tet," in May, some two hundred VC had infiltrated the district. From there they had launched mortar attacks against American and Vietnamese forces in the main part of the city. In reaction, the American commander charged with responding, Col. George Benson, had directed intense artillery fire and close air support into the district, destroying over five thousand dwellings, killing two hundred civilians, wounding two thousand, and generating forty thousand refugees.[4] While the district was under American fire, Charlie had gone there at considerable risk, verified the destruction, and reported back to Lansdale, who got the bombardment called off. Benson cursed Lansdale afterward for his interference. Ironically, in a previous assignment as military attaché in Indonesia, Benson had been largely responsible for helping that army undertake a successful civic action program with rural villagers. Now he saw no relationship between destroying in Vietnam a link of popular support for the army and government similar to that between the army and the people he had helped build in Indonesia.[5]

Despite the appalling destruction I saw when I toured the district, Vietnamese student volunteers were back helping the inhabitants rebuild. After the bombardment stopped, some VC still hung around; the inhabitants asked for arms, got them, and repelled the remaining VC themselves. Morale was being restored. Despite student and resident bitterness at the government and the Americans, the refugees were moving back in.[6]

It was a classic example of the bankruptcy of Westmoreland's approach. It also showed how hard it was for someone like Benson to think about consequences in a combat situation when his men were being fired on from an area full of civilians, to restrain conventional warfare instincts and instead find ways to respond other than employing massive firepower. The rules of engagement for this kind of war had to be clear, drilled into the military leadership, and enforced if pacification was to succeed over the longer term. The "you have to destroy it to save it" philosophy was dead wrong. So were conventional notions of force protection as a primary goal. The word was that Gen. Creighton Abrams, Westmoreland's successor, was appalled by the damage and subsequently prohibited action by artillery, bombing, or helicopter gunships within the city without his personal permission.[7]

My relatively few nights at the Cong Ly villa were punctuated by terrific cracking booms from 122-mm (about six-inch diameter) rockets that the VC were firing at random from the Saigon outskirts directly into the city. Unaimed, they were nevertheless an effective psychological weapon, causing considerable apprehension. No one knew where they were going to land. It only took a few moments for the VC to set up portable launchers and send the rockets on their way. There seemed to be no ready counter for this terror tactic. It was getting on everybody's nerves, and it was a reminder of how insecure the area surrounding Saigon was. I remember thinking, "Shades of Hop Tac!" when awoken by an explosion that did not sound too far away.

I got a close-up view of the explosive force of these rockets when I went to see Nguyen Van Buu, the Vietnamese businessmen who had lived across the street from us in 1962 and 1963. He was now out of jail and again operating some of his businesses, but on a much smaller scale. Buu was still occupying the same house, and he gave me a tour. A rocket had gone through an open window of the second story and hit the servant quarters behind, completely demolishing it. The explosion had killed a Catholic priest sleeping there and heaved a large reinforced-concrete roof beam about twenty feet into a nearby alley. Buu normally slept in the servant quarters, figuring it gave him better protection than the house, which fronted on the main street. When the priest came he had offered him his own more comfortable room in the servant quarters and moved back temporarily into the main house's second-story bedroom, through which the missile had flown.

There were some encouraging developments. General Abrams had recently taken over from General Westmoreland as head of MACV and was setting a new tone. The word of mouth around town was that in May, after the most recent mini-Tet operations, he had gone to the Second Field Forces headquarters at nearby Bien Hoa for a briefing. (Abrams would assume formal command in early June.) After silently sitting through the usual briefing about how U.S. forces had done so well during mini-Tet, he had stood up and said, "Gentlemen, we didn't win any goddam victories, we got our ass kicked." He then stomped out.[8]

Abrams had moved out of Westmoreland's palatial villa into a smaller house near MACV headquarters. He habitually wore field fatigues instead of the spit-and-polish uniform with resplendent ribbons, or sharply tailored fatigues, that had most often been Westmoreland's attire. Lansdale told me Abrams wanted to make the Vietnamese army and the local forces work, which Westmoreland never understood or was interested in. Also he wanted to humanize MACV and its command image. Instead of roaring out to the Vietnamese General Staff headquarters for meetings in a formal procession with sirens blazing like his predecessor had, Abrams was driving himself out unpretentiously in his own jeep for working sessions with the Vietnamese chief of staff, General Cao Van Vien. Instead of formally exchanging bland statements about how well things were going as Westmoreland had done, Abrams would begin by telling Vien his problems in a frank and personal way, which, of course, would get Vien talking about his own problems in the same way.

General Abrams would also address the security of Saigon as a priority. In a very short time he would stop the rocketing through aggressive day-and-night patrolling and by the stationing of helicopter gunships in continuous nighttime orbit over likely firing positions, among other tactics. Westmoreland had minimized the importance of protecting Saigon against rocketing, saying it was "an almost impossibility" and that anyway the rocketing was "of really no military consequence." Abrams understood that beyond the human cost, which he valued, an unhealthy siege mentality was developing within the Vietnamese leadership. He said publicly that the attacks would be stopped, and they were.[9]

From my old army psywar friend, Vuong, still a news stringer for Bob Shaplen of the *New Yorker,* I would get an inside view of President Thieu. Thieu was Diem and Nhu combined, except he was slower than Diem and not as smart as Nhu. His principal drawback was that he seemed to confide in no one, not even his brother or his closest political associate, whom he had appointed secretary for the presidency.

Thieu's leadership abilities remained largely untested. There were small signs that he was beginning to reach out to some civilian politicians, having asked retired general Tran Van Don, now a leading senator, to work with Prime Minister Huong to put their two political fronts into one group. Also, Thieu had announced he was going to arm what were termed "People's Self-Defense Forces," to be recruited from the civilian population, although the actual training and arming had not yet started.

More encouraging politically was the growth of the Vietnamese National Assembly and Senate into functioning bodies. The legislature was one element in the Vietnamese power structure that was trying to be responsive to the people and was learning how to represent them. Legislators from the Saigon districts affected by Tet and mini-Tet were leading the way in insisting that the population be armed for self-defense. The genesis of true political parties lay in two major blocs in the Senate and an incipient merger of blocs in the National Assembly. But the process would take time, support, and tolerance from the executive branch.

Just before I arrived for my June 1968 visit, an interesting sidelight was cast on the Viet Cong. Lansdale was approached by the National Liberation Front (NLF) through intermediaries. If the Americans would get rid of Thieu and Ky, we could name any provisional government we wanted for a two-year period to prepare for general elections. The NLF would immediately cease all attacks on Saigon and would be willing to dissolve itself. The purported rationale was that the southerners in the NLF wanted to regain control from Hanoi, which now had seized the initiative through the Paris peace talks. Lansdale told them the United States could not and would not overthrow the Vietnamese constitutional process that it had helped create. This demarche was probably a probe to feel out American terms for a ceasefire and an indication that the NLF was seriously preparing for an eventual test at the polls. I thought it could reflect a north/south split within the NLF, which, if it existed, was worth trying to exploit, if we had the skill to do so.[10]

I regretted missing Lansdale's farewell party, which happened two days after I left. It was largely impromptu. On actual count by Dave Hudson, more than three hundred people, mainly Vietnamese, showed up at a villa near the airport where Lansdale had been invited. It was a sentimental occasion, a goodbye to an American who they knew genuinely cared for them. Various Vietnamese leaders made remarks, and Lansdale decided to make a speech of his own. "What," he asked, "did they want to do for their own country? What kind of nation did they want?" He was disappointed, he said: "All you seem to want to do is be president and have everybody bowing to you and cheering as you smile and wave your hand. . . . It doesn't seem to go beyond that." Chastened, the Vietnamese looked at each other. Then one made a stirring speech about his country and what he wanted for it. Someone else congratulated him and said he didn't know the speaker believed that, that he had opposed him for twenty years when he should have been helping him. Lansdale said, "You people had better start working together or you're going to lose your country." He reflected later, "It was a very moving moment. Maybe at last some were learning the . . . lessons for building a nation."[11]

Afterward, Lansdale got a phone call asking him to come to the palace, where he found Thieu fuming. "The police tell me you're trying to start a revolution with all these politicians." "Goddamit, Thieu," Lansdale replied, "you know what I was doing? I was doing your job. You should be doing what I was doing. I'm a foreigner and you should never let a foreigner do your job as president." Lansdale recounted what happened and urged Thieu to make use of those men. "Call them in. Listen to them. Allow them to sound off with ideas." If they have good plans, he urged, put them to work carrying them out. His government would be better off. He and Thieu then calmed down and said a cordial goodbye.[12] It was vintage Lansdale—no one else could have talked to a Vietnamese leader that way and be listened to. But no single lesson in leadership would prove enough, as the next seven years would tell.

Part IV
THE FINAL ACT—
AND THE FUTURE

Chapter 22
Humphrey Loses, Nixon Takes Over

Returning to the United States in July 1968 was to come back to a country in severe turmoil. Parts of Washington remained in smoking ruins from the riots after Martin Luther King's death. Robert Kennedy was dead, and the antiwar movement had become a dominant force within the Democratic Party. Vietnam was obviously the critical issue on which the election would turn.

On the Republican side, Richard Nixon's attitude toward South Vietnamese political aspirations had been revealed during a trip to Saigon in 1966, when he had visited Lansdale. "What are you up to, Ed?" he had asked. "We want to help General Thang make this the most honest election ever held in Vietnam," Lansdale replied. (Thang had just acquired the job of organizing the constituent assembly elections.) Winking, laughing, and slapping his knee, Nixon replied, "Oh sure, honest, yes, honest, that's right, so long as you win!"[1] The election of Nixon seemed likely to bring manipulative cynicism to the Oval Office.

Despite the difficult times, I thought Vice President Humphrey understood the changes needed and offered hope for a way out without abandoning the South Vietnamese people to the communists. But would there be an opportunity for rational consideration of the true facts on the ground? The American people had never been given an adequate explanation of why we there, what was truly at stake, and how a different approach might have worked, because our leadership had never understood the war themselves. Instead we were trapped in unrealistic hopes for negotiations with the North Vietnamese, while they were determined to wait us out, not giving an inch of legitimacy to the South Vietnamese cause. Their demand was for a forced coalition with the National Liberation Front combined with complete American withdrawal—or nothing. They would continue to expend manpower, maximizing American casualties and waiting for American public opinion to turn completely against the war. This strategy had succeeded with the French; now it was America's turn.

In a memo to Humphrey after I got home, I ventured some advice. The United States should insist that the Vietnamese organize and arm the civilian population of Saigon; propose a program for gradual U.S. troop withdrawal, with the first troops to leave by October; not retaliate for rocket attacks against Saigon by bombing Hanoi (then being actively considered in some quarters); and avoid claims of progress or victory until real, measurable success was crystal clear. "The administration has grabbed at straws so many times in the past there is a real credibility gap," I added.[2] By this time, I had become the unofficial Vietnam advisor to Humphrey, having been appointed by Bill Connell as a "dollar-a-year man."[3] All I could do was to try to warn Humphrey, through Bill, about statements he might make that were likely to be undercut by Vietnamese realities.

TESTIFYING TO THE DEMOCRATIC CONVENTION
PLATFORM COMMITTEE

For reasons of faith and sentiment I did what I could to help Humphrey in his 1968 presidential campaign. His understanding of Vietnam offered hope. To try to ensure that he had a reasonable platform to run on, I paid my way out to Chicago to testify before the Democratic Convention Platform Committee on August 22. (I was not a delegate and did not attend the convention, which opened four days later.) I had heard the Platform Committee was completely divided between a majority who wanted out of Vietnam instantly, regardless of the consequences, and those who supported the administration's position that there had to be a negotiated solution that left behind a free South Vietnam.

I told the committee that although I was now a private citizen, I had been intimately involved in Vietnam since 1954 as a public servant and spoke from firsthand experience. "The Democratic Party," I said,

> instead of offering unrealistic panaceas for peace, should use straight talk to help our people better understand what the war is really about, to show them a realistic road toward an honorable solution, and to ask for their patient understanding and support. The Committee has already heard a number of solutions for peace in Vietnam, many of which use certain premises as justification for essentially abandoning our commitment there. I would like to examine these premises because I find them either wrong or unfair.

These premises were: that the war was diverting resources from more important needs at home; that it had impaired our prestige in the world; that a military victory was our objective; that it was purely a civil war, in which the VC was an independent and legitimate political force; that we had the right to impose a form of government on the noncommunist Vietnamese; and that Vietnam was unique, we would not have to face similar challenges elsewhere. I questioned the ethics of abandoning people in more desperate straits than threatened any American and the ethics of imposing a coalition government on the noncommunist Vietnamese—in effect, a mirror image of what the Soviets had just done, in Czechoslovakia during the "Prague Spring." The noncommunist part of Asia supported our standing by the South Vietnamese; Europe was not the world. I agreed that a military victory was not possible; the war was a political struggle in which Hanoi's communist leadership sought not to defeat us militarily but "to defeat the Vietnamese nationalists in Vietnam psychologically and politically and the U.S. at home." Facts on the ground demonstrated the National Liberation Front represented only a minority of the South Vietnamese. "Wars of national liberation" were likely to continue until it was clear to the communists they could not succeed. "We must and can find better ways of meeting this challenge," I said, "but it is not by quitting in Vietnam."

Our failure in Vietnam, I told the Platform Committee, was one of implementation. We had to correct this failure by making our deeds in prosecuting the war and helping the Vietnamese consistent with our own principles of self-government and of putting the welfare of the people first. We could do these things better, "by concentrating our support behind Vietnamese democratic political development, by cutting down the size of the American presence and by shaping our military efforts so that the primary emphasis falls on protecting people rather than killing them."[4]

I expected some open disagreement from the antiwar group on the committee, but they were quiet. I sensed that this was the first time many of them had heard a moral argument for staying with the South Vietnamese from someone who had been directly involved. Nonetheless, antiwar minds seemed impervious to argument. The committee adopted a platform that was workable only if we wanted to surrender the South Vietnamese. Given the national mood, it probably would have helped Humphrey electorally, but it would have drawn accusations of bad faith had he won. Accepting the NLF as an equal negotiating partner with the South Vietnamese government at that point would have spelled a rapid communist takeover. The "doves" thought the NLF was an independent force, when in fact it was completely controlled by the North Vietnamese. (After the 1975 North Vietnamese takeover, key members of the National Liberation Front, including its chairman, revealed that they were longtime covert members of the Vietnamese Communist Party. Subsequently, noncommunist NLF members were driven into exile or retirement.)[5] In any case, enough floor votes were mustered at the convention to defeat the committee's recommended platform but it widened the party split, which never got fully healed.

In the memo for Humphrey I concluded that he, running as his own man, desperately needed to develop a winning strategy for Vietnam. There were real experts on Vietnam in various places in Washington, some of them known as "mavericks," who would be willing to help develop such a strategy without publicity or expectation of future reward. They had "a deep commitment to their country and to the people of South Vietnam, a deeply held desire to make meaningful the expenditure of 25,000 American and countless Vietnamese lives and a willingness to sacrifice their own lives and careers if necessary to obtain a meaningful outcome." I suggested the vice president take the initiative in assembling such a group informally. If the idea appeared feasible, I would be happy to organize and direct its activities.[6]

A POLICY PAPER FOR THE NEW PRESIDENT

I got a verbal go-ahead from Bill Connell. Originally drafted for Humphrey, the paper evolved into a policy statement that could be used by whichever candidate won. After the convention, Humphrey's campaign had problems trying to disassociate him from Johnson's unpopularity and to show his independence. This effort revolved around stopping the bombing and starting peace talks in Paris. The campaign could not use comprehensive policy advice at this stage, Connell and I understood. We agreed that developing a proposed approach for the next administration was the most useful thing we could do.

We began a series of meetings in September. Sam Karrick, back from his service with Lansdale, agreed to serve as group coordinator. Participants included Sven Kraemer, then on loan from the Defense Department's International Security Affairs (ISA) office to the White House NSC staff; Maj. Charley Cook from ISA in the Pentagon, who had been in Vietnam; and Tad Cantrell, working for Assistant Secretary Bill Bundy at the State Department. Having worked for his father, Hadley Cantrell, founder of the Institute for International Social Research at Princeton, Tad had a feel for American public opinion. There were also Charlie Sweet and Dave Hudson, who had just returned from Saigon. Each of us had been frustrated by some aspect of how the war was being waged and how poorly it was being explained to the American public. The stakes were high. A serious reexamination and a new departure were essential. Lansdale, though worn out, agreed to serve as a catalyst and commentator.

We finished a final draft in late October as the presidential campaign wound down to what was for most of us a truly disappointing finish, with Humphrey surging at the end but too late to catch Nixon. Nixon's purported plan to end the war helped take him over the top.

There was no such plan: all the possibilities, including "Vietnamization," were already widely known to those with intimate knowledge of the conflict.

Our paper, "A Political Strategy for Viet-Nam," twenty-three pages long with an appendix on recommended actions, covered the current military and political situation in Vietnam, the mood of the American people, meaningful outcomes and alternative courses of action, a political strategy, and a conclusion.

A meaningful outcome was a "South Vietnam free from North Vietnamese attack, reasonably independent, relatively stable, responsive to the needs of the South Vietnamese people and increasingly able with allied help to assume the main burden of the fight against the South Vietnamese communists . . . moving forward sufficiently to allow de-Americanization and a gradual reduction in visible U.S. presence which would serve as a catalyst in the Vietnamese nation-building process and assuage an uneasy American public." Major liabilities were the uninspiring nature of South Vietnam's present leadership; the weakness of its political organizations, as well as the Viet Cong's determination and effectiveness; our inferior, not superior, position in the Paris peace negotiations; South Vietnamese shortcomings in confronting the communist political and military challenge; and the fact that a classic military victory alone would not necessarily lead to long-term political stability.

Alternatives were continuing to rely mainly on military pressure to influence the war's course and the Paris talks; stepping up military operations; or decreasing our effort unilaterally, regardless of what the other side did. Our recommended course was to pursue a political/military strategy designed to strengthen the South Vietnamese in their political confrontation with the National Liberation Front while phasing down the visible U.S. presence.

In our prior actions the United States had tried to make changes in ignorance or disregard of Vietnamese values, feelings, perceptions, and ways of doing things. Proposed actions had to improve Vietnamese military and political effectiveness in ways the Vietnamese would accept, support, and participate in.[7]

OCTOBER SURPRISE

Johnson's failure to produce a strong gesture toward peace in Vietnam was hurting Humphrey's campaign. In the middle of October, Humphrey was eight points down in the opinion polls, apparently headed for inevitable defeat. Staunch Democrats, turned off by the war, were not rallying around him. Some were even giving support to Nixon, by publicly condemning Humphrey. (John Kenneth Galbraith would proclaim after the election, "I'm proud I didn't vote for Hubert Humphrey.")[8] Finally, however, on October 31, President Johnson announced a complete halt in the bombing of North Vietnam and the initiation of peace talks in Paris, to begin on November 6, one day after the presidential election. There was an instant reaction in American public opinion. Humphrey's campaign began to breathe oxygen, and by November 2 the gap in the polls had closed to 40 percent Humphrey, 42 percent Nixon.

For some time the Americans and the South Vietnamese had conducted a delicate dance with regard to starting genuine peace talks with the North. The South Vietnamese needed to be treated as equals by the North, which the North was not willing to do. Thieu, like most South Vietnamese leaders, was deadly afraid that unless South Vietnam's status was recognized, such talks would elevate the National Liberation Front to coequal status with the Saigon government and force a coalition. "Coalition" was a dirty word to most noncommunist Vietnamese, who remembered Ho Chi Minh luring nationalist political groups and leaders into alliances and then betraying them.

A more personal factor was also involved. When Vice President Humphrey had visited newly elected President Thieu in 1967, he had told him time was running out on American public support for the war and that greater Vietnamese self-help was needed. Thieu had responded blandly that the United States would be there for a long time and had no option except to keep its troops at present levels. This had provoked Humphrey into interjecting, "Perhaps I haven't made myself clear" and repeating his warnings about American public opinion and the need for the Vietnamese to act. Later, sensing he may have gone too far, Humphrey asked Bunker, "Was I too tough on him?"[9] He had in fact broken a cardinal rule— never lecture a Vietnamese. The resentment generated always obscured the message, no matter how reasonable. Thieu began to view Humphrey unfavorably, if not as an enemy.

At the same time, Nixon had begun laying the groundwork to convince Thieu he was a staunch friend, first through a personal visit to Saigon in 1966, then by telling Vietnamese ambassador Bui Diem in New York in 1967 that if elected in 1968, he would "see that Vietnam gets better treatment from me than from the Democrats." During 1968, John Mitchell, Nixon's campaign manager, set up a sub-rosa link to Thieu through Anna Chennault, widow of the famous leader of the Flying Tigers in World War II. Publicly, she was chairwoman of Republican Women for Nixon; privately she transmitted messages from Mitchell (but directed by Nixon) to Thieu. Thieu was leery of Bui Diem, who he considered to be primarily loyal to Vice President Ky, so he sent his own messengers to Washington, to contact Mrs. Chennault. He also relied heavily on Kieu, his brother, who was the ambassador to Taiwan. Mrs. Chennault often sent messages to Thieu through aides and his brother.[10]

Thus, while the Johnson administration planning for talks with the North was going forward in Washington, Vietnamese thinking in Saigon was headed in the opposite direction. Thieu's main concern about the upcoming American elections was who was most likely to stand behind the South Vietnamese in refusing to concede anything to the communists. He believed that was Nixon, not Humphrey. This was not understood in Washington, where Johnson thought Bunker had the situation under control.

Henry Kissinger had warned the Nixon campaign that Johnson was likely to spring an "October Surprise," halting the bombing and starting peace talks. In anticipation, Nixon (through Mitchell and Chennault) began urging Thieu to stand fast against Johnson if he stopped the bombing and announced talks, or Humphrey would win the election, not Nixon. This was blatant interference, foreshadowing future Nixon White House illegal election activities.

By the time Johnson made his announcement on October 31, he had been unable to get an unequivocal indication of South Vietnamese intentions. He finessed the matter, declaring they were "free to participate." Thieu had said nothing to indicate he would not join the talks, and Bunker had taken this for assent. But in a speech to the Vietnamese National Assembly on Vietnamese National Day, November 1, Thieu declared, "South Vietnam deeply regrets not being able to participate in the present exploratory talks"; he received seventeen standing acclamations during his defiant address. Ambassador Bunker was completely surprised. South Vietnamese reaction to the speech was overwhelmingly favorable—they would not be dictated to by the Americans. Expectations that had lifted the Humphrey campaign received a dash of cold water, as the *Washington Post* headlined, "S. Vietnam Spurns Nov. 6 Talks."

Mitchell's conversations with Madame Chennault had been secretly recorded, at Johnson's direction, for over a month, as were the communications between the Vietnamese embassy and Saigon.[11] Humphrey's people wanted to reveal the information, but only Johnson was in a position to authorize a leak, and he did not. When Nixon won the election by only five hundred thousand votes, Humphrey thought Thieu's actions had cost him the election, and so did other seasoned observers. One was Theodore White, who believed that had the prospect for peace become clearer Humphrey would have won but that the ensuing confusion halted the momentum. "The tide of opinion that had begun to flow to Humphrey . . . began to flow back to Nixon."[12] The ultimate irony was that Kissinger's future secret negotiations with the North Vietnamese, behind the back of the South Vietnamese, would be an even greater betrayal than anything the more ethical Humphrey might have tried.

Again, the Americans had no one on the inside to know what Thieu truly intended. Vietnamese politics had again trumped American policy, this time with the aid of Nixon's hidden hand. The great disconnect between American officialdom and the Vietnamese continued.

NIXON AND KISSINGER

Surprisingly, the Vietnam war would go on for another seven years. The Nixon administration would pursue a policy of "Vietnamization," the accelerated training of the Vietnamese armed forces and the turnover to them of the fighting, combined with the gradual drawdown of American troops. General Abrams, now the American commander in Vietnam, would pursue a strategy different from Westmoreland's war of attrition, which had backfired. The emphasis changed to the protection of the civilian population, arming and supporting local forces better, doing away with free-fire zones, and concentrating on the support of Vietnamese pacification efforts, while emphasizing smaller and more flexible American operations against still-increasing North Vietnamese regulars. Pacification largely succeeded, but American combat losses continued at a rate unacceptable to the American public. The public turned more and more against the war, its opposition aggravated by such actions as the sudden invasion of Cambodia by American as well as South Vietnamese troops. Politically, the emphasis on stability versus democratic reform in Saigon only added to American popular disenchantment. The Vietnamese government was perceived as corrupt and dictatorial, hence unworthy of the continued sacrifice of American lives.

Nixon's focus on resolving the conflict through big-power politics and secret negotiations was not something that could be credibly explained to the American public, as the expenditure of American lives and treasure continued. The alternative of refocusing our efforts on helping the South Vietnamese construct a viable and attractive democratic political cause, which could have fueled a united will to resist and therefore have resonated with American opinion, was completely ignored. The result would not be "Peace with Honor," as Nixon had proclaimed, and for which Kissinger was awarded the Nobel Prize, but the collapse of South Vietnam under the assault of practically the entire North Vietnamese army and the imposition of communist tyranny, with tragic results for the South Vietnamese people.

Sven Kraemer seemed our best channel for getting high-level attention from the new Nixon administration for our policy paper. Henry Kissinger, about to be appointed as Nixon's national security advisor, had been a protégé of Sven's father, Fritz Kraemer, in the 1940s and had been Sven's professor at Harvard.[13] Kissinger did get the paper and presumably read it, but he never discussed it directly with Sven. Our conclusion was that it had never received serious consideration. The new Nixon administration took essentially the same bureaucratic approach as had Johnson, spiced up by "Vietnamization." South Vietnamese political development took a back seat, as did effective outreach to the American public—who would continue to be told, not engaged. The emphasis was on smoke and mirrors at the Paris peace talks, on maintaining South Vietnamese political stability as an end in itself, and on improving population security in South Vietnam. Despite Nixon's knowledge of his expertise, Lansdale was never asked for an opinion.

When our paper produced no discernable impact, I began to give up trying to influence Vietnam policy. While it would have been difficult even for Humphrey, had he been elected, to make the necessary changes in how the war was being fought and to emphasize the political side of the war, I believed we would have had a better than even chance with him to get things done differently. It was still possible, I believed, to show genuine political and pacification progress in Vietnam while positively engaging the American public in the process. I would have been ready to sell my firm for whatever it was worth and return to Vietnam. Lansdale, though jaded and aged by his disappointing experience, would have gone back to Saigon, with renewed energy. So would many others who had been most effective with the Vietnamese.

Humphrey's openness and belief in people was the opposite of Nixon secretiveness. He understood the critical need for South Vietnamese political reform. Had the South Vietnamese been able to show they were developing truly representative political institutions, had a positive change been made in the way the war was fought, accompanied by a steady drawdown of American troops, Humphrey might have been able to convince a substantial majority of the American people to persevere in seeking an honest way out. In General Abrams he would have had a general who was already changing the way the war was being fought and who understood and supported pacification. In Bunker he would have had an ambassador who, with a different set of instructions, would have supported a revived Lansdale mission focused on democratic reform, in conjunction with the revamped pacification efforts that were just beginning. But it was not to be.

A SIGNIFICANT POLITICAL MISTAKE

I never lost interest, however, in what was going on. In 1970, former lieutenant colonel Tran Ngoc Chau, now a national assemblyman, was persecuted by President Thieu. His immunity violated, he was tried and sentenced to jail, to be finally released less than a year before Saigon fell in 1975. Before his imprisonment Chau had been visited unexpectedly by his brother, Hien, an intelligence officer for the North Vietnamese. (Split families were not uncommon in South Vietnam.) Initially, Chau tried to convince his brother to abandon the communist cause, but Hien had come specifically to recruit Chau to join the National Liberation Front. They argued respectfully but heatedly in a series of secret meetings, with no resolution. Chau, who still had a tenuous relationship with the Agency, told at least one American case officer about his contacts. Then, in 1969, Hien was picked up by the Vietnamese government and confessed to talking to his brother. Chau fell under suspicion, because, out of a desire to protect his brother, he had not reported these conversations to his own government. That was the ostensible cause of, but not an excuse for, what followed.

Chau had been elected secretary general of the National Assembly, roughly equivalent to our Speaker of the House. He had attracted a bloc of followers whose votes could not be bought. He had also aroused Thieu's ire by attacking government corruption. Chau was desperate for a South Vietnamese political solution not tied to American negotiations with the North Vietnamese in Paris, which he found demeaning. He advocated having the National Assembly talk directly to the National Assembly of North Vietnam about a peaceful solution, thus taking the initiative away from the Americans. If, as he expected, the North

Vietnamese rejected the approach, the blame would be theirs and the South Vietnamese could recapture a sense of self-respect. Thieu and Chau had been quite close when both were at the military academy earlier in their careers, but now Thieu saw Chau as a direct challenge to his authority.

Americans on the scene who knew Chau well, such as John Paul Vann, attempted to intercede but were waved off by Ambassador Bunker. Thieu tried to get the newly created Supreme Court to strip Chau of his immunity as an assemblyman, but it refused. Thieu then bribed and threatened enough Assembly members to strip Chau's immunity, an extralegal procedure. The national police then invaded the National Assembly and arrested Chau on the floor as a communist collaborator, dragging him out after ripping off the National Order medal, his country's highest decoration, that he was defiantly wearing. He was tried and given a ten-year sentence. The Vietnamese Supreme Court later ruled his arrest and conviction unconstitutional, but Thieu would keep him in prison for four years.

This was widely covered by the American press. Elliot Richardson, then undersecretary of state, urged Bunker to intervene. Bunker reluctantly talked to Thieu, but Thieu would not budge; Bunker would not force the issue, telling some of the press privately that Thieu's actions were fully justified. Those in the United States who knew Chau tried to intervene, without success.[14] Nobody in the CIA would admit to knowing anything exculpatory. Chau's case became a political cause celèbre in the United States, to the effect that Thieu was just a dictator, thus driving another American public-opinion nail into Vietnam's coffin. It was a dispute that should have been mediated before Chau's defiance and Thieu's need to uphold his authority hardened into concrete.

As the 1970s progressed, my sense of commitment to what I viewed as the universal rights of the Vietnamese people to live in freedom made it impossible to join the antiwar movement, no matter how disappointed I was with my own government and Thieu's. I knew what the outcome of complete withdrawal, with no continuing support, would be. Nor could I join the hawks, whose focus was still on bringing the North Vietnamese to heel militarily. My sister and brother-in-law became peace activists and marched on Washington. We didn't talk about it.[15]

POLITICAL WEAKNESS, PACIFICATION PROGRESS

The 1971 South Vietnamese elections for president were perhaps the last chance for political reform and for the establishment of a viable political cause around which various political and religious factions could unite. It was also the last chance to modify the Vietnamese government's image in the eyes of the American public as a corrupt dictatorship unworthy of support. Unfortunately, the American focus was on regime stability, so we did not use our influence to bring about an open and competitive political process. Thieu wound up running unopposed. Both Big Minh and Ky were potential opposition candidates, but they were squeezed out by Thieu's rigging of the rules for candidate eligibility. Ambassador Bunker understood the adverse impact of a one-man election and argued within the Nixon administration against letting Thieu proceed with a blatantly unfair process. Kissinger's attitude was, "While Thieu's methods were unwise, neither Nixon or I was prepared to toss Thieu to the wolves: indeed short of cutting off all military and economic aid and thus doing Hanoi's work for it, there was no practical way to do so. We considered support for the political structure in Saigon not a favor done to Thieu but an imperative of our national interest."[16]

Throwing Thieu to the wolves was a false analogy. Even Bunker, who was a firm Thieu supporter, saw the need for a credible election. The truth was that Kissinger and Nixon wanted, at whatever cost to the Vietnamese body politic, a regime they could manipulate and control. Had Big Minh and Ky run, they probably would have split the vote and given Thieu the opportunity to win legitimately. The result of the one-man election was a further blossoming of one-man rule. In the words of Thieu's own ambassador to the United States at the time, "This would prove the most destructive and destabilizing factor of all."[17]

South Vietnamese political progress was sacrificed to the need to keep an essentially weak, often vacillating regime in place in order to facilitate the Paris negotiating process. When the Peace Accords were announced, it became clear that a substantial communist force, some 150,000 to 200,000 North Vietnamese regulars, had been allowed to remain in the South. If one understood the terms of the accords, there was little to celebrate. Larry Berman would sum it up in the title of his book about the peace negotiations: *No Peace, No Honor: Nixon, Kissinger, and Betrayal in Vietnam.*

Kissinger deserved no award, certainly not the Nobel Prize, except one given for deception. Despite the gains in pacification, the Vietnamese government remained vulnerable. Thieu improved his standing by pushing through real land reform and supporting pacification but never generated the widespread political support that a more genuine democratic effort could have engendered. While able to rally the nation during the 1972 Easter Offensive, his government offered too little political outreach and indulged in too much nepotism and corruption to sustain public confidence. The Vietnamese military and political understructures were still too dependent on American support and advice. As early as 1967, Bui Diem, Thieu's ambassador in Washington, had begun warning him that American support could not be expected to continue more than another five years. He was reading the signs in Congress and in American public opinion, but Thieu ignored him and persisted in thinking to the very end that America would never abandon Vietnam.

A stalemate à la Korea—the South Vietnamese bearing the brunt of the struggle, with U.S. air and logistical support—was not an impossible outcome. Pacification largely worked, with persistence and a changed approach and the support of General Abrams, and Bill Colby running CORDS.[18] By 1972, most of South Vietnam, particularly the Delta area, was not only pacified but peaceful. So was most of central Vietnam. The next year Senator Tran Van Don, accompanied by retired general Ton That Dinh, drove all the way from Saigon to Hue and back in a civilian car without any armed escort.[19] The North Vietnamese would later admit they suffered a severe reverse in the South Vietnamese countryside in the years after 1968, acknowledging that many of their bases had been wiped out in South Vietnam and that numbers of North Vietnamese and Viet Cong troops had been compelled to retreat to sanctuaries in Cambodia.[20]

During the North Vietnamese Easter Offensive of March 1972, the South Vietnamese army proved able, with American logistical and air support and advisors, but with no American combat troops, to hold Vinh Loc (only two days' march north of Saigon) with six thousand troops against a North Vietnamese force of almost twenty-eight thousand. With two divisions the army retook the northernmost province, Quang Tri, driving six invading North Vietnamese regular divisions back across the seventeenth parallel. Altogether, of the about two hundred thousand men the North Vietnamese mustered for their offensive, an estimated forty thousand were killed. They lost more than half their tanks and heavy artillery. This contrasted with an estimated eight thousand South Vietnamese killed. The defeat resulted in the easing out of Vo Nguyen Giap as the North Vietnamese commander.[21]

All American units and military advisors withdrew after the 1972 peace agreement, and supporting equipment, weapons, and ammunition, which had already been reduced, were more than cut in half for 1974 by the U.S. Congress. This left the Vietnamese army without adequate supplies and with severely reduced logistics. Without U.S. logistical support the army was not capable of moving rapidly enough to face any future North Vietnamese offensive, nor was the Vietnamese air force capable of bombing North Vietnamese units without being shot down by missiles.[22] There was still no sufficiently strong and experienced command structure in place, with consistently able combat commanders, for all key Vietnamese army units. Nor had the South Vietnamese been adequately organized, trained, or equipped to repel on its own an all-out North Vietnamese invasion.[23]

With adequate American aid as well as logistical and air support the South Vietnamese government under Thieu's leadership might possibly have sustained itself politically and militarily over the long run, but even so the regime suffered from institutional weakness, internal corruption, cronyism, and uninspired leadership. In 1974, little noticed by an American press no longer interested in Vietnam, a Catholic priest, Father Tranh Huu Thanh, launched the People's Anticorruption Movement. This unleashed an outpouring of popular rage at the corruption of Thieu's entourage, including his wife, at a time of galloping inflation and economic recession, caused mainly by cuts in American aid.

Bui Diem, back in Saigon as an independent newspaper publisher, was asked to draft a speech for Thieu that would help dissipate the anger and focus public opinion on the growing threat of an all-out North Vietnamese offensive in 1975. What Bui Diem actually wanted was for Thieu to initiate a dialogue with the opposition, which had broadened far beyond Father Thanh's original movement. But Thieu's speech acknowledged no problems, offered no conciliation; instead he talked about how the communists were against him and were behind all the trouble. Looking at Thieu on the television screen, Diem concluded that he was "unable to look beyond himself, even in this extremity."[24]

What was not accomplished was the development of a unifying political cause in South Vietnam in the form of representative and responsive national government under inspired leadership, something the average Vietnamese could feel was worth risking one's life to defend—and which might have changed American public opinion. Whether this critical failure could have been overcome by a different American and Vietnamese approach is a question to which there can be no definitive answer. Certainly, it was never seriously tried.

Chapter 23
Tragic Aftermath—and Why

Prior to the Peace Accords, Nixon had secretly promised President Thieu "to respond with full force should the settlement be violated by North Vietnam."[1] He also promised continued economic and military aid. In the meantime, the antiwar movement had grown so much that when Watergate led to the resignation of Nixon in 1974, Congress cut off further support. The Vietnamese were left alone, with the dwindling military supplies and equipment they had on hand and with no effective air support. The door was wide open for an outright invasion of the South by the full weight of the regular North Vietnamese army. That took place in 1975, and South Vietnam collapsed. North Vietnamese tanks coming all the way from Hanoi crashed the gates of the presidential palace in Saigon in April, while the remaining Americans and the relatively few Vietnamese who could—about 130,000 whom we rescued—fled for their lives. The sight was so shameful and pitiful that I couldn't watch it on TV for any length of time. Particularly disgraceful was the CIA station's reputed failure to destroy all its records. This allowed lists of CIA contacts, who were not necessarily agents, to fall into North Vietnamese hands—as death warrants.

MASS VENGEANCE

Left behind were some of my oldest and closest Vietnamese friends, Colonel Tran Ngoc Chau, General Le Van Kim, and Vo Van Hai, President Diem's former secretary. Chau was thrown into a reeducation camp (reportedly, the CIA's division chief in Washington, Ted Shackley, vetoed a field request to have him put on the evacuation list). When Chau finally got out of the camp he remained under house arrest until he and his family, under the ruse of being Vietnamese of Chinese descent, became "boat people," in a wandering saga worthy of Ulysses. By accident they would eventually be discovered on an Indonesian island and then be flown to the United States.

General Kim and his wife, Gaby, gave up waiting for an evacuation helicopter, which was late, and tried to flee by boat down the Saigon River, but they were caught. Their son, Phuoc, an aide to the acting minister of defense, Senator Tran Van Don, got out. I had no direct word about exactly what had happened to Kim until I happened to pick up an Italian news magazine at the Rome airport a few months after the fall of Saigon and casually opened it to an article about Vietnam. Staring at me was a photograph of one of the reeducation camps, with Kim in the foreground being harangued by a communist cadre. I stared in shock and deep chagrin. The image stayed with me for a long time.

Kim was confined for several years to a series of reeducation centers, winding up in a particularly severe camp near the Chinese border in North Vietnam, where he would have starved to death had not Gaby found her way north to grow some extra food for him outside the camp. Eventually he was released, and he and Gaby lived for a time in Saigon, in the servant's quarters of Gaby's mother's small house, where I had met surreptitiously with Kim in 1963. They would eventually be allowed to immigrate to France through the efforts of Phuoc, whose friends in the French economic aid program interceded. Kim came out with only the clothes on his back and the flip-flops on his feet. I saw him when he visited the United States in 1983, fifteen years after we had last seen each other in Saigon. We embraced, broke down, and openly cried.

Vo Van Hai died in a prison camp, where he was reportedly maltreated, sometime after the fall of Saigon. It took a long time for the feeling to recede that I should have found my way out to Vietnam and somehow helped save him and others like him.

First impressions of the North Vietnamese takeover appeared more benign than expected based on the mass executions in Hue during the 1968 Tet Offensive. More careful initially about their international image, the communists hid from view the executions—mainly of South Vietnamese intelligence, special police, provincial reconnaissance team personnel and nationalist political party members in the provinces, suspected spies for the Americans, and many former Viet Cong who were considered traitors not just for surrendering under the Chieu Hoi program but for actively fighting for the South Vietnamese side. In addition, all officials of the government and private businessmen above the rank of clerk and all officers of the South Vietnamese armed forces, as well as employees of the Americans, an estimated three to four hundred thousand, were soon rounded up and marched off to special indoctrination camps, the Vietnamese version of the Soviet Gulag. There many were kept as long as ten years, some for as long as seventeen, and a number died of deprivation and disease. Also arrested and held in prison for several years on "suspicion" were active supporters of the National Liberation Front who had neglected to join the movement formally.[2] Agriculture was collectivized, and more than a million city dwellers were driven out into "special economic zones" in the countryside, where they were expected to make a living. How many starved to death is unknown. It was a predictable reprise of what the Viet Minh had done after taking over the North in 1954 and 1955, except that there were no mass trials or executions of the so-called landlord class in the villages. Ordinary South Vietnamese soldiers and former government civilians were denied jobs, and their children were denied entrance to high schools and universities. Even South Vietnamese army cemeteries were uprooted. It was mass vengeance.

Then came the exodus of more than a million people by boat into the South China Sea toward the Philippines and into the Gulf of Thailand toward Thailand, Malaysia, and Indonesia. Those escaping were not only former regime families or supporters but ordinary farmers and fisherman as well. Ironically, among the boat people were also a number of National Liberation Front leaders, including Truong Nhu Tang, the NLF minister of justice, who were nationalists, not Communist Party members, first. The repression and the exodus that followed constituted a tragedy of immense proportions. For almost fifteen years after 1975, the Vietnamese people went through unshirted hell until the regime began giving in to the need for a market-based economy. The communist takeover of South Vietnam also sounded the death knell for 1,800,000 Cambodians and several hundred thousand Lao, including Hmong, executed or deliberately eliminated by maltreatment in camps, prisons, or the countryside following communist takeovers of those countries.

The South Vietnamese did not deserve that fate. They made many mistakes, but they did not have the advantage of almost two hundred years of democracy that we did. We made mistakes too, and I've always thought we should have known better. The current Vietnamese scene of peace and growing prosperity does not justify what the Vietnamese had to go through to get there. It only demonstrates the tremendous potential that they always had as a people to develop themselves and their country if given freedom and opportunity to do so. The war's ending also left us with a moral dilemma that we have yet fully to confront. After becoming so deeply involved and significantly hindering (as well as helping) the attempts of the South Vietnamese to defend themselves, were we right to abandon them in 1975, without at least providing as much help as we had in 1972, when they had repelled the previous North Vietnamese invasion? Can we say we acted like the great and generous nation we believe ourselves to be?

WHY WE FAILED IN VIETNAM

In an interview before his death, Gen. Maxwell Taylor concluded we had failed in Vietnam because "we didn't know ourselves. We thought we were going into another Korean war, but this was a different country. Secondly, we didn't know our South Vietnamese allies. We never understood them, and that was another surprise. And we knew even less about North Vietnam."[3] Former secretary of defense Robert McNamara, in his book *In Retrospect: The Tragedy and Lessons of Vietnam,* said our decision makers were "setting policy for a region which was terra incognita." But then he excuses the mistakes, on the ground that "our government lacked experts for us to consult to compensate for our ignorance." He recognizes General Lansdale as one expert but dismisses him, because he "was relatively junior and lacked broad geopolitical expertise."[4] McNamara simply rejected advice that did not conform to his preconceptions. No set of "experts" could have overcome that obstacle.

We failed to understand the "x factor"—the political and psychological nature of the struggle for the "hearts and minds," the feelings of the Vietnamese people. We failed to communicate with or understand the Vietnamese on a human level, often confusing increased numbers of staffers with greater influence. We underestimated the motivating power of Vietnamese nationalism, and we failed to comprehend the fanatical determination of an enemy willing to sacrifice its entire people until only the Politburo was left. We failed to comprehend the intimate connection between our actions in Vietnam and political support at home. Above all, we failed to understand that the South Vietnamese could never stand on their own unless they were able to develop a political cause as compelling as that of the communists. We thought in conventional World War II battlefield terms, when this conflict was at its heart a political one, a war of ideas and of the spirit. Within that framework, the failure lay with our leadership in Washington and on the ground. The decision makers didn't understand how much putting the right people in charge mattered.

This did not have to happen. At critical junctures, decisions were made in a vacuum about policy and whom to send to the field, decisions that doomed the enterprise to failure. Lansdale had posed a basic question: "How does a guy go about getting policy folks to understand the nature of the problem they are trying to solve?" If the policy makers at the top didn't listen or were unwilling to admit they didn't know or that they might be wrong, getting them to change, even in the face of setbacks, proved impossible. Their attitude was reflected in and reinforced by optimistic progress reports that had little basis in fact.

David Halberstam aptly caught the aura of the principal Vietnam advisors and decision makers for Kennedy and Johnson. The title of his epic *The Best and the Brightest* expressed not only how these men were viewed but how they saw themselves. Vice President Johnson, after returning from his first cabinet meeting in 1961, extolled the brilliance of the Kennedy team to the House Speaker, Sam Rayburn: "Well, Lyndon," Rayburn responded prophetically, "you may be right and they may be every bit as intelligent as you say, but I'd feel a whole lot better . . . if just one of them had run for sheriff once."[5]

Top policy makers in Washington, with egos inflated by meritorious careers, had a low tolerance for different views based on firsthand experience. The standardized flow of information up through the bureaucracy, telling details strained out, was too often distorted by an optimistic patina of progress. This was particularly true from the last half of 1963 through 1968, when we radically changed the course of the war and embarked on a path from which we could not walk back.

Our leaders in Washington and Saigon thought that they knew enough, from their personal experience in a context unrelated to Vietnamese reality, simply to issue prescriptions for Vietnamese problems they didn't understand. It was as if the top levels of officialdom were in thrall to a self-induced image of a mythical country that was hardly ever the real Vietnam, comfortable with the illusion that remedies coming from their self-contained bubbles would result in positive events on the ground. There was also underestimation of, and in some quarters even contempt for, Asians, the Vietnamese in particular. Too often this tendency played a role in our treating them as less than equal, undermining our assessments of Vietnamese capabilities and negating consideration of their concerns.

President Kennedy at least understood that the Vietnamese had to win the struggle themselves and had previously rejected any direct American troop involvement. Particularly poignant and certainly prophetic were the concerns he dictated in the Oval Office about Diem's assassination and the future, about the generals' ability to "stay together and build a stable government," about the possibility that public opinion would "turn on this new government as oppressive and undemocratic."[6] He had been stymied at a critical juncture by his own bureaucracy and domestic political concerns; perhaps he might have seen his way around that institutional blockage had he lived. He most certainly would have been highly skeptical that we could win the war on our own, with little reference to the Vietnamese.

President Johnson's practical political instincts deserted him on Vietnam. While challenging his advisors, the same top-level team that had gotten Kennedy into trouble, he was unwilling to seek informed alternative sources. He distrusted Lodge, thought he had been wrong about the coup against Diem, yet sent him back as ambassador. He bought the notions that we had to find a Vietnamese leader and just back him, that security was separate from the need for a popular base for government. His lack of experience in foreign affairs and military matters caused him to rely too heavily on McNamara and Westmoreland. McNamara, able to muster logical-sounding arguments buttressed with facts and figures, overwhelmed less tangible counter-arguments and persuaded almost everyone that he knew what he was talking about. By the time Johnson realized he did not, it was too late.

Absolutely fatal was the failure to explain openly and honestly to the American people what the war was about and what we were trying to achieve. Our lack of understanding and miscalculations at the top led us to justify a massive commitment of American troops as the best way to achieve a quick military victory. When victory failed to materialize and stalemate seemed to set in, public support was lost. The image of American boys sacrificing their lives while, it seemed, the South Vietnamese were profiteers, refusing to fight, was corrosive. Our complicity in creating this situation by failing to mitigate the adverse impact of our overwhelming presence on the cohesion of Vietnamese society was easy to overlook.

News of villages resisting the Viet Cong and of South Vietnamese troops fighting and losing their lives at a much greater rate than ours became muted background noise. The moral cause of helping the South Vietnamese defend themselves against the imposition of an alien and repressive doctrine dressed up as Vietnamese nationalism became confused. The American public took the conduct of the war, from bombing Vietnamese civilians to the My Lai massacre, as evidence that we were destroying the people we were supposed to help. Too often we amplified the image of the Vietnamese on our side as inconsequential. Instead of building them up, we tore them down.

What some were doing in Vietnam, particularly during the early Rural Affairs days, was work grounded in reality, supporting grassroots political, social, and economic development. Rural Affairs proved that part of the job could be done in a nonbureaucratic and effective way at the local level, but then rampant American bureaucracy, compounded by inept leadership, stepped in. Attempts to get Americans working together as a team degenerated into petty squabbles, until a truly combined rural reconstruction and security effort (that is, CORDS) came along—which did good work but whose massiveness overstimulated dependency. One experienced U.S. observer estimated that Vietnamese officials were obliged to spend half their time dealing with the Americans, leaving them little opportunity to do their own jobs.[7] By that time, while it was not too late to support effective pacification, it was too late to affect American public opinion. The South Vietnamese could not ultimately sustain themselves unless political reform and true self-governance prevailed at the top while also working its way up from the bottom. We were unwilling to risk the uncertainty inherent in supporting a more democratic political approach and opted instead for a false sense of stability tied to sustaining the political status quo.

Whether the South Vietnamese could have hung on after our withdrawal with all-out logistical and air as well as advisory support from us is an open question. It would have given them a better chance to survive in the short run, but in the long run they still needed to accomplish the democratic reforms necessary to unify their society and to develop a political cause capable of challenging the communists.

Chapter 24

Beyond Vietnam: Iraq, Afghanistan, and the Future

To old Vietnam hands, the occupation of Iraq in 2003, accompanied by the rise of the insurgency there, was a bad movie from the past. Our failure to understand the Iraqis or the genesis of the insurgency there—even that there *was* an insurgency—was a plotline much too familiar. The periodic pronouncements of "progress" brought back memories of Vietnam-era declarations of light at the end of the tunnel and victory around the corner. Overconfident self-deception was again loose in Washington.

From the enclave of administration leadership in Washington to the Green Zone in Iraq, an eerie resemblance exists with the way decisions were made and actions were taken during Vietnam, except that the removal from reality seems even greater this time. Big thinkers and high officials in Washington or in isolation in Baghdad believed we could conceive the desired end result, then direct the Iraqis to make it work. During the occupation, it was easy to picture Ambassador Paul Bremer's more realistic advisors coming out of Green Zone meetings thinking, like Lansdale in Saigon in 1965–68, that whatever country had been discussed it sure as hell wasn't Iraq. Hubris, ignorance, and political insensitivity reigned even more supreme than in Vietnam.

FAILING IN IRAQ AND AFGHANISTAN

Critics claim that our Vietnam experience is not applicable to Iraq, citing differences of history, culture, temperament, religion, religious rivalry, and ethnic division. They also point out differences between an insurgency in South Vietnam strongly supported with troops and weapons by North Vietnam, and an insurgency in Iraq with much less outside support but compounded by sectarian and ethnic divides. In fact, the widespread use of improvised explosive devices and suicide bombers to drive us out, sowing societal chaos and promoting sectarianism, did not exist in Vietnam. But these are tactical considerations. Some anarchy was inevitable, given Iraq's history, but a case can be made that our early moves had a lot to do with promoting it.

As the appointment of Lodge and Taylor undermined South Vietnamese political possibilities, so the arrival of Ambassador Bremer and the Washington-Baghdad Green Zone mindset undermined a successful transition to a functioning Iraqi self-government. Disbanding the Iraqi army en masse with no postwar employment, the wholesale firing of Baathist government employees (who had been forced to join Hussein's party to hang on to their jobs), and failure to keep state-owned factories operating provided fertile ground for insurgent recruitment. Bremer's time-consuming insistence on a complicated caucus system versus elections for a constituent assembly, over the opposition of Grand Ayatollah Ali Sistani, aroused suspicions that we intended to maintain control. This helped create a political vacuum, into which the Sunni insurgency and the Shiite militias grew.

Overarching in both Vietnam and Iraq was hubris at the top, combined with an unwillingness to listen to alternative views or to understand the enemy, the local people on our side, or our own limitations and capabilities. In Vietnam we were arrogant and largely ignorant about the country for too long, believing we, and not the South Vietnamese, could win the war. We followed a similar view in Iraq. It was up to us to put down the insurgency and write the political script for the Iraqis, who would then graduate into a secure and full-blown democracy. The ghost of the great Washington-Saigon disconnect returned to haunt us in the form of an even greater disconnect between Washington and Baghdad.

Hauntingly similar to Vietnam is the way we dealt with the insurgency during our first four years in Iraq. We started with a handicap, in that our troops were too few in number and had no coherent security mission. Then we wasted a year without training any substantial Iraqi forces while failing to recognize the insurgency, which we further inflamed by a blind "kick the door down" approach, all of this helping precipitate Abu Ghraib. After the invasion and the toppling of Saddam Hussein, we were going to provide security ourselves, à la Westmoreland. This ignored the cardinal counterinsurgency rule—you can't do it for them, they have to do it themselves. As General Abrams put it in 1971, "There's very clear evidence . . . in some things, that we helped too much. And we *retarded* the Vietnamese by doing it. . . . *We* can't run this thing. . . . *They've* got to run it. The nearer we get to that the better off *they* are and the better off *we* are."[1] Once training of the Iraqi army started, we concentrated on turning out numbers, paying insufficient attention to who they were, how their units were integrated, how they were going to operate and be led, and what they thought they were fighting for.

In dealing with American public opinion too, the Vietnam era has repeated itself. By combining the Johnson administration's failure to reach out with Nixon's secrecy and divisiveness, the George W. Bush administration created the worst of both. Bureaucratic infighting reached such a peak that the principals seemed to prefer fighting each other to confronting real enemies in the field. The confidence of the American people was lost, to such an extent that it may not be restorable within a time frame that might sustain the current counterinsurgency approach. It would be ironic, indeed tragic, if the first-rate team we finally assigned to Iraq, Ambassador Ryan Crocker and Gen. David Petraeus, turns out to have arrived too late, as was the case with Ambassador Bunker and General Abrams in Vietnam.

Whatever may happen in Iraq, however, there is still Afghanistan, which we have thus far aided mainly on the cheap. There the struggle to overcome a failed state and an impoverished country continues under resurgent Taliban pressure upon a still-fledgling government trying to do right by its people but afflicted with all the ills to which such governments are subject. The notion that we are going to kill enough Taliban to win the war still seems strong, although there are signs a broad counterinsurgency approach may be taking hold.[2] In the meantime, the miniscule Afghan army and police are being "ramped up," presumably with effective counterinsurgency training and advisory support, but local citizens must be enlisted in defending their own communities if security is to hold. Making the situation more difficult, in a way similar to Vietnam, is the Taliban's cross-border sanctuary in Pakistan.

We have demonstrated in Afghanistan the same self-centered tendency as we have in Iraq to think we can impose a made-in-Washington solution on someone else's country without adequately taking into account the state of mind and history of its peoples. Having made mistakes, we have compounded them by not dealing frankly with the American public about exactly where we went wrong and why, by not appealing for public understanding on the basis of a frank and rational explanation of what we can realistically achieve. Talking at, instead of with, the public about "democracy" and "staying the course," as against "cutting and running," has proven no more effective than calls for "maintaining U.S. credibility" and "peace with honor" were in Vietnam.

What Should Be Done

We are in for a long struggle to overcome the threat of radical Islamic extremism, whose virulence may take a generation to subside. The Iraq war may be one of a kind in its scale and in terms of how it got started, but we face a similar challenge in Afghanistan, and there are likely others to come. As with the Cold War, this different kind of war is at its heart an ideological, political, and psychological challenge. We cannot protect the American people by ducking this challenge and assuming it will just fade away if we change presidents. We must face it not with fear but with self-confidence that we, in conjunction with other rational and decent nations and their peoples, will prevail. Our heritage calls us not to retreat within ourselves into a homeland-security crouch but to look beyond our borders for opportunities for joint efforts to preserve and enhance mankind's better aspirations.

As a priority, we must reestablish our moral authority with policies and actions that reflect our best traditions, adhere to international law, and show "a decent respect to the opinions of mankind," to quote our Declaration of Independence. We will not prevail if we continue to respond primarily with weapons and money. They will not ultimately determine success—people will. We can only do this job with the willing help of other nations and peoples, and we must recognize that interdependency. We must be practical in our actions and modest about our achievements, and moreover, we must stand for something beyond our personal well-being and be willing to sacrifice for it more widely.

On Iraq, as war weariness affects us, should we not ask ourselves what we owe the Iraqi people for having occupied their country and helped precipitate the chaos? Do we not at least owe them some time (not an infinite amount) to pull themselves together? Is this not a commitment inherent in our having assumed the responsibility of an occupying power, however dubious the route followed to get there? In our inevitably reduced future role in Iraq, will we have gotten a security force on its feet through training and mentoring, not only combat effective but capable of self-sustainment without our logistical and air support? Or are we going to cut future assistance radically, as we did in Vietnam in 1974?

Those who think that precipitously pulling out of Iraq is going to enhance our prestige elsewhere, particularly in the Arab world, don't understand that constancy under difficult circumstances will be read as trustworthiness on both sides of the Israeli/Palestinian divide. There a satisfactory outcome depends in part on the reliability of the interlocutor. It will call for long-run engagement on our part, probably with peacekeeping troops on the ground, to make a two-state solution work.

Principles and Precepts

What, then, can we take as most relevant from our Vietnam experience and thus far from Iraq and Afghanistan? Certainly we have been taught that to maintain the support of the American public and that of allies, the government needs to live up to its goals, not undermine them by the means it chooses. We must assert and maintain our basic principles as Americans in whatever we do to help others defend and build their countries, whether it involves combat operations against terrorist groups or not. Instead of what we did at Guantanamo and allowed to happen at Abu Ghraib, we should be guided by rules we laid down in 1903 for the Philippine Constabulary, the national police force created at that time to maintain law and order in the face of an insurrection. Not only was the constabulary to comply with American justice rules of evidence, but "any member . . . who whips, maltreats, abuses . . . or tortures by the so-called 'water cure' [the waterboarding of the time], or otherwise any native of the Philippine Islands, or causes [such actions] is subject to imprisonment not to exceed five years, a fine . . . and a dishonorable discharge."[3]

Such precepts enunciated over a hundred years ago are even more valid today. What may appear expedient can be fundamentally flawed when not thought through and made consistent with our beliefs, as Abu Ghraib and Guantanamo have demonstrated. There are no shortcuts in this kind of struggle. The American public will not sustain misbehavior in the handling of prisoners or the abuse of civilians in Iraq or elsewhere, any more than they sustained My Lai in Vietnam. Without public backing no nation-building effort can be supported long enough to be effective, particularly when our own troops are at risk.

Some think that being successful at nation building and counterinsurgency is mainly a matter of adopting "good" policies. Certainly good policy sets the right framework, but more crucial is implementation on the ground. There we are badly lacking. Helping others to build responsible self-government with popular roots where there is little experience or tradition to sustain it means helping build effective institutions and civil society. This is very difficult and requires patience and time, as well as perseverance. We tend to look for "silver bullet" answers or to overwhelm the problem with top-heavy bureaucratic agencies isolated from and often disdainful of the people we are supposed to help—thus putting Parkinson's Law to work with a vengeance. One thinks of the Baghdad Green Zone and our new $750 million embassy compound the size of ten football fields for thousands of Americans, too many of whom will essentially be passing paper to each other.

Success in helping others build a nation under stress, under internal attack, depends mainly on human contact and understanding and the use of imagination and intelligence rather than simple brute force. Good personal relations are crucial. One key advisor can be worth more than several combat brigades. Personal intent, motivation, imagination, and the ability to build trust in those we are trying to advise counts for practically everything, particularly in the unhinged environment in which this kind of work takes place; willingness and ability to listen to and understand those we are trying to help is essential. Back in 1901, President William McKinley instructed Americans in the Philippines to treat the local people "with the same courtesy and respect for their personal dignity which the people of the United States are accustomed to require from each other."[4] Following that rule engenders friendship and trust. Breaking it creates distrust and resistance in the people we are trying to help and backfires with our own public. That this rule, along with civilized treatment of the Filipino insurrectionists, was not always followed in practice back then does not vitiate the principle underlying it.

Counterinsurgency effectiveness comes down to understanding the "x factor," acknowledging that the ultimate contest is not for physical terrain on the conventional battlefield but for the feelings of the civilian population, without whose support, or at least acquiescence, insurgencies cannot prosper. In Iraq we were guided instead, early on, by the nostrum that the only thing the Iraqis respected was force. A different set of rules should have been followed. The first of these, applying to the political, economic, and military aspects of counter-insurgency-*cum*-nation building, is that we cannot do this job ourselves, only the local people can. This makes us chafe, since it puts the outcome ultimately in the hands of local leaders whom we do not control. However, we can influence them wisely, provided we understand what and how to advise. At all times we should adhere to Lawrence of Arabia's prescription, "Better your allies do it tolerably than you do it perfectly. It is their war, and you are to help them, not to win it for them."[5]

Winning the support of the people as the only sure way to win the war is an equally important concept. This means: "So long as actions taken in the war contribute to winning the people, they contribute to winning the war." Conversely, "when they do not contribute to winning the people, they contribute to losing the war." The successful way is "winning the people first, winning the war second."[6] This is difficult stuff and against normal combat instincts. The usual rules of force protection—fire back reflexively if fired upon, no matter the surroundings—have to be changed and the changes enforced. Counterinsurgency cannot succeed if your principal object is to kill insurgents by whatever means available, particularly by using airpower and artillery against suspected insurgent locations that also harbor civilians. The confusion of means with ends was particularly prevalent in Vietnam, with our "search and destroy" operations. The killing of civilians in Iraq and Afghanistan by air strikes comes at a significant cost, as neither the Iraqis nor the Afghans accept our attempting to transfer the blame to the enemy for "hiding" among women and children. We must severely constrain these strike tactics.

The Right People

Our Vietnam, and now the Iraq and Afghanistan, experience tells us that we must be much more selective about the people, military and civilian, we send abroad to engage in counter-insurgency and nation building, particularly in an environment full of civil strife and political turmoil. Nation building is hard, and we must provide particularly effective people. Needed are committed volunteers who genuinely believe in helping others. Particularly needed is the right field commander. That person must be able to listen to, understand, and communicate with others whose ways of thinking may be quite different. Such persons must not be assigned on the basis of past political, administrative, or even military accomplishments largely unrelated to the complicated task at hand. Counterinsurgency combined with nation building is distinctly not a job for conventional civilian administrators or military commanders who, however much at home elsewhere in government or the armed forces, are fish out of water in revolutionary environments that place a premium on individual initiative, political sensitivity, and willingness to take reasonable risks. Even less is it a task for large bureaucracies.

Those at the very top of our government, particularly the president, must begin to understand that they cannot rely exclusively on a narrow circle of like-thinking advisors, particularly those lacking in practical field experience. Informal means should be used to reach periodically down to the working level, to get a realistic picture of actual conditions on the ground in countries we are assisting. Dissent, if based on facts and firsthand knowledge, must be listened to and evaluated. President Franklin D. Roosevelt's reaction to Gen. George Marshall's dissenting views in a meeting at the White House before World War II, when Marshall was only the deputy chief of staff of the army, should be remembered. Roosevelt was so impressed by Marshall's courage in speaking out and the intelligence of his arguments that he appointed him chief of staff.

While we no longer have a Lansdale with us, we do have his ideas and his approach, as well as more contemporaneous contributions from others, all valuable guidance, and we have other assets not available during his time. One of those is our recognition of the importance of human rights and the need to promote democracy as the only long-range answer to our own security. Another is the existence of nongovernmental organizations (NGOs), such as the National Endowment for Democracy, and the Republican and Democratic Institutes under that umbrella, specifically devoted to helping develop democratic institutions in other countries. There are other American NGOs devoted to grassroots development and peacemaking, that, if given space to operate and tacit endorsement, can sometimes do what our officials could not even if they were freer from existing bureaucratic hindrances. NGOs can be particularly helpful in countries where incipient descent into chaos needs to be headed off.

Changing Organization and Direction

Our armed forces are adapting themselves to the challenge of "asymmetrical warfare," but they cannot carry this burden alone. Their combat-driven conversion to counterinsurgency needs to be matched on the civilian side. Specifically, a currently understaffed State Department needs to go to war, beefing itself up to undertake political advisory efforts and participating in joint civil/military counterinsurgency and nation-building efforts beyond traditional diplomacy. The Agency for International Development (AID) needs to change radically to play an effective economic and social development role. The post–Cold War de-emphasis of the mission of the U.S. Information Agency should be reconsidered, as we gear up for another ideological contest. Islamic extremism can be defeated over the long run only by change within Islam itself, but we can do a much better job of supporting and fomenting moderation with a fully funded and more focused effort, as we did during the Cold War.

More needs to be done within the armed forces to speed up the preparation of soldiers capable of training and mentoring indigenous forces to combat insurgencies effectively. Particularly needed within the U.S. Army is an advisory corps, where such service can be pursued as a career, recognized on an equal basis with traditional combat specialties like the infantry and artillery.[7] Advisory tours should not be arbitrarily limited; also, substantial overlap by replacements is necessary if advisors are to be effective. Additional compensation may be needed, in terms of premium pay as compensation for longer rotation periods.

The proactive spirit that existed in the Foreign Service in Vietnam needs renewal.[8] Civilian participation should be expanded in provincial reconstruction teams in Iraq and Afghanistan, and these teams need greater coherence in what should be their primary mission: promoting local security, self-development, and self-government. To stimulate the needed level of commitment, civilian service in counterinsurgency should be both voluntary and specially recognized. Cross training in counterinsurgency with special emphasis on its political and social side is needed, as well as area and language training.

AID currently relies mainly on subcontractors, often unsuited for provincial reconstruction or development work, while its senior levels lack experience and orientation in that direction.[9] AID should be reorganized with a fresh set of rules, more dynamic leadership, and much greater flexibility to provide agricultural and other technical volunteers for decentralized rural development. Finally, the CIA needs to get back into political action as a team effort, but with a positive orientation, not just buying support.

Current nation building–*cum*-counterinsurgency efforts are still being implemented through separate agencies, often at odds with each other, while Washington fiddles. Radical restructuring at the highest level to carry out effective, *combined* counterinsurgency and nation building where it is needed, in a limited number of countries, seems necessary. A new organization with a relatively small staff could be set up directly under the president and supervised by the national security advisor, with the mission of coordinating support for such activities, with a direct line of command to combined missions in the field. In organizing and operating such combined field missions, the CORDS experience in Vietnam is highly relevant (albeit with a lighter footprint).[10] If this is adopted, Congress must be involved on a cooperative basis, making special provision for oversight. Funding procedures should be taken out of normal bureaucratic channels, to facilitate timeliness and on-the-spot relevance. We must cut through the bureaucratic swamp now impeding support from Washington. The Bush administration made a start by appointing a White House coordinator for Iraq and Afghanistan, but that is not sufficient.

CONCLUSIONS

We are likely engaged in a long and patience-testing struggle. We can accomplish nothing without the support of the American people. The executive branch must take the American people and their representatives, the Congress, into its confidence from the beginning. Concern about revealing our general intentions to our enemies must not be allowed to trump keeping the American people informed and involved through dialogue, not dictation or exaggeration, which only backfires. This calls for honesty and transparency in explaining what we are doing and why, and how tough it is, in terms the public can understand. It also means frankly acknowledging setbacks and difficulties, and talking *with* the American people, not at them. Congress has to be involved every step of the way to build bipartisan support; otherwise, trust is likely to be undermined no matter how noble the original cause. We need to develop public support for the long haul.

To work successfully in direct support of others whose history and culture are different from ours, our attitude needs to be the antithesis of hubris; it needs to be something best expressed by the old saying, "May God give us the grace to see ourselves as others see us." Do those ultimately responsible for building their own nation see us as friends—yes, even as brothers—who share their aspirations or as arrogant strangers trying to impose our ways? Are we perceived as primarily interested in furthering our own ends or as genuinely interested in the well-being of those we are trying to help? We are dealing with fellow human beings, not abstractions, no matter how different in appearance, religion, customs, and culture—never inanimate objects to be treated with disrespect and moved around a geopolitical chess board without human consideration.

Because of our native optimism, democratic ideals, and lack of cynicism, we Americans, and our nation as a whole, are better suited than we may now believe to the challenges we face in becoming involved in other countries under difficult circumstances. Because we have been so successful in the past as a nation, however, we cannot let feelings of innate superiority blind us or allow our predilection for bureaucracy strangle us. We must be very selective in finding, deploying, and wisely supporting capable individuals in the field while keeping the careerists, the time servers, and above all, large bureaucracies, at home.

Acknowledgments

Many, many people have contributed to this book: foremost my wife, Barbara, whose patience and extraordinary support, including the review of numerous drafts of the original manuscript, were essential to delivering a reasonably coherent version to the publisher. Behind her were our children, Rufus, Anne, Edward, and Patricia, whose encouragement provided vital moral support. I am also indebted to my sister, Lucretia Whitehouse, for reviewing the description of our family background.

I owe special thanks to Dr. Murray Brennan of Sloan-Kettering Memorial Hospital in New York City. His consummate skill literally saved my life in 1999, thus allowing me to write this book.

I wish to highlight the assistance of my indefatigable agent, Leona Schecter, and her husband, Jerry, who not only led me to the publisher but who also reviewed the manuscript, helped sharpen the text, and reduce its over-extensive length.

Then there were friends who read earlier versions and encouraged me to persevere: my Yale classmate Tony Schulte, who arranged for various editors to read initial drafts; author Al Santoli, who contributed comments and encouragement; and historian Larry Berman, who offered helpful advice.

One could not wish for a more cooperative and helpful publisher than the Naval Institute Press. I would like to single out Rick Russell, the director, who made the decision to publish the book, and Liz Bauman of the editorial staff, for reviewing and suggesting edits to the manuscript, helping select photographs, and arranging key meetings. Her thoughtful assistance and consistent, cheerful encouragement were vital. Chris Onrubia made a significant contribution with design and the handling of photographs, as did Susan Corrado with final editing and production and George Keating and Judy Heise with marketing and publicity. The mapmaking skills of Chris Robinson and information about the history and location of Saigon streets and installations provided by retired Foreign Service officer Jim Nach merit particular recognition.

A number of individuals at various libraries and repositories of documents provided very useful assistance. I owe special thanks to military historian Bob Sorley, who advised me on accessing the National Archives; Ted Gittinger, now retired, of the LBJ Library in Austin, Texas, for providing valuable historical perspective as well as copies of important interviews and documents; Stephen Plotkin of the JFK Library in Boston, Massachusetts, for documents and recordings concerning President Kennedy and Vietnam; Michael Hussey of the National Archives in College Park, Maryland, for assistance in locating State and Defense Department documents; and Chris Upham and my son Edward for their help in researching the Lansdale Papers at the Hoover Institution Library and Archives in Palo Alto, California.

Nick Arundel deserves mention for his recollections of the early 1954 days in Saigon, the late Demi Gates for his memories of 1955, the late Oggie Williams for his recollections of the 1956 period, and Ken Coate for information about his father, Bob Coate, and copies of Bob's personal letters. Also, my thanks to old friend Stu Methven for his recollections, to Elyette Conein and family for answering questions and letting me look at material about Lou Conein, to my brother-in-law Sven Kraemer for his recollection of our attempt to influence the Vietnam policies of whomever might win the 1968 presidential election, and to Steve Hosmer of RAND for his comments on the book's conclusions. In addition, particular thanks go to historian Ed Miller, for his review of and comments on the manuscript as well as his willingness to share some of his research into the files of the former Diem government, still preserved by the current Vietnam government.

I wish to acknowledge the contribution of the USOM Rural Affairs staff without whose inspiration this book would not have been possible. Special thanks for the foreword to this book go to Ambassador Richard Holbrooke, whose first overseas posting was with Rural Affairs. Among many Rural Affairs veterans who helped with their remembrances and material from their files, I wish to single out Bert Fraleigh, Tom Luche, Earl Young, and John O'Donnell, whose untimely death in 2003 left us bereft of his thoughtful and kindly presence. Another veteran of Rural Affairs, Vlad Lehovich, not only contributed remembrances but read the manuscript and provided valuable comments. Among the Vietnamese of Rural Affairs, particularly notable for his help was Lam Quang, former provincial assistant in Phu Yen Province, who became the first elected official of Vietnamese origin in the United States. I would also like to acknowledge the remembrances of the late Mark Huss, as well as those of Lt. Gen. Sam Wilson, USA (Ret.), and Jerry French, both of whom served on General Lansdale's staff when he was in the Pentagon, and of Cal Mehlert, who provided background information and photographs from his time in An Giang Province in the Delta. Retired congressman Frisco "Johnny" San Juan provided memories of Filipino help for South Vietnam and of the incomparable President Ramon Magsaysay.

I take special note of the contributions of Lieutenant Colonel Tran Ngoc Chau, former ambassador Bui Diem, and General Hoang Van Lac, whose recollections helped shape the narrative of this book. Their stories supplied important parts of the material as well as motivation for writing this book. Also, thanks go to Le Van Phuc, General Kim's son, who helped verify facts about Kim's life and career, and to Nguyen Thai for helping me identify individuals in some of the photos.

Finally I wish to acknowledge continuing inspiration from the writings and career of Gen. Edward G. Lansdale, whose thoughtfulness, insight, and devotion to the well-being of the Vietnamese people, experienced firsthand, were far removed from the caricatures presented by some in the press and in books. To sources of inspiration I would add the brave Vietnamese who struggled for a decent future for Vietnam, the Filipinos who assisted in the early days, members of the early Saigon Military Mission and of the later Saigon Liaison Office, and many other Americans, military and civilian, who served mainly in the field, sincerely devoting themselves to helping protect and better the lot of the average Vietnamese.

Notes

PREFACE

1. Cecil Currey, *Edward G. Lansdale: The Unquiet American* (Boston: Houghton Mifflin, 1988), 2. Confirmed by Lt. Gen. Sam Wilson USA (Ret.), then a lieutenant colonel on Lansdale's Pentagon staff who accompanied him to the meeting with McNamara. Lansdale was trying to explain the importance of such intangible factors as motivation in an insurgency struggle.

2. Bui Diem, "Reflections on the Vietnam War: The Views of a Vietnamese on Vietnamese-American Misconceptions, in *Looking Back on the Vietnam War: A 1990's Perspective on the Decisions, Combat and Legacies*," ed. William Head and Lawrence E. Grinter (Westport, Conn.: Praeger, 1993).

3. Dan Van Sung, *Dilemmas in Vietnam*, first written in July 1963, translated and republished in January 1964 with a foreword by C. T. R. Bohannon that Sung approved, bringing it up to date and specifically citing the USOM Rural Affairs program as contributing "to the true national revolution."

4. To some the very term "nation building" conjures up an image of arrogantly trying to build somebody else's nation for them. The approach the author learned was completely different. We were there to help the Vietnamese build a nation, not to build it for them.

PART I: PROLOGUE

1. Arthur J. Dommen, *The Indochina Experience of the French and the Americans* (Bloomington: Indiana University Press, 2001), 231, 242–43.

2. While Secretary of State Dulles and President Eisenhower were, though not optimistic, determined to try to stabilize South Vietnam, Secretary of Defense Charles Wilson, in a National Security Council meeting on October 25, 1954, declared, "The only sensible course of action was for the United States to get out of Indochina entirely and as soon as possible. The situation there was utterly hopeless." U.S. State Department, *Foreign Relations of the United States* (Washington, D.C.: 1952–54) [hereafter FRUS with year], vol. 13, Indochina, part 2, 2185.

3. Edward Lansdale, *In The Midst of Wars* (New York: Fordham University Press, 1991), 128.

4. The background of Lansdale's assignment to Vietnam is taken from his autobiography, *In the Midst of Wars;* Cecil Currey, *Edward G. Lansdale;* and from *The Pentagon Papers: The Defense Department History of United States Decisionmaking on Vietnam: The Senator Gravel Edition* (Boston: Beacon, 1971), vol. 1, doc. 95, "Lansdale Team Report on Covert Saigon Mission in 1954 and 1955," 573.

5. Taken from minutes of conversations held in Paris by the secretary of state and Foreign Minister Bidault with relation to "united action" in Southeast Asia, April 21, 1954, FRUS 1952–54, vol. 13, Indochina, part 1, 1332–33. This dismissive attitude toward Vietnamese nationalism was all too typical of French government opinion in general.

6. Edward Miller's thoroughly researched thesis, "Grand Designs: Vision, Power and Nation Building in America's Alliance with Ngo Dinh Diem, 1954–1960" (PhD dissertation, Harvard University, 2004), laid to rest the myth that Diem's appointment had been arranged by the United States.

7. Ambassador in France (Dillon), telegram to State Department, FRUS 1952–54, vol. 13, Indochina, part 2, 1609.

CHAPTER 1: SAIGON–*PANIER DE CRABES*

1. *Yale Banner* (New Haven, Conn.: Yale Banner, 1951), 303, 322.

2. Two years after his capture, Jack Downey emerged alive for a communist Chinese show trial that sentenced him to life in prison. He would finally be released in 1973 through the intercession of President Nixon after his historic visit to Beijing. The CIA published in 2007 the complete story of his being shot down, captured, and tried. On his return Jack went to Harvard Law School (having been rejected by Yale, to the acute disappointment of his class), married a Chinese woman then working in New Haven, had a son, became the utilities commissioner of Connecticut, was appointed a state judge in New Haven, and had a Juvenile Court building named after him. He is currently retired but still handling cases.

3. The CIA had a junior-officer training program under which they tracked the author while he enlisted just like any other recruit in the army (other services such as the Marines or the Navy were also possible). It was up to the author to get through basic training and officer candidate school on his own, after which the Agency could arrange for him to be detailed back to CIA, as a legitimate army officer. He would have to fulfill his army service obligation of two years as an officer before being considered for possible civil hire.

4. The author had remembered the major's warning but had no evidence of the specific combat event until he was given a copy of a front-page article from the *Wichita Evening Eagle* of August 7, 1954, headlined "Reds Take 5 Outposts in New Saigon Flare-up." The article was found by a member of the National War College staff at Fort McNair and given to the author at a seminar he gave in 2006 on the 1954–55 period of American involvement in Vietnam.

5. Transferred back to the United States in late 1948 to disappointing duty as an intelligence instructor at Fort Lowry, Colorado, Lansdale arranged a transfer in 1949 to the Office for Policy Coordination, the highly secret organization President Truman had created to fight the Cold War as the covert operations arm of the National Security Council. There he developed an approach to the Huk rebellion in the Philippines involving his return to the Philippines as an advisor to Ramon Magsaysay, then a congressman, soon to be appointed Philippine secretary of defense. Taking Magsaysay's ideas and his own, Lansdale put together a Magsaysay strategy and a plan to defeat the communist Huks. The essence of the plan was to win the support of the population away from the Huks by making democracy work through clean elections while radically changing the way the Philippine army operated, putting the well-being and the security of the population first while aggressively pursuing Huks who would not turn themselves in or surrender. Starting in late 1950, when the Huks were very close to winning, the process culminated in 1953 with Magsaysay's landslide election to the presidency and the voluntary surrender of Luis Taruc, the Huk's hardcore Stalinist leader, because he "no longer had anything to fight for." (This is only known case of a hard-core Moscow-trained communist political leader voluntarily giving up the cause until the fall of the Berlin Wall and the changes in Eastern Europe).

6. Lansdale's background comes from the author's memory, buttressed by Lansdale's *In the Midst of Wars,* and Currey's *Edward G. Lansdale.*

7. See Lansdale, *In the Midst of Wars,* 157–59; *Pentagon Papers,* vol. 1, doc. 95, 576; and Currey,

Edward G. Lansdale, 152. Lansdale established a friendly and more personal relationship; he was being called to the presidential palace for talks on a frequent basis, often daily when the series of political crises Diem faced became more and more acute. Diem would use Lansdale not only as a source of practical ideas but also as an independent check on what he was being told by his Vietnamese sources, including his brothers. In his internal report on the first year of the Saigon Military Mission (doc. 95 of the *Pentagon Papers*, vol. 2), Lansdale credited the plan he presented at their first meeting as the foundation for their friendship. Aspects of the plan that would have appealed to Diem were positive ideas about how to deal with immediate governance issues, such as the refugees and the territory being evacuated by the Vietminh, rather than focusing on more abstract political advice about handling the sects or broadening his government. Although the plan was never adopted per se, many of its ideas found their way into reality, such as setting up a special commission to deal with the refugees, using the army in a positive way to occupy the Vietminh evacuated areas, and organizing the veterans who were about to be discharged, as well as how Diem should reach out in a more personal way to the population. Lansdale's patience and informal manner were a considerable contrast to most of Diem's official callers, who seemed to talk down to him. His relationship with Diem would grow into a friendly and personal one in which he was used not only as a source of support and practical ideas but also as an independent check on what Diem was being told by others, including his brothers.

8. "Political action" was political advisory work; "military civic action" was about proper troop behavior and giving assistance to the civilian population; while "psychological warfare," as broadly defined in Vietnam, covered troop information and civic action instruction, overt public information and propaganda directed at the civilian population as well as overt and covert propaganda against the enemy, the Vietminh.

9. According to the description of Brigadier General de Castries given in the definitive book about Diem Bien Phu by Martin Windrow, *The Last Valley* (London: Cassel Military Paperbacks, 2005), he was a brave commander who cared about his men and did his best under difficult circumstances. There is no evidence that he ever requested air drops of luxuries for his mess at the expense of his troops. When his command post finally surrendered, the staff emerged mostly untouched while those defending the outposts were not only exhausted and covered with mud but many were gravely wounded. The subsequent death march of the prisoners and their segregation and brainwashing during captivity by the Vietminh deliberately pitted them against each other and heightened their sense of betrayal, a reason for the disdain felt by some against de Castries. When de Castries was repatriated he was so weighed down by feelings of shame, heightened by his captivity, that he asked, "Is it true that they want to shoot me?" (page 637). As for the courage of the Vietnamese at Dien Bien Phu, most fought quite bravely according to Windrow.

10. These stay-behind operations, in which the author was not involved, are described in *Pentagon Papers,* vol. 1, doc. 95. The release of the *Pentagon Papers* to the *New York Times* resulted in great notoriety for this aspect of Lansdale's efforts because the United States was covertly violating the Geneva Accords. These same operations are also described at greater length by Kenneth Conboy and Dale Andrade, *Spies and Commandos: How American Lost the Secret War in North Vietnam* (Lawrence: University Press of Kansas, 2000). However, in the latter, on page 4, Conboy and Andrade state, "Lansdale's primary mission became stay-behind resistance operations." This is not correct. Lansdale's primary mission remained trying to save South Vietnam from a communist takeover. These stay-behind activities were insurance against the possibility that the main effort might fail. The Vietnamese teams (one Dai Viet and one VNQDD) sent into North Vietnam were eventually compromised and finally picked up the North Vietnamese in 1958 and 1959. The operation was a failure. Similar operations were conducted elsewhere against the communist bloc with a low percentage of success. In China, a similar operation was doubled, causing the capture and show trial of the author's classmate Jack Downey when his agent pickup plane was shot down in Manchuria in 1952.

11. The author received his own copy of the Linebarger book in 1956 and has kept it in his library ever since, mainly for sentimental reasons. Published in 1948, it is still the best single book on the subject.

12. The correct way, according to Mao, to make the water (the people) hospitable to the fish (the guerrillas) in embattled areas was to treat the population the correct way through "three main rules of discipline," and "eight points for attention." The main rules were: "Obey orders in all your actions. Do not take a needle or a single piece of thread from the masses. Turn in everything captured." The eight points were: "Speak politely. Pay fairly for what you buy. Return everything you borrow. Pay for anything you damage. Don't hit or swear at people. Don't damage crops. Don't take liberties with women. Don't ill treat captives." Mao and subsequently the North Vietnamese enforced such instructions by "iron discipline" including execution if necessary. To encourage similar correct behavior on our side, it would prove necessary to provide intensive indoctrination with similar specifics, including the democratic notion that the troops were the servants, not the masters of the people. *The Selected Works of Mao Tse-tung*, vol. 4, 155–56, in *Mao Tse-tung Internet Library*, www.marx2mao.com/Mao/.

13. There are a number of variations of the story of Diem's encounter with Ho Chi Minh. This one was told the author by Vo Van Hai and is similar to the description in Anne Miller's unpublished biography of Diem. A more complete version with documentation appears in Edward Miller, "Vision, Power and Agency: The Ascent of Ngo Dinh Diem, 1945–54," *Journal of Southeast Asian Studies 35*, no. 3 (October 2004), 433–58. While the author agrees with most of Miller's conclusions about Diem, he disagrees with Miller that Diem, after the meeting with Ho Chi Minh, continued to entertain serious thoughts about joining the Vietminh in a government of "national union." The author believes Diem deliberately asked Ho for control of the security forces at their meeting as his price for joining because he knew that this was the one thing the communists would never give up. The earlier assassination by the Vietminh of his older brother, Ngo Dinh Khoi, and Khoi's young son was unforgivable.

14. The author remembers this quote quite well but has been unable to find a documented source.

15. Vuong and An were close friends. The author would see a lot of them over the 1954–56 period because of his advisory role to the Vietnamese army. Subsequently, the author saw them less often but remained friends. When they dropped by to see the author in Saigon, he would always learn something he didn't know before about the Vietnamese political scene.

16. Lucien Conein was born in France in 1921, the son of a disabled French army veteran of World War I and a mother whose sister had married an American soldier from Kansas City. He grew up in Kansas City. Restless after dropping out of high school, Conein ran away from home just before World War II, found his way to France, and enlisted in the regular French army in 1939. Shipped to the Belgium border in 1940, just as the German army rapidly advanced toward Paris, he joined a completely disorganized retreat. Winding up in the south of France without papers, he escaped from internment, enlisted in the Vichy French army, went to Algeria, and then transferred to a French artillery unit destined for Martinique. He landed in New York City, where he found his way back to Kansas City, got American citizenship, and volunteered for the American army in 1941. The OSS recruited him as a leader of one of the famous Jedburgh teams. He parachuted into southwestern France the day of the Allied invasion of southern France. As the war wound down in Europe, Conein was dropped into South China in 1945 to cross the Vietnam border to work with a Free French unit against the Japanese occupation. Eventually he would meet Ho Chi Minh and General Giap, as well as some of the officers of what was now the Vietnamese army when they had been ordinary soldiers in the resistance. This background is based on the *Kansas City Star*, September 20, 1998; an unpublished set of interviews of Conein by Stanley Karnow that the family allowed the author to see; and the *Washington Post*, obituary, June 6, 1998.

17. Banzon was the brother-in-law of President Magsaysay of the Philippines. While officially posted as the Philippine military attaché to Thailand, Magsaysay had sent him to Indochina as a military observer, accredited to the French. Magsaysay had adopted a policy of assigning abroad any of his wife's relatives who were already in the Philippine government to avoid even the appearance of nepotism or influence peddling. Banzon was deeply involved in the successful anti-Huk campaign when Magsaysay was secretary of defense and had both intelligence and psychological warfare experience.

18. Chargé at Saigon (McClintock) telegram to State, May 3, 1954, FRUS 1952–54, vol. 13, Indochina, part 2, 1460.

CHAPTER 2: MAKING A START

1. The most famous of Ho Chi Minh's betrayals was that of Phan Boi Chau, a prominent nationalist leader and rival, who was picked up in the late 1930s by the French Sureté based on a tip from Ho, was jailed, and died under arrest. See Philippe Devillers, *Histoire du Viet-Nam de 1949 à 1952* (Paris: Seuil, 1952), and Robert F. Turner, *Vietnamese Communism: Its Origins and Development* (Stanford, Calif.: Hoover Institution Press, 1975), 58–59.

2. See Bui Diem, with David Chanoff *In the Jaws of Victory* (Boston: Houghton Mifflin, 1987), 48–50, for a description of the situation in the Hanoi area at the time. When he went into hiding to escape the Viet Minh terror squads, Bui Diem believes there may have been French collaboration with the Vietminh in their campaign to eliminate other nationalists but says no one has been able to document it. He pointed out to the author in conversation in December 2007 that the French had had a tougher time negotiating with the noncommunist Vietnamese nationalists than with the communists and that they may have thought it was easier to reach an agreement with Ho Chi Minh, particularly if they helped him eliminate his rivals.

3. John Dos Passos, *The Living Thoughts of Tom Paine* (New York: Premier Books, 1963), 47. This famous quote supposedly responds to Benjamin Franklin's "Where Liberty is, there is my country."

4. Lansdale's characterizations might sound simplistic but on close examination often went to the heart of what needed doing.

5. Pham Xuan An got his friend (and the former head of the South Vietnamese central intelligence service) Dr. Tuyen onto practically the last American helicopter out as Saigon fell in 1975, even though An was a North Vietnamese spy and Tuyen was one of the most sought-after South Vietnamese for the North Vietnamese to interrogate and then execute. An was subjected to reindoctrination in Hanoi, probably owing to his having helped Tuyen escape. See Larry Berman, *Perfect Spy: The Incredible Double Life of Pham Xuan An,* Time *Magazine Reporter and Vietnamese Communist Agent* (New York: Collins, 2007), 218–26. Former NLF minister of justice Truong Nhu Tang, in his *A Vietcong Memoir: An Inside Account of the Vietnam War and Its Aftermath* (New York: Vintage, 1986), 130, claims that ARVN General Tran Van Trung hid his Vietcong cadre sister-in-law in his house and that ARVN chief of staff General Cao Van Vien protected two of his wife's nephews, who were sons of a communist cadre. According to Tang, "the war was replete with instances of friends and relatives protecting each other, even though they were fighting on opposite sides."

6. The genesis of Operation Brotherhood (OB) is described in Lansdale, *In the Midst of Wars,* and in *Pentagon Papers,* vol. 1, doc. 95. The fact that Lansdale and hence the CIA had given it financial and advisory support would serve as the basis for its denigration in some American and Filipino quarters in later years, when the Vietnam War became controversial. Particularly damaging in the eyes of its detractors was a memo which became public knowledge from *Pentagon Papers* (vol. 2, 643–49, doc. 100). OB was, in the author's experience, an immensely successful humanitarian

effort with significant positive psychological and political effects on the South Vietnamese. That the idea sprang out of a meeting between Oscar Arellano and Lansdale in Saigon or that it enjoyed CIA covert financial support should not detract from its accomplishments. The author had a lot of direct contact with OB in Vietnam and later in Laos and can say that no orders were ever issued by him or anyone else from Lansdale on down telling the Filipinos what to do. The Americans who were directly involved and the Filipinos who ran OB worked together like brothers. They shared the same goal, a free Vietnam. For a fuller history of Operation Brotherhood in Vietnam, see Miguel A. Bernard, *Adventure in Viet-Nam: The Story of Operation Brotherhood 1954–1957* (Manila: Operation Brotherhood International, 1974).

7. Some have assumed that the defeat of the Huks had very little significance or application elsewhere, because it was a movement "promoting essentially reformist—not in fact revolutionary objectives [which] could be countered with repression and a set of palliative measures that left a regressive social and economic system intact." See Thomas L. Ahern, Jr., *CIA and Rural Pacification in South Vietnam* (Langley, Va.: Center for the Study of Intelligence, declassified, 2007), 401–402. On the contrary, serious studies of the Huk movement show it was completely communist controlled, with the same revolutionary objectives of mobilizing the population and taking over the government as set forth in Maoist doctrine. Moreover, its supreme leader, Luis Taruc, was a Moscow-trained Comintern agent. As for leaving a "regressive system intact," Magsaysay as president was already addressing government corruption and abuses of power and had plans for land reform and for organizing a new third party for the next presidential election and subsequent congressional elections. Success in these plans could have opened the road for social and economic reform, but first the insurgency had to be defeated.

8. Professor Edward Miller, doing research in Ho Chi Minh City (Saigon) on Ngo Dinh Diem in 2001, found in Diem government files (folder 791, Office of the President, 1st Republic series, "Phu Tong Phong De Nhat Cong Hoa") an actual copy in English of the pilot national security operation for Long My, written by the author in 1954, "National Action Staff Study." A copy is in the author's files.

9. Currey, *Edward G. Lansdale*, 168; Lansdale, *In the Midst of Wars*, 183.

10. This would have reduced Diem's role to that of a complete figurehead and effectively turned control of his government over to the French, acting behind the scenes. General Xuan had been head of an earlier separate government of Cochin China, set up by the French.

11. A copy of the presidential directive on National Action (called "pacification" in this version in French) was provided to the author by Professor Miller and is in the author's files. Miller found it in folder 14651, Office of the Prime Minister series, Vietnam National Archives Center No. 2, Ho Chi Minh City, Vietnam. Most of the directive is very military in nature, except for the two-page annex at the end, which provided the principles to guide the actions of the Vietnamese armed forces during occupation operations, to include a proposed complaint and action system and general guidelines for troop behavior and for providing medical assistance, potable water and food to the population, and engaging in reconstruction. *Groupes administratifs mobiles* (administrative mobile groups) were to be organized by the civilian ministries to assist in setting up local government operations, but these were never adequately mobilized and deployed, for lack of qualified personnel. The military commanders of Operation Liberty and Operation Giai Phong wound up performing most of these civilian functions themselves at the beginning, with some assistance from a few civilian administrators who were themselves not very well qualified. The lack of adequate civilian support for these operations helped spark the implementation by Diem of the Civic Action program, headed by Kieu Cong Cung.

12. Lansdale, *In the Midst of Wars*, 204–205. Later, Collins could not recall the incident, but it was common knowledge among Lansdale's team at the time.

13. During the Huk campaign, when Magsaysay was secretary of defense, he and Lansdale actually lived in the same house together; according to Filipinos who observed the relationship up close, they were like brothers. It was a glimpse that there was something quite unusual about Lansdale in his ability to relate to Asians and to earn their friendship and trust. Because the Vietnamese were so reserved culturally, there would not be the same degree of intimacy, but there would develop a similar degree of trust and affection.

14. Cecil Currey in his biography of Lansdale (p. 364, endnote 21), recalls asking a Manila taxi driver in 1985 the same question and receiving an outburst that I might have thought contrived if I had not seen similar reactions. Currey's driver later said in a letter about Magsaysay's death, "He was mourned by the people so deeply in their heart. His grave is simple, like just for a common person. He is my only Guy; my only President like him could give every Filipino a social justice. Ever in my heart he is always alive. He is my only President, my only guy."

CHAPTER 3: A NATION BEGINS TO RISE

1. Chief of the National Security Division, Training Relations Instruction Mission (Lansdale), memorandum to the Special Representative in Vietnam (Collins), FRUS 1955–57, vol. 1, Vietnam, 3–8, January 3, 1955. In this memo Lansdale was asking for authority to coordinate a broad approach to saving South Vietnam, "national action," of which pacification was a part. In a handwritten, marginal note Collins wrote, "Designated Lansdale to coordinate our phases of program under General O'Daniel's direction." It is doubtful that Collins was completely aware of the broad charter this gave Lansdale.

2. Practically all Vietnamese leaders as well as the general population consulted a variety of soothsayers at some point in their lives. They were also affected by numerology, believing in good and bad days for such specific actions as starting a journey or building a house, based on particular days of the Vietnamese lunar month.

3. This psychological warfare effort receives summary mention in *Pentagon Papers,* vol. 1, doc. 95, 582, and in Lansdale's *In the Midst of Wars.* It was also cited in Halberstam's *The Best and the Brightest* (New York: Random House 1969), 278, presumably because of its exotic flavor. These activities came in for a lot of ex post facto criticism as either cynical or naïve, when most made practical sense in terms of the temper of the times and the low morale of the South Vietnamese, as well as their considerable reliance on fortune telling. Nobody thought such activities alone were going to win the struggle.

4. The airport's runway was reinforced by pierced-steel planking installed by the Japanese when they took over Indochina in 1941. At the start of the war in the Pacific, this airport and the one in Saigon launched the Japanese planes that sank the battleships *Prince of Wales* and *Repulse* off the coast of Malaya.

5. Phong was a thin, ascetic-looking Vietnamese around thirty-five, dressed informally in a plain white shirt and khaki trousers. Puffing impassively on a pipe, Phong told his story, speaking English haltingly with traces of a British accent. He had been a resistance leader in the general Rach Gia area for many years, having first led a youth group against the French when they returned to Rach Gia in 1945. When the Vietminh leadership tried to force him to join the Lao Dong (communist) party in 1952, he refused. He had been fighting for independence but not for a foreign doctrine that was against his traditions and religion. He quit the Viet Minh and became a farmer. With the aid of a shortwave battery radio and a dictionary he learned English by listening to the BBC every night for three years. Asked why he trusted us, he said he had read our history: Americans were not colonialists, otherwise we would not have given the Philippines its independence.

6. The author was not aware at the time of the historical origin of this drama and assumed it was

entirely Vietnamese, when in fact it was about a Chinese dynasty that ruled in northern Vietnam during the seventh to tenth centuries; also, the general was Chinese. The drama had become a Vietnamese story.

CHAPTER 4: A BUCKET OF EELS AND OPERATION GIA PHONG

1. Savani was also the author of *Visages et Images du Sud Viet-Nam* (Faces and Images of South Vietnam), which the author found informative shortly after his arrival in August 1954 for its firsthand description of the religious and ethnic groups in South Vietnam.

2. The subject of Trinh Minh Thé is fraught with controversy. The French tried to label him a merciless warlord. This was due in part to his controversial tactic of singling out key senior French officers for assassination which he claimed was more humane than the widespread killing which occurred from pitched battles. One bomb attempt went wrong and resulted in civilian deaths, an incident which became in Graham Greene's hands the leitmotif for the consequences of blind American naiveté, in *The Quiet American*. The other charge was that he was corrupt and thus was bought by Diem or Lansdale. See Ronald H. Spector, *Advice and Support: The Early Years, The U.S. Army in Vietnam* (Washington, D.C.: Center of Military History, 1985), 245, and Stanley Karnow, *Vietnam: A History* (New York: Penguin Books, 1984), 238. Currey's biography of Lansdale concludes that Lansdale had bribed Thé but notes the present author's objections (that Thé was unbribable) in a footnote. Joe Redick, Lansdale's assistant and interpreter, who was an essential party to all Lansdale meetings with Thé, agreed with the author. Joe Baker, Lansdale's administrative officer at the time, in a note to the author stated that he had transported considerable sums of local currency to the palace at Lansdale's direction, and he remembered that the payment for Thé's troops was to cover a month's back pay. Subsequently, some have questioned whether Lansdale was as important a link between Diem and Thé as his memoirs imply. There had been contacts between Diem and Nhu with Thé that preceded Lansdale's involvement. Skepticism about Lansdale's role, the author believes, stems at least in part from a difficulty in believing that Diem, or Thé, would invest that much trust in Lansdale, who after all was a foreigner. As the author saw it, for the Vietnamese to trust Lansdale as a go-between for delicate contacts and negotiations was not unusual. Also, as a practical matter neither Diem or his brother Nhu would have been able to travel to see Thé in Tay Ninh in September 1954, the time of Lansdale's first visit to Thé's redoubt. At this time the French were still completely hostile to Thé and would have killed him if they could have. As for the meetings in Saigon in which Thé would arrive in disguise to see Lansdale, as described in Lansdale's memoir, the author remembers being warned by Redick to stay away from Lansdale's house because of just such a meeting.

3. Secretary of state letter to the special representative in Vietnam (Collins), FRUS 1955–57, vol. 1, Vietnam, doc. 128, 270.

4. Operation Gia Phong was commonly called at the time by its Vietnamese name in French and English, because the translation in English, "Breaking Chains," was awkward. "Operation Liberty" was so-called in English and French rather than "Tu Do," because of the difference between the northern and southern Vietnamese pronunciation of *Do*. The author's text follows this practice.

5. A copy of the Short Course is in the author's files. The author considered it relevant enough to needs in Iraq to have provided it in late 2006 to a friend with close contacts in the Pentagon.

6. This incident is mentioned in Lansdale, *In the Midst of Wars*, 236, but in connection with the preparations for Operation Liberty, when it actually occurred during the preparations for Operation Giai Phong. The author failed to catch this when he reviewed Lansdale's memoir manuscript before its publication.

7. This incident is recounted in Howard Simpson, *Tiger in the Barbed Wire: An American in Vietnam*

1952–1991 (McLean, Va.: Brassey's (U.S.), 1992), 144–46. Simpson's book provides a firsthand account full of the flavor of Saigon and the war there in 1955.

8. This is the same Dave Smith who later became deputy chief, then acting CIA chief, of station in Saigon, during the 1963 coup period.

CHAPTER 5: THE BATTLE FOR SAIGON

1. FRUS 1955–57, vol. 1, Vietnam, See telegram 3828, 294–96, for Dulles' initial instructions and telegram 3837, 301, for the block placed on these instructions. Editorial note 145, on pages 301–303, gives the background of two important telegrams that Lansdale sent, the first in the morning before the fighting with the Binh Xuyen broke out (although skirmishing was probably already under way). David L. Anderson, in *Trapped by Success: The Eisenhower Administration and Vietnam, 1953–61* (New York: Columbia University Press, 1991), 112, cites Kenneth Young as telling journalist Robert Shaplen that Dulles sent the blocking telegrams as a result of Lansdale's first telegram. The second Lansdale telegram, sent the same day but in the late evening, arrived in time for a climatic meeting of the National Security Council that rejected Collins' proposal to dump Diem. What is not clear is how and when Lansdale learned that Collins was recommending that Diem be replaced despite his reassuring Lansdale before he left that policy remained in support of Diem. Lansdale's *In the Midst of Wars* cites Diem as his source of information about Collins' actions in Washington; however, he did not see Diem until the early afternoon, when he had already sent his earlier message recommending against Diem's replacement. As stated in the text, the author believes he was tipped off through CIA back channels from Washington; if so, he could not have said so in his book. (Faithful to his secrecy oath, Lansdale did not acknowledge his connection with CIA in his memoirs.) It should be noted that Lansdale in his memoirs describes sending his second key telegram a day later than he actually sent it, according to editorial note 145, ibid. When Lansdale wrote his memoir he had to rely on memory, as the diplomatic and Agency files were not available to him. Each member of his former team, including the author, was asked to review his manuscript for accuracy but by that time it was practically impossible to remember the precise, day-by-day order of events.

2. There would be much argument over who actually started the war between the army and the Binh Xuyen. It is clear that some skirmishing had started earlier than the shelling of the presidential palace. There would be second- and third-hand claims that Diem started it deliberately on Lansdale's advice, but this is unlikely. There were provocations on both sides. The author remembers that the inside word within the Lansdale team was that the Binh Xuyen started it.

3. John Gates was recruited by the Agency after graduating in 1950 from Harvard, where he had taken summer officer training in the Marine Corps. He had the choice of serving in the Marine Corps or going into the Agency. He chose the Agency and wound up in Madrid, where he ran an operation creating and selling anticommunist cartoon strips to Latin American publications. When the assignment to Vietnam opened it sounded interesting and was a way of fulfilling his military service obligations, so he took it. Now a somewhat boring but comfortable existence in Madrid suddenly looked pretty good.

4. Telegram MC 976-55 from the U.S. Army attaché is mentioned in FRUS 1955–57, Vietnam, vol. 1, editorial note 145, 299–300, and can be found in the National Archives, Department of State, Central Files, 752G.00/4-2855.

5. FRUS 1955–57, vol. 1, Vietnam, editorial note 145, 303.

6. Ibid., memorandum of discussion at the 246th meeting of the National Security Council, April 28, 1955, 312.

7. The specific reference to Collins' comments about Lansdale is found in doc. 167 (special representative in Vietnam [Collins], telegram to the Department of State, FRUS Vietnam, 1955–57, vol. 1, 353). Lansdale's team would hear informally from inside the Agency that his reporting as well as his arguments had been important factors in turning opinion around in Washington. Diem and the Vietnamese army were, of course, principally responsible for saving his government, and ultimately South Vietnam, at this critical moment. There is little doubt that had Collins succeeded the South Vietnamese would have wound up with a weak government with French fingerprints all over it, dependent on the Binh Xuyen for its existence and immersed in turmoil, as it would never have been accepted by Trinh Minh Thé or Diem. Diem could well have gone to central Vietnam or to Thé's home area (Nui Ba Den) to head a nationalist reaction against such a government.

8. So close did Trinh Minh Thé feel to Lansdale that he apparently told his wife that if anything happened to him she should seek Lansdale's help and protection. Lansdale became a kind of godfather for the children (they were Buddhists) and was best man at Thé's son's wedding in 1965. This bond with Thé's movement, the Lien Minh, and its leaders carried over to the author in 1963 because of his prior association with Lansdale. During the Buddhist crisis in 1963, General Van Thanh Cao, Thé's former deputy, treated the author as a close friend, asking for advice on the very delicate matter of how best to resolve that crisis. Before that the author had only seen Cao once, at the time of his initial inspection trip to Vietnam in June 1962.

9. The author would hear later that during the earlier attempted takeover of Greece the communists had also kidnapped youth and taken them along when they were forced to retreat into Yugoslavia.

10. Ton Tat Dinh, later promoted to general, would turn out to be a key figure in the 1963 coup against Diem, having joined the coup plotters while still having the confidence of Diem and Nhu. After 1975, Dinh arrived as a penniless refugee in the United States. The author remembers him working as kitchen help in a fast-food eatery in Washington, D.C.

11. Collins and Lansdale were at opposite ends of the spectrum in their opinion of and approach to the Vietnamese. Lansdale would characterize Collins' way of talking to Diem as that of a "country squire looking down his aristocratic nose at a bumpkin," for which Collins would unconsciously supply some evidence by later referring to Diem in an interview patronizingly as "a fine little man." See Anderson, *Trapped by Success,* 118, sourced by notes 86 and 87 of chapter 5.

12. Lansdale tried to introduce ranger training into the regular training courses that MAAG was beginning to give to the Vietnamese army, but it was too unconventional. Later, through Lansdale's initiative in giving Vietnamese officers ranger training in the Philippines, a ranger training course was started within the Vietnamese army, but it was to take several years before the army's force structure was modified, over American objections, to create ranger companies within each division, thus potentially providing some irregular-warfare capability.

13. Much was made after the fact of the idea that Diem's refusal to participate in consultations concerning the elections proposed by the Geneva Conference protocol justified the North Vietnamese insurgency in the South. Seen in the light of the situation at the time, however, Diem's position was reasonable, given the fact that the Vietnamese nationalist government existing at the time of the Accords had never signed the protocol, nor had any of the participating governments signed it. The North had a larger population than the South, an estimated fourteen million to twelve million, and to the communists "free elections" were a joke. Lansdale suggested informally that Diem could have gained a propaganda advantage by challenging the North on the "free" elections issue, but Diem felt that interference by various foreign countries in the process, particularly by the French and the International Control Commission, would work to the North's favor.

14. Martin Windrow, *The Last Valley* (London: Cassell, 2005), 653–55.

CHAPTER 6: CIVIC ACTION

1. This was the nearby area northwest of Saigon that the Vietminh and the Vietcong laced with underground tunnels and is now a major tourist attraction.

2. According to one embassy telegram, Diem is quoted by Collins as saying Cung had the rank of major in the Vietminh (FRUS 1955–57, vol. 1, Vietnam, 121). The author's description is based on Nguyen Dinh Thuan's description of Cung's having reached the rank of brigadier and also on what Cung told the author about his life and career in the Vietminh. He tended not to exaggerate but to understate.

3. The incident of Conein throwing bombs was first recounted by Zalin Grant, *Facing the Phoenix: The CIA and Political Defeat of the United States in Vietnam* (New York: W. W. Norton, 1991), 126, but that account is incomplete. In a later interview with the author, Conein's widow, Elyette, recalled that more than one bomb had been thrown but thought one of the bombs had been thrown into the yard of the American ambassador. The author's memory is that the bombs were directed at certain French officers, which made more sense, since the purpose was to get the renegade French to call off their campaign. If Conein did indeed lob one into our ambassador's yard it was based on a wild idea of his own, not on anything he may have discussed with Lansdale, because it was unnecessary and risky.

4. It was unfortunate the Vietnamese went overboard with the referendum. Lansdale had cautioned Diem not to exaggerate the vote totals and thus undermine the referendum's legitimacy. It was clear Bao Dai had become so identified with the French that there was no way he could have mustered a significant favorable vote, so there was no need to exaggerate the results. The whole operation was managed by Ngo Dinh Nhu with great zeal but poor judgment, with the result that it would be discounted in retrospect. Coloring the ballots to favor Diem psychologically could be considered a legitimate tactic, but stuffing the ballot boxes, which apparently happened, cannot. Reportedly the number of votes recorded was greater in the Saigon area than the number of registered voters, although not all the Catholic refugees from the North who voted had been previously registered. The 98 percent total for Diem looked artificial when the reality was, in the author's opinion, at least 80–20 against Bao Dai, so discredited was he.

CHAPTER 7: SOUTH VIETNAM STABILIZES—LAOS UP FOR GRABS

1. Additional background is contained in Lansdale, *In the Midst of Wars,* 339–45, and in Currey, *Edward G. Lansdale,* 181–84. The author was flattered that Lansdale took him into his confidence on the issue of the Can Lao, which was really about bringing politics and government out into the open and away from a clandestine and highly restrictive political approach. While the author does not entirely agree with Currey's more extreme comments about its deleterious effect, there is no doubt that the way the Can Lao functioned and the extent to which it was feared by many as well as exploited by opportunists was a significant contributing factor to Diem's loss of widespread political support and ultimate downfall. The party's monopolization of certain businesses, which paid for the privilege by helping finance the party, gave off the stench of corruption. It also brought out the worst side of tendencies to engage in political conspiracy, divisiveness, and envy. It functioned as a mechanism to ensure personal loyalty to Diem, not as a means of actually operating the government. In that it resembled the communist political commissar system, but without the iron discipline necessary for enforcement, and was entirely at odds with the democratic aspirations of the South Vietnamese constitution and of most civilians and many military officers.

2. On the way to Laos in February 1957, the author stopped by Saigon to see Vietnamese officials—such as Nguyen Dinh Thuan at the Ministry of Defense, and Kieu Cong Cung, the head of Civic Action—to ask in advance for some training support for the civic action program in Laos. He was

invited for dinner to Cung's house, where his host told him about the first shipment of USOM commodity support for Vietnamese Civic Action just arrived in Saigon. "Can you believe it?" he said. "Twenty-five thousand magnificent scissors."

3. USOM was apparently not happy with the way Michigan State University (MSU) had been brought into the picture through Wesley Fishel's contact with Diem and the fact that the MSU contract was directly with the Vietnamese government and not with USOM itself. Nevertheless, the MSU role in training, equipping, and advising the Civil Guard was hotly defended later by Ambassador Durbrow and USOM when Diem, with support from General Williams, tried to have the responsibility shifted to his Ministry of Defense, claiming that MSU was not effective. A contributing factor was MSU's recruitment of American big city police, who were out of place for the advisory role.

4. This incident remains very vivid in the author's mind. Like many sensitive actions at the time, it was never written up but was handled quietly, off the record. If written up, it would have gotten the State Department, Defense, and the CIA station formally involved and would have backfired. Making official demarches was not the way to handle such problems. Also, official policy at this time remained supportive of the Can Lao. After Lansdale left it did not take long for Nhu to extend Can Lao control into the army, with predictably divisive effects. While not directly provable, it could only have contributed to the discontent that provoked the paratrooper coup in 1960 and continuing discontent thereafter.

5. Bui Diem came from a northern mandarin family of great distinction and joined the nationalist Dai Viet party in 1945. Having survived the Vietminh purges of 1946, he continued his political activity, helping to found the Popular Nationalist Party in 1951 as a successor to the original Dai Viet. He became editor in chief of *Quoc Dan,* the successor party's newspaper in Hanoi. When Dr. Phan Huy Quat was appointed defense minister in the preceding government to Ngo Dinh Diem, Bui Diem was his chief of cabinet. He would eventually become South Vietnam's ambassador to the United States, from 1967 to 1973.

6. Harry Maurer interviewed Williams for his book *Strange Ground: Americans in Vietnam 1945–1975—An Oral History* (New York: Henry Holt, 1992). Williams' recollections are in the personal files of the author.

7. These letters are in the author's personal files.

8. Much has been made of this in critiques of the Diem government. The move to direct central government control denied local villagers their traditional voice in village government, a long-standing cultural tradition. A temporary suspension of existing village councils may have been justified on a case-by-case basis, but the government's edict was too sweeping and needlessly alienated local leadership, sweeping out the good with the bad and never resuscitating an improved version of the original tradition under Diem. Who exactly originated the idea and whether it was seen as a preliminary step to the later communist "Denunciation Campaign" was never clear to the author.

9. General Williams was something of an exception in that he had Diem's full confidence but unfortunately was charged with converting the Vietnamese army into regular divisions to oppose an overt North Vietnamese invasion across the seventeenth parallel, ignoring the more likely alternative of renewed guerrilla warfare.

10. The "domino theory" would be much criticized later after the fall of Saigon in 1975, because the only dominos that fell were Cambodia and Laos. That conveniently ignores the institutional weaknesses, the existence of active or incipient insurgencies, and the rising influence of communist parties and fronts in most of Southeast Asia that prevailed in the 1950s and into the 1960s. The takeover of South Vietnam, which could have easily occurred in 1956 had we withdrawn but did not occur until 1975, gave the rest of Southeast Asia time to gain institutional strength and to defeat local communist supported insurgencies in Malaysia, Singapore, and Thailand and to prevent a

communist coup in the case of Indonesia. No one bore greater witness to this than the longtime prime minister of Singapore, Lee Kuan Yu.

11. This was the author's first real encounter with prejudice by other U.S. agencies against CIA personnel in the field, and it was a surprise, although there had been hints of it in Vietnam. Somehow the climate of opinion among many, but not all, was that CIA employees were up to something underhanded and were averse to true economic or social development. No explanations that civic action was overt village development, not covert intelligence, were accepted. Negative attitudes were mainly lodged in USOM and PEO, the military assistance mission. One USOM employee was heard saying that the Lao "had just come down out of the trees." Nothing characterized this attitude more than the actions of a PEO employee's wife who had flown up from Bangkok to reside with her husband in Vientiane. After her plane landed she took one look from the plane's doorway at the ramshackle terminal and the hulks of abandoned aircraft nearby and refused to come down the boarding stairs. Never getting off, she insisted on flying back to Bangkok on the same plane.

12. The author's visit with Diem caused a storm, because he had not cleared it first with the U.S. ambassador, Elbridge Durbrow, who cabled an angry protest to Ambassador Parsons in Laos. The embassy had been notified that the author was coming with Oudone to see Civic Action, but the visit to Diem had come unexpectedly. Instructed to steer clear of the palace during future trips to Saigon, the author did so, confining himself to seeing old friends at home, like Nguyen Dinh Thuan from the Ministry of Defense, and Colonel Le Van Kim, who was by this time engaged in directing resettlement on the High Plateau. The old days of just informally dropping by to see Vietnamese officials had vanished.

13. U.S. aid regulations prohibited economic assistance to religious institutions. In Lao villages most Buddhist *wats* also served as primary schools. The first priority for improvement in many villages was replacing the thatch roofing of the *wats* with tin sheets. It was called "school repair."

14. Oun Sananikone, Oudone's uncle, exemplified the insouciance of senior Lao politicians who had been used to winning elections based on family name. He was a well-known Lao elder statesman with a good reputation from his independence movement (Lao Issara) days. He was also one of the few who managed to run alone on the government side in a district that consisted of the northern part of Vientiane Province. His opponent was none other than Souphanouvong himself, who used a Pathet Lao cadre to blanket the villages with propaganda. When the returns came in Oun had lost. He was particularly galled because a large village he had visited had voted against him. He returned after the election to complain. "I got you all this aid but you didn't vote for me." The villagers were quiet, looking puzzled. Finally, one said, "But you didn't ask us to vote for you."

15. Lansdale had recommended the author's award for his work on pacification with the Vietnamese army, accompanied by the unusual (for the CIA) citation, "His understanding and patience with Asians and his immense fund of kindly good humor made him an outstanding representative of the United States and the West." Allen Dulles smiled wryly when he read the citation to the author. Lansdale said he wrote that to teach others in the Agency what was important in working with Asians.

16. Fraleigh would become the author's deputy when he returned as an AID official to Saigon in 1962. Methven was already in Saigon as a case officer working with civilian irregular defense groups. The author would continue to see Henry Hecksher, his former station chief in Laos, over the years when he was in town from other assignments.

17. The author followed the integration of the Pathet Lao troops into the Royal Lao Army through Colonel Oudone Sananikone. The Pathet Lao remained, at their insistence, in two isolated camps, barring any personal contact with Lao army soldiers stationed nearby. The reason why became clear during a visit of a Pathet Lao delegation to Vientiane for a meeting with the Lao general staff.

A Pathet Lao noncom pulled a knife out of his belt and tried repeatedly to stick it into the armor of a parked Lao army tank, insisting that the tank was made of paper. Then he asked whether it ran and if it did, where the American driver was. A Lao soldier proceeded to drive the tank around, as a demonstration. The Pathet Lao noncom started arguing with the driver in Lao, insisting that the latter was an American. The driver replied, "I am talking to you in Lao; how can I be an American?" The Pathet Lao said heatedly he couldn't be Lao, the Americans ran everything in Laos. His indoctrination was so complete that he could not be convinced otherwise, demonstrating why the Pathet Lao leadership could never permit their troops to be truly integrated. Control would melt away as soon as the troops realized the truth. North Vietnamese techniques of indoctrination were just as thorough and would contribute to the fanaticism of the Vietcong in the future, particularly those reinfiltrated from the North.

18. Corruption stemmed primarily from the way USOM administered the commodity import program used to generate Lao *kip* to pay for the Lao army and civil service; Laos had almost no tax base or exports to support its national budget. To avoid inflation by directly introducing kip into the economy, the program exchanged it for dollars to pay for imports. The exchanged local currency was then used to pay for local government costs. Coached by some of the overseas Chinese, Lao merchants applied for import licenses, putting up the required kip at the official rate of thirty-five to one. They then either imported the commodity and sold it on the open market for what the kip was really worth—about a hundred to one—tripling their money, or sold the import license to someone else, at least doubling their money. There were few restrictions on what could be imported; cars and refrigerators were brought in, then taken back across the Mekong and sold in Thailand at free market prices. Many of the senior Lao politicians, whose families were in local commerce, were cashing in. This form of corruption was finally stemmed by devaluing the kip, but only after considerable political damage was done to the Lao government. It was a ripe target for Pathet Lao propaganda.

19. At a meeting between Prime Minister Souvanna Phouma and Secretary Dulles in January 1958, during a discussion about the then–newly agreed coalition with the Pathet Lao, Souvanna concluded, "Laos was therefore impermeable to communism." His reasons were: "Its Buddhism was strong," "it was under populated," and "the people lived in the traditions of the past." He said the experiment of coalition had succeeded "because the Pathet Lao were not communist." See FRUS East Asia–Pacific Region, Cambodia, Laos, vol. 16, 1958–60, memorandum of conversation, Department of State, Washington, January 13, 1958, 411–19. According to Impeng Suryadai, who had been Souvanna's chief of cabinet, these remained his core convictions. He seemed to have changed his mind based on later statements made to U.S. diplomats in the 1960s after Lao "neutralization" had occurred, and the communists had clearly taken advantage of it.

PART II: PROLOGUE

1. Ted Gittinger, interview of Lansdale, Lyndon Baines Johnson Library and Museum [hereafter LBJ Library], Austin, Texas, June 5, 1981.

2. There is evidence that the anticommunist denunciation campaign may have begun in 1956, but the author was not aware of it at the time. It was an approach that smacked too much of how communism operated for Lansdale and his team to feel comfortable with it. The author believes it may have started as a Can Lao–sponsored operation.

3. There were two CIA officers, George Carver and Russell Miller, with the coup forces. Carver was political, while Miller was involved in paramilitary training. Nhu apparently had an anonymous note sent to Carver threatening his safety which gave the station chief, Bill Colby, a rationale for remanding him.

4. The author was told by Joe Redick that he had attended in 1959 a formal dinner at the palace at which Durbrow insisted on personally translating President Diem's remarks from French to English, adding sarcastic asides in English that Diem clearly understood and obviously resented. Joe said the mutual dislike between the two was palpable.

5. *Pentagon Papers,* vol. 2, 126.

6. Saigon to State, April 22, 1960, FRUS 1958–60, vol. 1, 409.

7. The report which President Kennedy saw was Lansdale's memorandum for the secretary of defense, deputy secretary of defense, January 17, 2001 (Washington, D.C.: U.S. Defense Department, *United States–Vietnam Relations, 1945–67*), book 11, 1–12. The description of the key roles of ambassador and political advisor and their qualifications are taken from pages 3 and 4 of Lansdale's report. There were many other recommendations, but getting the right people out to Vietnam was key. The quote at the end describing the gist of Lansdale's approach comes from the *Pentagon Papers,* vol. 2, paragraph 3, 441.

8. There are different views about the role which Lansdale wished to play. Currey (*Edward G. Lansdale,* 227 and note 37, 393–94) believes Lansdale was shooting for the ambassadorship from the start. The author disagrees based on his conversations with Lansdale about this same subject. What Lansdale initially had in mind was similar to his previous operational roles, dealing with the Vietnamese informally with a political mandate and the support of a wise ambassador. He had hoped one of his few friends at State, Kenneth Young, would be appointed that ambassador. He could work with Young, he felt, the same way he had under Admiral Spruance in the Philippines and Donald Heath in Vietnam. When he realized Kennedy was serious about the ambassadorial posting and that Young was not going to Vietnam, he overcame his reservations about becoming a diplomat and communicated his acceptance. At one point the appointment appeared in the works. Lt. Gen. Sam Wilson (Ret.), on May 2, 2006, recalled receiving, on detached duty in the Philippines in 1961 for the filming of *Merrill's Marauders,* a message from Lansdale asking him to free himself for a visit to Saigon, where he expected to arrive soon as "chief of mission." Later Wilson received another message postponing the request. There was also a reported attempt to elevate him in rank and appoint him to take over the Military Advisory Group in Saigon, but this was hotly rejected by the Joint Chiefs, who did not regard him as "true military." After it became clear Lansdale was not going to be assigned out to Saigon he tried to have Defense take over the lead in coordinating and directing U.S. policy on Vietnam from Washington with himself playing a key role, but this too failed in the face of opposition from State. (See *Pentagon Papers,* vol. 2, 442–45.)

9. Currey, *Edward G. Lansdale,* 2, from an interview of Lansdale by Charles McCarry. Confirmed by author's conversation with Sam Wilson in 2006.

10. Lansdale interview by Ted Gittinger, LBJ Library, June 5, 1981. The conversation with Diem went this way. Lansdale asked Diem, "Do you really need them [the American troops] to stay alive?" Diem said, "You mean I shouldn't ask?" Lansdale asked again, "Do you need them?" Diem finally said no, and Lansdale suggested he stay with that.

11. Lansdale talked to the author about this before the latter went out to Saigon in 1962, but the author never saw a paper making this specific proposal. Lansdale was largely excluded from the preparation of Taylor's report for the president.

12. Saigon to State, October 25, 1961, FRUS 1961–63, vol. 1, 432. *Pentagon Papers,* vol. 2, 126, cites Diem asking four times for Lansdale's return. Cottrell, a senior State official on the Taylor mission, and Bill Bundy from Defense endorsed sending Lansdale, "but nothing happened."

13. FRUS 1961–63, vol. 1, 432. Original source is: John F. Kennedy Presidential Library and Museum [hereafter JFKL], National Security Files, Vietnam Country series.

14. Walter Rostow, *Diffusion of Power: An Essay in Recent History* (New York: Macmillan, 1972), 278–79.

CHAPTER 8: RETURN TO VIETNAM

1. Stephen T. Hosmer and Sibylle O. Crane, *Counterinsurgency: A Symposium April 16–20, 1962* (Santa Monica, Calif: RAND, 1962). The foreword of the 2006 edition quotes one of the prominent participants, General Frank Kitson, who rose to commander in chief of UK Land Forces, as saying about the symposium, "All our ideas were the same. Although we had no difficulty making our ideas understood to each other, we had mostly been unable to get our respective armies to hoist in the message."

2. On the way home at the end of 1955 the author had stopped off in Paris to see Secretary of State for Defense Dung and his assistant, Nguyen Dinh Thuan, who were there on an official Vietnamese mission negotiating the final status of French forces in South Vietnam. To his surprise he was met at the airport by a uniformed chauffeur from the French Ministry of Defense, who drove him to the hotel where the Vietnamese were staying in an official car with the tricolor flying on its fenders. The Vietnamese had named him an official visitor, and he was accorded all the amenities of the official delegation, including the cost of the hotel. After several days of sightseeing alone, and catting around town at night with the Vietnamese, the author left for the airport in the same chauffeured limousine. What the French thought was a mystery. Before leaving Paris, Thuan wanted only one favor. If asked, the author was to confirm that the Delegation had been hard at work in Paris. "Hard work—like in Paris," became a standing joke between Thuan, Dung, and the author. Taking some advantage of the French was enjoyable after their excoriation of SMM in Saigon.

3. JCRR had been started on the mainland before the communist takeover because the Chinese Nationalist ministries had been such a source of incompetence and corruption. Because it cut across bureaucratic lines, AID's technical divisions in Washington had successfully fought against using the idea elsewhere. Everyone who had served on Taiwan knew that, along with land reform, it had been key to the bottom-up agricultural revolution there.

4. This is still the case today, with our military advisors in Iraq and Afghanistan on fixed rotational assignments with little overlap. Lt. Col. John A. Nagl, author of *Eating Soup with a Knife,* a contemporary book about counterinsurgency, and commanding officer of a battalion at Fort Riley, Kansas, training transition teams for Iraq and Afghanistan, has proposed a permanent army Advisor Corps to address the importance of that function. This was earlier recommended by a RAND Corporation Study. See *The Army's Role in Counterinsurgency and Insurgency,* R-3947-A (Santa Monica, Calif.: November 1990), which also recommends the establishment of a counterinsurgency institute to train U.S. and foreign military and civilian personnel. The RAND study was met by indifference at the time.

5. Later more would be learned about VC techniques and motivation from captured documents translated and circulated within Rural Affairs. One such document was a VC cadre's account of how he personally turned one hamlet in the Delta into a VC stronghold over time. It showed the importance of the Vietcong cadre to the insurgent success and how motivated the cadre were by intense nationalism and by a sense of grievance against the Diem regime, which they were convinced was dominated by foreigners, the Americans. The lesson the author drew was that that the Vietnamese on our side had to develop an equally intense positive belief in their own political cause impelling them to make comparable sacrifices. Fear of communism alone was not going to be enough.

6. This area on the Cambodian side of the border would grow into the central command post for the National Liberation Front and for the Vietcong military command in the South.

7. While the Montagnards, who were of Indonesian stock, had no great love for the noncommunist

Vietnamese, because of neglect and Vietnamese resettlement on lands they felt had traditionally belonged to them, most feared the Vietcong more. (The Montagnards engaged in slash-and-burn agriculture, which obliged a seminomadic existence covering large swathes of territory which they regarded as traditionally theirs, not unlike our own native Americans.) On the other hand, it was clear the government could not hold the High Plateau–mountain area bordering Laos, containing the main routes of infiltration from the North as well as Vietcong bases going back to Vietminh times, without the support of the Montagnards.

8. See FRUS 1962–63, Vietnam, vol. 2, 470–72, for a complete memo of this conversation.

9. See the LBJ Library interview of Ambassador Nolting, November 11, 1962.

10. Part of the author's report to AID, "A Report on Counter-Insurgency in Vietnam," August 31, 1962, author's files.

11. Ibid.

12. Halberstam in *The Best and the Brightest,* 217, claims it was slide 869 that contradicted slide 11, but the author believes his own memory is more accurate. Given the attention McNamara gave the slides and the detailed questions he asked, 869 slides would have taken several days.

13. Buddhist Americans were generally viewed as a bit strange in those days, but that was not a view the author shared. Gard had seen combat as a major in the Marine Corps during World War II, serving with OSS near the end. He was currently teaching Buddhism at Yale. He knew firsthand all the prominent Vietnamese Buddhists and how they were organized. He thought they could be enlisted in rural development and he was very interested in going to Vietnam. Unfortunately, his security clearance application was rejected.

CHAPTER 9: STARTING RURAL AFFAIRS

1. Recollections of Tom Luche in an e-mail to the author in 2006.

2. From a conversation by the author with Amelie Burke, née Cecillon, on January 15, 2008. According to Amelie, Buu's main and most personal relationship was with Ngo Dinh Diem, not with his brother Ngo Dinh Can in central Vietnam, as has been assumed by some historians.

3. Bernie came from a well-to-do Shanghai family and was a talented young musician with the Shanghai Symphony just before the Japanese took over the City at the beginning of World War II. He then went to ground with a group of Chinese guerrillas on the Shantung Peninsula. After that he fought the Chinese communists and was close to the Kuomintang on Taiwan. His church connections brought him to Vietnam just as Lansdale was leaving in 1956. There he set up a communications system in the palace for President Diem and was instrumental in helping a Catholic priest from Taiwan, Father Hoa, organize his Binh Hung outpost in Camau, publicized by Lansdale's 1961 article in the *Saturday Evening Post.* When Bernie died in 1995, former CIA director Bill Colby and the author were pallbearers at his funeral. The author was never aware of any direct connection with the CIA.

4. The International Voluntary Services (IVS) was a nongovernmental organization that came into being in 1952 through the initiative of a committee supported by John Foster Dulles and headed by the U.S. Technical Cooperation Agency (now AID), with representatives from the Brethren, Mennonite, and Quaker denominations. The object was to form a private voluntary agency to send young secular technical-assistance volunteers overseas to share skills and techniques in agriculture and other technical areas with people in the underdeveloped world. Initial financial support came from remaining Point Four funds. The first volunteers went to Egypt, Jordan, Iraq, Nepal, and Laos. In the late 1950s the program expanded to Vietnam, Cambodia, Ghana, and Liberia. Exceptional early leadership was provided by Dr. John Nofsinger, who as a young man had been

a volunteer teacher during the American occupation of the Philippines. IVS continued operation until 2003, when it closed due to a lack of funding. It had had much of the same spirit as the Peace Corps (Nofsinger also served as an advisor to Sergeant Shriver during the Peace Corps startup).

5. Lam Quang and his family were evacuated to a refugee camp in the Philippines during the fall of Saigon in April 1975, eventually landing in Westminster, California, where he became a member of the city council, the first elected official of Vietnamese descent in the United States. In 2006 he was named by the Orange County newspaper as one of the hundred most influential citizens in the history of the county, including Spanish and Mexican times. He credits his early job with Rural Affairs as helping instill the self-confidence necessary to start his own business in Vietnam before the fall of Saigon and to become a leader in his community in the United States.

6. A copy of the "USOM *Provincial Representatives Guide,*" January 1963, author's files.

7. Some idea of the range of tasks undertaken by the provincial reps can be gleaned from a handwritten to-do list in the author's file, made by John O'Donnell for Kien Hoa Province and dated December 1964. "1. Get quarterly report from MAAG. 2. Get copy of voucher for relocation Binh Hai District (124 families). 3. Prepare report on health workers. 4. Prepare financial statement and monthly report for December. 5. Check supply records on PL 480 food and cement. 6. Location and power output of generators in Province. 7. Report for economic development team not yet ready. 8. Dredging projects; Relocation plans and requirements. 9. Discuss fertilizer plan. 10. Discuss gasoline problem. 11. List of militia and list of officials trained by hamlet. 12. Hamlet defense plan (Lt. Goff of MAAG). 13. Get rubber stamp with ink pad for hamlet dedications. 14. Discuss with Mr. Thanh 50,000 sweet potato cuttings, where can they be planted? 15. Chieu Hoi Center funds—self-help project. 16. Generator installation at Giao Hoa. 17 Giang Tram dispensary. 18. Village tool kits—which hamlets or villages? 19.Self-Help projects—visit all hamlets given money—Prepare report—plans for future use of money. 20. Truck to Saigon to pick up miscellaneous items. 21. Radio for Chieu Hoi center. 22. Ping pong set for Chieu Hoi Center. 23. Defense works for Chieu Hoi Center—responsive defense force. 24. Release table cloths for towels for Chieu Hoi Center. 25. Aspirant Duyet—has lousy training program, slapped a Hoi Chanh (returnee). 26. Reactivate Thoi Thuan agroville as resettlement area for Hoi Chanh who can't go home. Provide 3,000 piasters to build a house, 5 sacks cement, 5 pigs, plant sweet potato cuttings, bulgar wheat and cooking oil and 20 piasters a day for working to improve center, 50 ducks, 10 chickens. Assign one company of Civil Guard as security using agroville as base for patrols—clear surrounding area to make max use of air strikes for defense. 27. Need organization chart for land reform, NACO (agricultural credit), agriculture and livestock provincial services. 28. What is organization at village level? How many villages have committees? 29. How many hectares available through land reform program? How many hectares now completely owned? 30. Education—teacher training programs—self-help vs. official USOM sponsored?—teacher salaries. 31. Rural police—concept—Identification of VC agents. 35. 5 KW generator for ferry landings on the Hem Luong River."

8. Karnow, *Vietnam,* 617. See also Mark Moyar's *Phoenix and the Birds of Prey* (Annapolis, Md.: Naval Institute Press, 1997), 244–54, where he analyzes in some depth what the North Vietnamese had to say about the impact of Phoenix on the loss of their cadres in the countryside, directly and for other reasons related to pacification as a whole. Historian Thomas L. Ahern, Jr., in his *CIA and Rural Pacification in South Vietnam* in contrast, is skeptical about the lasting effect of Phoenix achievements, particularly after CIA support was withdrawn in 1972.

9. Born in the imperial capital of Hue in 1924, Chau came from a prominent family. His grandfather was a great scholar and a high-ranking dignitary at the imperial court. His father had been a province chief, and the family was well known and respected by the Ngo family. Because of that, as well as his performance, he had, as the author discovered, President Diem's confidence and consequently some discretion in the hamlet program, particularly as to not playing the numbers game.

10. A copy of Walton's proposal for population control is in the author's files. At the time, the author was also concerned that the proposed hamlet police force might be turned into an American-financed expansion of Ngo Dinh Nhu's Republican Youth movement, which was not popular.

11. The next day Brent had asked "What's this about your going to see Secretary Thuan with Colonel Bohannon in shorts and sandals?" saying Thuan had complained. The author explained about Bo's habits and promised no more visits to government offices without tie and coat. Thuan told the author he hadn't complained, he just couldn't resist teasing Brent about some of his eccentric employees. The author got Bo to buy a pair of long pants, a regular shirt and jacket, and even a pair of shoes. Bo settled for a string tie but continued to wear sandals unless protocol demanded otherwise. An old Filipino friend from his guerrilla days against the Japanese said that Bo was so tough he never wore shoes, just like his men, and retained the habit when he could get away with it.

12. The most complete history on Chieu Hoi the author has seen was put together by retired sergeant major Herb Freidman and can be found at www.sywarrior.com/ChieuHoiProgram.html.

13. The arrangement of using commercial transport may be seen as abetting the VC in some areas. On the contrary, it was practical recognition by the Vietnamese government, which knew what was going on, that some compromises had to be made for the greater good of getting relief and other supplies to where they were needed by the population. Payment of such tolls was not widespread, but it did happen. Otherwise all shipments would have required Vietnamese army trucks and guards, which were needed for military operations. MAAG was unable to move its barbed wire down to the provinces precisely because it would have diverted vehicles and boats from supporting military operations.

14. A copy of an untitled memorandum by the author, dated December 18, 1962, reporting on this meeting is in the author's files. The memorandum was likely directed to the mission director, Brent, with copies to the ambassador, the deputy chief of mission (DCM), Trueheart, and the CIA chief of station, Richardson.

15. The author's impressions are taken from his contact with Hilsman at the time and from his reading of Hilsman's "A Report on South Vietnam," of January 25, 1963, described as a memorandum from Hilsman and Forrestal to the president, see FRUS 1961–63, Vietnam, vol. 3, 49–62.

CHAPTER 10: AN UNEVEN PATH

1. An army regiment under Colonel Lu Lan was responsible for a significant victory in April 1963, against a unit of Vietcong regulars. In an operation called "Dan Thang 106," aided by timely information from friendly villagers, a regiment of the 25th Infantry Division cornered a sizeable unit of Vietcong main-force regulars in a coastal swamp in Quang Ngai, annihilating them. According to captured VC accounts, two factors were responsible for the defeat: the hostility of most of the villagers and the army's effective use of armored personnel carriers. The result was almost the direct opposite of Ap Bac, yet it went largely unreported by the foreign press. The Delta was only a few hours' drive away, while covering central Vietnam involved arranging a flight and staying overnight.

2. The *Times of Vietnam* was an English-language newspaper published daily in Saigon. Gene and Anne Gregory, an American couple, were its founders and owners as well as its publisher and editor, respectively. Many of its stories were such manifest plants by the president's brother Ngo Dinh Nhu and Madame Nhu that the paper was widely regarded as the government's mouthpiece. The day after the coup against Diem the *Times'* office was wrecked by mobs.

3. Ap Bac was seized on by American reporters at the time as conclusive evidence that the Vietnamese couldn't or wouldn't fight. American losses heightened its importance. It was amply reported in various dispatches of the time and acquired iconic status in Halberstam's *The Making of a Quaqmire*

and Neil Sheehan's A *Bright Shining Lie.* Lately, in Mark Moyar's revisionist *Triumph Forsaken: The Vietnam War 1954–1965* (New York: Cambridge University Press, 2006), the battle has been cast in a more positive light, and Colonel Vann, who was the principal American advisor, is accused of having positioned the helicopter landing zone in the wrong place. My reaction at the time was that the battle was overhyped and certainly not the conclusive demonstration of Vietnamese army incompetence, even cowardice, it was touted to be. Nonetheless, it was certainly promoted by the National Liberation Front and Hanoi as a decisive engagement proving they could hold their own against American-inspired tactics using helicopters and armored personnel carriers. (Pham Xuan An would be decorated for Ap Bac by the North Vietnamese for supplying information about American helicopter tactics.) However, in general the VC continued to avoid pitched battles if possible. General Cao was known to be flaky and not very competent as a corps commander, despite the belief at higher MACV levels that he was a superior soldier. Rural Affairs did not detect at the time any demoralizing effect on the Vietnamese army, nor did the battle seem to have any practical impact on the pacification battle going on at the local level in the provinces.

4. Reportedly Diem had chewed out General Cao earlier when he was a division commander over a particular battle in which eighteen South Vietnamese soldiers had been lost (although VC casualties were much greater), and this had affected his subordinate commanders. There was no evidence that specific orders to avoid combat losses as an important objective were ever issued, but it is certainly possible that word of Cao's chewing out had a chilling effect within his command.

5. The need to save face, in this case by delaying the transfer of Major Nhut, was related to avoiding offense to Diem's brother Bishop Thuc, who was reputed to be his strong supporter. Face-saving as a general Vietnamese practice was imbedded in a culture of avoiding public humiliation and shame. Direct, on-the-spot, public firings were rare, as they were thought to reflect badly not only on the persons fired but on their families and superiors. Changes were often delayed and given rationales not related to reality. Face-saving occurs in Western society, but the cultural context is different in Asia.

6. The author's memorandum, entitled "Vinh Long Province," dated March 26, 1963, to Mission Director Brent about the long walls, is in the author's files.

7. The author later discovered that Phuoc had told Denis Warner in 1962 about his draconian approach to families with VC connections. See Denis Warner, *The Last Confucian* (New York: Macmillan, 1963), 14–15.

8. One of these ideas was getting American small towns directly involved by adopting Vietnamese strategic hamlets. Lansdale's 1961 story in the May 1961 *Saturday Evening Post* about Father Hoa's Binh Hung village had led a town in New England to adopt it as a sister community. The editors of *Reader's Digest* were interested in doing a story on the concept if we could get it off the ground. We wanted to get the American public involved on a person-to-person basis. Burns in Phu Yen was enthusiastic about it, and so was Secretary of Defense Thuan. Stoney offered his office in AID/Washington as a transit point for correspondence and in-kind assistance. Unfortunately, the funding crisis intervened, then the Buddhist uprising, so nothing happened.

9. FRUS 1961–63, vol. 3, Vietnam, 254–56. The diplomatic record shows clearly that discussions with the Diem government had been going on for over a month while Rural Affairs was kept in the dark.

10. Memorandum to Director Brent from the author, prepared April 30, 1963, of twelve pages, "Financing and the Future of the Counter-Insurgency Effort in Vietnam," is in the author's files and is mentioned in footnote 5 to embassy telegram 959 to State (FRUS 1961–63, vol. 3, Vietnam, 255).

11. FRUS 1961–63, vol. 3, Vietnam, 256–58.

12. Letter from the author to Seymour Janow, May 4, 1963 (in the author's files), to which Janow finally

responded with a letter dated May 15, 1963 (also in the author's files), urging him not to resign and encouraging Rural Affairs to do its best to make the system work.

13. Memorandum, "Conversation with Counselor Ngo Dinh Nhu on 7 May 1963," May 14, 1963, to the director of USOM (Brent) from the author (copy in the author's files).

14. Memorandum, "Conversation with President Diem on 27 May 1963," June 20, 1963, to the director of USOM (Brent) from the author (copy in the author's files). Also in the author's files is a copy of the report on the strategic hamlets, "Informal Appreciation of the Status of the Strategic Hamlet Program," June 1, 1963. A copy in French was transmitted to the president by the author, initially in summary form and then at full length, with a province-by-province rundown. The author also gave a copy of this report and of a second one, prepared in September, to Colonel Lac, on an informal basis, for his review.

15. Luong was a friendly bureaucrat and mainly Lou Conein's contact. It was nevertheless important to cultivate him, which I did, but my main contact for getting things done was Colonel Lac. Luong seemed constantly to keep his finger in the wind to see which way it was blowing, and he was not known for bringing anything except good news to Diem.

16. The main remaining subjects discussed were resettled hamlets in the Delta being too far removed from the inhabitants' ricefields; overextension of the program in the Delta; what to do about An Xuyen (Camau) and Chuong Thien—two particularly difficult Delta provinces; how to deal with the Plaines de Joncs (Plain of Reeds)—the swampy area to the southwest of Saigon, which was a VC stronghold and the site of the battle of Ap Bac; the advisory role of the Americans; and the tendency in some provinces to establish isolated combat hamlets in contested areas without adequate security. To all the issues raised Nhu had practical responses, if sometimes veering into abstractions.

17. Minutes of this meeting were recorded and are contained in "Memorandum for the Record, 6/8/63, signed by the author, Subject: Rural Affairs Meeting with Counselor Nhu on 29 May 1963," author's files.

18. This contrasts with the impression given by Philip E. Catton's *Diem's Final Failure: Prelude to America's War in Vietnam* (Lawrence: University Press of Kansas, 2003), that there was a large gulf between the American and Vietnamese approaches to the Strategic Hamlet Program. Despite, the wooly nature of Nhu's views about the applicability of "personalism," he could also be pragmatic in terms of the need for rural development once he understood that it involved villager participation, not handouts. At the beginning it was certainly true that Diem and Nhu had unrealistic expectations of what could be achieved by the population on its own and did not understand the adverse reaction caused by the burden of unpaid labor and excessive relocation. While the regime made exaggerated public claims of progress to counteract foreign criticism of the regime, the author got the impression that both Diem and Nhu were a lot more realistic about the numbers game being played in the provinces than they let on. Had the Buddhist crisis not intervened, the author believes, substantial modifications would have been made in consolidating existing hamlets, ensuring better security and in governing attitudes. Another indication that our views were being listened to was the widespread distribution later in the summer, by Colonel Lac with Nhu's permission (despite the Buddhist crisis and the coup atmospherics), of a seventeen-page, critical examination of the hamlet program, written by Bohannon, called *Notes on Strategic Hamlets,* in Vietnamese and dated August 15, 1963 (English copy in author's files). This pamphlet stated that the key to the program's success lay in motivating the population to defend itself and that this could only be accomplished by providing the population "with continuing concrete evidence of government concern for their welfare; with convincing evidence that the government is their government." Bohannon concluded that it would take a sustained effort, with the changes he recommended, three to five years to succeed. Another Rural Affairs report prepared around the same time for

AID/Washington's consumption estimated success would take another three years ("Social and Economic Progress Achieved under the Counterinsurgency Program in Vietnam through August 1963" dated September 1963, copy in the author's files).

19. A copy of this order, entitled "Clear and Hold Operations" and dated February 1, 1963, prepared by the MACV J-5 staff with quiet collaboration from Rural Affairs, is in the author's files.

20. FRUS 1961–63, vol. 3, Vietnam, 247–53.

21. Letter to General Stilwell, July 15, 1963, transmitting two memos concerning ARVN incidents observed by Rural Affairs personnel in Binh Dinh and Phu Yen provinces (author's files).

22. Rural Affairs provincial reps were hearing from American military unit and sector advisors that Vietnamese army units in the Delta appeared to avoid engaging the Vietcong, who too often were slipping out of their grasp (the author's classified memo to General Stillwell, "Opinions of Military Advisors in the Delta Provinces," July 30, 1963, in the author's files). General Rowny, who was doing a survey of combat operations in the Delta, made a similar report at around the same time, but it never sparked an investigation by the MACV leadership.

23. A copy of this memorandum to Ambassador Nolting, "Bombs, Rockets, Shells, Popular Support and the U.S. Interest," August 6, 1963, is in the author's files. In a message to State from Nolting dated April 25, 1963 (FRUS 1961–63, vol. 3, Vietnam, 247–53), concerning interdiction operations by American aircraft, he gave a green light to such operations, claiming a close study of the subject had been done by his staff with the Second U.S. Air Force. The argument was even made that "it also seems highly questionable to conclude that individuals affected by Farmgate [U.S.] or VNAF [Vietnamese air force] interdiction strikes, even if these individuals are basically anti-VC or at least not wholehearted VC supporters, are going to become sympathetic to the VC." No consultation was conducted with either MAAG sector advisors or USOM provincial reps, who were the only ones with firsthand knowledge of the adverse effect of many of these operations. Years later after General Abrams took command of MACV in 1968, he developed similar reservations about the adverse impact of airpower and limited its use in populated areas (Lewis Sorley, *A Better War* [New York: Harcourt, 1999], 220–21). This issue remains alive in both Iraq and Afghanistan.

CHAPTER 11: THE BUDDHIST CRISIS

1. The author learned from Vo Van Hai, the president's secretary, in early January 1963 that there was a scandal involving his close friend, Nguyen Dinh Thuan. Dr. Tuyen, the head of Vietnamese central intelligence; the minister of social affairs, Nguyen Luong; the director general of social welfare, Nguyen Van Hung; and Thuan had been skimming proceeds from the national lottery by selling tickets on the black market. Diem could not decide what to do, in the face of advice from Nhu to cover it up. Hai speculated that Nhu had known about the scheme all along and had done nothing to prevent it since the threat of exposure gave him a hold over both Thuan and Tuyen. That certainly fit in with Nhu's way of thinking. In any case, word had leaked to others in the government and was undermining the president's authority and support. Despite Thuan's key role in the government, Hai said, he and others felt that justice had to be done or support for Diem would suffer a severe blow. The author took the information verbally to Nolting, who listened and said he would take it "under advisement." Luong and Hung quietly resigned, as their only apparent recourse. In Hoang Van Lac and Ha Mai Viet's *Blind Design: Why America Lost the Vietnam War* (self-published), 130–31, Lac states he knew about it and had been asked by Diem to take over as chief of police to conduct an investigation, which he gracefully avoided by pointing out he was already the commissioner for strategic hamlets and could not do justice to both jobs. Lac attributes the resignation of four of Diem's ministers around this time to the demoralizing effect of the scandal. Earlier in 1962, Thuan had confided to the author he had been obliged to cooperate with Dr.

Tuyen "in everything" in order to remain in the palace. What "everything" meant was now clearer. Unfortunately, Diem's failure to confront this issue depressed the morale of, and fanned discontent among, his supporters who were not part of Ngo Dinh Nhu's circle. In that sense it made Diem more vulnerable when the Buddhist crisis erupted.

2. Saigon, telegram to State, FRUS 1961–63, vol. 3, Vietnam, 314.

3. Frederick Nolting, *From Trust to Tragedy* (New York: Praeger, 1988), 109.

4. John Mecklin, *Mission in Torment: An Intimate Account of the U.S. Role in Vietnam* (New York: Doubleday, 1965), 157.

5. State Department, telegram to Saigon, June 11, 1963, FRUS 1961–63, vol. 3, Vietnam, 381–83.

6. Ibid., footnote 5, 386.

7. State Department, telegram to Saigon, June 19, 1963, FRUS 1961–63, vol. 3, Vietnam, 402–404; also Saigon to State, June 22, 1963, 411–13.

8. Saigon, telegram to State, June 25, 1963, FRUS 1961–63, vol. 3, Vietnam, 413–14.

9. Memorandum entitled "Recommendations for Immediate U.S. Action" from the author to chargé d'affairs Trueheart, dated July 5, 1963, is in the author's files, with a copy in the Lansdale papers at the Hoover Institution [hereafter HI], box 49, no. 1373. Jonathan Nashel, in *Edward Lansdale's Cold War*, 123, claims that the author sent this as a telegram to the State Department. In fact, however, he had no authority to send telegrams to Washington. Apparently Trueheart held off any action awaiting Ambassador Nolting's return, as indicated by a follow-up memo to Nolting from John Mecklin, cited in the note that follows.

10. John Mecklin, "Eyes Only" memorandum to Ambassador Nolting, July 12, 1963, referring to the author's memorandum of July 5 to Trueheart, author's files. Nashel, in *Edward Lansdale's Cold War*, 124, finds the idea that Lansdale could have made a significant difference "fantastic." The author saw it as developing a practical scheme acceptable to Diem for creating a "prestigious assignment" for Nhu abroad, bringing his brother Luyen to replace him, thus helping recover Vietnamese political support for Diem from the army and his former supporters, in the first instance, while also mollifying the Buddhists and eventually providing a political opening for Diem's noncommunist opponents—in short, a new start.

11. "Eyes Only" memorandum to Ambassador Nolting "Conversation with Secretary Thuan on 9 July 1963 and Recommended Action," July 10, 1963 (copy in author's files).

12. Director of the Vietnam Working Group (Kattenburg), memorandum to assistant secretary of state for far eastern affairs (Hilsman), "Luncheon with Lansdale," July 24, 1963, FRUS 1961–63, vol. 3, Vietnam, 527–28.

13. Memorandum for the record, "Conversation with President Diem on 19 July 1963," July 25, 1963, copies to Ambassador Nolting, Director Brent, and Chief of Station Richardson. Trueheart was also given a copy, although his name is not listed. A copy is in the author's files.

14. Memorandum for the record, "Conversation with General Van Thanh Cao on 11 July 1963," July 12, 1963, copies to Ambassador Nolting, Director Brent, DCM Trueheart, and Chief of CAS Richardson (copy in the author's files). Reference to this memo can be found in FRUS 1961–63, vol. 3, Vietnam, 489.

15. A paper dated July 30, 1963, entitled "How The Initiative Might Be Taken Away from the Buddhists," in English and French, is in the author's files. The French copy was given to Secretary Thuan.

16. Undated copy of this draft letter is in the author's files.

17. Memorandum of a telephone conversation between (Harriman) and (Hilsman), August 1, 1963, FRUS 1961–63, vol. 3, Vietnam, 550.

18. In his June progress report Burns had estimated that 75 to 80 percent of the province's population was already in secure strategic hamlets. Some four thousand Montagnard refugees and thirteen thousand Vietnamese refugees from VC-controlled areas had been resettled in hamlets, over three hundred *Hoi Chanhs* (VC returnees) had come in, there were over two thousand armed hamlet militias in being, and 218 hamlet committees had been elected. Only eight VC attacks against the hamlets had occurred in June, and no hamlets overrun. Also, 150 hamlet self-help projects were either under way or completed, and seventeen hamlet schools had been finished.

19. Nolting, *From Trust to Tragedy,* 121.

CHAPTER 12: AMBASSADOR LODGE INTERVENES

1. Saigon embassy, telegram to the Department of State, August 24, 1963, FRUS 1961–63, vol. 3, Vietnam, 613–14, author's files.

2. Saigon embassy, "Operational Immediate," limited-distribution telegram to the Department of State, August 24, 1963, FRUS 1961–63, vol. 3, Vietnam, 611–12, author's files. By the use of "respond" Thuan did not mean a coup but resistance to further moves by the Nhus.

3. Roger Hilsman, *To Move a Nation: The Politics of Foreign Policy in the Administration of JFK* (New York: Doubleday, 1967), 485.

4. Telegram from the embassy in Saigon to the Department of State, August 24, 1963, FRUS 1961–63, vol. 3, Vietnam, 620–21.

5. Department of State, Top Secret, "Operational Immediate" telegram to the embassy in Saigon, August 24, 1963, signed by Ball. There was controversy over whether this cable had been properly cleared or not. General Taylor's views are recorded in his memoir, *Swords and Plowshares: A Distinguished Soldier, Statesman, and Presidential Adviser Tells His Story* (New York: W. W. Norton, 1972), 292–94, while Hilsman has claimed in an oral history interview at the Kennedy Library that it had been cleared by the president and all representatives of the relevant agencies.

6. Lodge cable summarized in telegram from Forrestal to President Kennedy at Hyannis Port on August 25, 1963. Cited in *Pentagon Papers,* vol. 2, 735.

7. Acting secretary of state (Ball) to Lodge, August 25, 1963, FRUS 1961–63, vol. 3, Vietnam, 635.

8. Conein knew General Don, Kim's brother-in-law, extremely well and had met Kim a number of times but did not know him well enough for mutual trust. Kim, on the other hand was much closer to Big Minh, the senior and most respected general in the army, than he was to Don. Without Minh's leadership there would be no coup.

9. The author never wrote up this meeting, assuming Conein would keep Lodge, and presumably Richardson, informed.

10. A similar experience would happen to Vlad Lehovich at a lunch with Lodge in 1965. Vlad was in central Vietnam when Ambassador Lodge suddenly sent a small jet to bring him down to Saigon for lunch, having heard that Vlad was doing great work in the provinces. Vlad expected to be asked about his work, but instead Lodge spent the entire lunch telling stories about his pre–World War II days in the horse cavalry. Afterward, Vlad heard from an aide that Lodge had said, "That Lehovich boy, good fellow, you can have a real conversation with that young man."

11. Lodge's conversations with Diem and Nhu are summarized in telegrams to the Department of State of August 26 and August 27, 1963, FRUS 1961–63, vol. 3, Vietnam, 644–45 and 651–53.

12. Ibid., 671–72.

13. Central Intelligence Agency station Saigon, telegram to the Agency, September 2, 1963, FRUS 1961–63, vol. 4, Vietnam, 90–92.

14. This meeting with Kim and Bui Diem was reported verbally to Lodge but never recorded in writing.

15. The points listed as part of the discussion with Bui Diem are in the author's handwriting on a sheet of legal-size paper with the title "Main points of BD's program which the G's have agreed to," author's files.

16. FRUS 1961–63, vol. 4, Vietnam, 20–22.

17. President to the ambassador in Vietnam (Lodge), FRUS 1961–63, vol. 4, Vietnam, 35–36.

18. An account of both meetings with General Kim was sent by the CIA station to the Agency and is contained in FRUS 1961–63, vol. 4, Vietnam, 86–88.

19. A copy of the September 2, 1963, *Times of Vietnam* is in the author's files.

20. Memorandum to the ambassador, "Conversation with a usually reliable, well informed source on 2 September 1963," September 4, 1963, author's files.

21. Interview with the president, Hyannis Port, Massachusetts, September 2, 1963, FRUS 1961–63, vol. 4, Vietnam, 93–95.

22. Memorandum to the ambassador, "Information from a Reliable Vietnamese Journalist in Contact with Colonel Huong, Chief of Staff at the Presidency," September 1963, author's files.

23. FRUS 1961–63, vol. 4, Vietnam, 84–85.

24. The source is Pham Xuan An, who related his belief about the seriousness of Nhu's contacts with the North during a long discussion with the author in May 2002 at An's home in Saigon.

25. Memorandum to the ambassador, "Comments of Colonel Hoang Van Lac, Chief of the permanent Bureau of the Interministerial Committee on the Strategic Hamlets on 5 September," September 5, 1963, author's files.

26. Memorandum to the ambassador, "Conversation with Vo Van Hai on 6 September 1963," September 7, 1963, author's files.

27. Memorandum to the ambassador, "Conversation with Denis Warner, Australian Correspondent, on 5 September," September 5, 1963, author's files.

28. Memorandum to the ambassador, "Analysis of the Situation and Necessary Actions," September 5, 1963. The author classified it "Top Secret" but, considering the lapse of time and everything published since, the author has no reservations about making it public. The memo devotes considerable space to outlining a strategy to isolate Counselor Nhu and indicate U.S. displeasure with him, short of completely cutting economic aid. In the eyes of many Vietnamese, who were desperate to stop Nhu and ideally save Diem, the United States appeared to be acquiescing to Nhu's extreme actions and losing both prestige and influence; the extraordinary criticism being published in the *Times of Vietnam* was not being answered. Copy is in the author's files.

29. Oral history of John Michael Dunn at the LBJ Library.

30. See Harvey C. Neese and John O'Donnell, eds., *Prelude to Tragedy, Vietnam 1960–1965* (Annapolis, Md.: Naval Institute Press, 2000), 197–98, Colonel Tran Ngoc Chau's contribution, "My War Story: From Ho Chi Minh to Ngo Dinh Diem." Another Vietnamese who worked closely with Diem and Nhu, General Hoang Van Lac, was skeptical, in conversation with the author in 2006, over whether Diem could have been separated from Nhu. The author posed this question to Pham

Xuan An in Saigon in 2002. As a journalist and a spy for the North, An had a particularly well-informed inside view of the palace. He thought it possible and that only Lansdale could have done it. Larry Berman, researching his biography of An, asked the same question; An confirmed his previous opinion. An said Lansdale was the only American Diem trusted.

31. In central Vietnam, the Buddhist situation varied from province to province depending on how it was being handled by the province chief. There were no open clashes, however, and Colonel Chau's arrival in the important port city of Danang had defused an ugly situation there. The reported sudden appearance of a Buddhist "Sacred Fish" in Quang Nam Province was widely talked about and believed among Vietnamese sympathetic to the Buddhists. It was an enormous carp, having supposedly first appeared in July after the Buddhist incident in Hue, believed to be a disciple, or even a reincarnation, of Buddha. It began to attract large crowds. Troops were reportedly sent by Colonel Tung's Special Forces in Saigon to kill it by tossing grenades into the pond, wiping out everything except the giant fish, which, it was said, kept swimming. Its indestructibility was considered proof that it was indeed miraculous. People began arriving to drink water from the pond, including army soldiers. Local officials abandoned any further attempts to kill it. The fish's indestructibility was interpreted as a symbol of Buddhist resistance to the regime. Whether all this was true didn't matter—it was Vietnamese perceptions that mattered.

32. A copy of this report, "Second Informal Appreciation of the Status of the Strategic Hamlet Program," September 1, 1963, is in the author's files. The report was a twenty-four-page narrative frankly appraising how the program was being implemented in each of the thirty-four provinces of South Vietnam. While optimistic about overall progress except in the Delta, the report made clear that success could not yet be claimed and described the basic reasons why. The program failed in some provinces and succeeded in others mainly because of the attitudes and leadership abilities of the province chiefs. The report found the best progress in the middle part of the coastal zone of central Vietnam and the highland provinces (II Corps), some progress in I Corps in the northern part of central Vietnam, some progress in III Corps (the area to the immediate north and west of Saigon), and good progress in only two provinces in IV Corps (the Delta).

33. State Department, telegram to the embassy in Vietnam, FRUS 1961–63, vol. 4, Vietnam, 130.

34. Former political counselor of embassy in Vietnam (Mendenhall), memorandum to the deputy assistant secretary of state for far eastern affairs (Rice), August 16, 1962, FRUS 1961–63, vol. 2, Vietnam 1962, 596–601.

35. Memorandum to Colonel Lac, "Consolidation of the Strategic Hamlet Program in the Delta," September 4, 1963, author's files.

36. Alsop, *I've Seen the Best of It,* 459–62.

37. Saigon embassy, telegram to the State Department, FRUS 1961–63, vol. 4, Vietnam, 137–40. This meeting with Thuan, as recorded in the telegram, also reported on a recent meeting of the Inter-ministerial Strategic Hamlets Committee, featuring a report from the IV Corps commander, General Cao. Cao claimed that his troops were becoming more mobile when in fact the number of fixed posts had increased. He also recommended that more modern weapons, such as carbines, not be supplied to the Civil Guard and Self-Defense Corps but they be armed with locally made guns (for which no manufacturing capability existed). The memo did not include the Long An situation, which the author had briefed Bohannon about verbally and suggested he try to take up with Colonel Lac and with MACV.

38. Joseph Alsop, handwritten memorandum to Michael Forrestal, n.d., "Vietnam, General, 1963" folder, President's Office Files, box 128a, JFKL.

39. Harkins, "Eyes Only" cable to Taylor, MAC 1649, September 9, 1963, National Archives, Department of State, Central Files, POL. 27, VIET S.

40. Taylor, memorandum for the Honorable Dean Rusk, Secretary of State, August 23, 1963, Subject: "Attached Cable from General Harkins," National Archives, Department of State, Central Files, POL. 27, VIET S.

CHAPTER 13: MEETING PRESIDENT KENNEDY

1. While the attorney general was included on the list of persons in attendance compiled by Bromley Smith at the time, he was not in fact there, as evidenced by his not making any recorded contribution to the discussion. It was understood that he had been occupied with an urgent civil rights matter.

2. The most complete record of this meeting is found in "Memorandum of a Conversation, White House, Washington, September 10, 10:30 a.m.," FRUS 1961–63, vol. 4, Vietnam, 137–40, 161–67. This account is amplified by the author's memory and some rudimentary notes he made at the time plus a summary that he sent in a letter to Colonel Bohannon in Saigon shortly thereafter (in the author's files). There are different versions of this meeting in Hilsman's *To Move a Nation* and Halberstam's *Best and the Brightest.* There is apparently a tape at the JFK Library of at least part of this meeting, referred to as "Vietnam—Mendendall and Krulak Reports, Tape 109/A44," which according to JFKL personnel is not likely to be released until the end of 2009.

3. FRUS 1961–63, vol. 4, Vietnam, 169–71.

4. Ibid., 171–74.

5. Harkins, telegram to Krulak, MACV 1675, September 12, 1963, FRUS 1961–63, vol. 4, Vietnam, 194–95.

6. Copy of the *Times of Vietnam* of September 23, 1963, is in the author's files. Curiously in this same article, an interview with Peter Barnett of Australian Broadcasting quotes President Diem as defending the government's decision to build strategic hamlets rapidly, even if some were overextended. It was impossible to know whether the president really believed this (in view of increasing internal evidence that the program was in fact overextended) or whether he was simply warding off criticism of the regime. The author believes he was more aware of problems with the program than he let on publicly but that to say so at this time would have been an admission that maybe the war was not being won and that therefore the government was in trouble.

7. FRUS 1961–63, vol. 4, Vietnam, 199–201.

8. The Nolting quotes are from his oral history on file at the LBJ Library. The author's response is from memory.

9. The letters cited in this paragraph are in the author's files.

10. Currey, *Edward G. Lansdale,* 254.

11. The report in question actually estimated that sixty-nine strategic hamlets had been overrun in Long An in August. A copy of this report is in the author's files.

12. A copy of the September 1963, *Times of Vietnam* is in the author's files.

13. Ambassador in Vietnam (Lodge), letter to the secretary of state, September 13, 1963, FRUS 1961–63, vol. 4, Vietnam, 205–206.

14. Ibid., doc. 120, 240–41.

15. Paul Kattenburg on audiotape to Anne Blair, cited in her *Lodge in Vietnam* (New Haven, Conn.: Yale University Press, 1995), 88.

16. Lodge, letter to Rusk, September 24, 1963, National Archives, Department of State, Rusk Files, lot 72 D, Correspondence-L.

17. Assistant Director for Rural Affairs, United States Operation Mission, Vietnam (Phillips), memorandum, Subject: "Comments on the Necessity for an Advanced Decision to Introduce U.S. Forces in Viet-Nam," FRUS 1961–63, vol. 4, Vietnam, 249–51. Forrestal's comment about the author is in footnote 1, 249. Blair, *Lodge in Vietnam,* interprets a phrase from this memo about ensuring "necessary funds to go around Saigon" as referring to funds to support a coup, whereas the sentence read, "with the necessary funds to go around Saigon, if this is required, *to keep the Province program moving*" [italics added], which clearly referred to the Provincial Rehabilitation Program, as it was known in American circles—that is, the Strategic Hamlet Program. This was a continuation of the author's idea of trying to isolate and push the Nhus into exile while keeping the counterinsurgency program operating.

18. According to Daniel Ellsberg, this account was an outtake by the publisher from the manuscript of his book, *Secrets: A Memoir of Vietnam and the Pentagon Papers* (New York: Viking Penguin, 2002). This outtake was given to the author by Ellsberg, who reconfirmed his recollections over the phone in 2006. He said the account had originally been meant to fit in at the break on page 104, in chapter 7 of *Secrets.* The account was retold in Seymour Hersh's *The Dark Side of Camelot* (Boston: Little, Brown, 1997), 427–28, and subsequently described in Howard Jones' *Death of a Generation* (New York: Oxford University Press, 2003), 365.

19. From a conversation between the author and Ravenholt in the Philippines in 1996, confirmed over the phone by Ravenholt in June 2007.

CHAPTER 14: THE OVERTHROW OF DIEM

1. No description of Buu's proposal was written at the time; the account is from the author's memory.

2. William Bundy, letter to the author, October 7, 1963, author's files.

3. "Report of McNamara's 27 September Interview with Richardson," FRUS 1961–63, vol. 4, Vietnam, 301–303. McNamara used "Richardson" as a code name for Nguyen Dinh Thuan and refers to him in the text as "R" (see footnote 2). In the author's opinion this was a desperate but sincere attempt by Thuan to use McNamara to persuade Diem to change course before a coup occurred. Of course, that served his interests, but it also served the interests of the nation. His picture of the political situation and the consequences of the status quo were quite accurate.

4. A copy of the *Times of Vietnam* of September 17, 1963, is in the author's files. What made the author so angry was that having been trying to save Diem, he was now being singled out as an enemy. It showed the length Nhu was willing to go to on the basis of hearsay about what the author may have said about Colonel Tung during the meeting in Washington with President Kennedy on September 10. Evidence of Nhu's paranoia and the spurious "intelligence" he was receiving was contained in a history of the coup written by a former ARVN officer reputed to be close to President Diem and serialized in a Saigon newspaper in 1970. The installment, dated September 16, 1970, sent to the author by Mark Huss, related the following conversation in the palace, which would have occurred sometime after the author's return to Saigon from Washington in September 1963. "Mr. Ngo Dinh Nhu asked, 'Have you been following up closely on Rufus Phillips?' Colonel Tung replied, 'Phillips still has his secret contacts with the Xa Loi Pagoda.' Mr. Nhu then ordered, 'Try to collect solid roofs against that man. He must be expelled from the Country.'" The installment went on to identify the author correctly as holding "a high position in USAID" but also claimed he was "working for the CIA" and that "As Colonel Tung had a special intelligence net covering Phillips, a net which included many beautiful women, every activity of this man was closely observed." While Rural Affairs had some very attractive female Vietnamese employees, it is doubtful they were working directly for Tung and the author had absolutely no contact with the Buddhists. The installment

also related that Nhu had recently attended a dinner with the CIA station chief, Richardson, at a Saigon restaurant with Nhu claiming, "Richardson 'is a very understanding man. The man I'm worried about is Smith" (that is, Dave Smith, Richardson's deputy).

5. The author's letter to President Diem dated October 7, 1963, marked "Private" and "Personal," is in the author's files.

6. The climate of hyper-suspicion then prevailing within the American mission is probably what engendered the rumor that surfaced that the author was holding "press conferences." The only incident that might be termed a press conference had been an informal meeting with some of the American press at the author's house back in July. The no-holds-barred session was attended by Mal Browne of AP, Jim Robinson of NBC, Pete Kalisher of CBS, Dave Halberstam of the *New York Times,* Nick Turner of Reuters, and Neil Sheehan of UPI and some of our area and provincial reps. They told the reporters that the real war was being fought at the hamlet level, it wasn't being covered, and it was being won in many areas. Most minds were not changed, but the transparency and honesty of what was said came through and was appreciated. Rural Affairs acquired respect and earned considerable trust, which was not the case for much of local American officialdom. A memorandum for the record about this meeting, entitled "Press Conference," October 8, 1963, is in the author's files.

7. Mecklin, *Mission in Torment,* 223.

8. FRUS 1961–63, vol. 4, Vietnam, 423, footnote 5.

9. Ibid., 445.

10. In two previous interviews, one on record at the LBJ Library and the other at the Laubinger Library at Georgetown University (Foreign Affairs Oral History program), the author described Diem's question to him as, "Are the military planning a coup?" Or, "Is there going to be a coup against me?" In reflecting back on this meeting and Diem's typical style of posing questions, which was not direct but indirect and conditional, the author believes the formulation presented in the current text is correct. Diem's question in French was *"Pensez-vous qu'il y aura un coup?"* and the author's response was, *"Malheureusement que oui."* Because the coup followed so precipitously on the heels of this meeting it was never written up, but it remains burned into the author's memory. A superficial and inaccurate use of this exchange was made by Tim Weiner in *Legacy of Ashes: The History of the CIA* (New York: Doubleday, 2007), 218, extracted from the author's interview located in Foreign Affairs Oral History at the Georgetown University Library. Weiner misidentifies the author as CIA rather than AID, which would have been clear had he read the entire interview. Also, Lodge did not send the author to see Diem, which is clear in the same interview.

11. Tape recording of White House meeting, October 25, 1963, JFKL, Presidential Recordings Collection, Tape 117 A53 (cassette 3 of 3).

12. FRUS 1961–63, vol. 4, Vietnam, 449. Also see Tran Van Don, *Our Endless War: Inside Vietnam* (Novato, Calif.: Presidio, 1978), 98.

13. FRUS,1961–63, vol. 4, Vietnam, 442–46. The author is indebted to Anne Blair, who brings out in *Lodge in Vietnam,* page 67, that Lodge did not report Diem's admission that he couldn't govern without U.S. aid in this particular cable but only reported Diem's apparently negative reactions.

14. Ibid. One could speculate that Diem was merely trying to buy time, but this was not his way of doing things. Diem was not intentionally deceptive, particularly in dealing with Americans. Based on the author's impressions of his character, it is more likely he had finally concluded that a compromise had to be reached that would in time, and with some face-saving, require the removal of his brother from the regime.

15. Copy of this memorandum of conversation with Thuan is in the author's files.

16. This description is based on a synopsis of what the author regards as the most reliable accounts, especially Lou Conein's testimony to the Church Committee (see *Report of Proceedings of the Senate Select Committee to Study Governmental Operations with Respect to Intelligence Activities*, June 20, 1975, National Archives, RG 46, box 47 of Church Committee Records). Minh seems to have been motivated by rage over the loss of face when Diem had refused twice to speak to him over the phone. In addition, when Minh went to Gia Long Palace to accept Diem's surrender, he discovered that Diem had been hiding all the time in Cholon. He then intercepted the personnel carrier carrying Diem and Nhu and gave his bodyguard, Captain Nhung, the order on the spot to execute them. Needless to say, the author did not know until years later who was responsible and would have not been willing to talk to Minh after the coup had he known at that time that he was directly responsible. Conein refused to point fingers at the time and would not fully reveal his complete version of events even to his friends until he appeared before the Church Committee.

17. Taylor, *Swords and Plowshares*, 301.

18. Presidential Recordings, dictation by President Kennedy on November 4, 1963, item 52.1, JFKL.

CHAPTER 15: THE NEW REGIME

1. To deny the allegations and clear the air, the author prepared a memorandum for the record entitled, "Alleged Attempts to Give political Advice to the Generals," November 5, 1963, which concluded, "At no time was any political advice solicited nor did I render any." The original source of the supposed complaint by the generals was never identified. The author had no time to find out or interest in trying, although he suspected interagency rivalry at work. Copies were sent to Lodge, Trueheart, and Brent. A copy of this memorandum is in the author's files.

2. Hoang Van Lac, *Blind Design*, 174.

3. Informal memorandum to General Le Van Kim, November 7, 1963, "Some Thoughts on the Strategic Hamlet Program," author's files. On the same day the author sent another memorandum to Kim about Nguyen Van Buu asking that arrangements be made to keep his ships in operation (they were essential to transport Rural Affairs fertilizer and other supplies to central Vietnam); reporting that Buu was willing to place his troops entirely under military command while paying them up to date out of his pocket; and requesting that he be treated justly. The latter memo had no effect: his troops were almost immediately disbanded, leaving a considerable security gap, and the ships were seized, remaining idle for a considerable period of time.

4. Memorandum for the ambassador, "Conversation with General Le Van Kim on 13 November 1963," n.d., author's files.

5. Memorandum for the record, "Conversation with the Prime Minister on 13 November 1963," FRUS 1961–63, vol. 4, Vietnam, 596–599. A copy of this memorandum is in the author's files.

6. A copy of the Bohannon memo dated November 7, 1963, is in the author's files.

7. The author met informally with General Minh and General Kim, at Kim's request, at his house back in late February 1963. After exchanging memories of meeting in the Delta in 1955, Minh wanted to talk about the Strategic Hamlet Program. Denouncing it bitterly, he said it was alienating people in the Delta and was a Nhu pipe dream; President Diem was out of touch with reality and wouldn't listen to anyone. The army was poorly organized and using the wrong tactics. Many of the lessons learned about civic action in the early days had been lost. When asked what he thought should be done differently, he said stop supporting the Strategic Hamlet Program. The author said we (the Americans) were trying to make the program work. We understood there were problems in the Delta, but the basic idea of village self-defense was sound and working better in central Vietnam, where there was less resettlement. What were his suggestions? He said nothing would work

under Diem. His government was in a nose-dive. The author learned later that one of Minh's relatives had been forcibly resettled in a strategic hamlet in Long An Province and that he had called Colonel Lac directly to complain. As time went on it became apparent that much of Minh and Kim's criticism of the program in the Delta, as well as criticism of army operations and behavior, was on target.

8. Memorandum for the record, November 20, 1963, "Conversation with General Duong Van Minh on 18 November 1963," see FRUS 1961–63, vol. 4, Vietnam, 603–607, author's files.

9. The author had given Kim on November 12 another informal memo, entitled "The Province Chiefs" (copy in author's files), containing an evaluation of good and bad province chiefs. Afterward, the author concluded it had little or no effect; wholesale changes in the province chiefs were being made mainly by the corps commanders, and the good were being swept out with the bad because of association with the previous regime. Personal relations with the corps commanders were also an important factor.

10. FRUS 1961–63, vol. 4, Vietnam, 608–11. Lodge's remarks show that he saw no connection between the Vietnamese need to develop a consensus responding to the widespread desire for a more representative and responsive government as a unifying and inspirational political cause, as opposed to just getting "on with the war." This disconnect would consistently cripple any effective American approach to helping the Vietnamese.

11. Secretary of defense, memorandum to the president, Washington, D.C., November 23, 1963, FRUS 1961–63, vol. 4, Vietnam, 627–28.

12. Memorandum for the record of a meeting, Executive Office Building, Washington, D.C., November 24, 1963, FRUS 1961–63, vol. 4, Vietnam, 635–37.

13. Ibid., 645–47, para. 7.

14. Copy of this letter to Lodge is in the author's files.

15. Bui Diem and Chanoff, *In the Jaws of History,* 114.

16. Ibid. The memorandum covering McNamara's meeting with the generals (FRUS 1961–63, vol. 4, Vietnam, 716–19) gives a more diplomatic version of the exchange but makes clear that McNamara grilled the generals as if they were his subordinates. Also the author found it interesting that the need for Minh to address the public was taken up by both McNamara and McCone at this meeting. According to Lou Conein, Lodge had prodded Minh along similar lines in an earlier meeting, telling him that after Kennedy's assassination President Johnson had gone on TV to reassure the American people; Minh should do the same. Minh's reply was, "It sounds good; give us TV," a remark that he paraphrased during the meeting with McNamara. Unfortunately, this top-level political dialogue of the deaf would become almost the norm for the next two critical years.

17. Secretary of defense (McNamara), memorandum to the president, Washington, D.C., December 21, 1963, "Vietnam Situation," FRUS 1961–63, vol. 4, Vietnam, 732–35.

18. Joint Chief of Staff special assistant for counterinsurgency and special activities (Krulak), "Report on the Visit of the Secretary of Defense to South Vietnam 19–29 December 1963," FRUS 1961–63, vol. 4, Vietnam, 723.

19. Ibid., 745–47.

20. Ibid., 753–58.

PART III: PROLOGUE

1. Source previously cited in note 23 to chapter 10.

CHAPTER 16: EVENTS GO WRONG

1. Letter from Bohannon to author in author's files.

2. Ibid.

3. The note from Lodge and the letter from Dunn are in the author's files.

4. Embassy in Vietnam, telegram to State, January 10, 1964, FRUS 1964–68, vol. 1, Vietnam 1964, 16–22.

5. Ibid., 22–24.

6. Paper with these comments is in author's files.

7. Department of State, Central Files, POL. 27, VIET S.

8. Harkins oral history, LBJ Library. Also see Moyar, *Triumph Forsaken,* 294. As a side note, Lou Conein told Stanley Karnow he had been tipped off as early as December that Khanh was plotting a coup and had reported it but that no follow-up occurred. Conein then left to receive his medal in Washington.

9. Saigon, telegrams 1442, 1443, January 30, 1964, Department of State, Central Files, POL. 27, VIET S, and MAC 321 of January 30, 1964, LBJ Library, National Security File, Vietnam Country File, vol. 2. The "good riddance" quote comes from Bui Diem and Chanoff, *In the Jaws of History,* 114.

10. FRUS 1964–68, vol. 1, Vietnam 1964, 47–48. According to the accompanying footnotes this cable was actually drafted by Bill Moyers, based on recommendations he had made to President Johnson, and was sent jointly by Rusk and McNamara to Lodge. It and subsequent urgings from Lodge in Vietnam and from Washington that Khanh launch an immediate offensive against the VC completely ignored the political reality that Khanh's priority was to consolidate his own and the new military committee's hold on power, typical of the aftermath of any government overthrow.

11. Ibid., 45–47.

12. Ibid., editorial note, 56, and footnote 2 on 48.

13. Ibid., 54–55. In this cable Lodge concluded, "If Khanh is able, his advent to power may give this country one-man command in place of a junta. This requires a tough, ruthless commander. perhaps Khanh is it." It was a complete misreading of the Vietnamese political situation and of the ability of any Vietnamese to impose his will and rule by fiat even if that were desirable.

14. Saigon, telegram 1641 to secretary of state, February 27, 1964, National Archives, Department of State, Central Files, POL. 27, VIET S.

15. The author's letter to Lodge has been lost but is referred to in Bohannon's correspondence with the author at the time (in the author's files), which also described Lodge's reaction.

16. The paper pointed out, "The nature of the struggle was primarily political." What was needed was "a viable political plan of action which the Vietnamese believe is their own." The military actions which flow from the plan might "seem primarily defensive in character . . . , but they were "part of an overall political offensive." Also, "In addition to leadership, an idea worth fighting for" was necessary. That idea that existed in the minds of many Vietnamese was "essentially the idea or ideal of political democracy." It "had different meanings for the Vietnamese peasant than the GVN administrator and soldier. To the peasant it meant effective local self government aided and protected by forces of the government responsive to his security, political and economic needs. To the soldier and administrator it meant the establishment of democratic institutions and above all leadership which respects the basic rights of the people." "Growing tangible evidences of political democracy," were "absolutely essential to inspire the administrators and soldiers to respond

to the needs of the peasants." The political plan proposed eleven concrete actions. The first was to provide for election to a new National Assembly from "free electoral districts." Simultaneous with the start of assembly elections, the existing Council of Notables would begin work on a new constitution to be approved by a combination of appointed and elected council members. Khanh should proclaim a clear approach to combating the insurgency, something like Magsaysay's "all-out friendship" toward the population and the insurgents who cooperate, or "all-out force" against the die-hards. This "could be understood by peasant and soldier alike." A national complaint and action commission was proposed, as well as other specific actions for making pacification effective. Afterward, the only idea that survived was a national complaint and action agency, which the Vietnamese actually established, but then there was no close-in American advice or financial support, so it went nowhere, though badly needed. A copy of this paper is in the author's files.

17. National Defense University, Taylor Papers, T-36-71.

18. Wilfred G. Burchett, *Vietnam: Inside Story of the Guerilla War* (New York: International, 1965), 219. Burchett was an Australian communist who was permitted complete access to the communist side of the war in the South. Naturally biased against the South Vietnamese and the Americans, he is generally reliable when directly quoting statements by NLF and North Vietnamese leaders.

19. For the "Vietnam wants to lie down" or similar "Vietnam go to sleep" versions, see Bui Diem and Chanoff, *In the Jaws of History*, 114–15, and Tran Van Don, *Our Endless War*, 126. For the "ruptured duck" version the author is indebted to Dolf Droge, on the National Security Council staff at the time, who based it on McNamara's mispronunciation of "Vietnam" as "Veetnaam."

20. FRUS 1964–69, vol. 1, Vietnam, 134–39.

21. Charles L. Garrettson III, *Hubert H. Humphrey: The Politics of Joy* (New Brunswick, N.J.: Transaction, 1993), 172–73.

22. Ibid., acknowledgments, xiii.

23. Thao's tomb was visited in 2002 by the author's college classmate and friend Putney Westerfield, who had known and befriended Thao back in 1956. Westerfield had been a case officer in the regular Agency station at the time; see Ahern, *CIA and Rural Pacification in South Vietnam*, 20. Although it seems Thao was a North Vietnamese agent or perhaps even a double agent, the author believes his influence over the Diem government was limited and notes that none of the coup plots in which he was involved before and after Diem actually succeeded, although he was certainly a destabilizing influence. Former NLF Minister of Justice, Truong Nhu Tang in *A Vietcong Memoir* identifies Thao as clearly on their side and claims he was influential in getting Diem and Nhu to overextend the Strategic Hamlet Program, thus undermining it. The author believes the push by Diem and Nhu for instant results had more to do with wanting to show a quick turning of the tide to counteract South Vietnamese defeatism and to stop any American move toward neutralization. Tang also thought Thao had cut a deal with the VC in Kien Hoa Province to stay quiet when he was province chief there, but he offers no specific evidence, and Colonel Tran Ngoc Chau, who succeeded Thao as province chief, found no specific evidence of a Thao deal with the VC. Thao had imported into the province a number of Hoa Hao as district chiefs whom Chau had to replace for ineffectiveness. From June 1962 to November 1963, Thao was an inspector with the Strategic Hamlet Program, but Colonel Hoang Van Lac, who was in a position to know, describes Thao as having very little practical influence over the program. It seems probable his role has been posthumously exaggerated by the North Vietnamese to burnish their image of superiority by presenting a picture of the Saigon government as completely penetrated and under their secret influence.

24. Simpson, *Tiger in the Barbed Wire*, 164–65.

25. FRUS 1964–69, vol. 1, Vietnam, 477–84.

26. Ibid.

27. Ibid.

28. Ibid., 525.

29. General Clifton, memorandum for the president, June 25, 1964, "Comments on Senator Humphrey's Memorandum to the President on Southeast Asia," LBJ Library.

CHAPTER 17: GENERAL TAYLOR REPLACES LODGE

1. Halberstam, *Best and the Brightest,* 163.

2. A copy of the author's memorandum to Killen of July 9, 1964, "Vietnam," is in the author's files.

3. Neese and O'Donnell, eds., *Prelude to Tragedy,* 117.

4. Ibid., 232–33.

5. A copy of Fraleigh's letter to the author is in the author's files. Also see Neese and O'Donnell, eds., *Prelude to Tragedy,* 116–19, for Fraleigh's account of Killen's wrecking of Rural Affairs.

6. A copy of the letter from Director Bell is in the author's files.

7. Long afterward, a Rural Affairs Vietnamese assistant with close student and Buddhist contacts told me that Killen had actually called him in at the time and threatened to fire him. He said he told Killen, "You don't fire me. I can get a thousand students in front of your house tomorrow. Then I fire you."

8. Tran Van Don, *Our Endless War,* 128.

9. The account of the genesis of the provisional constitution and of the dispute that arose between Taylor and Khanh is based on conversations the author had with Conein when Conein returned to the United States in the fall of 1964 after being recalled by Taylor. Little of this found its way into official correspondence, except for the exchanges between Taylor and Khanh at Vung Tau, but there is little reason to doubt the essential veracity of Conein's account. It was vintage Taylor in terms of how he dealt with the Vietnamese. Why Taylor's staff was not more sensitive to the local political hazards of such a unilateral move by Khanh and did not warn Taylor, or if they did, why he ignored it, is not revealed by any written records that the author has been able to locate.

10. FRUS 1964–69, vol. 1, Vietnam, 682–85. Three days before his meeting with Khanh in Vung Tau, Taylor did express "concern over renewed instability which will result from these sweeping changes" (ibid., 672), but then at his subsequent meeting with Khanh gave him a go-ahead, saying any internal problems resulting from the new constitution were Khanh's affair. It was a comedy of errors that, unfortunately, and along with much else occurring in 1964, resulted in the further dissolution of effective Vietnamese government and hence would set the stage for massive American intervention.

11. Conein related the events surrounding his return to the United States to the author at the time. Sam Wilson was present in Saigon when Conein made his phone call to General Duc. He confirmed Conein's story about this to the author in 2006.

12. A copy of the memorandum, dated October 29, 1964, is in the Humphrey Collection at the Minnesota State Historical Society. Another is in the author's files, and it is described by Charles Garrettson in *Hubert H. Humphrey,* 160–61.

13. Neese and O'Donnell, eds., *Prelude to Tragedy,* 119–21.

14. Ibid., 123.

15. FRUS 1964–68, vol. 2, Vietnam, 444.

16. A complete copy of this paper is in the author's files and is substantially quoted in Garrettson, *Hubert H. Humphrey,* 183–84.

17. Ibid.

18. Ibid.

19. See also note 3 of this book's preface for a description of Sung's paper. Characterization of Vietnam as in the midst of revolution went at least as far back as Paul Mus's *Viet Nam: Sociologie d'une guerre,* originally published in 1952. Mus saw Vietnamese society as being in a state of turmoil and flux, cut loose from its Confucian roots and from its more recent colonial past. (I had first read Mus in 1954 and continued to think that "revolution" was the most accurate single-word description of the Vietnamese political scene.) This characterization was widely used by the Vietnamese themselves to describe the political and social situation and would be picked up by such writers as Bob Shaplen, who wrote influential articles about South Vietnamese politics for the *New Yorker* and entitled one of his books *The Lost Revolution.*

20. A copy of the complete article, published in the April 1965 edition of *Pageant,* is in the author's files.

21. Ibid.

22. Ibid. At the awards ceremony Father Hoa also said, "When fought as a conventional war we really have no chance to win. How can we explain to a mother when her child is burned by napalm; how can we expect a young man to fight for us when his aged father was killed by artillery fire? Indeed, how can we claim to be with the people when we burn their homes simply because those houses happened to be in communist controlled territory." Father Hoa's comments might seem somewhat "Pollyannaish," but he was a tough and realistic combat leader who understood how to win this particular kind of war. Unfortunately, after Diem's overthrow, Father Hoa fell into increasing disfavor with the succession of Vietnamese governments due mainly to uninformed accusations that he had received undeserved special support from Diem. In the confusion of Khanh's reign and American disconnection, the outside support upon which he depended for the transport of essential supplies gradually evaporated. Eventually, his presence became a sovereignty issue, and an inadequate Vietnamese commander was appointed, which resulted in the outpost's complete decline.

23. Karnow, *Vietnam,* 398–99. Taylor's telegram of December 20, 1964, describing the meeting did not give the details of what he said to the generals; see FRUS 1964–68, vol. 1, Vietnam, 1014–16. However, Taylor's offending words are described in a later message sent by Deputy Ambassador Johnson about his conversation with two Vietnamese officers, Thieu and Cang, who had been at the meeting with Taylor (ibid., 1053).

24. Ibid., 1058. President, telegram to the ambassador in Vietnam (Taylor). According to the footnotes this cable was drafted at the LBJ Ranch. Who suggested making use of the "specialized skills of men who are skillful with Vietnamese" is not clear.

25. FRUS 1964–68, vol. 2, Vietnam, 12–18.

26. This feeling was shared by individuals as different as Bui Diem, Colonel Chau, Colonel Lac, and General Kim, among others, but the hoped-for American interest in and support for Vietnamese political reform was not a priority for General Taylor. Writing about the American side of the aid equation, Colonel Lac stated, "If aid to Asian peoples is to be effective it must recognize Asian sensitivities and aim at the development, not of economic improvement alone, but of national patriotic spirit and just and democratic development." (Translation into English from Lac's book, *A Solution to the Problem of Vietnam,* published in Saigon in the spring of 1965. This excerpt is in the author's files.) With the exception of the pressure exerted by the Vietcong insurgency, many of the conditions cited as insurmountable handicaps by Taylor also existed in 1954 and 1955.

27. Taylor, *Swords and Plowshares,* 334.

28. FRUS 1964–68, vol. 2, Vietnam, doc. 17.

29. This memo, located at the LBJ Library, was cited by Taylor's son, John M. Taylor, in his biography of his father, *General Maxwell Taylor: The Sword and the Pen* (New York: Doubleday, 1989), 311 and 312, as evidence of backstabbing in Washington. Bundy's comments are a good description of Taylor's personality and make clear why he could not communicate effectively with the Vietnamese. When asked about it in 1987, McNamara said simply that General Taylor's performance as ambassador "had been superb at all times"; Bundy said, as he looked back, that "it was not the ambassador but the situation that was basically at fault." The truth was that the administration from the president on down had their doubts but had no way of replacing Taylor without demeaning him and having it appear the president had made a mistake. Taylor was simply unequipped by his personality and nature, as well as by the formality of his position, for the vital political side of his job and was too proud to admit he needed help. In this he very much resembled another American general dispatched to Vietnam as ambassador in 1954, J. Lawton Collins.

30. The author's favorable opinion about Quat's convictions is based on what Quat told Lansdale and the author during a 1964 visit to Washington as foreign minister when General Khanh was in power. He wanted understanding of American involvement, which he explained in great detail to Vice President Humphrey, in giving close-in political advice to General Khanh and others to rally the nation and push for a constitutional process. Neither his manner or his words indicated he thought this was a springboard to personal power. According to Bui Diem, who knew him extremely well, he was not that kind of person. Also according to Bui Diem, since Quat knew he lacked a political base in the south when he became prime minister in early 1965, he thought his greatest contribution was to get a process started that would lead eventually to civilian government.

31. Robert Shaplen, *The Lost Revolution: The U.S. in Vietnam, 1946–1966,* rev. ed. (New York: Harper and Row, 1965), 257. Shaplen went on to say (258), "American diplomats always seemed to want to deal only with the top men of the country, and they consequently missed a great deal of what was going on below the surface."

32. A complete text of this memo can be found in Garrettson's *Hubert H. Humphrey,* app. E, and in the author's files. Humphrey argued not about the military aspects of the bombing decision but about its political effect in the United States, which he thought was the best way to reach Johnson.

33. Carl Solberg, *Hubert Humphrey: A Biography* (New York, W. W. Norton, 1984), 274.

34. Garrettson, *Hubert H. Humphrey,* 186–87, based on an interview by Garrettson with Moyers.

35. National Security Files, LBJ Library, Vietnam Country File, box 40, vol. 30, 127d–27f.

36. Ibid., 127b.

37. Ibid., 127.

38. Bui Diem and Chanoff, *In the Jaws of History,* 137.

39. Lewis Sorley. *Honorable Warrior: Genereal Harold K. Johnson and the Ethics of Command* (Lawrence, Kansas: University Press of Kansas, 1998), 304.

CHAPTER 18: THE LANSDALE MISSION

1. Author's recollection from conversations with Lansdale in July 1965, also described in Currey, *Edward G. Lansdale,* 292.

2. Hoover Institution, Lansdale Collection [hereafter HI LC], box 99, folder 6. Extracts as quoted from Lodge's memo of instructions are contained in a thirty-seven-page chronology of the Saigon Liaison Office (SLO) activities.

3. The *Washington Evening Star* of July 19 had carried a story by John Wheeler headlined, "U.S. Bombs Kill Innocents," describing a friendly village destroyed by American airpower in support of the Vietnamese army because a Vietcong unit had temporarily occupied it. A U.S. officer was quoted as explaining, "We usually kill more women and kids than we do Vietcong but the government troops just aren't available to clean out the villages so this is the only way." Such articles generated anxiety among many of us that American units were likely to have an even greater adverse impact by their much greater firepower unless this line of thinking was changed.

4. Memos to the President, LBJ Library, National Security File, vol. 13. In expressing concern about the inevitable adverse effects on the civilian population of the way American units were likely to fight, Lansdale tried to alert Lodge to this problem, but it would be largely ignored for most of Westmoreland's tenure as commander of MACV.

5. Ibid. Accompanying memo of McGeorge Bundy transmitting Lodge's memo to President Johnson.

6. Some like Barry Zorthian, the head of JUSPAO in Saigon, who talked to Lansdale in Washington at the time, thought him incredibly naïve about what he could accomplish, because he would talk about inspiring a democratic revolution, changing the way the Vietnamese were fighting the war. To Zorthian, "Lansdale was one of these unrealistic, fuzzy-headed guys who were living in the past" (Grant, *Facing the Phoenix,* 265). To those whose main experience was in managing large burcaucracies Lansdale's approach would have sounded simplistic and naïve. His focus was entirely on persuading the Vietnamese to do the right thing for their country, using his ability to teach and to advise on what the right thing was, in terms the Vietnamese could accept as their own and act on. He knew only they could win the war, not us. It was not something which could be readily explained without sounding simplistic .

7. The new members included Mike Deutch, an ingenious economist/engineer who had worked as a consultant to the Pentagon; Daniel Ellsberg, one of McNamara's "whiz kids" in the Pentagon; Hank Miller from USIA, who had long been personally close to Lansdale; and Charles Choate, a Boston attorney in private practice who was an expert in constitutional law. Dave Hudson, whom I had recruited for Rural Affairs, was picked up locally at my suggestion as liaison with USOM Provincial Operations. Bert Fraleigh, back on duty with USOM, supported Lansdale by informing him about rural development problems and opportunities and participating in strategy sessions. Bernie Yoh, coming out on his own, functioned as an outside gadfly with good local Catholic connections until his freewheeling got him crosswise with influential Vietnamese. It is worth noting that for those with established government positions, going out to Vietnam with Lansdale was not going to enhance a career. It was obvious from prior experience that bureaucratic enemies would be generated. For those with families it was a considerable sacrifice, since dependents were no longer allowed in Saigon. For members of his original team, it was a display of loyalty based on firsthand knowledge of how effective Lansdale could be and how he dealt with those who worked for him.

8. Keyes Beech Oral History, LBJ Library.

9. Quote is from an anonymous source to Lou Conein, who passed it on to the author in 1966.

10. Corruption was an endemic problem that became worse with the succession of military governments. While it was mainly their wives and relatives who handled the business side of it, the husbands were complicit, of course. After the fall of Saigon, however, it was possible to measure most of those who had been corrupt by who arrived in exile largely penniless and who came with means. Among those who were known to have little or no means were General Ky, Generals Don, Lac, Lu Lan, Loan, and Ton That Dinh, and Bui Diem, in addition to those of course who got out later after being subjected to the North Vietnamese gulag, such as General Kim and Colonel Chau.

11. HI LC, box 55, folder September. The author briefed Lansdale the next day on this conversation, but the memo chronicling the meeting with Bui Diem on September 5 was not formally typed up until September 24.

12. Memorandum of conversation between General Cao (Cao Dai) and Rufus Phillips on September 10, 1965, ibid.

13. Two memorandums for the record on conversations with Lieutenant Colonel Chau, province chief of Kien Hoa Province, on September 11 and 12, subtitled "pacification" and "political," ibid.

14. Neese and O'Donnell, eds., *Prelude to Tragedy,* 199–200.

15. The author's very frank discussion with Chau about American strategy is recounted from memory; the account is generally the way Chau remembers it.

16. Huss, mentioned earlier as a source of information for the author, had worked previously for Lansdale in the Philippines, which facilitated a working link between Colonel Lac and Lansdale when the latter arrived back in Saigon in 1965. In 1964, the author and Lansdale persuaded Huss that his talents were underutilized selling cars in Baltimore and that he should join Rural Affairs in Saigon.

17. The author has not been able to find the cable in question in the National Archives, but Deutch claimed at the time that it had been sent as he described it.

18. Memorandum to Charles Mann, "USOM Support of Rural Construction (pacification)," September 23, 1965, HI LC, box 96, folder 6.

19. Lansdale, letter to the author, October 19, 1965, HI LC, box 54, folder Rufus Phillips (1).

20. Memorandum for the record, "Conversation with Bui Diem on 24 September 1965," September 24, 1965, HI LC, box 55, folder September.

21. Remembering what had been done with USIS help in making Bui Diem's film *Fire and Shadow* back in 1956, the author talked to teammate Hank Miller about Kim. Later Hank would tell the author he had talked to Barry Zorthian about Kim but that nothing came of it. Zorthian was too preoccupied with running his own bureaucracy and trying to manage difficult relations with the U.S. press. It would have taken an unusual degree of cooperation, mixing funding from the CIA with material support from JUSPAO, for Kim to make films, aside from clearing the way on the Vietnamese side. Such a cooperative approach was practically impossible in the prevailing bureaucratic atmosphere.

22. Memorandum to Lansdale, "Religious Reconciliation and Unity," September 28, 1965, HI LC, box 55, folder September.

23. Memorandum to Lansdale, "Thoughts on Rural Construction Concept and Organization," September 25, 1965, HI LC, box 55, folder September.

24. Letter to Lansdale (letter refers to "the Chief," who is Vice President Humphrey), October 5, 1965, HI LC, box 51, folder Correspondence, general.

25. Lansdale, letter, December 18, 1965, HI LC, box 54, folder Rufus Phillips (1).

CHAPTER 19: TRIUMPH OF THE BUREAUCRATS

1. FRUS 1964–68, vol. 4, Vietnam, 41–43.

2. Miscellaneous papers from the "Warrenton Meeting" are in the author's files, including Unger's presentation and presentations by various agencies and individuals.

3. Handwritten memo by the author in author's files.

4. Lou Conein, in his colorful and profane way, after he had heard about the meeting, would describe it as "the biggest American circle-jerk ever." The author felt like walking out after the first day. Had Conein been there, he wouldn't have lasted that long.

5. John Roche, memorandum for the president, November 4, 1966, LBJ Library, National Security File, Memos to the President.

6. Grant, *Facing the Phoenix*, 264. At this point, Lansdale had no further career ambitions except to help the Vietnamese succeed. For his previous "national security" efforts in the Philippines he had already received the nation's highest recognition, the National Security Medal (his was reportedly the third such award, after "Wild Bill" Donovan and J. Edgar Hoover), and the Distinguished Service Medal—twice.

7. Lansdale was given credit by some for much of the language of Ky's statement at the conference, but Bui Diem actually drafted it. Bui Diem and Lansdale were very close personally and met informally many times. Like much involving Lansdale and the Vietnamese, it was impossible to know where Lansdale stopped and the Vietnamese began. Expressions typical of Lansdale crept into Ky's speeches, such as the aim of democratic government being "to have something to fight for, not merely against communism, but for a nation of progress nurtured by personal liberty."

8. Currey, *Edward G. Lansdale*, 306.

9. Conversation between Sam Wilson and the author on June 8, 2006.

10. Lansdale, letter to Mike Deutch, June 22, 1966, HI LC, box 59, folder General. The author was sometimes abroad on business, so that Deutch, who was always in Washington was a recipient of letters intended for both when the author was absent.

11. Lansdale, handwritten note to Deutch, HI LC, May 15, 1966, box 54, folder Rufus Phillips (2), asking that it be shared with the author.

12. Drew Pearson, "Inside the White House" column, *Washington Post*, July 11, 1966.

13. In his oral history at the LBJ Library, Interview II, Lansdale relates that one of our officials, he did not say whom, actually asked Prime Minister (General) Ky, "Why don't you let me write out your policies the way Lansdale does in a cabinet meeting?" Lansdale had tried to explain to his fellow officials how he worked indirectly, but it just didn't take. Ky was, of course, offended by what the official said, and Lansdale was in the doghouse for several weeks until he was able to make it up to Ky.

14. Sometimes Lansdale went overboard to his own detriment in openly attacking others, particularly other agency types whom he felt were "shadow boxing" to make themselves look good. One outstanding example of his ability to get under the skin of others he felt were not up to their jobs was his behavior in a meeting between the Pentagon and the State Department over Vietnam policy in 1961. As related by Currey (232–33), Lansdale opened a meeting of the newly created joint agency task force on Vietnam he was chairing on behalf of Defense by stating, "I know the feelings of some of you. If you don't mind I'm going to take five minutes at the beginning. I'll tell you what you think of me and what I think of you. We'll get that out of the way. Then we'll get on with the business." This provoked extreme acrimony and undermined the Defense Department's bid to continue chairing the task force, which subsequently passed to the State Department. Other times his lashing out seemed justified, as when, for example, he got so upset with interagency bickering in a Mission Council meeting in Saigon under Lodge that he suggested the individuals engaging in it be sent out to fill body bags with dead American soldiers, "to let them learn what the hell Americans are doing in this country." See Al Santoli, *To Bear Any Burden* (Bloomington: Indiana University Press, 1999), 195–96.

15. See Karnow, *Vietnam,* 236, describing Lansdale as counting "on 'psychological warfare' techniques that resembled advertising techniques" and exuding "a brand of artless goodwill that overlooked the deeper dynamics of revolutionary upheavals, . . . oblivious to the social and cultural complexities of Asia." Karnow goes on to belittle Lansdale's approach to counterinsurgency in a training course as simple-minded and encapsulated by Lansdale's comment, "Communist guerrillas hide among the people. If you win the people over to your side, the communists guerrillas have no place to hide. With no place to hide, you can find them. Then, as military men, fix them . . . finish them." Karnow clearly didn't read the rest of the course. Winning the people over to one's side remains a central tenet of counterinsurgency, as set forth in the recently released U.S. Army and Marine Corps, *Counterinsurgency Field Manual* (Chicago: University of Chicago Press, 2007).

CHAPTER 20: REFUSING TO GIVE UP

1. Lansdale, memo to Ambassador Lodge, May 27, 1966, "The SLO Role," HI LC, box 52, folder April–May 66, General.

2. Lodge, memorandum SLO-Ed Lansdale, May 31, 1966, ibid.

3. Lansdale, handwritten note to Deutch (asking that it be shared with the author), May 15, 1966, HI LC, box 54, folder Rufus Phillips (2).

4. Daniel Ellsberg, *Papers on the War* (New York: Simon and Schuster, 1972), 195–96. This was recorded in a memo from Ellsberg to Lansdale at the time.

5. An's beat-up green Renault sedan, used to visit "Peace and Prosperity" village, is now displayed in a military museum in Hanoi, because he also used it to rendezvous with his couriers. See Berman, *Perfect Spy,* 174.

6. Memorandum to General Lansdale, "'Peace and Prosperity' Village, Gia Dinh Province: The Political War," August 21, 1966, HI LC, box 56, folder August 1–17, August 18–31, September.

7. See Berman's *Perfect Spy,* 179, in which Pham Xuan An confirmed the use of the "Peace and Prosperity Village" area as a staging ground for the 1968 Tet Offensive.

8. The author told Larry Berman, An's biographer, that he didn't see "how An could have ever bought into the Communist party line" (Berman, *Perfect Spy,* 71). An knew too much about the United States and about what the communists had done in the North after they took over in 1954 really to believe in communism as a creed. How he rationalized and maintained this schizophrenia remains a mystery. Maybe what it came down to was the fact that he had a familial duty to look after his mother and his own wife and children, and his mother would not leave Vietnam. Even if at any point he had wanted to abandon his role as a spy he couldn't have gone abroad with his wife and children, leaving his mother behind to face retribution, and he could not have remained in Vietnam, which would have put his life and that of his family and his mother in almost certain jeopardy. He would die of lung failure in 2006 from a lifetime of heavy smoking.

9. Bill Colby shared the same opinion of Vann—immeasurably effective but too much in command. See William Colby with James McCargar, *Lost Victory: A Firsthand Account of America's Sixteen-Year Involvement in Vietnam* (Chicago: Contemporary Books, 1989), 305.

10. Memorandum to Lansdale, "The An Giang Project," August 27, 1966, HI LC, box 56, folder August 1–17, August 18–31, September. The "sugar baby" watermelons were even more successful per square meter of tilled land than soybeans. Because these watermelons were perfectly round, like a full moon, they sold at a premium during Vietnamese New Year celebrations. Some farmers made enough money off this crop alone to begin replacing their straw huts with brick houses. When the Delta had been largely pacified by 1970–72, these crops had spread throughout the area and contributed to a wave of rural prosperity.

11. Some observers of the Vietnamese army believe that officers who had once been Vietminh were discriminated against by the majority who did not have that background. There may have been some of that, but the author does not believe it adversely affected Chau's career. Another reason for his not being promoted to general was his lack of participation in the coup against Diem, many of whose participants received instant promotions. He remained under some suspicion afterward because of his closeness to Diem.

12. The author distinctly remembers the memo he prepared for Lansdale about this meeting with Lac but has been unable to locate it in the Lansdale papers at the Hoover Institution. Page 26 of the SLO chronology in box 99, folder 6, of the Lansdale papers mentions the author's memorandum about his discussion with Lac on corruption.

13. Memo to Lansdale, August 30, "Conversation with General Le Van Kim on August 30, 1966," HI LC, box 59, Phillips Memoranda.

14. Lansdale oral history at LBJ Library, Interview II, gives a particularly vivid account of Lansdale's meeting with Ky and of Ky's willingness to meet with Thi, as well as how proud Westmoreland and Lodge were of their decision to back using force: "This was the way to settle things." Lansdale's comment was, "I hope to hell we don't fight the Russians this way or somebody else, because it's thoughtless. It really is. We're a brighter people than that, and I'd like to see us use some of our wisdom on these things."

15. See George M. Kahin, *Intervention* (New York: Alfred A. Knopf, 1986), 415–32, for a more complete description of the Buddhist revolt. The author does not agree with Kahin's characterization of the event as a defining moment in which the choices were a largely neutralist government with the Buddhists dominating an elected Assembly or the continued domination of the military. Had the United States been willing to take some political risks in advising Ky and acting as a go-between with Thi and the Buddhists, a more popular and unified national government might have emerged, capable of pursuing a better political strategy of undermining and overcoming the VC. This choice was largely Lodge's, who not only distrusted the motives of the Buddhists but had a deep-seated prejudice against elections, except as a public relations exercise, and a bias in favor of autocratic rule.

16. The author regarded the situation as sufficiently serious back in April to write Unger a memo saying he was hearing from Vietnamese friends that Ky had lost all moral authority and was likely to fail in the confrontation. With overt American support, Ky succeeded, but at a cost. Lodge pitched it in terms of Ky's having had no alternative except to use force; however, its use deepened the Buddhist split with the government and enhanced civilian distrust of the military while precipitating Tri Quang's hunger strike and placing the constituent assembly elections at risk. Although these elections would turn out to be a success, bitterness remained among the Buddhists about American interference, which would continue to undermine widespread political support for subsequent Vietnamese governments.

17. The SLO villa was the only American place in Saigon where many Vietnamese felt comfortable just dropping by and talking. These visits were sometimes inconvenient, but the benefits often outweighed the drawbacks. This was one of many small ways in which Lansdale would help the Vietnamese that seldom showed on the official scorecard.

18. Memorandum to Ambassador Lodge, "Conversation with Tri Quang on 2 September, September 3, 1966," HI LC, box 56, folder August 1–17, August 18–31, September.

19. Memorandum to William Jorden, "The Vietnam Elections—Ed Lansdale's Key Role," September 22, 1966, HI LC, box 59, folder Phillips.

20. R. W. Komer, letter to Lansdale, September 16, 1966, HI LC, box 56, folder August 1–17, August 18–31, September.

21. Lansdale, handwritten letter to Phillips, November 9, 1966, HI LC, box 59, folder Phillips (1).

22. Handwritten letter to Lansdale, November 26, 1966, HI LC.

23. Lansdale, memorandum, "The Battleground in 1967," November 8, 1966, Lansdale note to Walt Rostow and Rostow's note to President Johnson can be found at the LBJ Library, National Security Files, Memos to the President, box 11, vol. 15.

24. Memorandum to Ambassador Leonard Unger, "Comments on Ed Lansdale's Paper of 3 October 1966 entitled 'Future Plans,'" November 10, 1966, HI LC, box 59, folder Phillips.

25. Bohannon returned to Manila at the end of 1965, mainly because he disagreed with Lansdale's unwillingness to take on the bureaucracy in a frontal assault. Bo had a short fuse and couldn't stand bureaucracy, particularly being undercut by an establishment he viewed as composed of ignoramuses in how to fight the war. His attitude had generated complaints from all quarters. Conein had gone back with the CIA Saigon station in 1966. There he had gotten himself into trouble over an episode of boisterously throwing flower pots off the roof of the Brink's hotel onto the sidewalk below, where they sounded like grenades going off. He was subsequently banished to the most remote province in South Vietnam, Phu Bon, which he labeled "Phu Elba." Hank Miller had gone to the Philippines to head USIS there. Mike Deutch had left earlier because of conflicts with USOM. Ellsberg had transferred at his request over to Porter's pacification staff and Joe Baker had returned to CIA for an assignment in Paris.

26. See Roche's sarcastic memo to President Johnson of November 13, 1967, at LBJ Library, National Security File, Memos to the President. Roche had been away from Saigon for a year by this time, but he was echoing back-channel criticism of Lansdale by other detractors.

27. Memorandum to William Connell, "The Vietnamese Elections," July 25, 1967, author's files.

28. The real story was told the author long afterward by Bob's son, Ken Coate. Bob had been captured with another American after the Battle of the Bulge by Germans who decided to shoot them both. They were allowed to run for it. Coate was shot but not fatally, passing out in the snow, which staunched his wound and kept him from freezing to death. Somehow he made it back to American lines, where he was hospitalized, then sent back into action. He never knew what happened to the other man.

29. The author knew General Thieu's brother Kieu from the 1962–63 period and saw him at his request after the presidential election. His brother, Kieu said, intended to form an informal "brain trust" of selected advisors who would meet informally with selected Americans to work out ideas of what the new Thieu administration should do and how best to integrate American efforts. Unfortunately, this never came to fruition, and Thieu would continue to operate mainly as his own advisor. I told Kieu about Coate with the results as described. The meeting was an example of the access Lansdale and his group had to the Vietnamese and how if this access had been used proactively the Vietnamese government could be influenced in a positive direction. The memorandum of the author's conversation with Kieu, September 9, 1967, can be found in the Lansdale Collection, HI LC, box 59, folder Phillips.

30. The way Komer acted with the Vietnamese was often counterproductive. On one occasion, he reportedly insulted Thieu by pointing a finger at him in a way that was interpreted as giving an order in "an obscene manner" (Hoang Van Lac, *Blind Design,* 67). Lac also said, "Ambassador Komer can't even pacify himself. How can he lead the 'Hearts and Minds' program, pacifying the mass?" (301). The author would get an earful from Mark Huss about Komer's ineptness with the Vietnamese, which often came across as arrogance. Huss served as the principal liaison between Komer and Lac as the working-level point of contact for pacification.

31. George Wilson, "War's End in View—Westmoreland," *Washington Post* and, *Times Herald,* November 22, 1967.

32. Sorley, *A Better War*, 8. Sorley's account is based on an interview with General Donn Starry, who was present and heard it. Afterward Westmoreland would claim he never said it.

CHAPTER 21: CHANGE COMES LATE

1. Memorandum to the Vice President, "Report from Saigon—June 1968," n.d., HI LC, box 59, folder Phillips.

2. Ibid.

3. Bui Diem and Chanoff, *In the Jaws of History*, 276–77. In his description of this incident and the surrounding circumstances Bui Diem makes the ultimate point that "South Vietnamese corruption and political reform were simply not high on the American list of priorities . . . the emphasis was always elsewhere, on negotiations, and military moves and big-power diplomacy." Efforts were made to address corruption. At American urging a commission was set up to control corruption. Several province chiefs and lower-level military personnel were jailed, and one was even executed. Reading the official record gives the impression that something was being done about corruption. See Bunker's weekly report to the president of February 10, 1970, in Douglas Pike, ed., *The Bunker Papers* (Berkeley: University of California, Institute of East Asian Studies, 1990). Bunker says (vol. 3, 747) that he had "a very frank talk" with Thieu about corruption and that Thieu's response "was encouraging and constructive." However, corruption at the top was never faced or dealt with. See Stephen T. Hosmer, Konrad Kellen, and Brian M. Jenkins, *The Fall of South Vietnam* (New York: Crane Russak, 1980), 70.

4. This was reportedly authorized by Westmoreland. See Sorley, *A Better War*, 28.

5. Curiously, this was the same Benson I had met in the Pentagon in 1966. Recently back from Indonesia, he had expressed a keen interest in being assigned to help Lansdale in Saigon.

6. "Report from Saigon—June 1968." My reporting about District Eight particularly disturbed the vice president, according to Connell. Humphrey remembered it as a success story from his visit after the 1967 Vietnamese elections.

7. Sorley, *A Better War*, 28.

8. "Report from Saigon—June 1968." Abrams was reportedly disturbed not only that the VC had once again been able to penetrate Saigon during mini-Tet but also by the routinely upbeat nature of the stereotypical after-action military briefing, regardless of reality.

9. Sorley, *A Better War*, 24–25.

10. "Report from Saigon—June 1968."

11. Edward Lansdale Oral History, LBJ Library; Currey, *Edward G. Lansdale*, 323–24; also, told to the author by Dave Hudson after he left Saigon in 1968.

12. Ibid.

CHAPTER 22: HUMPHREY LOSES, NIXON TAKES OVER

1. The author was not present, but Lansdale told him about it afterward. It was like "having a pitcher of ice water dunked on you," he said. Also see Ellsberg, *Secrets*, 108. Ironically, Nixon as Ike's vice president had strongly supported Lansdale's efforts to ensure free Philippine congressional elections in 1951, which had severely undermined the communist Huks.

2. "Report from Saigon—June 1968."

3. Bill Connell, letter to author, author's files.

4. A copy of the author's presentation to the Democratic Convention Platform Committee is in the author's files.

5. Truong Nhu Tang, *Vietcong Memoir*, chaps. 21–24.

6. "Report from Saigon—June 1968."

7. A copy of this paper, "A Political Strategy for Viet-Nam," is in the author's files. Besides building on General Abrams' changed strategy of protecting the population, the paper focused on helping the Vietnamese make theirs a genuinely responsive government, including the armed forces, in attitude as well as in action. Immediate steps were to phase down and out those American programs that did not improve local security, Vietnamese administrative capabilities, or local economic and social development; to reduce the numbers of American advisors in AID and CORDS; and to establish joint Vietnamese-American commissions to oversee agricultural development and the economy. The recommended focus at home was to reestablish a dialogue with the American people. Rather than rationalizing why we acted, we needed to explain, in terms the American people could understand, what we were trying to achieve. We should talk with the public, not at it, practice understatement, involve the Congress, establish an interagency Vietnam information office, and set up as a medium for public involvement—a "blue ribbon" advisory committee with widespread participation by the Congress, the universities, the press, business, labor, and minorities.

8. Garrettson, *Hubert H. Humphrey*, 199.

9. Hubert H. Humphrey, *The Education of a Public Man* (New York: Doubleday, 1976), 349.

10. Nguyen Tien Hung and Jerrold L. Schecter, *The Palace File* (New York: Harper and Row, 1986), 23.

11. Bui Diem and Chanoff, *In the Jaws of History*, 244; Bui Diem says two messages he sent to Saigon had some relevance. One was dated October 23, 1968: "Many Republican friends have contacted me and urged us to stand firm"; another on October 27 said, "I am regularly in touch with the Nixon entourage." By "entourage" Bui Diem said he meant Anna Chennault, John Mitchell, and Senator John Tower. Thomas Powers, *The Man Who Kept the Secrets* (New York: Alfred A. Knopf, 1979), claimed that during the week which ended on the twenty-seventh, a cable was intercepted from the Vietnamese embassy in Washington to Saigon explicitly urging Thieu to "stand fast against any agreement until after the election." Bui Diem says in his memoirs that he could see how his October 27 message "in the charged re-election atmosphere . . . constituted circumstantial evidence for anybody to assume the worst," but he was not part of any deal. The author believes him, because he was not sufficiently trusted by Thieu to be a party for any explicit deal, if indeed one was made, as opposed to the circumstance of Thieu's already wanting to favor Nixon and being presented with a specific opportunity to help him get elected while increasing his own popularity in South Vietnam.

12. Theodore White, *The Making of the President 1968* (New York: Athenaeum, 1969), 446.

13. By fate, Sven Kraemer became the author's brother-in-law after meeting his future wife, Carla, Barbara's younger sister, at a restaurant celebration in October 1968 over the finishing of the policy paper—at least one positive outcome of this paper-writing exercise.

14. The author protested to the few people he knew still in the government and wrote a letter to Murray Chotiner, an inside advisor to Nixon, without result.

15. It was impossible to have a rational discussion with many peace activists. Their issue was never the real country of Vietnam or the real Vietnamese people; it was mainly us, the morality of warfare, the immorality of our government, and the draft.

16. Henry Kissinger, *White House Years* (Boston: Little, Brown, 1979), 1035.

17. Bui Diem and Chanoff *In the Jaws of History*. See pages 288–94 for a discussion of what happened and the importance Ambassador Diem placed on this issue. His failure to influence Thieu in a more democratic direction would be one of the main reasons for his resignation as ambassador (293–95).

18. See Colby, *Lost Victory*, chap. 16, "Pacification on the Offensive," and Sorley, *A Better War*, chap. 5, "Pacification," and chap. 13, "Victory." For a much more pessimistic view, see Ahern, *CIA and Rural Pacification in South Vietnam*, 410–413. Ahern maintains that the South Vietnamese never had the capacity to win over the rural population because of ingrained attitudes which "never sought to mobilize the countryside, but only to preserve the economic and social status quo." The author disagrees with this conclusion. Ahern correctly puts his finger on motivation as the key to determining which side was going to win but then consistently downgrades the noncommunist Vietnamese in this regard. Ahern also makes the case that the American (not exclusively CIA) approach was flawed by "misunderstanding of the nature of the challenge, and by the prevailing . . . confidence in the superiority of American material resources and managerial techniques." The author agrees this was a serious flaw, but it was not universally shared by all involved, as shown by episodes recounted elsewhere in this book.

19. Tran Van Don, *Our Endless War*, 229. The state of security in the provinces was attested to by many others, including NSC staffer Sven Kraemer. In an e-mail to the author on November 3, 2007, Sven stated he made nine visits to Vietnam during the 1969 to 1973 period. During three visits in 1973 he securely traveled all over Vietnam with a single interpreter and only one or two Vietnamese soldiers, who mainly drove.

20. Harry G. Summers and Stanley Karnow, *Historical Atlas of the Vietnam War* (Boston: Houghton Mifflin, 1995), 148. While this statement by North Vietnam's Nguyen Co Thach, who became foreign minister, apparently referred specifically to the Phoenix program, an examination of what happened would also give credit to the decimation of the VC cadre caused by Tet and the failed VC offensives that followed in 1968, as well as to the entire pacification effort including improved local self-defense, the Chieu Hoi program, improved ARVN operations, village elections, effective land reform—particularly in the Delta—and economic and social improvement. When combined with security, these factors helped turn most of the population away from the Vietcong.

21. Sorley, *A Better War*, 337–40.

22. Hosmer, Kellen, and Jenkins, *Fall of South Vietnam*, 137–50. As an example, only five out of thirty C-130s needed to transport troops and supplies were operable at any one time, due to a lack of spare parts. The number of rounds per infantryman going into combat was cut from four hundred to two hundred, affecting combat capability and morale. The average supply rate of artillery shells in 1975 was less than 10 percent of what had been supplied in 1972 during the Easter Offensive. Fuel shortages affected aircraft and vehicle operability.

23. The causes of the final collapse are many, but the lack of adequate time at the very end of the U.S. withdrawal after the accords to prepare the South Vietnamese army for an all-out North Vietnamese assault was one. The army was still dependent on American logistical support for the mobility necessary to confront the North Vietnamese on different fronts, and on American B-52 air support to destroy North Vietnamese troop concentrations and supply lines. Other causes were poor planning, the lack of an adequate and experienced command structure, the lack of a mobile reserve, disastrous withdrawal decisions that sparked panic (exacerbated by the co-location of dependents with the troops), and the lack of inspired, self-sacrificial leadership at the top, particularly by President Thieu, who became demoralized, perhaps in part because he had become so dependent personally on American support.

24. Bui Diem and Chanoff, *In the Jaws of History*, 329.

CHAPTER 23: TRAGIC AFTERMATH—AND WHY

1. President Nixon, secret letter to President Thieu, January 17, 1973, in Nguyen Tien Hung and Schecter, *Palace File*, 1–2. Three other secret letters from Nixon to Thieu made essentially the same commitment.

2. See Doan Van Toai and David Chanoff, *The Vietnamese Gulag* (New York: Simon and Schuster, 1986), for a general description of how National Liberation Front supporters who were not communists were thrown into prisons and "reeducation" camps and badly treated.

3. Karnow, *Vietnam*, 23. Taylor's statement was remarkable for its honesty in admitting his own failure to understand. Whether he ever concluded there were some who *did* understand the enemy and the South Vietnamese is not clear.

4. Robert McNamara, *In Retrospect: The Tragedy and Lessons of Vietnam* (New York Times Books, 1995), 32.

5. Halberstam, *Best and the Brightest*, 41. Rayburn was making the point that intellectual brilliance did not necessarily translate into practicality and that Johnson should not be overimpressed—which, unfortunately, continued after he took over as president.

6. Previously quoted from Presidential Recordings, Dictation by President Kennedy on November 4, 1963, item 52.1, JFKL.

7. Robert H. Miller, *Vietnam and Beyond: A Diplomat's Cold War Education* (Lubbock: Texas Tech University Press, 2002), 95–96. Miller spent over five years in our embassy in Vietnam during the 1960s. While the author does not agree with all of Miller's observations, this one is right on target.

CHAPTER 24: BEYOND VIETNAM: IRAQ, AFGHANISTAN, AND THE FUTURE

1. Lewis Sorley, *Vietnam Chronicles: The Abrams Tapes 1968–1972* (Lubbock: Texas Tech University Press, 2004), 633. Also cited in U.S. Army and Marine Corps, *Counterinsurgency Field Manual*, 50.

2. A piece in the *Washington Post* of August 12, 2007, by Nathaniel Fick, a former captain in the Marines, now a fellow at the Center for a New American Security, entitled "To Defeat the Taliban Fight Less, Win More," was very encouraging in the recounting of his experience in teaching counterinsurgency to Afghan soldiers in Kabul. The concepts expressed were something the author could have written from his Vietnam experience. Nevertheless, as reported in the news, there is still too much focus on the use of airpower in Afghanistan to combat the Taliban and on enemy body counts, while too many civilian casualties are incurred. At the time of writing this book, there seems to be no overall strategy for counterinsurgency-*cum*-nation building that blends the political, psychological, economic, and social aspects. The appointment of Gen. David H. Petreus as commander of U.S. Central Command could help rectify this.

3. *Manual for the Philippine Constabulary*, 1915, reproduced in 1963 for the USOM Office of Rural Affairs, page 226 of the original document. Copy in the author's files.

4. President McKinley's instructions to the commission [a civilian commission established in 1900 to set up the government of the Philippines], ibid., 238. The fact that some American troops violated the rules established for the constabulary and failed to treat Filipinos according to McKinley's instructions does not undermine their validity.

5. Extract from T. E. Lawrence, *Arab Bulletin*, August 1917. Author's copy is part of T. Malupit [C. T. R. Bohannon], ed., *Vietnam & Counterinsurgency: A Training Compilation* (n.p.: Eastern

Construction, October 1, 1967). Also cited in U.S. Army and Marine Corps, *Counterinsurgency Manual.*

6. "Bombs, Rockets, Shells and Popular Support." See note 23 in chapter 10.

7. The Marine Corps prides itself on preparing all of its officers and noncoms for counterinsurgency, but it should give special recognition as well to those who are particularly good at mentoring foreign forces.

8. In an opinion piece entitled "The Longest War," *Washington Post,* March 31, 2008, from Khost, Afghanistan, Ambassador Richard Holbrooke described the work of Kael Weston, a young Foreign Service officer, in bringing together disparate tribal elders, sheiks, mullahs, students, and former Taliban to resolve problems and correct misunderstandings—ideally, helping the Afghans to build self-sustaining local institutions. This type of involvement is precisely what is needed from younger Foreign Service officers. Holbrooke also points out responsibility will have to be given back to the Afghans if the effort is to be lasting, and this is likely to take a long time.

9. On January 24, 2002, the author sent Andrew Natsios, at the time the administrator of the U.S. Agency for International Development (AID), a letter recommending the decentralization of American aid to the provinces in Afghanistan based on the Rural Affairs experience in Vietnam. Though this letter was sent through a former member of Rural Affairs, then engaged at a high level within the State Department, the author never received either a written acknowledgement or a phone call. A similar idea would eventually emerge as the provincial reconstruction team almost two years later. Had it been started earlier, when Afghanistan was largely peaceful after the Taliban defeat, some of the problems now being experienced might have been headed off.

10. CORDS in Vietnam involved over seven thousand personnel with advisors at every level of the Vietnamese government, down to the districts in the provinces. While Bill Colby's leadership made this mass into a generally effective instrument, it also tended to create overdependence among the Vietnamese. The same effect could have been accomplished, in the author's opinion, by a much smaller organization involving a military advisory team, USOM rep, and USIS and CIA reps at the provincial level, much as Rural Affairs, in conjunction with the MAAG sector advisors, demonstrated in an earlier incarnation. This does not detract from Colby's performance, which was exceptional, or from the performance of most participants in CORDS.

Cast of Characters

VIETNAM 1954–68

THE VIETNAMESE

All Vietnamese are listed for convenience of identity by their first names first, while standard Vietnamese usage is to have the first name shown last. This is to assist the reader since in the text, after using the full name when persons are introduced they are usually referred to afterward by the first name. For example, Pham Xuan An is first mentioned by his full name and thereafter is most often referred to in the text as An. (The only exception is Ho Chi Minh, whose name was not a standard Vietnamese name but an alias meaning "the enlightened" and who is always referred to as "Ho.")

An, Pham Xuan. Southern Vietnamese journalist and spy for North Vietnam. Was an adjutant working in Vietnamese army psywar in 1954. Later went to the United States on a scholarship, studied journalism, worked for the Sacramento *Bee*, returned to Vietnam, and worked for a series of American journalists while being the top spy for the North Vietnamese. He and his close friend Nguyen Hung Vuong were stringers for Bob Shaplen of the *New Yorker*. Author spent several hours reminiscing with him in 2002 in Saigon. Subject of *Perfect Spy*, by Larry Berman, published in 2007. Died at the end of 2006.

Buu, Nguyen Van. Originally from central Vietnam, he was a prominent businessman with a coastal shipping fleet and cinnamon-growing and shrimp-raising concessions. His first wife was a niece of the Ngo brothers, and he was particularly close to Ngo Dinh Diem. Probably one of the funding sources for the Can Lao party. Had his own troops guarding his shrimp farms and the Bien Hoa–Vung Tau Highway, which connected Saigon to the coast, as well as guarding the cinnamon plantations in central Vietnam. In October 1963, he proposed kidnapping and exiling the president's brother, Ngo Dinh Nhu, in order to save President Diem. Jailed after the 1963 coup. Left for France before the 1975 fall of Saigon. Deceased.

Can, Ngo Dinh. Fourth of the Ngo brothers, he operated behind the scenes controlling the politics of central Vietnam under President Diem. After the coup against Diem he was granted refuge in the U.S. consulate in Hue but was turned over to the new government by Ambassador Lodge and jailed. He was eventually condemned by a military court under General Khanh and executed by firing squad.

Cao, Huyen Van. Born in South Vietnam. A major commanding the presidential guard for President Diem in the 1955–56 period, he became a brigadier general in charge of IV Corps area (the Delta) in late 1962. Exercised poor leadership during the battle of Ap Bac in early 1963. Remained in charge of IV Corps until the coup against Diem. Eventually retired and ran successfully for a seat in the Vietnamese Senate in 1971.

Cao, Van Thanh. Born in Tay Ninh Province in a Cao Dai family, he was the deputy commander to General Thrinh Minh Thé of the Cao Dai Lien Minh in 1954. Integrated into the Vietnamese army, he rose to the rank of brigadier general, but was regarded as a "political" general by most other ranking officers. During the 1962–63 period he served as a go-between for the Diem government with the Buddhists. He collaborated with the author in July 1963 on a scheme to resolve the Buddhist conflict, which was short-circuited by Ngo Dinh Nhu. Later he tried to help Lansdale work with various religious factions in 1965 to achieve unity.

Chau, Tran Ngoc. Born in central Vietnam to a prominent family, Lieutenant Colonel Chau was the people-oriented chief of Kien Hoa Province in 1962–63, responsible for the single most effective pacification effort under the Strategic Hamlet Program during that period, using his own original ideas. Appointed in July 1963 by President Diem to replace the mayor of Danang, he helped quiet the Buddhist rebellion in that part of central Vietnam. Returned to Kien Hoa as province chief in 1965. Subsequently ran the Revolutionary Development cadre school, where he had a dispute with the CIA over who should sponsor the school and resigned. In the 1967 elections he won a seat in the National Assembly from Kien Hoa Province, collecting over 40 percent of the vote against eleven other candidates. A leader in the National Assembly, he was thrown in jail by President Thieu in 1972, becoming a political cause célèbre among the Buddhists and in the United States. He was released in time to be jailed again by the North Vietnamese after the fall of Saigon. Finally released from prison in 1980, he and his family escaped by boat. Resides in the Los Angeles area and was a contributor to *Prelude to Tragedy*.

Cung, Kieu Cong. Of southern Vietnamese origin, Cung was a second lieutenant in the French army before World War II when he resigned and joined the southern resistance in 1946 against the French, rising to the rank of brigadier in the Vietminh. Because of his refusal to join the Communist Party, he had to go into hiding around 1952. Surfacing in 1955, he volunteered to help President Diem start Civic Action, an effort to put teams of workers into South Vietnamese villages to fill the vacuum left by the departing Vietminh. Failed to get significant U.S. economic aid despite efforts by Lansdale and the author during the early years of the Diem government to persuade the American economic mission that this type of activity should have a high priority. Died suddenly in 1958 of a heart attack.

Diem, Bui. Born in North Vietnam to a prominent family, was a nationalist political organizer from his student days. Became a Dai Viet political party organizer and journalist, then became chief of cabinet for Dai Viet leader, Phan Huy Quat, when he was defense minister in an early Bao Dai government, and prime minister in the post-Diem government in 1965. Later served as an advisor to Prime Minister Nguyen Cao Ky during the 1965–66 period and became South Vietnam's ambassador to the United States in 1968, serving until 1972. Friend of the author's since 1954. Author of *Into the Jaws of History*, one of the few books to give the Vietnamese side of the story of the Paris peace negotiations and the accords as well as an overview of what happened in Vietnam. Retired and lives in the Maryland suburbs of Washington, D.C.

Diem, Ngo Dinh. Arriving in July 1954 in Saigon as prime minister, he was elected president of South Vietnam in 1956, serving until his murder during the November 1963 coup. Born in 1901, the third of six brothers from an influential central Vietnam family of Catholics, he became the most prominent noncommunist nationalist who refused to cooperate with the French. Appointed as prime minister in 1954 by Bao Dai as a last gesture to Vietnamese nationalism, he was not manipulated into power by the Americans, but was a political leader in his own right. His qualities of strong character served him and his people well in the early days when he overcame the sect rebellion, got rid of French influence and proclaimed South Vietnam's independence. However, his authoritarian tendencies, absorption in detail, and proclivity to micromanage were drawbacks in later years, when his brother Ngo Dinh Nhu became dominant as his main political advisor and source of intelligence. His isolation helped undermine his support during the Buddhist crisis when he increasingly relied on Nhu's hard-line advice. He had a special relationship with General Lansdale, but was constantly frustrated in his efforts to get Lansdale back to Vietnam as an advisor. At the end, Nhu succeeded in alienating not only the leadership of the Vietnamese army but most of the civilians who had been among Diem's most ardent early supporters. His murder during the 1963 coup left a residue of bitterness, particularly among Vietnamese Catholics.

Don, Tran Van. Prominent Vietnamese army general, brother of the wife of General Le Van Kim and a close friend of Lucien Conein. Don came from a southern family but had been born in France, where his father was a doctor. After loyally supporting Diem during the early years, he became increasingly alienated and was a leader of the coup against Diem but was not involved in Diem's killing. Was chief of staff of the army during the first post–November coup government, then was exiled to Dalat when General Khanh took over. Retired and ran successfully for the South Vietnamese Senate in 1967, becoming a prominent political leader thereafter. Flew into exile in 1975 and wrote a book on his experiences, *Our Endless War,* published in 1978. Died in 1999.

Duc, Hoang Van. A southern Vietnamese, Duc as a lieutenant colonel led the Vietnamese army occupation of the Camau Peninsula during Operation Liberty in early 1955. Subsequently, promoted to general and made commander of the IV Corps in the Delta, he led an abortive coup in 1964 against the Khanh government. Eventually went insane and wandered around Saigon as a street person. Deceased.

Hai, Vo Van. Originally from central Vietnam, Hai was a longtime associate and private secretary to President Diem from the time he became prime minister in 1954. Frozen out of influence with Diem by Ngo Dinh Nhu after the 1960 paratrooper coup, he remained as personal secretary until the 1963 coup deposing Diem, when he retired quietly to his home. Jailed by the communists after the 1975 takeover, he died in prison. Was well known to the author.

Hinh, Nguyen Van. Named commander in chief of the Vietnamese armed forces in 1954 by Bao Dai. A French as well as Vietnamese citizen, he became involved in organizing a coup against Prime Minister Diem with covert French support in 1954 but was obliged to retire to France through a combination of Diem's maneuvering with Bao Dai and American efforts, led by Colonel Lansdale, to undermine the coup. Deceased

Ho Chi Minh. Born in central Vietnam in 1890, Ho traveled the world as a young man working at various jobs until he was recruited in Paris by the French communist party in 1920. Thereafter he went to Moscow for training, became a member of the Comintern, and founded the Indochinese Communist Party, whose ambitions extended beyond Vietnam. He did not return personally to Vietnam until 1941, when he began organizing the Vietminh as a patriotic front under communist control. Achieving spectacular success as the principal spokesman for independence in 1945, he led the initial war against the French. Behind his deceptive, fatherly façade he dedicated himself effectively to the communist takeover of Vietnam using nationalism and anticolonialism as tools. He remained president of North Vietnam from 1954 to 1969, when he died before he could see ultimate success.

Khanh, Nguyen. Of southern Vietnamese origin, he was an ambitious corps commander who executed a bloodless coup in January 1964 against the original coup group that overthrew Diem. Persuaded the Americans, particularly Ambassador Lodge, that he was the man to back but was not highly regarded by his own people. Attempted to proclaim his own constitution making himself president, then was forced to back down. Finally obliged to resign and go into exile in early 1965. Remained in the United States. Currently living in Texas.

Khiem, Tran Van. Brother of Madame Nhu and presidential palace plotter involved in drawing up assassination lists during the crisis between the American and Vietnamese governments over the treatment of the Buddhists. More than a bit crazy, he wound up shooting his mother and father, Tran Van Chuong and Madame Chuong, in Washington and then committing suicide.

Kim, Le Van. Originally from central Vietnam, as a colonel in the Vietnamese army General Staff he was initially in charge of planning for the occupations of areas to be evacuated by the Vietminh in 1955. Then he commanded the occupation of Interzone Five, with great success. The most brilliant of all Vietnamese staff officers, he enjoyed an extraordinary civilian career prior to World War II helping the great French movie director Marcel Pagnol. Successively appointed by Diem as head of the Military Academy in 1956, then in charge of resettlement in the Highlands, he fell out of favor after the 1960 paratrooper coup and was sidelined. Close to General Duong Van Minh, he was one of the main planners of the 1963 coup against Diem. He missed evacuation in 1975 and was put into a series of communist concentration camps, eventually released and permitted to go to Paris, where he resided until his death in 1990. Was a close friend of the author.

Khoi, Ngo Dinh. Eldest of the Ngo brothers, he was murdered by the Vietminh in 1945. While Ho Chi Minh disclaimed responsibility, Ngo Dinh Diem blamed him for the assassination. By some accounts Khoi had the greatest potential in the family for leadership, which is probably why he was eliminated, as were other prominent noncommunist nationalist leaders in the immediate post–world war period.

Ky, Nguyen Cao. From northern Vietnam, he was the commander of the air force and a member of the younger group of generals, along with Nguyen Van Thieu, called the "Young Turks," who took over after General Khanh. He became prime minister in June 1965, and General Thieu became chief of state. They were rivals for the presidency in the national election of 1967, when the generals picked Thieu as their candidate and Ky was forced to accept the nomination for vice president. Ky was evacuated to the United States in 1975.

Lac, Hoang Van. As a colonel in the Vietnamese army, originally from North Vietnam, he served as executive secretary of the Interministerial Committee on Strategic Hamlets in 1962 and 1963. Author worked closely with Lac, who continued to play a key role in successive pacification programs after the fall of Diem in 1963 and rose to the rank of major general. Was an extremely able staff officer who understood the need to win the support of the population for pacification to succeed. Evacuated in 1975, he lives in Houston, Texas, and currently heads a charity, Children Support Association, that brings badly burned Vietnamese children to the United States for treatment. The charity also drills water wells in poor Vietnamese villages throughout present-day Vietnam. Author of *Why America Lost the Vietnam War,* an analysis and personal account, and a contributor to *Prelude to Tragedy*.

Luyen, Ngo Dinh. The youngest of the Ngo brothers, Luyen had friends in the Vietnamese army and among the political opposition to Diem. He served the Diem government, mainly in diplomatic missions abroad, and would have been a more open and convivial replacement for Ngo Dinh Nhu if that could have been arranged.

Minh, Duong Van. A southern Vietnamese, "Big" Minh was the most popular general in the Vietnamese army. Led the forces that put down the Binh Xuyen rebellion in Saigon and defeated the other dissident sect forces in the Delta in 1955. Good field commander but failed after the 1963 coup against Diem to assert leadership. Remained reluctant chief of state during most of the Nguyen Khanh period in 1964. Eventually retired. Was potential candidate against General Thieu in the 1971 presidential campaign. In 1975, he was designated as president at the last minute to surrender to the North Vietnamese. Allowed by the communists to retire without incarceration. Died in 2006.

Nhu, Ngo Dinh. President Diem's younger brother and political advisor, he also supervised the regime's central intelligence service. Prime instigator and backer of a secret political party, the Can Lao, that controlled the inner core of government and army personnel loyal to Diem and Nhu. An intellectual of verbal virtuosity, he propounded "Personalism," an obscure quasi-religious doctrine of French origin designed as an ideological counterpoint to communism but whose main instrument, the Can Lao, operated in practice somewhat like the Communist Party. Was a divisive influence, hypersuspicious of others. and principally responsible for isolating Diem from many of his earlier supporters. Tended toward political paranoia and was easily aroused to fits of anti-Americanism, some of it justified by clumsy American actions. He and his wife, Madame Nhu, became the principal focus of dislike by Vietnamese army officers and many civilians and was in the end a prime cause of President Diem's overthrow.

Phuoc, Le Van. A southern Vietnamese colonel, he was the chief of Vinh Long Province, where he promoted a security policy of building long walls inside of which the population would be relocated and controlled. Extremely authoritarian and punitive in his approach to pacification. Had a run-in with the author which resulted in his policy of long walls being rejected by Counselor Nhu and the Strategic Hamlet Committee. Later moved to Saigon and was involved in coup and anticoup plotting with Madame Nhu's brother, Tran Van Khiem, prior to the coup against Diem.

Quang, Tri. Buddhist monk from central Vietnam who led the rebellion against President Diem. Extremely good political organizer and agitator. Became a thorn in the side of successive Vietnamese governments after Diem's overthrow. Unlike several other Buddhist monks, who were killed by the communists when they took over in 1975, he was allowed to retire to a monastery. Some Americans thought he was procommunist, but he was not, despite opposing a series of Vietnamese governments in the 1964–66 period.

Quat, Phan Huy. A medical doctor by profession, Quat was the longtime leader of the northern faction of the Dai Viet nationalist party. Was defense minister in the Vietnamese government in 1953 preceding that of Diem. Became prime minister in 1965 for about six months after General Khanh was deposed but was unable to unite the various political and religious factions. Although one of the most experienced of the civilian politicians available after the 1963 coup against Diem, he never had a strong political base of his own.

Sung, Dan Van. Northern Vietnamese intellectual and member of the Dai Viet Party. Influential because of his writings. Became a member of the General Assembly in later South Vietnamese governments after 1967. A strong voice for South Vietnamese democracy and unity.

Thao, Pham Ngoc. A colonel in the South Vietnamese army from southern Vietnam, he was probably an agent for the North Vietnamese. He became influential as a province chief under Diem, then played an outsider role, often as an agent provocateur in a succession of governments. Organized his own coup against Diem in 1963 but was persuaded to hold off by the generals to permit their coup to go forward. Involved behind the scenes in several coup attempts thereafter; he was finally arrested by President Thieu and subsequently killed. Was a favorite of many Americans and spent some time in the United States assigned to the Vietnamese embassy in Washington.

Thé, Trinh Minh. Cao Dai leader with an independent "third force," the Lien Minh, in Tay Ninh Province in 1953 and 1954. He integrated 2,500 of his troops into the Vietnamese army under Prime Minister Diem in 1955, splintering the sect opposition. Became a friend and confidant of Lansdale who served as a conduit between Thé and Diem. Natural leader who fought the French and the Vietminh at the same time. Was killed leading his troops against the Binh Xuyen during the war for Saigon in 1955.

Thieu, Nguyen Van. Vietnamese army general from southern Vietnam, he was elected president in 1967 on a joint ticket with General Ky as vice president; was reelected as the sole candidate in 1971, squeezing out potential opposition by rigging the election rules. He was a strong supporter of pacification and land reform, which were effective during his administration. Secretive by nature, he tended to rely on a small inner circle of supporters and advisors. Refused to tackle widespread corruption that plagued and undermined his government. By refusing to go to Paris for negotiations in late 1968, he helped tip the U.S. presidential elections to Nixon instead of Humphrey. Overly dependent on American support to save South Vietnam and his regime, Thieu had good intentions but was too small a man for the job. Lived in London after the fall of Saigon. Deceased.

Tho, Nguyen Ngoc. A southerner who served as vice president under President Diem, he was gradually eliminated from any influential role in Diem's government during the late 1950s and early 1960s by Ngo Dinh Nhu. Had many influential contacts in the Delta but was not effectively used by Diem to cement relationships with the Cao Dai and Hoa Hao after their forces were defeated in 1955. He was close to General Duong Van "Big" Minh and served as prime minister in the first government that followed the 1963 coup against Diem.

Thuan, Nguyen Dinh. From northern Vietnam, he was originally chief of cabinet to Tran Van Dung when Dung became secretary of state for defense in the Diem government in 1955. Worked his way up to secretary of state and assistant secretary of defense under President Diem from about 1960 until the 1963 coup. He was the third-most influential person in the Diem government, after Diem and Nhu, and extremely able. Often serving as buffer between Diem and the Americans, he was a close friend and confidant of the author. Went into exile in France in November 1963, after the coup.

Thuc, Ngo Dinh. The second of six brothers, Thuc rose to become archbishop of Hue, where he ill served President Diem by arrogantly flaunting the supposed superiority of his church over the Buddhists, thus abetting, if not directly causing, the Buddhist crisis of May 1963. He joined Ngo Dinh Nhu in advocating a hard line against the Buddhists, which undermined Diem's support and his government. Through the apostolic delegate's intercession, Thuc was sent abroad later in 1963, but the damage had been done.

Tuan, Bui Anh. (Not to be confused with Professor Bui Anh Tuan.) VNQDD nationalist and journalist from North Vietnam. Helped with propaganda operations against the Vietminh and in support of the South Vietnamese government in 1954 and 1955. He eventually worked in the Vietnam press office of the Diem presidency and as a private journalist. Escaped to the United States during the fall of Saigon in 1975.

Vien, Le Van. Binh Xuyen general who started out as a taxi driver in pre–World War II Saigon and worked his way up to warlord and head of a paramilitary force that ensured the security of the Saigon–Cap St. Jacques road during the French-Vietminh war. Subsequently led his forces, with French behind-the-scenes support, in an unsuccessful rebellion against the Diem government in 1955, then went into exile in France. During the 1954–55 period the Binh Xuyen, under his command, controlled the national and the Saigon police as well as all gambling and most of the prostitution and opium dens in Saigon. Deceased.

Vuong, Nguyen Hung. Of South Vietnamese origin, he was a second lieutenant on the Vietnamese army psywar staff in 1954, when the author first met him. He was involved in several occupation operations (Camau and Interzone Five) in 1955, working with Vietnamese army psywar companies in conjunction with the author. Later became a freelance journalist, worked for Bob Shaplen of the *New Yorker* and was Pham Xuan An's closest friend. He did not know at the time about An's secret connection to the North Vietnamese. Was evacuated to the United States, where he died in the 1980s.

THE AMERICANS IN VIETNAM

Abrams, Creighton. Commanding general of MACV from July 1968 to 1972, replacing General Westmoreland. He changed the operational emphasis to protection of the population as the primary goal. No longer were the Americans trying to win the war themselves; the new doctrine was that the Vietnamese had to do it themselves, with our support. By the time of his departure, most of the South Vietnam countryside was pacified and the American troops under his command had declined from over five hundred thousand to around fifty thousand. Deceased.

Alsop, Joseph. Influential national columnist and reporter, writing mainly on foreign affairs, during the 1952–68 period, and making periodic trips to Vietnam. Cousin of Franklin D. Roosevelt and personally close to President Kennedy and his administration. Deceased.

Arundel, Arthur. U.S. Marine Corps captain. Transferred from the CIA mission in Korea in August 1954 to become a roommate of the author at that time. Tour was up when he returned to the United States in December 1954. Mustered out of the Marine Corps, he became a correspondent with CBS News in Washington, later pioneered *All News All the Time* Broadcasting in the United States, and founded a large Virginia newspaper chain. He lives today near The Plains, Virginia.

Bohannon, Charles T. R. Retired army lieutenant colonel who led guerrillas in the Philippines against the Japanese during World War II; became part of Lansdale's team in defeating the Huks from 1950 to 1953, then backstopped the Saigon Military Mission from Manila between 1954 and 1956. In late 1962 he came to Saigon on contract to USOM/Rural Affairs where he helped get the Chieu Hoi (surrender) program off the ground while also influencing the hamlet program through his *Notes on the Strategic Hamlet,* printed in August 1963. He had previously collaborated with Napoleon Valeriano on a book about defeating the Huks in the Philippines, *Counter-Guerrilla Operations: The Philippine Experience.* (Praeger, 1962) Returning to Manila in 1964, he came back to Vietnam with the Lansdale mission in 1965. Deceased.

Brent, Joseph. USOM/Saigon mission director from August 1962 until July 1964. Generally supported Rural Affairs, despite objections from the technical divisions of the mission. Deceased.

Bundy, William. Assistant secretary of defense for international security affairs from 1961 to 1964, after service with the CIA. Became deputy assistant secretary of state for Far Eastern affairs replacing Roger Hilsman in 1964, serving in this post until 1968. Was a key contact for the author in 1963 and during 1965–68 period. Generally sympathetic to Lansdale's mission under Lodge but was locked into Johnson's decision-making process. He was willing to listen to contrary views. Deceased.

Bunker, Ellsworth. U.S. ambassador to Vietnam from 1967 until 1973. Strong supporter of President Nguyen Van Thieu. Generally regarded as the best ambassador the United States ever had in Vietnam. Deceased.

Burns, Robert. Former U.S. Army captain who became USOM/Saigon Rural Affairs provincial representative in Phu Yen Province from 1962 to 1963. Later became a regional rep in 1964 and was forced to resign by a new USOM mission director, James Killen, in the fall of 1964. He stayed on in Vietnam as a private businessman until 1975. Deceased.

Collins, J. Lawton. General Collins, known as "Lighting Joe" for his quick reactions in World War II, was appointed as President Eisenhower's special representative and ambassador to South Vietnam in late 1954 until May 1955. Consistently talking down to the Vietnamese, he was highly influenced by the French commissioner general and commander, Paul Ely, who was bitterly anti-Diem. He became convinced that the Vietnamese army would not support Diem and that Diem had to be replaced, which he almost succeeded in effecting during a trip to Washington in April 1955. His lack of political understanding of the Vietnamese eerily foreshadowed a similar mindset by General Maxwell Taylor as ambassador in 1964. Deceased.

Conein, Lucien. Long history of involvement in Vietnam from end of World War II as an OSS agent, then as a member of Lansdale's Saigon Military Mission from 1954 to 1956, then as a member of CIA station from 1962 intermittently until 1969. Served as part of the Lansdale mission in 1965, reverting back to the CIA station in 1966. Was the sole liaison between Lodge and the generals during the plotting and carrying out of the coup against Diem in November 1963. Deceased.

Dunn, John Michael. U.S. army colonel who was the principal assistant and right-hand man for Ambassador Lodge, arriving with him in Saigon in July 1963. Served as Lodge's assistant until June 1964. Later rose to rank of brigadier general and served as military aide to Vice President Agnew. Deceased.

Durbrow, Elbridge. U.S. ambassador to Vietnam from 1957 until 1961. Had a miserable relationship with President Diem. Led a country team in Saigon plagued by bitter infighting between agencies. Deceased.

Fippen, William. Deputy chief of USOM/Saigon in 1962, when Rural Affairs was organized with his strong support. Had been in charge of the mission since the previous chief, Arthur Gardiner, resigned in 1961. Deceased.

Fishel, Wesley. An assistant professor at Michigan State University, Fishel became an early friend of Ngo Dinh Diem in 1950 and helped build support for him in the United States. Early on in 1954 he became an advisor to Diem in Saigon, helping him communicate with the American embassy, while he and Lansdale worked informally together. He returned to teaching at Michigan State in the fall of 1954 but kept a close watch on U.S. policy toward Diem. Fishel headed a Michigan State advisory mission in Vietnam from 1956 to 1958, and subsequently became embroiled in accusations by the antiwar movement that his Saigon advisory mission had been nothing but a CIA front. Deceased.

Fraleigh, Albert "Bert." Dynamic AID employee who was very successful in Taiwan with the resettlement of Chinese Nationalist veterans from 1950 on. As Rural Affairs deputy in Saigon from 1962 to 1964, he launched an unprecedented rural development effort, resulting in the first South Vietnam rice exports in 1963 since the beginning of the Vietcong insurgency. Opposed Killen's dismantling of Rural Affairs and was fired. Nevertheless, came back to Vietnam in 1965 to assist with refugees and then to develop model accelerated agricultural development programs. Resides on the Olympic Peninsula in Washington state.

Gates, John. Marine Corps first lieutenant detailed to the CIA and on duty with the Saigon Military Mission under Lansdale in Saigon from 1955 to end of 1956. Worked closely with the author. Deceased.

Habib, Philip. Head of the political section of the U.S. embassy in Saigon under Ambassador Lodge from 1965 to 1967. Later involved in peace negotiations in Paris. Had a distinguished career as a senior diplomat in the Foreign Service heading up Middle East and Central American peace negotiations in later administrations. Engaged in intense turf warfare with Lansdale in Saigon during the 1965–67 period. Deceased.

Harkins, Paul. First commanding general of MACV in Saigon. Served from 1963 through the first half of 1964. Replaced by William Westmoreland. Generally regarded as ineffective at best. Deceased.

Heath, Donald. U.S. ambassador to Vietnam in the 1953–54 period. Provided strong support for Lansdale, despite his doubts about the viability of Ngo Dinh Diem. Deceased.

Holbrooke, Richard. His first job as a newly minted Foreign Service officer was with USOM/Rural Affairs, serving as provincial rep in Ba Xuyen Province in the Delta from late 1963 to 1964. Later served in the embassy in Saigon, back in Washington, and in Paris on matters involving Vietnam. Had an extremely distinguished career in the State Department, becoming ambassador to the United Nations and Germany, among other important posts. Resides in New York City.

Jorgensen, Gordon. CIA station chief in Saigon during 1964–66. Had served under Lansdale in Saigon as his deputy during 1955–56 and was station chief in Laos from 1960 to 1962. Deceased.

Karrick, Sam. In 1954–55 period was a regular army lieutenant colonel in MAAG, assigned to the National Security Division, under Lansdale, of the joint American-French military mission, TRIM. Later was detached from the Pentagon and served as the executive officer of the Lansdale mission (SLO) from 1966 to 1968. Deceased.

Killen, James. Appointed USOM/Saigon mission director in July 1964. Largely dismantled the Rural Affairs office and programs, including the joint provincial sign-off system for pacification funding just when it was most needed during the era of chaotic Vietnamese politics from 1964 to 1965. Served a year and was replaced by Charles Mann in 1965. Deceased.

Lansdale, Edward. An army intelligence officer, who switched to the air force after World War II, he was assigned to the Office of Policy Coordination (the covert action arm of the nascent CIA) in 1948. Sent to the Philippines, where he helped Secretary of Defense Ramon Magsaysay defeat the communist Huk rebellion and then be elected president. In 1954 he was assigned to Saigon to try to save South Vietnam after the Geneva Accords cut the country in half. There he became a confidential advisor to Ngo Dinh Diem and helped to create an independent South Vietnam. An unorthodox thinker and operator and a strong advocate for democracy, he was constantly at odds with the American bureaucracy, which managed to keep him out of Vietnam when his presence might have saved Diem in 1963. Retiring as a regular air force major general in 1963, he returned to Vietnam as special assistant to Ambassador Lodge in 1965 but was never able to carve out a prime political-action role in what had become a huge, largely mindless American operation. From 1965 to 1968, he helped bring limited democracy to Vietnam and change the American pacification approach but was never utilized to his full potential. For his service in the Philippines Lansdale was the third recipient after Gen. "Wild Bill" Donovan, OSS chief, and Gen. Bedell Smith, first head of the CIA, of the U.S. National Security Medal. Died in 1987.

Lodge, Henry Cabot. Former Republican senator from Massachusetts and ambassador to the United Nations under Eisenhower, Lodge was appointed ambassador to Vietnam by President Kennedy in July 1963. Advocated and supported the coup by the Vietnamese generals against Diem. Served as ambassador until July 1964, when replaced by General Taylor, then reappointed by President Johnson to replace Taylor in 1965. Took Lansdale with him as a special assistant in 1965 but failed to support him. Served until April 1967. Had a patronizing attitude toward the Vietnamese. Deceased.

Mecklin, John. Former *New York Times* correspondent who became head of the U.S. Information Service in Saigon in 1962. Left in 1964. Supported return of Lansdale but also advocated the direct intervention of U.S. troops in Saigon to support the coup by Vietnamese army generals against Diem. Deceased.

Melvin, George. U.S. Army lieutenant colonel who replaced Sam Karrick in the National Security Division of TRIM under Lansdale in 1955. Recruited as a regional rep for Rural Affairs in 1962. Served until 1964, when transferred to Laos. Transferred back to Vietnam in 1965 as part of the Lansdale mission. Deceased.

Methven, Stuart. After service in Laos, transferred as CIA case officer to the Saigon station in 1962. Supported Special Forces operations with the Montagnards and Vietnamese provincial pacification operations. Worked in close collaboration with Rural Affairs. Retired from the CIA after becoming chief of station in Zaire. Has a book out in the fall of 2008 about his CIA career, *Laughter in the Shadows,* published by the Naval Institute Press. Lives in Belgium.

Nolting, Frederick. American ambassador to Vietnam, replacing Durbrow in 1961. Achieved good personal relations with Diem but was unable to affect the outcome of the Buddhist crisis when his advice to Diem counseling conciliation was overcome by Nhu's hard line. He was replaced by Henry Cabot Lodge in July 1963. Deceased.

O'Daniel, John "Iron Mike." U.S. Army lieutenant general in charge of MAAG from 1954 through 1956. He believed in the Vietnamese army when its willingness to take on the Binh Xuyen in 1955 was being questioned. Strong supporter of Lansdale during the 1954–55 period. Deceased.

O'Donnell, John. Rural Affairs provincial representative in the Delta. Of part Hawaiian ancestry, with an instinctive understanding of the Vietnamese, he was singularly effective in supporting Colonel Tran Ngoc Chau, the Kien Hoa Province chief, and in developing counterinsurgency doctrine. Left Rural Affairs because of Killen. Deceased.

Redick, Joseph. Lansdale interpreter and aide during the 1954–56 period. Later voluntarily returned to assist Lansdale again in 1965 as part of the Saigon Liaison Office. Resides in the Shenandoah Valley of Virginia.

Reinhardt, Frederick. The American ambassador who succeeded General Collins in 1955, serving a two-year term during the early years of the Diem government. Deceased.

Richardson, John. CIA station chief in Saigon from 1962–63. Close to Ngo Dinh Nhu and Colonel

Tung, head of the Vietnamese Special Forces. Not trusted by Lodge and eventually forced out when his cover was blown to an American newspaper, possibly by Lodge himself. Deceased. Subject of book by his son, John, *My Father the Spy.*

Sharpe, Lawrence. Navy lieutenant who attended U.S. Army psywar school at Fort Bragg with two key Vietnamese officers who were later involved in coup plotting against Prime Minister Diem in 1954. Lansdale had Sharpe transferred from the Seventh Fleet on temporary duty to Saigon, where he helped Lansdale frustrate the Hinh coup attempt. Lives in Pennsylvania.

Simpson, Howard. Handled press for the U.S. Information Agency in Saigon during the 1953–55 period. Blew the whistle on the French connection with the Binh Xuyen in 1955 when no one in the embassy wanted to listen. Returned as a press advisor to General Nguyen Khanh in 1964. Deceased.

Smith, David. Part of the Saigon Military Mission, arriving as an army first lieutenant in December 1954. Worked closely with the author supporting Vietnamese army pacification operations while also providing invaluable support for Operation Brotherhood. Later became deputy chief of station in Saigon in 1962 and was acting chief during the coup against Diem in November 1963. Deceased.

Stilwell, Richard. U.S. Army brigadier general in 1963 in charge of G-3 (operations) at MACV. Important contact for Rural Affairs but generally supportive of the Harkins and Westmoreland approach to the war. Subsequently, when taking over MAAG in Thailand in 1967, he took a different, people-oriented approach to the Thai government's successful counterinsurgency campaign against communist-supported guerrillas there. Deceased.

Sweet, Charles. International Volunteer Services (IVS) social worker who helped develop the slum areas on the south side of the Saigon River and whose reporting got the devastation of that area by American bombs and artillery fire called off in 1968. Lives in rural Virginia.

Taylor, Maxwell. Four-star general who served as army chief of staff under Eisenhower. Intellectually brilliant and polished, he was designated by President Kennedy as his senior military advisor after the Bay of Pigs and then served as chairman of the Joint Chiefs for Kennedy and for Johnson until 1964, when he accepted the post of ambassador to Vietnam, where he was not effective with the Vietnamese. Deceased.

Trueheart, William. As deputy chief of mission in Saigon from 1962 to 1963, ably handled U.S. counterinsurgency coordination. Was chargé when Ambassador Nolting went on home leave and the Buddhist rebellion got out of hand in May–June 1963. Served briefly under Lodge and then returned to the United States. Deceased.

Unger, Leonard. Deputy assistant secretary of state for Far Eastern affairs and head of the Vietnam Coordinating Committee in 1965 and 1966. Previously U.S. ambassador to Laos. The author dealt with him as the main source of official Washington support for Lansdale's Saigon Liaison Office. Deceased.

Vann, John Paul. Lieutenant Colonel Vann was the American military advisor to the Vietnamese 5th Division during the battle of Ap Bac in 1963. He disagreed with General Harkins about the way the war was being fought, retired, and was hired by USOM Rural Affairs, returning to Vietnam in 1964 as a civilian. Later became the CORDS senior advisor to the Vietnamese army II Corps and was extraordinarily effective until he died in a helicopter crash in 1972. Principal subject of *A Bright Shining Lie,* by Neil Sheehan.

Westmoreland, William. Served as deputy chief of MACV under General Harkins, then took over as the commanding general in 1964. Served until 1968, when he returned to the United States and became army chief of staff. Was largely responsible for the war of attrition against the Vietcong using American troops in large-unit operations with conventional tactics. Sidelined the Vietnamese army and neglected pacification. Deceased.

Williams, Ogden. CIA career case officer, he arrived in Saigon in 1955 as Lansdale's interpreter and aide, staying on through 1957 as liaison with the palace and the Ministry of Defense. Hired by AID in 1962, he supported Rural Affairs in Washington initially and then in Saigon in 1963 and 1964. Deceased.

Williams, Samuel "Hanging Sam." Army lieutenant general who took over MAAG from General O'Daniel in 1956. He was responsible for implementing Washington policy converting the Vietnamese army into a conventional force of regular divisions to resist an overt North Vietnamese invasion across the seventeenth parallel. At odds with Ambassador Durbrow, he supported Diem in wanting MAAG to train and equip the Civil Guard. Deceased.

Yoh, Bernard. Originally from Shanghai, became a guerrilla against the Japanese during World War II, then fought the communists. Became a U.S. citizen, was close to the Vatican and Opus Dei, operated with the support of the Roman Catholic Church as an anticommunist advisor and polemicist. Helped Father Hoa establish his outpost in Camau in 1959. Was an ex officio member of the Lansdale mission during the 1965–66 period. Deceased.

Young, Earl. Initially started as Rural Affairs provincial rep in Phu Bon Province, under very primitive conditions in late 1962. Moved in July 1963 to Long An Province, just south of Saigon, where he witnessed the Strategic Hamlet Program's disintegration during the Buddhist crisis and the continuing pacification failures of 1964, though Lodge had given Long An a high priority. Returned to the army and retired as a lieutenant colonel. Lives in the San Diego area.

Zorthian, Barry. Head of the U.S. Information Service in Saigon beginning in 1964. Went on to head JUSPAO, a much larger organization coordinating the American mission's information flow and dealing with the press from 1965 through 1968. Also assisted the Vietnamese Government with public information and propaganda, which tended to take less of his attention as direct American troop involvement grew. Lives in the Washington, D.C., area.

THE AMERICANS IN WASHINGTON

Bell, David. Director of USAID from 1963 to 1965. Strong supporter of the Rural Affairs approach to counterinsurgency in 1963 but then failed to rein in or replace USOM/Saigon director James Killen when it became clear he was destroying Rural Affairs. Deceased.

Bundy, McGeorge. President Kennedy's national security advisor beginning in 1962, staying on under Johnson through 1967. Was intellectually brilliant but never understood the human side of the Vietnam conflict. Deceased.

Bundy, William. Brother of McGeorge, served in the CIA, then was assistant secretary of defense from 1961 to 1964, when he became the assistant secretary of state for the Far East. Second-tier advisor to President Johnson and willing to listen to contrary opinions but went along with the Westmoreland/McNamara policy of bombing and of trying to win the war with American troops. Deceased.

Connell, William. Administrative assistant to Senator, subsequently Vice President, Humphrey from 1963 through 1968. Main conduit to Humphrey for the views of the author and of Lansdale. Lives in the Maryland suburbs of Washington, D.C.

Forrestal, Michael. National security staff advisor directly handling Vietnam for President Kennedy and subsequently for President Johnson, until 1966. Was initially open to listening to unconventional views about Vietnam but then became an advocate for the coup against Diem and a supporter of bombing North Vietnam and introducing U.S. troops. Deceased.

Harriman, Averell. Assistant secretary of state for Far Eastern affairs from 1961 to April 1963, when he became under secretary of state for political affairs. Negotiated Laos neutrality. Strongly favored coup against Diem, in open opposition to Secretary McNamara and General Taylor during 1963, thereafter deputy secretary of state for political affairs. Subsequently a negotiator with the North Vietnamese in Paris, favoring a neutralist approach to solving the Vietnam conflict. Deceased.

Hilsman, Roger. Based on his limited guerrilla experience in World War II, considered himself an expert on counterinsurgency. Served as director of intelligence and research at State Department until April 1963, when he became assistant secretary for Far Eastern Affairs until January 1964, when he resigned under pressure from President Johnson. He was a strong supporter of the coup against Diem, drafting the famous cable of August 24 that Lodge interpreted as authorizing Washington support for a coup by the Vietnamese generals. Lives in New York state.

Humphrey, Hubert. U.S. senator from Minnesota, vice president from 1964 to 1968. Unsuccessful candidate for the presidency against Nixon in 1968. Reelected to the U.S. Senate two years later. Strong backer of the Lansdale approach to the war and of the Lansdale mission but pushed aside by President Johnson after opposing the bombing of North Vietnam. Deceased.

Janow, Seymour. Assistant director for the Far East of USAID from 1962 to 1963. Responsible for hiring the author to study how AID might participate in counterinsurgency, recruited the author for, and supported him in, the leadership of USOM/Saigon Rural Affairs. Deceased.

Jorden, William. Former journalist who was a special assistant to Averell Harriman. Frequent visitor to Vietnam and strong supporter of the return of Lansdale to Vietnam in late 1963 and 1964 to assist Ambassador Lodge. Later transferred to the White House staff of President Johnson and helped Johnson write his biography. A peripheral advisor on Vietnam policy. Deceased.

Komer, Robert. Formerly with CIA, joined national security staff of President Kennedy, became White House coordinator for pacification in 1965 for President Johnson, and was sent to Saigon in 1967 as the first director for CORDS, the combined American military-civilian group in Vietnam supporting Vietnamese pacification. Nicknamed "the Blowtorch." Deceased.

Krulak, Victor. Marine Corps major general, sent to Vietnam by President Kennedy in September 1963 to survey whether the Buddhist crisis was affecting the war, came back with optimistic report that the war was being won. Appointed by the Joint Chiefs to a special "counterinsurgency" position, he was able to shoulder Lansdale aside and become a favorite of Secretary McNamara. Later admitted he had been mistaken about how the war should be fought. Deceased.

McCone, John. Republican industrialist with no practical intelligence experience, appointed by President Kennedy to head the CIA after the Bay of Pigs. Strongly resisted Lodge's attempt to have Lansdale appointed the Saigon chief of station in September 1963. Deceased.

McNamara, Robert. Peripatetic secretary of defense appointed by President Kennedy in 1961, and continuing under President Johnson until 1968, when he resigned to become head of the World Bank. Principal architect along with General Westmoreland of the strategy and tactics followed in Vietnam under President Johnson, including the bombing of North Vietnam and the deployment of American ground forces in active combat against the Vietcong. Generally recognized as the single most influential advisor to Johnson on the war. Lives in New York City.

Mendenhall, Joseph. Former political counselor in the American embassy during the tour of Ambassador Durbrow from 1959 to 1961. Became very anti-Diem from that period, and, serving in the State Department from 1962 through 1964, exerted behind-the-scenes influence supporting the 1963 coup. He was sent to Saigon on the same mission as General Krulak in September 1963 and returned with a pessimistic report so different from Krulak's that President Kennedy asked whether both had been to the same country. Reportedly living in Nevada.

Rostow, Walter. Senior foreign policy advisor to President Kennedy in 1961–62. Became involved in Vietnam, headed up the Taylor-Rostow mission to Vietnam in 1961. Strong advocate that the president send Lansdale to Vietnam. A hawk during the Johnson administration. Deceased.

Stoneman, Walter. Head of the Vietnam affairs office in USAID/Washington from 1962 to 1968. Strong, effective supporter of Rural Affairs operations and personnel. Tried unsuccessfully to mitigate the changes in the Saigon mission under Killen. Deceased.

Unger, Leonard. Ambassador to Laos until 1964, then deputy assistant secretary for the Far East in the State Department, where he also coordinated Vietnam affairs from 1965 to 1966. Was designated as the main source of support for the Lansdale mission in the 1965–68 period but was not influential. Deceased.

OTHERS

Arellano, Oscar. Filipino chairman of Operation Brotherhood from its inception in 1954. Architect by profession, he was active in the Manila Jaycees and from 1954 on devoted himself full-time to directing Operation Brotherhood. Impulsive but indefatigable in supporting OB and in expanding its services into related social welfare fields. Effectively directed the transition of OB from Vietnam to Laos. Deceased.

Banzon, Joe. Colonel in the Philippine army and first military attaché to Vietnam. Instrumental in assisting Operation Brotherhood and in supporting Vietnamese army pacification operations as well as introducing the author to pacification and military civic action during the 1954–55 period. Deceased.

Hoa, Nguyen Loc. Chinese priest with guerrilla experience against the Japanese and then against the Chinese communists. Father Hoa immigrated to Vietnam from Taiwan in the late 1950s and established a combat village in the Camau Peninsula. He recruited Vietnamese of Chinese descent from the slums of Cholon, who made up most of his counter-guerrilla fighters. Received Magsaysay Prize in 1964 for his successful efforts in "defending freedom." His combat village was taken over by successive Vietnamese governments after Diem, and he retired to Taiwan. Deceased.

Magsaysay, Ramon. Popular, dynamic secretary of defense in the Philippines during the successful campaign against the communist Huks from 1950 to 1952. Ran for president against the corrupt Quirino regime in 1953 and won in a landslide. Close friend and confident of Lansdale. Completely undermined Huk popular support by restoring Filipino faith in democratic government. He strongly supported efforts to buttress the shaky Vietnamese government under Ngo Dinh Diem in 1954–55. Died in a plane crash in 1957.

Romain-Defosses, Jacques. Lieutenant colonel in the French army with seventeen years' service in Vietnam, he was appointed deputy to Lansdale in the TRIM National Security Division, where he gave genuine assistance in coordinating French support of the Vietnamese army occupation operations in Camau and central Vietnam. One of the few French officers at the time sympathetic to the Vietnamese. Deceased.

San Juan, Frisco "Johnny." Graduating from the Philippine Military Academy in 1941, he became a guerrilla leader against the Japanese and early organizer of Philippine veterans after World War II. Subsequently, he assisted Magsaysay in the Defense Department and became head of the Complaints and Action Commission in Magsaysay's presidency. Also headed the Freedom Company's efforts to provide Filipino advisors to South Vietnam. After Magsaysay's death he converted the Freedom Company into Eastern Construction, providing maintenance technicians for the Vietnamese and the Lao armies, while also supporting political development in Laos and the Chieu Hoi (surrender) program in Vietnam. Lives in Metro Manila in the Philippines.

Shaplen, Robert. *New Yorker* writer of articles about Vietnam, he was the most knowledgeable American journalist about Vietnamese politics. Published several books about Vietnam, including *The Lost Revolution*. Used Pham Xuan An and Nguyen Hung Vuong as his assistants in gathering political information. Only American journalist during the1960s in touch with what was happening with the Vietnamese, whereas most of his press colleagues focused almost exclusively on the Americans. Deceased.

Thompson, Sir Robert. Knighted for his work in defeating the communist insurgency in Malaya, Thompson headed a small British advisory mission in Vietnam. Commonly thought of as the godfather of the Strategic Hamlet Program, he was influential in promoting the defended village concept, but his ideas of completely separating the population from the insurgents—which worked in Malaya, in large part because the insurgents were mainly Chinese—were not applicable in Vietnam. Continued to be consulted by the Johnson and Nixon administrations, he rightly supported a more unconventional approach to the war. Deceased.

Valeriano, Napoleon. Colonel Valeriano was a very successful leader of the 7th Battalion Combat Team against the Huks when Magsaysay was secretary of defense. Parodied by Stanley Karnow in his *In Our Image: America's Empire in the Philippines* as a commander of "swashbuckling units called 'skull squadrons' for their practice of beheading suspected Huks," but that was not the case at all. When Magsaysay became president in 1953, Valeriano became commander of the presidential guard. In 1954 and 1955, Valeriano was an advisor to Diem's presidential guard, helping make it a capable and loyal force. Coauthor with Bohannon of *Counter-Guerrilla Operations: The Philippine Experience*, Valeriano became a U.S. citizen and worked for the Defense Department and the CIA. Deceased.

Warner, Denis. Australian journalist with experience in reporting on the French-Vietminh war and the subsequent Diem government's operations against the Vietcong in the 1960–63 period. Was the source of information about schemes by Madame Nhu's brother to take over the government in 1963, including a hit list of Americans to be assassinated. Published a book about Diem and Vietnam in 1963, *The Last Confucian*.

LAOS 1957–59

THE LAO

Phouma, Souvanna. Crown prince and prime minister of Royal Lao government from 1956 to 1958, when he was the principal advocate of a coalition government with the communist-controlled Pathet Lao, headed by his half-brother Crown Prince Souphanouvong. When supplementary elections for the National Assembly were dominated by the Pathet Lao, Souvanna Phouma was replaced as prime minister by the more openly anticommunist Phoui Sananikone. With the neutralization of Laos proposed by the Kennedy administration, Souvanna would return as prime minister where he remained until the fall of Saigon and the subsequent communist takeover of Laos in 1975. With a French wife, he was much under the influence of the French, retiring to France in 1975. Deceased.

Ratikoun, Ouane. Chief of staff of the Lao army from 1956 to 1960, when deposed by the Cong Le coup. Came from humble origins and rose through the ranks. Strong advocate of American training of the army, which never materialized until it was too late. Taken captive when the Pathet Lao took over in 1975, he starved to death in a reeducation camp.

Sananikone, Oudone. Lieutenant colonel detached from the Lao army to become Commissioner of Civic Action in 1957, working under Prime Minister Souvanna Phouma. Got the program under way despite bureaucratic obstruction and difficulty in recruiting suitable personnel. In 1958 he ran the Lao side of Operation Booster Shot, delivering aid to the villages. One of the original organizers of the Committee for the Defense of the National Interests (CDNI), a group of younger reform-minded Lao who were also anticommunist. Eventually became a major general in the Lao army and was abroad in 1975 when the communists took over. Came to the United States with most of his family. Deceased.

Souphanavong. Crown Prince Souvanna's half-brother and leader of the Pathet Lao, for which he was an effective figurehead. Briefly headed a ministry in the 1958 Lao coalition government but was never in control of the Pathet Lao movement, which continued to be run by the North Vietnamese from behind the scenes. Deceased.

THE AMERICANS

Clark, Milton. Affable CIA chief of station in Vientiane from 1956 to 1957. Gave strong support to Civic Action and to the author. Deceased.

Cool, John. With a doctorate in anthropology was in charge of USOM/Vientiane provincial operations in 1958–59, when he opposed Civic Action and Operation Brotherhood. Offended the Lao and almost lost his job but was saved by author's intercession. Representative at the time of the worst kind of bureaucratic obstructionism. Current whereabouts unknown to the author.

Fraleigh, Albert "Bert." Came to Laos from Taiwan to boost rural development but was not supported by the USOM/Vientiane mission. (See the entry on Fraleigh under "Vietnam 1954–1968/The Americans" for more background.)

Hecksher, Henry. Replaced Milt Clark as Lao CIA station chief in late 1957. More dynamic and active than Clark, had initial difficulty in adjusting to the slow pace of Laos but became effective in political action with the Lao, including Prime Minister Phoui Sananikone, until Ambassador Smith began undercutting him. His conflicts with Smith became a cause célèbre and were cited as a reason for President Kennedy's order in 1961 making ambassadors clearly in charge of all mission activities. Deceased.

Methven, Stuart. CIA case officer who replaced the author in Laos in 1959. (See the entry on Methven under "Vietnam 1954–1968/The Americans" for more background.)

Miller, Hank and Anne. Hank Miller was the chief of USIS in Laos from 1956 to 1960. He and his wife, Anne, ran an open house for Lao and foreign visitors. They were the first to reach out to the Lao and incorporate them into what the Americans were doing. Hank was a member of the Lansdale mission to Vietnam from 1965 to 1967. Both deceased.

Parsons, Graham. American ambassador to Laos from 1955 to 1957. Opposed the coalition government. Very supportive of civic action. From 1958 to 1961 served in the State Department in Washington, where he became a prime mover in convincing Rusk to block the nomination of Lansdale as ambassador to Vietnam. Deceased.

Smith, Horace. American ambassador to Laos from 1958 to 1960. Convinced that the French really understood the Lao, he was pompous and prejudiced against the younger Lao leaders and thought the older Lao politicians knew best. Carried on a feud with Hecksher over the CIA station's operations and influence. On one occasion was ordered out of Laos temporarily by the State Department to prevent him from frustrating U.S. policy but was allowed to serve out his tour. Deceased.

Glossary

AID	Agency for International Development (also USAID)
amah	nursemaid
Annam	central part of Vietnam and largest of the three historical regions of the country, with Hue as its capital
ao dai	Vietnamese female dress
ARVN	Army of the Republic of Vietnam (also Vietnamese army)
Binh Xuyen	gangster sect in Saigon area
bonze	Buddhist priest or monk
Can Lao	secret political organization within the GVN civil service and army controlled by Ngo Dinh Nhu, President Diem's brother
Cao Dai	religious sect located mainly in the Tay Ninh area of South Vietnam
case officer	CIA intelligence or political action staff officer operating in the field, usually under official cover
CAT	Civil Air Transport (owned by the CIA but often on contract to Defense Department and other U.S. government agencies, furnished air support for resupplying French forces in Dien Bien Phu, evacuating Vietnamese refugees from the north in 1954–55, and air operations in Laos in the early days)Became Air America.
CDNI	Committee for the Defense of the National Interests (pressure group of younger Lao civil service and military leaders)
cha gio	Vietnamese spring rolls
Chieu Hoi	Vietnamese government surrender program ("open arms")
Cholon	Chinese quarter of Saigon
CIA	Central Intelligence Agency (also referred to as "the Agency")
CIDG	Civilian Irregular Defense Group
CINCPAC	Commander in Chief, U.S. Pacific Command
civic action	Vietnamese and Lao government programs sending teams to work in rural villages, also the practice of soldiers helping the civilian population

Civil Guard	provincial-level security forces, later called Regional Forces (RF)
Cochin China	southernmost of the three historical regions of Vietnam with Saigon as its capital (a colony under the French while Tonkin and Annam were protectorates, which the French ruled indirectly through mandarin administrations)
CORDS	Civil Operations and Revolutionary Development Support (combined group controlling U.S. pacification operations)
Dai Viet	Vietnamese nationalist political party
dong	Vietminh currency in 1954–55
DRV	Democratic Republic of North Vietnam
ECA	Economic Cooperation Administration (predecessor to International Cooperation Administration [ICA])
G-5	Vietnamese army psychological warfare staff
G-6	irregular warfare
General Assembly	elected Lao legislative body under their parliamentary system
Gia Long	palace used by Ngo Dinh Diem during first few months after his arrival in 1954, and again after 1960 when part of the main Independence Palace (Doc Lap) was destroyed during the 1960 paratrooper coup and a new palace was under construction
GVN	government of South Vietnam
hamlet	a cluster of homes, several hamlets make up a village
hamlet militia	hamlet self-defense forces under the Strategic Hamlet Program, later referred to as People's Self Defense Forces
Hoa Hao	religious sect centered in the southwest Delta
Hoi Chanh	returnees under the Chieu Hoi surrender program
Huks	communist guerrilla movement (Hukbalahap) in the Philippines
ICA	International Cooperation Administration, predecessor to USAID
ICC	International Supervisory and Control Commission, composed of Poles, Canadians, and Indians, set up to supervise the Geneva cease-fire agreement
ISA	Office of International Security Affairs in the U.S. Defense Department
IVS	International Volunteer Services
JCS	Joint Chiefs of Staff (U.S.)
JGS	Joint General Staff of the Vietnamese armed forces
JUSPAO	Joint U.S. Public Affairs Office
kip	Lao currency
Lien Minh	separate Cao Dai movement, headed by General Trinh Minh Thé

LST	landing ship, tank
MAAG	Military Assistance Advisory Group (U.S.)
MACV	Military Assistance Command, Vietnam (U.S.)
MAP	Military Assistance Program (U.S.)
MNR	Movement for National Revolution (President Diem's political party)
Montagnards	indigenous tribes of Indonesian origin living in the mountains and High Plateau of South Vietnam
My	"America" or "American" in Vietnamese
National Assembly	elected Vietnamese legislative body
NATO	North Atlantic Treaty Organization
nipa	Type of thatching used on roofs of Filipino huts
NLF	National Liberation Front (communist-controlled South Vietnamese political front)
NSC	National Security Council (U.S.)
nuoc mam	Vietnamese fish sauce
OB	Operation Brotherhood (International Jaycees sponsored Filipino medical volunteers during 1954–56 in Vietnam and later in Laos)
OCB	Operations Coordination Board (working group, subsidiary to NSC, composed of agency representatives under President Eisenhower, inactive during Kennedy administration)
PEO	Program Evaluation Office (U.S. military advisory group in Laos)
PF	Popular Forces village-level security forces
Phap	"French" in Vietnamese
phi	Vietnamese word for a spirit, good or evil
Phoenix	program aimed at killing or capturing hard core VC cadre
PL	Pathet Lao (Lao communist front group)
PL-480	Public Law 480 authorizing the Food for Peace Program
prov rep	USOM provincial representatives under Rural Affairs and subsequently under USOM Office of Provincial Operations
psywar	psychological warfare
SDC	Self-Defense Corps, village-level security forces, later called Popular Forces
SDECE	Service de Documentation Extérieure et de Contre-Espionage (French Foreign Intelligence Service)
SEATO	South-East Asia Treaty Organization
SLO	Saigon Liaison Office, Lansdale advisory group under the U.S. ambassador, 1965–68

SMM	Saigon Military Mission, covert CIA mission in Saigon, 1954–56, separate from the regular CIA station
station	shorthand reference for regular CIA station in Vietnam and Laos
STEM	Special Technical and Economic Mission (predecessor to USOM/Saigon)
Tet	Vietnamese lunar New Year, also refers to the VC offensive launched on January 31, 1968
Thich	honorific before name of Buddhist monk
Tonkin	northernmost of the three historical regions of Vietnam, with Hanoi as its capital.
TRIM	Training Relations Instruction Mission (American-French)
USAID	U.S. Agency for International Development (also AID)
USIA	U.S. Information Agency
USIS	U.S. Information Service (local office of USIA)
USOM	U.S. Operations Mission (local office of USAID)
VC	Vietcong
Vietcong	Vietnamese communists, also spelled Viet Cong
Vietminh	communist-controlled political and guerrilla movement against the French and the Bao Dai governments, also spelled Viet Minh
VNQDD	Viet Nam Quoc Dan Dan, Vietnamese nationalist political party
wat	Buddhist temple in Laos and Thailand

Note on Sources

My sources, in addition to my memory and the historical record, are my personal files, letters, notes, and other records, including copies of memorandums of conversations, written at the time. These files, notes, letters, and other documents will all be donated to the Vietnam Archive at the Vietnam Center at Texas Tech University once this book has been published. A number of memoranda written by me are to be found in the various volumes about Vietnam in the Foreign Relations of the United States series. Descriptions of events in which I was not directly involved are documented by notes, as are messages and statements by various principal actors.

As background for and checks upon my memory and interpretation of the events of the earlier 1954–56 period, a number of books and other materials were particularly helpful (full publication data for cited works appear at first mention in the notes). In particular these were Edward Lansdale's *In the Midst of War;* Cecil Currey's biography, *Edward G. Lansdale: The Unquiet American* (about which, see below); and the abridged version of the *Lansdale Team Report on Covert Saigon Mission in 1954 and 1955* contained as document 95 in the *Pentagon Papers;* and the *Foreign Relations of the United States 1952–1954*, Indochina, vol. 13, part 2, and 1955–1957, vol. 1, Vietnam. Other useful books and publications were *The Smaller Dragon,* by Joseph Buttinger, for early Vietnam history and general background; Howard Simpson's *Tiger in the Barbed Wire,* for its descriptive flavor and details of the times; Ronald H. Spector, *Advice and Support: The Early Years, the U.S. Army in Vietnam,* for the military record; Edward G. Miller's article "Vision, Power and Agency: The Ascent of Ngo Dinh Diem," in the *Journal of Southeast Asian Studies*, and his Harvard PhD thesis, "Grand Designs: Vision, Power and Nation Building in America's Alliance with Ngo Dinh Diem, 1954–1960," for correcting much of the record about Diem, though it lacks adequate information about Lansdale's actions and motivations; David L. Anderson, *Trapped by Success: The Eisenhower Administration and Vietnam, 1953–61,* for general background (but not interpretation); an unpublished biography of Ngo Dinh Diem by Anne Miller, for background; *Visages et Images du Sud-Viet-nam,* by Major A. M. Savani, and *Sociologie d'une Guerre,* by Paul Mus, for background; *Le Mal Jaune,* by Jean Larteguy, interesting for what it tells of the French attitude toward the Americans and Lansdale in particular; unpublished interviews with Lucien Conein, belonging to the Conein family, for background; Bui Diem, *In the Jaws of History;* Miguel A. Bernard, *Adventures in Viet-Nam: The Story of Operation Brotherhood 1954–1957,* for the story of the selflessness of devoted Filipino doctors and nurses; and Joseph Alsop's *I've Seen the Best of It,* for his take on events of those days; as well as numerous newspaper and magazine articles from that period.

The main sources of background information for the in-between years of 1957 to 1961 in Vietnam and from 1957 through 1959 in Laos are the memory of the author; his personal records, letters, and notes from interviews; of course, information from pertinent volumes of *Foreign Relations of the United States* covering Vietnam from 1957 through 1961 and Laos for the years 1957–59; a paper written by Ambassador Horace Smith about his Laos experience, on file at the LBJ Library, in Austin, Texas; and documents at the Hoover Institution in Palo Alto, California. A useful general reference book for the Lao period was Arthur J. Dommen, *The Indochinese Experience of the French and the Americans.*

The later period in Vietnam, from 1962 on through 1968, is documented in more detail by specific memoranda and other source materials in the author's files; material from the various editions of the *Foreign Relations of the United States;* documents from the National Archives; records at the LBJ Library; records at the JFK Library in Boston; and documents at the Hoover Institution. Books that were particularly useful as references in no order of importance were: *Foreign Relations of the United States,* all volumes about Vietnam covering the years 1962 through 1968; *The Pentagon Papers, Senator Gravel Edition,* for important official memoranda, messages, and reports of this period; *The Lost Revolution,* by Robert Shaplen, on South Vietnamese politics; *From Trust to Tragedy,* by Frederick Nolting, for his perspective on Diem and the tragedy of his demise; *To Move a Nation,* by Roger Hilsman, for a distinctly different Washington perspective; *In Retrospect: The Tragedy and Lessons of Vietnam,* by Robert McNamara, for what he still fails to understand about his own mistakes; *Blind Design,* by Hoang Van Lac, for a Vietnamese perspective from direct experience; *Our Endless War,* by Tran Van Don, for another Vietnamese perspective; *In the Jaws of History,* by Bui Diem, for a balanced view of the South Vietnamese and American sides; *Vietcong Memoir,* by Truong Nhu Tang, for inside views on how the NLF saw things and what happened to those who ate the North Vietnamese salt; *War without Guns,* by George Tanham, for an early account of Rural Affairs provincial representatives at work in the countryside; *War Comes to Long An,* by Jeffrey Race, for its insight about how the Vietcong worked at the village level; *Diem's Final Failure,* by Philip E. Catton, for its detailed, if sometimes misinterpreted, history of the Strategic Hamlet Program; *Secrets: A Memoir of Vietnam and the Pentagon Papers,* by Daniel Ellsberg, for its insight into how Lodge frustrated Lansdale and the democratic process in Vietnam; *The Two Vietnams* (revised edition), by Bernard Fall, for general background (influenced by the French view that only they really understood Vietnam); *Mission in Torment,* by John Mecklin, for his firsthand account of travails with the American press; *The Last Confucian,* by Denis Warner, for details about the earlier (1961–62) period of the war; *The Best and the Brightest,* by David Halberstam, for its analysis of the New Frontiersmen and Vietnam policy making in Washington (Halberstam is particularly acute about McNamara); *Facing the Phoenix,* by Zalin Grant, for its distinctive political take on the struggle within South Vietnam and on Tran Ngoc Chau; *Intervention,* by George McT. Kahin, for its description of the mishandling of the second Buddhist uprising; *Hubert H. Humphrey: The Politics of Joy,* by Charles L. Garretson III, for its inside rundown on what Humphrey really thought about the war and his unsuccessful efforts to influence President Johnson; *Lodge in Vietnam,* by Anne Blair, for details about Henry Cabot Lodge; *A Death in November,* by Ellen J. Hammer, for its description of the coup (although she mischaracterizes my own position); *Kennedy in Vietnam,* by William J. Rust, for its details about the policy and decision making that supported the coup against Diem; *Dereliction of Duty,* by H. R. McMaster, for its reaction to the failure of various services chiefs to stand up for their convictions; *A Better War* and *Vietnam Chronicles: The Abrams Tapes 1968–1972,* both by Lewis Sorley, for its estimable assessment of how different a leader Abrams was from Westmoreland and of the way in which Abrams changed to a more successful strategy while simultaneously drawing down all U.S. forces; *Lost Victory,* by William Colby, for its description of CORDS and the successes of the pacification campaign in Vietnam after the war had been lost at home; *CIA and Rural Pacification in South Vietnam,* by Thomas L. Ahern, Jr., of the Center for the Study of Intelligence, for a more pessimistic view of the pacification effort; *The Palace File,* by Nguyen Tien Hung and Jerrold L. Schecter, for details of how Nixon and Kissinger dealt with the South Vietnamese; *Once a Warrior King,* by David Donovan, for its intimate picture of what life was like for an American military advisor at the village level in a Delta province; *The Fall of South Vietnam,* by Stephen T. Hosmer, Konrad Kellen, and Brian M. Jenkins, for details from South Vietnamese sources about the 1975 collapse; and *No Peace, No Honor* and *Perfect Spy,* both by Larry Berman, for first elucidating the charade of Nixon's and Kissinger's "peace with honor," then illuminating the life of an ambiguous but highly successful spy for the North Vietnamese.

Prelude to Tragedy: Vietnam 1960–1965, edited by Harvey Neese and John O'Donnell, deserves special mention for its firsthand accounts of Vietnamese and Americans who struggled on the ground to win. This book was motivated to a considerable degree by the ignorance and arrogance of Secretary of Defense Robert McNamara, who said in his book *In Retrospect: the Tragedy and Lessons of Vietnam* that our government lacked "experts" on Vietnam. *Prelude to Tragedy* constitutes an informed, firsthand account by eight actors on the ground, including myself, of what went wrong and what could have gone right with the war, mainly during the period covered by the title. Although the eight authors sounded similar themes from their varied experience, by its nature the book could not adequately cover a more comprehensive history of events, even though its introduction and conclusion provided a summary context; nor was there space for everything I wanted to recount and explain. My part had been written from memory, and there were some errors in it. Building as it does on what I had written in *Prelude to Tragedy,* this book, *Why Vietnam Matters,* is more thoroughly researched and covers a considerably longer time frame.

There is also Stanley Karnow's *Vietnam: A History*, used as a general reference for most Vietnam history courses. Marred by an overly dismissive caricature of Diem, an underrating of the South Vietnamese in general and of counterinsurgency efforts like the Strategic Hamlet Program in particular, a flippant view of some Americans, and an overadmiring picture of the Vietcong and the North Vietnamese, it nevertheless contains much valuable firsthand reporting from interviews and eyewitness observations. To its credit, the book pulls no punches when describing North Vietnamese and Vietcong brutality and the degree to which the insurgency was communist controlled.

For those curious to explore more about Lansdale's thinking and ways of operating, Cecil Currey's *Edward G. Lansdale: The Unquiet American* and Lansdale's own *In the Midst of Wars,* are the best sources, in addition to his personal papers at the Hoover Institution in Palo Alto. While there is some fictionalization in Lansdale's story telling as reported in both books, Currey's biography was based on extensive research and interviews with many who knew Lansdale and worked with him, and it is full of revealing details. Some writings about Lansdale, such as Professor Jonathan Nashel's *Edward Lansdale's Cold War,* tend to pick out bits and pieces of his record to prove an ideological point without giving a rounded portrait and fail to understand the context of the societies and countries, the Philippines and Vietnam, in which Lansdale was operating. The same could be said of Karnow's dismissive description of Lansdale in *Vietnam: A History,* as exuding "a brand of artless goodwill that overlooked the deeper dynamics of revolutionary upheavals . . . oblivious to the social and cultural complexities of Asia."

Finally, for a description of American errors and mistakes made in Iraq, see *Fiasco,* by Thomas Ricks; *Imperial Life in the Emerald City,* by Rajiv Chandrasekaran; and *Squandered Victory: The American Occupation and the Bungled Effort to Bring Democracy to Iraq,* by Larry Diamond.

Index

About the Author

Rufus Phillips, born in 1929, was raised in rural Charlotte County, Virginia, near Appomattox. Graduating from Yale in 1951, he joined the CIA in 1952 and then enlisted in the U.S Army. Detailed back to the CIA, in 1954 he began his deep involvement in Vietnam affairs of some fourteen years as part of the Saigon Military Mission, headed by the "legendary" Col. Edward G. Lansdale. He received the CIA's Intelligence Medal of Merit in 1955 for his service as sole adviser to two Vietnamese army pacification operations in 1955. In 1962, as an employee of the U.S. Agency for International Development (AID), he returned to Saigon to organize and lead a special office, called Rural Affairs, whose mission was counterinsurgency. Obliged to return home in November 1963 to take over the family engineering business, he remained a consultant to AID and the State Department from 1964 to 1968, making extended visits to Vietnam and serving as an informal adviser to Vice President Hubert Humphrey. Phillips contributed to *Prelude to Tragedy: Vietnam 1960–1965*, edited by Harvey Neese and John O'Donnell and published by the Naval Institute Press (2001). He lives with his wife, Barbara, in Northern Virginia.

THE NAVAL INSTITUTE PRESS is the book-publishing arm of the U.S. Naval Institute, a private, nonprofit, membership society for sea service professionals and others who share an interest in naval and maritime affairs. Established in 1873 at the U.S. Naval Academy in Annapolis, Maryland, where its offices remain today, the Naval Institute has members world-wide.

Members of the Naval Institute support the education programs of the society and receive the influential monthly magazine *Proceedings* or the colorful bimonthly magazine *Naval History* and discounts on fine nautical prints and on ship and aircraft photos. They also have access to the transcripts of the Institute's Oral History Program and get discounted admission to any of the Institute-sponsored seminars offered around the country.

The Naval Institute's book-publishing program, begun in 1898 with basic guides to naval practices, has broadened its scope to include books of more general interest. Now the Naval Institute Press publishes about seventy titles each year, ranging from how-to books on boating and navigation to battle histories, biographies, ship and aircraft guides, and novels. Institute members receive significant discounts on the Press's more than eight hundred books in print.

Full-time students are eligible for special half-price membership rates. Life memberships are also available.

For a free catalog describing Naval Institute Press books currently available, and for further information about joining the U.S. Naval Institute, please write to:

Member Services
U.S. NAVAL INSTITUTE
291 Wood Road
Annapolis, MD 21402-5034
Telephone: (800) 233-8764
Fax: (410) 571-1703
Web address: www.usni.org